T0295592

Pricing Insurance Risk

Pricing Insurance Risk

Theory and Practice

Stephen J. Mildenhall and John A. Major

This edition first published 2022

Registered Office
John Wiley & Sons, Inc., 111 River Street, Hoboken, NJ 07030, USA

Editorial Office
111 River Street, Hoboken, NJ 07030, USA

For details of our global editorial offices, customer services, and more information about Wiley products visit us at www.wiley.com.

Wiley also publishes its books in a variety of electronic formats and by print-on-demand. Some content that appears in standard print versions of this book may not be available in other formats.

Library of Congress Cataloging-in-Publication Data
Names: Mildenhall, Stephen J., author. | Major, John A., author.
Title: Pricing insurance risk : theory and practice / Stephen J Mildenhall, John A Major.
Description: Hoboken, NJ : John Wiley and Sons, 2022. | Includes bibliographical references and index.
Identifiers: LCCN 2021062792 (print) | LCCN 2021062793 (ebook) | ISBN 9781119755678 (hardback) | ISBN 9781119755692 (pdf) | ISBN 9781119756521 (epub) | ISBN 9781119756538 (ebook)
Subjects: LCSH: Risk (Insurance) | Risk management.
Classification: LCC HG8054.5 .M55 2022 (print) | LCC HG8054.5 (ebook) | DDC 368–dc23/eng/20220111
LC record available at https://lccn.loc.gov/2021062792
LC ebook record available at https://lccn.loc.gov/2021062793

Cover Design: Wiley
Cover Image: © zef art/Shutterstock

Set in 9.5/12.5pt STIXTwoText by Integra Software Services Pvt. Ltd, Pondicherry, India

SKY10063981_010524

Dedicated to our wives, Helen and Diane

Contents

Preface

Pricing Insurance Risk is a topic of great concern to actuaries, especially property-casualty actuaries, our primary audience. But it is also relevant to those working in other fields, including risk management and Enterprise Risk Management, capital modeling, catastrophe modeling, financial regulation, and solvency assessment. Insurance risk is managed through pooling, unlike financial risk that is managed through hedging. The title could have been Pricing Non-Hedgeable Risk.

The book came about through a confluence of supporting factors. We had worked independently for many years on the problem of defining the value of risk management and risk transfer (especially in the context of property catastrophe risk) and "escaping the efficient frontier." Don Mango brought us together to work with him and Jesse Nickerson to present a multipart tutorial on spectral risk measures at the Casualty Actuarial Society Spring 2018 meeting. The tutorial was so successful that we felt it deserved a wider audience and set about developing a monograph: "Spectral Risk Measures for the Working Actuary." As we proceeded to refine our thinking and presentation, we realized there was so much more to be explained. Three and a half years and 1200 git commits later, we had this book.

The literature is rich with good answers to many fundamental questions about insurance risk that are consistent with finance theory and relatively easy to apply. Much is known, in the sense of being out there in the literature, but too much is not *widely* known by people who would benefit from that knowledge. Actuarial education and practice in this area lags the state of the art. We have encountered actuaries struggling with ill-defined terminology and concepts with multiple names. We have seen confusion wrought by inappropriate application of finance theories (remember the underwriting beta?). Our newly minted US Fellows are often ignorant of the latest developments because they are not on the exam syllabus and there has not been an easy way to incorporate them.

This book presents these good answers in one systematic and comprehensive source for the first time, making them much more accessible to actuaries and other practitioners. With this book we intend to raise the bar in actuarial education, enable clear communications, and improve the efficiency of actuaries everywhere by delivering a fresh map of the conceptual territory. We wish we could take credit for the theory we present, but most of it is around twenty years old. We are simply reporting the work of others.

Insurance pricing is multidisciplinary, combining actuarial science and risk theory, probability and statistics, finance and economics, accounting and law. As we organized and synthesized a body of literature as nearly as old as the industry itself to tell the story of insurance pricing, we tried to be sensitive to its historical development—a play some of which we watched unfold in real time. It is a story we both found fascinating. From defining underwriting profit and a reasonable target profit in the 1920s to arguments about investment income in the 1960s. From systematic risk and option pricing theory applications in the 1980s to a more insurance-specific model in the 1990s. And most recently to the introduction of coherent, convex, and even star-shaped risk measures. We hope the reader has time to appreciate the giants on whose shoulders we are lucky enough to stand and can join us in taking in the spectacular vistas of the meaning, quantification, and management of risk they have revealed.

In putting together this book we tried to stay reasonably rigorous without getting lost in a theorem-proof wilderness. We feel strongly that knowing how to use a technique is not helpful if you are unsure that it is valid to use in the first place! We include technical remarks and provide pointers into the literature (about 300 bibliographic references) for those who want a more thorough understanding of "why." For the practitioner, we included nearly 100 examples and 150 exercises. The Learning Objectives at the end of each chapter summarize what we hope the reader will take away from it. **Bold** words and phrases introduce terminology that is used throughout the book.

We aimed this book primarily at property-casualty actuaries, at minimum two years of experience as a student actuary with basic knowledge of insurance coverage and structuring, and having passed the beginning mathematics exams. We expect readers with different backgrounds will still be able to get something from the book. A lot of the insurance and finance terminology is only an internet search away. Mathematics background should include calculus and basic probability—sample spaces, discrete vs. continuous random variables, normal and lognormal distributions, integration by parts, etc. Of course, for an in-depth understanding, more background, especially in probability theory, is better.

The manuscript was prepared using free software. It was written in Markdown and converted to TeX using Pandoc. TikZ was used for the figures and diagrams, and all the graphs and plots were made using Python, Pandas, and Matplotlib. We used R for the statistical analysis and to double check Python (they always agreed). Spreadsheets were used for the discrete examples. We both remember when computers booted from (genuinely) floppy disks. The existence of so much free software, of such a high quality, is an unexpected joy.

We owe a debt of gratitude to many people. In academia, keeping us accurate, we thank Dani Bauer, Stuart Klugman, Andreas Tsanakas, Ruodu Wang, Shaun Wang, and George Zanjani. In business, keeping us real, we thank Avi Adler, John Aquino, Neil Bodoff, Julia Chu, Andrew Cox (1978–2021), Dan Dick, Paul Eaton, Bryon Ehrhart, Kent Ellingson, Stephen Fiete, Bob Fox, Jonathan Hayes, Greg Heerde, Wouter Heynderickx, Rodney Kreps, Morton Lane, Mike McClane, Tessa Moulton, Parr Schoolman, Paul Schultz, Jason Trock, Gary Venter, Steve White, and Rebecca Wilkinson.

Special thanks go to Don Mango for starting this all; to Jesse Nickerson for his early involvement in the research and his comments on drafts; and to Yuriy Krvavych and Lawrence McTaggart for their comments on drafts. Richard Goldfarb stands out for particular thanks, having provided very detailed and pertinent feedback that resulted in numerous improvements. Stephen: I would like to recognize the influence of Glenn Meyers and Richard

Derrig (1941–2018) early in my career—they taught me how to think about pricing insurance risk. I am enormously grateful to my wife, Helen, who started proofreading the manuscript at a late stage and found herself learning the material in a crash course. Her fresh perspective and unyielding commitment to clarity helped improve the presentation in uncountably many ways. John: I would like to thank Jack Caron, Bernie Shorr, and Aaron Stern for opening doors.

1

Introduction

In order to make insurance a trade at all, the common premium must be sufficient to compensate the common losses, to pay the expense of management, and to afford such a profit as might have been drawn from an equal capital employed in any common trade.
Adam Smith, *The Wealth of Nations* (Book 1, Ch X, Part I, 5th Edition, 1789)

1.1 Our Subject and Why It Matters

Pricing insurance risk is the last mile of underwriting. It determines which risks are accepted onto the balance sheet and makes an insurer's risk appetite operational. It is critical to successful insurance company management.

As the last mile, pricing depends on all that has come before. Actuaries and underwriters have analyzed and classified the risk, trended and developed losses, and on-leveled premiums to pick a best-estimate prospective loss cost. Accountants have allocated fixed and variable expenses. Simulation models place the new risk within the context of the company's existing portfolio. The mechanics of all this work is the subject of much of the actuarial education syllabus: experience and exposure rating, predictive analytics, and advanced statistical methods. That is not the subject of this book! All of that prior effort determines the expected loss, and we take it as a given. Pricing adds the *risk margin*—to afford capital a reasonable return. The risk margin is our subject.

Since risk margins are often small, how is it they deserve a whole book? Because risk considerations have an outsized market impact. True, personal property may only earn a single-digit margin. But that business often relies on reinsurance priced with margins of 50% or more. When the reinsurance markets fail or become stressed—as seen after Hurricane Andrew and the Northridge earthquake, for example—the tail of high-risk-margin business wags the dog of much larger property lines. Risk margins are critical to the functioning of the insurance market. Even for lines with thin margins, the collective risk and return decisions of firms have profound macro impacts over time such as the secular increases in homeowners pricing over the last twenty years.

Pricing Insurance Risk: Theory and Practice, First Edition. Stephen J. Mildenhall and John A. Major.

We emphasize *insurance risk*. We do not discuss credit risk nor operational risk. We have only a little to say about asset risk and nothing about interest rate risk. Market risk, underwriting cycles, competitive threats? Sorry, all off-topic. We are focused on the risk of losses arising from insurance contracts. We lean heavily towards a property-casualty perspective and, within that, towards catastrophe risk; however, the principles we lay out apply to any insurance risk. This is not a book about Enterprise Risk Management (ERM) although we do have a few words to say about optimization and portfolio management.

The goal of this book is to demonstrate how to

1. compute a reservation price (technical premium, required premium) for the **portfolio**, and
2. allocate it to portfolio **units** (policies, lines of business, etc.) in a defensible manner

starting from a model of the insured risks. These pricing techniques have powerful applications. They allow us to assess the performance of different units, evaluate needed reinsurance, and optimize overall strategy.

1.2 Players, Roles, and Risk Measures

Figure 1.1 shows the participants in the insurance pricing problem. Insureds, left, pay premiums to the insurer and in turn receive loss payments. The regulator, on top, observing the risk that the insurer is taking on, imposes asset requirements. Investors, right, provide capital and in turn receive the residual value (remaining assets) after losses are paid.

Insureds buy insurance because of their aversion to risk and because they are required to do so to drive a car, buy a house with a mortgage, etc. Regulators play a social policy role, addressing three principal concerns. First, to ensure mandated third-party insurance provides effective protection. Second, to manage the externality of losses exceeding assets. And third, to prevent insureds being fleeced by excessive premiums. The first concern is present in any tort-based system. We loosely identify the second as European and the third as

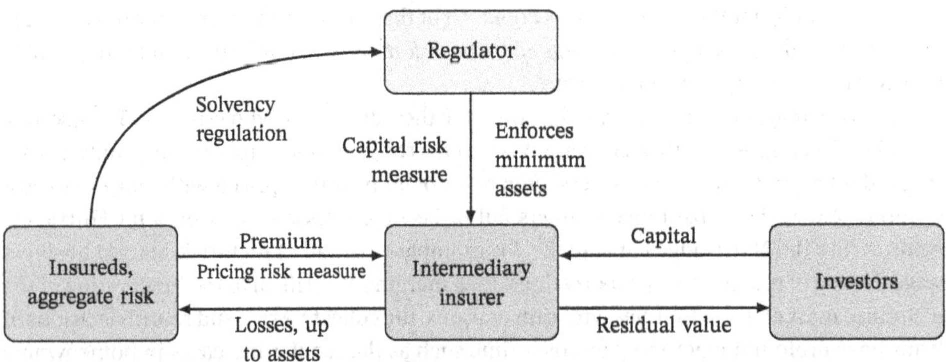

Figure 1.1 Players and their roles. The regulator applies a capital risk measure to determine required insurer assets. The pricing risk measure gives the cost of investors' capital. Assets in excess of losses are paid to investors as the residual value of the business.

American. We focus on the second concern, asset adequacy. Our development of technical premiums naturally aligns with the third fairness consideration if we assume that capital markets require fair returns.

Investors indirectly determine premiums because premiums plus capital add up to and fund assets, Figure 1.2. Investors' willingness to provide capital to insurers translates into a pricing risk measure, which the insurer applies to the covered risks. *Premium and asset levels are separate problems and need separate tools.*

Two important questions arise from insurance company promises to pay certain sums of money contingent on random events.

1. Are there sufficient assets to honor those promises?
2. Are investors being adequately compensated for taking on those risks?

Crucially, we need to talk about not one but *two* different risk measures to answer these questions.

Question 1 concerns risk tolerance and is usually answered by an economic capital model. It determines the assets necessary to back an existing or hypothetical portfolio at a given level of confidence. This exercise is also reverse engineered: given existing or hypothetical assets, what are the constraints on business that can be written?

We can imagine a regulator—interpreted broadly as an external authority—considering a portfolio of risks that the insurer proposes to cover. The regulator specifies the amount of assets the insurer must hold to cover the risk. If there is a shortfall after losses are realized, it will be made up by parties external to the insurer, e.g., a guarantee fund or other government entity, or the insureds themselves insofar as they are not reimbursed for claims. The regulator seeks to minimize the nonpayment externality, balanced with a desire for economical insurance.

A **capital risk measure** is applied to economic capital model output to quantify the level of assets the insurer must hold. Value at Risk (VaR) or Tail Value at Risk (TVaR) at some high confidence level, such as 99.5% or 1 in 200 years, are both popular, but other possible measures exist.

Question 2 concerns risk pricing or risk appetite. We must determine the expected profit insureds need to pay in total to make it worthwhile for investors to bear the portfolio's risk. Regulated insurers are invariably required to hold capital on a regulated balance sheet. We generally assume a funding constraint where premium and investor supplied capital are the only sources of funds. Then, the **pricing risk measure** determines the split of their asset funding between premium and capital.

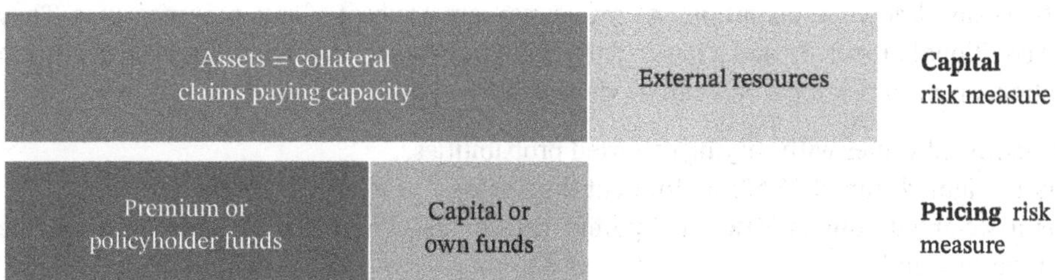

Figure 1.2 The different roles of capital and pricing risk measures.

The capital and pricing risk measures should not be confused. Historically, capital risk measures have been studied in the context of finance and regulation, e.g., Artzner *et al.* (1999). In contrast, actuaries have studied pricing risk measures as premium calculation principles (Goovaerts, De Vylder, and Haezendonck 1984). The recent popularity and focus on coherent risk measures has overshadowed actuarial premium calculation principles and led to some confusion about the two distinct purposes of risk measures. Much of the recent literature implicitly or explicitly refers to the capital domain only. However, practitioners dealing with issues such as business unit performance, premium adequacy, and shareholder value are operating in the pricing domain. Taking a risk measure suitable for one use and applying it to the other invites unexpected and confusing results. Instead, we must understand how the capital and pricing measures work together in a complex, nonlinear manner to determine technical prices.

The top-down pricing process we have described may not seem commonplace, although those working in catastrophe reinsurance should find our process familiar. Most individual risk pricing actuaries can legitimately claim to use a bottom-up approach. Nevertheless, deep within almost every company lies a corporate financial model functioning exactly as we describe. It asks: How much capital is needed? What is the cost of that capital? What overall margin is necessary? And, how should it be allocated to each unit?

1.3 Book Contents and Structure

The book has four main parts: one on measuring risk, one about portfolio pricing, one about pricing units within a portfolio, and one addressing advanced topics. The high level overview we provide here supplements the introductory paragraphs in each chapter.

1.3.1 Part I: Measuring Risk

Part I is about **risk**. What is risk, and how can it be measured and compared? We discuss the mathematical formalism and practical application of representing an insured risk by a random variable. We define a risk measure as a functional taking a random variable to a real number representing the magnitude of its risk. We give numerous examples of risk measures and the different properties they exhibit.

Some properties are more or less mandatory for a useful risk measure, and they lead us to coherent risk measures. Coherent risk measures have an intuitive representation, providing us with some guidance on forming and comparing them. Spectral risk measures (SRMs)—also known as distortion risk measures—are a subset of coherent measures. They have additional properties and a particularly straightforward representation via a distortion function. Spectral risk measures can be viewed in four equivalent ways:

1. as expected values with varying distorted probabilities,
2. as a weighted sum of TVaRs at different thresholds,
3. as a weighted sum of VaRs at different thresholds, where the weights have specific properties, and
4. as the worst expected value across a set of different probability scenarios.

Spectral risk measures alter or distort the underlying pattern of probabilities and compute expected values based on the new probabilities, analogous to the effect of stochastic discount factors in modern finance. The distorted probability treats large losses as more likely, creating a positive pricing margin. TVaR is the archetypal SRM. It is simple yet powerful and has many desirable properties. We gain analytical insights into the nature of SRMs because they are all weighted averages of TVaRs. For example, we can allocate any SRM-derived quantity by bootstrapping a TVaR allocation.

1.3.2 Part II: Portfolio Pricing

Part II is about **portfolio pricing**, where the entire portfolio is treated as a single risk. Risk is related to return, suggesting we should apply a risk measure to portfolio losses and use the result to indicate a price. Our principal goal is to determine what price is sufficient for assuming the portfolio risk. Secondary goals include understanding, making inferences about, and calibrating to, market prices.

Insurance is characterized by risk transfer through risk pooling. Figure 1.1 combines all insureds into one portfolio. It shows how the capital and pricing risk measures interact to determine the insurer's risk pool premium. Part II of the book treats the cash flows on the lower right, between the insurer and the investors.

We are aware that pricing actuaries and underwriters do not set premiums; markets do. However, the aggregate effect of individual company risk-return decisions drives quotes and acceptances in the market. When we talk about setting premiums, we understand it in the framework of evaluating market pricing or offering a quote.

How are the parameters of a pricing model determined? This is a difficult question that must be answered to put theory into practice. We provide examples showing how different parametrization methods perform, link pricing to capital structure, and calibrate an SRM to catastrophe bond pricing.

1.3.3 Part III: Price Allocation

Insurers must allocate a portfolio price and margin to its constituent units to sell policies and run their business. **Price allocation** is the topic of Part III.

We examine how units contribute to portfolio risk. For example, the models may show several outcomes that lead to insolvency. Which units are the drivers of losses in those scenarios? Parallel questions can be asked of other, less catastrophic, levels of loss.

Having computed technical premiums as distorted expected values, we can then apply the same distorted probabilities to unit losses, based on their co-occurrence with the total portfolio losses, to allocate the premiums to units. This technique provides a high degree of consistency and synchronization in calculating technical premiums by unit.

There is a particular approach to handling business unit performance assessment and reinsurance decision making that makes use of a capital measure, typically VaR or TVaR, but appears not to make use of a pricing metric. This approach is rooted in return on risk-adjusted capital style financial logic. It takes two steps: allocate capital and then assign a cost of capital *hurdle rate* that every unit must meet on its allocated capital. All decisions, such as reinsurance purchases, use the same cost of capital as a benchmark.

Practitioners recognize that this approach tends to place uncomfortably large burdens on catastrophe exposed units relative to units that do not participate much in solvency threatening events. In addition, when applied to reinsurance purchasing, it tends to favor, almost without exception, deals that operate at high levels of loss with low probabilities. We show that the problem here stems from the implicit use of what we call the Constant Cost of Capital (CCoC) SRM. The overall hurdle rate for the entire portfolio may not be appropriate for every unit. What is needed is a pricing risk measure—*different* from CCoC—that responds to varying levels of riskiness with different required rates of return. Whereas Part II discusses the construction of such measures, Part III discusses how to deploy them.

1.3.4 Part IV: Advanced Topics

The last part of the book touches on five topics that go beyond the coverage of previous chapters: asset risk, reserves, going concern and franchise value, reinsurance optimization, and portfolio optimization.

1.3.5 Further Structure

Parts II and III divide portfolio pricing from allocation considerations. Within each part, we further distinguish **classical** from **modern** approaches, and **theory** from **practice**. The hierarchy, reflected in the sequence of eight core chapters, is:

- Chapters 8 and 9: classical portfolio pricing theory and practice,
- Chapters 10 and 11: modern portfolio pricing theory and practice,
- Chapters 12 and 13: classical price allocation theory and practice, and
- Chapters 14 and 15: modern price allocation theory and practice.

Our dividing line between classical and modern is 1997, the average publication date of three highly influential papers. Relating to Part I: Artzner *et al.* (1997) introduced coherent risk measures and revolutionized thinking about measuring risk. Relating to Part II: Wang (1996) introduced the premium density and developed the theory of pricing by layer. And, relating to Part III: Phillips, Cummins, and Allen (1998) rigorously derived financial prices in a multiline company accounting for default. The classical versus modern bifurcation serves a convenient organizational purpose but should not be taken too seriously.

Classical pricing is predominantly actuarial and risk theoretic. A stability requirement, often linked to the probability of eventual ruin, determines required assets. There is no direct consideration of the cost of capital. On the other hand, modern approaches combine risk theory with financial and mathematical economics and decision science. They relate risk to the investors' return and the cost of capital and pay attention to uncertainty and risk under pooling. They leverage powerful mathematics to understand intuitively reasonable risk measures.

1.4 What's in It for the Practitioner?

This book is intended to be a practitioner-friendly reference as well as providing a theoretical framework. Our methods must have a firm theoretical foundation to justify their real world application. Many topics are inherently technical and require a mathematical background to understand fully. At the same time, the methods we describe can and should be implemented in practice. We have structured the book so readers eager to get their hands dirty can do that more easily. Throughout Parts II and III, we alternate theoretical and practical chapters. The Practice chapters present a range of simple numerical examples and apply all the methods we propose to three realistic Case Studies.

We also pay more attention to institutional arrangements—the way things get done—than the typical theoretical presentation. Different forms of capital, capital compared to equity, accounting, and the mechanism of default, especially equal priority, all play essential roles. Furthermore, we address certain standard practices in the industry and subsume them within our analytical framework so the reader can better appreciate their properties and behavior.

Over the years we have found that putting these tools and techniques into practice raises the following questions.

Which risk measure should I use? A common followup question asks if the risk measure should be sensitive to the tail of the distribution or volatility in the body, which translates into a concern about solvency vs. quarterly earnings. As always in modeling, the measure must be appropriate to the intended purpose. Our framework separates the amount of capital from its cost: the capital risk measure is necessarily tail focused, whereas the pricing risk measure captures investor return expectations. Additionally, the connection between capital *structure* and the *pricing* risk measure is a fundamental insight.

How do I reconcile and manage different economic and regulatory views of risk? Often followed by, "Who cares? We manage to [Rating Agency's] capital model". We agree: you don't care. The rating agency model is a binding constraint on the *amount* of capital for many insurers. You control the form and influence the *cost* of capital. Again, two risk measures. It isn't a question of reconciliation; it is a question of understanding each measure's distinct purposes.

Should pricing target a return on all capital, or can there be *excess capital*? Genuinely excess capital is exceptionally rare. Our model produces a cost of capital specific to each company, which varies with the amount of capital. A better capitalized company has a lower percentage cost of capital, other things being equal, because higher layer capital is less stressed and exposed to risk. As a result, the problem of applying a uniformly high cost of capital, producing uneconomic premiums, should not occur. The *frictional costs* of capital are, however, constant for all layers of capital. Indeed, they could be increasing if the management of overcapitalized companies has an incentive to engage in frivolous, self-aggrandizing activities.

How do I determine the cost of capital? Does it vary by unit? The risk cost of capital is the weighted average cost over the actual capital used. Debt and reinsurance have known costs. The cost of equity capital is normally estimated using a peer study. The cost of capital varies by unit according to which capital layers each unit consumes. The frictional cost of capital typically does not vary by unit.

Can risk margins ever be negative? Classical and modern approaches to pricing are unanimous that the risk margin must be positive for the portfolio. However, negative margins are appropriate for some units within the portfolio. They occur for units that are hedges, with losses arising more in situations where the portfolio has lower losses and less when the portfolio has more significant losses. The common practice of paying a positive margin for ceded reinsurance proves the point: the outward cash flow (premium) is greater in expectation than the inward cash flow (recovery). Looking at expectations makes reinsurance seem inappropriate, but the key to the value of reinsurance (or any hedge) is *when* those cash flows occur.

How do I use a risk measure to determine reservation prices? Chapter 10 and Chapter 14 show how pricing and capital risk measures combine to determine premiums. Chapter 20 offers some more advanced considerations.

The reader will recognize a gap between our simplified models of insurance operations and the complexity of the real world. The practitioner who has mastered Parts I, II, and III and is starting to think seriously about implementing risk measures will likely come up with numerous "What about...?" questions. The following more advanced questions commonly arise for insurers with functioning and integrated risk pricing systems. They are addressed in Part IV.

How do I handle asset risk? How do I incorporate risky assets in the model? How much capital does asset risk consume? Should I treat asset risk in a fundamentally different way from insurance risk? We conclude that an additional degree of freedom emerges, but not to any good use. Section 8.8 discusses the impact of asset risk on pricing and the market value of equity in an option pricing model. Chapter 16 shows that investing in a risky asset typically *lowers* the fair price (and quality) of insurance being sold.

How do I price for reserve risk? I write business that takes years to settle. It is unrealistic to assume all losses are paid in one year. How do I incorporate reserves into the model? Reserve volatility consumes underwriting capacity. However, our model shows that the allocated margins are small when reserves arc stable. In a sense, reserves can provide ballast for the prospective portfolio. IFRS and other accounting conventions have begun to require a risk margin for reserves for better earnings recognition. We discuss the Solvency II Cost of Capital Risk Margin and a real option approach to reserves in Chapter 17.

How do I manage a going concern? I don't manage for just one year and then dissolve the business; I manage a going concern with brand recognition and franchise value. How does that change the model? Chapter 18 outlines the theory of *optimal dividends* and a simple model of franchise value.

How can I optimize ceded reinsurance purchases? I can see how assumed reinsurance can be treated as selling another line of business, but how do I think about ceded reinsurance?

More specifically, how should I go about optimizing it? Chapter 19 discusses how to evaluate and optimize a ceded reinsurance program.

How can I optimize my insurance portfolio? I used to think about optimizing my capital usage against capital constraints. Now I think I should be optimizing my cost of capital, but that doesn't seem to be what you are recommending. Is there a disconnect here? Chapter 20 explores the complex interaction of cost allocation, benefit allocation, and premium regulation. It uncovers some unavoidable market distortions.

1.5 Where to Start

If you have read this far, you likely have a pricing problem. It may be embedded in a broader effort—business unit assessment or portfolio optimization or strategic planning—but it comes down to a pricing problem at its core. At a high level, our recommendations sound simple:

1. Establish your asset requirement.
2. Establish your portfolio cost of capital.
3. Select and calibrate a consistent spectral risk measure.
4. Use what we call the natural allocation to allocate the margin to each unit.

These recommendations presume a lot of work has already been done: gathering and organizing relevant data, developing a mathematical model or numerical tabulation (simulated sample) of the portfolio risks, establishing loss cost estimates for the units, etc. As we said, pricing is the last mile.

The asset requirement should be easy to determine since an external authority usually promulgates it. However, it may require some work to compute, using a standard (e.g., regulatory) capital risk measure. If you find no obvious binding capital constraint, remember that *management's* risk tolerance is irrelevant; only the *owner's* risk tolerance matters. Try to divine it. This step can be incredibly challenging for mutual companies. If you are engaged in an optimization project, then a capital risk measure is necessary because you will have to what-if the capital requirement. If the problem involves the current portfolio only, say a business unit profitability assessment or reinsurance purchase decision, you need only calculate current required assets.

The portfolio cost of capital may similarly be handed down from on high. It can be expressed as a rate of return or a monetary margin amount; these are interchangeable representations. In the unlikely case you get to set your portfolio profitability target, you need to examine your firm's balance sheet—fortunately, this is required in the next task.

Selecting and calibrating a pricing risk measure—specifically a spectral risk measure—is the biggest challenge. We have evolved away from our early fondness for particular parametric SRMs (especially the ones we invented). We now recommend using bespoke nonparametric or semiparametric distortion functions to more closely mirror actual funding costs. It may be that you are not modeling the entire firm's portfolio but only a part of it.

If you do not have access to the whole company risk profile, fear not. You should treat the task as if the parent company is the investor and the portfolio is the company—even though this is a case of suboptimizing. The point here is that the SRM gives *shape* to how the overall required margin is distributed across layers of assets at risk. More specific advice on selecting a distortion function is given in Section 11.5.

With these inputs in hand, allocating margin via the natural allocation is almost a trivial numerical exercise.

Of course, we hope you will read the whole book eventually, but we are not so naïve as to assume you have the time to sit down and read it cover to cover. It takes a lot more to explain and understand *why* than *how*. Why spectral risk measures make sense and do not violate the received wisdom of finance theory, and why the natural allocation is justified in being treated as canonical and not merely one of many equally acceptable alternatives—these issues take many more pages than explaining the mechanics of computation. We hope you will appreciate the why and read the whole book. But if you want to jump ahead to a quick grasp of the how, we recommend the following. Make sure to do enough of the exercises as you go along to feel secure that you "get it."

- Read about the insurance market and Ins Co., our model company, in Chapter 2.
- Review the introductory material on risk measures in Chapter 3. This should be material you already know. But do pay special attention to the Lee diagram in Section 3.5.
- Some of the material on VaR and TVaR in Chapter 4 may be new to you, so make sure you are comfortable with the basics.
- Section 5.1 lays out the big picture of how Ins Co. approaches the task of analyzing its capital and pricing needs.
- Read the practical applications in Chapter 6 and Guide to the Practice Chapters, Chapter 7.
- Read about classical risk theory in Section 8.4 and the DCF model in Section 8.7. This will help tie the later material back to material you likely have already seen.
- See how classical premium calculation principles work out on our case studies in Section 9.1.
- Read the sections in Chapter 10, Modern Portfolio Pricing Theory, down through Section 10.8. This is core theory about SRMs.
- Read and work examples in Chapter 11, Modern Portfolio Pricing Practice, down through Selecting a Distortion in Section 11.5. Read this last section twice and bookmark it for the day you need to select a distortion for your own purposes.
- Browse Classical Price Allocation Theory, Chapter 12, down through Loss Payments in Default, Section 12.3. This is material that should be more or less familiar to actuaries.
- See how classical price allocation works out on our Case Studies in Chapter 13.
- Read the first two sections in Chapter 14, Modern Price Allocation Theory. This covers the natural allocation of a coherent risk measure, properties and characterization of allocations, computational algorithms, and comments on selecting an allocation. This is the core theory about allocating SRMs. If you are looking for ways to visualize multidimensional risk, read Section 14.3, especially Section 14.3.7, as well.

- Read Modern Price Allocation Practice, Chapter 15. This is essential “how-to” material.
- If reserves feature prominently in your project, you may want to read Chapter 17 in Part IV. This also covers the Solvency II risk margin in Section 17.3.
- If reinsurance purchasing features prominently in your project, you may want to read Chapter 19.
- If you are working with portfolio optimization, you may want to read Chapter 20.

2

The Insurance Market and Our Case Studies

In this chapter, we outline the operation of the insurance market as we model it and describe the hypothetical Ins Co. used in our examples. We then introduce a Simple Discrete Example and three more realistic Case Studies which are used throughout the book to illustrate the methods presented in the theory chapters.

2.1 The Insurance Market

Insurers are **one period, limited liability** entities with no existing liabilities. We consider multi-period insurers in Part IV only. The insurer is called **Ins Co.** It sells insurance **policies** to **insureds** or **policyholders**. Policyholder and insured are treated as synonyms, and both include **claimants**. Ins Co.'s **portfolio** is the collection of policies it writes. The length of the period is usually one year. Its length is relevant only because of the time value of money, since interest is a rate per year.

Policyholder liabilities are any amounts Ins Co. owes to policyholders. The two biggest are loss reserves and unearned premium reserves. We incorporate reserves in Part IV only. In property-casualty insurance, loss reserves cover claims that have been incurred but not paid, whether reported or not. In life insurance, liabilities include policy values for long duration contracts.

Assets are the total financial resources owned by Ins Co. that it can use to meet its policyholder liabilities. A regulator usually stipulates **required assets**, a minimum amount of assets that Ins Co. must hold; see Section 1.2.

Ins Co., like all firms, finances its assets by issuing **liabilities**. It sells policies, creating policyholder liabilities, in exchange for premiums, and it raises capital from **investors** by selling them its residual value (equity) or other promises (debt, reinsurance).

Investors can be shareholders when Ins Co. is a stock company or insureds when it is a mutual company or debt holders or reinsurers.

Insurers are **intermediaries** between insureds and investors. Intermediary always means an insurance company intermediary, and never an agent or broker.

Pricing Insurance Risk: Theory and Practice, First Edition. Stephen J. Mildenhall and John A. Major.

Portfolio components are referred to as **units**. A unit can be a single policy or a group of policies or be defined by line, geography, branch, business unit, or other characteristics. Unit can also represent the segmentation between reinsurance ceded losses and retained losses.

Ins Co.'s **aggregate loss** is the sum of losses from its portfolio over one period.

Ins Co.'s operations are controlled by eight variables: **(expected) loss**, **premium**, **assets**, **margin**, **capital**, **loss ratio**, **cost of capital**, and **leverage**. The first five are monetary quantities, and the last three are unitless ratios. They obey five relationships:

1. premium equals loss plus margin,
2. assets equal premium plus capital, which we call the **asset funding constraint**,
3. loss ratio equals loss divided by premium,
4. cost of capital equals margin divided by capital, and
5. asset leverage equals assets divided by premium.

Figure 2.1 lays out these variables and relationships. Monetary quantities are the vertices, the bold diagonal lines correspond to the ratios, and the two shaded triangles signify the asset and premium sum conditions.

Premium is the amount charged for providing insurance. Premium is net of (i.e., excludes) underwriting expenses but includes an allowance for risk called the **margin**. Profit, profit load, profit margin, risk margin, and risk load are all synonyms for margin.

Premium is the critical variable; it is the foundation of the schematic. It is the bridge between investor cash flows on the left and insurance cash flows on the right. At the expected outcome, premium is shared, with margin flowing to investors and expected loss to the insured.

Policyholders are liable for their expected loss—as Adam Smith pointed out in 1789; by "common loss" he means expected loss. Financing the remaining assets is the **shared liability** of policyholders and investors. The shared liability equals assets minus expected loss, or equivalently capital plus expected margin. **Pricing apportions the shared liability to policyholders and investors.**

The **loss ratio** is the ratio of loss to premium. Because premiums exclude expenses, a 90% loss ratio includes a healthy margin. The premium **markup** is the inverse expected loss ratio,

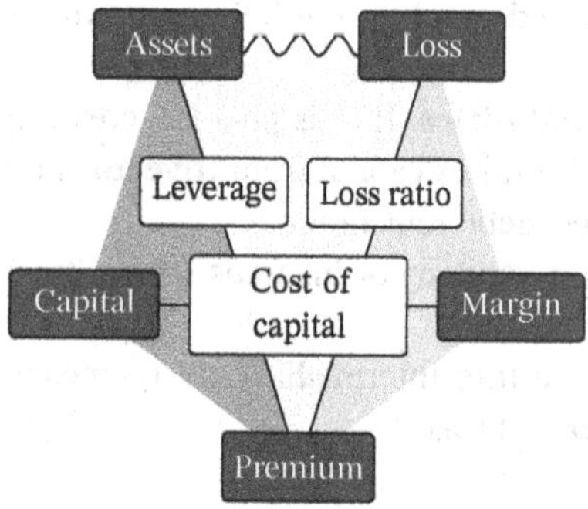

Figure 2.1 The eight variables that control insurance operations and five relationships between them.

the ratio of premium to expected loss. Catastrophe bond pricing often quotes markups rather than loss ratios. **Premium leverage** refers to the ratio of premium to capital.

The margin is distinct from the **contingency provision**, which the Actuarial Standards Board (2011) defines as a correction for persistent biases in ratemaking. It says the "contingency provision is not intended to measure the variability of results and, as such, is not expected to be earned as profit."

A **catastrophe** or **catastrophe event** refers to an single event causing loss to multiple units, such as a hurricane, typhoon, earthquake, winter storm, terrorist attack, or pandemic. A **catastrophe loss** is the total loss across all units from a catastrophe event. A **catastrophe unit** means a unit prone to catastrophe losses. A **catastrophe risk** is a peril likely to result in catastrophe losses. Catastrophe risks tend to attract large margins, making them particularly interesting.

At various points we mention **catastrophe models**. These are computer simulation tools used to estimate potential catastrophe losses from an insurance portfolio. Mitchell-Wallace *et al.* (2017) provides helpful background about the operation and use of catastrophe models.

Losses in a **thick-tailed** unit have a high coefficient of variation, are right-skewed and leptokurtic (high kurtosis), and have a significant probability of assuming a very substantial value. Catastrophe losses are usually thick-tailed.

A **long-tailed** unit has a slow payout pattern, meaning claims are not settled until many years after they occur.

Reinsurance is a type of insurance, so we say insurance to cover both, and reinsurance if that is all we mean. Cedents cede business to reinsurers.

The accounting distinction between capital and equity causes unnecessary confusion.

Capital refers to funds intended to assure the payment of obligations from insurance contracts, over and above reserves for policyholder liabilities. Capital is also referred to as **net assets**. The book value of capital depends on accounting conventions. Capital is usually regulated by statute. **Surplus** is a synonym for capital used in US statutory accounts.

Equity is the value of the owner's residual interest. In a stock company, it is called shareholder's equity. Accounting equity is typically lower than capital since debt can be included in capital but not equity. Equity also has a market value for public stock companies, based on the value of shares outstanding. Equity levels are not regulated. Accounting equity can be negative. The market value of equity is always non-negative because of limited liability.

2.2 Ins Co.: A One-Period Insurer

In this section, we introduce the hypothetical insurer called **Ins Co.**, that we use as the base for our theory and examples. Ins Co. is a limited liability company that intermediates between insureds and investors.

Ins Co.'s customers are **insureds** who are subject to risks they wish to insure, for the three reasons explained in Section 8.1.1. Insureds who use insurance for risk transfer or financing are sensitive to insurer quality and possible default because it correlates with their own misfortune (Merton and Perold 1993; Froot 2007).

Ins Co. is owned by **investors** who provide risk bearing capital. The investor group overlaps with the insured group in a mutual insurer. Investors may be risk averse. They often have limited capacity to evaluate insurance risk, giving insurers a competitive advantage in risk assessment and pricing (Froot and O'Connell 2008).

Ins Co. exists for **one period**. It comes into existence at time $t = 0$ and lasts for one period. Ins Co. has no initial liabilities. At $t = 0$ it writes one or more single-period insurance contracts and collects premiums from its insureds. At the same time, it raises capital from investors by selling them all or part of its uncertain $t = 1$ residual value. Ins Co.'s liabilities can be structured as a combination of equity, debt, or reinsurance.

When Ins Co. writes a policy, it collects premium at $t = 0$ and earns it over the period. We assume all other transactions occur at the end of the period. Therefore all the premium is earned and available to pay claims at $t = 1$. There is no need to consider an unearned premium reserve because there are no intermediate cash flows or solvency tests between $t = 0$ and $t = 1$.

At time $t = 1$, Ins Co. pays any claims due and gives any residual value to its investors. If Ins Co.'s assets are insufficient to pay the claims, then it defaults. Investors have **limited liability**: they lose their original investment but owe nothing more.

The length of the policy period is relevant because it determines the investors' cost to fund the insurer. At $t = 0$ the investors must pay-in the capital, i.e., cause cash to be transferred into a separate legal entity. They may incur a time-based funding cost. Since funding costs are expressed per year, it is usual to use a one-year time period.

Premiums cover expected losses and loss adjustment expenses, the cost of capital, and frictional capital costs. All other expenses are outside the model. The epigraph to Chapter 1 shows that Adam Smith was already aware of the cost of capital for insurers in 1789, and wrote about it in a surprisingly modern manner.

Table 2.1 summarizes the aggregate cash flows between Ins Co., investors, and policyholders. At $t = 0$ all amounts are fixed. At $t = 1$ the random loss outcome X is revealed. The model can include stochastic asset returns.

In an unregulated insurance market, insured relative risk aversion interacts with investor opportunity costs of capital to determine the amount of assets supporting the risk and the split of those assets into premium and capital. In a regulated market, the amount of assets is determined, or at least heavily influenced by a regulator (or quasi-regulatory rating agency), but the market still determines the *split* of funding between premium and equity.

2.3 Model vs. Reality

The reader should bear in mind:

- Man plans, and God laughs (old Yiddish saying)
- Anything that can go wrong, will go wrong (Edward Murphy)

- The map is not the territory (Alfred Korzybski)
- All models are wrong but some are useful (George E.P. Box)

All the analysis presented in this book presumes we know the objective probability distribution underlying the phenomenon being studied. Cue laughter. This conceit is particularly pernicious when coupled with management optimism and its attempts at optimization.

To make the results *useful*, sensitivity analysis must be part of the effort. Perturb the assumptions in a realistic manner and repeat the risk measure calibration, capital calculation, margin allocation, etc. Then do it again. Coherent risk measures are all about taking the worst case among a set of alternatives. The alternatives reflect our uncertainty about event probabilities by positing different values. Lift this strategy to the entire engagement. Generate a set of assumptions and look across the set of answers. Only then will you know whether the best estimate is robust or fragile. With that caveat, we proceed, assuming that we have a tin opener as the joke about economists has it.

2.4 Examples and Case Studies

In this section we introduce a Simple Discrete Example and three more realistic Case Studies. These are used throughout the book to illustrate the various methods presented in the theory chapters.

We include simple examples to familiarize practitioners with the computations required to implement the methods we cover. The Cases aim to help practitioners develop an intuition for how each method prices business, informing their selection of an appropriate method for an intended purpose without resorting to trial and error.

The Cases share several common characteristics.

- Each includes two units, one lower risk and one higher.
- Reinsurance is applied to the riskier unit.

Table 2.1 Investor and insured transactions with Ins Co. at $t = 0{,}1$. In the last row $X \wedge a' = \min(X, a')$.

View	Total		Loss		Margin		Capital
At issue, $t = 0$							
Insured	Premium	=	Expected loss cost	+	Margin		
Investor	Capital	=					Capital
Ins Co. Total	Assets	=	Expected loss cost	+	Margin	+	Capital
expected	a	=	$\mathsf{E}[X]$	+	M	+	Q
At expiration, $t = 1$							
Ins Co. Total	Assets	=	Loss outcome			+	Residual value
random	$a' = a(1+r)$	=	$X \wedge a'$			+	$(a' - X)^+$

- Total unlimited losses are calibrated to ¤100. (The symbol ¤ denotes a generic currency.)
- Losses are in ¤ millions, although the actual unit is irrelevant.

For each Case Study:

- Figures 2.2, 2.4, and 2.6 show densities. The horizontal axis shows loss amount. In each figure the top row shows gross losses and the bottom row shows net. The left column uses a linear scale and the right a log scale.
- Figures 2.3, 2.5, and 2.7 show bivariate plots of one unit against the other. The three plots show the gross and net logdensities, and the right plot shows a scatter plot of a sample. The two units are assumed independent. These plots show where the bivariate distribution is concentrated.

We strongly recommend that the reader reproduce the Examples and Cases. We suggest a general-purpose programming language such as R or Python, although SQL or even a spreadsheet suffices, with a bit of ingenuity. See Section 2.4.5 for a discussion of the implementation we used.

2.4.1 The Simple Discrete Example

Ins Co. writes two units taking on loss values $X_1 = 0, 8$, or 10, and $X_2 = 0, 1$, or 90. The units are independent and sum to the portfolio loss $X = X_1 + X_2$. The outcome probabilities are $1/2, 1/4$, and $1/4$, respectively, for each marginal. The nine possible outcomes, with associated probabilities, are presented in Table 2.2. The output is typical of that produced by a catastrophe, capital, or pricing simulation model—albeit much simpler.

Exercise 1. Recreate Table 2.2 in a spreadsheet (or R or Python). Compute and plot the distribution and survival functions, $\Pr(X \le x)$ and $\Pr(X > x)$ for X.
Solution. Since the data is discrete, the answers are step functions. The survival function is

$$S(x) = \begin{cases} 0.75 & 0 \le x < 1 \\ 0.625 & 1 \le x < 8 \\ 0.5 & 8 \le x < 9 \\ 0.4375 & 9 \le x < 10 \\ 0.3125 & 10 \le x < 11 \\ 0.25 & 11 \le x < 90 \\ 0.125 & 90 \le x < 98 \\ 0.0625 & 98 \le x < 100 \\ 0 & 100 \le x. \end{cases} \tag{2.1}$$

□

Table 2.2 Simple Discrete Example with nine possible outcomes.

X_1	X_2	X	P(X_1)	P(X_2)	P(X)
0	0	0	1/2	1/2	1/4
0	1	1	1/2	1/4	1/8
0	90	90	1/2	1/4	1/8
8	0	8	1/4	1/2	1/8
8	1	9	1/4	1/4	1/16
8	90	98	1/4	1/4	1/16
10	0	10	1/4	1/2	1/8
10	1	11	1/4	1/4	1/16
10	90	100	1/4	1/4	1/16

Table 2.3 Discrete Example estimated mean, CV, skewness and kurtosis by line and in total, gross and net. Aggregate reinsurance applied to X_2 with an attachment probability 0.25 (¤20) and detachment probability 0.0 (¤100).

	Gross			Net		
Statistic	X_1	X_2	**Total**	X_1	X_2	**Total**
Mean	4.500	22.750	27.250	4.500	5.250	9.750
CV	1.012	1.707	1.435	1.012	1.624	0.991
Skewness	0.071	1.154	1.131	0.071	1.147	0.794
Kurtosis	−1.905	−0.667	−0.649	−1.905	−0.673	−0.501

Loss statistics are shown in Table 2.3. The table includes the impact of aggregate reinsurance on the more volatile unit X_2 limiting losses to 20 and show a gross and net view for some exhibits. Others are left as Practice questions.

2.4.2 Tame Case Study

In the Tame Case Study, Ins Co. writes two predictable units with no catastrophe exposure. We include it to demonstrate an idealized risk-pool: it represents the best case—from Ins Co.'s perspective. It could proxy a portfolio of personal and commercial auto liability.

To simplify simulations and emphasize the underlying differences between the two units, the Case Study uses a straightforward stochastic model. The two units are independent and have gamma loss distributions with parameters shown in Table 2.4.

The Case includes a gross and net view. Net applies aggregate reinsurance to the more volatile unit B with an attachment probability 0.2 (¤56) and detachment probability 0.01 (¤69).

Table 2.4 Loss distribution assumptions for each Case Study. The Hu/SCS Case combines a Poisson frequency and lognormal severity.

Case	Unit	Distribution	Mean	CV	Frequency	μ	σ
Tame	A	Gamma	50	0.10			
	B	Gamma	50	0.15			
Cat/Non-Cat	Non-Cat	Gamma	80	0.15			
	Cat	Lognormal	20	1.0		2.649	0.833
Hu/SCS	Hu	Aggregate	30	10.923	2	−0.417	2.5
	SCS	Aggregate	70	0.736	70	1.805	1.9

Table 2.5 Tame Case Study estimated mean, CV, skewness and kurtosis by line and in total, gross and net. Aggregate reinsurance applied to B with an attachment probability 0.2 (¤56) and detachment probability 0.01 (¤69).

	Gross			Net		
Statistic	**A**	**B**	**Total**	**A**	**B**	**Total**
Mean	50.000	50.000	100.000	50.000	49.084	99.084
CV	0.100	0.150	0.090	0.100	0.123	0.079
Skewness	0.200	0.300	0.207	0.200	−0.484	−0.169
Kurtosis	0.060	0.135	0.070	0.060	−0.474	−0.157

Table 2.6 Cat/Non-Cat Case Study estimated mean, CV, skewness, and kurtosis by line and in total, gross, and net. Aggregate reinsurance applied to Cat with an attachment probability 0.1 (¤41) and detachment probability 0.005 (¤121).

	Gross			Net		
Statistic	**Cat**	**Non-Cat**	**Total**	**Cat**	**Non-Cat**	**Total**
Mean	20.000	80.000	100.000	17.786	80.000	97.786
CV	1.000	0.150	0.233	0.737	0.150	0.182
Skewness	3.972	0.300	2.539	3.139	0.300	1.351
Kurtosis	35.933	0.135	19.173	55.220	0.135	16.336

Loss statistics based on a Fast Fourier Transform (FFT) approximation (see Section 2.4.5) are shown in Table 2.5. The FFT approximation is essentially exact and it is used for all graphics and illustrations. Simulation can also be used. Table 4.6 shows various VaR, TVaR, and EPD levels. See the important comment in Section 2.4.5 regarding computational methods.

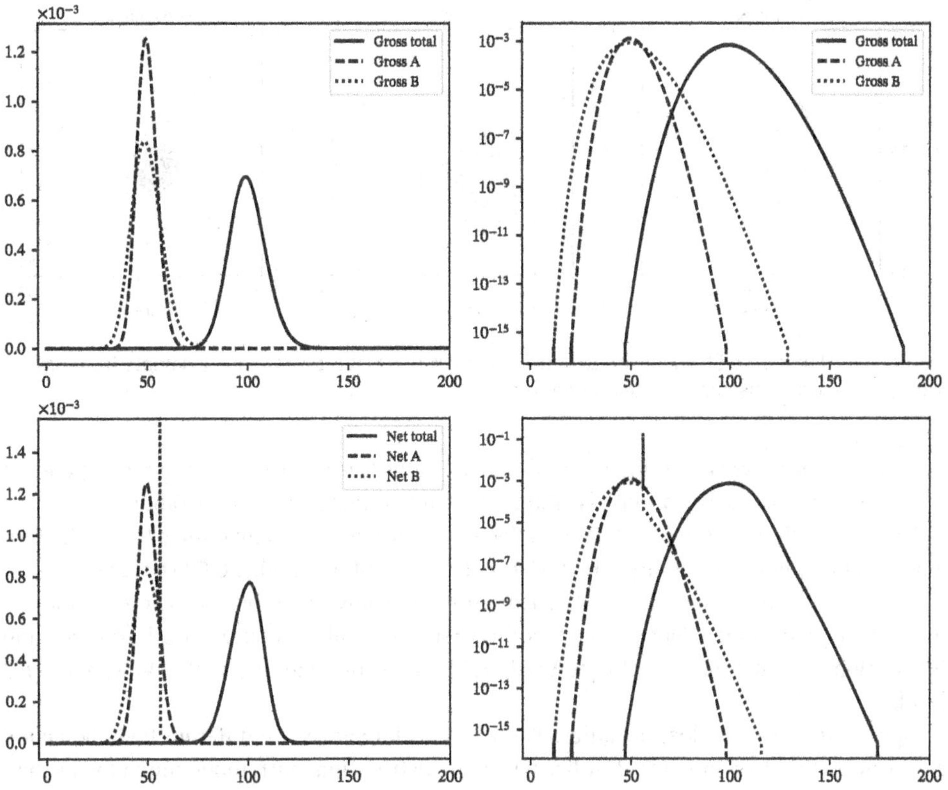

Figure 2.2 Tame Case Study, gross (top) and net (bottom) densities on a nominal (left) and log (right) scale.

Figure 2.2 shows the loss densities. The spike in the lower left plot is caused by the reinsured unit B hitting its limit, which produces a probability mass. Its magnitude is clear on the lower right, log scale, plot. The tail behavior of the two units is similar. Both have log concave gross densities. Figure 2.3 shows the bivariate plots. The outcomes are tightly clustered about their expected values.

2.4.3 Catastrophe and Non-Catastrophe Case Study

In the Cat/Non-Cat Case Study, Ins Co. has catastrophe and noncatastrophe exposures. The noncatastrophe unit proxies a small commercial lines portfolio. Balancing the relative benefits of units considered to be more stable against more volatile ones is a very common strategic problem for insurers and reinsurers. It arises in many different guises:

- Should a US Midwestern company expand to the East coast (and pick up hurricane exposure)?
- Should an auto insurer start writing homeowners?
- What is the appropriate mix between property catastrophe and noncatastrophe exposed business for a reinsurer?

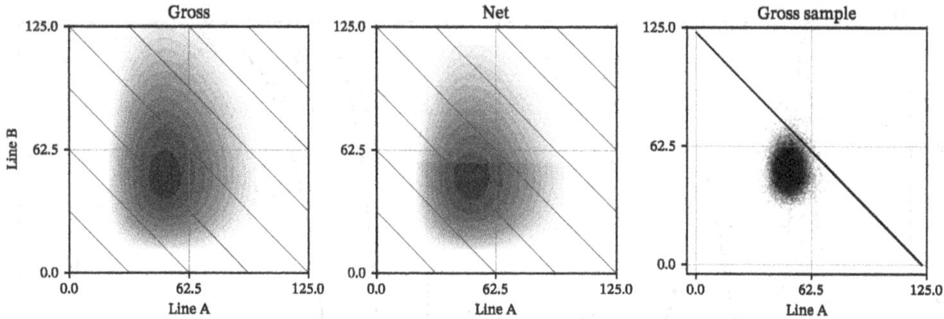

Figure 2.3 Tame Case Study, bivariate densities: gross (left), net (center), and a sample from gross (right). Impact of reinsurance is clear in net plot.

This Case uses a stochastic model similar to the Tame Case. The two units are independent and have gamma and lognormal distributions with parameters shown in Table 2.4.

The Case includes a gross and net view. Net applies aggregate reinsurance to the Cat unit with an attachment probability 0.1 (¤41) and detachment probability 0.005 (¤121).

Loss statistics based on an FFT approximation are shown in Table 2.6. The FFT approximation is good, though not as exact as the first case, and it is used for all graphics and illustrations. Simulation can also be used. Table 4.7 shows various VaR, TVaR, and EPD levels.

Figure 2.4 shows the loss densities. The top left plot shows the different body behavior. Non-Cat is close to symmetric. Cat has a peaked distribution, with mode much lower than mean. The spike in the net plots is caused by claims generating a limit loss to the reinsurance on Cat. The different tail behavior of the two units is evident, especially on a log scale. noncat has a log concave density whereas Cat is eventually log convex. The impact of reinsurance is clear. It introduces a point mass at the aggregate attachment for Cat. The total distribution is still continuous. Figure 2.5 shows the bivariate plots. The left plot emphasizes the different tail behavior; Non-Cat remains localized close to its mean while Cat decays very slowly (vertically).

Table 2.7 Hu/SCS Case Study estimated mean, CV, skewness, and kurtosis by line and in total, gross, and net. Per occurrence reinsurance applied to Hu with an attachment probability 0.05 (¤40) and detachment probability 0.005 (¤413).

	Gross			Net		
Statistic	**Hu**	**SCS**	**Total**	**Hu**	**SCS**	**Total**
Mean	29.727	69.133	98.860	18.987	69.133	88.121
CV	10.923	0.736	3.324	16.246	0.736	3.548
Skewness	121	24.900	116	137	24.900	132
Kurtosis	27	9	26	32	9	31

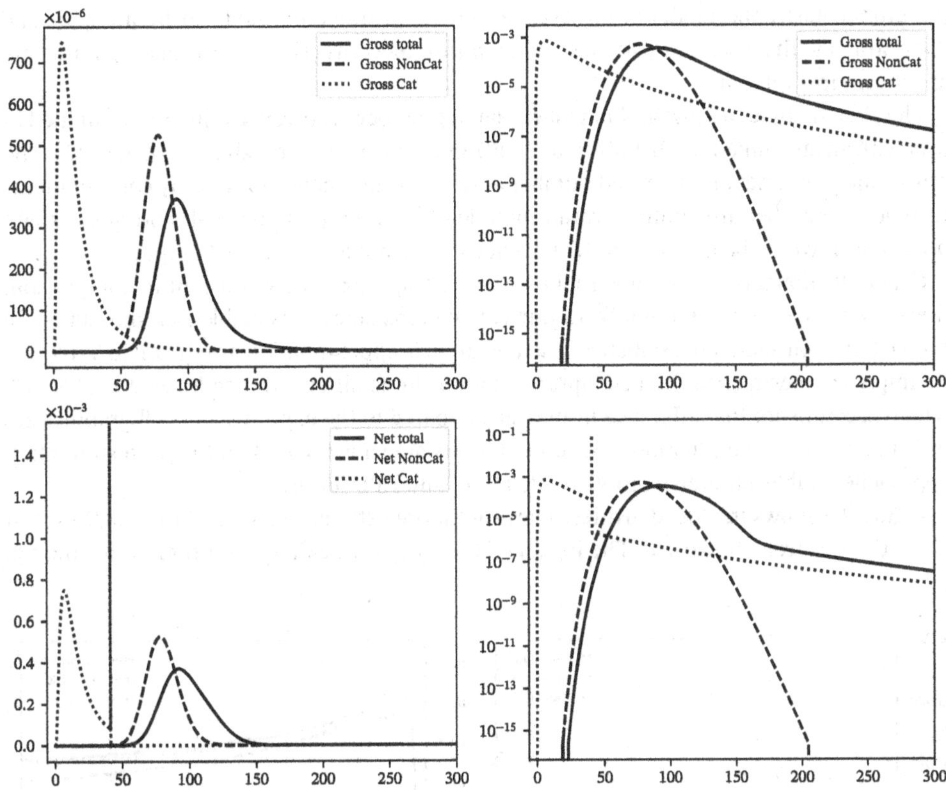

Figure 2.4 Cat/Non-Cat Case Study, gross (top) and net (bottom) densities on a nominal (left) and log (right) scale.

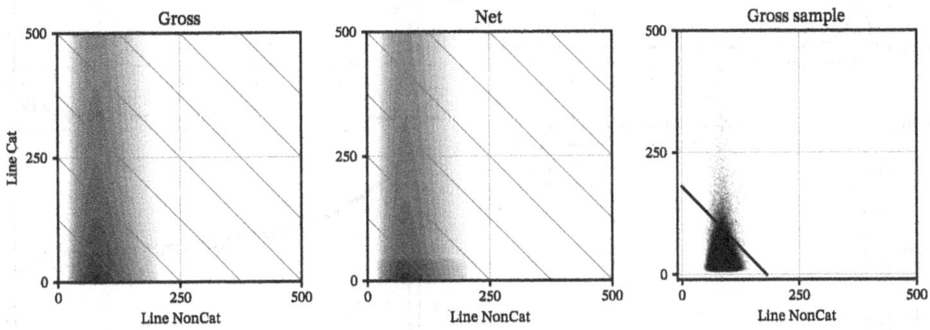

Figure 2.5 Cat/Non-Cat Case Study, bivariate densities: gross (left), net (center), and a sample from gross (right). Impact of reinsurance is clear in net plot.

2.4.4 Hurricane and Severe Storm Case Study

In the Hu/SCS Case Study, Ins Co. has catastrophe exposures from severe convective storms (SCS) and, independently, hurricanes (Hu). In practice, hurricane exposure is modeled using a catastrophe model. We proxy that using a very severe lognormal distribution in place of the gross catastrophe model event-level output. Both units are modeled by an aggregate distribution with a Poisson frequency and lognormal severity. The key stochastic parameters are shown in Table 2.4.

The Case includes a gross and net view. Net applies per occurrence reinsurance to the Hu unit with an attachment probability 0.05 (¤40) and detachment probability 0.005 (¤413). The reinsurance assumes an unlimited number of free reinstatements, to simplify computations. In practice, the net distribution would include inuring property per risk and quota share programs. It would be taken from the net catastrophe model event-level output.

Other attritional (i.e., noncatastrophe) losses are approximately constant in comparison, therefore we can exclude them from our calculations since reasonable risk measures are translation-invariant,. Loss statistics based on an FFT approximation are shown in Table 2.7. To improve convergence the FFT approximation limits all occurrence losses to 1.2×10^9, which accounts for the difference in means compared to the expected 100. All graphics are based on the FFT computation, but computations are shown based on FFT and simulation approaches. Table 4.8 shows various VaR, TVaR, and EPD levels.

Figure 2.6 shows the loss densities. These are more extreme versions of the Cat/Non-Cat Case. Cat is extremely skewed. The lognormal severity is thick-tailed for both units, though

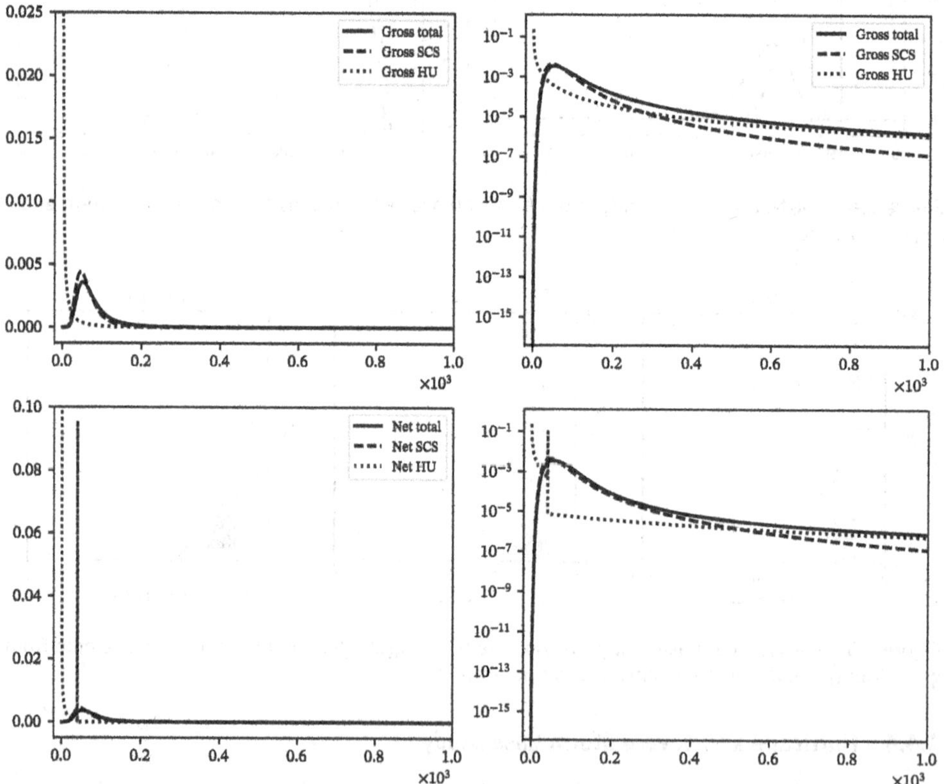

Figure 2.6 Hu/SCS Case Study, gross (top) and net (bottom) densities on a nominal (left) and log (right) scale.

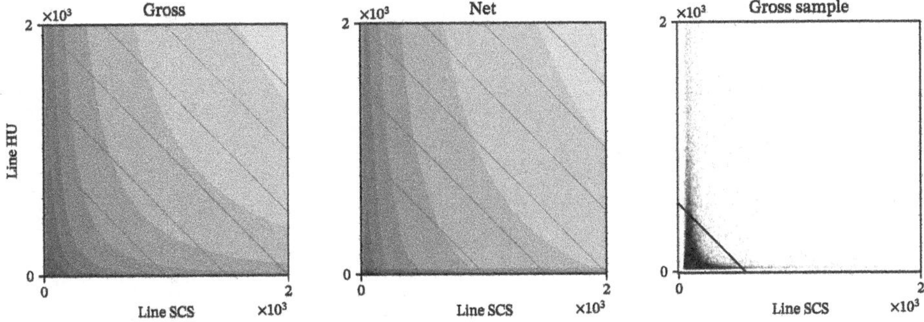

Figure 2.7 Hu/SCS Case Study, bivariate densities: gross (left), net (center), and a sample from gross (right). Impact of reinsurance is clear in net plot.

Cat is thicker. Figure 2.7 shows the bivariate plots. The right-hand plot shows the pinched behavior typical of thick-tailed distributions. A large loss combined with a small loss is the most likely nontrivial outcome. The distribution is clustered around the axes.

2.4.5 Computational Methods

All of the computations we show were completed in Python, R, or a spreadsheet—and sometimes all three. **All of the simple discrete examples are easy to replicate in a spreadsheet.** There is no *conceptual* jump from the spreadsheet examples to the R and Python Case Studies, just an increase in the numerical complexity. Once you can implement in a spreadsheet, you understand well enough to program, or instruct a programmer to create, a production implementation.

We implemented the Case Studies using Fast Fourier Transforms (FFTs) because they are fast and precise. You do not have to worry about simulation errors or wait for simulations to complete. The FFT method is described in Wang (1998a) and Mildenhall (2005). FFT methods are extremely powerful but have a fatal flaw: they assume all marginal distributions are independent. For our examples, this flaw is irrelevant. Although the Case Studies assume independent marginals for convenience, **all of the methods and algorithms still apply when the marginals are not independent**. Its flaw makes FFTs unsuitable for most production applications, and we know that most readers do not use FFTs. Remember: you can implement the Case Studies in any programming language or simulation tool. Just be aware that your answers will vary from those we show due to simulation errors.

2.5 Learning Objectives

1. Describe the cash flows in a one-period Ins Co.
2. Implement the Discrete Example in a spreadsheet to replicate numerical computations.
3. Program the Case Studies and replicate the numerical computations.

2.5 Learning Objectives

Part I

Risk

3

Risk and Risk Measures

In this chapter, we define and classify risk. We explain different ways to use a random variable to represent a risky outcome. We introduce the Lee diagram and use it to represent expected loss, limited loss, and excess loss. We define a risk measure and explain how it codifies a risk preference. Finally, we characterize risk measures, discuss their applications in pricing and capital management, and consider their potential functional forms.

3.1 Risk in Everyday Life

Every day, we take action, sometimes without being sure of the outcome. Some actions result from decisions we make, while others are inescapable. Some uncertain outcomes are well-defined such as with a lottery ticket or card game, but most are ill-defined: What kind of career would I have with a bachelor's degree in statistics? What will my retirement be like with this amount of savings? Some are purely monetary, others related to health, family, politics, or world events. Bernstein (1996) summarizes how the modern world emerged, in part, because we developed better ways to understand and decide between actions with uncertain outcomes.

Our risk preferences have economically meaningful consequences. A decision depends on the riskiness of the outcome and the risk attitude of the decision maker (Diamond and Stiglitz 1973). When we act on our own behalf we are free to choose how to act; when we act as an agent we are required to act in a manner consistent with certain standards of behavior. There is substantial interest in decision theory: making consistent and considered choices between alternative courses of action with uncertain outcomes. Decision theory is a fundamental part of economics, finance, management, risk theory, and actuarial science.

Quantitative decision theory relies on numerical risk measures. A risk-based capital formula and an insurance pricing model are two examples of numerical risk measures. The definition, specification, and classification of risk measures is a central problem of actuarial science, with a long history (Borch 1962; Bühlmann 1970; Goovaerts, De Vylder, and Haezendonck 1984).

Pricing Insurance Risk: Theory and Practice, First Edition. Stephen J. Mildenhall and John A. Major.

3.2 Defining Risk

The International Organization for Standardization (ISO) Guide 73:2009 defines **risk** to be **the effect of uncertainty on objectives**, where an **effect** is a deviation from what is expected. Risk is caused by **events** which have **consequences**. The pivotal word in the definition is **uncertainty**, which ISO defines as "the state, even partial, of deficiency of information related to, understanding or knowledge of, an event, its consequence, or likelihood."

We use the ISO definition of risk. Insurers also use **the risk** to refer to the peril (earthquake, fire, flood, etc.) that may cause a loss and use **a risk** as a synonym for an account, case, insured, contract or policy, or for the subject of a policy.

There is a fundamental distinction between speculative risk and pure risk. A **pure risk** or **insurance risk** has a potential bad outcome but no good outcomes. It is a possible loss with no chance of gain. Insurance policies are designed to put the insured, at best, in the same position they would have been without a loss (in order to avoid morale hazard). A **speculative risk** or **asset risk** has both good and bad outcomes; it can be a loss or a gain. Reframing can convert a pure risk into a speculative one. The loss on an insurance policy is a pure risk. But the net position, premium less loss and expense, is a speculative risk.

An uncertain outcome that involves a choice is called a **prospect**. A prospect is relative to a reference point. The uncertainty in your bonus is relative to what you expect, not zero. Business is evaluated relative to plan, not insolvency. This can make the distinction between pure and speculative risks a matter of definition; an insurer can focus on the policy loss payments (pure risk) or on the net position of premium less losses (speculative risk). The existence of different reference points can also lead to framing bias problems, described in Kahneman (2011).

A prospect with outcomes denominated in a monetary unit is called a **financial risk**. An insurance loss, the future value of a stock or bond, and the present value of future lifetime earnings are examples of financial risks.

A financial risk can have **timing** uncertainty, **amount** uncertainty, or both. It can involve:

- Payment of a known amount at a random time, e.g. benefit payment on a whole or term life insurance policy.
- Payment of a random amount at a known time, e.g. payment on a pure endowment policy, which pays if the insured survives to a certain age or payment of a year-end employee bonus if the employer profit target is met.
- Payment of a random amount at a random future time, e.g. loss payment on a typical property-casualty insurance policy.

Insurance contracts can reduce timing or amount uncertainty, or both, for example by specifying payment dates or applying limits and deductibles to loss amounts. Accounting rules often require that reinsurance contracts transfer both timing and amount risk.

Risk is **time separable** if a measure of the magnitude of the risk of an amount at a future time can be expressed as the product of (1) the magnitude of the risk of the amount if immediately due, times (2) a discount factor. In this book we will assume risk is time separable. Under time separability a risk measure becomes a measure of amount risk. (Timing risk and discounting are discussed in Chapter 8.)

3.3 Taxonomies of Risk

In this section, we describe different ways to classify risk. Here, we are talking about classifying generic types of risk in the abstract, not about classifying insureds in the sense of rating class plans. It is generally not productive to dwell excessively on abstract risk classifications, but it is useful to be aware of them and to establish a common vocabulary.

The US Risk Based Capital framework for Property/Casualty insurers classifies risks into the following categories Obersteadt (2017):

- R0: Asset risk—subsidiary insurers
- R1: Asset risk—fixed income
- R2: Asset risk—equity
- R3: Credit risk
- R4: Underwriting risk—reserves
- R5: Underwriting risk—premium
- RCAT: Catastrophe risk (earthquake and hurricane).

The European Solvency II Standard Formula for the Solvency Capital Requirement classifies risks as:

- Underwriting risk, including premium, reserve, and catastrophe risk
- Default (counterparty) risk, including diversified and nondiversified counterparties
- Market risk, including interest rate, equity, real estate, spread, currency, concentration, and illiquidity risks
- Operational risk.

Some Enterprise Risk Management frameworks categorize risks as:

- Health and safety risks
- Reputational risks
- Operational risks
- Strategic risks
- Compliance risks
- Financial risks.

Insurance-focused ERM lists may add:

- Asset risk
- Credit risk

- Market risk
- Underwriting risk
- Reserving risk
- Catastrophe risk.

This book focuses on pure underwriting, reserving, and catastrophe risks. For property-casualty insurance, the others tend to be background risks that are hard to distinguish between units and therefore not relevant to pricing.

The next three sections categorize risk according to the following dimensions:

- Diversifiable (idiosyncratic) vs. systematic (including catastrophe)
- Systemic vs. nonsystemic
- Objective vs. subjective probability and uncertainty.

3.3.1 Diversifiable Risk

Insurance is based on **diversification**, where the risk of the sum is less than the sum of the risks. It is important to understand whether a risk is **diversifiable**, also known as **idiosyncratic**. Risks diversify when each unit is small relative to the total and their losses exhibit a material degree of independence from one another. A **diversification benefit** occurs when adding independent units to a portfolio increases its risk by much less than what the standalone risks represent. The central limit theorem ensures that pooling is an effective mechanism to manage diversifiable risk.

The opposite of diversifiable risk is **nondiversifiable**, also known as **systematic** risk. The failure to diversify usually means that there is a common underlying cause or other source of **dependence risk** to multiple unit losses, or there is a single unit heavily influencing the total loss. Catastrophes affecting multiple units simultaneously are an example of the former. A catastrophe line of business with outsize losses compared to the other lines is an example of the latter. The presence of systematic risk means there is less diversification benefit than in its absence.

Dependence risk between units can manifest itself in different ways, some more dangerous than others. It is easy to identify in a simulation context: where are you sharing variables? Variables resimulated in each iteration for each unit diversify, at least to some extent. Any variable whose value is shared between units introduces dependence and systematic risk. Weather and loss trend assumptions are examples of shared variables.

Remark 2. In finance, systematic risk usually refers to the common variation of stock prices over time whereas idiosyncratic risk refers to the deviation of individual stock prices from the common movement. By adding many stocks to a portfolio, idiosyncratic risk—but not systematic risk—can be diversified away. This leads to pricing principles where only systematic risk matters because the well-diversified investor can make idiosyncratic risk "go away."

In Section 12.4 we will see that this simplification does not apply to the problem of pricing insurance risk. □

Example 3. You live in a Dystopian Dictatorship and are a member of a group of 100 prisoners. Evil Leader decides to execute 1% of the prisoners. EL considers two approaches. Execute each prisoner with a 1% probability or with 1% probability execute all prisoners. The number of deaths is diversifiable in the former approach and nondiversifiable in the latter. The expected number of executions is the same for each approach. □

Remark 4. The discounting impact of timing remains even when amount risk diversifies. Timing risk tends to be quite tame since payout patterns follow a predictable claim settlement process, regulated by the cadences of medicine and law. The historical development of insurance pricing reflects this distinction: in many cases amount risk is largely irrelevant but estimating the appropriate discount rates and investor and insured cash flows remains paramount; see the discounted cash flow and internal rate of return models in Chapter 8. □

3.3.2 Systemic Risk

Systemic risk affects a financial system consisting of many interacting agents or firms and is created by that system's operation or structure. It occurs when an event causes a chain reaction of consequences. So-called systemically important financial institutions or SIFIs—those deemed *too big to fail*—generate systemic risk. They are so interconnected and interwoven in the financial system that the failure of one would have dire consequences for all. Systemic risks are often triggered by exogenous shocks such as the oil crisis of the 1970s or the failure of Long-Term Capital Management. The October 1987 Black Monday crash and Global Financial Crisis (GFC) of 2008 are two examples where losses from systemic risk emerged suddenly but endogenously. Systemic risk is linked to complex webs of contracts, collateral valuation, and duration transformation, where the system relies on a fragile confidence that can quickly erode. Systemic risks are by nature nondiversifiable (Brunnermeier and Oehmke 2013)

Property-casualty insurers are not usually regarded as systemically important financial institutions, although some large life insurers and AIG were designated as SIFIs by the Financial Stability Board after the GFC. A large, highly connected reinsurer could generate systemic risk if, for example, its failure would cause knock-on insolvencies. Insurers themselves are generally not regarded as systemically risky because they have liquid assets and illiquid uncallable liabilities (Chen *et al.* 2013).

The interaction of rating plans as another example of systemic risk for insurers. Adverse selection against a rating plan can cause realized rates to be lower than expected, through a combination of adverse selection and winner's curse. The effect is on premium rather than loss.

In a catastrophe, many insureds are subject to the same occurrence. Such risks are *systematic* (nondiversifiable) but not *systemic*. The risk arises as the result of an outside event and is not caused or exacerbated by the operation of the system.

Example 5. The October 1987 Black Monday stock market crash was a largely unexpected and sudden global decline in share prices. The Dow Jones Industrial Average fell 22.6% in one day. It was partially caused by the widespread use of portfolio insurance, which triggered sell orders in a declining market. Long-Term Capital Management was a hedge fund that failed in 1998 due to a combination of high leverage and exposure to the 1997 Asian financial crisis and 1998 Russian financial crisis. Its history is told in Lowenstein (2000). □

3.3.3 Types of Uncertainty

Probabilities can be objective or subjective. **Objective** probabilities are amenable to precise determination. They are usually based on physical symmetry (coin toss, dice roll) or repeated observations. Objective probability applies the law of large numbers, the central limit theorem, Bayesian statistics, and credibility theory to make precise predictions about samples. Insurance is largely based on objective probabilities from repeated observations (loss data).

Subjective probabilities provide a way of representing a degree of belief. They follow the same rules as objective probabilities and have proven a powerful way to impose order and consistency in economics and finance. Subjective probabilities are applied to nonrepeatable events: an election, a horse race, or an economic outcome. Subjective probability is also used with game theory, nonadditive probability, and behavioral science to make predictions and understand uncertainty. Insurance largely avoids pricing based on subjective probabilities, as the problems with creating markets for terrorism and cyber risks attest.

The differences between objective and subjective probabilities, and their relations to the development of probability and adjacent theories in judgment, psychology, physics, inference, and statistics, are discussed in Diaconis and Skyrms (2018).

It is usual to distinguish **process risk** in the face of a well-defined (objective) probability model from **uncertainty** when there is no probability model or even no clearly defined set of possible outcomes. Process risk is also called a **aleatoric** uncertainty, derived from the Latin *alea* or dice. Uncertainty is sometimes called **Knightian uncertainty** after the economist Frank Knight. **Epistemic** uncertainty is caused by a knowledge gap, possibly one that could in principle be filled.

Parameter risk is intermediate between process risk and uncertainty. It refers to a known model with unknown parameters. Actuaries often use Bayesian models to introduce (and sometimes remove) parameter risk. There is a blurred line between parameter risk and uncertainty. For example, a parameter can be used to select between competing models.

A situation of **unknown unknowns** represents an extreme form of uncertainty.

These concepts and relationships are summarized in Figure 3.1.

Example 6. When the US National Science Foundation decided to fund the LIGO search for gravitational waves there was epistemic uncertainty since no one knew for sure whether

Risk	Aliases	Description and Examples	Theories	Management
Objective Probabilities: Repeated Events				
Process	Aleatory diversifiable event idiosyncratic irreducible error roulette lottery	Known model and parameters; iid events; e.g. unusually high frequency, or large or catastrophe loss; actual economic activity, inflation, loss trend, weather	**Probability:** law of large numbers; law of iterated logarithm; central limit theorem; Berry-Esseen theorem; large deviation theory; Pollaczeck-Khinchine formula	Capital; diversify over large book; underwriting guidelines and policy limits; excess of loss or aggregate stop loss reinsurance
Parameter	Contagion estimation bias model bias nondiversifiable standard error	Known model, unknown parameters; non-iid severity, e.g. expected economic activity, inflation, loss trend, weather	**Statistics:** classical linear models; GLMs; time series; Bayesian statistics; credibility; data science and predictive analytics; machine learning; neural networks	Data and analytic sophistication; capital; temporal diversification; underwriting guidelines; multiyear quota share, aggregate stop loss reinsurance
Subjective Probabilities: Unique Events				
Uncertainty	Ambiguity butterfly effect epistemic horse race Knightian model	Knowable but unknown, ignorance and indolence; unknowable; unknown unknowns; e.g. adverse selection; nonstationary parameters, distracted driving; social inflation; independent and indistinguishable	**Finance, economics, chaos theory:** subjective probabilities; nonadditive probabilities; multiple priors; maximin utility	Product design; behavioral underwriting; capital; quota share; front or line-slip facility, off-balance sheet, sidecars
Market Interactions and Responses				
Systemic	Contagion fire sale liquidity risk market crash run on bank	Risk caused by (re)actions of market participants; significantly affects banks; e.g. premium risk, winner's curse; irresponsible competition and underwriting cycle, mass tort claim contagion	**Network and catastrophe theory:** phase shifts; turbulence; long-range correlation; thick-tailed, stable distributions	Marketing; public signaling; management and strategy; regulation; ORSA and ERM; capital; quota share; front or line-slip facility, off-balance sheet, sidecars

Figure 3.1 Taxonomy of insurance-related risk.

gravitational waves existed. If they did exist, experiments to detect them would still be subject to process risk: the chance none would be detected because no events producing gravitational waves occur during the observational period. There is even operational risk, that the detector malfunctions and misses an event. P.S. It appears they do exist! □

3.4 Representing Risk Outcomes

A risky outcome can be labeled explicitly by describing the facts and circumstances causing it. Or we can identify the outcome with its value. Or we can identify it with the probability of observing no larger value.

This section explores the mechanics, pros, and cons of these three representations. We call them the explicit, implicit, and dual implicit representations, respectively.

3.4.1 Explicit Representation

Finance theory is based on the notion of a security which pays one monetary unit in just one particular **state of the world**, known as an **Arrow-Debreu** security (see Section 8.6 for more). Of course, the state of the real world at any instant in time would be unimaginably complex to try to describe, so in practice, abstractions are used.

Example 7. We can imagine a narrower context where actuaries are trying to understand the loss experience of their personal auto physical damage portfolio over the past year. A spreadsheet describes each claim in terms of

- Policy number
- Date and time of loss
- Dollar value of damage
- Policy terms: deductible, limit
- GPS location of accident
- Vehicle make, model, year, and VIN
- Driver name, gender, age
- Other vehicle(s) involved
- Description of accident
- Link to photos of damage
- Link to adjuster report
- Link to police report

This is already getting unwieldy, but it is still not enough to *fully* explain what happened. Fortunately, the impossible is not necessary. To adequately identify each event, it is enough to note

- Policy number
- Vehicle VIN

- Date and time of loss
- GPS location of accident

because this is enough to put a unique identifier on each claim. More information may be required to assess the adequacy of the existing rate plan, but that's a different question. □

With sufficient detail of identifying variables, we have an **explicit representation** of risk outcomes. Mathematically, we represent the set of all possible variable value combinations as a set Ω called the sample space, and we characterize one particular combination of values as an element or sample point $\omega \in \Omega$. Other attributes not necessary for event identification, such as the amount of damage and driver name, are *functions* of that unique event identifier ω. If such functionally dependent information exists somewhere in a claim database or other data source, then it can be retrieved and associated with the event.

Example 8. As another example, consider the actuaries responsible for the commercial multiperil line of business. They are looking at their exposure to hurricanes and earthquakes. A simulation study results in a spreadsheet with the following columns:

- Nine-digit simulated catastrophe identifier
- Hurricane/earthquake flag
- Hurricane landfall lat-lon, velocity vector, wind speed, and radius to maximum winds
- Earthquake epicenter lat-lon, peak ground acceleration, and Modified Mercali Index value
- Multiperil portfolio gross loss
- Multiperil portfolio net loss after reinsurance

This information enables the actuaries to start to understand where their peak exposures are.

On another floor of the same building, the actuaries responsible for commerical auto physical damage have a similar file, except losses refer to the commercial auto portfolio. But *the same nine digit catastrophe identifier is used.* This means that the Enterprise Risk Management folks (in yet another building) can take those two spreadsheets and merge them together to see results across the entire commercial property book of business. Without this linkage, the dependence of results across the two lines of business would be a mystery. □

The strength of explicit event representation is that it enables outcomes to be linked across a book of business, thus dependence risk can be modeled without making assumptions. It is useful when events are not too numerous and affect significant portions of the portfolio. When events are very numerous and affect only small portions of the portfolio, explicit event representation does not provide enough benefit to justify its greater complexity.

To summarize: the **explicit representation** uses a random variable $X(\omega)$ defined on a sample space Ω of interpretable sample points, such as typhoon landfall and windspeed, or earthquake epicenter and magnitude. It is the most detailed representation and allows for easy aggregation, critical in reinsurance and risk management. It can distinguish between different events even if they cause the same loss outcome. It suffers from being arbitrary, especially regarding the detail communicated by the sample points, and the complexity of defining events, especially for high volume lines where it is unrealistic to tie an event to each individual policyholder.

3.4.2 Implicit Representation

The **implicit representation** identifies an outcome with its value, creating an **implicit event**.

The implicit representation relabels the sample space by identifying the event $\{X = x\}$ with the sample point x, creating a new random variable on the sample space of outcome values. It is easy to understand but hard to aggregate because there is no way to link outcomes. There is no easy way to specify dependence, which explains the interest in copulas, mathematical objects used to specify the dependence structure between two or more random variables. It is impossible to distinguish between implicit events that cause the same loss outcome.

The implicit representation defines a probability on the new outcome sample space by $\mathsf{P}_X(A) := \mathsf{Pr}(X \in A)$ for $A \subset \mathbb{R}$. P_X is uniquely determined by the **distribution function** $F(x) := \mathsf{Pr}(X \le x)$.

When risk is solely a function of loss outcome, rather than the cause of loss, it can be appropriate to work with implicit events.

Example 9. Ins Co. actuaries working with the homeowners line of business use the same catastrophe model as the commercial lines folks, but their spreadsheet has only the following columns:

- Hurricane/earthquake flag
- Homeowners portfolio loss

This information allows them to compute the probability distributions of losses, in total and also conditional on type of peril. However, it is insufficient to tie back to the commercial lines experience. The primary identifying feature for an event is the loss amount. □

Example 10. Ins Co. wants to purchase California earthquake reinsurance. The reinsurer needs explicit (event ID, event loss) model output, so it can aggregate its exposure. But Ins Co. can evaluate its reinsurance programs using implicit events (loss amount, probability). □

3.4.3 Dual Implicit Representation

The implicit representation is a useful simplification. But there are situations where we can simplify it further. If we don't care about the monetary outcome but care only about the rank of the outcomes, we can use the **dual implicit representation** and identify an outcome $X = x$ with its **nonexceedance probability** $p = F(x) = \mathsf{Pr}(X \le x)$. Equivalently, we can relate x with $s = S(x) = \mathsf{Pr}(X > x)$, its **exceedance probability.** We work with the former and call it a **dual implicit event.**

Identifying an outcome with its probability is scale invariant and straightforward. It is easy to make comparisons: no matter the range of X, $F(X)$ lies between 0 and 1. In fact, for continuous X, $F(X)$ is uniformly distributed between 0 and 1—the basis of the inversion method for simulating random variables.

The dual implicit representation has the same disadvantage as the implicit: it is hard to aggregate. In addition, it suffers from being relative to an often unspecified reference portfolio. After Hurricane Katrina, news reports described it from a 25 year (relative to all US landfalling hurricanes) to a 400-year event (storms along a similar track).

Example 11. Investors and rating agencies assess bonds by their estimated probability of default. They are using a dual implicit representation of the bond. □

Example 12. Although catastrophe models generally simulate explicit events, the results are often summarized by exceedance probability. Rating agency and regulatory capital models charge for catastrophe risk using events defined by exceedance probability, rather than objective event. □

Example 13. The homeowners reinsurance actuaries in Ins Co. get a spreadsheet similar to the commercial lines simulation output, with losses arranged in ascending order. Their concern is identifying where various proposed reinsurance programs attach and exhaust (Section 3.5.3). They flag various rows with notations such as *program 1 attaches*, *program 2 exhausts*, etc. Since the rows are in ascending loss order, they can count rows above or below a particular notation and calculate the probability of attachment and exhaustion. They prepare a report that focuses on these probabilities without mentioning the actual dollar loss amounts. □

Remark 14. The mapping from p back to x is defined by the inverse of the distribution function. Spreadsheet programs provide several, including: `BETA.INV`, `CHISQ.INV`, `F.INV`, `GAMMA.INV`, `LOGNORM.INV`, `NORM.INV`, and `T.INV`. □

3.4.4 Dictionary between the Three Representations

All three representations are used in insurance. The explicit representation could be a specific claim file, as a claim adjuster sees it. Its implicit representation identifies it with its loss amount and ignores other details. And its dual implicit representation identifies it with its nonexceedance probability level. Many explicit events can have the same loss amount or probability level. The probability depends on the reference portfolio. Table 3.1 summarizes the three ways of representing a risk. The last row shows how to compute expected values in each representation, the subject of the next section.

Example 15. Lloyd's uses an explicit event approach to measure risk because of its intended use of the results. Each syndicate at Lloyd's reports to the Corporation of Lloyd's their estimated losses from 16 specific Realistic Disaster Scenarios (RDS), such as a Miami-Dade Florida Windstorm or Japanese Typhoon. The Corporation then aggregates them *over all syndicates* to determine its total exposure. If Lloyd's merely asked each syndicate for its 100 year or 250 year loss, it would be unable to determine its aggregate exposure. Rating agencies and regulators evaluate companies on a standalone basis. They do not need to aggregate exposure in this way, and so a dual implicit event, such as a VaR or TVaR loss amount at an extreme return period, fits their intended purpose. The RDS system is described in Lloyd's (2021). We discuss it further in Sections 5.1 and 5.A. □

Table 3.1 Representing risks: event definitions and natural sample spaces.

Facet	Random variable	Distribution function	Quantile function
Notation	X	F	F^{-1}
Events	Explicit	Implicit	Dual implicit
Sample space	Ω	$\mathbb{R} = (-\infty, \infty)$	$[0,1] \subset \mathbb{R}$
Sample point	$\omega \in \Omega$	Outcome, x	Probability or rank, p
Probability	Pr	$P_X(a,b] = \mathsf{P}(X \in (a,b]) = F(b) - F(a)$	Uniform
Mean $\mathsf{E}[X]$	$\int_\Omega X(\omega)\mathsf{Pr}(d\omega)$	$\int_0^\infty (1-F(x))dx = \int_0^\infty x dF(x)$	$\int_0^1 F^{-1}(p)dp$

3.5 The Lee Diagram and Expected Losses

Graphical methods are widely used in mathematics and statistics to visually present ideas which would otherwise be abstruse.

Lee, *The Mathematics of Excess of Loss Coverages* (1988)

In this section, we present the Lee diagram and use it to illustrate different ways to compute expected and layer losses.

3.5.1 The Lee Diagram

Lee diagrams are introduced in Lee (1988), a famous actuarial science paper. Lee diagrams are a constructive visualization of several important actuarial concepts, and we use them extensively.

Figure 3.2 reproduces the original Lee diagram. It shows claims sorted by ascending size along the horizontal axis and outcome amount on the vertical axis.

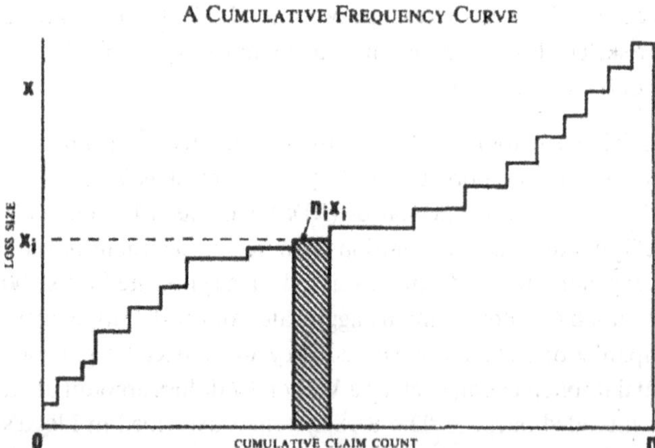

Figure 3.2 The original Lee diagram. Source: Lee (1988). Reproduced with permission of the Casualty Actuarial Society.

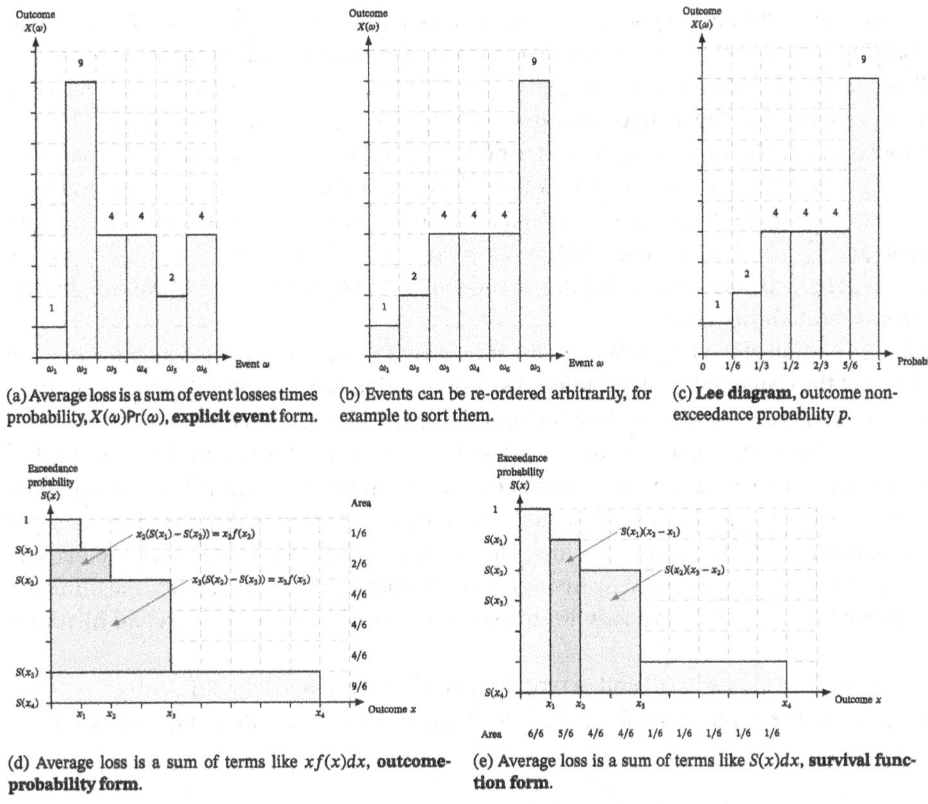

(a) Average loss is a sum of event losses times probability, $X(\omega)\Pr(\omega)$, **explicit event** form.

(b) Events can be re-ordered arbitrarily, for example to sort them.

(c) **Lee diagram**, outcome non-exceedance probability p.

(d) Average loss is a sum of terms like $xf(x)dx$, **outcome-probability form**.

(e) Average loss is a sum of terms like $S(x)dx$, **survival function form**.

Figure 3.3 Different ways of computing expected losses for a sample discrete distribution. Each event is equally likely.

A **Lee diagram** plots outcome x on the vertical axis and probability of nonexceedance $p = F(x)$ on the horizontal (label) axis. It is a plot of the dual implicit representation because it labels an event by $F(x)$. The probability $F(x)$ is equivalent to the event rank, between 0 (smallest) and 1 (largest). The Lee diagram can be obtained from the distribution function by reflecting its graph in a 45 degree line through the origin, or (more simply) from the survival function by rotating its graph by 90 degrees counterclockwise about the origin. After rotating, the horizontal axis shows the exceedance probability in reverse order, which is the same as the nonexceedance probability. Figure 3.3 panel (c) shows another Lee diagram.

3.5.2 Expected Losses and the Lee Diagram

Consider a simple discrete space $\Omega = \{\omega_1, \dots, \omega_6\}$ with six equally likely sample points. Let X be the loss random variable defined on Ω with outcomes $1, 9, 4, 4, 2$, and 4.

The mean loss is 4, which can be seen by summing the losses, 24, and dividing by the number of outcomes or as the probability weighted sum of outcomes $1/6 + 2/6 + 4/2 + 9/6$. Five ways of looking at X are illustrated in Figure 3.3.

Figure 3.3 panels (a) and (b) show the explicit representation. The outcomes are labelled by sample point. The two views illustrate that sample points do not have a natural ordering.

We can compute the mean by summing over sample points, $\mathsf{E}[X] = \sum_{\omega\in\Omega} X(\omega)\mathsf{Pr}(\omega)$. Event probabilities correspond to bar widths. We call this the **event-outcome form**.

Panel (c) is a Lee diagram. Compared to panel (b), it uses dual implicit labels for each outcome—its probability of nonexceedance $\mathsf{Pr}(X \le x)$—in place of explicit events.

Panel (d) plots the survival (exceedance probability) function, $S(x)$, against the outcome x. The width of the vertical bars equals the difference of the sorted outcome values. Using (d), we can compute the mean in the usual way as the sum-product of loss outcome and probability: $\sum_i x_i \mathsf{Pr}(X = x_i)$, since $\mathsf{Pr}(X = x_i) = \mathsf{Pr}(X > x_{i-1}) - \mathsf{Pr}(X > x_i) = S(x_{i-1}) - S(x_i)$. Each area is exactly the same as in (c), just rotated by 90 degrees clockwise. We call this the **outcome-probability form**.

The orientation of the Lee and event-outcome diagrams stresses that the outcome loss is a function of the event rank or description. Lee's orientation is more natural in many contexts than panels (d) or (e), and is used throughout the remainder of the book.

Panel (e) shows the same function as (d), but uses horizontal bars with heights equal to outcome probabilities, i.e. the differences of the survival function. Using (e), we can compute the mean as $\mathsf{E}[X] = \int_0^\infty S(x)dx$, by considering the chances each width-one outcome layer on the horizontal axis is used to pay a loss. The first layer is always used because all outcomes are ≥ 1. The second layer is used by five out of six outcomes, so 5/6 probability, the third and fourth by 4/6, etc. There is no possibility of a loss above 9. We call this the **survival function form**.

The total areas in panels (d) and (e) are the same but are divided up differently.

Converting the expressions for $\mathsf{E}[X]$ into integral form yields three equations for the mean:

$$\mathsf{E}[X] = \int_\Omega X(\omega)\,\mathsf{P}(dx) = \int_0^\infty xdF(x) = \int_0^\infty S(x)dx. \tag{3.1}$$

The first integral corresponds to panels (a) and (b), the second to (d), and the last to (e). When X has a density f, $\int_0^\infty xdF(x) = \int_0^\infty xf(x)dx$. Using $xdF(x)$ is more general than $xf(x)dx$ and allows for jumps in F, see Appendix A.4. We prefer to use $xdF(x)$ unless the density exists and needs emphasizing.

The equivalence between the last two expressions in Eq. (3.1) relies on integration by parts, $\int udv = uv - \int vdu$, applied with $u = x$ and $v = S$,

$$\begin{aligned}\int_0^\infty xdF(x) &= -xS(x)\Big|_0^\infty + \int_0^\infty S(x)dx \\ &= \int_0^\infty S(x)dx\end{aligned}$$

since $xS(x) \to 0$ as $x \to \infty$ when X has a mean. Note that $dS = -dF$, accounting for the sign change.

Remark 16. The expression $\int_0^\infty S(x)dx$ for the mean is well known to life actuaries via the expression $e_x = \sum_t {}_tp_x$ for curtate future lifetime in terms of survival functions. The average future lifetime is the sum of the probability of surviving to each future age. Count the birthdays! □

Exercise 17. Figure 3.3 does not show the implicit representation. Plot it. What are the horizontal and vertical axes? □

Exercise 18. Let X be a Bernoulli random variable defined on $\Omega = [0, 1]$ by $X(\omega) = 0$ for $\omega < 0.4$ and $X(\omega) = 1$ for $\omega \geq 0.4$. What are $\mathsf{P}(X = 0)$, $\mathsf{P}(X = 1)$, and $\mathsf{E}[X]$? Plot X and its distribution and survival functions, and its Lee function. Clearly label all axes and the value of each function at any jump points. Repeat the exercise for Y defined by $Y(\omega) = 0$ if $\omega \in [0, 0.1) \cup [0.25, 0.35) \cup [0.5, 0.6) \cup [0.75, 0.85)$ and $Y(\omega) = 1$ otherwise.

Solution. X and Y define different random variables but they have the same distribution and survival functions, and the same implicit and dual implicit representations. They are both Bernoulli(0.6) variables, with $\mathsf{P}(X = 0) = 0.4$, $\mathsf{P}(X = 1) = 0.6$, and mean $\mathsf{E}[X] = 0.6$. Figure 3.4 shows the requested plots. Strictly, the vertical segments are not part of the function graphs. The dot indicates the value of each function at jumps. □

Exercise 19. A model produces 100 equally likely events that it labels by an event identifier. The events define a sample space $\Omega = \{0, \dots, 99\}$ and probability $\Pr(\{\omega\}) = 1/100$. The model defines two identically distributed, dependent random variable outcomes

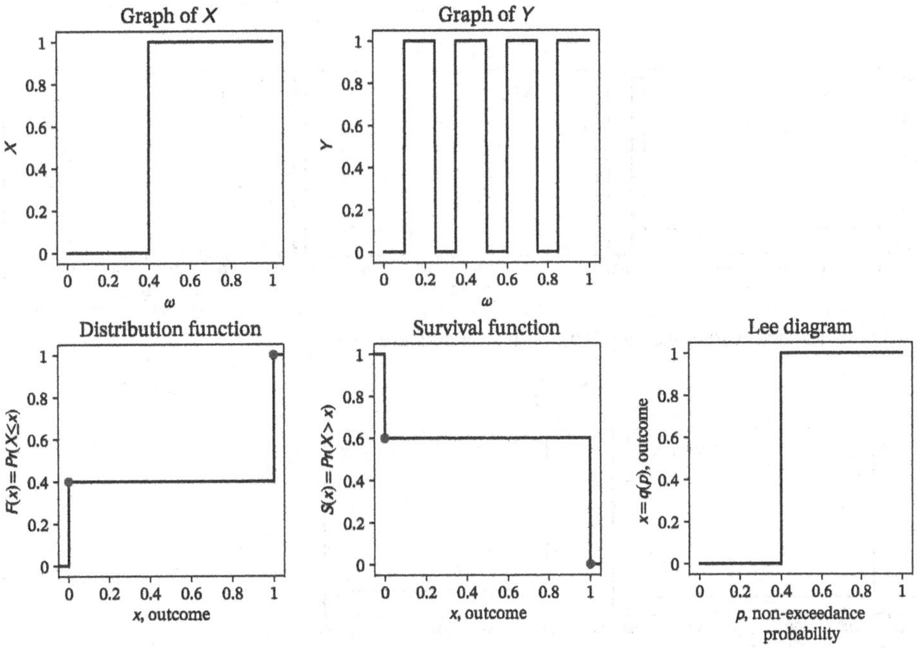

Figure 3.4 The random variables, distribution and survival functions, and Lee diagram for two identically distributed Bernoulli random variables.

$$X_1 = \begin{cases} 100 & 0 \le \omega < 90 \\ 1000 & 90 \le \omega < 95 \\ 0 & 95 \le \omega < 100 \end{cases} \quad \text{and} \quad X_2 = \begin{cases} 100 & 0 \le \omega < 90 \\ 0 & 90 \le \omega < 95 \\ 1000 & 95 \le \omega < 100 \end{cases}$$

with sum

$$X = \begin{cases} 200 & 0 \le \omega < 90 \\ 1000 & 90 \le \omega < 100. \end{cases}$$

1. Create the model in a spreadsheet and confirm $\mathsf{E}[X] = 28$ and $\mathsf{E}[X_i] = 14$.
2. Plot X_1, X_2, and X as functions of $\omega = 0, 1, \dots, 99$.
3. Plot the survival functions, as functions of the outcome x.
4. Plot the Lee diagrams, as functions of probability p.
5. Are the random variables different? The survival functions? The Lee diagrams?

We return to this example in Chapter 15.

Solutions. Figures 3.5–3.7 show the random variables, the survival functions, and the Lee diagrams. The random variables are all distinct, but the survival function and Lee diagrams for each line are the same. □

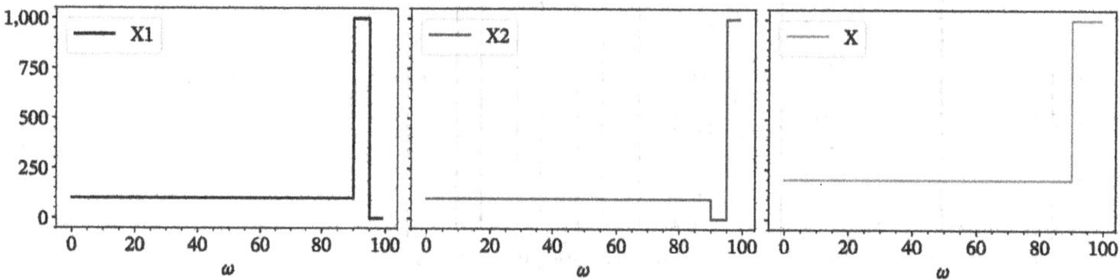

Figure 3.5 Random variables, functions of an explicit state.

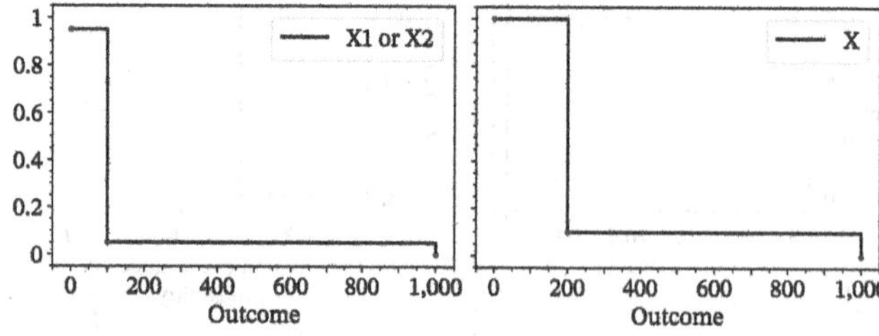

Figure 3.6 Survival functions of the outcome.

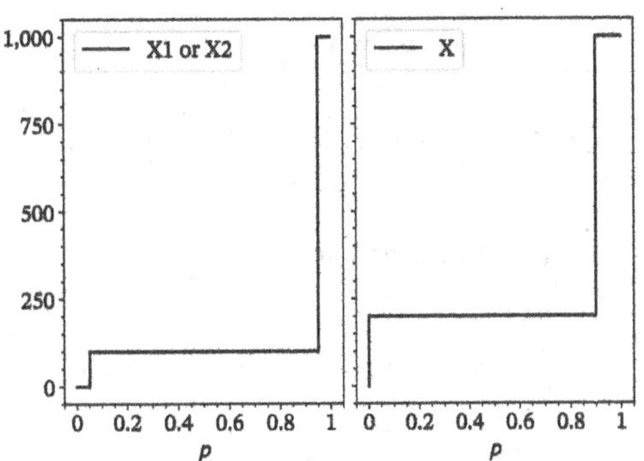

Figure 3.7 Lee diagrams, function of a dual implicit state.

Remark 20. The relationships illustrated in Figure 3.3 are a discrete version of the formula for integration by parts. Consider approximating Riemann sums to the integral of the survival function. Let $0 = x_0 < x_1 < \cdots < x_n < \cdots$, be a fine, but not necessarily equally spaced, dissection of the positive reals. We get two equivalent representations of $\mathsf{E}[X]$ by

$$\int_0^\infty S(x)\,dx \approx \sum_{i\ge 0} S(x_i)(x_{i+1} - x_i) \tag{3.2}$$

$$= \sum_{i\ge 0} x_{i+1}(S(x_i) - S(x_{i+1})) \tag{3.3}$$

$$= \sum_{i\ge 1} x_i f(x_i')(x_i - x_{i-1}) \tag{3.4}$$

$$\approx \int_0^\infty x f(x) dx, \tag{3.5}$$

using Taylor's theorem to write $S(x_{i-1}) - S(x_i) = S(x_i - (x_i - x_{i-1})) - S(x_i) = -S'(x_i')(x_i - x_{i-1}) = f(x_i')(x_i - x_{i-1})$, for some $x_{i-1} \le x_i' \le x_i$. □

Exercise 21. Confirm the change in indexing between Eq. (3.2) and Eq. (3.3) is correct by looking at panels (d) and (e). □

Technical Remark 22. In addition to the outcome-probability and survival function forms, there is a third, dual implicit outcome expression

$$\mathsf{E}[X] = \int_0^1 F^{-1}(p) dp$$

by change of variable substitution $F(x) = p$, $f(x)dx = dp$. This view replaces the probability defined by X with the uniform probability dp on $[0, 1]$. □

Technical Remark 23. Figure 3.8 relates integral expressions for the mean and the different ways of representing risk presented in Section 3.4. When F is absolutely continuous it has a density, giving the usual $\int x f(x) dx$ representation of the mean in the second to last line. □

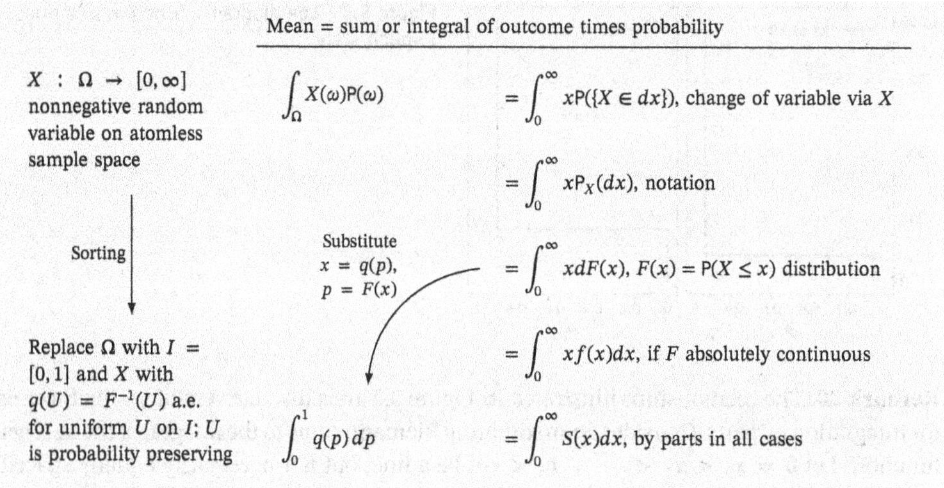

Figure 3.8 Different ways of computing the mean for a random variable X, with $\mathsf{E}[|X|] < \infty$.

3.5.3 Layer Notation

It is common to use limits and deductibles to transform the insured loss. If X is a loss random variable, then applying a **deductible** d transforms it into

$$(X-d)^+ = \begin{cases} 0 & X \le d \\ X-d & X > d \end{cases}$$

and applying a **limit** of l transforms it to

$$X \wedge l = \begin{cases} X & X \le l \\ l & X > l. \end{cases}$$

These notations are shorthand: for example, $X \wedge l$ is the random variable with outcome $(X \wedge l)(\omega) = X(\omega) \wedge l$ at sample point $\omega \in \Omega$.

When a policy has both a limit and a deductible, the limit is applied after the deductible. Applying a limit and a deductible creates what is called a limited **excess of loss layer** or simply a **layer**. Many reinsurance contracts and specialty lines policies are **tranched** into a coverage **tower** consisting of multiple layers, written by multiple insurers. (A tranche means *a piece cut off* or *a slice*.) In this context, a layer is sometimes identified with its limit and the deductible is called the **attachment** of the layer. A layer that attaches at 0 is called **ground-up**; all others are **excess**. Layers in a tower are typically arranged with no gaps.

Example 24. An aggregate reinsurance tower to ¤100M could be structured as a ¤10M retention, layer 1: ¤10M excess 10M, layer 2: ¤30M excess 20M, and layer 3: ¤50M excess 50M.

The cedent retains losses in excess of ¤100M. (Note: ¤30M excess 20M refers to a layer with a limit of ¤30M that attaches at ¤20M.) □

Example 25. Structured finance tranches asset-backed securities (MBS, CDO, etc.) in an analogous way. The tranches are generally determined to achieve a certain ratings defined by probability of default, meaning they have a dual implicit definition. □

It is convenient to introduce the notation L_d^{d+l} for the layer with limit l in excess of attachment d. The layer pays

$$L_d^{d+l}(x) := \begin{cases} 0 & x \le d \\ x-d & d < x \le d+l \\ l & d+l < x \end{cases} \tag{3.6}$$

for a **subject loss** x. The **detachment** or **exhaustion** point of the layer is $d+l$. The cover can be written succinctly as

$$L_d^{d+l}(x) = (x-d)^+ \wedge l.$$

The notation L_d^{d+l} mimics integrals, with the attachment and detachment points as sub- and super-scripts, and makes it easy to add them: $L_0^{l_1} + L_{l_1}^{l_1+l_2} = L_0^{l_1+l_2}$.

We use the two equivalent expressions $L_0^l(X)$ and $X \wedge l$ interchangeably for a ground-up cover.

The expected loss and premium for a layer divided by the layer's limit are called **loss on line** and **rate on line**, respectively.

When applied to a random loss X, $L_d^{d+l}(X)$ becomes a random variable.

Exercise 26. Using multiple layers it is possible to create any continuous indemnity function that increases with subject loss. Describe in words and plot payments from the following towers as functions of the subject loss $0 \le x \le 1000$.

1. $L_0^{500}(x)$
2. $L_{250}^{\infty}(x)$
3. $L_{250}^{1000}(x)$
4. $0.5L_{250}^{500}(x) + 0.75L_{500}^{750} + L_{750}^{1000}$
5. Which of (1)–(4) has the same payouts as a call option? What is its strike?
6. Write the payout function for a put option in terms of L functions.

Solution. (1)–(4) See Figure 3.9. Cover (4) includes co-participations or coinsurance clauses, where some layers are only partially placed. (5) L_{250}^{∞} has the same payout as a call option with strike 250. (6) A put option with strike k has payout function equal to $k - L_0^k$. □

Remark 27. Limits and deductibles can be applied per claimant, claim, occurrence, or in the aggregate. We assume the reader is familiar with these concepts. The exact meaning of a limit and deductible is defined by that of X. In this book X almost always represents aggregate loss on a portfolio. □

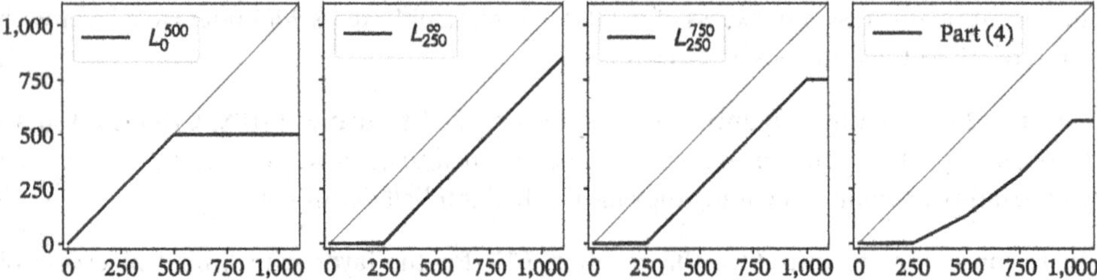

Figure 3.9 Sample layering functions for Exercise 26.

3.5.4 Computing Layer Losses with the Lee Diagram

The Lee diagram makes it easy to visualize different loss layers and write down their expected values using survival-function form expectations. We use a for a height on the vertical axis because it usually represents assets available to Ins Co. for paying claims. Alternatively it can represent an attachment point.

Figure 3.10 illustrates several significant actuarial quantities in a Lee diagram.

- The area $\mathsf{E}[(X-a)^+]$ equals the unconditional **excess loss cost** for losses in excess of the attachment a. It is called the **insurance charge** in US retrospective rating plans. When a represents assets it is called the **insolvency put** or **expected policyholder deficit** (EPD). In finance, the excess loss cost corresponds to the expected payout of a **call** option and a is called the **strike price**.

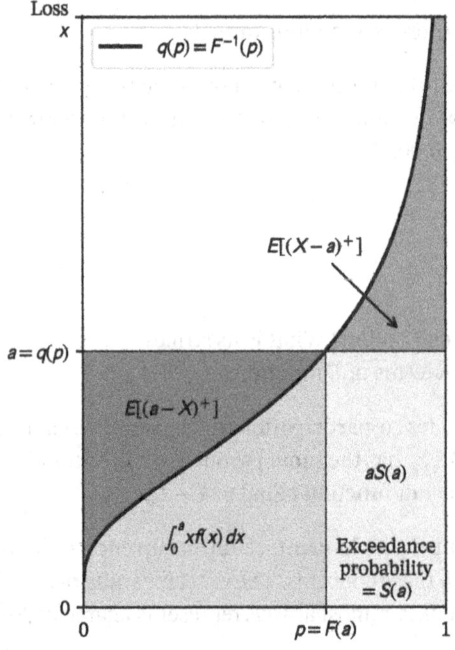

Figure 3.10 Insurance variables in a Lee diagram.

- The **limited expected value** up to a level a is the expected value with a limit a on losses. It is given by

$$\mathsf{E}[X \wedge a] = \int_0^a S(x)\,dx = \int_0^a x\,dF(x) + aS(a), \tag{3.7}$$

  the sum of the two shaded areas at the bottom, to the right of the curve. The integral is a Riemann-Stieltjes integral if X has a mixed distribution. Limited expected values are used to compute increased limits factors.
- The **expected loss**, $\mathsf{E}[X]$ is the sum of the three shaded areas under the curve.
- $\mathsf{E}[(a-X)^+]$ is the **insurance savings** or the investor's **residual value**, or, in finance, the expected value of a **put** option.

The diagram makes obvious a **put-call parity**-like relationship

$$\mathsf{E}[X] + \mathsf{E}[(a-X)^+] = a + \mathsf{E}[(X-a)^+]. \tag{3.8}$$

The shaded area under the curve plus the put equals the strike plus the call. (Put-call parity in finance is more subtle as it relates to prices not mathematical expectations.) In insurance retrospective rating terminology Eq. (3.8) says that the expected losses plus the savings equals the attachment (entry ratio) plus the expense (Kallop 1975).

Exercise 28. Show that $\mathsf{E}[(a-X)^+] = \int_0^a F(x)dx$ by computing $(a-X)^+ = a-(X \wedge a)$ and by using integration by parts. Identify the relevant areas on the Lee diagram. □

3.5.5 Algorithm to Evaluate Expected Loss for Discrete Random Variables

The algorithm in this subsection is very basic. We present it to establish an approach to working with discrete random variables that we generalize in subsequent chapters.

We present an algorithm to compute $\mathsf{E}[X]$ in two ways, based on Eq. (3.1),

$$\mathsf{E}[X] = \int_0^\infty x dF(x) = \int_0^\infty S(x)dx. \tag{3.9}$$

The two integrals correspond to the areas shown in Figure 3.11, panels (a) and (b), respectively. In (a), dF equals minus the backward difference of S, and in (b) dx equals the forward difference of x.

Follow these steps to evaluate Eq. (3.9).

Algorithm Input: X is a discrete random variable, taking finitely many values $X_j \geq 0$, and $p_j = \mathsf{P}(X = x_j)$.

Algorithm Steps

1. **Pad** the input by adding a zero outcome $X = 0$ with probability 0.
2. **Group by** X_j and sum the corresponding p_j.
3. **Sort** events by outcome X_j into ascending order. Relabel events $X_0 < X_1 < \cdots < X_m$ and probabilities $p_0, \dots, p_m$.

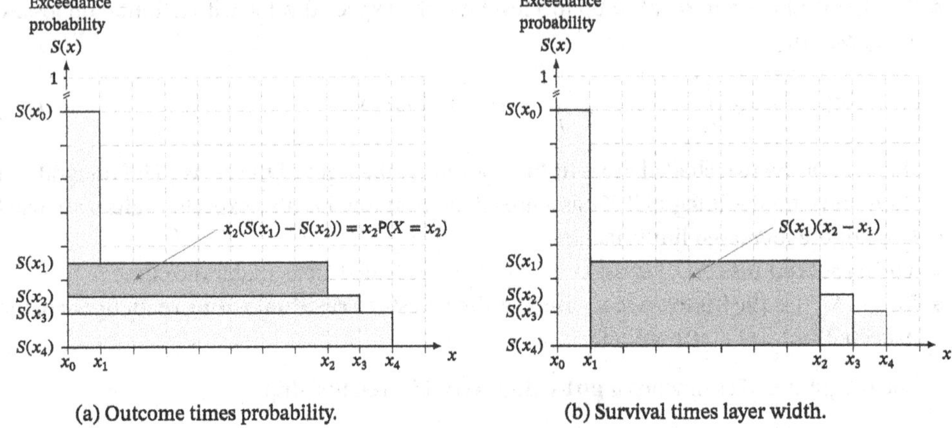

(a) Outcome times probability.

(b) Survival times layer width.

Figure 3.11 Two ways of computing expected loss from a discrete sample.

4. **Decumulate** probabilities to compute the survival function $S_j := S(X_j)$ using $S_0 = 1 - p_0$ and $S_j = S_{j-1} - p_j$, $j > 0$.
5. **Difference** the outcomes to compute $\Delta X_j = X_{j+1} - X_j$, $j = 0, \dots, m-1$.
6. **Outcome-probability sum-product:**

$$\mathsf{E}[X] = \int_0^\infty x dF(x) = \sum_{j=1}^{m} X_j \mathsf{P}(X = X_j). \tag{3.10}$$

7. **Survival function sum-product:**

$$\mathsf{E}[X] = \int_0^\infty S(x) dx = \sum_{j=0}^{m-1} S_j \Delta X_j. \tag{3.11}$$

Comments.

a. Step (1) treats 0 as special because the second integral in Eq. (3.9) starts at $X = 0$. The case where the smallest outcome is > 0 is illustrated in Figure 3.12. Now $S(x) = 1$ for $0 \le x < X_1$ and $\int_0^\infty S(x)dx$ includes the shaded dashed rectangle of area X_1. Step (1) allows us to systematically deal with any discrete data. It adds a new outcome row only when the smallest observation is > 0.
b. After Step (3), the X_j are distinct, they are in ascending order, $X_0 = 0$, and $p_j = \mathsf{P}(X = X_j)$.
c. In Step (4), $S_m = \mathsf{P}(X > X_m) = 0$ since X_m is the maximum value of X.
d. The forward difference ΔX computed in Step (5) replaces dx in various formulas. Since it is a forward difference ΔX_m is undefined. It is also unneeded.
e. Step (6) computes the first integral in Eq. (3.9). It is a sum because X is discrete and has a probability mass function, like a Poisson, rather than a density, like a normal—explaining why we use the notation $dF(x)$, not $f(x)dx$. The sum starts at $i = 1$ because $X_0 = 0$. Notice that $\mathsf{P}(X = X_j) = S_{j-1} - S_j$ is the negative backward difference of S.

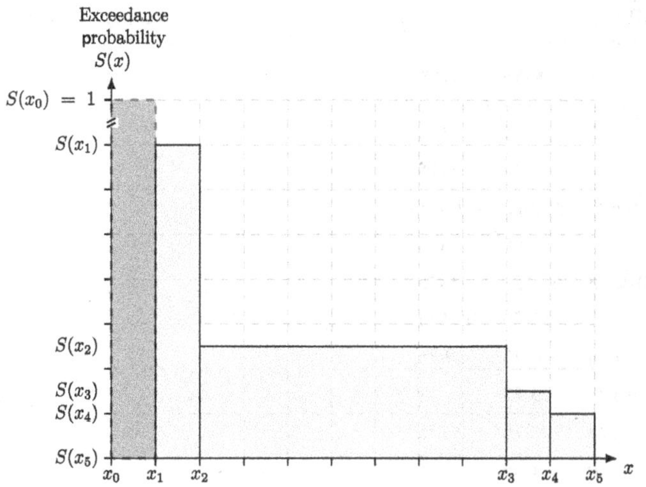

Figure 3.12 Accounting for the effect of adding 1 to each outcome.

Table 3.2 Simple Discrete Example with nine possible outcomes, ordered by portfolio loss X, with layer width ΔX and exceedance probability S.

j	X	ΔX	$P(X) = \Delta S$	S	$X \Delta S$	$S \Delta X$
0	0	1	0.25	0.75	0	0.75
1	1	7	0.125	0.625	0.125	4.375
2	8	1	0.125	0.5	1	0.5
3	9	1	0.0625	0.4375	0.563	0.4375
4	10	1	0.125	0.3125	1.25	0.3125
5	11	79	0.0625	0.25	0.688	19.75
6	90	8	0.125	0.125	11.25	1
7	98	2	0.0625	0.0625	6.125	0.125
8	100		0.0625	0	6.25	
Sum			1		27.25	27.25

f. Step (7) computes the second integral in Eq. (3.9). The sum starts at $i = 1$, corresponding to the first vertical bar in Panel (b) that extends from $X_0 = 0$ to X_1 and has height $S(X_0)$.
g. Note the index shift between Eqs. (3.10) and (3.11).
h. Both Eqs. 3.10 and 3.11 are exact evaluations. The approximation occurs when the underlying distribution being modeled is replaced with the discrete sample given by X. □

Exercise 29. Apply the Algorithm to X defined by the Simple Discrete Example, Section 2.4.1.

Table 3.3 Solution to Exercise 30.

j	X	ΔX	$\mathsf{P}(X) = \Delta S$	S	$X\Delta S$	$S\Delta X$
0	0	100	0	1	0	100
1	100	1	0.250	0.75	25	0.75
2	101	7	0.125	0.625	12.625	4.375
3	108	1	0.125	0.5	13.5	0.5
4	109	1	0.0625	0.4375	6.8125	0.4375
5	110	1	0.125	0.3125	13.75	0.3125
6	111	79	0.0625	0.25	6.9375	19.75
7	190	8	0.125	0.125	23.75	1
8	198	2	0.0625	0.0625	12.375	0.125
9	200		0.0625	0	12.5	
Sum					127.25	127.25

Solution. The sorted data, starting with $X_0 = 0$, is shown in Table 3.2. From now on we label the outcomes X_j as shown there.

Table 3.2 shows event rank $j = 0, \dots, m = 8$, and the columns S and ΔX from Steps (4) and (5). For future applications, it is important we can recover $\mathsf{P}(X = X_j)$ as a difference of S_j. This is easy: $\mathsf{P}(X = X_j) = \Delta S_j := S(X_{j-1}) - S(X_j)$ is the jump at X_j and ΔS_0 is the jump at $X_0 = 0$, i.e, $1 - \mathsf{P}(X > 0)$. It is the negative backward difference because S is the survival function. Finally, the table shows two computed columns: $X\,\Delta S$ and $S\,\Delta X$. The totals show that Steps (6) and (7) give the same result for $\mathsf{E}[X]$, 27.25. □

Exercise 30. Apply the Algorithm to $X + 100$.

Solution. Step (1) now introduces the 0 row, see Table 3.3. □

Exercise 31. The loss outcomes are all distinct in Table 3.2. When there are ties, Step (3) is needed. Recompute the table if X_1 can take values 1, 9, 10. □

The algorithm's computations can be visualized using a Lee diagram, as shown in Figure 3.13. The horizontal axis shows events and their cumulative probabilities (in 1/16ths and decimals). The width of each event corresponds to its objective probability, ΔS in the table. The vertical axis shows potential outcomes from 1 to 100. The horizontal black lines show the outcome X for each event. In this case, there are nine events with nine distinct outcomes. The shaded area shows the chances each unit of assets is needed to fund an event. For example, the 99th and 100th units are only at risk from (or needed to fund) event $j = 9$, which has outcome 100 (upper right-hand corner). We might say these units are potentially *consumed* by event $j = 9$. The eight units 91–98 are at risk from events $j = 8$ and $j = 9$. The step heights of the shaded area correspond to ΔX in the table and ΔX_7 for row $j = 7$ is shown. At the bottom of the graph, the first unit of assets is needed to fund events $j = 2$ through 9. Event $j = 1$ has a zero loss, which does not require any assets. The plots in Figure 3.11 show the same function (different data values) rotated by 90 degrees to make the interpretation as $\int S(x)dx$ clearer.

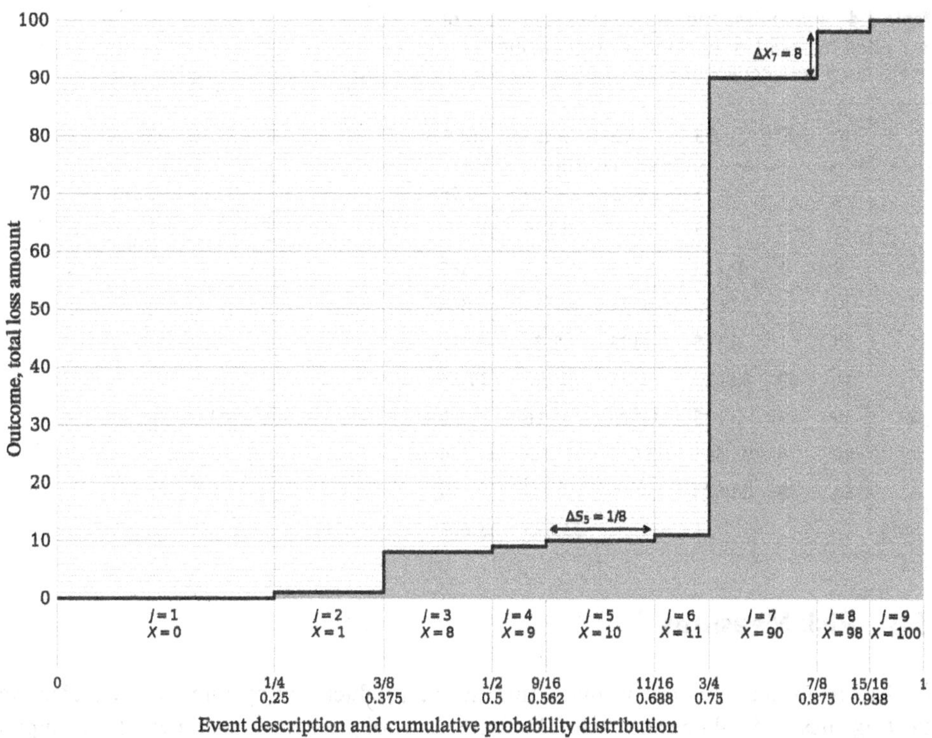

Figure 3.13 Lee diagram showing relationship between different asset layers and the events they fund.

Given the increasing sequence X_j, it is convenient to define $\mathrm{j}(a) = \max\{j : X_j < a\}$ and $\mathrm{j}(0) = 0$. It is the index of the largest observation strictly less than a. For example, $\mathrm{j}(90) = 6$ and $\mathrm{j}(91) = 7$. It is used in calculations as follows. To compute the limited expected value of X at $a > 0$, the survival function form evaluates

$$\mathsf{E}[X \wedge a] = \int_0^a S(x)dx = \sum_{j=0}^{\mathrm{j}(a)-1} S_j \Delta X_j + S_{\mathrm{j}(a)}(a - X_{\mathrm{j}(a)}) \tag{3.12}$$

because ΔX_j is the forward difference. It computes the integral as a sum of horizontal slices, e.g. the ΔX_7 block in Figure 3.13. For $a = 0$ obviously $\mathsf{E}[X \wedge 0] = 0$. For $a = \infty$, j is set to $j + 1$, where j is the maximum index with $S(X_j) > 0$, resulting in the unlimited $\mathsf{E}[X]$.

The outcome-probability form is

$$\mathsf{E}[X \wedge a] = \sum_{j>0} (X_j \wedge a)\Delta S_j = \sum_{j=1}^{\mathrm{j}(a)} X_j \Delta S_j + a S_{\mathrm{j}(a)}. \tag{3.13}$$

It computes the integral as a sum of vertical slices, e.g. the ΔS_5 block in Figure 3.13.

When $a = 80$, Table 3.4 shows the above calculations through the simple expedient of replacing X values with $X \wedge a$ and recomputing other columns that depend on X. Notice that columns involving S still use X's survival function. Numbers changed from Table 3.2 are displayed in bold.

Table 3.4 Computing the limited expected value of X, limited to $a = 80$. X' refers to $X \wedge a$ but values related to S are unchanged.

j	X'	$\Delta X'$	ΔS	S	$X'\Delta S$	$S\Delta X'$
0	0	1	0.25	0.75	0	0.75
1	1	7	0.125	0.625	0.125	4.375
2	8	1	0.125	0.5	1	0.5
3	9	1	0.0625	0.4375	0.563	0.438
4	10	1	0.125	0.3125	1.25	0.313
5	11	**69**	0.0625	0.25	0.688	**17.25**
6	**80**	**0**	0.125	0.125	**10**	**0**
7	**80**	**0**	0.0625	0.0625	**5**	**0**
8	**80**	**0**	0.0625	0	**5**	**0**
Sum			1		**23.625**	**23.625**

3.6 Risk Measures

An ice cream manufacturer wants to introduce a product that customers will prefer over existing ones. It would be very helpful to have a way of predicting customer ice cream preferences. As far as a customer is concerned their preference may be very simple and intuitive: "this brand tastes better!" That preference is not expressed in a way that the manufacturer can use to predict customer responses to a new product. However, through taste tests the manufacturer is able to determine general principles which do predict the preferences of most customers. For example, most customers prefer ice cream with a higher fat content and natural rather than artificial ingredients. This information is a good start but ideally the ice cream manufacturer can find a way to represent it numerically—an ice cream measure, if you will—which will enable them to analyze it much more easily.

Risk preferences have many parallels with ice cream preferences. Both are somewhat idiosyncratic and personalized—but some general principles about them can be determined, although it is harder for risk since there is no simple taste test to elicit risk preferences. Like ice cream manufacturers, risk management professionals would benefit from having a risk measure that quantifies a true risk preference and allows them to predict how individuals act. In this section, we try to find such risk measures. It is important to note that risk preferences are opposite to ice cream preferences in the sense that better ice cream is preferable, whereas more risk is not.

Formally, a **risk measure** is a real-valued functional on a set of random variables that quantifies a risk preference—the way an individual or group of individuals decides risk questions. The random variables represent risks, and the risk measure conducts a taste test; given two, it predicts which one is preferred, i.e. has lower risk. A risk capital formula, such as NAIC RBC or Solvency II SCR, and a classification rating plan are archetypal risk measures. Section 6.5 provides a compendium of other standard risk measures.

3.6.1 Risk Preferences and Risk Measures

A **risk preference** models the way we compare risks and how we decide between them. It captures our intuitive notions of riskiness and converts them into a form we can use to predict future preferences. Using the ice cream analogy, the manufacturer needs to convert "this tastes better" into a series of preferences about ice cream ingredients, which can be used to predict the desirability of a new product.

Risk preferences are defined on a set of loss random variables $\mathcal{S}$. We write $X \succeq Y$ if the risk X is **preferred** to Y. If $X \succeq Y$ and $Y \succeq X$ we are neutral between X and Y.

A risk preference for insurance loss outcomes needs to have the following three properties.

1. **Complete** (COM) for any pair of prospects X and Y either $X \succeq Y$ or $Y \succeq X$ or both, that is, we can compare any two prospects.
2. **Transitive** (TR) if $X \succeq Y$ and $Y \succeq Z$ then $X \succeq Z$.
3. **Monotonic** (MONO) if $X \le Y$ in all outcomes then $X \succeq Y$.

The second property ensures the risk preference is logically consistent. The third reflects the reality that large positive outcomes for losses are less desirable than small ones. If $X \succeq Y$ then X is generally smaller or tamer than Y. The third property also ensures the risk preference takes into account the volume or size of loss, even when there is no variability. For example a uniform random loss between 0 and ¤1 million is preferred to a certain loss of ¤1 million, even though the former is variable and the latter is fixed.

Example 32. $X \succeq Y$ iff $\mathsf{E}[X] \le \mathsf{E}[Y]$ defines a risk neutral preference. $X \succeq Y$ iff $\mathsf{E}[X] + \mathsf{SD}(X) \le \mathsf{E}[Y] + \mathsf{SD}(Y)$ defines a mean-variance risk preference. Notice the order of the inequalities in both cases. □

A **risk measure** is a numerical representations of risk preferences. If $\mathcal{S}$ and the preference $\succeq$ have certain additional properties then it is possible to find a risk measure $\rho : \mathcal{S} \to \mathbb{R}$ that **represents** it, in the sense that

$$X \succeq Y \iff \rho(X) \le \rho(Y). \tag{3.14}$$

The reversed inequality arises because ρ measures risk, and less risk is preferred to more.

The risk measure collapses a risk preference into a single number. It facilitates simple and consistent decision making. We consider risk measures and risk preferences in more detail in Chapter 5.

Exercise 33. Based on your own views of risk, write down a few properties you believe a consistent risk preference should exhibit. For example, if you prefer X to Y what can you say about $X + W$ vs. $Y + W$ for another risk W? □

3.6.2 Volume, Volatility, and Tail Risk

Risk measures quantify the following three characteristics of a risk random variable.

1. **Volume:** a smaller risk is preferred. The mean measures volume.

2. **Volatility:** a risk exhibiting less volatility (or variability) is preferred. Variance and standard deviation measure volatility. We use the word '*volatility*' in a sense parallel to *stock price volatility*. Volatility is two-sided.
3. **Tail:** a risk with a lower likelihood of extreme outcomes is preferred. The level of loss with a 1% probability of exceedance is a tail risk measure. Tail risk is one-sided.

These characteristics overlap.

A risk measure must reflect volume because we want it to mirror a risk preference satisfying the MONO axiom, smaller risks are preferred to larger ones—even if the small risk is volatile and the large risk is certain. A measure of variability or tail risk that ignores volume is called a measure of **deviation**. The eponymous standard deviation is the, well, standard example. Adding the mean to a measure of deviation creates a risk measure.

Risk-based capital (RBC) formulas are risk measures. Many of them are volume based. They compute target capital by applying factors to premium, reserve, or asset balances. The factors vary according to the risk of each element. Examples include NAIC RBC, the Solvency II Solvency Capital Requirement standard formula, and most rating agency capital adequacy models. Classification rating plans are also risk measures. They compute a premium as a function of risk characteristics, such as building value and location, construction, occupancy, protection, and use for property insurance.

A risk measure sensitive to volatility quantifies mild to moderately adverse outcomes: outcomes frequent enough that most actuaries see examples during their careers. Management is often concerned with quarterly results volatility and can suppose investors are similarly troubled. Standard deviation quantifies volatility risk very well, and a *two deviations from the mean* rule of thumb turns out to be a surprisingly accurate estimate of a 20-year event in many situations.

Tail risk represents something so extreme it may or may not be experienced during a career, nevertheless it must always be considered possible. A tail risk catastrophe event often doubles or triples the previous worst historical event.

Variability and tail risk are distinct. An outcome of winning ¤1 million or ¤3 million has variability, but much less tail risk for most people than the possibility of gaining or losing ¤1 million. The variability of the two is the same but the tail risk is different. Risk is always relative to a base.

In Section 5.2 we enumerate several mathematical properties that risk measures should have, providing another way to characterize them.

3.6.3 Applications of Risk Measures

Insurance company operations are governed by the interaction of two risk measures: a capital risk measure setting the needed amount of capital and a pricing risk measure determining its cost. These two roles should not be confused.

A **capital risk measure** determines the assets necessary to back an existing or hypothetical portfolio at a given level of confidence. This exercise is also reverse engineered: given existing or hypothetical assets, what are the constraints on business that can be written?

Capital risk measures are used by management to determine economic capital, by a regulator to determine a minimum capital requirement, and by a rating agency to opine on the adequacy of held capital. Value at Risk (VaR) or Tail Value at Risk (TVaR) at some high confidence level, such as 99.5% or 1 in 200 years, are both popular, but other possible measures exist. These are both explored in Chapter 4.

A **pricing risk measure** determines the expected profit insureds need to pay in total to make it worthwhile for investors to bear the portfolio's risk. Pricing risk measures are called **premium calculation principles** (PCP) in actuarial texts (Goovaerts, De Vylder, and Haezendonck 1984). It is not expected that the loss be less than *premium* with a high degree of confidence—capital provides the cushion. But the premium must include a margin sufficient for the insurer to raise the needed capital cushion.

Risk measures typically have at a free parameter encoding their conservatism. As a result, there are two modes of use:

- Given a level of conservatism, they *determine* a premium or capital requirement.
- Given price or capital requirement, they *evaluate* its implied level of conservatism.

For example, a capital risk measure can be applied to capital model output to *determine* the amount of capital needed to be sufficient for 99% of outcomes. Or, it can *evaluate* what percentage of outcomes a given amount of capital covers.

By **determine** capital or premium, we mean to derive a technical or benchmark quantity—usually the actual held capital or market premium differ. The benchmark value can be used to evaluate an actual one.

The capital and premium applications both determine a monetary quantity, so it is helpful if the risk measure is denominated in monetary units. The mean and standard deviation are monetary but variance or probability of default are not. If the risk measure is not monetary, then we need an undesirable extra step get to the answer.

In practice, the capital and pricing applications usually require different risk measures with different properties. Capital risk measures must be sensitive to tail risk to ensure solvency. Management, concerned with solvency and earnings risk, often looks for pricing risk measures that are sensitive to volatility. They can bemoan the fact that tail risk measures fail to *see* volatility risk, just as measures of height fail to quantify weight. As we discuss in Section 4.1, the solution is to use two risk measures. The interplay of the pricing and capital risk measures is a central theme of the book.

Example 34. You have a flight to catch and want to allow sufficient time for your trip to the airport. George Stigler, a winner of the 1982 Nobel Prize in economics, said, "If you never miss the plane, you're spending too much time in airports." How much time do you allow?

If you're going on vacation you are very concerned about missing your flight. You don't want to lose any vacation time—there's only one flight per day—and you'll pay the cost of flight changes. You use a conservative capital risk measure approach. You build in a big time margin so that even in extreme traffic conditions you still make it to the airport on time.

If you're returning from a business trip you are much more concerned about wasting time—your company will pay for flight changes, and there's a flight every hour. You use a similar approach to a pricing risk measure. You consider the average journey times you

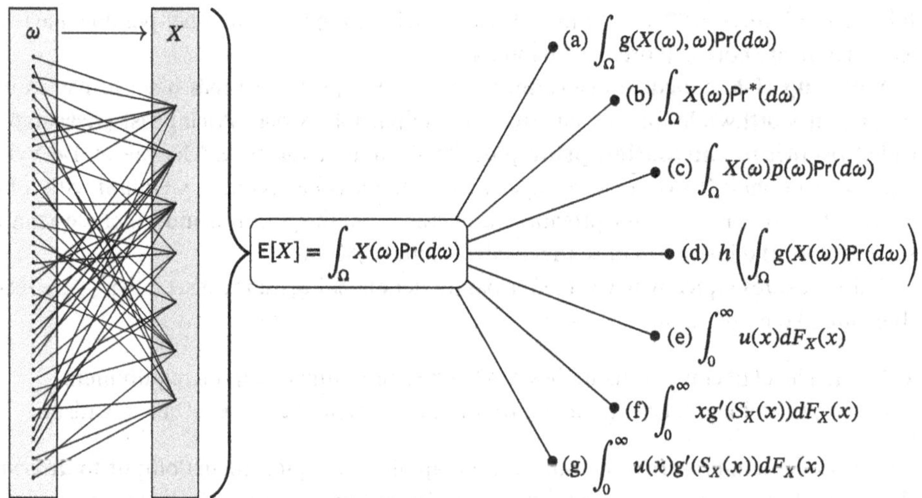

Figure 3.14 Potential functional forms for risk measures inspired by the expected value. The left shows the stochastic model, with many different states of the world mapping to the same loss outcome. These extensions overlap: a given risk measure can often be written in multiple ways.

have experienced, factoring in the time of day, day of the week, and weather, and add a small margin for minor traffic issues. □

Example 35. Stress tests are often used as a risk measure: what are my results in a stressed environment? Again, there are capital and pricing flavors. Lloyd's Realistic Disaster Scenarios, Example 15, define a capital stress test. They quantify the impact of extreme but realistic events. By ensuring adequate capital to pay all claims from RDS events, Lloyd's can communicate its risk paying capacity to a nontechnical audience. Setting capital using a risk measure equal to the worst outcome over the RDS set achieves this goal. Insurers can use alternative climate scenarios in catastrophe models to stress test pricing. These act to increase mean event frequency. An insurer may want to price with a margin reflecting the uncertainty in expected mean frequency. Here, the stress test applies to pricing. □

3.6.4 Risk Measure Functional Forms

What functional forms should we consider for a risk measure? The representation of $\rho(X)$ should be related to the potential outcomes described by X. The most basic summarization of X is the mean, which is the probability weighted sum of outcomes

$$E[X] = \int_\Omega X(\omega)\Pr(d\omega) = \int xdF(x). \tag{3.15}$$

There are many different ways we could generalize the mean; see Figure 3.14.

a. Adjust outcomes by a factor depending on the outcome value and the explicit sample point ω. In finance the sample point is often called *the state of the world* or simply the state.
b. Adjust the probabilities to create a new measure. The new measure can make previously impossible events possible and vice versa.
c. Scale existing probabilities to create a new measure using a function of the explicit sample point (i.e. a random variable) p with $p(\omega) \geq 0$ and $\mathsf{E}[p] = 1$. A specific scenario has this form. In this case events which are impossible under the original probability remain impossible. This approach is developed in Section 8.6.
d. Adjust with a function of loss and not ω. Standard deviation has this form, $h(x) = \sqrt{x}$ and $g(x) = (x - \mu)^2$.
e. Adjust outcomes independently of ω and leave probability unchanged. If the function u is increasing and convex then this form is called an **expected utility risk measure**. When outcomes can take positive and negative values we can adjust them with an S-shaped **value function** (Kahneman and Tversky 1979). The value function reflects attitudes to changes in wealth rather than final wealth.
f. Adjust probabilities by a function of the **rank** of the loss, but leaves the loss amount unchanged. This form is called **dual utility theory** and leads to spectral risk measures; see Section 10.7. (The function $g : [0,1] \to [0,1]$ must satisfy $g(0) = 0$ and $g(1) = 1$. It is used to adjust probabilities. Integration by parts shows that $\int_0^\infty xg'(S(x))dF(x) = \int_0^\infty g(S(x))dx$ since $d(g(S(x)))/dx = -g'(S(x))\, dF/dx$. $S(x)$ is the rank of x.)
g. A combination of (e) and (f) leads to **rank-dependent utility** (Machina, Teugels, and Sundt 2004; Quiggin 2012). Other attempts to adjust probabilities independent of ω are hard and often lead to measures that do not uniformly prefer more of a good to less, counter to any intuitive notion of behavior (Quiggin 2012; Section 4.8).

Adjusting probabilities rather than outcomes retains the original units of X, which is desirable for applications.

In methods (e)–(g), the result depends only on the distribution of X, not its value on each ω. Risk measures with this property are called **law invariant**; see Section 5.2.13. Most of the risk measures studied in detail in this book are law invariant.

Having created a risk measure, we can apply another function to the result. For example, we can load for operational and unmodeled risk by increasing the result by a fixed percentage.

We can create several different risk measures using a variety of techniques and then compute their weighted average, or their maximum. We can further adjust according to our belief in each. Using these processes allows us to create what *appears* to be a bewildering array of risk measures (Section 6.5); we are likely to confuse our clients—and ourselves. We say appears because, under the skin, there are far fewer than the table suggests. The situation is analogous to zoology; the number of individual species in the zoo is daunting, but a visit to the natural history museum reveals underlying similarities under the skin. In our case, the powerful classification theorem for coherent risk measures in Section 5.4 provides the skeleton. This controls the complexity and guides our selection.

Ultimately, the choice of risk measure must be appropriate for its intended application. More advice is given in Chapter 6, and Section 11.5.

Exercise 36. Your student actuary proposes a new adjustment

$$\rho(X) = \int_{\Omega} v(X(\omega))\mathsf{Pr}(d\omega). \tag{3.16}$$

You tell them it is already in our list. Which item is it? □

Exercise 37. Which risk measure forms (a)–(g) address each of the following management, regulator, or investor concerns?

1. Insolvent is insolvent: I don't care about the cause.
2. Differentiate a loss from a catastrophe peril from a loss from a noncatastrophe peril.
3. Incorporate different opinions about what is possible.
4. Avoid an outsize loss relative to peers.
5. Reflect ambiguity and estimation risk in probabilities. □

3.7 Learning Objectives

1. Define a risk and a financial risk.
2. Define and distinguish between timing and amount uncertainty, volume, and volatility, process risk and uncertainty, an insurance risk and a speculative risk, a diversifiable and nondiversifiable risk.
3. Define and give examples of systemic risks and distinguish them from systematic (nondiversifiable) risks.
4. Differentiate between objective and subjective probabilities.
5. Distinguish between process risk and uncertainty and parameter risk.
6. Define a catastrophe risk in an insurance context.
7. Define and identify the explicit, implicit, and dual implicit representations of risk.
8. Create a Lee diagram from a sample of losses or a loss distribution or a loss random variable.
9. Identify expected losses, excess losses, limited losses, put and call values, insurance charge and insurance savings, and policyholder deficit on a Lee diagram.
10. Compute expected losses, excess losses, limited losses, put and call values, insurance charge and insurance savings, and policyholder deficit given a distribution function.
11. Explain how put call parity is the same as insurance savings plus expense equals entry plus loss.
12. Explain and use different expressions for calculating the mean $\mathsf{E}[X]$.
13. Compute expected losses from a random variable, a density or probability mass function, a distribution function or a survival function. Relate the expressions to different stochastic models of risk.
14. Define a risk preference and a risk measure and explain the connection between the two.
15. Characterize risk measures by their sensitivity to volume, volatility, and tail risk.

16. Explain the two principal insurance applications of risk measures, to pricing and capital.
17. Explain how a risk measure can be used to determine premium or capital and to evaluate them.
18. Explain the term *determine premium*.
19. Explain seven different ways that expected value can be extended to create a risk measure.

4

Measuring Risk with Quantiles, VaR, and TVaR

In this chapter, we introduce quantiles, the fundamental building block for many risk measures. Quantiles get renamed value at risk (VaR) when used as a risk measure. We discuss the properties of VaR in detail. We then introduce tail value at risk (TVaR) as an extension of VaR that addresses certain of its technical shortcomings. We pay careful attention to problems caused by discrete and mixed distributions, which are a reality in actuarial work.

4.1 Quantiles

In Section 3.4.3 we used the inverse distribution function to take a dual implicit event, defined by a probability of non-exceedance p, to an outcome x. In doing so, we glossed over the problem that distribution functions do not always have a well-defined inverse. They can have jumps (discrete and mixed distributions) and flat spots (which can occur for any kind of distribution). Quantile functions define an inverse that works in all cases. They are needed whenever we work with discrete variables, such as simulation model output.

4.1.1 Definition and Examples

A quantile function is inverse to the distribution function $F(x) := \mathsf{Pr}(X \le x)$. For each $0 < p < 1$, it solves $F(x) = p$ for x, answering the question,

> which x has non-exceedance probability equal to p?

Or, said another way,

> which x has exceedance probability equal to $1 - p$?

When the distribution function is continuous and strictly increasing there is a unique such x. It is called the p-quantile, and is denoted $q(p)$. The resulting function $q(p) = F^{-1}(p)$ is called the quantile function; it satisfies $F(q(p)) = p$.

As we just mentioned, two issues arise when defining quantiles.

Pricing Insurance Risk: Theory and Practice, First Edition. Stephen J. Mildenhall and John A. Major.

First, the equation $F(x) = p$ may fail to have a *unique* solution when F is not strictly increasing. This can occur for any F. Is corresponds to a range of *impossible* outcome values.

Second, when F is not continuous, the equation $F(x) = p$ may have *no solution*: F can jump from below p to above p. Simulation and catastrophe models, and all discrete random variables have discontinuous distributions.

These two situations are illustrated in Figure 4.1. The distribution F has a flat spot between 0.9 and 1.5 at height $p = 0.417$. At $x = 1.5$ it jumps up to $p = 0.791$. The "inverse" to F at $p = 0.417$ could be any value between 0.9 and 1.5—illustrated by the lower horizontal dashed line. The inverse at any value $0.417 < p < 0.791$ doesn't exist because there is no p so that $F(p) = 0.6$. However, any rational person looking at the graph would agree that the answer must be $x = 1.5$, where the black dashed line intersects the vertical line $x = 1.5$.

Figure 4.1 illustrates that when F is not continuous and $F(x) = p$ has no solution because p lies is within a jump, we can still find an x so that

$$\Pr(X < x) \le p \le \Pr(X \le x). \tag{4.1}$$

$\Pr(X < x)$ equals the height of F at the bottom of the jump and $\Pr(X \le x)$ at the top. (Turning this around, we can also say $\Pr(X \ge x) \ge 1 - p \ge \Pr(X > x)$.) At a p with no jump, $\Pr(X = x) = 0$, $\Pr(X < x) = p = \Pr(X \le x)$, and we have a well-defined inverse, as the lower line at $p = 0.283$ illustrates.

Eq. (4.1) motivates the following definition.

Definition 1. *Let X be a random variable with distribution function F and let $0 < p < 1$. Any x satisfying*

$$\Pr(X < x) \le p \le \Pr(X \le x)$$

is a p **quantile** *of X. Any function $q(p)$ satisfying*

$$\Pr(X < q(p)) \le p \le \Pr(X \le q(p)) \tag{4.2}$$

for $0 < p < 1$ is a **quantile function** *of X.*

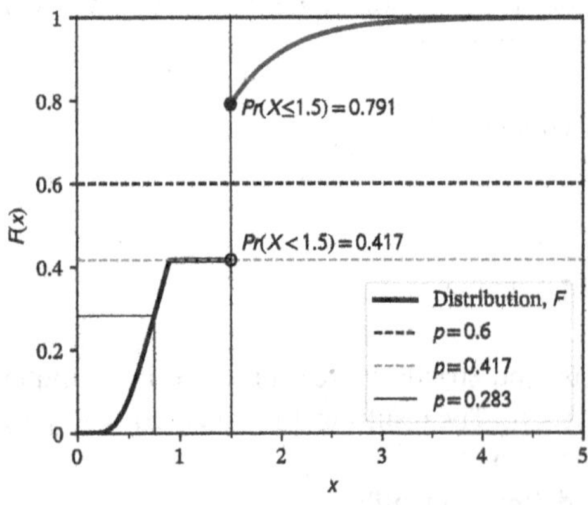

Figure 4.1 The two ways a distribution function can fail to have a well-defined inverse: (1) a flat spot (lower dashed line) at p = 0.417, and (2) within a jump (upper dashed line). Generated by a lognormal $\mu = 0$, $\sigma = 1$ distribution with values between 0.9 and 1.5 set to 0.9.

Exercise 38. What are the 0.1 and 1/6 quantiles for the outcomes of the fair roll of a six-sided die?

Solution. There are six outcomes $\{1, 2, 3, 4, 5, 6\}$ each with probability 1/6. The distribution function jumps at each outcome.

1. For $p = 0.1$ we seek x so that $\Pr(X < x) \leq 0.1 \leq \Pr(X \leq x)$. We know $0 = \Pr(X < 1) < \Pr(X \leq 1) = 1/6$ and therefore $q(0.1) = 1$. It is good to rule out other possible values. If $x < 1$ then $\Pr(X \leq x) = 0$ and if $x > 1$ then $\Pr(X < x) \geq 1/6$, showing neither alternative satisfies the definition of a quantile.
2. For $p = 1/6$ we seek x so that $\Pr(X < x) \leq 1/6 \leq \Pr(X \leq x)$, which is satisfied by any $1 \leq x \leq 2$. If we pick $x = 1$ then $0 = \Pr(X < 1) < 1/6 = \Pr(X \leq 1)$. If we pick $1 < x < 2$ then $\Pr(X < x) = 1/6 = \Pr(X \leq x)$. If $x = 2$ then $\Pr(X < 2) = 1/6 < \Pr(X \leq 2) = 1/3$. □

In Figure 4.1, the vertical segment at $x = 1.5$ between $p = 0.417$ and $p = 0.791$ is not strictly a part of F's graph, because a function must associate a *unique* value to each x in its domain. However, filling in the vertical segment makes it easier to locate inverse values by finding the graph's intersection with the horizontal line at p and is recommended in Rockafellar and Royset (2014). From now on, we always *fill in* jumps in this way, treating the added segment as part of the graph.

Figure 4.2 illustrates three general behaviors a mixed distribution function can exhibit. Each row corresponds to a mixed distribution, differing only in the location of a probability mass. The continuous part of the distributions accounts for 0.5 probability and is uniform from 0 to 2 and 8 to 10. The probability mass of 0.5 is located at 2 in the top row, 5 in the middle, and 8 in the bottom. The first column shows the densities, with the triangle indicating the location of the mass. (Although the triangle is small, it represents half the probability.) The second column shows the distribution function F. And the third column shows the quantile function q.

Since the distribution and quantile functions are inverse, their graphs are reflections of one another in a 45-degree line through the origin. The distribution function is continuous from the right, hence the location of the probability masses indicated by the circles. In the top row $F(2) = 0.75$ because of the mass $\Pr(X = 2) = 0.5$.

The value of the quantile function is unambiguous except where F is flat, at $p = 0.75$ and $p = 0.25$. Consider the top row where the mass occurs at $x = 2$. For any $p \neq 0.75$ a horizontal line at p intersects the graph of F (including vertical segments) at a unique point, which defines $q(p)$. The $p = 0.75$ quantile is any value x satisfying $\Pr(X < x) \leq 0.75 \leq \Pr(X \leq x)$. Looking at the top middle plot shows any value $2 \leq x \leq 8$ is a 0.75 quantile, i.e. any value in the horizontal segment of the distribution graph or vertical segment of the quantile graph. There are two natural choices we can make: $x = 2$ and $x = 8$. In general, define

- The **lower quantile** function $q^-(p) := \sup \{x \mid F(x) < p\} = \inf \{x \mid F(x) \geq p\}$, and
- The **upper quantile** function $q^+(p) := \sup \{x \mid F(x) \leq p\} = \inf \{x \mid F(x) > p\}$.

The lower and upper quantiles both satisfy the requirement of Eq. (4.2) to be a quantile function. The lower quantile is left continuous. The upper quantile is right continuous. The

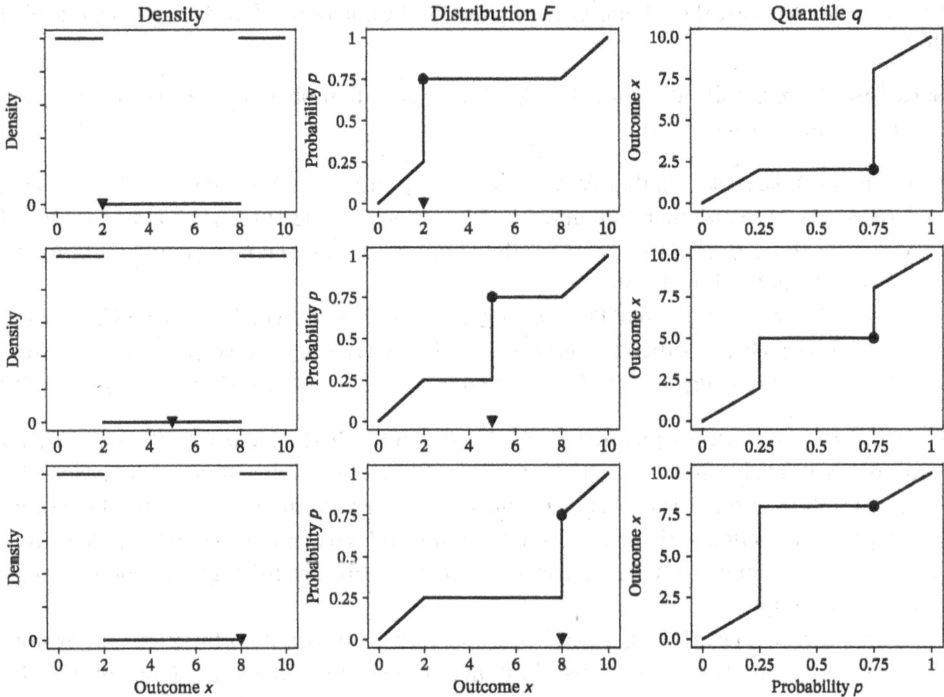

Figure 4.2 Three types of discontinuous behavior illustrated for the density (left column), distribution (middle), and quantile functions (right) of X. The distribution function is continuous from the right because it is $\Pr(X \leq x)$, as illustrated by the dots showing the values at jump points. The quantile's dots are carried over from the distribution function. The actual value of the quantile function at jump points can be chosen as any point in the range that satisfies Eq. (4.2). The upper (resp. lower) quantile picks the top (resp. bottom) point and is continuous from the right (resp. left).

ambiguity about the value of $q(0.75)$ is irrelevant in the sense that an exact value $p = 0.75$ never occurs (occurs with probability zero) in simulations.

Remark 39. In Figure 4.1, the fact that the jump occurs at the end of the flat spot is a coincidence. For mixed distributions, jumps can occur anywhere along F and not just after flat spots. Discrete distributions are stair-stepped functions meaning jumps always occur after flat spots. Continuous distributions don't have jumps. □

Example 40. The Lee diagram, Section 3.5.1, is a plot of the quantile function. □

Example 41. The spreadsheet `BINOM.INV(num_trials, prob_success, p)` evaluates the inverse of the discrete binomial distribution functions. The documentation says it "Calculates the *smallest* value for which the cumulative binomial distribution is greater than or equal to a specified criteria." Therefore it returns the lower quantile of the binomial and `=BINOM.INV(1, 0.5, 0.5)=0`. □

Example 42. Figure 4.3 illustrates different random variables with the same distribution and quantile functions. □

Example 43. Let X_1, X_2 be independent standard normal distributions and $X = X_1 + X_2$. Then X has a normal distribution with variance 2. It is easy to write down and compute the distribution and quantile functions of all these variables. The quantile functions, $q_{X_i}(p) = \Phi^{-1}(p)$ and $q_X(p) = \sqrt{2}\Phi^{-1}(p)$, are one-to-one mappings between $(0,1)$ and $\mathbb{R}$. However, there are infinitely many solutions ω to $X(\omega) = x$, given by $X_1 = t$ and $X_2 = x - t$ for $t \in \mathbb{R}$. These solutions have probability zero (zero length) and are all mapped to the value $q(F(x))$ in the quantile view. This example shows the loss of information entailed by moving from the random variable X, where for a given ω the decomposition $X(\omega) = X_1(\omega) + X_2(\omega)$ is known explicitly, to q or F, where it is not. This loss of information is one reason that aggregation of distribution functions is difficult. □

Remark 44. A quantile (or QQ) plot compares the quantiles of two distributions. They are used in statistics to evaluate distribution fits. A Lee diagram is a QQ plot of X against a uniform distribution. We do not use QQ plots in this book. □

Technical Remark 45. Sometimes it is convenient to extend q to take argument $0 \le p \le 1$. In that case we must allow the values $\pm\infty$. For example, if X is lognormal then $q(0) = 0$ but $q(1) = \infty$. □

4.1.2 Algorithm to Compute Quantiles

Algorithm Input: A distribution function F and a probability level $0 < p < 1$.
Follow these steps to determine the p quantile of F.

Algorithm Steps

1. **Determine** where a horizontal line at height p intersects the graph of the distribution function, including vertical segments.
2. **If** there is a unique intersection, then it is the unique quantile.
3. **Else** there is an interval of intersection (F is horizontal) and

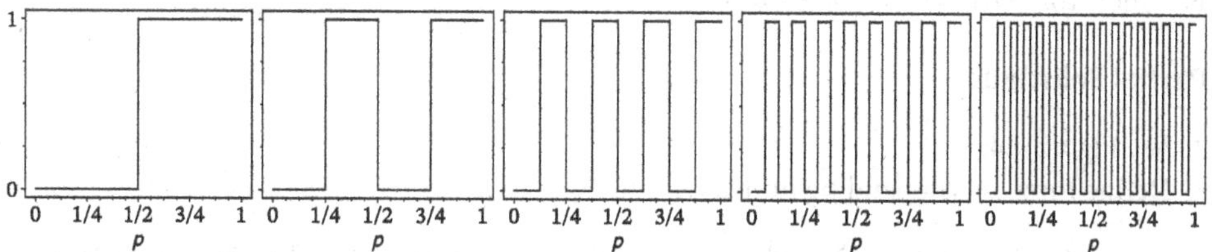

Figure 4.3 Five independent Bernoulli random variables with $p = 0.5$ defined on $\Omega = [0,1]$. The quantile functions for all five distributions look like the first plot on the left, albeit with different interpretations for the vertical axis. The plots illustrate that two random variables with the same distribution or quantile function can be very different.

- The left end (smallest value) is the lower quantile,
- The right end (largest value) is the upper quantile, and
- Any value in between is a legitimate quantile.

The actual selection in Step (3) refers to an event with a probability zero of occurring. The lower quantile has the smallest absolute value when the flat interval lies to the right of zero (losses, using the actuarial sign convention), and the upper quantile has the smallest absolute value when it lies to the left of zero (wealth, using the accounting sign convention).

Exercise 46.

1. A Bernoulli outcome takes values 0 and 1 with probability 0.5. Carefully describe all quantiles.
2. Carefully draw the distribution and quantile function for the outcome of rolling a fair die.
3. Catastrophe model output has outcomes 0, 10, 90, and 100 with probabilities 0.97, 0.01, 0.01, and 0.01. Carefully describe the distribution function and quantile function. What number would you report as the 0.99 quantile? As the 0.996 quantile?
4. Show that $q^-(p) = \sup\{x \mid \Pr(X < x) < p\}$ and $q^+(p) = \sup\{x \mid \Pr(X < x) \le p\}$. Verify that all three definitions for lower and upper quantiles agree.
5. Show that $F(x) \ge p \iff q^-(p) \le x$, and $F(x) < p \iff q^-(p) > x$. Draw diagrams!
6. Show that $q^-(F(x)) \le x$ with equality if F is strictly increasing and $F(q^-(p)) \ge p$ with equality if F is continuous.
7. Let X be a loss random variable with a finite mean. Show that q is a p quantile for X if and only if it minimizes the (convex) objective function

$$b(c) = p\,E[(X-c)^+] + (1-p)\mathsf{E}[(c-X)^+].$$

8. What is the quantile function for X having an exponential distribution with mean 100?
9. What is the quantile function for X having a Pareto distribution with shape parameter 1.5 and scale parameter 1000?
10. Show that F is continuous iff q^- is strictly increasing and that q^- is continuous iff F is strictly increasing.
11. Show that $\Pr(q^-(F(X)) \ne X) = 0$.

Partial Solutions.

2. See Figure 4.4.
3. Define three sets depending on p as

$$A = \{x \mid \Pr(X \le x) < p\},\quad B = \{x \mid \Pr(X < x) < p\},\quad C = \{x \mid \Pr(X \le x) \ge p\}.$$

Let $q_A(p) = \sup A$, $q_B(p) = \sup B$ and $q_C(p) = \inf C$. Since $\Pr(X < x) \le \Pr(X \le x)$ it follows $A \subset B$ and therefore $q_A \le q_B$. C lies to the right of B because the distribution function is nondecreasing. Therefore $q_B \le q_C$. The three functions are equal if $q_C \le q_A$. If $y \le q_C(p)$ then $y \notin C$ so $\Pr(X \le y) < p$. Hence $y \in A$ and so $y < q_A(p)$ as required.

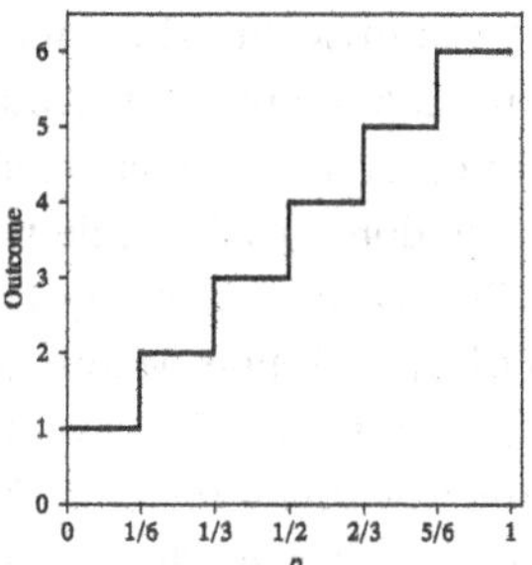

Figure 4.4 Quantile function for the outcomes of the fair roll of a six-sided die, including vertical segments.

4. Follows from the definition of q^-. If x_0 satisfies $F(x_0) \geq p$ then $x_0 \in \{x \mid F(x) \geq p\}$. By definition $q^-(p) = \inf\{x \mid F(x) \geq p\}$ and therefore $x_0 \geq q^-(p)$. Since F is increasing and continuous from the right $\{x \mid F(x) \geq p\}$ is closed. Therefore, if $x_0 \geq q^-(p)$ then $x_0 \in \{x \mid F(x) \geq p\}$ and so $F(x_0) \geq p$. □

4.1.3 Simulation Using Quantile Functions

The quantile function can be used to simulate values from X. Let U be a uniform random variable, meaning $\mathsf{Pr}(U \leq \omega) = \omega$ for $\omega \in [0, 1]$. Consider the new random variable $q^-(U)$, which takes the value $q^-(U(\omega))$ at ω. Then $q^-(U)$ has the same distribution as X since $\{p \mid q^-(p) \leq x\} = \{p \mid p \leq F(x)\}$ by Exercise 46, Part 5, and therefore

$$\begin{aligned}\mathsf{Pr}(q^-(U) \leq x) &= \mathsf{Pr}(U \leq F(x)) \\ &= F(x) \\ &= \mathsf{Pr}(X \leq x)).\end{aligned}$$

This relationship underlies the **inversion method** of simulation. It is true for any quantile function, not just q^-, see Follmer and Schied (2016, p. A.19). It does not require that X have a continuous distribution.

The fact that X and $q(U)$ have the same distribution explains why quantiles are so important as risk measures: they capture the same information as X about *outcomes*. All that is lost is the labeling of the sample points, which is not usually a problem for regulators since they are more concerned with the fact of insolvency than its particular cause.

Technical Remark 47. When F is continuous, $F(X)$ is uniform and can be used in place of U. If X is also strictly increasing then F and q are inverse functions and $X = q(F(X))$. This result can be extended to non-continuous X on an atomless probability space. Ryff (1970) shows there exists a random variable U on the same space with a uniform distribution on $(0, 1)$ so that $X = q(U)$ almost surely. This is a much stronger condition than the first result, which just says $q^-(U)$ and X have the same distribution. Ryff's U is equal to $F(X)$ where F is continuous and adds a term $\mathsf{P}(\{\omega \mid X(\omega) = X(\omega_0), \omega \leq \omega_0\})$ at ω_0 if $\mathsf{P}(X = X(\omega_0)) > 0$, i.e. if ω_0 is in a flat spot of X (jump of F). □

Technical Example 48. Imagine the US coast from Port Isabel, Texas to Lubec, Maine stretched out to a straight line and scaled to $[0, 1]$. The coast is about 3700 miles long. Using four decimal places is sufficient to measure the landfall location of a hurricane. The remaining digits in a random $\omega \in [0,1]$ can be used to encode information about a hurricane's direction, central pressure, radius of maximum wind speed, and other salient characteristics. Running each event through a catastrophe model produces a random variable X defined on $\Omega = [0,1]$ giving the corresponding insured loss outcome. The graph of X is very fractured, with peaks at locations corresponding to Houston, New Orleans, Mobile, Miami, etc. Assuming all loss amounts are distinct, we can also sort events by outcome. The event at physical location ω moves to a place a proportion $F(X(\omega))$ of the way down the list. Thus $\omega \mapsto \psi = F(X(\omega))$ gives a reordering of the coast line according to event size. The graph of X on this reordered map is an increasing function, with the value $q(\psi)$ at ψ. □

4.2 Value at Risk

4.2.1 Motivation

You are planning to host dinner for a group of friends at Ye Olde World restaurant. Olde World has great food but accepts only cash. How much cash should you take? You want to be *reasonably confident* that you have *enough* cash. In symbols, let X be a random variable that models your bill for this group of friends and a your cash on hand, then you want

$$\Pr(X \le a) \ge 0.95, \tag{4.3}$$

to be 95% (say) sure that you will have enough money. $X \le a$ means you have enough cash, and ≥ 0.95 puts a lower bound on your confidence. The smallest amount a you can take satisfying Eq. (4.3) is called the 0.95-VaR of the restaurant bill. It is exactly the lower quantile $q_X^-(0.95)$ of X defined in Section 4.1.1.

Why do you select 95% confidence? There is a cost to you of holding cash. If you need to withdraw a substantial amount, you have the inconvenience of multiple trips to the ATM or even an interaction with a bank teller. If you have too much cash left over, you have to re-deposit it at the bank. You select 95% because it balances your fear of embarrassment at failing to meet your obligations against the inconvenience to you of holding too much cash. It is an individual choice—part of your risk preference.

4.2.2 Definition and Examples

When a quantile is used as a risk measure it gets a special name: Value at Risk (VaR). Delbaen (2000) says "VaR is the most widely used instrument to control risk."

Definition 2. *The* p **Value at Risk** *or* **VaR** *of a loss random variable* X *equals the lower* p*-quantile,* $q^-(p) = \inf\{x \mid F(x) \ge p\}$. *It is denoted* $\mathsf{VaR}_p(X)$.

Thus l is $\mathsf{VaR}_p(X)$ if it is the smallest loss such that the probability $X \le l$ is $\ge p$. This is sometimes phrased: the smallest loss so that $X \le l$ with confidence at least p. *Smallest loss* allows for the case F is flat at p. *Probability* $\ge p$ allows for jumps in F.

VaR has several advantages. It is simple to explain, can be estimated robustly, and is always finite. It is widely used by regulators, rating agencies, and companies in their internal risk management. Its principal disadvantage is occasionally suspect performance concerning diversification; see Section 4.2.5.

Exercise 49. X is a random variable defined on a sample space with ten equally likely events. The event outcomes are $0, 1, 1, 1, 2, 3, 4, 8, 12, 25$. Compute $\mathsf{VaR}_p(X)$ for all p.

Solution. The graph is shown in Figure 4.5. Follow the algorithm for computing a p-quantile: fill in the vertical segments in the graph of the distribution function. Draw a horizontal line at height p and find its intersection with the completed graph. There is a unique solution for all p except $0.1, 0.4, 0.5, \dots, 0.9$. Consider $p = 0.4$. Any x satisfying $\mathsf{Pr}(X < x) \le 0.4 \le \mathsf{Pr}(X \le x)$ is a 0.4-quantile. By inspection the solutions are $1 \le x \le 2$. VaR is defined as the lower quantile, $x = 1$. The 0.41 quantile is $x = 2$. VaRs are not interpolated in this problem specification. The loss 25 is the p-VaR for any $p > 0.9$. □

Exercise 50. Based on grouped data, you are given the following information about a continuous random loss X. Compute $\mathsf{VaR}_p(X)$ for all p.

Loss, x	$F(x) = \mathsf{Pr}(X \le x)$
0	0.1
1	0.4
2	0.5
3	0.6
4	0.7
8	0.8
12	0.9
25	1.0

Solution. In this framing, we are given values of the distribution function of X and explicitly told X is continuous. In the absence of other information, it is appropriate to use an ogive (piecewise linear) approximation to the empirical distribution function (Klugman, Panjer, and Willmot 2018). To compute VaRs, again apply the algorithm to the ogive, producing Figure 4.6. □

Technical Remark 51. Many books and papers define VaR for asset random variables rather than loss random variables. Asset modeling uses the accounting sign convention that positive is good, making left tail quantiles bad with p close to 0. For loss random variables, right tail quantiles, with p close to 1, are bad. VaR for an asset random variable uses the upper quantile, and it is generally negative. (Note: the quantile with the smallest absolute value is selected.) VaR for an asset random variable Y is defined as $-q^{-}_{-Y}(1-p)$. To avoid ambiguity, it is often written slightly differently, e.g. as V@R. We consider VaR only for loss random variables in this book. □

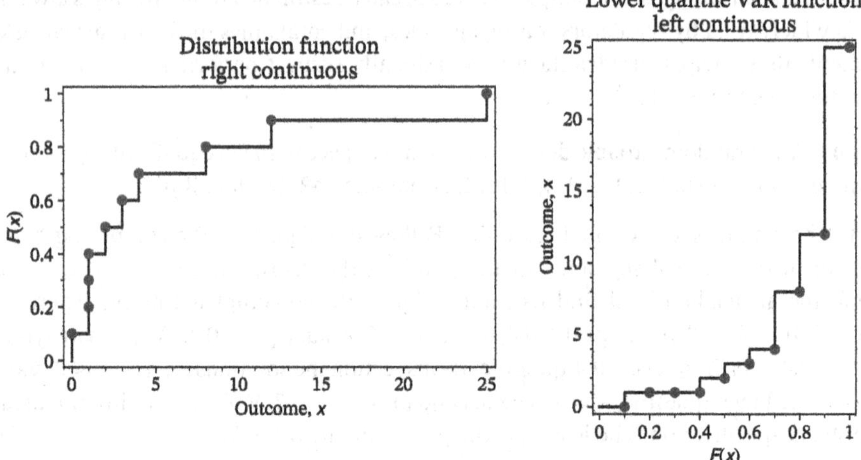

Figure 4.5 Left: the distribution function F corresponding to 10 equally likely samples 0, 1, 1, 1, 2, 3, 4, 8, 12, and 25. The distribution function is right continuous and so the jumps occur at the observations. Right: the corresponding VaR or lower quantile function, which is left continuous.

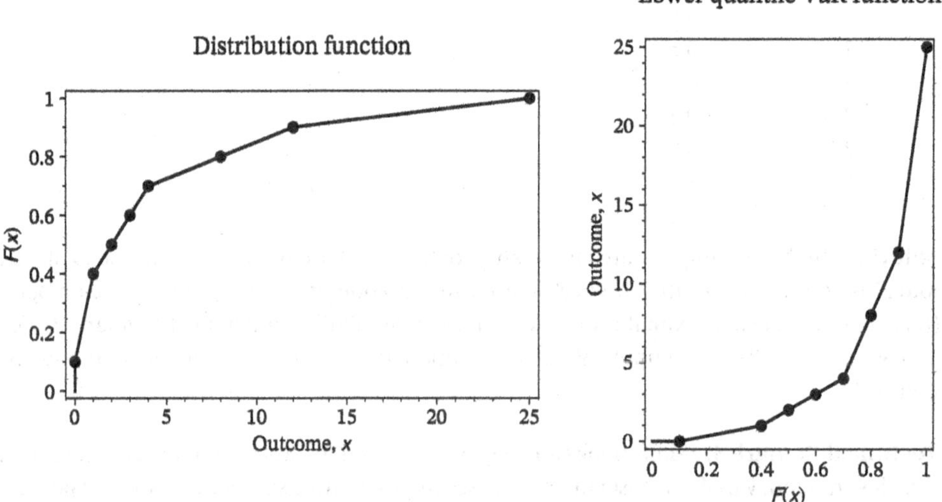

Figure 4.6 Left: the interpolated distribution function F; right: the corresponding VaR or lower quantile function for the sampled distribution points.

Table 4.1 Standard return periods and their probability representation.

VaR threshold	Exceedance probability	Return period	Applications
p	$1-p$	$1/(1-p)$	
0.99	0.01	100 years	
0.995	0.005	200 years	Solvency 2
0.996	0.004	250 years	AM Best, S&P, RBC
0.999	0.001	1,000 years	

4.2.3 Return Periods

VaR points are often quoted by **return period**, such as a 100 or 250 year loss, rather than by probability level. Return periods are more evocative—though perhaps also more confusing. It is necessary to know the time period over which losses are aggregated to convert to the return period. Actuarial applications almost always use one year, but banking applications typically consider one trading day (250 trading days corresponding to a year). We assume X represents aggregate losses over one year.

By definition, the exceedance probability $\mathsf{Pr}(X > \mathsf{VaR}_p(X))$ of p-VaR is less than or equal to $1-p$, meaning at most a $1-p$ probability per year. If years are independent, then the average waiting time to an exceedance is at least $1/(1-p)$. (The waiting time has a geometric distribution, with parameter p. Let $q = 1-p$. The average wait time is $q+2pq+3p^2q+\cdots = q(1+2p+3p^2+\cdots) = 1/q$.)

Standard return periods and their probability representation are shown in Table 4.1.

When X represents aggregate annual losses, the statement $x = \mathsf{VaR}_{0.99}(X)$, $p = 0.99$ means

- x is the smallest loss for which $X \le x$ with an annual probability of at least 0.99, or
- x is the smallest loss with an annual probability at most 0.01 of being exceeded.

The statement "A loss of size x or greater is expected to occur once every 100 years" suggests there is a quota of one loss per 100 years. It is clearer to say, "There is a 1% chance per year of a loss of size x or greater occurring."

4.2.4 Aggregate and Occurrence Probable Maximal Loss and Catastrophe Model Output

All of our discussion so far relates to *aggregate* loss over one year. Occurrence flavored quantiles and closely related occurrence PMLs are also used. These have different meanings and computations that we describe here.

Probable maximal loss or **PML** and the related **maximum foreseeable loss** (MFL) originated in fire underwriting in the early 1900s. The PML estimates the largest loss that a building is likely to suffer from a single fire if all critical protection systems function as expected. The MFL estimates the largest fire loss likely to occur if loss-suppression systems fail. For a large office building, the PML could be a total loss to 4 to 6 floors, and the MFL could be a total loss within four walls, assuming a single structure burns down. McGuinness (1969) discusses PMLs.

Today, PML is used to quantify potential catastrophe losses. Catastrophe risk is typically managed using reinsurance purchased on an occurrence basis and covering all losses from a single event. Therefore insurers are interested in the annual frequency of events greater than an attachment threshold, leading to the occurrence PML.

To describe occurrence PMLs, we need to specify the stochastic model used to generate events. It is standard to use a homogeneous Poisson process, with a constant event intensity λ per year. The number of events in time t has a Poisson distribution with mean λt. If X is the severity distribution (size of loss conditional on an event) then the number of events per year above size x has Poisson distribution with mean $\lambda S(x)$. Therefore the probability of one or more events causing loss x or more is 1 minus the probability that a Poisson($\lambda S(x)$) random variable equals zero, which equals $1 - e^{-\lambda S(x)}$. The ***n* year occurrence PML**, $\mathsf{PML}_{n,\lambda}(X) = \mathsf{PML}_{n,\lambda}$, is the smallest loss x so that the probability of one or more events causing a loss of x or more in a year is at least $1/n$. It can be determined by solving $1 - e^{-\lambda S(\mathsf{PML}_{n,\lambda})} = 1/n$, giving

$$S(\mathsf{PML}_{n,\lambda}) = \frac{1}{\lambda}\log\left(\frac{n}{n-1}\right) \implies \mathsf{PML}_{n,\lambda} = q_X\left(1 - \frac{1}{\lambda}\log\left(\frac{n}{n-1}\right)\right)$$

(if $S(x) = s$ then $F(x) = 1 - s$ and $x = q_X(1-s) = \mathsf{VaR}_{1-s}(X)$). Thus, *the occurrence PML is a quantile of severity at an adjusted probability level*, where the adjustment depends on λ. See Example 54 for an application of these results.

Converting to non-exceedance probabilities, if $p = 1-1/n$ (close to 1) then $n/(n-1) = 1/p$ and we obtain a relationship between the occurrence PML and severity VaR:

$$\mathsf{PML}_{n,\lambda} = q_X\left(1 + \frac{\log(p)}{\lambda}\right) = \mathsf{VaR}_{1+\log(p)/\lambda}(X). \tag{4.4}$$

Catastrophe models output a sample of N loss events, each with an associated annual frequency λ_i and an expected loss x_i, $i = 1, \dots, N$. Each event is assumed to have a Poisson occurrence frequency distribution. The associated severity distribution is concentrated on the set $\{x_1, \dots, x_N\}$ with $\Pr(X = x_i) = \lambda_i/\lambda$, where $\lambda = \sum_i \lambda_i$ is the expected annual event frequency. It is customary to fit or smooth X to get a continuous distribution, resulting in unique quantiles.

Remark 52. Severity VaR (quantile) and occurrence PML are distinct concepts, related by Eq. (4.4). However, **aggregate PML** is often used as a synonym for aggregate VaR, i.e. VaR of the aggregate loss distribution. □

Let A equal the annual aggregate loss random variable. A has a compound Poisson distribution with expected annual frequency λ and severity random variable X. X is usually thick-tailed. Then, as we explain shortly,

$$\mathsf{VaR}_p(A) \approx \mathsf{VaR}_{1-(1-p)/\lambda}(X). \tag{4.5}$$

Eq. (4.5) is a relationship between aggregate and severity VaRs.

Eq. (4.5) and Eq. (4.4) combine to give an estimate for aggregate VaRs in terms of occurrence PMLs with no simulation. Thus for large n and a thick-tailed X occurrence PMLs and aggregate VaRs contain the same information—there is not *more information* in the aggregate, as is sometimes suggested.

The approximation Eq. (4.5) follows from the equation

$$\mathsf{Pr}(X_1 + \cdots + X_n > x) \to n\mathsf{Pr}(X > x) \text{ as } x \to \infty \tag{4.6}$$

for all n, which holds when X is sufficiently thick-tailed. See Embrechts, Klüppelberg, and Mikosch (1997), Corollary 1.3.2, for the details.

Example 53. This example presents a useful **VaR Heuristic**. When X_0 is a thin-tailed random variable and X_1 is an independent thick-tailed variable VaR for the total $X = X_0 + X_1$ can be approximated

$$\mathsf{VaR}_p(X) \approx \mathsf{E}[X_0] + \mathsf{VaR}_p(X_1). \tag{4.7}$$

A distribution is thin-tailed if it is bounded or has a log concave density. The normal is log concave. Figure 2.4, top right, shows that the noncat unit in the Cat/noncat Case is log concave. A distribution is thick-tailed if $S(x) \approx kx^{\alpha}$ for some constant k, or more generally if it is **subexponential**, Section 6.3. Figure 2.4, top right, shows the Cat unit is subexponential above a threshold, where it becomes log convex. When X_0 is log concave and X_1 subexponential, as is evident in Figure 2.5, X_0 can be regarded as constant over the range of X_1 and so Eq. (4.7) follows.

Table 4.2 applies Eq. (4.7) to the gross portfolio. The heuristic is a very accurate approximation across a wide range of probabilities in this case. □

Table 4.2 $\mathsf{VaR}_p(X)$ estimated as $\mathsf{E}[X_0] + \mathsf{VaR}_p(X_1)$ for the gross cat and noncat example, $\mathsf{E}[X_0] = 80$.

p	$\mathsf{VaR}_p(X_1)$	Approximation	$\mathsf{VaR}_p(X)$	Error
0.5	14.1	94.1	96.1	−0.021
0.75	24.8	104.8	109.5	−0.043
0.9	41.1	121.1	126.0	−0.039
0.95	55.6	135.6	139.9	−0.031
0.975	72.3	152.3	156.0	−0.024
0.99	98.1	178.1	181.1	−0.017
0.996	128.7	208.7	211.1	−0.012
0.999	185.3	265.3	267.2	−0.007
0.9995	218.9	298.9	300.6	−0.006
0.9999	312.7	392.7	394.0	−0.003

Table 4.3 Estimated occurrence and aggregate PML points for a simple model of US Hurricane risk. Frequency Poisson with mean 1.74. Severity lognormal with mean USD5 billion and $\sigma = 2.58$. Amounts in USD millions at 2018 price levels. Return periods n in years.

n	p	Adj p	Occ PML	Sev VaR	Agg VaR	Est VaR	Error
2	0.500	0.602	348	179	420	763	0.816
5	0.800	0.872	3,350	1,572	3,940	3,971	0.008
10	0.900	0.939	9,783	4,892	11,080	10,467	−0.055
20	0.950	0.971	23,420	12,490	25,620	24,107	−0.059
25	0.960	0.977	30,196	16,412	32,720	30,873	−0.056
50	0.980	0.988	62,630	35,870	66,180	63,256	−0.044
100	0.990	0.994	121,162	72,473	125,760	121,714	−0.032
200	0.995	0.997	222,461	137,948	228,020	222,931	−0.022
250	0.996	0.998	268,049	167,935	273,900	268,492	−0.020
500	0.998	0.999	466,816	300,935	473,500	467,178	−0.013
1,000	0.999	0.999	787,463	520,108	794,820	787,752	−0.009

Example 54. A simple model of US hurricane losses uses a lognormal severity distribution X with mean USD5 billion ($\mu = 21.315$) and $\sigma = 2.58$—hence the choice of σ in the Hu/SCS Case. The historical record 1851–2018 for hurricane landfalls shows the annual number of landfalls is consistent with a Poisson distribution N with mean 1.74. Table 4.3 shows the following.

- Return period n and corresponding probability level p.
- The adjusted p value, Adj p, used to compute the occurrence PML from Eq. (4.4).
- The occurrence PML points, Occ PML, computed using Eq. (4.4).
- VaR points from severity, Sev VaR, computed as quantiles of the lognormal severity. Note the difference between occurrence PML and severity VaR.
- VaR points for A, the aggregate distribution, Agg VaR. These are the same as aggregate PML points. They are computed using a Fast Fourier Transform approximation. They could also be estimated using simulation, possibly with importance sampling.
- The approximate aggregate VaR points, Est VaR, computed using Eq. (4.5).
- The error in the approximation. The approximation is excellent for larger return periods.

□

Exercise 55.

1. What happens to the difference between occurrence PML and severity VaR as the expected claim count λ becomes larger and larger?
2. Your management believes the historical record understates event frequency today. They suggest $\mathsf{E}[N] = 2.0$ is more appropriate. Recompute the occurrence PMLs given in Table 4.3.

3. Your management believes there is also the potential for demand surge and suggests the average loss should be USD6 billion. Again, recompute the occurrence PMLs.
4. Your management believes in *event clustering* and feels that a Poisson distribution for events is inappropriate. They want to use an over-dispersed model and suggest a negative binomial with variance equal to three times the mean. Recompute the occurrence PMLs once more. What arguments can you make against event clustering? Download the NOAA data and perform a chi-squared goodness of fit analysis of the Poisson model. What distribution would you recommend?
5. Build a simulation model to estimate the aggregate PMLs.
6. How do you compute two-year PML points rather than one year?
7. Why is occurrence reinsurance more common than aggregate reinsurance? □

4.2.5 The Failure of VaR to be Subadditive

Consider random variables X_1, X_2 and $X = X_1 + X_2$ with outcomes laid out in the next table.

Event	Probability	F	X_1	X_2	X
1	0.98	0.98	0	0	0
2	0.01	0.99	1000	100	1100
3	0.01	1	150	1100	1250

The $p = 0.99$ quantile for X is any loss x so that $\mathsf{Pr}(X < x) \le 0.99 \le \mathsf{Pr}(X \le x)$. From the table it is clear $1100 \le x \le 1250$. Value at risk is the least quantile: $\mathsf{VaR}_{0.99}(X) = 1100$. Similarly, $\mathsf{VaR}_{0.99}(X_1) = 150$ and $\mathsf{VaR}_{0.99}(X_2) = 100$. Thus we find

$$\mathsf{VaR}_{0.99}(X_1 + X_2) > \mathsf{VaR}_{0.99}(X_1) + \mathsf{VaR}_{0.99}(X_2).$$

This example shows that controlling VaR for each X_i does not necessarily control the total VaR, a highly undesirable outcome. A good risk measure should allow control of the total through control of the parts. That is, it should be **subadditive** and satisfy

$$\rho(X_1 + X_2) \le \rho(X_1) + \rho(X_2). \tag{4.8}$$

Coherent risk measures (Artzner *et al.* 1999) were created to address VaR's failure to be subadditive. Coherent risk measures are defined in Section 5.2.14.

McNeil, Embrechts, and Frey (2005) describe three ways VaR can fail to be subadditive.

1. When the dependence structure is of a particular, highly asymmetric form.
2. When the marginals have a very skewed distribution.
3. When the marginals are very heavy-tailed.

We examine each case in more detail.

Case 1: Failure of subadditivity driven by dependence structure

Surprisingly, given two nontrivial marginal distributions X_1 and X_2 and a confidence level p it is **always possible** to find a dependence structure where subadditivity fails! Dependence trumps characteristics of the marginal distributions.

Positive dependence between variables increases the risk of their sum. Therefore, a reasonable first guess is that the worst possible dependence structure occurs when X_1 and X_2 are comonotonic, i.e. we pair the largest value of X_1 with the largest value of X_2, second largest of X_1 with second largest of X_2 and so forth. This pairing produces the riskiest sum in many senses: it has the greatest variance and worst TVaR characteristics. However, it does not fail VaR subadditivity at any threshold p. It results in VaR being strictly additive: the p percentile of the sum is simply the sum of the p percentiles of X_1 and X_2. There is no diversification benefit, but there is also no failure of subadditivity either. The worst p-VaR pairing of X_1 and X_2 has a more subtle form.

How should we combine observations from X_1 and X_2 so that the value at risk of the sum is as large as possible? For example, given samples $x_{1,i}, x_{2,i}, i = 1, 2, \dots, 10000$ how should we form pairs $(x_{1,i}, x_{2,k(i)})$ so that 0.99-VaR of the samples $x_{1,i} + x_{2,k(i)}$ from $X_1 + X_2$ is as large as possible? The function $k(i)$ defines a shuffle of $\{1, 2, \dots, 10000\}$ as i varies. We want the 100th largest observation of $X_1 + X_2$ to be as large as possible.

The first thing to observe is that we should pair only the 100 largest observations of X_1 with the 100 largest observations from X_2. If we have a candidate pairing that does not satisfy this condition, we can make a better candidate by swapping any pairings using observations outside the top 100 with unused top 100 entries.

How should we pair the top $n = 100$ entries? The crossed pairing is an obvious contender: pair the largest X_1 with the 100th X_2, the second-largest X_1 and 99th X_2, and so forth, ending with the 100th X_1 and the largest X_2. Order tied elements arbitrarily. The crossed pairing makes sense: it does not waste any large values by needlessly pairing them together. It is easy to see that if we are trying to pair 2 values from X_1 and X_2 it is the correct answer; see Figure 4.7. The crossed pairing is also the optimal answer for any number of sample points.

When all the samples from X_1 and X_2 above their respective p-VaRs are different, the crossed pairing gives an easy way to demonstrate subadditivity violation because each term in the crossed pairing is greater than the sum of the individual VaRs! There are several important points to note about this failure of subadditivity.

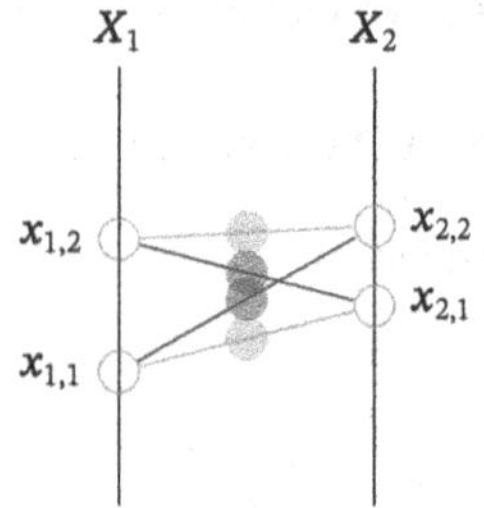

Figure 4.7 Crossed (darker) and uncrossed or comonotonic (gray) combinations of $(x_{1,1}, x_{1,2})$ and $(x_{2,1}, x_{2,2})$. The filled dark circles represent the aggregate assuming crossed dependence and filled gray assuming uncrossed. The maximum minimum value is the lower dark circle corresponding to the crossed arrangement.

- The dependence structure does not have extreme right tail dependence; it exhibits the exact opposite. It is not the *worst* way to combine two distributions; it just gives the highest p-VaR.
- The dependence structure is tailored to a specific value of p and does not work for other ps. It produces relatively thinner tails for higher values of p than either the comonotonic copula or independence. In this sense, it is a peculiar example: it creates risk only at a particular p.
- The dependence structure works for any nontrivial marginal distributions X_1 and X_2—it is universal.
- The implied dependence structure specifies only how the larger values of X_1 and X_2 are related; for values below the p-VaRs of X_1 and X_2 any dependence structure can be used.

It is a general theorem, first proved independently by Makarov (1982) and Rüschendorf (1982) that an analog of the crossed arrangement gives the maximum VaR for any two distributions X_1 and X_2, and not just for equally likely discrete samples.

The crossed pairing is hard to generalize to three or more marginal distributions. Whereas it is easy to create maximal positive dependence for any number of variables (the comonotonic copula), it is much harder to create maximal negative dependence. If X_1 and X_2 are negatively correlated and X_2 and X_3 are negatively correlated then X_1 and X_3 tend to be positively correlated. The Rearrangement Algorithm gives a way to approximate the worst VaR outcome in higher dimensions; see Section 4.2.6.

Exercise 56. You are given variables X_1, X_2 defined a sample spaces with 10 equally likely events. X_1 takes values $0, 0, 1, 2, 3, 6, 10, 18, 36, 52$ and X_2 values $0, 0, 0, 1, 2, 5, 8, 12, 23, 40$.

1. What are the 0.7-VaRs of X_1, X_2?
2. Describe the joint distribution of X_1, X_2 with the greatest 0.7-VaR. What is the range of variances of the sum?
3. Describe the joint distribution of X_1, X_2 with the greatest variance. What is the 0.7-VaR of the sum? □

Case 2. When the marginals have a skewed distribution

Case 1 involves dependent random variables. VaR can also fail to be subadditive for two iid random variables.

Let X_1 and X_2 be iid exponential distributions with mean 1. $X_1 + X_2$ has a gamma distribution with shape parameter 2 and scale 1. It is easy to see $\mathsf{VaR}_{0.7}(X_i) = -\log(0.3) = 1.204$. For the sum, $\mathsf{VaR}_{0.7}(X) = 2.439 > 2 \times 1.204 = 2.408$. Note $\mathsf{VaR}_{0.7}(X) =$ `GAMMA.INV(0.7, 2, 1)` in a spreadsheet. VaR for other p are shown in Table 4.4. VaR is not subadditive for $p < 0.7$.

Exercise 57. Determine the exact range of values of p where VaR is subadditive on two independent unit exponential distributions. □

Case 3. When the marginals are very heavy-tailed

Case 2 shows independent, thin-tailed variables can fail to be subadditive for a range of p. Case 3 shows that thick-tailed iid distributions can fail to be subadditive for all p above a threshold, which is a more serious breach.

Table 4.4 The sum of two independent mean 1 exponential distributions is not subadditive for $p < 0.7$ because the difference $2\mathrm{VaR}_p(X_1) - \mathrm{VaR}_p(X)$ is negative.

p	$\mathrm{VaR}_p(X_1)$	$2\mathrm{VaR}_p(X_1)$	$\mathrm{VaR}_p(X_1 + X_2)$	Difference
0.5	0.6931	1.386	1.678	−0.2921
0.6	0.9163	1.833	2.022	−0.1897
0.7	1.204	2.408	2.439	−0.03127
0.8	1.609	3.219	2.994	0.2246
0.9	2.303	4.605	3.89	0.7155
0.95	2.996	5.991	4.744	1.248
0.99	4.605	9.21	6.638	2.572
0.999	6.908	13.82	9.233	4.582

Suppose X_1, X_2 are iid and continuous with quantile function q, and let $\bar{q}(s) = q(1-s)$ and $\bar{q}_{X_1+X_2}(s) = q_{X_1+X_2}(1-s)$. With this notation $\Pr(X_i > \bar{q}(s)) = s$. Then, if s is small

$$\Pr(X_1 + X_2 > \bar{q}(s/2)) \ge \Pr(\max(X_1, X_2) > \bar{q}(s/2)) = \frac{s}{2} + \frac{s}{2} - \frac{s^2}{4} \approx s \tag{4.9}$$

and so $\bar{q}_{X_1+X_2}(s) \ge \bar{q}(s/2)$.

When X_i is leptokrutic (has a very peaked distribution with thick tails), the most likely outcome is one large observation and one small and the bivariate distribution is concentrated along the axes. Eq. (4.9) is then close to an identity and implies

$$\bar{q}_{X_1+X_2}(s) \approx \bar{q}(s/2). \tag{4.10}$$

Subadditivity requires $\mathrm{VaR}_p(X_1 + X_2) \le \mathrm{VaR}_p(X_1) + \mathrm{VaR}_p(X_2)$, i.e. $\bar{q}_{X_1+X_2}(s) \le 2\bar{q}(s)$. Assuming Eq. (4.10) this is equivalent to $\bar{q}(s/2) \le 2\bar{q}(s)$.

When

$$\Pr(X > x) = kx^{-\alpha} \tag{4.11}$$

for large enough x and some $k > 0$, Feller (1971), VIII.8. proves that the survival function of $X_1 + X_2$ decays at the same rate. Eq. (4.11) implies $\bar{q}(s) = (k/q)^{1/\alpha}$ and subadditivity holds if and only if

$$\bar{q}(s/2) \le 2\bar{q}(s) \iff \left(\frac{k}{q/2}\right)^{1/\alpha} \le 2\left(\frac{k}{q}\right)^{1/\alpha} \iff 2^{1/\alpha} \le 2 \iff \alpha \ge 1.$$

Thus, subadditivity fails for Pareto or stable distributions with $\alpha < 1$, two well-known examples of distributions with extremely thick tails and no mean. The Cauchy distribution is the boundary, $\alpha = 1$. If X_i are iid Cauchy then $X_1 + X_2 \sim 2X$ and so VaR is additive.

In general, distributions where $\bar{q}(s/2) \ge 2\bar{q}(s)$ do not have a mean because

$$\mathsf{E}[X] = \int_0^1 \bar{q}(s)ds = \int_0^{s_0} \bar{q}(s)ds + \int_{s_0}^1 \bar{q}(s)ds \ge \sum_{n\ge 0} \frac{s_0}{2}\bar{q}(s_0) + \int_{s_0}^1 \bar{q}(s)ds = \infty,$$

using Riemann sums to approximate the first integral along a partition $s_0/2^n$. (The area between $s_0/2^{n+1}$ and $s_0/2^n$ is $> (s_0/2^{n+1})2^n\bar{q}(s_0) = s_0\bar{q}(s_0)/2$ for every n.)

Case 3 is the risk equivalent of playing Russian roulette: you do not lower your risk by taking the average outcome of two shots. If the outcome can be truly terrible, then you want to experience it as few times as possible.

By Eq. (4.6) (or Feller's result), thick-tailed distributions satisfy

$$\mathsf{Pr}(\max(X_1, X_2) > x) \to 2\mathsf{Pr}(X_1 > x)$$

as $x \to \infty$, and so $\bar{q}_{X_1+X_2}(s) \approx \bar{q}(s/2)$. This behavior is common in insurance catastrophe data. Bad catastrophe loss years are driven by a single bad event much more frequently than by multiple events: 1992 Andrew, 1994 Northridge, 2005 Katrina, 2011 Tohoku (economic loss).

In Case 3, subadditivity fails for all p greater than a threshold, unlike Cases 1 and 2, where it holds for large enough p. A sample from a Case 3 distribution gives bounded variables where VaR fails to be subadditive for p in some range. This type of behavior is common when working with catastrophe simulation model output.

Exercise 58. You simulate ten equally likely outcomes for two units and obtain $X_1 = 0,0,0,0,1,1,2,3,20,400$ and $X_2 = 0,0,0,0,1,1,1,4,24,500$. The two samples are independent, giving 100 samples for $X_1 + X_2$.

1. Compute VaR_p for $p = 0.01, 0.02, \ldots, 0.99$ for each line and in total.
2. For which values of p is VaR subadditive? □

4.2.6 Worst-Case VaR and the Rearrangement Algorithm

We can be required to aggregate marginal distributions without a complete understanding of their dependency structure. For example, we may be working with capital model output and different risks that have been modeled independently or quasi-independently. The worst-VaR sum is useful in these circumstances.

The Rearrangement Algorithm (RA) is a practical and straightforward method to determine the worst-VaR sum. The RA works by iteratively making each marginal crossed (counter-monotonic) with the sum of the other marginal distributions. It is easy to program and suitable for problems involving hundreds of variables and millions of simulations.

The Rearrangement Algorithm was introduced in Puccetti and Ruschendorf (2012) and subsequently improved in Embrechts, Puccetti, and Ruschendorf (2013).

The Rearrangement Algorithm

Algorithm Input: Input samples are arranged in a matrix $\tilde{X} = (x_{ij})$ with $i = 1, \ldots, M$ rows corresponding to the simulations and $j = 1, \ldots, d$ columns corresponding to the different marginals. VaR probability parameter p. Accuracy threshold $\epsilon > 0$ specifies convergence criterion.

Algorithm Steps

1. **Sort** each column of $\tilde{X}$ in descending order.
2. **Set** $N := \lceil(1-p)M\rceil$.
3. **Create** matrix X as the $N \times d$ submatrix of the top N rows of $\tilde{X}$.
4. **Randomly permute** rows within each column of X.
5. **Do Loop**
   - **Create** a new matrix Y as follows. **For** column $j = 1, \dots, d$:
     - **Create** a temporary matrix V_j by deleting the jth column of X
     - **Create** a column vector v whose ith element equals the sum of the elements in the ith row of V_j
     - **Set** the jth column of Y equal to the jth column of X arranged to have the opposite order to v, i.e. the largest element in the jth column of X is placed in the row of Y corresponding to the smallest element in v, the second largest with second smallest, etc.
   - **Compute** y, the $N \times 1$ vector with ith element equal to the sum of the elements in the ith row of Y.
   - **Compute** x from X similarly.
   - **Compute** $y^* := \min(y)$, the smallest element of y.
   - **Compute** $x^* := \min(x)$.
   - **If** $y^* - x^* \geq \epsilon$ **then** set $X := Y$ and **repeat** the loop.
   - **If** $y^* - x^* < \epsilon$ **then break** from the loop.
6. **Stack** Y on top of the $(M-N) \times d$ submatrix of $M-N$ bottom rows of $\tilde{X}$.
7. **Output**: The result approximates the worst VaR_p arrangement of $\tilde{X}$.

Only the top N values need special treatment; all the smaller values can be combined arbitrarily because they aren't included in the worst-VaR rearrangement. Given that X consists of the worst $1-p$ proportion of each marginal, the required estimated VaR_p is the least row sum of Y, that is y^*. In implementation, x^* can be carried forward as the y^* from the previous iteration and not recomputed. The statistics x^* and y^* can be replaced with the variance of the row-sums of X and Y and yield essentially the same results.

Embrechts, Puccetti, and Ruschendorf (2013) report that while there is no analytic proof the algorithm always works, it performs very well based on examples and tests where we can compute the answer analytically.

Exercise 59. Compute the worst $\mathsf{VaR}_{0.99}$ of the sum of lognormal distributions with mean 10 and coefficient of variations 1, 2, and 3 by applying the Rearrangement Algorithm to a stratified sample of $N = 40$ observations at and above the 99th percentile for the matrix X.

Solution. Table 4.5 shows the input and output of the Rearrangement Algorithm. □

The table illustrates the worst-case VaR may be substantially higher than when the marginals are perfectly correlated, here 45% higher at 352.8 vs. 242.5. The form of the output

Table 4.5 Starting X is shown in the first three columns x_0, x_1, x_2. The column Sum shows the row sums $x_0 + x_1 + x_2$ corresponding to a comonotonic ordering. These four columns are all sorted in ascending order. The right-hand three columns, s_0, s_1, s_2 are the output, with row sum given in the Max VaR column. The worst-case $\mathsf{VaR}_{0.99}$ is the minimum of the last column, 352.8. It is 45% greater than the additive VaR of 242.5. Only a sample from each marginal's largest 1% values is shown since smaller values are irrelevant to the calculation.

x_0	x_1	x_2	Sum	s_0	s_1	s_3	Max VaR
49.0	85.6	107.9	242.5	87.1	124.6	141.1	352.8
49.4	86.6	109.5	245.6	70.8	113.6	169.3	353.7
49.9	87.7	111.2	248.8	98.8	127.9	127.4	354.1
50.3	88.9	112.9	252.1	79.9	118.8	155.5	354.1
50.7	90.0	114.7	255.5	83.1	107.1	164.3	354.5
51.2	91.3	116.6	259.1	92.1	139.7	122.8	354.6
51.6	92.6	118.6	262.8	67.7	135.4	151.5	354.7
52.1	93.9	120.6	266.6	108.8	116.1	129.8	354.7
52.6	95.3	122.8	270.7	62.8	105.1	186.9	354.8
53.2	96.7	125.0	274.9	63.9	170.6	120.6	355.0
53.7	98.3	127.4	279.3	69.2	111.3	174.6	355.1
54.3	99.9	129.8	284.0	72.7	144.5	138.1	355.3
54.9	101.5	132.4	288.8	59.9	101.5	194.1	355.5
55.5	103.3	135.2	293.9	127.5	103.3	125.0	355.8
56.1	105.1	138.1	299.3	60.8	162.6	132.4	355.9
56.8	107.1	141.1	305.0	66.3	109.1	180.5	355.9
57.5	109.1	144.4	311.1	61.8	149.8	144.4	356.0
58.3	111.3	147.9	317.5	65.0	155.8	135.2	356.0
59.1	113.6	151.5	324.3	74.8	121.6	159.7	356.1
59.9	116.1	155.5	331.5	77.1	131.5	147.9	356.5
60.8	118.8	159.7	339.3	59.1	179.9	118.6	357.5
61.8	121.6	164.3	347.7	58.3	99.9	202.0	360.1
62.8	124.6	169.3	356.7	57.5	191.1	116.6	365.3
63.9	127.9	174.6	**366.4**	56.8	98.3	210.9	366.0
65.0	131.5	180.5	377.0	56.1	96.7	221.0	373.9
66.3	135.4	186.9	388.7	55.5	205.1	114.7	375.4
67.7	139.7	194.1	401.5	54.9	95.3	232.7	382.9
69.2	144.5	202.0	415.7	54.3	223.3	112.9	390.5
70.8	149.8	210.9	431.6	53.7	93.9	246.3	393.9
72.7	155.8	221.0	449.5	53.2	92.6	262.5	408.2

(Continued)

Table 4.5 (*Continued*)

x_0	x_1	x_2	Sum	s_0	s_1	s_3	Max VaR
74.8	162.6	232.7	470.1	52.6	248.7	111.2	412.5
77.1	170.6	246.3	494.0	52.1	91.3	282.3	417.7
79.9	179.9	262.5	522.3	51.2	288.1	109.5	448.8
83.1	191.1	282.3	556.5	51.6	90.0	307.2	448.9
87.1	205.1	307.2	599.4	50.7	88.9	340.0	479.6
92.1	223.3	340.0	655.5	50.3	87.7	386.6	524.6
98.8	248.7	386.6	734.1	49.9	366.9	107.9	524.7
108.8	288.1	461.1	858.0	49.4	86.6	461.1	597.2
127.5	366.9	615.7	1110.1	49.0	85.6	615.7	750.3

columns shows the two part structure. There is a series of values up to 356 involving moderate sized losses from each marginal with approximately the same total. The larger values of the rearrangement are formed from a large value from one marginal combined with smaller values from the other two.

The bold entry 366.4 indicates when the comonotonic sum of marginals exceeds the worst 0.99-VaR arrangement.

Performing the same calculation with $N = 1000$ samples from the largest 1% of each marginal produces an estimated worst VaR of 360.5.

There are several important points to note about the Rearrangement Algorithm output and the failure of subadditivity it induces. They mirror the case $d = 2$.

- The dependence structure does not have right tail dependence.
- In Table 1, the comonotonic sum is greater than the maximum VaR sum for the top 40% observations, above 366.4. The algorithm output is tailored to a specific value of p and does not work for other ps. It produces relatively thinner tails for higher values of p than the comonotonic copula.
- The algorithm works for any nontrivial marginal distributions—it is universal.
- The implied dependence structure specifies only how the larger values of each marginal are related; any dependence structure can be used for values below VaR_p.

The Rearrangement Algorithm gives a definitive answer to the question "Just how bad could things get?" and perhaps provides a better base against which to measure diversification effect than either independence or the comonotonic copula. While the multivariate structure it reveals is odd and specific to p, it is not wholly improbable. It pinpoints a worst-case driven by a combination of moderately severe, but not extreme, tail event outcomes. Anyone who remembers watching their investment portfolio during a financial crisis has seen that behavior before! It is a valuable additional feature for any risk aggregation software.

4.2.7 When Is VaR Subadditive?

Cases 1–3 and the Rearrangement Algorithm focus on the failures of VaR. They show it is possible to make VaR subadditivity fail at a particular p for any pair of input distributions, with a solution with a thinner-than-worst-case tail for larger p. Failure for all $p \geq p_0$ requires very thick-tailed distributions. The former situation is somewhat contrived. The latter is real for catastrophe risk insurance.

Danielsson and Jorgensen (2013) report that VaR subadditivity holds for log-concave (thin-tailed) distributions. They also show that iid variables with tails like $x^{-\alpha}$ for $\alpha > 1$ are subadditive for p sufficiently close to 1.

VaR is used in a variety of regulatory and rating agency applications, including EU Solvency II and US Risk Based Capital (RBC) calculations. It should not be rejected just because it can fail in certain situations. Despite its occasional failures, VaR has many advantages: it is simple, easy to explain, exists for all random variables (even those without a mean), and can be robustly estimated. An awareness of how VaR can fail to be subadditive arms the user to address its shortcomings. Computing p-VaR for various thresholds, rather than relying on a single value, provides a more robust risk measure than a single VaR point and is a recommended practice.

4.3 Tail VaR and Related Risk Measures

4.3.1 Motivation

The next meeting of your Ye Olde World restaurant dining group is the Potluck Special, where the bill is paid by a random member of the group. There are 25 people in the group. As you walk to the ATM you recall your VaR rule of thumb and think, "I want to be 95% sure I can cover my obligation. But wait. There are 25 people in the group, so there is only a 4% chance I'll have to pay. I don't need to withdraw any cash." You turn on your heels and head to the restaurant cash-less, but still reasonably confident that you have enough cash. A few steps later though, you pause. "That doesn't seem prudent. *If* I am unlucky, and am selected to pay the tab, I'll look a fool." In part, TVaR was created to address this problem.

4.3.2 Definition of TVaR

Tail value at risk (TVaR) is the conditional average of the worst $1 - p$ outcomes. Since quantiles sort the outcomes, we can compute TVaR using the following definition.

Definition 3. *Let X be a loss random variable and $0 \leq p < 1$. The p-**Tail Value at Risk** is the conditional average of the worst $1 - p$ proportion of outcomes*

$$\mathsf{TVaR}_p(X) := \frac{1}{1-p}\int_p^1 \mathsf{VaR}_s(X)\,ds = \frac{1}{1-p}\int_p^1 q^-(s)\,ds.$$

In particular $\mathsf{TVaR}_0(X) = \mathsf{E}[X]$. *When* $p = 1$, $\mathsf{TVaR}_1(X)$ *is defined to be* $\sup(X)$.

TVaR is defined in terms of q^-, that is, dual implicit events. The actual sample space on which X is defined is not used. Recall, $\mathsf{VaR}_p(X)$ refers to the lower quantile $q^-(p)$, Definition 1.

TVaR is a well-behaved function of p. It is continuous, differentiable almost everywhere, and equal to the integral of its derivative (fundamental theorem of calculus). It takes every value between $\mathsf{E}[X]$ and $\sup X$. TVaR has a kink at jumps in F and is differentiable elsewhere.

Next, we compute TVaR for some continuous random variables, and then we discuss the complexities that occur for mixed and discrete random variables.

Remark 60. The definition and terminology TVaR is not consistent in the literature. TVaR is also known as conditional value at risk (CVaR), average value at risk (AVaR), and expected shortfall (ES). We always use the name TVaR. □

Example 61. The Swiss Solvency Test is based on 99-year TVaR. Basel III has adopted TVaR (Chang *et al.* 2019). □

4.3.3 TVaR of a Normal Random Variable

Let X be normal μ, σ and write $q_X(p) = \mu + \sigma z_p$, where $z_p = \Phi^{-1}(p)$ is the p percentile of a standard normal. Then

$$\mathsf{TVaR}_p(X) = \mu + \frac{\sigma\phi(z_p)}{1-p} \tag{4.12}$$

since

$$\begin{aligned}(1-p)\mathsf{TVaR}_p(X) &= \frac{1}{\sqrt{2\pi}\sigma}\int_{q(p)}^{\infty} y e^{-(y-\mu)^2/2\sigma^2}\,dy \\ &= \frac{1}{\sqrt{2\pi}}\int_{z_p}^{\infty} (\mu + \sigma x)e^{-x^2/2}\,dx \\ &= \mu(1-p) + \sigma e^{-z_p^2/2}/\sqrt{2\pi} \\ &= \mu(1-p) + \sigma\phi(z_p),\end{aligned}$$

on substituting $x = (y-\mu)/\sigma$ in the first integral.

Since $\mathsf{VaR}_p(X) = \mu + \sigma\Phi^{-1}(p)$, the difference $\mathsf{TVaR}_p(X) - \mathsf{VaR}_p(X) = \sigma(\phi(\Phi^{-1}(p))/(1-p) - \Phi^{-1}(p)) \to 1$ as $p \to 1$. It is independent of μ. TVaR is 14.6% larger than VaR when $p = 0.99$, 9% at $p = 0.999$, and 6.4% at $p = 0.9999$.

Exercise 62. Show that the limited expected value at a of a normal μ, σ random variable equals $a(1-p) + \mu p - \sigma\phi(z_p)$ where $p = \Phi((a-\mu)/\sigma)$. □

4.3.4 TVaR of a Lognormal Random Variable

Let X be lognormal with parameters μ and σ. X has density $f(x) = (\sqrt{2\pi}x)^{-1}\exp(-(\log(x)-\mu)^2/2\sigma^2)$. Let $q(p) = e^{\mu+z_p\sigma}$ be the p-VaR of X. Then

$$\begin{aligned}(1-p)\mathsf{TVaR}_p(X) &= \frac{1}{\sqrt{2\pi}\sigma}\int_{q(p)}^{\infty} x\exp\left(-\frac{(\log(x)-\mu)^2}{2\sigma^2}\right)\frac{dx}{x} \\ &= \frac{1}{\sqrt{2\pi}}\int_{z_p}^{\infty} e^{\mu+y\sigma}e^{-y^2/2}\,dy \\ &= \frac{e^{\mu+\sigma^2/2}}{\sqrt{2\pi}}\int_{z_p}^{\infty} e^{-(y-\sigma)^2/2}\,dy \\ &= \mathsf{E}[X]\Phi(\sigma - z_p)\end{aligned}$$

via substitution $y = (\log(x)-\mu)/\sigma$, $x = e^{\mu+y\sigma}$ and completing the square, $y^2 - 2\sigma y = (y-\sigma)^2 - \sigma^2$.

Exercise 63. Your Ye Olde World bill is modeled by X lognormal with mean ¤2500 and CV 0.2. Compute $\mathsf{VaR}_{0.95}(X)$ and $\mathsf{TVaR}_{0.95}(X)$ on a regular night where you pay the bill, and a Pot Luck night where you have a 0.04 chance of paying the bill and 0.96 chance of paying nothing. If you pick up the bill on Pot Luck night and have TVaR cash, what is the probability you have enough? What is your conditional cash shortfall? Discuss the implications. What about 0.99 values? At what probability level does the TVaR on a Pot Luck night exceed the expected bill?

Solution. The lognormal parameters are $\mu = 7.8044$ and $\sigma = 0.1980$. Using a spreadsheet, $\mathsf{VaR}_{0.95}(X) = 3395$ on a regular night and 0 on a Pot Luck night, as we observed. Using the formula for TVaR we get $\mathsf{TVaR}_{0.95}(X) = 3699$. On a Pot Luck night, your payment is $Y = 0$ with a probability of 0.96 and $Y = X$ with a probability of 0.04. Therefore, $\mathsf{TVaR}_{0.95}(Y) = 0.8\mathsf{E}[X] = 2000$. There is only a 0.152 chance you have enough cash if you do pick up the bill. Your conditional shortfall is $\mathsf{E}[X \mid X > 2000] - 2000 = \mathsf{TVaR}_{F(2000)}(X) - 2000 = 624$. You are mildly embarrassed but can cover the bill by borrowing from a prudent friend who also brings TVaR cash. If all the other diners bring VaR cash, the group will have a big problem, and your embarrassment will be acute. The rest of the exercise is similar. □

Exercise 64. Compare the behavior of TVaR and VaR for a lognormal random variable, as a function of p and σ. □

4.3.5 TVaR for Variables with Density $c(\alpha)x^\alpha g(x)$

If X is continuous and has a density that can be factored as $c(\alpha)x^\alpha g(x)$ where $g(x)$ does not involve powers of x alone or α, then

$$\begin{aligned}\mathsf{TVaR}_p(X) &= \frac{1}{1-p}\int_{q_p}^{\infty} xc(\alpha)x^\alpha g(x)\,dx \\ &= \frac{c(\alpha)}{c(\alpha+1)}\frac{1-F(q(p);\alpha+1)}{1-F(q(p);\alpha)}\end{aligned}$$

where $F(x;\alpha)$ is the distribution function with parameter α and $1-p$ is written as $1-F(q(p));\alpha)$ to emphasize the symmetry. The gamma, generalized gamma, transformed gamma, and generalized beta distribution (Cummins *et al.* 1990) are examples with the specified form.

Gerber and Shiu (1994) compute the TVaR for the exponential of an exponential family distribution. Landsman and Valdez (2005) consider general formulas for computing the TVaR of exponential family distributions.

4.3.6 Algorithm to Evaluate TVaR for a Discrete Distribution

Follow these steps to determine $\mathsf{TVaR}_p(X)$.

Algorithm Input: X is a discrete random variable, taking N equally likely values $X_j \geq 0$, $j = 0, \dots, N-1$. Probability level p.

Algorithm Steps

1. **Sort** outcomes into ascending order $X_0 < \cdots < X_{N-1}$.
2. **Find** n so that $n \leq pN < (n+1)$.
3. **If** $n+1 = N$ **then** $\mathsf{TVaR}_p(X) := X_{N-1}$ is the largest observation, exit;
4. **Else** $n < N-1$ and continue.
5. **Compute** $T_1 := X_{n+1} + \cdots + X_{N-1}$.
6. **Compute** $T_2 := ((n+1) - pN)x_n$.
7. **Compute** $\mathsf{TVaR}_p(X) := (1-p)^{-1}(T_1 + T_2)/N$.

These steps compute the average of the largest $N(1-p)$ observations. Step (6) adds a pro rata portion of the $\lfloor N(1-p) \rfloor$ largest observation when $N(1-p)$ is not an integer. For instance, if $N = 71$ and $p = 0.95$, then $Np = 67.45$ and $n = 67$, giving $\mathsf{TVaR}_p = 20(0.55x_{67} + x_{68} + x_{69} + x_{70})/71$.

Exercise 49 Continued. Recall, X is a random variable defined on a sample space with ten equally likely events and outcomes 0, 1, 1, 1, 2, 3, 4, 8, 12, 25. Compute $\mathsf{TVaR}_p(X)$ for all p. Is it a piecewise linear function?

Solution. For $p \geq 0.9$, $q(p) = 25$ and $\mathsf{TVaR}_p(X) = 25$. For $0.8 \geq p < 0.9$

$$(1-p)\mathsf{TVaR}_p(X) = \int_p^1 q^-(s)ds = \int_p^{0.9} q^-(s)ds + \int_{0.9}^1 q^-(s)ds$$
$$= (0.9-p) \times 12 + (1-0.9) \times \mathsf{TVaR}_{0.9}(X),$$

for $0.7 \geq p < 0.8$

$$(1-p)\mathsf{TVaR}_p(X) = (0.8-p) \times 8 + (1-0.8) \times \mathsf{TVaR}_{0.8}(X),$$

and so forth. The TVaR function is shown on the left in Figure 4.8. TVaR is not piecewise linear. For example, for $0.8 \leq p < 0.9$, $\mathsf{TVaR}_p(X) = (12(0.9-p) + 2.5)/(1-p)$. (Disclosure: the figure approximates TVaR linearly.) □

Remark 65. In Exercise 50 we computed VaR for the continuous version of X. We can compute the corresponding TVaR by integrating it. The result is shown on the right in Figure 4.8. □

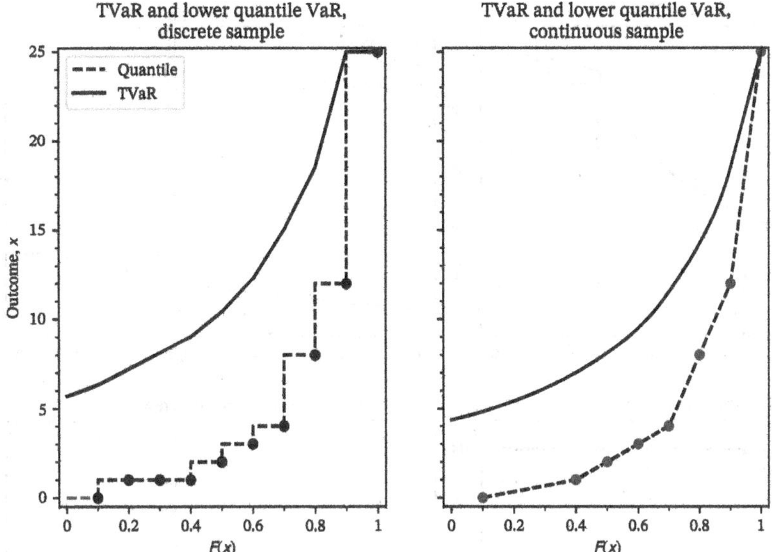

Figure 4.8 Left: TVaR (solid) and quantile (dashed) functions determined by the discrete example in Exercise 49; right: continuous sample, based on Exercise 50.

Exercise 66. Extend the TVaR algorithm to the case where the sample observations are not all equally likely. □

4.3.7 VaR and TVaR for the Case Studies

In this subsection we present the VaR and TVaR values for the Discrete Example and Case Studies introduced in Chapter 2.

First, there is a series of four four-panel plots showing VaR, TVaR, and bounded TVaR (explained below). In each graphic:

- the left column shows gross loss and the right net, and
- the top row uses a probability horizontal scale and the bottom row a log return period $(1/(1-p))$ scale.

These are Figures 4.9–4.12. VaR in the discrete case is a stair-step function; the others are continuous. TVaR is continuous in all cases. TVaR is strictly greater than VaR in all cases except the discrete case with capped losses. In that case TVaR and VaR become equal when they reach the asset limit. The return period view expands the tail of the distribution, making it easy to read off losses for 100-, 1000-, and 10,000-year return periods. It is a very convenient visualization.

Bounded TVaR is the TVaR of limited losses $X \wedge a$, for the asset levels shown. It is the TVaR of insured payments, allowing for default. It is visibly different from TVaR only for the Cat/Non-Cat and Hu/SCS Cases on the return period scale.

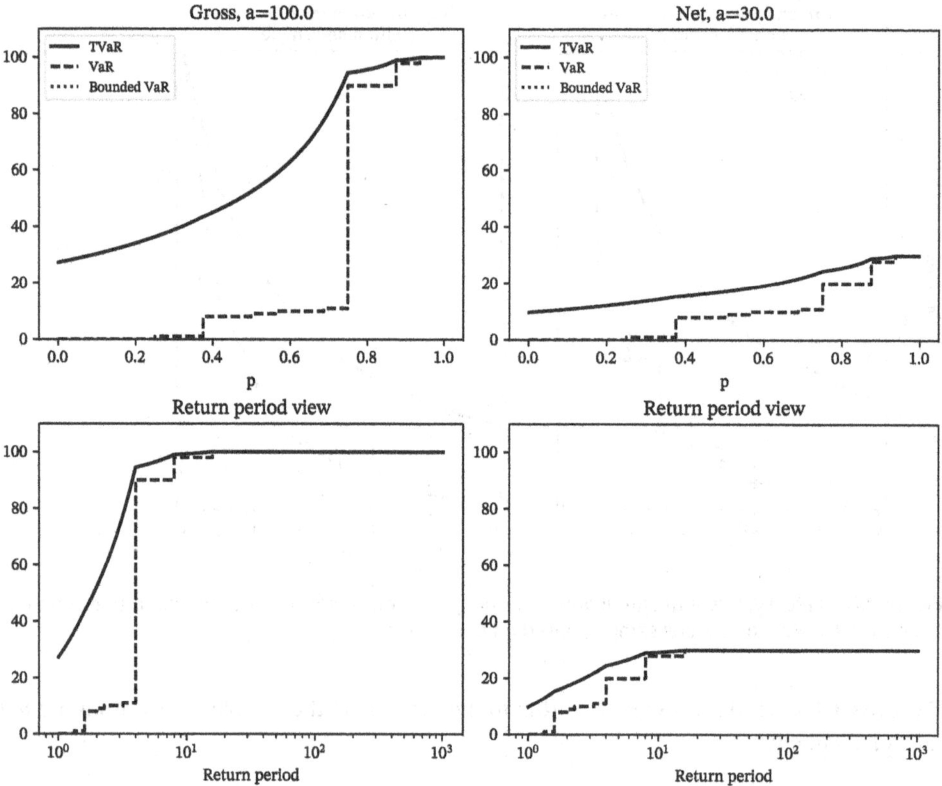

Figure 4.9 Discrete example, TVaR, and VaR for unlimited and limited variables, gross (left) and net (right). Lower view uses a log return period horizontal axis.

Next, there is a series of three tables presenting the VaR and TVaR values at critical return periods, by unit and in total, and showing the diversification benefit by comparing the total with the sum of the units. These are also shown on a gross and net basis. The tables include the EPD capital (described in Exercise 69). There is no table for the Discrete Example. These tables show the radically different tail behavior of the different units. The tables are Tables 4.6–4.8

Remark 67. Li and Wang (2019) compare VaR and TVaR and introduce PELVE: probability equivalent level of VaR and expected shortfall (TVaR). PELVE is defined as a constant c so that $\mathsf{TVaR}_{1-c\epsilon}(X) = \mathsf{VaR}_{1-\epsilon}(X)$ for small ϵ and a loss random variable X. The paper finds that PELVE is typically larger than 2.5, so replacing $\mathsf{VaR}_{0.99}$ with $\mathsf{TVaR}_{0.975}$ (as the Basel Committee on banking regulation has proposed) leads to an increase in measured risk. The appropriateness of PELVE $c = 2.5$ can be assessed from Table 4.6. □

Exercise 68. Use Table 4.6 to estimate the PELVE constant c for each unit and in total. Repeat with the other two Case Studies using Tables 4.7 and 4.8. What conclusions can you draw? □

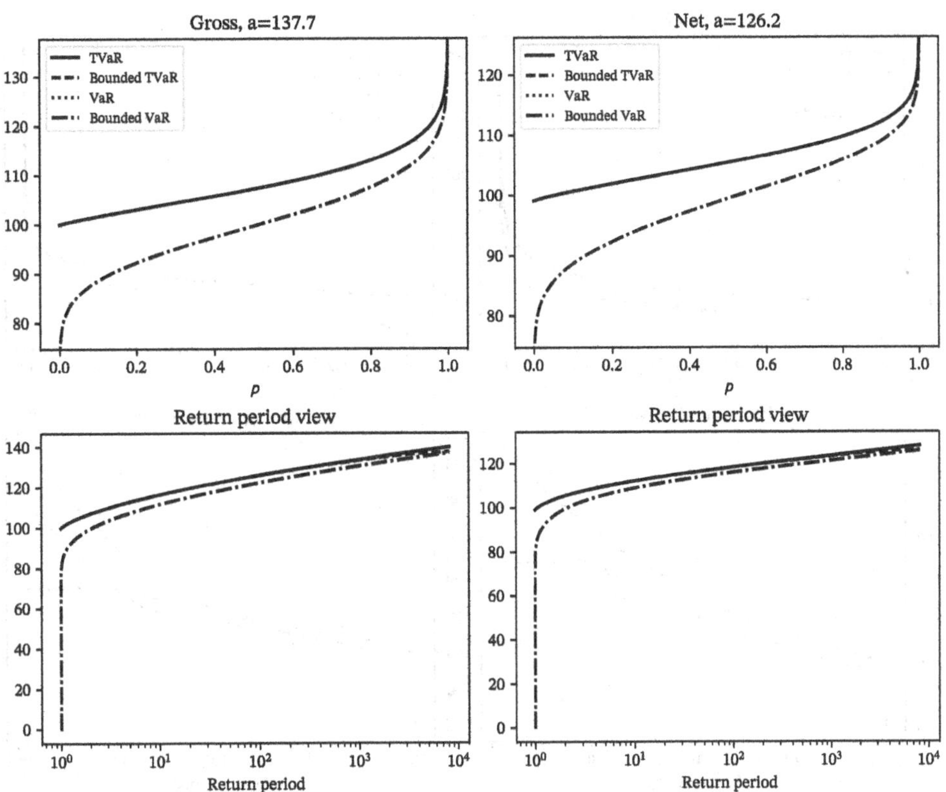

Figure 4.10 Tame Case Study, TVaR, and VaR for unlimited and limited variables, gross (left) and net (right). Lower view uses a log return period horizontal axis.

4.3.8 CTE and WCE: Alternatives to TVaR

TVaR is one of three similar risk measures. In this subsection we define the other two and compare them. They are:

1. Tail value at risk (TVaR) is the conditional average of the worst $1 - p$ outcomes.
2. Conditional tail expectation (CTE) refers to the conditional expectation of X over $X \ge \mathsf{VaR}_p(X)$.
3. Worst conditional expectation (WCE) refers to the greatest expected value of X conditional on a set of probability $> 1 - p$.

The formal definitions of CTE and WCE are as follows.

Definition 4. *Let X be a loss random variable and $0 \le p < 1$.*

1. $\mathsf{CTE}_p(X) := \mathsf{E}[X \mid X \ge \mathsf{VaR}_p(X)]$ *is the* **(lower) conditional tail expectation.** *The upper CTE equals* $\mathsf{E}[X \mid X \ge q^+(p)]$.
2. $\mathsf{WCE}_p(X) := \sup\{\mathsf{E}[X \mid A] \mid \Pr(A) > 1 - p\}$ *is the* **worst conditional expectation.**

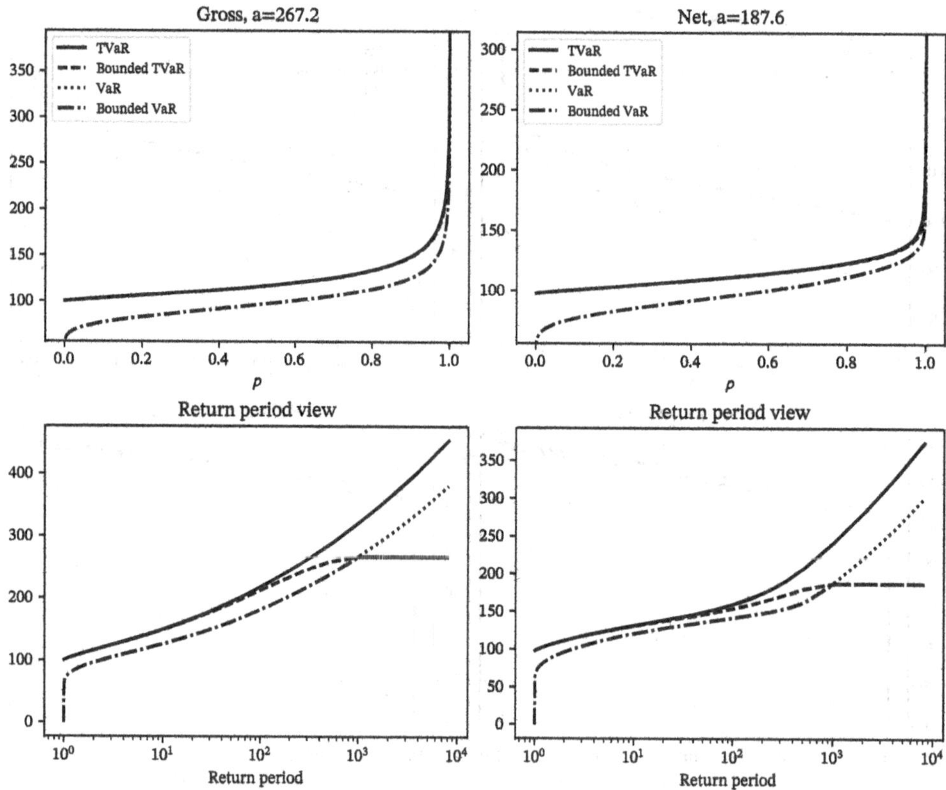

Figure 4.11 Cat/Non-Cat Case Study, TVaR, and VaR for unlimited and limited variables, gross (left) and net (right). Lower view uses a log return period horizontal axis.

Like TVaR, CTE is defined in terms of quantiles, and the sample space on which X is defined is not used. In contrast, WCE works with the original sample space and relies on its events. Some actuarial papers refer to CTE as tail value at risk, e.g. Bodoff (2007).

For continuous random variables TVaR, CTE, and WCE are all equal, and they are easy to compute. The distinctions between them arise for discrete and mixed variables when p coincides with a mass point. Figure 4.13 illustrates the problem that can occur. The left-hand plot computes TVaR when X is continuous. In this case, F and q^- are continuous, $F(q^-(p)) = p$ and $q^-(F(x)) = x$ for all x and p, and $q^- = q^+$. Set $x_0 = q^-(p_0)$ the p_0-VaR of X. Then, by definition,

$$\mathsf{TVaR}_{p_0}(X) = \frac{1}{1-p_0}\int_{1-p_0}^{1} q^-(s)ds = \frac{A+B}{1-p_0},$$

where A, B refer to areas in the plot. It is necessary to divide by $1 - p_0$ because TVaR is conditional. The rectangle A has area $(1-p)x_0$, and B has area

$$\mathsf{E}[X1_{X\geq x_0}] - (1-p)x_0 = \mathsf{E}[(X-x_0)1_{X\geq x_0}] = \mathsf{E}[(X-x_0)^+]$$

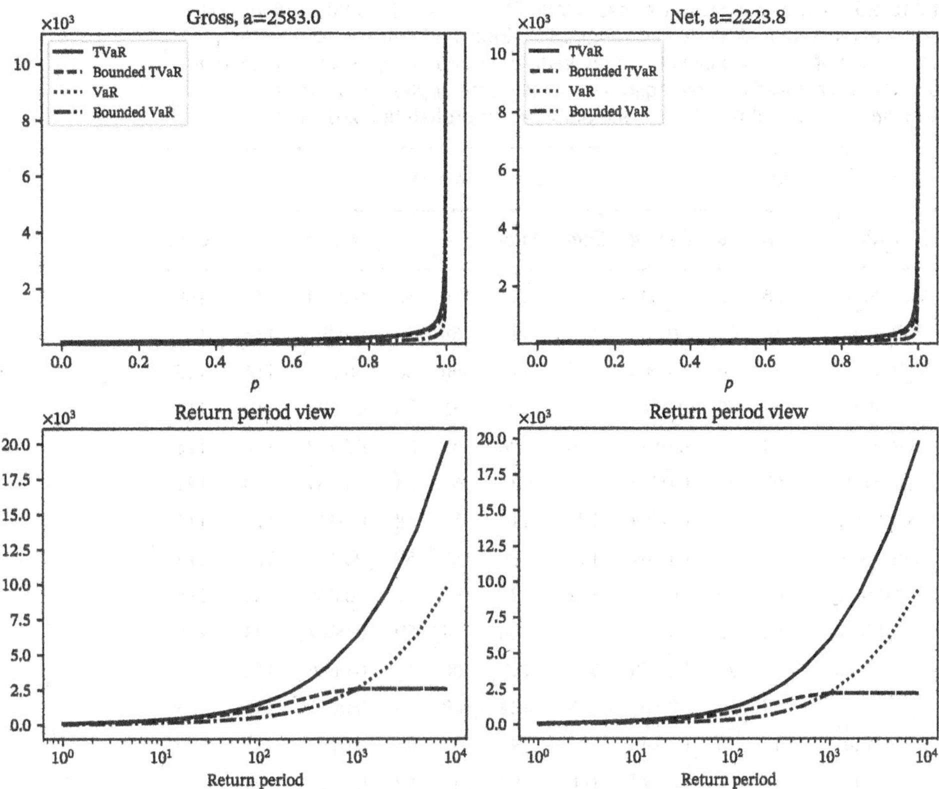

Figure 4.12 Hu/SCS Case Study, TVaR, and VaR for unlimited and limited variables, gross (left) and net (right). Lower view uses a log return period horizontal axis.

equal to the expected unconditional excess loss above x_0. Therefore TVaR equals CTE:

$$\mathsf{TVaR}_p(X) = x_0 + \mathsf{E}[X - x_0 \mid X \ge x_0] = \mathsf{E}[X \mid X \ge x_0] = \mathsf{CTE}_{p_0}(X). \tag{4.13}$$

Note that $\mathsf{E}[X \mid X \ge x] = \mathsf{E}[X1_{X\ge x}]/\mathsf{Pr}(X \ge x)$ by definition. In the continuous case, $X \ge x$ is the same as $X > x$.

The middle and right plots of Figure 4.13 illustrate the more complicated case where X has a probability mass at x_0. The mass is $p_+ - p_-$ and p_0 is deliberately chosen so that $p_- < p_0 < p_+$. As a result $x_0 = q^-(p_0)$ but $F(x_0) = p_+ > p_0$.

From the definition

$$\mathsf{TVaR}_{p_0}(X) = \frac{B + C + D}{1 - p_0}.$$

To compute $\mathsf{CTE}_{p_0} = \mathsf{E}[X \mid X \ge x_0]$, observe first that $\mathsf{Pr}(X \ge x_0) = p_-$ is larger than it should be because of the mass. Second, remember that $X \ge x_0$ defines a **subset of events** $\{p \ge p_-\}$ on the horizontal axis and not a subset of outcomes on the vertical axis, as the

Table 4.6 Tame Case Study estimated VaR, TVaR, and EPD by line and in total, gross, and net. EPD shows assets required for indicated EPD percentage. Sum shows sum of parts by line with no diversification and benefit shows percentage reduction compared to total. Aggregate reinsurance applied to B with an attachment probability 0.2 (¤56) and detachment probability 0.01 (¤69).

	Gross					Net				
Statistic	**A**	**B**	**Benefit**	**Sum**	**Total**	**A**	**B**	**Benefit**	**Sum**	**Total**
VaR 90.0	56	60	0.041	116	112	56	56	0.0344	113	109
VaR 95.0	58	63	0.053	121	115	58	56	0.0296	115	111
VaR 97.5	60	66	0.063	126	119	60	56	0.026	116	113
VaR 99.0	62	69	0.0743	131	122	62	56	0.0224	119	116
VaR 99.6	64	72	0.0843	136	126	64	59	0.0452	124	118
VaR 99.9	67	76	0.0974	143	131	67	64	0.0754	130	121
TVaR 90.0	59	64	0.0568	123	117	59	58	0.0444	117	112
TVaR 95.0	61	67	0.0664	128	120	61	59	0.0477	120	114
TVaR 97.5	62	69	0.075	132	123	62	59	0.048	122	116
TVaR 99.0	64	72	0.0849	137	126	64	59	0.0464	124	118
TVaR 99.6	66	75	0.0938	141	129	66	62	0.0666	128	120
TVaR 99.9	69	79	0.106	148	134	69	66	0.0931	135	123
EPD 10.0	45	46	0.0146	92	91	45	45	0.0122	91	90
EPD 5.0	49	51	0.0277	100	97	49	49	0.0232	98	96
EPD 2.5	52	55	0.0397	107	103	52	52	0.0323	104	101
EPD 1.0	55	59	0.0536	114	108	55	54	0.0392	109	105
EPD 0.4	57	63	0.0656	120	113	57	55	0.0407	113	108
EPD 0.1	60	68	0.081	128	119	60	56	0.0374	117	112

notation suggests. Then, it follows that

$$\begin{aligned}
(1-p_-)\mathsf{CTE}_{p_0} &= A+B+C+D \\
&= A+(1-p_0)\mathsf{TVaR}_{p_0} \\
\implies \mathsf{CTE}_{p_0} &= \frac{A}{1-p_-}+\frac{1-p_0}{1-p_-}\mathsf{TVaR}_{p_0} \\
&= \frac{p_0-p_-}{1-p_-}x_0+\frac{1-p_0}{1-p_-}\mathsf{TVaR}_{p_0} \\
&< \mathsf{TVaR}_{p_0}
\end{aligned}$$

because $x_0 < \mathsf{TVaR}_{p_0}$ and the weights sum to 1. We can rearrange this expression to give two more representations for TVaR

Table 4.7 Cat/Non-Cat Case Study estimated VaR, TVaR, and EPD by line and in total, gross, and net. EPD shows assets required for indicated EPD percentage. Sum shows sum of parts by line with no diversification and benefit shows percentage reduction compared to total. Aggregate reinsurance applied to Cat with an attachment probability 0.1 (¤41) and detachment probability 0.005 (¤121).

	Gross					Net				
Statistic	**Cat**	**Non-Cat**	**Benefit**	**Sum**	**Total**	**Cat**	**Non-Cat**	**Benefit**	**Sum**	**Total**
VaR 90.0	41	96	0.0857	137	126	41	96	0.132	137	121
VaR 95.0	56	101	0.117	156	140	41	101	0.108	142	128
VaR 97.5	72	105	0.138	177	156	41	105	0.0901	146	134
VaR 99.0	98	111	0.152	209	181	41	111	0.0686	152	142
VaR 99.6	129	115	0.156	244	211	49	115	0.0919	164	151
VaR 99.9	185	122	0.151	308	267	106	122	0.215	228	188
TVaR 90.0	65	102	0.122	168	149	43	102	0.108	146	131
TVaR 95.0	83	107	0.139	190	167	64	107	0.233	171	139
TVaR 97.5	104	111	0.149	215	187	75	111	0.267	185	146
TVaR 99.0	135	116	0.153	251	218	81	116	0.232	197	160
TVaR 99.6	172	120	0.15	292	254	92	120	0.177	213	181
TVaR 99.9	240	127	0.141	366	321	160	127	0.187	287	242
EPD 10.0	46	74	0.253	120	96	30	74	0.128	104	92
EPD 5.0	65	82	0.338	147	110	35	82	0.139	117	103
EPD 2.5	87	88	0.407	175	124	39	88	0.135	127	112
EPD 1.0	123	94	0.464	217	148	48	94	0.172	142	122
EPD 0.4	165	100	0.491	265	178	91	100	0.46	192	131
EPD 0.1	245	108	0.496	353	236	173	108	0.776	281	158

$$\mathsf{TVaR}_{p_0} = \frac{1-p_-}{1-p_0}\mathsf{CTE}_{p_0} - \frac{p_0-p_-}{1-p_0}x_0 \tag{4.14}$$

$$= \frac{1-p_+}{1-p_0}\mathsf{CTE}_{p_+} + \frac{p_+-p_0}{1-p_0}x_0. \tag{4.15}$$

Exercise 49 Continued. Compute $\mathsf{CTE}_p(X)$ for all p. When does it equal $\mathsf{TVaR}_p(X)$?

Solution. For $0.8 \le p < 0.9$, $\{X \ge q(p)\} = \{X \ge 12\}$ and $\mathsf{CTE}_p(X) = (12 + 25)/2 = 18.5$. For $0.7 \le p < 0.8$, $\mathsf{CTE}_p(X) = (8 + 12 + 25)/3 = 15$, and so forth. Figure 4.14 plots CTE_p, TVaR_p, and $q(p)$. CTE equals TVaR at each observation. (TVaR is computed exactly in this plot, making its curvature evident.) □

WCE depends on what events we allow. If the range $[p_-, p_+]$ is collapsed into a single **atom**, meaning an event whose sub-events all have probability 0 or $p_+ - p_-$, then WCE equals the CTE because the whole of the atomic event is included in any sets A used in the supremum. The atom forces the test sets A to be *too big*, which *lowers* CTE.

Table 4.8 Hu/SCS Case Study estimated VaR, TVaR, and EPD by line and in total, gross and net. EPD shows assets required for indicated EPD percentage. Sum shows sum of parts by line with no diversification and benefit shows percentage reduction compared to total. Per occurrence reinsurance applied to Hu with an attachment probability 0.05 (¤40) and detachment probability 0.005 (¤413).

	Gross					Net				
Statistic	**Hu**	**SCS**	**Benefit**	**Sum**	**Total**	**Hu**	**SCS**	**Benefit**	**Sum**	**Total**
VaR 90.0	44	111	0.0283	154	150	40	111	0.195	152	127
VaR 95.0	95	139	0.113	234	211	40	139	0.125	180	160
VaR 97.5	190	174	0.181	364	308	40	174	0.03	215	208
VaR 99.0	428	237	0.223	665	544	56	237	−0.136	293	340
VaR 99.6	899	326	0.217	1,225	1,007	527	326	0.22	853	700
VaR 99.9	2,488	541	0.173	3,029	2,583	2,116	541	0.195	2,657	2,224
TVaR 90.0	247	167	0.149	414	360	188	167	0.289	355	276
TVaR 95.0	430	211	0.175	641	546	635	211	1	846	411
TVaR 97.5	728	267	0.183	995	841	859	267	0.755	1,126	642
TVaR 99.0	1,404	369	0.173	1,773	1,511	1,032	369	0.146	1,401	1,223
TVaR 99.6	2,604	514	0.153	3,119	2,704	2,232	514	0.163	2,747	2,361
TVaR 99.9	6,209	856	0.122	7,065	6,298	5,837	856	0.128	6,693	5,932
EPD 10.0	3,438	100	6	3,538	523	5,761	100	16	5,860	341
EPD 5.0	8,140	141	4	8,282	1,684	12,591	141	7	12,732	1,646
EPD 2.5	16,268	204	3	16,473	4,491	23,178	204	4	23,382	4,821
EPD 1.0	32,660	342	2	33,003	12,538	42,058	342	2	42,401	13,623
EPD 0.4	53,156	583	0.99	53,739	27,010	63,020	583	1	63,603	28,891
EPD 0.1	82,900	1,278	0.465	84,178	57,464	90,444	1,278	0.535	91,722	59,739

In general

$$\mathsf{VaR}_p(X) \le \mathsf{CTE}_p(X) \le \mathsf{WCE}_p(X) \le \mathsf{TVaR}_p(X).$$

When $F(q^-(p)) = p$, the last two inequalities are equalities. If the probability space is atomless then $\mathsf{WCE}_p(X) = \mathsf{TVaR}_p(X)$, see Follmer and Schied (2016) Corollary 4.54 and 4.68. The set A that achieves the maximum WCE value need not be unique. The WCE representation of TVaR is an expected value with respect to the conditional probability $\mathsf{Q}(B) = \mathsf{P}(A \cap B)/\mathsf{P}(A) = \mathsf{P}(A \cap B)/(1 - p_0)$. The idea of computing TVaR using a different probability is the basis of all the allocations discussed in Chapter 14. In that context, the non-uniqueness of A causes particular problems.

Exercise 69. In Section 3.5.4 we defined the expected policyholder deficit (EPD) with assets a to equal $\mathsf{E}[(X-a)^+]$. It is the area B in the left plot of 4.13, and area D in the middle plot. Show that

$$\mathsf{E}[(X-a)^+] = (1 - F(a))(\mathsf{TVaR}_{F(a)}(X) - a). \tag{4.16}$$

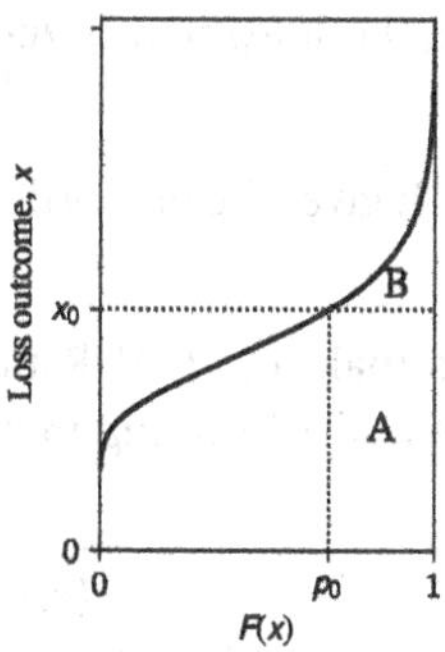

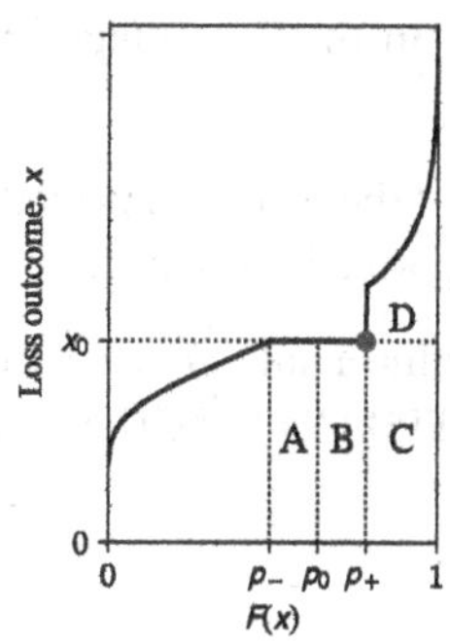

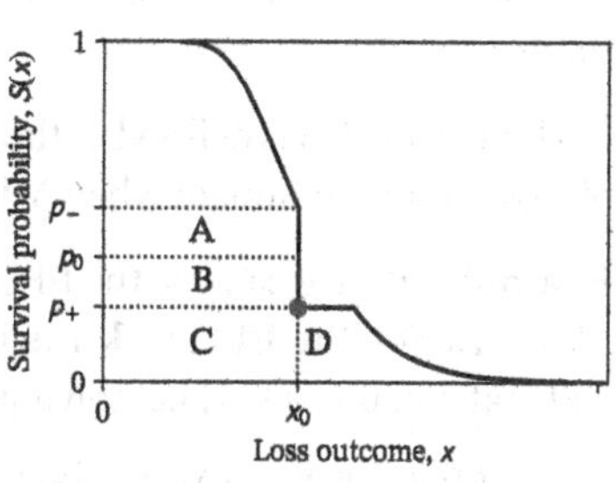

Figure 4.13 Left: the graph of $q^-(p) = \text{VaR}_p(X)$ against p to compute TVaR for a continuous random variable; middle: for a variable with point mass, the dot indicates q^- is continuous from the left; right: rotated version of middle plot showing $S(x)$ against x, with the dot indicating continuity from the right. With a point mass, $x_0 = q^-(p_0)$ but $F(x_0) = p_+$ and $F(q^-(p_0)) = p_+ > p_0$. The discontinuous jump in q^- at D does not affect the conclusions.

Figure 4.14 TVaR, CTE, and quantile functions for X.

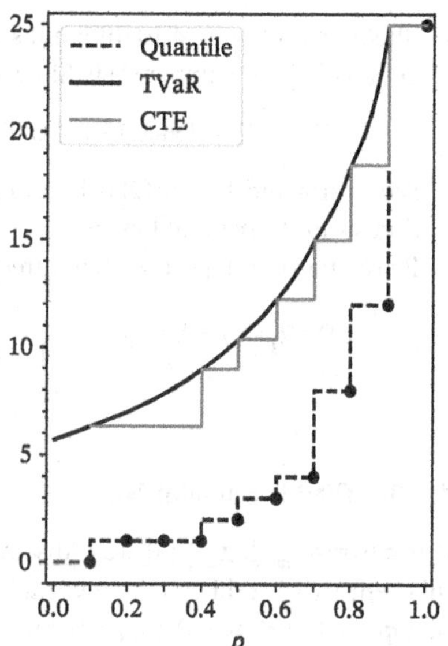

Solution Substituting $F(x) = p, x = q^-(p)$ gives

$$\begin{aligned}
\mathsf{E}[(X-a)^+] &= \int_a^\infty (x-a)dF(x) \\
&= \int_a^\infty x dF(x) - a(1-F(a)) \\
&= \int_{F(a)}^1 q^-(p)dp - a(1-F(a)) \\
&= (1-F(a))(\text{TVaR}_{F(a)}(X) - a).
\end{aligned}$$

A possible mass at $x = a$ is irrelevant in the first integral because the integrand is zero there. □

The **EPD ratio** is defined as the ratio of the EPD to expected losses. It gives the proportion of losses that are unpaid when X is supported by assets a.

Example 70. We can use the EPD to define a tail risk measure that is analogous to VaR and TVaR. Define the **EPD risk measure** $\mathsf{EPD}_s(X)$ to be the amount of assets resulting in an EPD ratio of $0 < s < 1$, i.e. solving

$$\mathsf{E}[(X - \mathsf{EPD}_p(X))^+] = s\mathsf{E}[X]. \tag{4.17}$$

The EPD risk measure is a stricter standard for smaller s. It accounts for the degree of default relative to promised payments, making it attractive to regulators. It is used to set risk-based capital standards in Butsic (1994) and as a capital standard in Myers and Read Jr. (2001). □

Exercise 71. Expain the behavior of EPD capital relative to VaR and TVaR. □

Exercise 72.

1. Illustrate on Figure 4.13 different sets A of probability p_0 so that $\mathsf{TVaR}_{p_0}(X) = \mathsf{E}[X \mid A]$.
2. Let CTE^+ denote upper CTE. Show that

$$\mathsf{CTE}_p(X) \le \mathsf{TVaR}_p(X) \le \mathsf{CTE}_p(X)^+.$$

   See Acerbi and Tasche (2002b), Corollary 5.2, and remember the accounting sign convention swaps upper and lower.
3. By reference to Figure 4.13, or directly from the integral definition of TVaR, show that

$$\mathsf{TVaR}_p(X) = \mathsf{VaR}_p(X) + \frac{1}{1-p}\mathsf{E}[(X - \mathsf{VaR}_p(X))^+]. \tag{4.18}$$

□

4.3.9 TVaR Is Subadditive

It is surprising that TVaR was "discovered" as a subadditive (Eq. (4.8)) risk measure only this century (Acerbi 2002). How can we see TVaR is subadditive? Naively, we might hope that $q_{X_1+X_2}(p) \le q_{X_1}(p) + q_{X_2}(p)$, but that is not true because VaR can fail to be subadditive. We need more ingenuity.

Exercise 73. Show if f and g are functions defined on Ω then $\sup_{\omega\in\Omega}(f(\omega) + g(\omega)) \le \sup_{\omega\in\Omega} f(\omega) + \sup_{\omega\in\Omega} g(\omega)$. □

Exercise 74. Given a collection of additive functions f_i, $f_i(x + y) = f_i(x) + f_i(y)$, defined on Ω, show that the function defined by $\sup_i f_i$ is subadditive. □

Embrechts and Wang (2015) give seven different proofs of subadditivity. The shortest runs as follows. Suppose X_1, X_2, and $X_1 + X_2$ are all continuous. This implies that the underlying probability space is atomless. Subadditivity follows from the WCE expression for TVaR using Exercise 74 because each conditional expectation is additive.

Here is a sketch of their most direct proof. It follows the common theme of ordering the sample space to make X increasing.

If X has a continuous distribution function, then it is well known that $F(X)$ is a uniform variable and $X = q(F(X))$. $F(X)$ acts like a unique ordering of events. When X is not continuous, it has probability masses, and there is no unique analog of $F(X)$. However, we can create a non-unique analog.

Exercise 75. Given a random variable X, let V be a uniform random variable independent of X. Define a random variable $U_X = F(X-) + V(F(X) - F(X-))$ (meaning $U_X(\omega) = F(X(\omega)-) + V(\omega)(F(X(\omega)) - F(X(\omega)-)))$, where $F(x-) = \lim_{t\uparrow x} F(t)$ is the value of F at x from the left and so $F(X) - F(X-)$ is the jump. In most cases there is no jump and $F(X) - F_X(X-) = 0$. Show that $X = q(U_X)$ for almost all ω. □

U_X can be regarding as ordering X. Using Exercise 75, substituting $t = U_X(s)$ and using the fact U_X is uniform,

$$\mathsf{TVaR}_p(X) = \frac{1}{1-p}\int_p^1 q(t)dt = \frac{1}{1-p}\mathsf{E}[q(U_X)1_{U_X \ge p}] = \frac{1}{1-p}\mathsf{E}[X1_{U_X \ge p}].$$

We claim that $\mathsf{E}[q(U_X)1_{U_X\ge p}]$ has the greatest possible value among expressions of the form $\mathsf{E}[XB]$ where B is in $\mathcal{B}_p$, the set of Bernoulli$(1-p)$ random variables. Then

$$\mathsf{TVaR}_p(X) = \frac{1}{1-p}\sup_{B\in\mathcal{B}_p}\{\mathsf{E}[XB]\}$$

and subadditivity follows from Exercise 74. It remains to show $\mathsf{E}[X1_{U_X\ge p}] \ge \mathsf{E}[XB]$ for all $B \in \mathcal{B}_p$. Since U_X is uniform, $\mathsf{E}[1_{U_X\ge p}] = \mathsf{E}[B]$. Therefore $\mathsf{E}[X(1_{U_X\ge p} - B)] = \mathsf{E}[(X-m)(1_{U_X\ge p} - B)]$ for all m. Take $m = q(p)$. Then

- if $q(U_X) > m$ then $X \ge m$, $U_X > p$, $1_{U_X\ge p} = 1$ and $\mathsf{E}[(X-m)(1_{U_X\ge p} - B)] \ge 0$,
- if $q(U_X) < m$ then $X \le m$, $U_X < p$, $1_{U_X\ge p} = 0$ and $\mathsf{E}[(X-m)(1_{U_X\ge p} - B)] \ge 0$ since both terms are ≤ 0, and
- if $q(U_X) = m$ then $X = m$, $\mathsf{E}[(X-m)(1_{U_X\ge p} - B)] = 0$.

Thus $\mathsf{E}[X(1_{U_X\ge p} - B)] = \mathsf{E}[(X-m)(1_{U_X\ge p} - B)] \ge 0$ as required.

4.3.10 TVaR as Solution to an Optimization Problem

TVaR has two representations in terms of optimization problems.

The first was introduced in Rockafellar and Uryasev (2002). They showed that VaR and TVaR solve the optimization problems

$$\begin{aligned}\mathsf{TVaR}_p(X) &= \min_x\{x + (1-p)^{-1}\mathsf{E}[(X-x)^+]\}\\ \mathsf{VaR}_p(X) &= \operatorname{argmin}_x\{x + (1-p)^{-1}\mathsf{E}[(X-x)^+]\}.\end{aligned}$$

The first line says that TVaR balances the cost of providing capital, x, against the cost of a shortfall, $\mathsf{E}[(X-x)^+]$, where the shortfall cost is weighted by $1/(1-p) > 1$. The closer p is to 1, the greater weight put on potential default scenarios resulting in a more conservative value for x. The second line means that VaR_p is the argument's value that minimizing the expression in braces.

These relationships are clear from Figure 4.15. The optimized expression can be written $(1-p)^{-1}\min_x x(1-p) + \mathsf{E}[(X-x)^+]$, cf. Eq. (4.13). Consider the area being minimized. If $x_l < x = \mathsf{VaR}$, the area includes the additional dark triangle from $\mathsf{E}[(X-x_l)^+]$. If $x_h > x = \mathsf{VaR}$, the area includes the additional dark triangle from $x_h(1-p)$. Only at $x = \mathsf{VaR}$ do these two terms disappear. The minimizing argument is $x = \mathsf{VaR}$. Rockafellar and Uryasev (2002) called the result CVaR and used it in an efficient linear programming algorithm to perform portfolio optimization over multiple CVaR constraints.

The second is presented in Follmer and Schied (2016) Theorem 4.52. It says that

$$\mathsf{TVaR}_p(X) = \max\{\mathsf{E}[XZ] \mid Z \geq 0, Z \leq (1-p)^{-1}, \mathsf{E}[Z] = 1\}$$

for $0 \leq p < 1$. We call the random variables Z **scenario functions**. (They are also called test functions.) They are densities for risk-adjusted probabilities: Z is positive and integrates to 1. They define different scenarios that could occur. The requirement $Z \leq (1-p)^{-1}$ means that the risk-adjusted probability cannot increase the objective probability by more than a factor $(1-p)^{-1}$. For an atomless probability space, the extreme points of the set of scenario functions are precisely $1_A/\mathsf{Pr}(A)$ for $\mathsf{Pr}(A) = 1-p$, i.e. the functions used in WCE; see (Delbaen, 2002, Example 4.2).

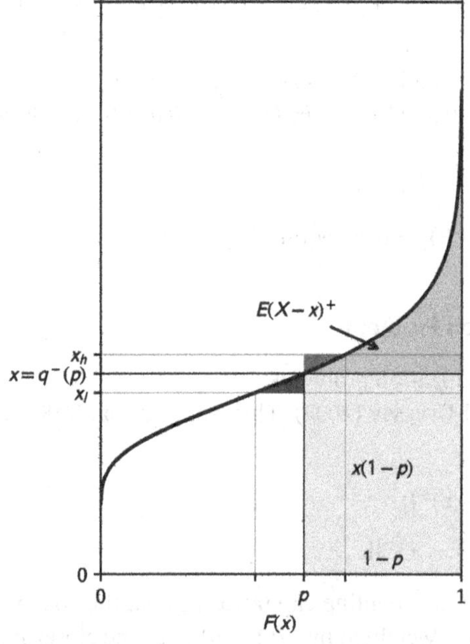

Figure 4.15 VaR and TVaR as solutions to an optimization problem. Graph shows loss outcome $q^-(p)$ vertically against p horizontally. TVaR is sum of light shaded areas divided by $1-p$.

4.3.11 Summary: The Different Manifestations of TVaR for a Continuous Variable

In mathematics, important concepts have many different manifestations. The numerous ways of computing TVaR attest to its importance. For a continuous loss random variable X we have collected eight different expressions:

$$
\begin{aligned}
\mathsf{TVaR}_p(X) &= \frac{1}{1-p}\int_p^1 q(s)ds \\
&= q(p) + \frac{1}{1-p}\int_{q(p)}^{\infty} S(x)\,dx \\
&= q(p) + \frac{1}{1-p}\int_{q(p)}^{\infty} xdF(x) \\
&= q(p) + \frac{1}{1-p}\mathsf{E}[(X-q(p))^+] \\
&= \mathsf{E}[X \mid X \ge q(p)] \\
&= \max_Z \{\mathsf{E}[XZ] \mid Z \ge 0, Z \le (1-p)^{-1}, \mathsf{E}[Z]=1\} \\
&= \min_x \{x + (1-p)^{-1}\mathsf{E}[(X-x)^+]\} \\
&= \sup \{\mathsf{E}[X \mid A] \mid \mathsf{Pr}(A) > 1-p\}.
\end{aligned}
$$

Writing

$$
\mathsf{E}[X \mid A] = \frac{1}{\mathsf{Pr}(A)}\int_A X(\omega)\mathsf{Pr}(d\omega)
$$

draws out the connection between the first and last representations. The last says TVaR is the worst expected loss over a set of probability scenarios that assume just an event of probability $1-p$ occurs.

See Artzner *et al.* (1999), Acerbi and Tasche (2002b), Acerbi and Tasche (2002a), Rockafellar and Uryasev (2002), Delbaen (2000), Delbaen (2002), Cherny and Orlov (2011), and Follmer and Schied (2016) for more details on the various manifestations of TVaR.

Exercise 76.

1. Explain each of these expressions for TVaR given above in words.
2. Validate the second and third expressions. Hint: use integration by parts. When F is absolutely continuous and has a density f, $\int xdF(x) = \int xf(x)dx$.
3. What are the relationships between the eight expressions when X is not continuous? Hint: you must separately consider X defined on an atomless probability space and one with atoms. Any finite sample space has atoms. □

4.4 Differentiating Quantiles, VaR, and TVaR

Given reference variables $X_1, \dots, X_n$ define a **homogeneous portfolio** by $X(\mathbf{v}) = \sum_i v_i X_i$, $\mathbf{v} = (v_1, \dots, v_n)$. Often X_i are interpreted as asset returns and $X(\mathbf{v})$ is the value of a portfolio with investment v_i in asset i. It can also represent losses on a portfolio with participation or volume in unit i given by v_i. Let $S_{\mathbf{v}}(t) = \Pr(X(\mathbf{v}) > t)$ be the survival function of $X(\mathbf{v})$ and $q_{\mathbf{v}}(p)$ be the p quantile of $X(\mathbf{v})$.

Major (2004) and Tasche (2001) contain the following expressions, which are valid whenever the underlying distributions are sufficiently well behaved. For example, they hold when the X_i have a jointly differentiable density.

The derivative of the survival function is

$$\frac{\partial S_{\mathbf{v}}(t)}{\partial v_i} = \mathsf{E}[X_i(1) 1_{\{X(\mathbf{v})=t\}}] = \mathsf{E}[X_i(1) \mid X(\mathbf{v}) = t] f_{\mathbf{v}}(t) \tag{4.19}$$

where $f_{\mathbf{v}}$ is the density of $X(\mathbf{v})$.

The derivative of $q_{\mathbf{v}}(p) = \mathsf{VaR}_p(X(\mathbf{v}))$ with respect to v_i is

$$\frac{\partial q_{\mathbf{v}}(p)}{\partial v_i} = \mathsf{E}\left[X_i(1) \mid X(\mathbf{v}) = q_{\mathbf{v}}(p)\right]. \tag{4.20}$$

The derivative of tail value at risk is

$$\frac{\partial \mathsf{TVaR}_p(X(\mathbf{v}))}{\partial v_i} = \mathsf{E}[X_i(1) \mid X(\mathbf{v}) > q_{\mathbf{v}}(p)]. \tag{4.21}$$

Tasche also gives expressions for derivatives of the shortfall and its powers.

$X(\mathbf{v})$ is called a homogeneous portfolio because its shape, as a probability distribution, depends only on $\mathbf{v}$ up to a positive constant. The distributions $X(\mathbf{v})$ and $X(\lambda\mathbf{v})$, $\lambda > 0$, are scalar multiples of one another.

4.5 Learning Objectives

1. Define a quantile.
2. Compute lower and upper quantiles given a discrete, continuous, or mixed distribution or a sample from a distribution.
3. Given the graph of a distribution function and p, identify $q(p)$ on the horizontal axis.
4. Give examples to illustrate how quantiles can fail to be unique.
5. Use quantiles to simulate from a random variable via the inversion method.
6. Define VaR and compute it given a discrete, continuous, or mixed distribution, or given a sample from a distribution.
7. Explain VaR to your management.
8. Translate between VaR expressed with probability level and return period.
9. Distinguish between VaR, aggregate PML, and occurrence PML.
10. Compute aggregate PML and occurrence PML given catastrophe model output.
11. Define a subadditive risk measure.

12. Explain what it means that VaR can fail to be subadditive, construct examples showing the failure, and describe its importance in risk management.
13. Describe three common cases where VaR fails to be subadditive.
14. Describe the Rearrangement Algorithm and apply it, given a multivariate sample.
15. Define TVaR and compute it given a discrete, continuous, or mixed distribution or a sample from a distribution.
16. Explain and illustrate the eight different ways of computing TVaR for continuous random variables.
17. Distinguish between TVaR, CTE, and WCE, both conceptually and through examples.
18. Compute TVaR using a Lee diagram.
19. Use a Lee diagram to distinguish TVaR from CTE.
20. Use a Lee diagram to explain how TVaR solves an optimization problem and the importance of VaR in the solution.
21. Apply formulas for the differentials of quantiles, VaR, and TVaR for the homogeneous portfolio.

5

Properties of Risk Measures and Advanced Topics

The generalised scenarios method is the universal coherent risk measurement method: it requires thinking before calculating, which can only improve risk management.
Artzner, Delbaen, Eber, and Heath, *Thinking Coherently*

In this chapter, we relate insurance loss scenarios to probability scenarios and provide motivation for our interest in coherent risk measures. Then, we enumerate mathematical properties a risk measure may possess and discuss how each helps represent real world risk preferences. Anyone using a risk measure should check it against these properties to ensure it is fit for purpose. We describe risk preferences and the famous Rothschild-Stiglitz characterization of increasing risk. We explain why firms' decision-making is different from individuals and how traditional utility theory is inadequate. Dual utility, related to spectral risk measures, is presented as a suitable alternative. We detail the close relationship between law invariance and second-order stochastic dominance. We explain how to represent coherent risk measures with probability scenarios (the generalized scenarios of the epigraph) and present Delbaen's theorem on directional derivatives, which has important implications for allocation. Two appendices cover realistic disaster scenarios and different modes of convergence for random variables.

5.1 Probability Scenarios

In this section, we explain the connection between insurance events, realistic disaster scenarios, probability events, and generalized probability scenarios, and show how they lead to coherent risk measures.

Artzner *et al.* (1999) have exerted a tremendous influence on the theory and practice of risk measurement. That paper has been cited in more than 10,000 other works. When its authors say that generalized scenarios are a *universal method* we should take note. What, exactly, do

Pricing Insurance Risk: Theory and Practice, First Edition. Stephen J. Mildenhall and John A. Major.

they mean? To see, we need to go back through our definitions and distinguish different uses of the word *event*.

In insurance and catastrophe modeling, an *event* describes a set of circumstances likely to result in insurance losses: a hurricane footprint or earthquake fault location. Or, at a micro-level, a cluster of bad traffic. It is a single occurrence (that may cause multiple claims across a portfolio). We call these occurrences **insurance events** and label them $E_1, \dots, E_N$, for some large N. To have a concrete example, let E_1 describe a category 5 hurricane making landfall in Miami. Whether an insurance event causes a loss depends on the portfolio exposed to it.

Lloyd's defines a **realistic disaster scenario** (RDS, see Section 5.A) as an insurance event that is potentially disastrous (e.g., category 3 or greater windstorm or Richter scale 7.5 or greater earthquake) but plausible (e.g., similar to one in the historical record). The insurance event E_1 is an RDS.

In probability theory, we start with the sample space Ω. Sample points in Ω describe different states of the world in our model. To a probabilitist, an *event* is a subset of Ω. It defines a range of states of the world. To distinguish from insurance events, we call these **probability events.**

A sample point $\omega \in \Omega$ defines a single state of the world by noting which insurance events occur during a year—we are setting up an annual aggregate view in catastrophe modeling language. (We can create different sample points to handle multiple occurrences of the same insurance event, but for simplicity, assume each event occurs at most once.) We write $\omega = (1, 0, 0, 1, 0, 0, \dots)$ where 1 or 0 in the kth place indicates whether or not the insurance event E_k occurs. For ω, events E_1 and E_4, and possibly others, occur. When Ω is discrete, as it is here, we can assume that any subset of Ω defines a probability event.

The probability event corresponding to years where E_1, the Miami hurricane, occurs is given by the set of all ω that start with 1

$$B(E_1) := \{(1, ?, ?, \dots) \in \Omega\}.$$

In general, define $B_k := B(E_k)$ to be the set of all sample points where the insurance event E_k occurs, i.e., those with the value 1 in the kth place.

So far, we have not used the probability function. A probability function P gives the likelihood of any probability event. The probability of a single sample point $\omega \in \Omega$ means $\mathsf{P}(\{\omega\})$, the probability of the associated probability event. Assume we are given an objective (or best estimate) probability function, P.

We can now define the **conditional probability scenario** associated with an insurance event E_k and the probability function P. It is the probability function Q_k equal to P conditional on B_k. Using Bayes' theorem, for any probability event A

$$\mathsf{Q}_k(A) := \frac{\mathsf{P}(A \cap B_k)}{\mathsf{P}(B_k)}.$$

By construction $\mathsf{Q}(B_k) = \mathsf{P}(B_k)/\mathsf{P}(B_k) = 1$. Thus the probability function Q_k treats E_k as though it is certain to occur. Each RDS defines a Q_k in this way.

How do we apply a conditional probability scenario? We need one last ingredient to add to the insurance events and conditional probability scenarios: an insurance portfolio against which we assess losses. The catastrophe modeling and actuarial departments estimate the losses, in total and by unit, from each insurance event. Total losses define a random variable X on Ω. The outcome $X(\omega)$ gives losses in the state of the world ω. Remember, $X(\omega)$ is an annual aggregate loss, and it includes both severe catastrophe events and all attritional losses. X_j denotes losses from unit j and $X = \sum_j X_j$.

Now we can apply a conditional probability scenario the same way we use any probability function: to compute expected values. P defines the best estimate expected value.

But, *why* do we apply a conditional probability scenario in this way? Q_k defines our best estimate probability in states of the world where the insurance event E_k occurs. Prudent risk management dictates that we should have the financial resources to pay our claims after the occurrence of any reasonable disaster. Based on historical events and management or regulator efforts, we can define a set of different RDSs, say r in all. Then, setting capital using the risk measure

$$\rho_c(X) := \max\{E_{\mathsf{Q}_1}[X], \dots, E_{\mathsf{Q}_r}[X]\} \tag{5.1}$$

provides an easy-to-communicate solvency standard: "We can pay claims from these realistic insurance events. . . ." But wait, there's more. As an unexpected bonus, we show in Section 5.2 that ρ_c has several desirable properties as a risk measure—plot spoiler: they are the coherent risk measures.

We have already encountered two risk measures of the form ρ_c: the mean corresponds to the set {P}, associated with $B = \Omega$, and TVaR can be computed using a P-conditional distribution, conditioned on a set of probability $1 - p$; see Section 4.3.8.

Thus far, our discussion has been focused on capital risk measures. What about the pricing application? We need to go back to P. We are taking it as given in our construction of Q_k. What if it is wrong? For capital applications, some uncertainty in P may not matter. If we want to estimate a VaR or TVaR and we perturb P and keep the same mean (it is our best estimate), some perturbations result in higher TVaR and some lower. But the tail of X usually changes slowly and nearly linearly and these perturbations average out. The TVaR with and without "P-uncertainty" won't differ by much.

The risk in pricing is different. Here we are concerned about the risk in our estimate of the mean $\mathsf{E}[X]$, not the risk in an *outcome* like an RDS. Uncertainty about P can be categorized as follows:

1. Statistical uncertainty: P is an estimate subject to the usual problems of estimation risk, and
2. Information uncertainty: P is based on a limited and filtered subset of ambiguous information.

Statistical uncertainty is the domain of cost estimation and determining the best estimate expected loss. It concerns estimates of objective probabilities. In an ideal world, it diversifies across the portfolio and is managed by the law of large numbers.

Information uncertainty is much more pernicious and unavoidable than statistical uncertainty. It reflects information asymmetry between the insured and insurer and between the insurer and investor. It concerns risk aversion and estimates of subjective probabilities.

We can create probability scenarios to reflect information uncertainty, and these need not be conditional expectations of P; see Example 77. They are the **generalized** scenarios of the epigraph.

Why do we apply generalized scenarios? For the same reasons as capital. We select many relevant generalized scenarios, compute expected losses using each, and take the maximum. A single generalized scenario can reflect events such as insureds being systematically miss-classified, adverse selection, or incorrect judgmental parameter selections rather than specifying catastrophes. These events are all included as part of the state of the world. Taking the maximum expectation gives us confidence that the premium will exceed **expected losses,** even in an adverse information scenario. Unlike capital, this is a statement about the mean, not the actual outcome.

Finally, in Section 5.4 we show all risk measures satisfying the coherent properties are of the form ρ_c if we allow generalized (non-conditional) probability scenarios. This situation is truly the best of all possible worlds. The risk measure ρ_c:

- is intuitive and easy to communicate,
- can be used for capital and pricing,
- has properties as a risk measure that are aligned with rational risk preferences, and
- any measure with those properties is a ρ_c for some set of probability scenarios.

The problem of defining ρ_c is reduced to selecting the appropriate set of RDSs (for capital) or generalized scenarios (for pricing). We call the set of probability scenarios $\mathcal{Q}$, setting up an equivalence $\rho_c \leftrightarrow \mathcal{Q}$. Notice the parallels here with the need for two risk measures from the Introduction, Section 1.2, and the two roles of risk measures in Section 3.6.3.

We use **probability scenarios** in this book to refer to both conditional probability scenarios and the generalized ones.

Before leaving this section and jumping into the mathematical properties of risk measures, we introduce a spreadsheet schematic to summarize how they are computed. The end of the chapter describes the connections between the properties of ρ_c and the scenario set $\mathcal{Q}$.

Example 77. This example shows that not all probability scenarios arise as conditional probabilities. Let $\Omega = \{\omega_1, \omega_2, \omega_3, \omega_4\}$ have four states and $\mathsf{P}(\{\omega_i\}) = 1/4$ for each. Then Q assigning probabilities 1/8, 1/8, 1/8, and 5/8 is not a conditional probability. □

Example 78. Ins Co. has a set of probability scenarios it uses for capital management (defined as conditional probabilities given the occurrence of an RDS) and another set of generalized probability scenarios for pricing. Ins Co.'s board has publicly announced that Ins Co. intends always to hold capital sufficient to pay losses from any capital scenario. To quantify this risk, Ins Co. computes ρ_c per Eq. (5.1).

It is helpful to have a spreadsheet implementation in mind to see how $\rho_c(X)$ works. To that end, we describe Ins Co.'s **Capital** and **Risk** (CAPRI) spreadsheet. CAPRI is provided by the economic capital modeling team working in conjunction with the catastrophe modeling team. CAPRI is part of a larger model and evaluates prospective underwriting risk only. It has three types of input:

1. **Sample Space** specifying states of the world. These identify everything (in theory) that happens in a future model year. Sample points are labeled by ω in a sample space Ω. In the language of Example 8, ω is a code we can use to look up additional information in other databases that specify the future state precisely. A single ω encodes whether each given insurance event occurs, tying back to catastrophe model output. In our spreadsheet, Ω is a single column with a huge number n of rows. In theory, all companies model with the same Ω; after all, it includes everything.
2. **Outcomes**. The outcomes are an estimate of the loss by unit from each event. There are m units, and m is usually between 10 and a few hundred; think business units or profit centers. Outcomes comprise a large array in the CAPRI spreadsheet that we name $\boldsymbol{X}$ with n rows and m columns. In addition, the **Sum** column gives the total loss across units by event. The outcome data array is specific to Ins Co.'s portfolio.
3. **Scenarios**. Ins Co. modelers provide a column P giving their best estimate probability for each probability event. If the probability events are a random sample, then their best estimate is simply that all events are equally likely, with P-probability equal to $1/n$. As discussed, *capital* applications generally define probability scenarios as P conditional probabilities, and *pricing* applications use generalized scenarios. The appropriate scenario set depends on the intended purpose of the modeling. $\mathcal{Q}$ is an alternative set of probabilities, each labeled Q_k and consisting of a column of non-negative numbers that sum to 1. The first scenario is P, and there are $r-1$ others.

Figure 5.1 is a schematic of the CAPRI spreadsheet. The top blocks of numbers show Ω, encoding the occurrence or non-occurrence of each insurance event. (The block is wide because CAPRI pulls in a brief state description for convenience, but they play no role in the calculations.) Next, CAPRI shows the unit losses $\boldsymbol{X}$ and total losses $\boldsymbol{\Sigma}$. And finally, the columns of scenario probabilities, $\mathcal{Q}$. Remember:

- Ω has n rows and 1 column, and is fixed for all users,
- $\boldsymbol{X}$ is an $n \times m$ array, with n rows and m columns, and $\boldsymbol{\Sigma}$ is a single column, both specific to Ins Co.'s portfolio, and
- $\mathcal{Q}$ is an $n \times r$ array, with n rows and r columns, and is specific to the analysis.

The calculations in CAPRI occur at the bottom block of numbers, labeled *Scenario expectations and risk*. Here CAPRI takes the matrix product `=MMULT(TRANSPOSE(Q), X)`, giving the expected loss to each unit from each probability scenario, an $r \times m$ array. The scenarios label the rows. The row sums compute the total portfolio expected loss from each scenario across all units. Finally, CAPRI measures risk using the maximum expectation among the scenarios, since Ins Co wants to hold enough capital to cover any one of them. Taking the `=MAX` for each column gives $\rho(X_j)$, the stand-alone risk by each unit, and $\rho(X)$, the maximum of the total column, gives the total measured risk for Ins Co.'s portfolio. □

Remark 79. Elsewhere, we use $X_{j,i}$ to store outcomes by unit by sample point, the transpose of $X_{i,j}$ shown here. □

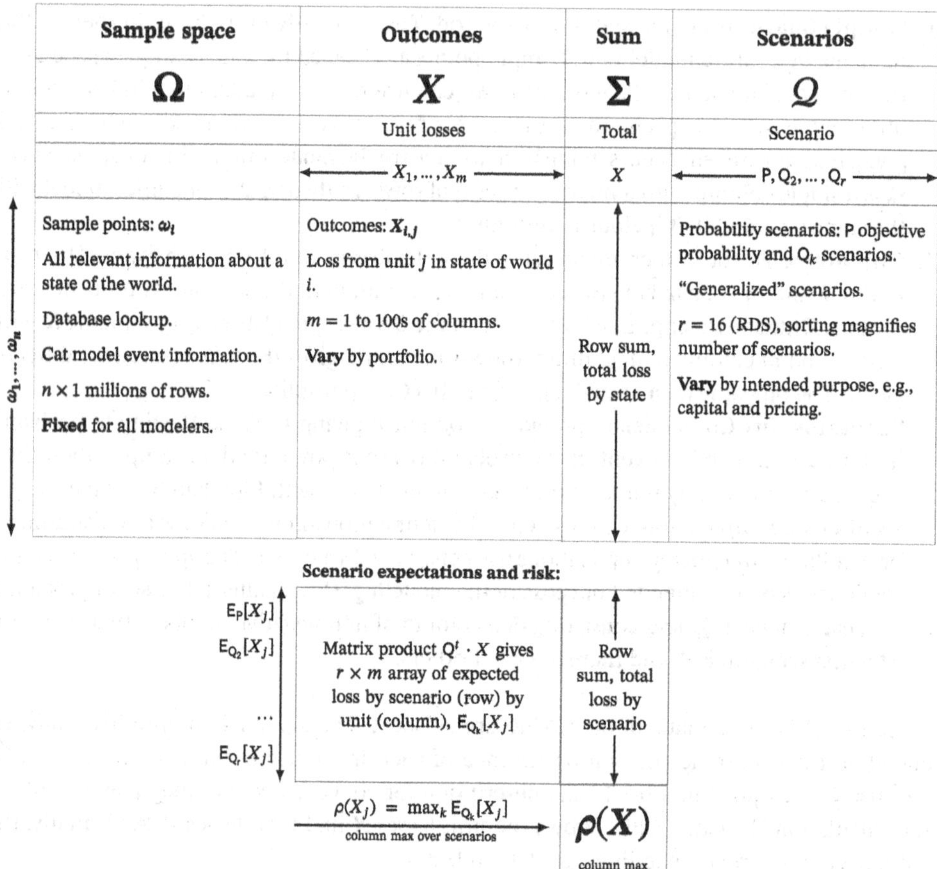

Figure 5.1 The basic structure of Ins Co.'s capital and risk pricing spreadsheet (CAPRI), showing the three types of input: sample space of states of the world, outcomes, and probability scenarios.

5.2 Mathematical Properties of Risk Measures

In this section we define different mathematical properties a risk measure can possess. Figure 5.2 is a schematic representation of the more significant connections between the properties defined in this section.

Throughout, ρ denotes a generic risk measure and ρ_c that given by Eq. (5.1) and associated with the set of probability scenarios $\mathcal{Q}$. We make several comments about the behavior of ρ_c, which usually involve noting the behavior of $\mathsf{E}_{\mathsf{Q}}[\cdot]$ for a probability scenario Q. We assume that ρ represents the risk preference $\succeq$, meaning $X \succeq Y$ iff $\rho(X) \le \rho(Y)$, see Section 3.6.1.

Risks use the actuarial sign convention: large positive values are bad. X and Y represent random variables on the sample space Ω, c a fixed risk, and $\lambda \ge 0$ a constant. There is no

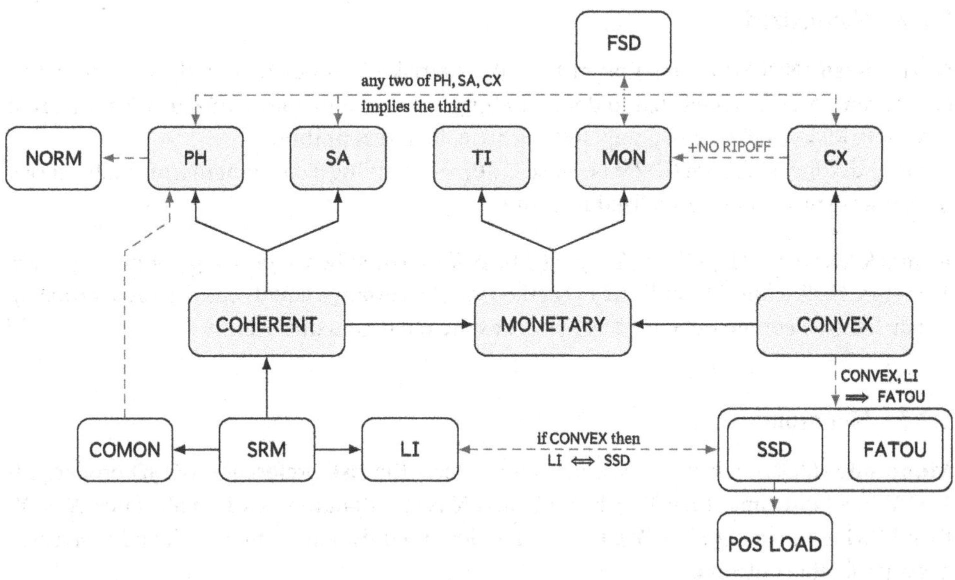

Figure 5.2 Relationships between properties of risk measures. Properties defining coherent and convex risk measures are in gray. A solid line indicates a definition, for example, a monetary risk measure is monotone and translation invariant. A cell is defined by all solid lines emerging from it, reading the arrows as implies. Dashed lines indicate implications, for example, positive homogeneous implies normalized. Monotone is almost equivalent to FSD.

separate consideration of time value; either work with present values and assume that time preferences are separable, or treat all risks as due immediately.

5.2.1 Translation Invariant

Translation invariant (TI) means $\rho(X + c) = \rho(X) + c$. Increasing a loss by a constant c increases the risk by c. To be TI requires ρ is denominated in monetary units, so $\rho(X) + c$ makes sense.

The mean, VaR, TVaR, and a scenario loss are TI. All ρ_c risk measures are TI because $\mathsf{E}_{\mathsf{Q}}[X + c] = \mathsf{E}_{\mathsf{Q}}[X] + c$. Standard deviation, variance, and all higher central moments are not TI because, for example, $\mathsf{Var}(X + c) = \mathsf{Var}(X)$. Factor-based measures are not TI because the factor is applied to the constant. Risk-based capital and rating agency capital models are often factor based. TI is sometimes called **cash invariant** or **translation invariant**.

If a risk X is written for premium P, ignoring expenses, the insurer has a net risk $X - P$. Given a TI capital risk measure ρ, capital to support the net position equals assets to support the risk minus the premium: $\rho(X - P) = \rho(X) - P$. Thus we can speak interchangeably of determining capital (net position) or assets (loss position).

TI allows measured risk to be decomposed into a *best estimate* and *risk margin*: $\rho(X) = \rho(\mathsf{E}[X] + X - \mathsf{E}[X]) = \mathsf{E}[X] + \rho(X - \mathsf{E}[X])$.

5.2.2 Normalized

Normalized (NORM) means that $\rho(0) = 0$. The risk of an outcome with no gain or loss equals zero. A risk is preferred to doing nothing according to a normalized risk measure if $\rho(X) \le 0$. Risks preferred to doing nothing are called **acceptable.**

All ρ_c risk measures are NORM because $\mathsf{E}_{\mathsf{Q}}[0] = 0$. Adding a constant to a normalized risk measure creates a non-normalized measure.

Remark 80. Given TI, $\rho(X - \rho(X)) = \rho(X) - \rho(X) = 0$ and hence $\rho(c) = \rho(0 + c) = \rho(0) + c$. Therefore NORM and TI imply $\rho(c) = c$: the risk of a certain c equals c, a desirable property. In particular, a certain debt of c has risk c, despite having no uncertainty. □

5.2.3 Monotone

Monotone (MON) means the risk measure reflects the risk preference MONO property: if $X \le Y$ in all outcomes then $X \succeq Y$. If the loss X is less than the loss Y in all states, $X \le Y$, then MON requires $\rho(X) \le \rho(Y)$. It says more loss is equivalent to more risk and represents a less preferable outcome.

All ρ_c risk measures are MON because $\mathsf{E}_{\mathsf{Q}}[X] \le \mathsf{E}_{\mathsf{Q}}[Y]$ when $X \le Y$.

Thinking fast, it is difficult to imagine a reasonable risk measure not satisfying MON. The mean, VaR, TVaR, and scenario losses all do. However, thinking slow, we realize that standard deviation and higher central moments are not monotone. For example if X is uniform(0, 1) and $Y \equiv 1$ then $X \le Y$ but $\sigma(X) > \sigma(Y) = 0$.

The related **no rip-off** property says that if $X \le c$ then $\rho(X) \le c$. Monotone risk measures have the no rip-off property.

5.2.4 Positive Loading

Positive loading means that $\rho(X) \ge \mathsf{E}[X]$. The closest one author has seen two actuaries to coming to blows was a heated debate at a research conference about the virtues of the positive loading condition. The other author found himself in a similarly heated debate, but fortunately in a teleconference. These debates usually confuse a positive loading for an entire portfolio (which we all agree is necessary) with a positive loading allocated to a part of a portfolio (which we mostly don't regard as necessary). Reinsurance can be regarded as an allocation with a negative loading.

Whether or not ρ_c has the positive loading property depends on $\mathcal{Q}$. Generally, the larger $\mathcal{Q}$ the more likely ρ_c has a positive loading. A small $\mathcal{Q}$ corresponds to measuring risk by looking at a few scenarios, a process that is easy to game—by finding gaps in the scenarios.

5.2.5 Monetary Risk Measures

A **monetary risk measure** (MRM) satisfies MON and TI. Most of the risk measures we consider are monetary; variance is not (units: ¤-squared). All ρ_c risk measures are monetary.

5.2.6 Positive Homogeneous

Positive homogeneous (PH) means that $\rho(\lambda X) = \lambda\rho(X)$ for $\lambda \geq 0$. It implies ρ is scale invariant. All ρ_c risk measures are PH because $\mathsf{E}_\mathsf{Q}[\lambda X] = \lambda\mathsf{E}_\mathsf{Q}[X]$.

PH is a controversial axiom. Long-Term Capital Management, and other similar experiences suggest risk varies with scale. Artzner *et al.* (1999) comment

> If position size directly influences risk (e.g., if positions are large enough that the time required to liquidate them depends on their sizes) then we should consider the consequences of lack of liquidity when computing the future net worth of a position. With this in mind, Axioms SA [Section 5.2.8] and PH, about mappings from *random variables* into the reals, remain reasonable.

In asset modeling, X represents return and λ is position size. In insurance modeling, the meaning of λX is less clear. When $\lambda < 1$ it can be regarded as a partial placement or quota share, but $\lambda > 1$ is problematic because of laws against over-insurance, Mildenhall (2017).

VaR, standard deviation, and scenario losses are all PH. Variance is not, though it is degree 2 homogeneous because $\mathsf{Var}(\lambda X) = \lambda^2\mathsf{Var}(X)$. The Esscher transform is not PH.

PH implies NORM since $\rho(0) = \rho(0 \times X) = 0 \times \rho(X) = 0$.

5.2.7 Lipschitz Continuous

Lipschitz continuous means that the difference in risk between two random variables is at most the maximum of the absolute value of the difference of their outcomes:

$$|\rho(X) - \rho(Y)| \leq \sup_{\omega\in\Omega} |X(\omega) - Y(\omega)|.$$

The maximum of the quantity on the right is called the **supremum norm** (or uniform norm) of $X - Y$, written $||X - Y||$. Lipschitz continuity follows by applying MON and TI to the inequalities $X \leq Y + ||X - Y||$ and $Y \leq X + ||X - Y||$.

Lipschitz continuous is a stronger condition than continuous, therefore ρ is also continuous with respect to the supremum norm.

5.2.8 Subadditive

Subadditive (SA) means $\rho(X + Y) \leq \rho(X) + \rho(Y)$. SA corresponds to a common-sense view of diversification: the risk of the pool is at most the sum of the risk of the parts. It is sometimes described by saying *mergers do not increase risk*. It is not without controversy, as regulators can find too much diversification benefit, (Dhaene *et al.* 2008).

Suppose ρ is SA and NORM. If X and Y are acceptable on a stand-alone basis, meaning they are preferred to nothing $\rho(X), \rho(Y) \leq 0$, then

$$\rho(X + Y) \leq \rho(X) + \rho(Y) \leq 0.$$

Thus, if X and Y are acceptable, then their sum $X + Y$ is also acceptable. As a result, Ins Co. can effectively manage its total exposure by managing its exposure by unit. The ability to manage bottom up in this way is a very useful property for a risk measure to possess.

The mean and TVaR are SA. VaR is not SA, as we saw in Section 4.2.5. All ρ_c are also subadditive because

$$\max\{E_Q[X+Y]\} = \max\{E_Q[X] + E_Q[+Y]\} \le \max\{E_Q[X]\} + \max\{E_Q[Y]\}.$$

SA implies $\rho(0) \ge 0$ because $\rho(0) = \rho(0+0) \le \rho(0) + \rho(0)$.

Exercise 81. Is variance subadditive? Standard deviation? □

Technical Remark 82. Let MON$'$ be the property: if $X \le 0$ for all outcomes then $\rho(X) \le 0$, i.e., a certain gain involves no risk. It is an alternative formulation of monotone.

1. If NORM and SA then MON is equivalent to MON$'$. To see why, let $X \le 0$. Then by MON and NORM $\rho(X) \le \rho(0) = 0$. Conversely if $X \le Y$ then $\rho(X) = \rho(X-Y+Y) \le \rho(X-Y)+\rho(Y)$. Hence $-\rho(X-Y) \le \rho(Y) - \rho(X)$. By MON$'$ $\rho(X-Y) \le 0$ and the result follows.
2. If TI, MON, SA, PH, and $a \le X \le b$ then $a \le \rho(X) \le b$. To see why, first note that PH implies NORM and so we can use MON$'$. If $X \le b$ then $X-b \le 0$ so $\rho(X-b) = \rho(X)-b \le 0$ and $\rho(X) \le b$. If $X \ge a$ then $a - X \le 0$ so $0 \ge \rho(-X+a) = \rho(-X) + a \ge -\rho(X) + a$. □

5.2.9 Sublinear

Sublinear means PH and SA both hold. Sublinear pricing risk measures have a positive bid-ask spread. Bid and ask prices are important in Section 10.4.

When ρ is a pricing risk measure, $\rho(X)$ is the **ask** price to pay X and $-\rho(-X)$ is the **bid** price to receive X. The ask price contains a positive margin if $\rho(X) \ge \mathsf{E}[X]$: premium exceeds expected loss payments; the bid prices does if $-\rho(-X) \le \mathsf{E}[X]$: premium paid is less than loss recoveries received. If the pricing functional ρ is homogeneous, rather than just *positive* homogeneous, then $-\rho(-H) = \rho(H)$ and it is impossible for both the bid and ask prices to contain a positive margin.

However, if ρ is sublinear, then both prices can contain a margin. To see this, first note $0 = \rho(0)$ by PH. Then

$$0 = \rho(X - X) \le \rho(X) + \rho(-X) = \rho(X) - (-\rho(-X)) = \text{ask} - \text{bid}$$

by SA, showing that sublinear functions always exhibit a non-negative **bid-ask spread**. Figure 5.3 shows the graph of $\rho(kX)$ against k for ρ from Example 83. $\rho(kX)$ has a kink at $k = 0$ and lies above the graph of the straight line $\mathsf{E}[kX] = k\mathsf{E}[X]$ for all k, showing the positive margin in both the bid and ask prices.

Example 83. Ins Co. underwrites weather insurance. It offers the *Hot August* policy that pays ¤1 if the average temperature during August in Metropolis is above 35C. It is very popular with utilities, who use it to hedge their generating costs when they need to meet high demand. Using historical data, suitably adjusted for global warming and urbanization, Ins Co. estimates the probability of a hot August is $p = 0.1$. Ins Co. also offers the *Cold August* policy that pays if the average is below 35C. It is popular with ice cream vendors and air conditioner salespeople. Obviously, the probability of a cold August is $1 - p = 0.9$.

Ins Co. prices a Bernoulli risk B_p with probability p of loss as $\sqrt{p}$ and extends pricing to be TI. Notice that $1 - B_p = B_{1-p}$. Thus, Ins Co. quotes $\sqrt{0.1} = 0.316$ for H and $\sqrt{0.9} = 0.95$ for $C = 1 - H$, so both prices contain a positive margin. Next, $\rho(-H) = \rho(C) - 1 = -0.05$ and so $\rho(H) > -\rho(-H)$, showing these prices include a positive bid ask spread. □

Technical Remark 84. Figure 5.3 shows that $\rho(kX)$ lies above the two *linear* functions $k \mapsto k\rho(X)$ and $k \mapsto k\rho(-X)$ (the continuations of the steeper and shallower thick lines, respectively). Suppose the domain of ρ is a real vector space V of random variables. Define a linear function $l(kX) = k\rho(X)$ on the vector subspace V_X of V generated by X, i.e., on kX for $k \in \mathbb{R}$. By construction, $l(kX) \le \rho(kX)$ for all k. The Hahn Banach theorem guarantees the existence of a linear function L_X, defined on all of V that extends l in the sense that $L_X(v) = l(v)$ for all $v \in V_X$, and that is dominated by ρ, $L_X(v) \le \rho(v)$, for all $v \in V$. We can use functions like L_X to represent ρ. Let V^* be the set of real-valued linear functions on V and define

$$\mathcal{L}_\rho = \{L \in V^* \mid L(X) \le \rho(X)\ \forall X \in V\}.$$

Then

$$\rho(X) = \max\{L(X) \mid L \in \mathcal{L}_\rho\} \tag{5.2}$$

because $L_X \in \mathcal{L}_\rho$ and $L_X(X) = \rho(X)$ by construction. This powerful idea, proved in this context by Kalkbrener (2005), is expanded in Section 5.4 . When ρ is suitably continuous, L_X is also continuous and it can be interpreted as a risk-adjusted linear pricing functional. □

5.2.10 Comonotonic Random Variables

Two random variables X and Y are **comonotonic** if $X = g(Z)$ and $Y = h(Z)$ for increasing functions g and h and a common variable Z. Comonotonic variables provide no hedge against

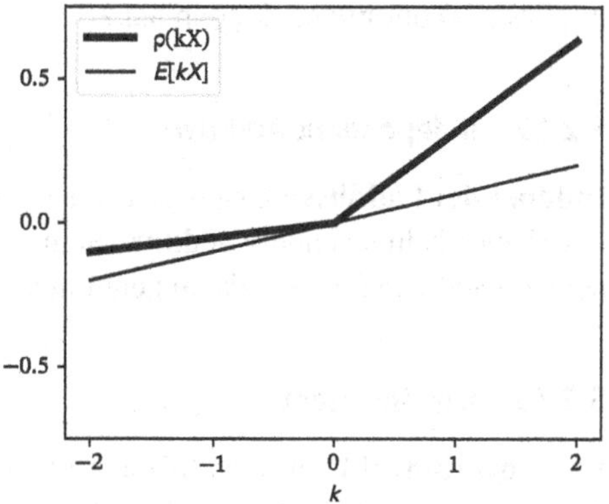

Figure 5.3 The graph of $\rho(kX)$ against k for a nonlinear functional ρ lies above the graph of $E[kX]$.

one another. According to Denneberg (1994), comonotonic is an abbreviation for *common monotonic.*

It can be shown that X and Y are comonotonic iff $(X(\omega_1) - X(\omega_2))(Y(\omega_1) - Y(\omega_2)) \geq 0$ for all $\omega_1, \omega_2 \in \Omega$, i.e., the two differences have the same sign. Samples from (X, Y) lie in the first (north east) or third (south west) quadrant.

Example 85. If X and Y are different excess layers of the same risk Z they are comonotonic. This follows because the indemnity (layering) functions are increasing. □

Example 86. If X and Y are random variables with quantile functions q_X and q_Y, and U is a uniform variable then $q_X(U)$ and $q_Y(U)$ are comonotonic and have the same marginal distributions as X and Y, respectively. At the opposite extreme, $q_X(U)$ and $q_Y(1-U)$ are anti-comonotonic. □

Exercise 87.

1. Show that X is comonotonic with any constant, i.e., if $Y = c$ then X and Y are comonotonic. (Recall that increasing means nondecreasing; see Appendix A.4.)
2. If X and Y are comonotonic, what can you say about the correlation between X and Y? □

5.2.11 Comonotonic Additive

Comonotonic additive (COMON) means $\rho(X + Y) = \rho(X) + \rho(Y)$ if X and Y are comonotonic. Since comonotonic variables do not diversify, there should be no diversification credit.

VaR, TVaR, and the weighted average of two TVaRs at different thresholds are COMON. Variance is not, nor is absolute semideviation; see Example 237.

Whether ρ_c is comonotonic additive depends on properties of $\mathcal{Q}$. In Remark 230 we identify the precise conditions needed.

Exercise 88. Show that COMON and MRM imply PH.

Solution. Since $\rho(nX) = \rho(X + \cdots + X) = \rho(X) + \cdots + \rho(X) = n\rho(X)$ and $\rho(X/n) = \rho(n(X/n))/n = \rho(X)/n$, PH holds for positive rational λ. The result follows because MRM implies ρ is continuous, Section 5.2.7. □

5.2.12 Independent Additive

Independent additive means $\rho(X + Y) = \rho(X) + \rho(Y)$ if X and Y are independent.

Variance is independent additive. Standard deviation is not. Gerber (1974) studies independent additive functionals. In general, ρ_c is not independent additive.

5.2.13 Law Invariant

Law invariant (LI) means $\rho(X)$ is a function of the distribution F of X, i.e., if X and Y have the same distribution function, then $\rho(X) = \rho(Y)$. Law invariant risk measures do not depend on the cause of loss or the particulars of the event generating it. Law invariance is also called **objectivity**. A law invariant risk measure can assess risk given an implicit or dual implicit representation; it does not need the explicit.

VaR, TVaR, and standard deviation are LI.

LI is motivated by the fact that an entity's risk of insolvency depends only on its distribution of future change in surplus—the cause of loss is irrelevant. Law invariance, coupled with continuity in distribution, enables risk to be estimated statistically, from an empirical sample or model fit of X. Law invariance is therefore deemed appropriate for regulatory capital risk measures.

LI may not be appropriate in pricing applications. For example, Florida hurricane risk is generally more expensive to insure than auto liability, even if it has the same distribution. The CAPM is another example where the underlying scenarios matter. Its pricing formula is not LI: stocks with the same distribution of returns but different correlations to the market have different target returns.

Whether ρ_c is law invariant depends on properties of $\mathcal{Q}$. Suppose $\mathcal{Q}$ consists of the conditional probability scenario defined by a single insurance event E (e.g., one Realistic Disaster Scenario). Then ρ_c is not law invariant. To see why, consider X and Y, random variables with identical distributions, where X models losses from a portfolio exposed to E and Y from a portfolio independent of (with no loss from) E. Then $\rho_c(X)$ equals the conditional expected loss from X given E occurs but $\rho_c(Y) = \mathsf{E}[Y]$.

In the discrete case, ρ_c is law invariant if $\mathcal{Q}$ is **closed under rearrangements**. Suppose that all events have equal P-probability. Then $\mathsf{Q} \in \mathcal{Q}$ is simply a column of non-negative numbers that sum to 1—a column of probabilities in a spreadsheet. By saying $\mathcal{Q}$ is closed under rearrangements we mean that all Q' created by rearranging the rows of Q are also in $\mathcal{Q}$. (A rearrangement is a probability preserving transform.) A similar rule applies in general, (Jouini, Schachermayer, and Touzi 2006).

When $\mathcal{Q}$ is closed under rearrangements, we can create a huge number of different Q by specifying a few fundamental ones and rearranging them. When we compute $\rho(X)$ we select the Q that is comonotonic with X, resulting in the highest $\mathsf{E}_{\mathsf{Q}}[X]$. The selected Q has the same sort order as X. When $\mathcal{Q}$ is closed under rearrangements we are guaranteed it contains this comonotonic Q. These conclusions follow from the Hardy-Littlewood inequality.

Example 89. Figure 4.3 shows five different Bernoulli(0.5) random variables. We can use them to better understand law invariance. Consider $\mathcal{Q}_1$ defined by all conditional probability scenario functions of the form $\mathsf{Q}(A) = 2\mathsf{P}(A \cap B)$ for $B \subset [0,1]$ with $\mathsf{P}(B) = 0.5$. Here P is the usual uniform probability on $[0,1]$. Let $\mathcal{Q}_2$ contain just $\mathsf{Q}_2(A) = 2\mathsf{P}(A \cap (0.5,1])$, the conditional probability scenario defined by the event $(0.5,1]$. Let ρ_1, ρ_2 be the two associated coherent risk measures. Then ρ_1 is law invariant (in fact, it equals $\mathsf{TVaR}_{0.5}$) but ρ_2 is not. Thus $\rho_1(X_i) = 1$ for the five X_i in Figure 4.3. However, $\rho_2(X_1) = 1$ but $\rho_2(X_i) = 0.5$ for $i = 2,3,4,5$. By taking different A in $\mathcal{Q}_2$ we can generate any values from 0 to 1 for individual X_i but they will eventually average to 0.5. $\rho_1(X)$ picks out a set B customized to X (law invariant) whereas $\rho_2(X)$ uses a fixed set (not law invariant). □

Example 90. Bühlmann (1980) introduced the idea of an **economic premium principle**, depending on a risk random variable X and a random variable describing the state of the market Z. He proposed $\mathsf{E}[Xe^{\pi Z}]/\mathsf{E}[e^{\pi Z}]$ as an example. It is not law invariant because it depends on the correlation between X and Z. Similarly, $\rho_2(X) = \mathsf{E}[X] + \mathsf{cov}(X, Z)$ is not law invariant. See also Winter (1994). □

5.2.14 Coherent

A **coherent** (COH) risk measure is monotone, translation invariant, positive homogeneous and subadditive, MON, TI, PH and SA. Coherent risk measures were introduced in Artzner *et al.* (1999). Coherent risk measures sought to address the problem that VaR ignores the degree of insolvency and is not subadditive. Unlike VaR, coherent measures need not be law invariant. For example $\mathsf{E}_{\mathsf{Q}}[X]$ for a fixed probability scenario Q is coherent but not law invariant. Huber (1981) already contains many of the concepts underlying a coherent risk measure, albeit in another context.

We have seen that all ρ_c risk measures are coherent—hence the subscript c. In fact, all coherent risk measures arise as ρ_c for suitable $\mathcal{Q}$; see Section 5.4 .

Example 91. TVaR, an average of TVaRs at different thresholds, the worst loss from a specified set of scenarios, and the worst loss overall are all coherent. Variance and VaR are not coherent. □

Exercise 92. Which of the four conditions for a coherent risk measure holds for variance? Which for standard deviation? □

5.2.15 Spectral

A coherent, law invariant, comonotonic additive risk measure is called a **spectral risk measure** (SRM). These play a central role in Parts II and III, and are discussed later in this chapter and at length in Chapters 10, 11, 14, and 15. When we define SRMs in Section 10.7 we use a more constructive definition but show that it is equivalent to this one.

5.2.16 Convexity Property

A risk measure has the **convexity** (CX) property if ρ is a convex function

$$\rho(\lambda X + (1-\lambda)Y) \le \lambda\rho(X) + (1-\lambda)\rho(Y)$$

for $0 \le \lambda \le 1$. The convexity property reflects the reality that a pooled combination of X and Y is less risky than the pooled results of two separate portfolios because the risks can offset one another in the pool. In contrast, any diversification benefit is lost in two stand-alone portfolios.

In Section 5.2.18 we define a convex risk measure to be one with the convexity property as well as TI and MON.

Remark 93. If ρ is convex, then the function $f(t) = \rho(tX)$ is a convex function of t for each X. □

5.2.17 Quasi-Convexity

A risk measure is **quasi-convex** (QCX) if

$$\rho(\lambda X + (1-\lambda)Y) \le \max(\rho(X), \rho(Y))$$

for $0 \le \lambda \le 1$.

Remark 94. Assuming TI, CX is equivalent to QCX. CX implies QCX since $\lambda\rho(X) + (1-\lambda)\rho(Y) \le \max(\rho(X), \rho(Y))$. Conversely since TI implies $\rho(X - \rho(X)) = 0$, QCX implies

$$\rho(\lambda(X-\rho(X)) + (1-\lambda)(Y-\rho(Y))) \le \max(\rho(X-\rho(X)), \rho(Y-\rho(Y))) = 0.$$

Combining the monetary terms and using TI again gives

$$\rho(\lambda(X-\rho(X)) + (1-\lambda)(Y-\rho(Y))) = \rho(\lambda X + (1-\lambda)Y) - (\lambda\rho(X) + (1-\lambda)\rho(Y))$$

and the result follows. □

5.2.18 Convex

A **convex** (CONVEX) risk measure is monotone, translation invariant and has the convexity property, TI, MON, and CX. Deprez and Gerber (1985) introduced convex risk measures, and they are studied in detail in Follmer and Schied (2016). All coherent risk measures are convex.

Convex risk measures share many properties with coherent measures, including respecting a diversification property, but without assuming PH. They allow larger risk positions to become more risky. In fact, a convex risk measure scales super-linearly once $\lambda > 1$, as Remark 95 shows.

Section 5.4 characterizes all coherent and convex risk measures, making it easy to define other measures that are convex but not coherent.

Remark 95. NORM and CONVEX imply

$$\begin{cases} \rho(\lambda X) \le \lambda\rho(X) & \text{for } 0 \le \lambda \le 1 \text{ and} \\ \rho(\lambda X) \ge \lambda\rho(X) & \text{for } 1 \le \lambda. \end{cases} \tag{5.3}$$

To see this, first let $\lambda < 1$ and consider $\rho(\lambda X + (1-\lambda)\rho(X))$. By TI

$$\rho(\lambda X + (1-\lambda)\rho(X)) = \rho(\lambda X) + (1-\lambda)\rho(X).$$

By CX and since NORM, TI imply $\rho(c) = c$,

$$\rho(\lambda X + (1-\lambda)\rho(X)) \le \lambda\rho(X) + (1-\lambda)\rho(\rho(X)) = \rho(X).$$

Therefore $\rho(\lambda X) \le \lambda\rho(X)$. If $\lambda > 1$, let $\nu = 1/\lambda$ and $Z = \lambda X$. Then $\rho(\nu Z) \le \nu\rho(Z)$ which is equivalent to $\rho(X) \le \rho(\lambda X)/\lambda$.

This result says that size matters: there is an increasing risk to a large position. There are numerous examples of this phenomenon in asset markets. □

Remark 96. Assuming MON, NORM, and TI, any two of CX, PH, and SA implies the third. □

Proof: To derive CX is obvious. To derive PH: Let $1 < \lambda = k + f$ where $k \geq 1$ is an integer and $0 \leq f < 1$. Then by Eq. (5.3) and SA

$$\begin{aligned}\lambda\rho(X) &\leq \rho(\lambda X) = \rho(kX + fX)\\ &\leq \rho(kX) + \rho(fX) \leq k\rho(X) + \rho(fX)\\ &\leq k\rho(X) + f\rho(X) = \lambda\rho(X)\end{aligned}$$

and so all inequalities must be equalities. If $\lambda < 1$, apply to $X = Y/\lambda$. To derive SA: write $\rho(X+Y) = \rho(\lambda(X/\lambda) + (1-\lambda)(Y/(1-\lambda))))$. □

Example 97. The exponential risk measure $c^{-1}\log \mathsf{E}[e^{cX}]$ is convex, but it is not coherent because it is neither PH nor SA. □

Remark 98. VaR has the advantage of always being finite. Can we find a convex or coherent risk measure that is finite for all risks? Alas, no. There are no risk measures offering both guaranteed finiteness and good diversification behavior for unbounded random variables (Delbaen 2009). Any coherent risk measure takes the value ∞ for some unbounded random variable. □

5.2.19 Acceptance Sets

The **acceptance set** of a risk measure is the set of risks preferred to doing nothing. If ρ is coherent, and hence normalized, the risk of nothing is $\rho(0) = 0$ and the acceptance set $\mathcal{A} = \{X \mid \rho(X) \leq 0\}$. If ρ is a capital risk measure, then

$$\rho(X - a) = \rho(X) - a \leq 0 \iff \rho(X) \leq a,$$

in words: X is acceptable provided it is supported by assets at least equal to $\rho(X)$. Note that $X - a$ is the risk of X *supported by* a. If ρ is a pricing risk measure $\rho(X)$ similarly determines the minimum acceptable premium for X.

A coherent risk measure can be recreated from an acceptance set by setting $\rho(X)$ equal to the minimum amount of assets required for $X - a$ to be acceptable:

$$\rho(X) = \min\{a \mid X - a \in \mathcal{A}\}.$$

Figure 5.4 shows five acceptance sets. In each sub-figure, the acceptance set is the shaded area between the solid black lines. Random vectors are treated like vectors in the plane. These sets illustrate the following properties.

a. A **convex cone** acceptance set based at 0 determines a PH risk measure. If X is acceptable then any positive multiple λX is also acceptable, because the ray from 0 through X is within the cone.

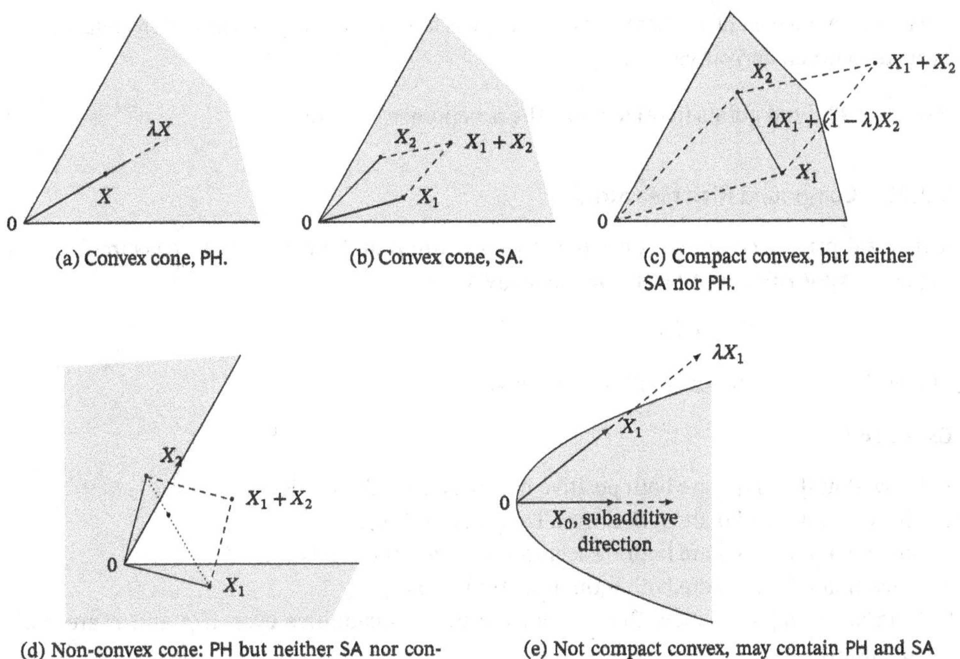

(a) Convex cone, PH.

(b) Convex cone, SA.

(c) Compact convex, but neither SA nor PH.

(d) Non-convex cone: PH but neither SA nor convex (dotted line does not lie in shaded region).

(e) Not compact convex, may contain PH and SA cone. PH in direction X_0 but not X_1.

Figure 5.4 Acceptance sets and corresponding risk measure properties. Shaded region represents the acceptance set. Black lines represent the boundary; unbounded region have no boundary line. Only (c) is bounded. The origin is marked with 0. (a) A convex cone is PH, the line λX is contained in the shaded region $\mathcal{A}$ and (b) is also SA, the sum of two points in $\mathcal{A}$ is again in $\mathcal{A}$. (c) A compact convex $\mathcal{A}$ is neither PH nor SA, but the line joining two points in $\mathcal{A}$ is in $\mathcal{A}$. (d) A non-convex cone is PH but not SA. (e) A non-compact convex $\mathcal{A}$ can be SA and PH in some directions but not others.

b. A convex cone determines a SA risk measure. If X_1 and X_2 are acceptable then the sum X_1+X_2 is too. Subadditivity follows because $\rho(X_1+X_2) \le \rho(X_1)+\rho(X_2) \le 0$ if $\rho(X_i) \le 0$.
c. A **convex** acceptance set determines a risk measure with the convexity property CX, but one that need not be PH or SA. In this case the shaded set is bounded, note the black lines all around the border. Clearly any ray from 0 through a point in $\mathcal{A}$ eventually leaves it—because it is bounded—showing it is not PH. The points shown have the property that $X_1 + X_2 \notin \mathcal{A}$, showing it is not SA. CX requires only that the line segment joining X_1 and X_2 is in $\mathcal{A}$, which follows for a convex risk measure because

$$\rho(\lambda X_1 + (1-\lambda)X_2) \le \lambda\rho(X_1) + (1-\lambda)\rho(X_2) \le \max(\rho(X_1), \rho(X_2)) \le 0.$$

d. A non-convex cone is PH but the labeled points show the failure of SA.
e. An acceptance set can be PH in some directions (X_0), but not others (X_1). In this case, $\mathcal{A}$ is convex but neither PH nor SA

The acceptance set of a coherent risk measure is a convex cone. It is completely determined by its directional derivatives at 0.

Exercise 99. Find points in (e) to show the acceptance set is not SA. □

5.2.20 Compound Risk Measures

real world pricing combines a pricing risk measure ρ and a capital risk measure a into a single **compound pricing risk measure** given by

$$\rho_a(X) := \rho(X \wedge a(X)).$$

The next exercise investigates properties of ρ_a.

Exercise 100.

1. Show that if ρ and a are both positive homogeneous then so is ρ_a.
2. Show that if ρ and a are both normalized then so is ρ_a.
3. Show that if ρ and a are both translation invariant then so is ρ_a.
4. Show that if ρ and a are both monotone then so is ρ_a.
5. Find an example to show that ρ_a can fail to be subadditive even if ρ and a are both subadditive.
6. Is ρ_a coherent if ρ and a are both coherent?
7. Is ρ_a convex if ρ and a are both coherent?
8. Explain why the failure of subadditivity in (5) is less likely to occur as the capital standard becomes stricter (lower probability of default).

Solutions.

1. Positive homogeneous: $\rho_a(kX) = \rho(kX \wedge a(kX)) = \rho(kX \wedge ka(X)) = \rho(k(X \wedge a(X))) = k\rho(X \wedge a(X)) = k\rho_a(X)$.
2. Normalized: $\rho_a(0) = \rho(0 \wedge a(0)) = \rho(0 \wedge 0) = \rho(0) = 0$.
3. Translation invariant: $\rho_a(X + c) = \rho((X + c) \wedge a(X + c)) = \rho((X + c) \wedge (a(X) + c)) = \rho((X \wedge a(X)) + c) = \rho((X \wedge a(X))) + c = \rho_a(X) + c$.
4. Monotone: if $X \le Y$ then $a(X) \le a(Y)$ and therefore $X \wedge a(X) \le Y \wedge a(Y)$. The claim follows.
5. Example: ρ_a fails to be subadditive when $X+Y$ diversifies effectively and pooled insurance is higher quality despite being more leveraged. It is then reasonable that the pool premium is higher. The normal distribution gives an explicit example. Take $\rho = \mathsf{E}$ to be objective expected value (risk-neutral pricing) and a to be 0.99-TVaR. If X_1, X_2 are iid standard normal, then $a(X_i) = 2.665$ and $a(X) = 3.769$. The corresponding LEVs, $\mathsf{E}[X \wedge a(X)]$ are -0.0012 for each unit and -0.00002 in total. Thus $\rho_a(X) > 2\rho_a(X_1)$. The probability each unit has a loss above its TVaR asset level is 0.996, but for the total it is 0.9999, indicating higher quality insurance and explaining the higher price.
6. No, it is not necessarily subadditive by part 5.
7. It is not convex because PH and convex implies SA, but by Example 5 we know the compound measure is not coherent.

8. As assets increase $X \wedge a(X)$ gets closer to X. □

5.2.21 Star-Shaped

Subadditivity is justified by the mantra that mergers do not create risk. Positive homogeneity can be rationalized, in part via an expected valuation adjustment for illiquid positions. The introduction of convex risk measures was motivated by the observation that subadditive risk measures can give too much credit for (often failing) mergers (Dhaene *et al.* 2008) and also by liquidity issues for large positions. More recently, **star-shaped** risk measures (Castagnoli *et al.* 2021), have emerged. These require $\rho(kX) \ge k\rho(X)$ for $k > 1$, the bad part of Remark 95. Convex risk measures and VaR are both star-shaped.

5.2.22 Risk, Deviation, Regret, and Error

A **deviation** is a sublinear (PH, SA) functional $\mathcal{D}$ that satisfies $\mathcal{D}(X+c) = \mathcal{D}(X)$ and $\mathcal{D}(X) \ge 0$ for all X and > 0 if X is not constant (Rockafellar, Uryasev, and Zabarankin 2006). In contrast, TI means $\rho(X + c) = \rho(X) + c$. Deviations do not measure volume. Standard deviation is a deviation. Variance is not because it is not PH.

Given a law invariant coherent risk measure ρ, $\mathcal{D}(X) = \rho(X) - \mathsf{E}[X]$ defines a deviation measure. Conversely, given $\mathcal{D}$, $\mathcal{D}(X) + \mathsf{E}[X]$ represents a monetary risk measure. Deviations separate the volume and variability parts of a risk measure. Volume is always measured by $\mathsf{E}[X]$, but there are many ways to measure volatility and tail risk.

More generally, Rockafellar and Uryasev (2013) distinguish four measures for a loss random variable X that they describe as sitting in a **risk quadrangle**:

1. **risk** ρ: the overall hazard of X,
2. **deviation** $\mathcal{D}$: the non-constancy or uncertainty in outcome of X,
3. **regret** $\mathcal{V}$: the regret or pain in facing (assuming, holding) X, and
4. **error** $\mathcal{E}$: the non-zeroness or size of X.

Error and regret are linked through some **statistic**, $\mathcal{S}$. All of these quantities are interconnected,

$$\rho(X) = \mathsf{E}[X] + \mathcal{D}(X), \quad \mathcal{D}(X) = \rho(X) - \mathsf{E}[X],$$
$$\mathcal{V}(X) = \mathsf{E}[X] + \mathcal{E}(X), \quad \mathcal{E}(X) = \mathcal{V}(X) - \mathsf{E}[X],$$
$$\rho(X) = \max_x\{x + \mathcal{V}(X - x)\}, \quad \mathcal{D}(X) = \min_x\{\mathcal{E}(X - x)\},$$
$$\text{argmin}_x\{x + \mathcal{V}(X - x)\} = \mathcal{S}(X) = \text{argmin}_x\{\mathcal{E}(X_x)\}.$$

The expression for risk in terms of regret and deviation in terms of error are optimizations. The expressions for the statistics in terms of minimum regret or minimum error are estimation problems.

Exercise 101. Identify risk, deviation, regret, and error, and validate the optimization and estimation equations in the following cases.

1. $\mathcal{S}(X) = \mathsf{E}[X]$, $\rho(X) = \mathsf{E}[X] + c\mathsf{Var}(X)$, $\mathcal{D}(X) = c\mathsf{Var}(X)$, $\mathcal{V}(X) = \mathsf{E}[X] + c\mathsf{E}[X^2]$ and $\mathcal{E}(X) = c\mathsf{E}[X^2]$.
2. What if $\rho(X) = \mathsf{E}[X] + c\sigma(X)$ is standard deviation based?
3. $\mathcal{S}(X) = \mathsf{VaR}_p(X)$, $\rho(X) = \mathsf{TVaR}_p(X)$, $\mathcal{D}(X) = c\mathsf{TVaR}_p(X - \mathsf{E}[X])$, $\mathcal{V}(X) = \frac{1}{1-p}\mathsf{E}[X^+]$ and $\mathcal{E}(X) = \mathsf{E}[(pX^+ + (1-p)X^-)/(1-p)]$. □

5.3 Risk Preferences

Risk preferences are difficult to elicit (Ruhm *et al.* 2005). Therefore, it is helpful to know if there are any statements that hold for all reasonable preferences, no matter the decision maker's exact proclivities. It is particularly helpful if these statements can be verified from the distribution or quantile function.

The easiest property to analyze is the preference for smaller losses, which we discuss first. Then we discuss the famous Rothschild and Stiglitz (1970) definitions of increasing risk.

Throughout this section, all random variables are defined on a sample space Ω with event set $\mathcal{F}$ and probability function P. X and Y are loss random variables, where large positive values are bad.

5.3.1 The Preference for a Smaller Loss

X should be preferred to (or deemed less risky than) Y by *any* risk preference if

$$X(\omega) \le Y(\omega) \text{ for all } \omega \in \Omega. \tag{5.4}$$

Risk preferences with this property are called **monotonic** (MONO); see Section 3.6.1. A risk measure that respects MONO is monotone, MON, Section 5.2.3.

If Eq. (5.4) holds then $F_X(x) \ge F_Y(x)$ for all x and $q_X(p) \le q_Y(p)$ for all $0 \le p \le 1$. Unfortunately, the converse is not true, as the next example shows.

Example 102. Bäuerle and Müller (2006) give the following example, illustrated in Figure 5.5. Let $\Omega = \{\omega_1, \omega_2\}$ with $\Pr(\{\omega_1\}) = 1/3$ and $\Pr(\{\omega_2\}) = 2/3$ and consider

$$X(\omega_1) = 3,\ X(\omega_2) = 1,\ Y(\omega_1) = 2,\ Y(\omega_2) = 4.$$

Then $F_X \ge F_Y$ and $q_X \le q_Y$ but $X(\omega_1) > Y(\omega_1)$. Since the probabilities of ω_1 and ω_2 are different there do not exist two different random variables with the same distribution on Ω. There are no nontrivial probability preserving transformations of Ω, i.e., no innocuous reorderings. Therefore it is impossible to find different versions of X, Y that are event-by-event monotone. □

If $F_X(x) \ge F_Y(x)$ for all x, or equivalently $q_X(p) \le q_Y(p)$ for all $0 < p < 1$, then X precedes Y in **first-order stochastic dominance**, FSD, written $X \preceq_1 Y$.

If $X \preceq_1 Y$, and X and Y are defined on a sample space with no atoms, then it is possible to define X', Y' with the same distribution functions as X, Y so that $X'(\omega) \le Y'(\omega)$ for all ω. (This fact explains why FSD and MON are described as *almost equivalent* in Figure 5.2.) The

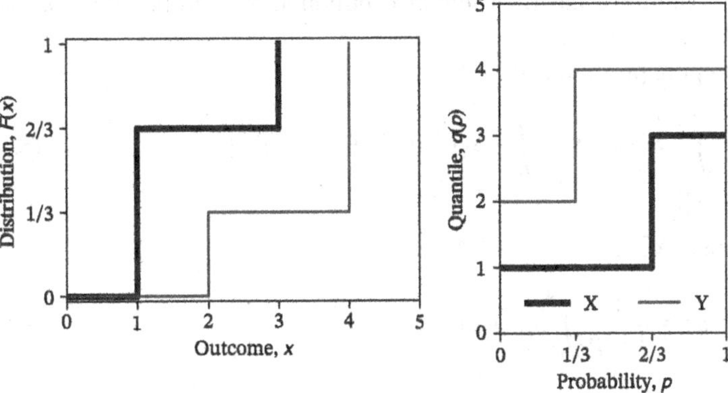

Figure 5.5 The distribution (left) and quantile function (right) for X and Y in Bäuerle and Müller's example.

failure to find such X', Y' in Example 102 is caused by the atoms in Ω. They make it possible to identify a sample point and an outcome, which destroys law invariance.

FSD can be characterized using utility functions that act on outcomes: $X \preceq_1 Y$ iff

$$\mathsf{E}[u(X)] \le \mathsf{E}[u(Y)]$$

for all increasing u. It can also be characterized using dual utility functions that acts on probabilities: $X \preceq_1 Y$ iff

$$\int_0^\infty g(S_X(x))dx \le \int_0^\infty g(S_Y(x))dx \tag{5.5}$$

for all increasing $g : [0,1] \to [0,1]$. Using integration by parts to write

$$\int_0^\infty g(S_X(x))dx = \int_0^\infty x dF_g(x),$$

where $F_g(x) = 1 - g(S_X(x))$, and

$$\mathsf{E}[u(X)] = \int_0^\infty u(x)dF_X(x),$$

draws out the parallels between the utility and dual utility characterizations. Utility adjusts the outcomes $x \leftrightarrow u(x)$ whereas dual utility adjusts the probabilities $S(x) \leftrightarrow g(S(x))$. These adjustments are partially motivated by the functional forms given in Section 3.6.4, specifically, (e) and (f).

5.3.2 The Definition of Increasing Risk

Characterizing *increasing risk* is difficult. To focus on risk and not amount, assume that $\mathsf{E}[X] = \mathsf{E}[Y]$. Here are five possible ways Y can be considered more risky than X.

1. Y has the same distribution as $X + Z$, where Z is a *noise* term with $\mathsf{E}[Z \mid X] = 0$.

2. Y is a dilation of X, meaning X has the same distribution as Y conditional on partial information, $\mathsf{E}[Y \mid \mathcal{F}']$, for $\mathcal{F}' \subset \mathcal{F}$.
3. Y has higher stop loss pure premiums than X:

$$\mathsf{E}[(Y-a)^+] = \int_a^\infty S_Y(x)dx \ge \int_a^\infty S_X(x)dx = \mathsf{E}[(X-a)^+] \tag{5.6}$$

   for all attachments $a \ge 0$.
4. Y has higher TVaRs than X:

$$\frac{1}{1-p}\int_p^1 q_Y(t)dt \ge \frac{1}{1-p}\int_p^1 q_X(t)dt \tag{5.7}$$

   for all $0 \le p < 1$.
5. Y has higher variance than X: $\mathsf{Var}(Y) \ge \mathsf{Var}(X)$.

It is a remarkable fact, largely due to Rothschild and Stiglitz (1970), that definitions (1)–(4) are equivalent and are *different* from (5). As a result, there is no universal risk ranking that all economic agents agree because some might care about properties (1)–(4) and some about variance.

Exercise 103. Find a uniform distribution U and a Pareto distribution X with $\mathsf{E}[U] = \mathsf{E}[X]$ and $\mathsf{Var}(U) > \mathsf{Var}(X)$. Use it to deduce that (5) is a different definition of increasing risk to (1)–(4). □

Wang and Young (1998) show that (3) is characterized by the behavioral statement (6) and (4) by the dual statement (7).

6. X is preferred to Y by every increasing, convex (not concave, see discussion of signs in Appendix A.2) utility function u,

$$\mathsf{E}[u(X)] \le \mathsf{E}[u(Y)]. \tag{5.8}$$

7. The distorted expected value of X is lower than Y

$$\int g(S_X(x))dx \le \int g(S_Y(x))dx, \tag{5.9}$$

   for all increasing, concave $g : [0,1] \to [0,1]$.

When any of the equivalent conditions (1)–(4) holds then we say X precedes Y in **second-order stochastic dominance** (SSD), and write $X \preceq_2 Y$.

In (1), the noise term has unconditional mean zero because $\mathsf{E}[Z] = \mathsf{E}[\mathsf{E}[Z \mid X]] = 0$. It is important that $X + Z$ and Y are required only to have the same distribution; they are not necessarily equal state by state. Z is not necessarily independent of X, although it is uncorrelated because $\mathsf{E}[XZ] = \mathsf{E}[X\mathsf{E}[Z \mid X]] = 0$. Y can be thought of as a lottery ticket which pays an amount with expected value X. Risk averse individuals prefer the certain amount over the lottery. Z could be degenerate for some X and introduce uncertainty for others or it could be symmetric or asymmetric, but it introduces potential uncertainty for all outcomes.

It is easy to see (1) and (2) are equivalent. Given (1), take $\mathcal{F}'$ to be all subsets defined by outcomes of X. Then $\mathsf{E}[Y \mid \mathcal{F}'] = \mathsf{E}[Y \mid X] = \mathsf{E}[X + Z \mid X] = X + \mathsf{E}[Z \mid X] = X$. Conversely, given Y and $\mathcal{F}'$, let $X = \mathsf{E}[Y \mid \mathcal{F}']$ and $Z = Y - X$. Then $\mathsf{E}[Z \mid X] = 0$ and $Y = X + Z$. Finer $\mathcal{F}$ corresponds to more information, which is riskier because it allows a greater range of outcomes. Risk aversion can be interpreted as a preference for risks whose outcome is determined by less information and are therefore more easily known. The simplest case is $\mathcal{F}' = \{\emptyset, \Omega\}$, when $\mathsf{E}[Y \mid \mathcal{F}'] = \mathsf{E}[Y]$ is constant.

Exercise 104. Explain why (1)–(4) implies that parametric insurance with basis risk is suboptimal for risk averse insureds. □

Example 105. Let X be a random variable modeling prospective losses from an insurance policy. Decompose the sample space Ω into $\Omega_0 \times \Omega_1$, where Ω_0 captures information about the policy available at $t = 0$, when it is underwritten, and Ω_1 information not revealed until the end of the policy period, when claims are paid. For a personal auto (motor) policy Ω_0 includes information about the driver's experience, location, vehicle type, use, and driving record, as well as proxy data such as credit record. Ω_1 captures data about trips and traffic and the weather, as well as specific information about accidents. $\mathcal{F}$ is generated by $\mathcal{F}_0 \times \mathcal{F}_1$. Underwriting is the process of obtaining the best possible estimate of $\mathsf{E}[X \mid \mathcal{F}_0]$. By definition, information in $\mathcal{F}_1$ is not available to the underwriter. In this light, Rothschild-Stiglitz says that using incomplete information $\mathcal{F}_0' \subset \mathcal{F}_0$ to rate the policy increases risk. In general, unknown but knowable information is very risky: it is the basis of adverse selection. □

In (1) it is possible to determine the distribution of Z explicitly given X and Y. For discrete distributions this is done through a series of mean preserving spreads, which move probability from an outcome to a larger one and a smaller one. For general distributions, Machina and Pratt (1997) give an algorithm to determine the distribution of Z conditional on X. Their method shows that $Z \mid X$ can always be taken as a simple two point distribution with mean zero.

Although variance and standard deviation are almost miraculously useful in probability and statistics, these examples show they give a different view of risk compared with another plausible and intuitively appealing definition. They are less useful as general purpose risk measures, largely because they weight upside and downside symmetrically.

Example 106. Variance can be useful when considering small risks. If X is a risk with mean zero, u an increasing, concave utility function, and w initial wealth, then we can compute the **certainty equivalent cost** of X by solving $\mathsf{E}[u(w - X)] = u(w - c)$ for c. If X takes only small values, then we can apply Taylor's theorem around w to get $-\sigma^2 u''(w) \approx -cu'(w)$ and so $c \approx -\sigma^2 u''(w)/u'(w)$. The term $-u''(w)/u'(w)$ is called the **Arrow-Pratt coefficient of absolute risk aversion**. The second-order term captures the Jensen's inequality effect of local convexity where upside and downside do not balance. □

Remark 107. Definitions (1)–(4) are not a complete risk preference because some pairs of random variables cannot be ranked. Conditions (3) and (4) must hold uniformly, for all x or p. □

5.3.3 Preferences over Risk Pools

Section 3.4 introduced three ways of representing a risk or prospect. There is a natural way to combine two risks in each representation.

1. **Explicit:** A sum of random variables, using the underlying dependence structure.
2. **Implicit:** A mixture of distribution functions. Mixtures do not pool components: the result comes from one distribution or the other. This method leads to utility theory.
3. **Dual Implicit:** A mixture of quantile functions, which assumes pooling but with comonotonic dependence. It leads to dual utility theory.

The risk combinations given by (2) and (3) are different approximations to (1), which gives the actual, state by state, sum. (2) and (3) are different in subtle ways, as we explain next.

In combination (2), for $0 \le p \le 1$ we form the mixture distribution function

$$F_M = pF_X + (1-p)F_Y.$$

F_M can be interpreted as the distribution function of a **compound lottery** which takes an outcome from F_X with probability p and from F_Y with probability $1-p$. An outcome from the mixture distribution F_M is simulated in three steps.

1. Simulate uniform random $U, V, 0 \le U, V \le 1$.
2. If $U \le p$ return $F_X^{-1}(V) = q_X(V)$.
3. If $U > p$ return $F_Y^{-1}(V) = q_Y(V)$.

Notice that M involves no pooling of results from X and Y: the result is either a sample from X or a sample from Y. It is does not correspond to how insurance risks are pooled.

Consider a choice between two lotteries:

- A: a risk X with probability p and Z with probability $1-p$ or
- B: a risk Y with probability p and Z with probability $1-p$.

To an underwriter, lottery A insures risk X or Z based on the toss of a coin with probability p of heads, and B similarly with Y and Z. If Y is preferred to X then B should also be preferred to A because if the coin comes up heads the underwriter insures the preferred risk and if tails the same risk. The preference for A over B when X is preferred to Y is called the **independence axiom**.

Combination (3) relates to a choice between two quota share portfolios

- C: an outcome from X multiplied by a weight w plus an outcome from Z multiplied by $1-w$ or
- D: an outcome from Y multiplied by a weight w plus an outcome from Z multiplied by $1-w$.

Choice C has exposure to an outcome from X **and** Z whereas in A the outcome is X **or** Z. It could be that X is preferred to Y but that Y is a hedge against Z, and D is preferred to C. However, if we assume the worst possible dependence, where X and Z, and Y and Z are comonotonic, then C should always be preferred to D. We can build a comonotonic proxy with the same distributions by replacing each variable with its quantile function:

- C_c: simulate a random p and form $wq_X(p) + (1-w)q_Z(p)$ or
- D_c: simulate a random p and form $wq_Y(p) + (1-w)q_Z(p)$.

The subscript c indicates a comonotonic version of the risks: C_c is a draw from a model where X and Y are comonotonic. It is important the same p is used to draw both samples.

The **dual independence axiom** requires that if X is preferred to Y and Z is any third risk then C_c is preferred to D_c. It is an alternative to the independence axiom and it underlies dual utility theory. It is more appropriate for insurance because it uses outcomes that are pooled.

Technical Remark 108. There is a sleight of hand in the independence axiom that is described by Segal (1992). He points out that the two stage compound lottery A is identified with the one-stage lottery $pX + (1-p)Z$. For these to be equally attractive the decision maker must care only for the probabilities of final outcomes and not for the way uncertainty is resolved, an assumption known as the **reduction of compound lotteries** (ROCL). □

5.3.4 Problems with Utility Theory as a Model of Firm Decision Making

The expected utility representation has some undesirable properties when applied to firms.

- Firms do not have diminishing marginal utility of wealth: shareholders are insatiable.
- Firm preferences are not relative to a wealth level, they are absolute.
- Utility theory combines attitudes to wealth and to risk.
- Utility functions are not linear and so expected utility is not a monetary risk measure.
- Utility theory is based on combination through mixing, with no pooling, counter to the operation of insurance.

Dual utility theory addresses these shortcomings of expected utility.

Diminishing utility of wealth and risk aversion are very different. To encode firm decision-making we need a theory that separates wealth from risk. The dual utility model has this property. Yaari (1987) comments that

> Under the dual theory, maximization of a linear function of profits can be entertained simultaneously with risk aversion. How often has the desire to retain profit maximization led to contrived arguments about firms' risk neutrality?

Adjusting probabilities is linear in outcomes: the adjusted value of a sum of random variables is the sum of the individual adjusted values.

The utility method of adjusting outcomes is linear in probabilities: the utility of a mixture of distributions is the weighted average of the utilities. As a result individuals are **ambiguity neutral**: they replace ambiguous probabilities with their expected values. However, there is evidence that insurance premiums are driven in part by ambiguity aversion. Risks, such as terrorism, where loss probabilities are unknown or very hard to estimate, are deemed to be uninsurable.

Spectral risk measures are well suited for use as a risk measure for insurance purposes since they correspond to dual utility theory. We outline the theory of their use in Part II.

Tsanakas and Desli (2003) give a nice description of the actuarial issues with utility theory. The explanations in this section are taken in part from Wang and Young (1998) and Machina, Teugels, and Sundt (2004).

5.3.5 Law Invariance and Second-Order Stochastic Dominance

It is a surprising fact that a convex risk measure is law invariant if and only if it respects SSD. Rothschild-Stiglitz makes a strong case that SSD is a natural condition for a risk measure. However, law invariance is also a strong condition, with possibly unpalatable side-effects (Castagnoli, Maccheroni, and Marinacci 2004).

To see the equivalence, suppose first that ρ respects SSD and X has the same distribution as Y. Then $X \preceq_2 Y$ and $Y \preceq_2 X$ and therefore $\rho(X) = \rho(Y)$, showing ρ is law invariant. Conversely, suppose that ρ is law invariant and $X \preceq Y$. Then using the fact that $\mathcal{D} := \{X \mid X \preceq_2 Y\}$ is the closure of the convex hull of $\mathcal{E} := \{Y \circ T \mid T \text{ PPT}\}$ (Ryff 1967), we can write X as a limit of X_n where each X_n is a convex combination of $Y \circ T_i$ for probability preserving T_i with weights $w_i \geq 0$, $\sum w_i = 1$. Then

$$\begin{aligned}
\rho(X_n) &= \rho(\sum_i w_i Y \circ T_i) \\
&\leq \sum_i w_i \rho(U \circ T_i) \\
&= \sum_i w_i \rho(Y) \\
&= \rho(Y)
\end{aligned}$$

using the convex property and the law invariance of ρ. The result follows because ρ is continuous by Section 5.2.7, and so $\rho(X) \leq \lim \rho(X_n)$. The set $\mathcal{E}$ is the set of extreme points of $\mathcal{D}$ and the set of all random variables with the same distribution as Y, (also Ryff). See Svindland (2014) for more details on these topics.

5.4 The Representation Theorem for Coherent Risk Measures

In Sections 5.1 and 5.2 we explain the strengths of coherent risk measures of the form

$$\rho(X) = \max_{\mathsf{Q} \in \mathcal{Q}} \mathsf{E}_{\mathsf{Q}}[X] \tag{5.10}$$

where $\mathcal{Q}$ is a set of probability scenarios. We show they are intuitive and easy to communicate, we can use them for capital and pricing, and their properties align with realistic risk preferences. We describe Eq. (5.10) as a **representation** of ρ by $\mathcal{Q}$.

In this section we show the converse is true: all coherent risk measures have the form Eq. (5.10) for some $\mathcal{Q}$. This representation theorem is our trip to the natural history museum promised at the end of Section 3.6.4. Under the skin, all coherent risk measures have the same bone structure.

5.4.1 Handicapping Probability Scenarios

There is a *very* broad range of *possible* probability scenarios that could be included in Ω and we might deem some more plausible than others. We always have a base P best estimate probability. Probability scenarios that are *distant* from P in some suitable sense are unlikely and should be de-emphasized.

We can reflect this relative weighting by handicapping each scenario using a **handicapping function** α on the set of all scenarios. (In the literature α is called a **penalty function**.) Larger values of $\alpha(\mathsf{Q})$ correspond to less plausible Q, and if $\alpha(\mathsf{Q}) = \infty$ then Q is ignored altogether. We can generalize Eq. (5.10) by considering

$$\rho(X) = \max_{\mathsf{Q}\in\Omega} \mathsf{E}_{\mathsf{Q}}[X] - \alpha(\mathsf{Q}), \tag{5.11}$$

which de-emphasizes scenarios deemed improbable by α. Risk measures given by Eq. (5.11) are convex, Section 5.2.18. The handicapping function α can be calibrated using a notion of distance from P such as entropy; see Example 109.

Figure 5.6 illustrates computing $\rho(\lambda X)$ for a single X and range of λ, when ρ is defined by Eq. (5.11). Each thin line shows

$$\mathsf{E}_{\mathsf{Q}}[\lambda X] - \alpha(\mathsf{Q}) = \lambda \mathsf{E}_{\mathsf{Q}}[X] - \alpha(\mathsf{Q})$$

for a different $\mathsf{Q} \in \Omega$, as λ varies on the horizontal axis. The thick line shows the maximum value for each λ, i.e., $\rho(\lambda X)$. The intersection of each thin line with the vertical line at $\lambda = 0$ equals $\alpha(\mathsf{Q})$. If $\alpha \equiv 0$, then ρ is coherent, all the thin lines pass through the origin, and the maximum is swept out by the two lines with steepest absolute value slope—it forms a cone, as we noted in Figure 5.4, panels (a) and (b). Compare also with Figure 5.3.

What is the effect of α in Eq. (5.11) on the properties of ρ? Because $\alpha(\mathsf{Q})$ is constant, ρ is no longer positive homogeneous if $\alpha \not\equiv 0$ since

$$\mathsf{E}_{\mathsf{Q}}[\lambda X] - \alpha(\mathsf{Q}) \neq \lambda(\mathsf{E}_{\mathsf{Q}}[X] - \alpha(\mathsf{Q}))$$

when $\alpha(\mathsf{Q}) \neq 0$. The failure of positive homogeneity is clear from Figure 5.6: the graph is not a cone. How bothered are we by the failure of positive homogeneity? In fact, we should review how attached are we to each of the four properties of coherence: MON, TI, SA, and PH.

MON, that uniformly larger losses are riskier, is unimpeachable. (Remember we are measuring total risk; not the risk of X as part of a pool where a larger risk may be acceptable because of its hedging benefit.) TI, that adding a certain amount to a risk increases risk by that amount, is logical and makes for a practical risk measure that can measure assets or capital interchangeably, Section 5.2.1. So far, no debate.

There is also general agreement that pooling and diversification lowers risk, but how? At this point the unanimity ends: we have coherent and convex flavors. The coherent option interprets pooling benefit using positive homogeneity and subadditivity, whereas the convex option interprets pooling benefit using the convexity property, Section 5.2.16. In theory, the convex risk measure treatment of diversification makes them the preferred choice. In

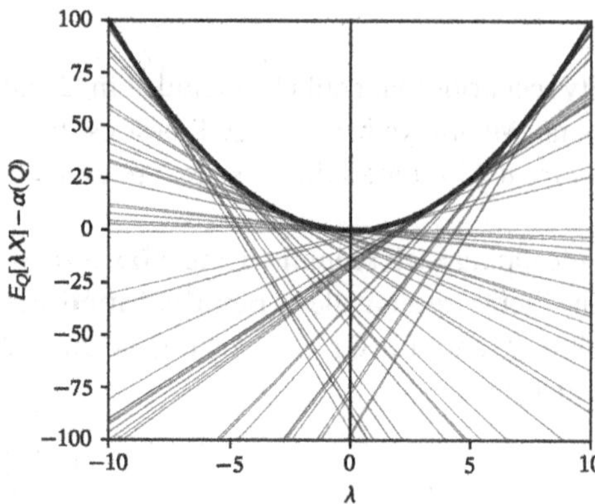

Figure 5.6 The impact of α on $\rho(X)$ defined by Eq. (5.11). Each thin line corresponds to a different probability scenario $Q \in \mathcal{Q}$.

practice, theoretical purity must be balanced against other considerations that we describe in Chapter 6.

Extending the fact that **all coherent risk measures** have the form Eq. (5.10), **all convex risk measures** have the form Eq. (5.11), subject to certain minor restrictions. Both common sense risk evaluation and mathematics lead to the same functional forms.

Example 109. Define a penalty function by

$$\alpha(Q) = E_Q\left[\log \frac{dQ}{dP}\right]$$

the **entropy** of Q with respect to P, the expectation of the log likelihood. Clearly $\alpha(P) = 0$ and α increases as Q becomes less similar to P. It is possible to show that for $k > 0$

$$E_Q[X] - \frac{1}{k}\alpha(Q) \le \frac{1}{k}\log E[e^{-kX}]$$

and that the upper bound, over all Q absolutely continuous with respect to P is attained by the probability with density $e^{-kX}/E[e^{-kX}]$. Thus

$$\rho(X) = \frac{1}{k}\log E[e^{-kX}]$$

is an convex risk measure. It is called the **entropic risk measure**. It is convex but not coherent. □

5.4.2 Properties of the Handicapping Function for Coherent Measures

How do properties of α relate to those of ρ? Let's assume ρ has the form Eq. (5.11) and see what can we deduce about α when we assume that ρ is coherent. There are three important properties.

Property 1. $\alpha(Q) \ge 0$ for all Q.

PH implies that $\rho(0) = 0$. Therefore, $\max_Q E_Q[0] - \alpha(Q) = \max_Q -\alpha(Q) = -\min_Q \alpha(Q) = 0$, as required. □

Before stating the second property, we need to make an additional assumption about ρ. We assume that $\rho(X) = \rho(Y)$ when $X = Y$ except on a set of P-probability zero. Recall that Q is absolutely continuous with respect to P, written $Q \ll P$, if $P(A) = 0$ implies $Q(A) = 0$.

Property 2. If $\alpha(Q) < \infty$ then Q is absolutely continuous with respect to P.

Suppose $Q \not\ll P$, so there is a set A with $Q(A) > 0$ but $P(A) = 0$. Consider the risk $X_n = n1_A$. By the additional assumption, $\rho(X_n) = \rho(0) = 0$ for all $n \geq 0$ because X_n and 0 differ only on a A. Therefore

$$0 = \rho(X_n) = \max_{Q' \in \Omega} E_{Q'}[n1_A] - \alpha(Q') \geq nQ(A) - \alpha(Q)$$

for all n, which is a contradiction unless $\alpha(Q) = \infty$. □

Property 3. If $\alpha(Q) < \infty$ and there is a risk X so that $\rho(X) = E_Q[X] - \alpha(Q)$ then $\alpha(Q) = 0$.

If $\rho(X) = E_Q[X] - \alpha(Q)$ then Q achieves the max in Eq. (5.11) for X. Suppose $\alpha(Q) < \infty$. Since ρ is PH, $\rho(\lambda X) = \lambda\rho(X)$ and therefore

$$\lambda E_Q[X] - \alpha(Q) \leq \lambda\rho(X) \implies \lambda(E_Q[X] - \rho(X)) \leq \alpha(Q) \implies \lambda\alpha(Q) \leq \alpha(Q)$$

for all $\lambda \geq 0$, which implies $\alpha(Q) = 0$ as required. □

Property 3 says that for a coherent risk measure, probability scenarios are deemed to be possible, when $\alpha(Q) = 0$, or impossible, when $\alpha(Q) = \infty$, and there is no further intermediate handicapping. Thus ρ is defined by $\Omega = \{Q \mid \alpha(Q) = 0\}$, and these are the only probability scenarios it considers. All other scenarios are ignored.

Properties 2 and 3 show that a coherent risk measure $\rho(X) = \max_{Q \in \Omega} E_Q[X]$ corresponds to a scenario set $\Omega = \{Q \mid Q \ll P,\ \alpha(Q) = 0\}$. It is the worst expected outcome over a set of scenarios that are all absolutely continuous with respect to P, and are all taken equally seriously.

We have shown how coherent risk measures correspond to sets of scenarios Ω. The details are presented more formally in Section 5.4.3.

Remark 110. Eq. (5.10) is sometimes called the **multiple priors** view. Resist the temptation to put a Bayesian prior on Ω. The scenarios in Ω usually reflect ambiguity and it is not possible to rank their likelihoods. In fact, the particular Q applied to evaluate $\rho(X)$ is determined by X, not selected randomly. It is better to think of the priors as being chosen by adverse selection, deliberately against your best interests, rather than by chance. In particular, the law of large numbers need not apply. These topics are explored further in Gilboa and Schmeidler (1989), Marinacci (1999), and references therein. □

5.4.3 Representation Theorem for Coherent Risk Measures in Detail

We now give a more formal statement of the representation theorem for coherent risk measures. We follow Follmer and Schied (2016), except they work from an asset perspective and use the accounting sign convention, Appendix A.2, which reverses the roles of continuity from above and below. This section is quite technical; it is aimed at readers who "want a more thorough understanding of *why*."

We work on the standard atomless probability space $(\Omega, \mathcal{F}, \mathsf{P})$, $\Omega = [0,1]$, $\mathcal{F}$ is the Borel σ-algebra generated by all open sets in Ω, and P is a reference probability. A risk is a random variable, a function $X : \Omega \to [0, \infty) \subset \mathbb{R}$ so that $X^{-1}(A) \in \mathcal{F}$ for all open $A \subset \mathbb{R}$.

L^∞ denotes the set of (essentially) bounded risks, where we identify two risks that differ on a set of probability zero. $\mathcal{M}$ is the space of probabilities on $(\Omega, \mathcal{F})$ and $\mathcal{M}(\mathsf{P})$ those that are absolutely continuous with respect to P.

In order to state the representation results, we need to describe the possible behavior of $\rho(X_n)$, where X_n is a convergent sequence of risks. (Section 5.B defines different notions of convergence for random variables.) Two examples show the range of possible behaviors.

Example 111. Let $X_n(\omega) = 1$ if $\omega < 1/n$ and 0 otherwise, and let $X = 0$. Then $X_n \downarrow X$ almost surely (i.e., for all ω in a set of probability one). Since $X_n(0) = 1$ for all n, the convergence is not pointwise. If $\rho(X) = \sup(X)$ then $\rho(X_n) = 1$ for all n, but $\rho(X) = 0$. Thus $\rho(X_n) \nrightarrow \rho(X)$ and continuity from above fails. Note that $\rho(X) \le \lim \rho(X_n)$. □

Example 112. Let $X_n(\omega) = 0$ if $\omega < 1/n$ and 1 otherwise, and $X = 1$. Then $X_n \uparrow X$ almost surely. Now $\rho(X_n) = 1$ for $n \ge 2$ and $\rho(X) = 1$. Thus $\rho(X_n) \to \rho(X)$ and ρ is continuous from below for this example. □

In general, ρ is **continuous from above** if $\rho(X_n) \downarrow \rho(X)$ when X_n is a decreasing sequence that converges to X almost surely, and ρ is **continuous from below** if $\rho(X_n) \uparrow \rho(X)$ when X_n is an increasing sequence that converges to X almost surely. The two examples show that ρ can be continuous from below but not above. It is possible to show that continuity from above implies continuity from below and that continuity from below is equivalent to the **Fatou condition**, that $\rho(X) \le \liminf \rho(X_n)$ for any bounded X_n converging almost surely to X. It means that if we control the risk of each X_n then we have also controlled the risk of X.

We can now state the important **representation theorem for coherent risk measures.**

Theorem 1. *Let $(\Omega, \mathcal{F}, \mathsf{P})$ be an atomless standard probability space. (a) Let ρ be a coherent risk measure on L^∞ and suppose ρ is continuous from below. Then there is a closed, convex set of probability scenario functions $\mathcal{Q}$ so that*

$$\rho(X) = \sup_{\mathsf{Q} \in \mathcal{Q}} \mathsf{E}_{\mathsf{Q}}[X]. \tag{5.12}$$

(b) Let ρ be a coherent risk measure on L^∞ and suppose ρ is continuous from above. Then there is a closed, convex set of probability scenario functions $\mathcal{Q}$ so that

$$\rho(X) = \max_{\mathsf{Q} \in \mathcal{Q}} \mathsf{E}_{\mathsf{Q}}[X]. \tag{5.13}$$

(c) The following are equivalent:

1. *ρ is a law invariant, coherent risk measure on L^∞,*

2. There is a compact, convex set $\mathcal{M}_\rho$ of probabilities on $[0,1]$ such that

$$\rho(X) = \max_{m\in\mathcal{M}_\rho} \int_{[0,1]} \mathsf{TVaR}_p(X) m(dp). \tag{5.14}$$

(d) ρ is law invariant, coherent, and comonotonic additive iff it has a representation Eq. (5.14) where $\mathcal{M}_\rho = \{m\}$ consists of a single probability. In that case

$$\mathcal{Q} = \{\mathsf{Q} \in \mathcal{M}(\mathsf{P}) \mid Z = \frac{d\mathsf{Q}}{d\mathsf{P}} \textit{ satisfies } \int_t^1 q_Z(s)ds \le g(1-t)\}.$$

Proof: (a) is Follmer and Schied (2016) Theorem 4.33 and (b) is Corollary 4.38. See also Delbaen (2002). For (c), Svindland (2010) shows ρ has the Fatou property and hence is continuous from below. Then the result follows from Kusuoka (2001) or Follmer and Schied (2016) Section 4.5. For (c) the result follows from Kusuoka (2001) or Follmer and Schied (2016) Section 4.7. Part (d) follows from Follmer and Schied (2016) Section 4.7. □

It is helpful to identify each element in $\mathcal{Q}$ with its Radon-Nikodym derivative $Z = d\mathsf{Q}/d\mathsf{P} \ge 0$. Z is a random variable and acts like a density, in that

$$\mathsf{Q}(A) = \int_A Z d\mathsf{P}. \tag{5.15}$$

The function Z integrates to one with respect to P because $\int Zd\mathsf{P} = \int d\mathsf{Q}/d\mathsf{P}\, d\mathsf{P} = \int d\mathsf{Q} = 1$. Conversely, given $Z \ge 0$ with $\mathsf{E}[Z] = 1$, Eq. (5.15) defines a probability scenario Q (but not necessarily one in $\mathcal{Q}$). We met the same concept in Section 3.6.4 (c), when discussing possible functional forms for risk measures.

Using the Radon-Nikodym derivative, $\mathcal{Q}$ can be identified with a set of random variables Z on Ω satisfying $Z \ge 0$, $\int Zd\mathsf{P} = 1$, and certain other properties depending on ρ. If ρ is continuous from above then know that for each X there is at least one Q so that $\rho(X) = \mathsf{E}_\mathsf{Q}[X]$. These scenarios are very important, motivating the following

Definition 5. *Let ρ be a coherent risk measure associated with the set $\mathcal{Q}$ of probability scenarios. Given a risk X, any $\mathsf{Q} \in \mathcal{Q}$, with Radon-Nikodym derivative Z satisfying*

$$\rho(X) = \mathsf{E}_\mathsf{Q}[X] = \mathsf{E}[XZ]$$

is called a **contact function for ρ at X**.

Section 5.5 shows that contact functions can be identified with the derivative of ρ at X.

Example 113. The risk measure $\rho = \sup$ illustrates the difference between cases (a) and (b) in Theorem 1. If $X(\omega) = 1-\sqrt{1-\omega^2}$ (a quadrant of a circle, radius 1 centered on $(0,1)$), then $\sup X = 1$, achieved at $\omega = 1$. But we cannot write $\sup X = \mathsf{E}[XZ] = \int XZ$ for a density function Z. Such a Z needs to be the density of the Dirac delta distribution at 1, which does not exist. Thus, for the sup risk measure, the sup in case (a) cannot be replaced by a max. However, we can approximate the putative Z as closely as we chose using density functions. Part (b) says that when ρ is continuous from above it is always possible to replace the sup with a max. Example 1 shows sup is continuous from below, but not above, so only part (a) applies. Theorem 1 says that the behavior in Example 111 is the only kind that can occur: if the risk measure *picks out points* then it is not continuous from above, otherwise there is some density Z so that $\rho(X) = \mathsf{E}[XZ]$. □

Example and Exercise 114. This example is not used elsewhere. In certain strange cases, a monetary risk measure can fail to be continuous from below. Take $\Omega = \{0, 1, 2, \dots\}$ and let P be a Poisson probability distribution on Ω (the specifics of P are irrelevant, as long as $\mathsf{P}(\{n\}) > 0$ for all n). Define a new function Q on subsets of Ω by

$$\mathsf{Q}(S) = \begin{cases} 0 & S \text{ is finite} \\ \mathsf{P}(S) & \text{otherwise.} \end{cases}$$

Show that Q defines a finitely additive probability, that is, it has the properties of a probability except that it is only additive for finitely many disjoint subsets of Ω rather than countably infinitely many. (Note $1 = \mathsf{Q}(\Omega) \neq \sum_n \mathsf{Q}(\{n\}) = 0$.) Define a risk measure by $\rho(X) = 0$ if $\{n \mid X(n) \neq 0\}$ is finite and $\rho(X) = \sum_n X(n)\mathsf{P}(n)$ otherwise. ρ can be regarded as $\mathsf{E}_{\mathsf{Q}}[X]$. Now, let $X_n = 1_{\{0,1,\dots,n-1\}}$ and note that $X_n \uparrow 1$. By definition, $\rho(X_n) = 0$ for all n, because X_n has finite support, but $\rho(1) = 1$. Therefore ρ is not continuous from below. Theorem 1 can be extended for probabilities that are not continuous from below by allowing $\mathcal{Q}$ to include all finitely additive probabilities like Q. When $\Omega = [0, 1]$ there are analogous, though more bizarre, probabilities like Q required to create a representation. □

Example 115. As we saw in Section 4.3, the scenarios defining TVaR_p are all probability functions with density $\leq 1/(1-p)$. For a given X, the selected Q just scales up the objective probabilities of the worst $1-p$ outcomes of X by $1/(1-p)$. TVaR gives a regulator view; all the focus is on bad outcomes. But the focus is balanced in the sense that the worst $1-p$ outcomes all have their probability increased by the same factor. It does not fixate on one or two really bad outcomes. □

There is also a convex risk measure version of Theorem 1, giving a formal statement about when Eq. (5.11) holds. The interested reader can look it up in Follmer and Schied (2016).

To evaluate a coherent risk measure on a particular random variable X we need to solve the maximization problem

$$\max_{\mathsf{Q}\in\mathcal{Q}} \mathsf{E}_{\mathsf{Q}}[X] = \max_{Z\in\mathcal{Q}} \mathsf{E}[XZ], \tag{5.16}$$

where the second expectation is with respect to P using Radon-Nikodym derivatives.

The famous Hardy-Littlewood inequality, (Follmer and Schied 2016) A.24, states that

$$\int_0^1 q_Z(s)q_X(1-s)ds \leq \mathsf{E}[XZ] \leq \int_0^1 q_Z(s)q_X(s)ds. \tag{5.17}$$

The maximum value of $\mathsf{E}[Z\tilde{X}]$ over all random variables $\tilde{X}$ with the same distribution as X occurs for the comonotonic coupling of Z and X. We have already encountered this in the Rearrangement Algorithm Section 4.2.6. The left-hand inequality says the least value of the expectation occurs when the variables are anti-comonotonic: the largest aligned with the smallest, second largest with second smallest etc. Note the roles of Z and X are interchangeable. When ρ is law invariant, we can use Eq. (5.17) to solve Eq. (5.16) very easily, by finding Z comonotonic with X.

Example 116. In Section 4.3.9, the variables X and $1_{U_X \ge p}$ are comonotonic and a special case of the Hardy-Littlewood inequality is proved to establish that TVaR is subadditive. □

In fact, ρ is law invariant if and only if the set of probability scenarios $\mathcal{Q}$ given by Theorem 1 case (c) is closed under **rearrangements** of Ω (Jouini, Schachermayer, and Touzi 2006; Svindland 2010). Closed under rearrangements means that if $Z \in \mathcal{Q}$ then $Z \circ T \in \mathcal{Q}$ for all probability preserving transformations of Ω. The PPT can be selected to sort events by the outcome X—a familiar step in some actuarial analyses.

5.5 Delbaen's Differentiation Theorem

Previewing Chapters 12 and 14, Delbaen's Differentiation Theorem says that the marginal and natural (generalized co-measure) approaches to capital allocation are the same when ρ is suitably differentiable. It is a significant result and has not been given the prominence it deserves, in our opinion.

Delbaen's Differentiation Theorem connects contact functions and differentials of risk measures. We follow Delbaen (2000), Section 8 closely. We continue to work on a standard probability space Ω with a reference probability P. L^1 denotes the set of integrable random variables on Ω defined up to sets of P-probability zero and L^∞ the set of (essentially) bounded functions. An integrable, positive $Z \in L^1$ with $\mathsf{E}[Z] = 1$ defines the density of a probability scenario that is absolutely continuous with respect to P and the linear operator on L^∞, $X \mapsto \mathsf{E}[XZ]$.

In order to explain Delbaen's Theorem, we begin by reviewing some properties of convex functions. A **convex function** $f : \mathbb{R} \to \mathbb{R}$ satisfies

$$f(\lambda x + (1-\lambda)y) \le \lambda f(x) + (1-\lambda) f(y)$$

where $0 \le \lambda \le 1$. For example, $f(x) = x^2$ and $f(x) = |x|$ are convex functions. $f(x) = \sin(x)$ is not. The maximum of a set of convex functions is again convex. Convex functions on $\mathbb{R}$ are extremely well behaved. They have a limited number of points of discontinuity and are differentiable except at possibly countably many points. Try drawing a convex function that is not continuous: it can jump up only at the boundary of its domain. Where it is not differentiable it can only have a kink. Convexity implies the graph of a convex function lies entirely above any tangent line when it is differentiable, and above any line between its left and right tangent lines when it is not. These latter properties are illustrated in Figure 5.7.

If f is differentiable at x_0 then its derivative $f'(x_0)$ has the property

$$f(x) \ge f(x_0) + f'(x_0)(x - x_0)$$

for all x. The equation on the right is the tangent line at x_0, so the inequality says a convex function lies above its tangent line. If f is not differentiable at x_0, we can compute its left (resp. right) derivative $f'_-(x) = \lim_{h\uparrow 0}(f(x+h) - f(x))/h$ (resp. $f'_+(x) = \lim_{h\downarrow 0}(f(x+h) -$

Figure 5.7 A typical real valued convex function with tangent lines and support lines. Solid thin lines are tangent lines. The dashed lines crossing at x^* show the left and right tangent lines. Much of the intuition from this picture follows through to convex functions defined on other domains. On the right, the function is discontinuous and jumps to $+\infty$ at x^{**}.

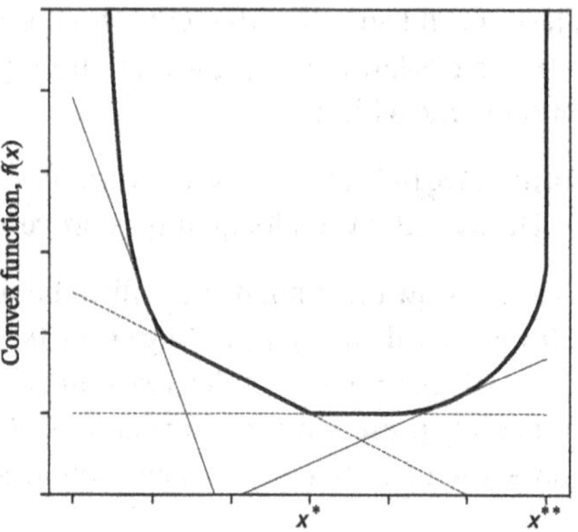

$f(x))/h)$ and use these to define left and right tangent lines. Again, f lies above both lines. Both f'_- and f'_+ exist for all x, both are nondecreasing, and $f'_-(x) \le f'_-(y) \le f'_+(y)$ for $x < y$, see Borwein and Vanderwerff (2010), Theorem 2.1.2.

A **subgradient** to f at x_0 is a real number s so that $f(x) \ge f(x_0) + s(x - x_0)$ for all x. If f is differentiable at x_0 then $s = f'(x_0)$ is the only subgradient. When it is not differentiable, the set of subgradients is the interval $[f'_-(x_0), f'_+(x_0)]$. These definitions can be extended to any convex function. The set of subgradients at x_0 is called the **subdifferential** and is denoted $Df(x_0)$. (Delbaen refers to the set of subgradients as the subgradient, op. cite p. 31.)

We can extend these concepts to a convex risk measure ρ. The derivative of ρ is a linear function of the form $X \mapsto \mathsf{E}[XZ]$ for some random variable Z. The condition $f(x) \ge f(x_0) + f'(x_0)(x - x_0)$ becomes

$$\rho(X) \ge \rho(X_0) + \mathsf{E}[(X - X_0)Z].$$

The **subdifferential** to ρ at X_0 is defined to be the set

$$D\rho(X_0) = \{Z \in L^1 \mid \rho(X) \ge \rho(X_0) + \mathsf{E}[(X - X_0)Z],\ \forall X \in L^\infty\}.$$

If we write $X = X_0 + Y$ then the condition defining $D\rho(X_0)$ becomes $\rho(X_0 + Y) \ge \rho(X_0) + \mathsf{E}[YZ]$, for all $Y \in L^\infty$.

The subgradients to ρ are just the contact functions we introduced in Section 5.4.3. Assume that ρ is continuous from below and let $\mathcal{Q}$ be the set of scenarios associated with ρ by Theorem 1, part (a).

Lemma 1. *A function $Z \in D\rho(X_0)$ if and only if $Z \in \mathcal{Q}$ and $\rho(X_0) = \mathsf{E}[X_0Z]$, that is, the subgradients are exactly the contact functions.*

Proof: Suppose $Z \in \mathcal{Q}$ and $\rho(X_0) = \mathsf{E}[X_0Z]$. Then for all Y

$$\begin{aligned}\rho(X_0 + Y) &= \sup_{Z' \in \mathcal{Q}} \mathsf{E}[(X_0 + Y)Z'] \\ &\ge \mathsf{E}[(X_0 + Y)Z]\end{aligned}$$

$$= \mathsf{E}[X_0Z] + \mathsf{E}[YZ]$$
$$= \rho(X_0) + \mathsf{E}[YZ]$$

and so $Z \in D\rho(X_0)$. This is the easy direction: contact functions are subgradients.

Conversely, let $Z \in D\rho(X_0)$. First we claim Z is a probability density, i.e., $Z \geq 0$ and $\mathsf{E}[Z] = 1$. This can be seen as follows. If $Y \leq 0$ then $X \geq X + Y$ and so $\rho(X) \geq \rho(X+Y) \geq \rho(X) + \mathsf{E}[YZ]$. Note that unlike subadditivity, the subdifferential gives helpful inequality $\rho(X+Y) \geq$ something. Hence $\mathsf{E}[YZ] \leq 0$, i.e., $\mathsf{E}[(-Y)Z] \geq 0$ for $-Y \geq 0$ and so $Z \geq 0$. Now take $Y = c \in \mathbb{R}$. Then by translation invariance $\rho(X) + c = \rho(X+c) \geq \rho(X) + \mathsf{E}[cZ]$, and so $c \geq \mathsf{E}[cZ]$. If $c \geq 0$ this implies that $\mathsf{E}[Z] \leq 1$ and if $c \leq 0$ that $\mathsf{E}[Z] \geq 1$. Hence $\mathsf{E}[Z] = 1$. We conclude Z is a probability density.

Next we show $Z \in \mathcal{Q}$ and $\rho(X_0) = \mathsf{E}[X_0Z]$. Let $\lambda \in \mathbb{R}^+$. Then by definition of the subdifferential and for any Y, using positive homogeneity,

$$\begin{aligned}
&\rho(X_0 + \lambda Y) \geq \rho(X_0) + \lambda\mathsf{E}[YZ] \\
\implies &\rho(X_0/\lambda + Y) \geq \rho(X_0)/\lambda + \mathsf{E}[YZ] \\
&\implies \rho(Y) \geq \mathsf{E}[YZ]
\end{aligned}$$

as $\lambda \to \infty$ and so $Z \in \mathcal{Q}$. Here we use the fact ρ is continuous with respect to the uniform topology. Finally let $Y = -X_0$,

$$\begin{aligned}
0 = \rho(0) &= \rho(X_0 - X_0) \\
&\geq \rho(X_0) - \mathsf{E}[X_0Z] \\
\implies &\mathsf{E}[X_0Z] \geq \rho(X_0)
\end{aligned}$$

and so $\rho(X_0) = \mathsf{E}[X_0Z]$. □

Theorem 2 (Delbaen). *If $D\rho(X_0) = \{Z\}$ is a singleton and ρ is continuous from above then*

$$\lim_{\epsilon \to 0} \frac{\rho(X_0 + \epsilon Y) - \rho(X_0)}{\epsilon} = \mathsf{E}[YZ]. \tag{5.18}$$

The function ρ is **Gâteaux differentiable** at X_0 when the limit in Eq. (5.18) exists. The limit is a **directional derivative**, because it applies only in the direction Y. A stronger notion of differentiability, called Fréchet differentiability, requires the limit to exist for all Y. A function of two variables with a tangent line in every direction is Gâteaux differentiable. But if the tangent lines have unbounded slope in some direction it is not Fréchet differentiable. $f(x, y) = x^3/(x^2 + y^2)$ for $(x, y) \neq (0, 0)$ and $f(0, 0) = 0$ is Gâteaux differentiable at $(0, 0)$ but not Fréchet differentiable. Gateaux derivatives are not necessarily linear.

Proof: The subdifferential is a singleton iff ρ is Gateaux differentiable by Borwein and Vanderwerff (2010), Cor 4.2.5. By Smulian's theorem (op. cit. Thm. 4.2.11), if Z_ϵ is the contact function for $X_0 + \epsilon Y$ (meaning $\rho(X_0 + \epsilon Y) = \mathsf{E}[(X_0 + \epsilon Y)Z_\epsilon]$) then $Z_\epsilon \to Z$ weakly (meaning $\mathsf{E}[XZ_\epsilon] \to \mathsf{E}[XZ]$ for all test functions X in L^∞). Therefore we can bracket $\rho(X_0+\epsilon Y) - \rho(X_0)$ using the definition of a subgradient at X_0 on the left and the fact that $\rho(X_0) \geq \mathsf{E}[X_0Z_\epsilon]$ on the right:

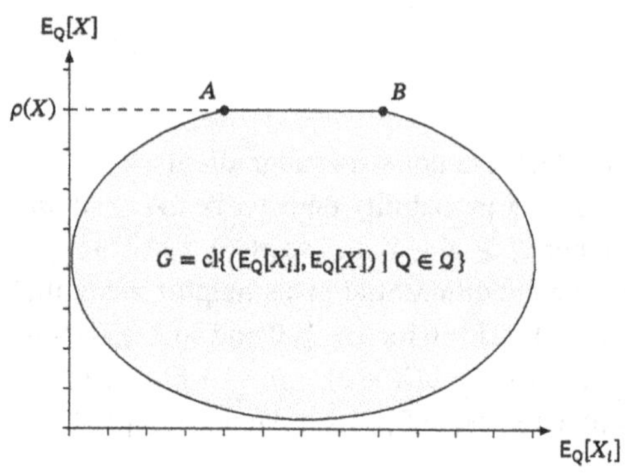

Figure 5.8 Cherny's generator set for X_1, X for a risk measure ρ represented by measures $\mathcal{Q}$.

$$\begin{aligned}
\epsilon \mathsf{E}[YZ] \le \rho(X_0 + \epsilon Y) - \rho(X_0) &= \mathsf{E}[(X_0 + \epsilon Y)Z_\epsilon] - \rho(X_0) \\
&= \epsilon \mathsf{E}[YZ_\epsilon] - (\rho(X_0) - \mathsf{E}[X_0 Z_\epsilon]) \\
&\le \epsilon \mathsf{E}[YZ_\epsilon]
\end{aligned}$$

$$\implies \mathsf{E}[YZ] \le \frac{\rho(X_0 + \epsilon Y) - \rho(X_0)}{\epsilon} \le \mathsf{E}[YZ_\epsilon].$$

The result follows because $\mathsf{E}[YZ_\epsilon] \to \mathsf{E}[YZ]$ as $\epsilon \to 0$ by weak convergence. □

Carlier and Dana (2003) discuss differentiation of spectral risk measures as Choquet integrals and shows they are differentiable at X iff q_X is increasing. Marinacci and Montrucchio (2004) link derivatives to Gâteaux derivatives. In both cases, the derivative equals $g'(S_X)$ with a suitable adjustment when g has a kink, and when it has a mass at zero, see Section 14.1.5.

Delbaen's theorem can be visualized using generator sets, introduced in Cherny (2008). For ρ defined by the closed convex set of probabilities $\mathcal{Q}$, let G be the closure of the convex hull of $\{(\mathsf{E}_\mathsf{Q}[X_i], \mathsf{E}_\mathsf{Q}[X]) \mid \mathsf{Q} \in \mathcal{Q}\}$. G is convex. $\rho(X)$ is the highest point in G. Figure 5.8 illustrates the case where the subdifferential at X is not a singleton. The flat line between A and B corresponds to the values $\mathsf{E}_\mathsf{Q}[X_1]$ for all probabilities where $\rho(X) = \mathsf{E}_\mathsf{Q}[X]$. To find a contact function for $X + tX_1$ solve

$$\rho(X + tX_1) = \sup_{\mathsf{Q}\in\mathcal{Q}} \mathsf{E}_\mathsf{Q}[X + tX_1] \tag{5.19}$$

$$= \sup_{\mathsf{Q}\in\mathcal{Q}} (1, t) \cdot (\mathsf{E}_\mathsf{Q}[X], \mathsf{E}_\mathsf{Q}[X_1]) \tag{5.20}$$

$$= \sup_{g\in G} (1, t) \cdot g \tag{5.21}$$

where $\cdot$ denotes the dot product. For $t > 0$ (respectively $t < 0$), we find the supremum by moving a line with slope $-t$ toward G from the extreme upper right-hand point (resp. upper left-hand point) in the graphic until it is tangent to G. The supremum is achieved at the tangent point B (resp. A). Any probabilities corresponding to points in the segment AB also achieve the supremum. The generator set makes it clear why ρ is not differentiable at X and shows that if we restrict the limit in the directional derivative to $t \downarrow 0$ (resp. $t \uparrow 0$) the limit gives the largest (resp. smallest) derivative in direction X_1.

Remark 117. The directional derivative Eq. (5.18) extends the homogeneous portfolio derivatives contemplated in Section 4.4. The latter are taken along directions equal to portfolio components, whereas directional derivatives can be taken along any direction. Essentially, the difference is between

$$\lim_{\epsilon\to 0} \frac{\rho(X_0 + \epsilon X_1) - \rho(X_0)}{\epsilon} \tag{5.22}$$

for *any* X_1 and

$$\lim_{\epsilon\to 0} \frac{\rho(X_0 + \epsilon X_0) - \rho(X_0)}{\epsilon}. \tag{5.23}$$

Eq. (5.23) equals $\rho(X_0)$ when ρ is TI. □

Exercise 118. Suppose X_i are normal μ_i, σ_i, $i = 0, 1$, with correlation r and that ρ equals TVaR_p. Use Eq. (4.12) to show the directional derivative Eq. (5.22) equals

$$\mu_1 + r\sigma_1 \frac{\phi(\Phi^{-1}(p))}{1-p}.$$

Compute the homogeneous portfolio derivative Eq. (5.23). □

5.6 Learning Objectives

1. Distinguish between an insurance event and an event in probability theory.
2. Define and distinguish between a conditional probability scenario and a generalized probability scenario.
3. Explain how to create a conditional probability scenario from a realistic disaster scenarios.
4. Create a basic CAPRI-like spreadsheet and explain its purpose.
5. Define each property listed in Section 5.2.
6. Distinguish between a risk measure and a measure of deviation.
7. Give examples of risk measures satisfying and not satisfying each property.
8. Distinguish between coherent and convex risk measures, with reference to their treatment of diversification.
9. Explain how a coherent risk measure is represented as the worst over a set of scenarios.
10. Explain and illustrate the purpose of a handicapping function.
11. Define and compute a contact function given a coherent risk measure and random variable.
12. Define and identify first-order stochastic dominance. Illustrate on a Lee diagram.
13. Define and identify second-order stochastic dominance. Illustrate on a Lee diagram.
14. Define and apply Rothschild-Stiglitz's characterization of risk; give an example showing variance provides a different view of risk.
15. Explain the shortcomings of utility theory as a model of firm decision making.
16. Distinguish between the mixture of distribution functions and quantile functions as models to combine risks.

17. Describe the connection between law invariance and second-order stochastic dominance.

5.A Lloyd's Realistic Disaster Scenarios

In this section, we briefly describe Lloyds's Realistic Disaster Scenarios (RDS) explain their connection to probability scenarios in some detail. It is an expanded version of the discussion in Section 5.1.

Lloyd's of London uses a scenario approach to assess risk. It is based on a set of sixteen explicitly defined realistic disaster scenarios, Lloyd's (2021). For each event Lloyd's provides

- a definition of the physical event, with a map showing the footprint or storm track;
- the assumed industry insured loss for property, split by primary class of business;
- additional lines of business that managing agents are recommended to consider;
- where applicable, a catalogue of major infrastructure (i.e., ports) that may be affected by the event; and
- where applicable, supplementary information that managing agents are required to provide (i.e., offshore energy).

The compulsory RDS set includes a Florida hurricane, a Gulf of Mexico hurricane, two East Coast US hurricanes (in one scenario, stressing reinsurance), a European windstorm, Japanese, New Madrid, San Francisco, and Los Angeles earthquakes, a UK flood, and two separate New York terrorism events.

As described in Example 15 Lloyd's uses an explicit event RDS approach to measure risk because it must aggregate the results across all syndicates to determine its total exposure.

How does an RDS define a probability scenario? It replaces the objective probability with its value conditional on the occurrence of the RDS, using Bayes' theorem. Recall, Bayes' says that $\mathsf{P}(A \mid B) = \mathsf{P}(A \cap B)/\mathsf{P}(B)$ for events A and B. The details of how that is achieved are instructive to see in detail and run as follows.

We can write each possible state $\omega \in \Omega$ as (ω', ω'') where $\omega' = 1$ indicates that RDS_k occurs and $\omega' = 0$ that it doesn't, and ω'' describes everything else in ω that is not related to the RDS. The event where RDS_k occurs is given by

$$B_k := \{\omega \in \Omega \mid RDS_k \text{ occurs in state } \omega\} = \{(1, \omega'') \mid (1, \omega'') \in \Omega\} = \{1, \text{any } \omega''\}.$$

The last expression is suggestive shorthand.

Further, we can separate total losses into $X = X' + X''$, where X' equals losses from RDS_k and X'' equals all other losses. Then, given any probability function P, we can compute $\mathsf{E}_{\mathsf{P}}[X]$ by conditioning on B_k:

$$\begin{aligned} \mathsf{E}_{\mathsf{P}}[X] &= \mathsf{E}_{\mathsf{P}}[X' + X'' \mid B_k]\mathsf{P}(B_k) + \mathsf{E}_{\mathsf{P}}[X' + X'' \mid B_k^c]\mathsf{P}(B_k^c) \\ &= \mathsf{E}_{\mathsf{P}}[X' \mid B_k]\mathsf{P}(B_k) + \mathsf{E}_{\mathsf{P}}[X'' \mid B_k]\mathsf{P}(B_k) + \mathsf{E}_{\mathsf{P}}[X'' \mid B_k^c]\mathsf{P}(B_k^c) \\ &= \mathsf{E}_{\mathsf{P}}[X' \mid B_k]\mathsf{P}(B_k) + \mathsf{E}_{\mathsf{P}}[X''] \end{aligned} \tag{5.24}$$

where B_k^c is the complement of B_k, the outcomes where RDS_k does not occur. By definition, $X' = 0$ for all states in B_k^c.

The probability scenario Q_k is the probability function of P **conditional on** B_k, which by Bayes' rule equals

$$\mathsf{Q}_k(\omega', \omega'') = \mathsf{P}(\omega', \omega'' \mid B_k) = \begin{cases} \dfrac{\mathsf{P}(\omega', \omega'')}{\mathsf{P}(B_k)} & \omega' = 1 \\ 0 & \omega' = 0 \end{cases}$$

because $(\omega' = 1, \omega'') \in B_k$ and the case $\omega' = 0$ is not. The scenario probability Q_k says the RDS is certain to occur, $\mathsf{Q}_k(B_k) = \mathsf{P}(B_k)/\mathsf{P}(B_k) = 1$.

At this point, it is easiest to assume that X'' and RDS_k are independent, which is usually reasonable and is standard practice. As a result, $\mathsf{E}_{\mathsf{Q}_k}[X''] = \mathsf{E}_{\mathsf{P}}[X'']$.

The random variable X' depends only on whether RDS_k occurs. It can be written

$$X'(\omega', \omega'') = \begin{cases} x' & \omega' = 1 \\ 0 & \omega' = 0, \end{cases}$$

where x' equals the estimated scenario loss (catastrophe model output) given the event occurs. Companies report x' as their RDS value for scenario k.

Using Eq. (5.24) to compute expected losses using Q_k gives

$$\begin{aligned} \mathsf{E}_{\mathsf{Q}_k}[X] &= \mathsf{E}_{\mathsf{Q}_k}[X' \mid B_k]\mathsf{Q}_k(B_k) + \mathsf{E}_{\mathsf{Q}_k}[X''] \\ &= X'(\omega' = 1) \times 1 + \mathsf{E}_{\mathsf{P}}[X''] \\ &= x' + \mathsf{E}_{\mathsf{P}}[X''] \\ &= (x' - \mathsf{E}_{\mathsf{P}}[X']) + \mathsf{E}_{\mathsf{P}}[X], \end{aligned}$$

where we add and subtract $\mathsf{E}_{\mathsf{P}}[X']$ in the last line.

Thus, Q_k replaces the P-expected RDS loss with its estimated outcome value x', conditional on its occurrence. By their nature, scenarios are improbable and $\mathsf{E}_{\mathsf{P}}[X']$ is usually small, so the difference $x' - \mathsf{E}_{\mathsf{P}}[X]$ is close to the reported value x'. Lloyd's knows the industry loss for each RDS and can estimate the amount by which its total loss will exceed expected for the scenario given x'.

The coherent risk measure corresponding to a set of RDSs corresponds to $\mathcal{Q} = \{\mathsf{Q}_k\}$ across each scenario and is given by $\rho(X) = \max_k \mathsf{E}_{\mathsf{Q}_k}[X]$. The value it reports for X equals the objective expected loss of X increased by assuming the worst RDS even occurs, where *worst* is defined relative to the portfolio underlying X.

5.B Convergence Assumptions for Random Variables

In this appendix we describe the convergence of random variables used in Section 5.4 and elsewhere. It is often necessary to know how a risk measure behaves when it is applied to a sequence of random variables, for example when considering derivatives or computing marginal risk for allocation applications. In order to do that we need to understand how sequences of random variables converge, which is a deep topic. In this section we give a brief introduction, highlighting examples of the different behaviors that can occur. Many of the examples below are taken from Stoyanov (2013).

There are several different notions of convergence for random variables.

1. X_n converges to X **pointwise** if $X_n(\omega) \to X(\omega)$ for all ω.
2. X_n converges to X **almost surely** or **almost everywhere** if $X_n(\omega) \to X(\omega)$ for almost all ω, i.e., for all ω in a set of probability 1. Thus, almost sure convergence requires $\Pr(\{\omega \mid X_n(\omega) \to X(\omega)\}) = 1$.
3. X_n converges to X in **probability** if for any $\epsilon > 0$ we have $\Pr(|X_n(\omega) - X(\omega)| > \epsilon) \to 0$ as $n \to \infty$.
4. X_n converges to X in **distribution** or **law** or **weakly** or in the **weak* topology** if $F_n(x) \to F(x)$ for all x for which $F(x)$ is continuous, where F_n, F are the distribution functions of X_n, X.
5. X_n converges to X in the L^1**-norm** if $\int |X_n(\omega) - X(\omega)|\,\mathsf{P}(d\omega) \to 0$ as $n \to \infty$. More generally, for $p \geq 1$ there is convergence for the L^p**-norm** if $\int |X_n(\omega) - X(\omega)|^p\,\mathsf{P}(d\omega) \to 0$.
6. X_n converges to X in the **sup-norm** if $\sup_\Omega |X_n - X| \to 0$.

Pointwise is the strongest notion and obviously implies almost sure convergence. Almost sure convergence implies convergence in probability, which implies convergence in distribution. L^1 convergence implies convergence in probability; Figure 5.9 lays out the relationships schematically. L^p convergence implies L^r convergence for $p \geq r \geq 1$. sup-norm convergence can be regarded as a special case of L^p as $p \to \infty$. Notice that since probability spaces have total probability (measure) 1, we are concerned about large values of X only . Random variables never fail to be integrable because of small values of X. (On $[1, \infty)$ the variable $X(x) = 1/x$ is divergent, but $[1, \infty)$ does not have finite measure.)

Convergence in distribution is special to probability theory. It is equivalent to a number of other conditions, spelled out in the *Portmanteau theorem* (Billingsley 1986). In particular, on a standard probability space, convergence in distribution is equivalent to $\Pr(X_n \in A) \to \Pr(X \in A)$ for all events A whose boundary has probability zero and to $\mathsf{E}[g(X_n)] \to \mathsf{E}[g(x)]$ for all bounded, continuous functions g. The last condition partially explains the condition for convergence in distribution using Fourier transforms (moment generating functions), since $g(x) = e^{2\pi i x\theta}$ is bounded for fixed θ.

The relationships between the different modes of convergence are best understood by considering examples.

Examples 119.

1. Convergence in probability but not almost surely.
   - X_n independent with $\Pr(X_n = 1) = 1/n$ and $\Pr(X_n = 0) = 1 - 1/n$; $X = 0$. $X_n(\omega) \to 0$ requires that all X_n for $n \geq N$ equal zero, which has probability $\prod_{n\geq N}(1 - \frac{1}{n}) = 0$ (take logs and use $\log(1 - 1/n) < -1/n$ and the fact $\sum_n 1/n$ diverges).
   - (Typewriter sequence.) Each integer $n \geq 1$ can be written uniquely as $n = 2^m + k$ for $0 \leq k < 2^m$. Let $X_n(\omega) = 1$ if $\omega \in [k2^{-m}, (k+1)2^{-m}]$ and 0 otherwise, and $X = 0$. Then

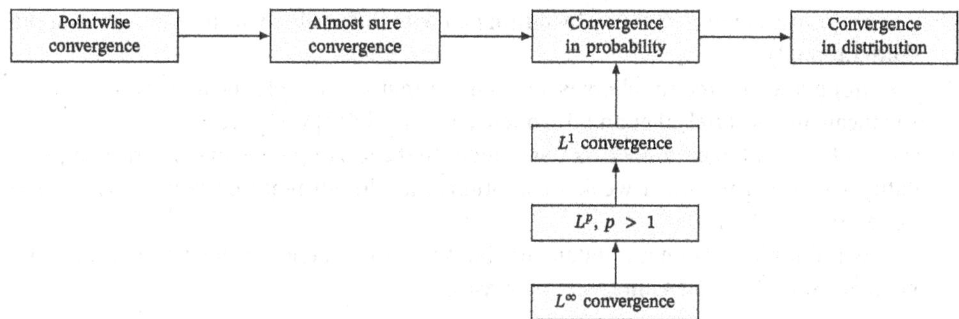

Figure 5.9 Different modes of convergence for random variables.

X_n converges to X in probability but not almost surely (for given ω, $X_n(\omega) = 1$ for one k for each m and is zero otherwise, hence it takes the values 0 and 1 infinitely many times and so $X_n(\omega)$ does converge for any ω).

2. Convergence in distribution but not in probability.
   - Let $X_n = X$ be Bernoulli and $Y = 1 - X$. Then X_n tends to X and Y in distribution (they have the same distribution) but not in probability because $\Pr(X_n = Y) = \Pr(X = Y) = 0$. Just as law invariant risk measures do not *see* the actual events, convergence in distribution does not consider explicit events.
   - The same example works if X is any nontrivial, symmetric random variable, and $Y = -X$.
   - Let X_n be uniform on k/n for $k = 0, 1, \dots, n-1$ and X be uniform on $[0, 1]$. Then X_n converges to X in distribution (the distribution of X_n is a finer and finer stair-step function converging to the distribution of X) but not probability (the distribution of X_n is supported on rational numbers, which have probability zero.)
3. L^1 convergence or almost sure but not both.
   - $X_n(\omega) = n$ if $\omega < 1/n$ and 0 otherwise converges to $X = 0$ almost surely but not in L^1, since $\int X_n = 1$ for all n but $\int X = 0$. Note X_n is unbounded; if X_n is dominated by an integrable function then Lebesgue's dominated convergence theorem ensures L^1 convergence.
   - The typewriter sequence has L^1 convergence but not almost sure convergence, since $\int X_n \to 0$. In fact, it converges in L^p for all $p < \infty$. It does not converge in L^∞ since $\sup X_n = 1 \neq \sup X = 0$.
4. Equivalent formulations for convergence in distribution.
   - The test function g must be continuous. Let $X_n = 1/n$ with probability $1 - 1/n$ and 1 otherwise. X_n converges to 0 in probability (for all $\epsilon > 0$, $\Pr(X_n > \epsilon) \to 0$ as $n \to \infty$). Let $g(x) = 0$ for $x \leq 0$ and $g(x) = 1$ for $x > 0$. For all n, $g(X_n) = 1$, but $g(0) = 0$.
   - Test sets A must have a boundary of probability zero. Apply the third (uniform) example from (2) to $A = \mathbb{Q} \cap [0, 1]$, the rationals in $[0, 1]$. $\Pr(X_n \in A) = 1$ for all n, but $\Pr(X \in A) = 0$. In this case the boundary of A is the set of all irrational numbers, which has probability 1 (the rationals have probability zero: they can be covered by an open set

of arbitrarily small probability by putting an open interval of width $\epsilon/2^{n+1}$ around the nth rational).

5. The strong law of large numbers is a statement that the sample mean converges to the true mean almost surely. For an iid sequence it holds iff $\mathsf{E}[|X_1|] < \infty$.
6. The weak law of large numbers is a statement that the sample mean converges in probability, which is true under weaker conditions that do not require the mean exists, see (Feller, 1971, p. 235).
7. The central limit theorem is a statement about the convergence of the distribution of the mean of a sample as the sample size increases. □

6

Risk Measures in Practice

In this chapter, we cover some practical considerations involved in choosing a risk measure. We outline the characterization method of selecting a risk measure and touch on the challenge of quantifying tail risk. We cover the importance of considering the intended purpose and users of the risk measures and then focus specifically on pricing and capital risk measures. There is a compendium of commonly used risk measures at the end of the chapter, for reference.

6.1 Selecting a Risk Measure Using the Characterization Method

Young (2006) identifies three ways risk measures can be selected:

1. **Ad hoc method:** start with a seemingly reasonable risk measure and rationalize it by establishing it has the properties desired (or argue against it based on its undesirable properties).
2. **Economic method:** use a rigorous economic theory to select a risk measure.
3. **Characterization method:** start with a list of desirable properties and then determine which risk measures have those characteristics.

Percentage loading (constant underwriting margin) and percentage of standard deviation are examples of favorite ad hoc methods.

Economic methods include utility-based approaches that set up and solve an optimization problem. Young describes the economic methods as "perhaps the most rigorous method that an actuary can use," but they tend to be hard to apply in practice.

We set up the characterization method in Section 5.2 by analyzing different properties and find that coherent and convex measures align well with our intuitions about risk. Both have a clear axiomatic characterization, in addition to an intuitive scenario interpretation, and a tractable representation, Sections 5.1 and 5.4. They are clear theoretical winners—at least, until we shine the light of reality on them, which we turn to now.

Pricing Insurance Risk: Theory and Practice, First Edition. Stephen J. Mildenhall and John A. Major.

These are the most important properties of a risk measure from a practical point of view.

- **Monotone** and **translation invariance** are essential for the measure to reproduce intuitive concepts of risk. Both are theoretically and practically sound.
- **Diversification** must be reflected, which coherent and convex measures do in different ways, Section 5.4.1.
- **Allocation:** a risk measure applied in aggregate must allow a practical allocation to its parts. Coherent risk measures perform well in this regard.
- **Theoretic soundness** and consistency with a general theory is desirable. For example, is the measure consistent with an arbitrage free market? Again, coherent measures perform well.
- **Explainable:** we must be able to explain any risk measure in order to "sell" it to users. Coherent measures perform well in this regard; see Section 5.1. The users will not want to use a risk measure they do not understand.

Emmer, Kratz, and Tasche (2015) address the best risk measure to use in practice. They discuss further desirable properties.

- **Elicitability:** the risk measure can be estimated by regression-like techniques.
- **Robustness** or **continuity:** a small change in inputs should result in a small change in measured risk, i.e., the measured risk is continuous in the data.
- **Backtesting:** measured risk is, and can be shown to be, consistent with observations.

They conclude that VaR's failure to be subadditive may not be a severe issue in practical applications. The fact VaR ignores the tail is more serious but makes it more robust. Considering VaR for a range of thresholds, rather than just one, ameliorates tail-insensitivity. TVaR is subadditive and tail-sensitive but hard to elicit and hard (but not impossible) to backtest.

Example 120. Here is an example of the characterization method. Wang and Zitikis (2019) recently showed that TVaR is the only monotone, law invariant measure that is suitably continuous (if $X_n \to X$ pointwise and X_n are acceptable then X is acceptable) and which offers no reward for concentration (NRC). NRC means that the risk measure is additive on a tail event, an event that aggregates all bad outcomes. Jouini, Schachermayer, and Touzi (2008) distinguish NRC from risk measures which are more conservative for tail risks, which they call strictly risk averse conditionally on lower tail events. These require a strictly increasing weighting of tail events, whereas TVaR weights tail events equally. In a sense, TVaR is cautious, but risk neutral, for the worst outcomes. □

6.2 Risk Measures and Risk Margins

In addition to the desirable properties listed in Section 6.1, the characteristics of the risk measures we select should be consistent with the characteristics of risk margins.

Five desirable characteristics of risk margins are identified in Risk Margin Working Group of the International Actuarial Association (2009).

1. The less that is known about the current estimate and its trend, the higher the risk margins should be.
2. Risks with low frequency and high severity have higher risk margins than risks with high frequency and low severity.
3. For similar risks, contracts that persist over a longer time-frame have higher risk margins than those of shorter duration.
4. Risks with a wide probability distribution have higher risk margins than risks with a narrower distribution.
5. To the extent that emerging experience reduces uncertainty, risk margins decrease, and vice versa.

The report goes on to discuss different approaches to estimating risk margins. These include:

1. Outcome methods, such as VaR and TVaR, which we discuss in Chapter 4,
2. Cost of capital methods, Section 17.3,
3. Discount-related methods, Section 8.7,
4. Explicit assumptions, and
5. Conservative assumptions.

6.3 Assessing Tail Risk in a Univariate Distribution

Recall that risk measures quantify three characteristics of univariate distributions: volume (location), volatility (scale), and tail, Section 3.6.2.

The mean measures volume and the standard deviation measures volatility, when the first and second moments exist.

Tail risk is the hardest of the three to quantify. The standard deviation is a poor measure of tail risk and even the question "Is this distribution *thick-tailed*?" is complex. Here are eight gradations of tail-thickness.

1. **No mean:** These distributions are killers. They break all the rules. VaR is not subadditive for distributions with no mean, Section 4.2.5. The law of large numbers does not apply. They are impossible to insure. Sums of iid variables may converge to a stable distribution with $\alpha \leq 1$.
2. **Mean, but no variance:** Still very-thick-tailed. The law of large numbers applies but the central limit theorem does not. Sums of iid variables may converge to a stable distribution with $1 < \alpha < 2$.
3. **Mean and variance, but only finitely many moments:** The law of large numbers and central limit theorem both apply. Higher moments, such as skewness and kurtosis, may exist. Kurtosis is very sensitive to extreme tails (compare the values in Table 2.6 and Table 2.7).
4. **All moments exist, but subexponential:** A distribution is **subexponential** if its survival function decays slower than an exponential, meaning $e^{kx}S(x) \to \infty$ for all $k > 0$. A subexponential distribution with moments of all orders are still extremely thick-tailed.

They are not characterized by their moments (it is possible to make a perturbed lognormal with the same moments as a lognormal). Subexponential distributions are discussed in Embrechts, Klüppelberg, and Mikosch (1997).

5. **Exponential tail:** The exponential distribution tail can be regarded as dividing thick from thin. If you work with the exponential you soon discover it has a surprisingly awkward tail thickness. The exponential has the memoryless property (constant hazard rate): $\mathsf{E}[X \mid X > x] = x + \mathsf{E}[X]$ for all $x \geq 0$. As a survival distribution, it does not exhibit aging.
6. **Super-exponential (faster than exponential) tail:** These distributions are thin-tailed. They have all moments and the central limit theorem and law of large numbers apply. Their extreme values are well understood and described by large deviation theory. Their moment generating function is analytic (differentiable) at 0, which allows classical theorems from risk theory, such as the Cramer-Lundberg approximation, to apply.
7. **Log-concave density:** The normal has a log-concave density, proportional to $-x^2$. These distributions are very well behaved, with sample averages tightly clustered around the sample mean. Risk in a portfolio of log-concave densities is entirely driven by dependency risk.
8. **Bounded:** There is obviously no tail risk in a bounded distribution. Since $\log(0) = -\infty$, bounded densities can be regarded as log-concave.

A plot of the log survival function against either loss or log loss is an effective way to assess tail behavior. The plot against loss shows whether or not the tail is subexponential: does it lie above or below a straight line? Against log loss it identifies classical power-law behavior, indicating only finitely many moments exist.

Exercise 121. Categorize the normal, uniform, beta, lognormal, gamma, inverse gamma, log gamma, Pareto, power-law stable, inverse Gaussian, exponential, Weibull, Poisson, and negative binomial distributions according to the eight gradations above. □

6.4 The *Intended Purpose:* Applications of Risk Measures

Our choice of risk measure should reflect its intended purpose and users.

The ASB Actuarial Standard of Practice No. 56, *Modeling*, states

> When the actuary designs, develops, or modifies the model, the actuary should confirm, in the actuary's professional judgment, that the capability of the model is consistent with the **intended purpose**.
>
> **Intended purpose:** The goal or question, whether generalized or specific, addressed by the model within the context of the assignment.
>
> **Intended User:** Any person whom the actuary identifies as able to rely on the model output.

Model: A simplified representation of relationships among real world variables, entities, or events using statistical, financial, economic, mathematical, non-quantitative, or scientific concepts and equations. A model consists of three components: an information input component, which delivers data and assumptions to the model; a processing component, which transforms input into output; and a results component, which translates the output into useful business information.

Section 3.6.3 identified pricing and capitalization as two applications of risk measures. Within each, risk measures can have a range of intended purposes.

- Individual risk pricing: quoting and evaluation of market pricing.
- Classification rate making: setting profit margins and allocation of cost of capital.
- Portfolio management: reinsurance purchasing, portfolio optimization, ORSA, insurance vs. asset risk split, strategic planning.
- Capital: determining risk capital or evaluating held capital.

The intended purpose determines the level of detail of modeling, whether it is stand-alone or as part of a portfolio, and the appropriate time period for modeling.

Risk measures can have different intended users, each with different concerns.

- Underwriter or pricing actuary: price adequacy, price competition, fair allocation of cost of capital.
- Insurer management and ERM function: relative performance, portfolio optimization, retention and reinsurance strategy, capital structure, signaling competence to external users.
- The insured: value of insurance, total cost of risk, solvency of insurer.
- Regulator: setting binding objective minimum capital standards.
- Rating agency: evaluating actual capital.
- Reinsurer: pricing inwards business, often with substantial catastrophe risk and potential aggregations.
- Investor (equity or debt): balance and compare risks and returns, solvency, franchise value, dilution.

Each application applies a risk measure to a different stochastic variable.

- Pricing: prospective amount and timing uncertainty, but ignoring reserves, which are a sunk cost.
- Management: underwriting income, net income, comprehensive income (change in surplus), and cash flow. Group and legal entity views.
- Regulation: default or impairment risk encompassing all sources of risk at a legal entity level.

Next we focus on specific considerations for selecting pricing and capital risk measures, taking their respective users and purposes into account.

6.4.1 Pricing Risk Measures

Pricing risk measures are also called premium calculation principles (PCPs). The following should be considered in selecting a PCP.

- **Explainable**: Ideal PCPs have a reasonable, transparent, and explainable basis and are consistent with theory. No one wants to use a method they do not understand.
- **Estimable**: PCP parameters should be easy to estimate from market prices.
- **Computable**: PCPs should be easy and efficient to compute.
- **Robust**: PCP values should be robust to the ambiguity in the underlying risk distributions.
- **Allocation**: Aggregate PCPs should have a natural and logical allocation methodology.
- **Optimal**: Insurers want to ensure their portfolios are efficient and close to optimal. PCPs should behave well when used in optimization algorithms. In this regard, convex risk measures are particularly helpful.
- **Diversification**: PCPs should respect insurance risk diversification. Additive functionals are not consistent with the purpose and operation of insurance.
- **Law invariant**: Classical PCPs are law invariant. Law invariance can be violated through the use of a reference portfolio, for example, in catastrophe risk portfolios.
- **Theoretically sound**: PCPs should be consistent with economic, financial theory, and behavioral considerations.

6.4.2 Capital Risk Measures

Capital risk measures are used by management to estimate economic capital, by regulators to determine minimum capital standards, and by rating agencies to set target capital standards and to assess the adequacy of held or adjusted capital.

In the 1990s the NAIC introduced risk-based capital standards and the EU introduced Solvency I. These were factor-based formulas that determined minimum capital standards based on statutory accounts. They were volume driven, applying factors to premium and reserve balances, asset values, and so forth. They use risk-sensitive capital factors. At the same time, rating agencies introduced parallel capital adequacy ratio models that took the same approach as the regulatory models and added a VaR-based catastrophe risk charge. All of these models use net premiums and reserves, giving an explicit benefit to reinsurance.

Actuaries explored using non-monetary measures of capital adequacy such as expected policyholder deficit ratio (Butsic, 1994; Myers and Read Jr., 2001).

Banks monitored their trading exposures using VaR models that estimated the daily risk to proprietary trading portfolios.

Artzner *et al.* (1999) introduced coherent risk measures, a watershed in capital modeling. It addressed the failure of VaR to be subadditive, Section 4.2.5. Subadditivity is deemed reasonable on the basis that "a merger does not create risk" and because it allows a bottom-up approach to risk management. Controlling a subadditive risk measure at a unit level provides control over the total, whereas VaR does not.

The natural desire that risk measures are monotone rules out standard deviation. Subadditivity also rules out semideviation from the mean.

Dhaene *et al.* (2008) suggested that subadditive risk measures could provide too great a credit for diversification. This fact, coupled with concerns over positive homogeneity, led to the introduction of convex risk measures (Föllmer and Schied, 2011).

Today, most capital standards are based on volume (RBC), VaR (Solvency II), TVaR (Swiss Solvency Test, Basel III), or on a blend of volume charges for non-modeled risks and VaR or TVaR for modeled natural catastrophe risks.

Castagnoli *et al.* (2021) states that almost all risk measures in use today are law invariant, except for specific scenario tests such as Lloyd's Realistic Disaster Scenarios (RDS). Law invariance is objective, depending only on the entity's loss potential, and enables the statistical estimation of risk.

Considerations for selecting a capital risk measures are similar to those for selecting PCPs. Here we highlight some differences:

- **Robustness to regulatory arbitrage** is very important; see Wang (2016). Measures should balance complexity against the data available, just as predictive modeling controls for over-fitting by looking at out of sample accuracy.
- **Simplicity** and **explainability** are paramount, to help the regulator communicate their objectives to different stakeholders.
- **Standardization** and reliance on public data enables comparison across entities.
- **Backtesting**: it should be possible to determine if a portfolio was managed to a risk measure tolerance. Are breaches reasonably explained by chance?
- Portfolio **optimization** against a regulatory standard is very important for insurers. TVaR-constrained optimization can be converted into a linear programming problem (Rockafellar and Uryasev, 2002), for example. Convex risk measures have good optimization behavior. Methods that compute the shadow costs of constraints are particularly helpful.

Heyde, Kou, and Peng (2007) consider properties of an ideal regulatory capital risk measure and emphasize measures that are robust. They conclude that VaR "though simple, is not irrational."

Since the early 2000s, the finance community has broadly agreed to use risk measures that combine volume and deviation denominated in monetary units. Risk for the total value of liabilities, usually over a one-year timeframe, is compared to available assets.

6.5 Compendium of Risk Measures

Table 6.1 shows example risk measures and families of risk measures. A specific risk measure can appear multiple times in the table. Mean value, utility, exponential, and Esscher measures are discussed more in Section 8.4.1. A **norm** $||X||$ is a function with length-like properties. The p-norm $||X||_p = \mathsf{E}[|X|^p]^{1/p}$, $p \geq 1$. It measures the length or size of X. As p increases the norm becomes more and more focused on the largest values of X. For higher-order measures $p > 1$.

Table 6.1 A compendium of risk measures.

Name	Expression	Notes
Moment Based		
Mean	$\mathsf{E}X$	c
Standard deviation	$\sigma(X) = \mathsf{E}[(X - \mathsf{E}X)^2]^{1/2}$	d
Sharpe ratio risk measure	$\mathsf{E}X + \lambda\sigma(X)$	
Variance	$\sigma(X)^2$	
semivariance	$\mathsf{E}[X] + c\mathsf{E}[(X - \mathsf{E}X)^2 1_{X>\mathsf{E}[X]}]$	
Higher noncentral moments, $n \geq 3$	$\mathsf{E}[X^n]$	
Higher central moments, $n \geq 3$	$\mathsf{E}[(X - \mu)^n]$	
Higher moments, skewness, kurtosis	various	
Quantile, p-VaR	$q^-(p) = \mathsf{VaR}_p(X)$	
Maximum loss, VaR_1	$\max(X)$ or $\sup(X)$	c
Probability of default above assets a	$\Pr(X > a)$	
Risk-based capital and regulatory		
RBC-based on premium factors	Sum product factors and values,	
RBC factors + VaR (revised NAIC RBC)	with possible covariance adjustment	
Risk-adjusted probabilities		
Risk-adjusted expected value	$\mathsf{E}_\mathsf{Q}[X]$	c
Worst scenario outcome (RDS)	$\max_\mathsf{Q} \mathsf{E}_\mathsf{Q}[X]$	c
Likelihood-adjusted worst scenario	$\max_\mathsf{Q} \mathsf{E}_\mathsf{Q}[X] - \alpha(\mathsf{Q})$, α penalty function	cx
Stop loss premium	$\mathsf{E}[(X - x)^+]$	
TVaR or expected shortfall	$\frac{1}{1-p}\int_{1-p}^{q} \mathsf{VaR}_s(X)ds$	c
TCE, tail conditional expectation	$\mathsf{E}[X \mid X \geq \mathsf{VaR}_p(X)]$	c, 1
WCE, worst conditional expectation	$\sup\{\mathsf{E}[X \mid A] \mid \Pr(A) > 1 - p)\}$	c, 2
xVaR or excess VaR	$\mathsf{xVaR}_p(X) := \mathsf{VaR}_p(X) - \mathsf{E}[X]$	d, 9
xTVaR or excess TVaR	$\mathsf{xTVaR}_p(X) := \mathsf{TVaR}_p(X) - \mathsf{E}[X]$	d, 9
Absolute semi deviation	$\mathsf{E}[(X - \mathsf{E}X)^+] = \lVert(X - \mathsf{E}X)^+\rVert_1$	
Dutch	$\mathsf{E}X + \lambda \lVert(X - \mathsf{E}X)^+\rVert_1$	c, 3
Higher-order (mean) deviation	$\mathsf{E}X + c \lVert X - \mathsf{E}X\rVert_p$	c, 4
—from target τ	$\mathsf{E}X + c \lVert X - \tau\rVert_p$	5
Higher-order semideviation	$\mathsf{E}X + c \lVert(X - \mathsf{E}X)^+\rVert_p$	c, 6
—from target τ	$\mathsf{E}X + c \lVert(X - \tau)^+\rVert_p$	5
Two-sided deviation, $\alpha > 1, 0 \leq \beta \leq 1$	$\mathsf{E}X + \inf_x\{\alpha_1\mathsf{E}[(x - X)^+] + \alpha_2\mathsf{E}[(X - x)^+]\}$	c, 7

(Continued)

Table 6.1 (Continued)

Name	Expression	Notes
Average absolute deviation from the median	$\mathsf{E}X + c\,\|X - MX\|$, MX the median	10
Generic coherent	$\sup_\mathsf{Q} \mathsf{E}_\mathsf{Q}[X]$	c
Generic convex, α likelihood penalty	$\sup_\mathsf{Q}(\mathsf{E}_\mathsf{Q}[X] - \alpha(Q))$	cx
Other		
Expected policyholder deficit percentage	$\mathsf{E}[(X-a)^+]/\mathsf{E}X$	
Expected policyholder deficit capital, $\mathsf{EPD}_p(X)$	Solve $\mathsf{E}[(X-a)^+] = p\,\mathsf{E}X$ for a	
Zero utility, u increasing, $u(0)=0$	Solve $\mathsf{E}[u(R-X)] = 0$ for R	8
Exponential	$c^{-1}\log \mathsf{E}[e^{cX}]$	cx
Mean value, given a function f	Solve $f(R) = \mathsf{E}[f(X)]$ for R	
Esscher transform	$\mathsf{E}[Xe^{hX}]/\mathsf{E}[e^{hX}]$	

Abbreviations

c: coherent

cx: convex

d: measure of deviation.

Notes

1. TCE is the same as TVaR for continuous variables but can differ, and fail to be subadditive, for mixed or discrete X. See Section 4.3.
2. WCE equals TVaR on an atomless probability space, but can differ, and fail to be subadditive, when the space has atoms.
3. Heerwaarden and Kaas (1992) define the Dutch risk measure as a two parameter family $\mathsf{E}X + \lambda_1 \|(X - \lambda_2 \mathsf{E}X)^+\|_1$. However, it is not TI when $\lambda_2 \neq 1$. It is monotone and subadditive when $0 \le \lambda_1 \le 1$. The Dutch principle is not comonotonic additive.
4. See Shapiro, Dentcheva, and Ruszczyski (2009), Example 6.18.
5. Deviation from target is not TI if the target does not scale.
6. Higher-order semideviation generalizes the Dutch principle. These measures are considered in Fischer (2003), so we call them Fischer measures, and Shapiro, Dentcheva, and Ruszczyski (2009), Example 6.20. They are coherent for $1 \le p \le \infty$ and $0 \le \lambda \le 1$.
7. See Shapiro, Dentcheva, and Ruszczyski (2009), Example 6.16.
8. Zero utility premium is TI iff the utility function is exponential utility (Goovaerts, De Vylder, and Haezendonck, 1984).
9. Excess forms of risk measures convert between required assets and required capital by subtracting the mean. Accounting conventions usually require the mean (or *best estimate*) is separately identified as a policyholder liability.
10. Average absolute deviation from the median is considered by Denneberg (1990).

6.6 Learning Objectives

1. Describe eight different measures of tail thickness and use them to categorize a given distribution function.
2. Describe how different risk measures address volume, volatility, and tail risk.
3. Describe and give examples of the ad hoc, characterization, and economic methods of classifying risk measures.
4. Describe the two principal uses of risk measures and the intended users for each.
5. Enumerate desirable properties of a pricing risk measure and explain how they can be applied to guide the selection of a suitable measure.
6. Enumerate desirable properties of a capital risk measure and explain how they can be applied to guide the selection of a suitable measure.

7

Guide to the Practice Chapters

In Parts II and III, the Practice Chapters 9, 11, 13, and 15 contain many simple examples and illustrations using the three Case Studies introduced in Chapter 2. These have different objectives. The simple examples can (and should) be replicated in a spreadsheet and are intended to build the reader's computational skills. The Case Studies are intended to build the reader's intuition regarding the different methods' behaviors.

We apply various classical and modern risk measures—our semi-serious division between classical and modern is 1997. These risk measures are listed in Table 7.1, which also shows some of their important properties using definitions from Section 5.2.

We consider pricing measures in conjunction with a value at risk capital risk measure. In addition, we consider TVaR and EPD capital risk measures in conjunction with the hard-to-classify constant cost of capital (CCoC) pricing measure. CCoC methods are explained in Sections 8.7.4 and 12.1.

In Chapter 9 the classical PCPs are applied stand-alone and in total to illustrate how premium varies with the shape of risk and to show the impact of diversification by comparing the sum of stand-alone premiums to the total premium.

In Chapter 11 we apply CCoC methods, with and without default, and stand-alone and in total, to show the impact of tail risk on pricing. The examples show that these methods are very sensitive to tail risk. We also apply the CCoC, proportional hazard, Wang, dual moment, TVaR, and blended SRMs (all defined in Sections 11.2 and 11.3) to distinguish their different loss ratio, leverage, and return characteristics across a range of risks.

In Chapter 13 we apply CCoC methods with a range of ad hoc allocations. These methods include most variants of standard US practice for regulated lines.

In Chapter 15 we give the SRM allocation of premium and capital. These examples include simple but powerful graphical illustrations that make it easy to communicate which lines contribute the most to the overall portfolio risk.

Chapters 11 and 15 both start with very detailed algorithms extending Section 3.5.5 that explain how to apply SRM pricing methods. Again, the examples are intended for you to replicate in a spreadsheet before examining the Case Studies.

We calibrate each Case's pricing to the same gross portfolio premium across all methods to ensure comparability. The baseline premium generates a 10% return on capital at the 99.99% VaR capital level for Tame and a 10% return at 99.9% VaR capital for Cat and Non-Cat and

Pricing Insurance Risk: Theory and Practice, First Edition. Stephen J. Mildenhall and John A. Major.

Table 7.1 Risk measures applied to the Case Studies. The Two-measure block applies the spectral pricing risk measures associated with a CCoC, proportional hazard, Wang, dual moment, TVaR, and blended distortion function, combined with a VaR capital risk measure.

Name	Formula	TI	MON	PH	SA	CX	COH	CONVEX	COMON	Allocation
Classical										
Net	$\mathsf{E}[X]$	●	○	●	●	●	○	○	●	Additive
Expected value	$\mathsf{E}[X](1+\pi)$	○	○	●	●	●	○	○	○	Additive
VaR	$\mathsf{VaR}_\pi(X)$	●	●	●	○	○	○	○	●	coVaR
Variance	$\mathsf{E}[X]+\pi\mathsf{var}(X)$	○	○	○	○	●	○	○	○	Covariance
Standard deviation	$\mathsf{E}[X]+\pi\mathsf{SD}(X)$	○	○	●	●	●	○	○	○	Comeasure $\mathrm{cov}(X_i,X)/\sigma_X$
Semivariance	$\mathsf{E}[X]+c\mathsf{E}[(X-\mathsf{E}X)_+^2]$	●	○	○	○	●	○	○	○	Comeasure
Exponential	$\pi^{-1}\log\mathsf{E}[e^{\pi x}]$	●	●	○	○	●	○	●	○	Tsanakas, Aumann-Shapley
Esscher	$\mathsf{E}[Xe^{\pi X}]/\mathsf{E}[e^{\pi X}]$	●	○	○	○	○	○	○	○	Comeasure
Dutch	$\mathsf{E}[X]+\pi\mathsf{E}[(X-\mathsf{E}X)^+]$	●	●	●	●	●	●	●	○	Comeasure
Fischer	$\mathsf{E}[X]+\pi\mathsf{E}[((X-\mathsf{E}[X])^+)^2]^{1/2}$	●	●	●	●	●	●	●	○	Comeasure
Modern										
CCoC	$\mathsf{E}[X]+d(\max(X)-\mathsf{E}[X])$	●	●	●	●	●	●	●	●	Natural
TVaR	$\mathsf{TVaR}_\pi(X)$	●	●	●	●	●	●	●	●	Natural
Spectral	$\rho_g(X)$	●	●	●	●	●	●	●	●	Natural
Capital measures										
VaR assets	$\mathsf{VaR}_\pi(X)$	●	●	●	○	○	○	○	●	Pro rata, equal risk, comeasure
TVaR assets	$\mathsf{TVaR}_\pi(X)$	●	●	●	●	●	●	●	●	Pro rata, equal risk, comeasure
EPD assets	$\mathsf{EPD}_\pi(X)$									Pro rata, equal risk
Two-measure										
CCoC and a	$\mathsf{E}[X\wedge a]+d(a-\mathsf{E}[X\wedge a])$	●	●	●	○	○	○	○		Lifted natural
Spectral and a	$\rho_g(X\wedge a)$	●	●	●	○	○	○	○		Lifted natural

Table 7.2 Pricing summary by Case. Tame Case uses a 0.9999 capital standard; Cat/Non-Cat and Hu/SCS use 0.999. Cost of capital is 0.10.

	Tame		Cat/noncat		Hu/SCS	
Statistic	**Gross**	**Net**	**Gross**	**Net**	**Gross**	**Net**
Loss	100.00	99.08	99.95	97.73	95.15	84.41
Margin	3.42	2.46	15.21	8.17	226.2	194.5
Premium	103.4	101.5	115.2	105.9	321.3	278.9
Loss ratio	0.967	0.976	0.868	0.923	0.296	0.303
Capital	34.23	24.64	152.1	81.68	2,262	1,945
Rate of return	0.1	0.1	0.1	0.1	0.1	0.1
Assets	137.7	126.2	267.2	187.6	2,583	2,224
Leverage	3.02	4.12	0.757	1.3	0.142	0.143

Table 7.3 Details of reinsurance for each Case. Reinsurance is applied to the most volatile unit.

Item	Discrete	Tame	Cat/noncat	Hu/SCS
Reinsured Line	X2	B	Cat	Hu
Reinsurance Type	Aggregate	Aggregate	Aggregate	Per occurrence
Attachment Probability	0.25	0.2	0.1	0.05
Attachment	20	56.17	41.11	40.25
Exhaustion Probability	0	0.01	0.005	0.005
Limit	80	12.91	79.64	372.4

Hu/SCS. Table 7.2 shows the resulting premium and other relevant descriptive statistics. Expected losses allow for possible default. The way the baseline premium is determined is not important as long as the pricing is calibrated consistently.

Each Case Study applies reinsurance to the more volatile unit. Table 7.3 shows the line, limit, attachment, and type of reinsurance applied. Occurrence reinsurance is applied with unlimited, free reinstatements. The model does not compute reinsurance premium. Net premium is computed by applying the pricing functional to net losses. The model can be used to determine whether or not a proposed reinsurance premium lowers the total cost of risk, net plus ceded vs. gross.

Part II

Portfolio Pricing

8

Classical Portfolio Pricing Theory

> *Thousands of insurance premiums are calculated every day. About everyone agrees that the "pure premium" can only be the mathematical expected value of the risk amount. But insurance companies cannot survive by merely charging pure premiums. Loadings taking into account the variability of the risk, i.e. its stochastic character, are necessary. Unfortunately no general principle for loaded premiums has been experienced or proven to be the uniformly best one. The practitioners do not even seem to agree about the prerequisites of a good premium calculation principle!*
>
> Goovaerts, de Vylder, and Haezendonck, *Insurance Premiums*

In this chapter, we take a chronological look at classical portfolio pricing after laying some necessary groundwork.

We begin the chapter by describing the services supplied by insurance companies, isolating the risk-bearing services for which capital is needed and whose pricing we describe in this book. We discuss the types of capital available to an insurer and its accounting and statutory underpinnings.

Our chronological presentation of classical portfolio pricing follows. We start with classical actuarial premium calculation principles (PCPs). We describe early pricing models that incorporate investment income and relate margin to capital. We continue with a detailed treatment of financial pricing that treats an insurance contract as a security. We survey the financial theory of asset valuation and then apply it to insurance in its discounted cash flow (DCF) and option pricing guises. At the end of the chapter, we consider whether the assumptions underlying financial pricing models are realistic.

8.1 Insurance Demand, Supply, and Contracts

In this section, we describe the role of an insurance company and the specific services it supplies to meet insurance demand. We isolate the risk-bearing services for which the provision of capital is needed and that comprise the insurance risk we are pricing in this book. We also cover the essential features of insurance contracts.

Pricing Insurance Risk: Theory and Practice, First Edition. Stephen J. Mildenhall and John A. Major.

8.1.1 Demand

Demand for insurance services can be broken into three types.

1. **Risk transfer** is the classic motivation for risk averse individuals to purchase insurance. The insured is exposed to a risk which they wish to avoid. Diversification allows them to do this by pooling their risk with other insureds. Risk pooling is the magic ingredient of insurance; diversification through pooling is the closest to a free lunch that finance allows. Risk pooling for short-tailed, property-casualty lines is inter-insured, intratemporal. It shares losses in one period between a pool of risks.
2. **Satisfying** demand, a phrase from Kunreuther, Pauly, and McMorrow (2013): the insurance policy satisfies certain statutory, regulatory, or contractual requirements in order for the insured to carry out another desired activity. Financial responsibility laws for driving an automobile and employer liability laws are examples of statutory requirements. A debt contract requiring insurance collateral protection is an example of a contractual requirement. Insurance purchased wholly or in part for satisfying requirements accounts for at least 60% of global property-casualty premium, according to Aon Benfield (2015).
3. **Risk financing**: the insured seeks to finance uncertain future contingencies in an efficient manner. Risk financing requirements are driven by accounting, regulation, and tax law. Under GAAP, an obligation cannot be expensed, and is not tax deductible, unless it is reasonably certain in timing and amount. A contingent future payment to settle a lawsuit may not meet these requirements and so may not be a deductible expense. Entities use insurance-based risk financing to convert contingent, nondeductible liabilities into certain, deductible amounts. Risk financing is typically performed for a single entity over time: it is intertemporal, intra-insured. Risk financing is used to fund reasonably certain losses in a cost efficient manner. Large deductible and retrospectively rated policies, self-insured retentions, and captives are used to satisfy risk financing demand.

Insurance that is purchased to meet a satisfying requirement generally needs to be issued by a regulated entity, especially if it is third-party, because judgment-proof buyers have no interest in the quality of insurance and simply purchase the cheapest allowable cover (Cummins, 1988). Insurers with on-balance sheet capital exist primarily to meet such demand.

8.1.2 Supply

Ins Co. collects premium from customers and supplies services in return. Insurance services include sales, marketing, risk surveys and loss control, customer billing and support, underwriting and pricing, claims adjusting, risk bearing, and investment management services (Figure 8.1). These services are bundled in different ways. Managing a **risk pool** involves two critical functions. The first is controlling access to the pool through underwriting and pricing, and the second is ensuring the pool is solvent by funding risk-bearing assets through the sale of liabilities. These two critical functions are the heart of an insurance company, and we abbreviate them **Pool Co.** and **Capital Co.** Underwriting assures pool members they are

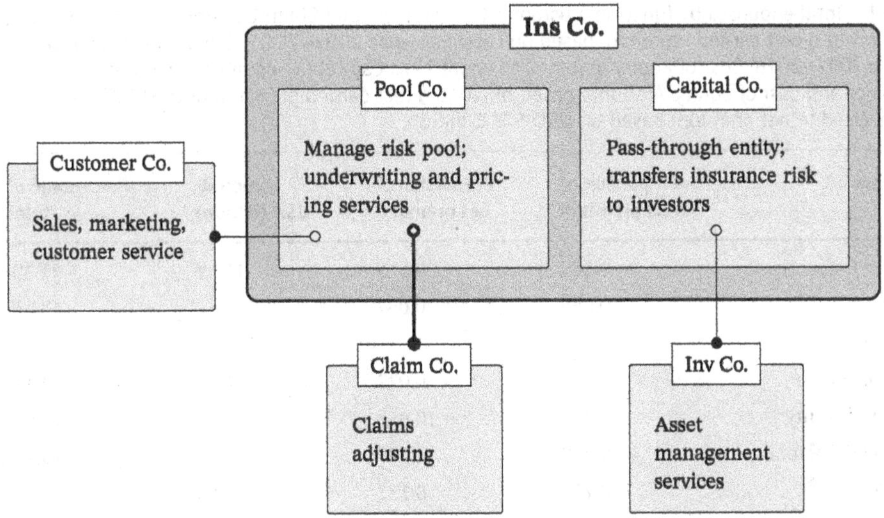

Figure 8.1 Services provided by an insurance company. Claim services are usually bundled within Ins Co., indicated by the thick line.

all treated fairly. To manage incentive conflicts Pool Co. and Capital Co. are usually one entity, Ins Co., which normally also bundles Claim Co. to adjust claims.

The market includes a wide variety of service combinations.

- Customer Co. functions are bundled in a direct writer, or handled by independent agents and brokers.
- Managing general underwriters can provide stand-alone Pool Co. services.
- Reinsurance and sidecar arrangements can provide stand-alone Capital Co. services.
- Third-party claims adjuster Claim Cos. are common, especially for large accounts.
- Independent Inv Cos. that provide asset management services for the pool's assets are very common, particularly for smaller insurers.

This book's title, *Pricing Insurance Risk*, refers to pricing the services provided by **Capital Co.** (Part II) and the allocation to each unit done by **Pool Co.** (Part III). All other services can be priced separately and have stand-alone comparables in the market. **Premium** covers only the cost of risk transfer. We assume that all other expense components are charged separately. Inv Co. expenses are usually netted out of investment income.

To assess the relative importance of each activity, Cummins and Weiss (2013) recommend measuring the output of an insurer using the value-added approach. Activities are taken to add significant value if they are given significant operating cost allocations. Table 8.1 shows a value breakdown on this basis, using operating costs from US statutory accounting data. The magnitude and split of these expenses should be no surprise. In practice capital costs are split between on-balance sheet costs, estimated via a cost of capital, and the cost of reinsurance.

Table 8.1 Total expenses by function. Customer Co., Pool Co., and Claim Co. functions shown as a percentage of direct earned premium, based on calendar years 2009–2016; Reinsurance expense based on 2002–2016; Cost of equity assumed to equal 12%. Capital Co. equals the sum of reinsurance and cost of equity. Amounts based on 2016 direct earned premium of USD 602.6 billion and converted to net premium based on USD 529.1 billion.

Component	Proportion of direct premium	Proportion of net premium	Amount, USD (billion)	Percentage of total
Customer Co.	0.189	0.215	113.9	41.3%
Pool Co.	0.085	0.097	51.2	18.6%
Capital Co.				
Reinsurance	0.019	0.022	11.4	4.1%
Cost of equity	0.050	0.057	30.1	10.9%
Capital Co. total	0.069	0.079	41.6	15.1%
Claim Co.	0.115	0.131	69.3	25.1%
Total	0.458	0.522	276.0	100.0%

Why do insurers exist? In a perfect complete market there is no convincing rationale, as we explain in Section 8.6. Insureds would contract directly with investors. In reality, in an imperfect market underwriting is costly and requires an accumulation of private loss data. Insurer capital is costly and risk pools allow it to be used more efficiently. Long-lived risk pools signal management competence to investors, lowering the cost of capital. Finally, mandatory insurance laws are effective only if they require insurance be purchased from well-capitalized insurers.

Figure 8.2 shows how insureds interact with Pool Co., which transfers risk to Capital Co., which finances risk bearing capacity by selling residual value rights to investors. Part II of the book is concerned with transactions on the right of the figure, where portfolio risk is managed. Part III deals with the left, where the total cost is allocated to policyholders.

8.1.3 Insurance Contracts

Insurance contracts must be written so that claims are clear and objective, easy to adjust, and discourage fraud. A contract is specified by delineating the circumstances under which it responds and the amount it pays. The amount is a random variable, a function of the underlying outcome.

A basic requirement of insurance is that it pays no more than the subject loss. The insured should never profit from an insurance claim.

Parametric insurance policies pay based on an explicit event outcome, defined by an objective physical description such as a hurricane intensity and landfall or earthquake magnitude and epicenter. Parametric insurance is easy to underwrite because it does not depend on the characteristics of the insured. However, they are hard to design to ensure that the insured has a loss only when a claim is triggered—to prevent the insured from profiting

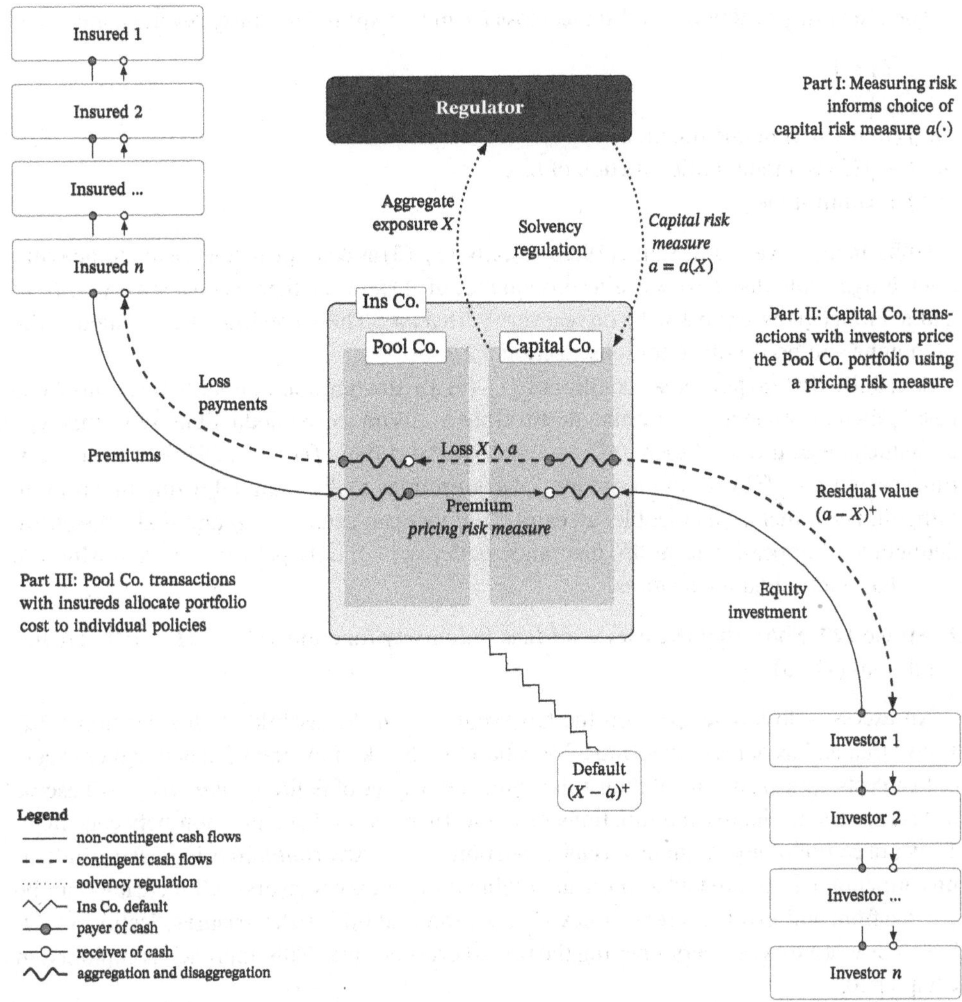

Figure 8.2 Interactions between the product and capital markets determine premium and asset levels. $X \wedge a$ indicates actual loss payments, given by the lesser of losses X and assets a. Contracts are not shown; they flow counter to cash.

from a claim. The insured is also exposed to **basis risk**: a mismatch between their subject loss and the insurance recovery.

For these reasons, the majority of insurance responds on a dual-trigger basis: an objective event occurs and it causes an economic loss to the insured. The **indemnity payment** is a function of an underlying **subject loss** amount suffered by the insured. Indemnity is a function of an implicit event, Section 3.4. Policies apply an **indemnity function** to the subject loss that combines limits and sublimits, occurrence, aggregate deductibles, and so forth.

The indemnity function f and subject loss L can be required to satisfy several conditions:

1. $f(L) \le L$.
2. $f(L) \ge 0$.
3. $f(L)$ is a monotonic function of L.
4. $L - f(L)$ is a monotonic function of L.
5. f is continuous.

Huberman, Mayers, and Smith (1983) describe (1)–(3) as basic principles of insurance contract design. Note that $f(0) = 0$ as a consequence of (1) and (2): there is no recovery without a loss. From (2) there can also be no recovery with a loss. These conditions are related to the monotone and no rip-off conditions, Section 5.2.3.

Schedules that do not satisfy conditions (1)–(5) are uncommon in nonlife insurance. The best known example is a **franchise deductible** or disappearing deductible. With this type of deductible d, if $L < d$ then $f(L) = 0$ but if $L > d$ then $f(L) = L$. Thus f is not continuous and $L - f(L)$ is not monotone. Discontinuities make claim adjusting much more difficult. For franchise deductible, an extra ¤1 of loss can cause $L > d$ and make the entire deductible disappear. A term life insurance policy, which only pays if you die during the term, has nonmonotonic features.

Exercise 122. Show that the **excess of loss** indemnity function $f(L) = (L - a)^+$ satisfies conditions (1)–(5). □

An excess of loss cover pays on the tail event $L > a$. Rothschild-Stiglitz, Section 5.3.2, shows that excess of loss covers are a basic building block of insurance, since higher excess of loss costs appears as one of their three equivalent ways of defining *more risky*. All excess of loss covers are increasing functions of L and there is no diversification between them. They are comonotonic random variables, Section 5.2.10. Any *continuous* increasing indemnity function can be created as a linear combination of excess layers—all securities can be created from options at different strikes. Comonotonic additive risk measures, Section 5.2.11, are additive on excess layers, opening the way to price by layer. This approach is exploited in Chapter 10.

An Arrow-Debreu security (Section 8.6), although natural in finance, is not a natural insurance cover. The corresponding indemnity function satisfies conditions (1) and (2), but not (3)–(5). It would not be offered in the insurance market and it is not a cover our theory tries to price. It cannot be created from a linear combination of excess of loss layers because it is not continuous in the subject loss.

Raviv (1979) shows that the Pareto optimal indemnity function for risk averse individuals has a deductible and coinsurance above the deductible. The insurance payment is an increasing and continuous function of the subject loss.

8.2 Insurer Risk Capital

This section discuses different types of insurer risk capital. It starts with some basic accounting and legal background.

8.2.1 Assets and Liabilities

Liabilities fund assets. Liabilities are sources of funds; assets show how they are used.

Assets are things you own or are owed. Assets are created when a tangible or intangible product or promise is received in exchange for cash or other consideration paid. An outward (ceded) reinsurance contract creates an asset, the reinsurer's promise to pay losses, in exchange for ceded premium. Not all assets are reported in financial statements. Brand value or ownership of renewals, for example, are not included.

Liabilities are things you owe. Liabilities are created when a promise is made in exchange for cash or other consideration received. A bank deposit liability is a promise to repay in exchange for a cash deposit or loan issuance. An insurance policy is a promise to pay losses in exchange for premium. A catastrophe bond is a promise to pay the bond's face value plus interest if no loss occurs in exchange for cash collateral. The amount of cash received for a liability equals its **market value**. Financial reporting takes a more comprehensive approach to booking liabilities than assets.

8.2.2 Insurer Insolvency, Default, and Priority Rules

It is necessary to understand the legal operation of default and insolvency in order to appreciate different types of liabilities and capital. Regulation typically allows a struggling insurer to enter a period of conservation or rehabilitation, where it is placed under regulatory supervision and control as it tries to improve its position. But if these fail, it is put into liquidation. In liquidation, the assets and liabilities are managed separately: the first to maximize their value and the second to ensure an orderly discharge of obligations. Liquidation is managed by a receiver. Policies are canceled. The receiver establishes a **fixing date**, which acts as a deadline for filing claims against the assets.

Pledged assets, such as collateral, are separated. Claims against the remaining assets are sorted into **classes** by **priority** (a.k.a. **pecking order**) that are paid in a waterfall. Within each class all claimants are treated equally. Skeel (2018) says "The equality of creditors norm is widely viewed as the single most important principle in American bankruptcy law."

The exact priority table is specified by statute. In the US, it varies by state. For example, in some states unearned premium has the same priority as insurance claims. Claimants senior to debt are sometimes called **general creditors**. All statutes give a high priority to insured loss claims. Claims include first party claimants and liability claimants whose claims were covered under one of the insurer's policies.

The NAIC Insurance Receivership Model Act Section 801 lists the following priority of distribution. This act has been implemented near-verbatim by many states.

- Class 1. Administrative expenses.
- Class 2. Guarantee association expenses.
- Class 3. All claims under policies of insurance including third-party claims... claims under non-assessable policies for unearned premium. Obligations arising out of reinsurance contracts and obligations to insurance pools (other than direct claims under policies) are not covered in class 3.

- Class 4. All claims under policies of insurance for mortgage guaranty, financial guaranty, or other forms of insurance offering protection against investment risk, or warranties. [Hence mortgage is written in a monoline company.]
- Class 5. Federal government claims.
- Class 6. Debts due employees.
- Class 7. Claims of other unsecured creditors not included in Classes 1 through 6, including claims under reinsurance contracts, claims of guaranty associations for assessments not paid by the insurer, and other claims excluded from Classes 3 or 4 above, unless otherwise assigned to Classes 8 through 13.
- Class 8. Claims of any state or local government.
- Class 11. Surplus notes, capital notes or contribution notes, or similar obligations.
- Class 13. Claims of shareholders or other owners arising out of their capacity as shareholders.... Claims in this class shall be subject to any subordination agreements, related to other claims in this class, that existed prior to the entry of a liquidation order.

Given two classes, the one paid first is **senior** and the one paid second is **subordinated**. The priority table essentially makes insurance claims the most senior claims since receiver's expenses are normally quite small.

Proceeds from assets sales are distributed by priority class, starting with the most senior. Money flows down a waterfall schedule. Since insolvency means liabilities are greater than assets, there are insufficient assets to pay all claimants and so the funds from asset sales are eventually exhausted. Senior priorities are paid in full. Claimants in a midpriority class have their claims pro rated, and claimants in subordinate classes receive nothing. All claimants within each class are treated equally: either they are all paid in full, or their claims are all pro rated down by the same percentage, a process called **equal priority**, or they are paid nothing. Debt holders describe their loss using the **loss given default** percentage.

Common equity is always the lowest priority, most subordinated, class.

Example 123. Ins Co. becomes insolvent with assets of ¤1000. There are no receiver's expenses.

- Given ¤800 insurance claims and ¤300 debt outstanding, claims are paid in full and debt holders paid at a rate 2/3 per ¤1.
- Given ¤1100 insurance claims and ¤300 debt outstanding, claims are pro rated down by a factor 10/11 and debt holders receive nothing. □

When claims for insurance losses and claims for unearned premium have equal priority, unearned premium becomes a claim and reduces the amount available to pay loss claims. However, many US states rank claims for insurance losses above claims for unearned premium in insolvency. (Premium is in the same priority as claims, and not available to pay claims, in: AL, AZ, CA, CO, CT, DE, HI, IA, IL, KS, KY, MT, NC, NH, NJ, NY, OH, OK, OR, PA, RI, TX, UT, VT, WA, WV, and WY.) In that case, we can assume all assets are available to pay claims at intermediate times, with the proviso that any unearned premiums be deducted from net assets prior to distributing the residual value of the firm to shareholders.

A new insurer like Ins Co. has starting assets equal to capital paid-in plus any debt raised. An insurance contract generates an asset for premium, either cash received or premium payable, and an exactly offsetting policyholder liability for unrecognized revenue, called the unearned premium reserve. Thus capital, or net assets, is unchanged after the policy is written. For Ins Co., we circumvent the issue of unearned premium reserves by assuming there are no interim solvency tests between the beginning and end of the operating period. As a result, assets available to pay claims equal starting capital plus premium. Certain regulatory regimes, including Solvency II, require management be able to demonstrate the solvency of their concerns *at all times*, so this assumption is not realistic in all geographies.

National Assocation of Insurance Commissioners (2016) describes the liquidation process in detail for US insurers.

8.2.3 Capital vs. Equity

Capital equals assets net of (minus) all liabilities **owed to policyholders**. The largest policyholder liabilities are loss reserves and unearned premium reserves. In many US states, claims on direct policies have a higher priority than those on reinsurance assumed contracts, but both count as policyholder liabilities. Capital determines an insurer's solvency from the policyholder's perspective, hence statutes regulate minimal capital. An entity can have negative capital but positive accounting equity or market value because of limited liability.

Our definition of capital is consistent with Actuarial Standards Board (2011), *Treatment of Profit and Contingency Provisions and the Cost of Capital in Property-Casualty Insurance Ratemaking*. It defines capital as "The funds intended to assure payment of obligations from insurance contracts, over and above those funds backing the liabilities." It says that

> Capital plays several roles in an insurance transaction, including providing the initial investment in physical plant and equipment and providing working capital. However, the primary role is to assure payment of obligations from insurance contracts, over and above those funds backing the liabilities.

Equity is the value of the owner's residual interest in the firm. It equals assets net of liabilities **owed to all parties** except owners. For a stock company it is called shareholders' equity. In a publicly traded company, equity has a **market value** in addition to various accounting values. The **price-to-book** ratio compares the market and accounting values of equity.

Issuing debt subordinate to policyholder claims but senior to the claims of shareholders increases capital but not equity. Issuing mortgage debt to purchase a home office does not change capital or equity because the asset is pledged as collateral for the loan. Mortgage debt is not subordinate to policyholder claims.

Both equity and capital depend on the specific accounting valuation standards; see Section 8.3.

Capital and equity are liabilities that fund assets and are shown on the liability side of the balance sheet. Non-equity capital, such as debt, is shown explicitly as a liability, whereas equity is separated from more senior liability holders.

Surplus is a US synonym for capital. US statutory accounting balance sheets report the amount of **policyholder surplus** rather than shareholder equity. Historically, policyholder surplus was further split into paid-in capital and net surplus. Owners could contribute to either account. Retained earnings grew net surplus. A new company would be organized with an amount of capital and a separate amount of surplus. Dividends could not be paid out of capital.

Capital has a number of other meanings it is good to be aware of to avoid confusion. The first three are identified by Kieso, Weygandt, and Warfield (2010).

1. **Corporate finance** takes capital to be total assets of the firm, for example capital as plant and equipment.
2. **Legally**, capital is a portion of stockholders' equity that is required by statute to be retained in the business for the protection of creditors. This explains the terminology statutory capital, minimum capital requirements, and solvency capital.
3. **Accountants** use capital to mean owners' equity, i.e. the value of the owner's residual interest under particular accounting assumptions. Equity is distinct from legal capital and may be greater or less than capital.
4. Merton and Perold (1993) define **risk capital** to be "the smallest amount that can be invested to insure the value of the firm's net assets against a loss in value relative to the risk-free investment of those net assets." **Net assets** equal what we call capital: assets net of policyholder liabilities.
5. **Cash capital** is the cash required up front to execute a transaction. It can be large, e.g. to buy a building, or small, e.g. to open a futures position. In insurance it is sometimes called **face capital**. In Mango (2005) it drives the occupancy cost.
6. **Working capital** is cash capital plus other operating expenses.
7. Brealey and Myers (1981) define **working capital** as the difference between current assets and current liabilities and the cumulative capital requirement as the total cost of plant and equipment, financed on a short- and long-term basis.
8. **Regulatory capital** is capital as we have defined it but measured according to a particular statutory accounting standard.

To reiterate, in this book capital refers to assets net of policyholder liabilities and equity refers to the owner's residual value, i.e. assets net of all liabilities.

8.2.4 Types of Insurer Capital

Insurers have access to many different types of capital. Management works to fund capital as efficiently as possible by issuing appropriate liabilities. The optimal capital structure is linked to the shape of the insurer's loss distribution.

Common equity: By law all stock companies must include a lowest priority ownership interest called common shareholders. They bear the ultimate risk and receive the benefit of success. There can be no priority between common shareholders, although they can differ in other ways, such as voting rights. They are the lowest priority class—last in line to be paid in the event of default. They own the residual value of the firm after everyone else has been paid. They have governance rights and appoint the board of directors and management. They can be paid dividends but are not guaranteed any specific payout. They generally have rights to share in any new issues of stock of the same class (the preemptive right). **Franchise value**, including intangible assets such as brand name and renewal rights, is an important part of the value of equity. It is reflected in the market value of equity but not in its accounting value.

The accounting value of common equity is generally reported in three categories:

1. **Capital stock**: equals the **par value** or **stated value** of shares issued.
2. **Additional paid-in capital**: equals the excess of amounts paid-in over par value. It is created when shares are sold at a price higher than par.
3. **Retained earnings**: cumulative undistributed earnings.

Legally, dividends can be paid out of retained earnings but under many laws they may not be paid out of paid-in capital.

Common stockholders generally control the insurer and profit the most if it is successful. They also bear the most risk. Other forms of capital are created to appeal to different types of investor.

Shareholders' liability is limited to the amount of their investment, except if they buy stock under par, which is why par tends to be low. Historically par was higher and not all equity capital was paid-in. In that situation investors were liable for calls on promised capital that had not been paid-in, leading to obvious collection problems.

Mutual insurance companies have a different legal form to stock companies. They are owned by policyholders who have a **noncertificated** ownership interest. They collectively own the equity, just as shareholders do. However, they do not have transferable share certificates and they can only act **collectively** and not individually. A policyholder cannot separately sell their interests. Policyholders have many of the same rights as shareholders, for example they appoint management. A mutual company is generally created under a separate section of the insurance code. The differences between mutual and stock insurance companies can make it challenging for a mutual company to determine its cost of capital. See Powell (2017) for more details about mutual insurers.

Reinsurance capital: Insurers have access to a special form of capital called reinsurance. Reinsurance is usually presented as an income statement transaction: premium and losses are ceded to the reinsurer. It can also be regarded as the sale of the residual value in a specified portion of business to a special class of investors called reinsurers. The reinsurer pays by contributing capital in-kind. At the end of the contract the residual value is transferred to the reinsurer by extinguishing their liability to pay claims.

Reinsurance functions as off-balance sheet capital because regulatory capital formulas operate on a net basis. It is easy to determine the capital equivalence of some forms of reinsurance such as catastrophe occurrence. It is more difficult for others such as casualty quota share. Reinsurance can be issued as an insurance-linked security, such as a catastrophe bond or industry loss warranty.

Collateralized reinsurance capital amounted to nearly USD 100 billion in 2021 and represents about 40% of catastrophe reinsurance protection according to the broker Aon plc. This suggests that reinsurance provides around USD 250 billion of capital globally to bear catastrophe risk, with the US consuming a significant proportion of the total.

Debt capital stands above equity in priority in the event of default. When it is subordinate to insureds' claims it creates capital. In the US, such debt is called a **surplus note**. Surplus notes provide a way for mutual companies to raise capital. Debt can be further tranched into different priorities, such as senior, junior, and mezzanine. It can be collateralized, for example a mortgage. Debt pays a specific coupon that is a tax deductible expense. Failure to pay the coupon or to repay debt when due puts the issuer into default and gives the debtholder the right to take it over.

The US industry makes relatively little use of surplus notes. In 2016, the US PC industry debt to total capital ratio was only 1.7%, stock companies 1.2% and mutual companies 1.8%. Reciprocals used 5.0% surplus notes. Debt is more commonly issued by stock holding companies but contributed as equity to operating insurance subsidiaries. Publicly traded insurers typically have debt to total capital ratios of between 10% and 30%.

Debt can be issued as a security or provided by a bank loan. A bank letter of credit provides contingent debt that is used in some cases to provide regulatory capital.

Preferred equity blends characteristics of debt and equity. It sits above common equity but below debt in priority. It typically pays a specified dividend, but payment can be suspended without triggering default.

Comparison of types of capital. Table 8.2 compares equity, reinsurance, and debt forms of capital. Reinsurance and equity cannot trigger default, whereas failure to pay debt coupons or repay principal does.

Capital structure: Insurance companies combine different forms of capital to fund the assets they need to bear insurance risk. A simple all-equity and a more realistic structure are shown in Figure 8.3. The right-hand diagram is a schematic because most reinsurance cannot be placed at a specified position in the capital tower. The insurer on the right has sufficient assets to pay ¤10B claims, through the use of debt, equity, and reinsurance. However, it is technically insolvent when claims exceed ¤8.5B because the owner's equity is exhausted. In that case, claims would be paid in full but some debt holders would not.

Table 8.2 Comparison of types of insurer capital.

Dimension \ Form	Equity	Reinsurance	Debt
Cost	High	Variable	Variable
Cost certainty	Residual	Contractual	Known
Tax deductible	No	Yes	Yes
Repayment obligation	No	No	Yes
Triggers default	No	No	Yes

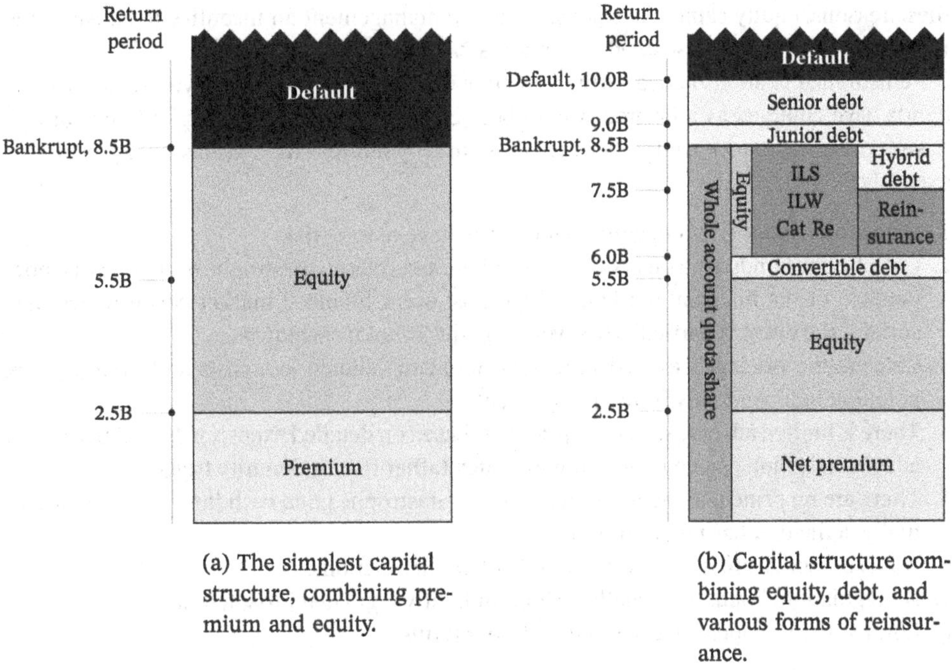

(a) The simplest capital structure, combining premium and equity.

(b) Capital structure combining equity, debt, and various forms of reinsurance.

Figure 8.3 A simple (left) and realistic capital structure (right).

8.2.5 Why Insurer Equity Capital Is Expensive

There are several reasons why insurer equity capital is expensive:

1. **Principal-agent problem**: investors and management do not have perfectly aligned incentives. Insurance is opaque and investors find it very difficult to monitor management. This is especially true for nonstandard lines of business.
2. No independent validation of insurance pricing: insurance is **not expertizable.** Catastrophe risk, where pricing can be evaluated using independent third-party models, is an exception.
3. Equity requires a **long-term commitment** to a cyclical business. Public securities markets provide an exit, but valuations may follow the underwriting cycle.
4. Returns are **left-skewed**. Investors prefer right-skewed returns with a big upside, such as technology stocks (Froot, 2007).
5. **Regulatory minimum capital standards** can force an insurer into supervision before it is technically insolvent. Regulation restricts dividend payments and other capital withdrawals from regulated entities.
6. Returns to investors may be subject to **double taxation**, because the insurer pays corporate taxes and dividend distributions are also taxed. As a result, investors incur an extra tax expense by holding income producing assets in an insurer legal entity.

Principal-agent problems are common to all entities with delegated management. The remaining reasons are peculiar to, or worse for, insurers than other businesses. For all these reasons, equity capital is expensive, giving management an incentive to consider the non-equity alternatives discussed in Section 8.2.4.

Reinsurance is an attractive form of insurer capital. Over the last 30 years, catastrophe bonds have emerged as a favored way to bear catastrophe risk. Catastrophe bonds offer a lower cost of insurance capital because they directly address the reasons equity capital is expensive.

1. Catastrophe bonds are not equity and do not have market risk.
2. Catastrophe bonds are a diversifying, zero-beta asset class: catastrophe occurrence is independent of the financial market, though post-event financial market performance may suffer if the event is particularly severe, e.g. the Tohoku earthquake.
3. Catastrophe pricing is expertizable; investors can validate loss costs and quantify risk potential independently from management.
4. There is limited adverse selection: pricing is based on detailed exposure data. If necessary, adverse selection can be managed with index rather than indemnity triggers.
5. There are no principal-agent problems since catastrophe bond cash flows are all contractually defined: it has no discretion.
6. No taxes: bonds are usually written in tax-free jurisdictions.
7. No regulation: bonds are usually written in lightly regulated jurisdictions.
8. Limited tenor: bonds have defined, 3–5-year terms.

For all of these reasons, most insurers choose to bear some of the catastrophe tail risk in their insurance portfolios using traditional or catastrophe bond reinsurance rather than equity capital. Offsetting these benefits, catastrophe bonds are illiquid and trade in a thin secondary market.

8.2.6 Estimated Cost of Insurer Equity Capital

Actuarial Standards Board (2011), *Treatment of Profit and Contingency Provisions and the Cost of Capital in Property-Casualty Insurance Ratemaking* recommends the following practices relating to the Basis for Cost of Capital Estimates (emphasis added):

> In estimating the cost of capital, the actuary should consider the relationship between risk and return. The methods used for estimating the cost of capital should reflect the risks involved in the risk transfer under consideration. These risks may include insurance, investment, inflation, and regulatory risks, as well as diversification, debt structure, leverage, reinsurance, market structure, and other appropriate aspects of the social, economic, and legal environments. Thus, **the cost of capital is likely to vary from one insurer to another**. The actuary should recognize that the capital which is needed to support any risk transfer has an opportunity cost regardless of the source of capital or the structure of the insurer.

The cost of equity capital is material. According to Cummins and Weiss (2013) the cost of equity capital for US property-casualty insurers is 13%. In total, they report that capital costs amount to 42% of noncapital expenses.

Several studies estimate the cost of equity capital for property-casualty insurers, including Cummins and Phillips (2005), Exley and Smith (2006), Hitchcox *et al.* (2006), Wen *et al.*

(2008), Risk Margin Working Group of the International Actuarial Association (2009), Salzmann and Wüthrich (2010), Cummins *et al.* (2010), Möhr (2011), Floreani (2011), Cummins and Weiss (2013), and Meyers (2019a). These studies produce a broad range of estimates: from 10% to 12% using a CAPM beta model to 17% to 18% using the Fama-French three factor model. Cummins and Weiss (2013) selects a 13.2% cost of capital. In a recent study, Barinov, Xu, and Pottier (2020) considers a multiyear model, reporting that the systematic risk of insurers increases during crises, and that insurance-specific factors, such as underwriting cycles, do not have a statistically significant impact.

Comparing the *expected* cost of equity to *actual* realized returns shows that historically the US property-casualty industry has achieved lower returns, at least on a statutory basis. Between 2001 and 2016 the compound average ROE based on net income to average equity has been 7.3%, 8.0% since 2003, and 8.5% over the last five years. Including changes in unrealized gains and losses, the average ROE since 2001 is 7.9%, 8.8% since 2003, and 9.3% over the last five years.

8.2.7 Weighted Average Cost of Capital

All non-equity capital has an explicit or estimable cost, such as the debt coupon rate or reinsurance premium less expected recoveries. The **weighted average cost of capital** or **WACC** is determined by combining the cost of all forms of capital. The capital benefit from reinsurance can be estimated by considering the reduction in regulatory capital it affords. The cost of equity capital can be estimated using an academic study, Section 8.2.6, or by a peer study considering historical returns, volatility, and observed price-to-book ratios. Return on equity must be high enough to support a reasonable valuation. The next table shows a typical WACC computation. For reinsurance, the cost is ceded premium minus expected recoveries (losses and ceding commissions) and lost investment income. The costs shown are after-tax costs. Debt interest and reinsurance expenses are both tax deductible.

Form of Capital	Amount	Cost
Senior debt	500	0.035
Junior debt	500	0.055
Reinsurance	1,000	0.085
Target ROE	2,500	0.15
WACC	**4,500**	**0.112**

The target ROE, the return on equity capital, drives the WACC since equity capital is usually the most significant proportion of capital, and equity is the most expensive form of capital.

8.2.8 Optimal Capital Structure

Determining the optimal capital structure is an important question in corporate finance. The Modigliani-Miller theorem says that firm value is independent of the mix of debt and equity in a perfect market because an investor can mimic the behavior of a leveraged firm synthetically. In reality, the market is not perfect, most notably because debt interest expense is tax deductible whereas stock dividends are not.

Two important theories of capital structure are the **trade-off theory** and **pecking order theory**. Trade-off argues the debt and equity mix trades off the costs and benefits of each, notably the expense of equity (Section 8.2.5) against the right of debt holders to force bankruptcy. Pecking order agues that informational asymmetries between management and owners makes equity more expensive, favoring internal (retained earnings) financing.

In a study of insurers, Dhaene *et al.* (2017) find that retained earnings are more important and debt is less important for insurers than for other industries, largely because of informational expenses.

Shiu (2011) considers the interaction of reinsurance and capital structure, finding that more leveraged insurers purchase more reinsurance. Cummins, Dionne, and Gagne (2008) analyze the costs and benefits of reinsurance, more as a factor of production than part of financing. As expected, they find that reinsurance reduces the volatility of loss ratio, but at a cost.

Insurer capital structure is a widely discussed topic; see Cummins and Doherty (2002), Hitchcox *et al.* (2006), and Froot (2007) for more.

8.3 Accounting Valuation Standards

Capital and equity depend on the accounting standard used to value assets and liabilities. Insurers are subject to a variety of valuation standards, the three most important being:

1. Statutory or regulatory standards, such as US NAIC, EU Solvency II, APRA.
2. Financial reporting standards, such as GAAP and IFRS.
3. Rating agency standards, such as Standard and Poor's and AM Best's.

Statutory standards generally use conservative valuations. They apply low valuations to assets and disallow or limit items such as goodwill that may never generate cash flow. They apply high valuations to liabilities, disallowing discounting (US Statutory) or adding risk loads (Solvency II, APRA).

Figure 8.4 shows the relationships between market value, shareholder equity, policyholder surplus, and statutory capital.

8.3.1 Default Risk, Accounting Value, Economic Value, and Cash Flow

Policyholders are exposed to default risk because insurers have finite resources. When portfolio losses are greater than the insurer's assets it defaults and insureds do not receive the payments they have been promised. Correctly accounting for default risk requires that estimates be based on the whole distribution of potential outcomes and not just expected values. A better capitalized insurer has a higher fair value premium because it pays more losses; it has a lower expected policyholder deficit. Historically, discounted cash flow models applied discount rates that reflected nondiversifiable risk, but they did not account for the impact

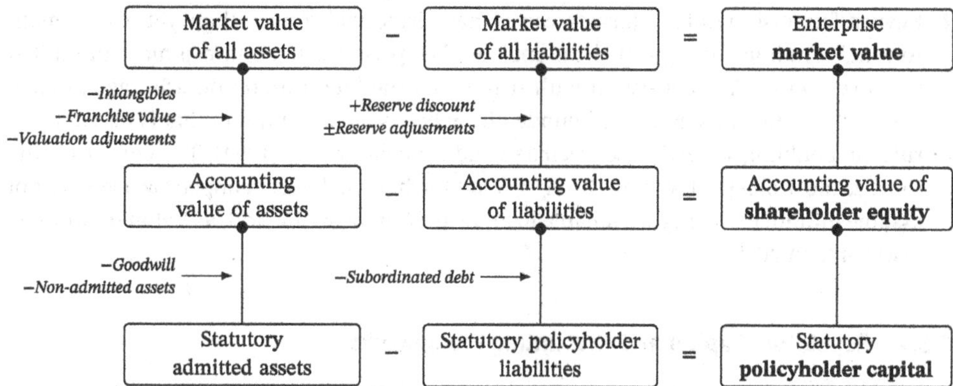

Figure 8.4 Capital, surplus, and equity under market value, accounting and statutory accounting views. Common adjustments are shown in italics. For example, reserves are undiscounted under US GAAP and the market view of loss reserves may differ from management's.

of idiosyncratic risk on loss payments. Later option pricing models took default risk into account.

The relationship between accounting measures and true economics is often questioned. Accounting begins by tracking cash flows but then overlays accrual adjustments in an attempt to match revenue and expense more closely. Depending on its objectives, it can also take a conservative approach to asset valuation. Both types of adjustment can drive a wedge between accounting and economic value.

Pricing and risk models often use an economic accounting or a risk capital balance sheet in order to correct for perceived shortfalls of accounting. For example, Merton and Perold (1993) create a risk capital balance sheet, Sherris (2006) an economic balance sheet, and Myers and Read Jr. (2001) and Erel, Myers, and Read (2013) a market value balance sheet.

Ultimately, cash is king and it makes sense to adjust accounting to reflect true economics, but these adjustments must not overlook the following two important considerations.

1. Accounting conventions have *real world consequences*. A company defaults based on its accounts, not a hypothetical risk balance sheet. Investor owners do not bounce back from company insolvency: they are wiped out, even if the company continues after a reorganization. (AIG was forced into government ownership on the basis of mark-to-market asset valuation adjustments and collateral calls, not an inability to pay claims.) Insurers face an even stricter standard than accounting solvency. Regulators have the right to appoint a conservator and take over the running of an insurer when its statutory capital falls below prescribed minimum levels, creating an *effective ruin* while still technically solvent. Minimum capital levels are often quite low, but statutory capital uses conservative accounting and statutory capital can be materially lower than financial capital. The regulatory take-over option creates a drag on value for owners that can be important in a multiyear, franchise value model; see Froot, Venter, and Major (2004) and Major (2009). As a result, statutory and financial accounting have a direct effect on cash flows, and hence economics, and it is necessary to track both to model economic value correctly.

2. Keynes famously wrote "Markets can remain irrational longer than you can remain solvent." Trading through an irrational market period can require almost unlimited resources, which is inconsistent with reality and the literature on no-arbitrage pricing. Generally trading processes are bounded from below, an assumption that is necessary to rule out doubling strategies; see Delbaen and Schachermayer (1994). The concern is the same as the problem of trading through default: what if it doesn't happen? Models cannot assume infinite financing is available to an insurer in the real world, as Lehman Brothers discovered in 2008.

8.3.2 Regulatory Capital and Accounting Frameworks

Every major developed economy regulates insurance. Regulation focuses on solvency and emphasizes risk-based capital standards (Cummins and Phillips, 2009). This section gives a high-level summary of some of the important differences in accounting treatments.

Solvency II. Solvency II considers a balance sheet consisting of assets, liabilities, and own funds, (EIOPA and Authority, 2014). It uses market valuation of assets and books liabilities on a best estimate basis plus a risk margin. Own funds comprises three parts.

1. Minimum Capital Requirement (MCR) below which the entity withdraws from the market. It is the lowest acceptable capital level.
2. Solvency Capital Requirement (SCR) estimated via the standard formula, internal model, or combination.
3. Free assets, or amounts in excess of SCR.

Solvency II uses a one-year stability criterion. Article 101 of the Solvency II Directive states, "The Solvency Capital Requirement (SCR) shall correspond to the Value-at-Risk (VaR) of the basic own funds of an insurance or reinsurance undertaking subject to a confidence level of 99.5% over a one-year period."

Table 8.4 Comparison of solvency frameworks across select jurisdictions.

Region	Assets	Liability	Risk Metric
US	US SAP	US SAP	Various
EU	IFRS based	Market consistent	VaR
Switzerland	Market consistent	Market consistent	TVaR
China	IFRS based	DCF	VaR
Japan	Japan GAAP	Market consistent	VaR
Canada	IFRS based	DCF	TVaR/VaR
Australia	IFRS based	DCF	VaR
Brazil	IFRS based	DCF (LAT Test)	VaR
Singapore	IFRS based	DCF	VaR
Mexico	IFRS compatible	DCF	VaR
S. Africa	IFRS based	DCF	VaR

NAIC Statutory Accounting (SAP). US Statutory Accounting is a **liquidation basis** accounting. Regulators evaluate the balance sheet to determine if enough funds exist to pay current and future policyholder benefits. **Non-admitted assets** consists of items that are not liquid or that cannot be readily converted to cash to pay policyholder benefits. They are not counted as assets. Insurer liabilities are booked on a net basis. Policy acquisition expenses are earned when written.

Generally Accepted Accounting Principles (GAAP). US GAAP follow US statutory treatment for loss reserves: they are booked as management's best estimate on a nominal basis with no risk adjustment. However, unlike statutory accounting, the GAAP reserve liability is gross of reinsurance, and reinsurance recoverables are booked as a separate asset. GAAP allows acquisition expenses to be deferred, unlike statutory accounting. This creates the deferred acquisition expense asset.

International Financial Reporting Standards (IFRS). IFRS accounting is more market value oriented than GAAP. Loss reserves are valued on a discounted basis including a risk adjustment. Under IFRS 17, the risk adjustment for nonfinancial risk should reflect "…the compensation an entity requires for bearing the uncertainty about the amount and timing of the cash flows that arises from nonfinancial risks as the entity fulfills insurance contracts." As a result, profits on an insurance policy are earned over the payout period of reserves, rather than being fully earned at the end of the policy period.

Rating Agency Evaluations. Rating agencies adjust statutory or GAAP financials in their internal capital models. Common adjustments include:

- The removal of goodwill and intangible assets that never turn into cash.
- The addition of discount in loss reserves when reserves are booked on a nominal basis.
- The explicit quantification of catastrophe risk using a model evaluation. Net, after-tax losses at a 100- or 250-year return period are used, on either an occurrence or aggregate basis.

8.3.3 Taxes

Tax is extremely complex. It varies by geography and changes frequently. It requires its own dedicated book to treat in detail. Here are some basic modeling guidelines.

- A very simple approach to tax is to convert the cost of capital into a pre-tax cost and then to ignore it.
- Use the correct marginal rate for each cash flow. For example, if underwriting losses and capital gains are taxed at different rates then the different marginal rates should be applied to each.
- Beware tax loss carry forwards. They require future operating income to realize. They are generally nontransferable. Under US statutory accounting they are only admitted if the insurer passes certain stringent tests. For example, they are limited as a proportion of surplus.
- Follow the precepts of discounted cash flows (DCF). Look at the timing of tax payments. Discount them at the appropriate rates depending on whether they apply to risky or risk-free cash flows.

8.4 Actuarial Premium Calculation Principles and Classical Risk Theory

Having laid important groundwork in the earlier sections of this chapter, we can now begin our chronological presention of Classical Portfolio Pricing.

In this section, we present some common actuarial **premium calculation principles** (PCPs). These give a risk theoretic solution to pricing that is typically concerned with solvency, the probability of ruin, or risk attitudes. Unlike financial models, the premium is not directly linked to the cost of capital.

8.4.1 Actuarial Premium Calculation Principles

Bühlmann (1970) and Goovaerts, De Vylder, and Haezendonck (1984) define a **classical** or **objective** or **actuarial** premium calculation principle to be a functional that determines premium from a loss distribution—rather than a random variable. Classical PCPs are therefore law invariant, Section 5.2.13. Law invariance assures that premium can be estimated from a statistical fit to the underlying loss distribution. It is objective in the sense of only depending on the insured's estimated loss distribution and not other variables such as the cause of loss or the state of the market.

Expected value is the simplest classical PCP. It is justified by the law of large numbers. It is fair and consistent with finance in a risk neutral world. It is not universally adopted because of the **Fundamental Theorem of Risk Theory**, which says that an insurer charging the expected loss rate is guaranteed to fail in a finite length of time regardless of its starting surplus. Since no one wants to buy insurance from, or work for, an insurer guaranteed to have a finite life expectancy, risk loads are positive.

There are a large number of law invariant risk measures that can be used as classical PCPs. In the following formulas, π corresponds to a safety level or loading, with higher π producing higher premiums. An annotation (IPm.n) refers to the relevant section of Goovaerts, De Vylder, and Haezendonck (1984) (a whole book about classical PCPs) and (K.a) to Kaas *et al.* (2008), Section 5.3. See also Laeven and Goovaerts (2008).

1. **Net** premium (K.a): $P = \mathsf{E}[X]$.
2. **Expected value** or **constant loading** premium (IP2.3, K.b): $P = \mathsf{E}[X] + \pi\mathsf{E}[X]$.
3. **Maximum loss** premium (IP2.4, K.i): $P = \mathsf{E}[X] + \pi \max(X)$.
4. **Value at Risk** or **Percentile** premium (K.h): $P = \mathsf{VaR}_\pi(X)$. VaR fails positive loading, which is a serious drawback. VaR is a generalization of maximum loss.
5. **Tail Value at Risk** premium: $P = \mathsf{TVaR}_\pi(X)$.
6. **Variance** premium (IP2.5, K.c): $P = \mathsf{E}[X] + \pi\mathsf{Var}(X)$.
7. **Standard deviation** premium (IP2.6, K.d): $P = \mathsf{E}[X] + \pi\mathsf{SD}(X)$.
8. **Semivariance** premium (IP2.7): $P = \mathsf{E}[X] + \pi\mathsf{Var}^+(X)$, where $\mathsf{Var}^+(X) = \int_{\mathsf{E}[X]}^\infty (x - \mathsf{E}[X])^2 f(x)dx$ is the positive semivariance.
9. **Mean value** premium (IP2.8, K.g): P solves $f(P) = \mathsf{E}[f(X)]$, where f is a continuous, strictly increasing function defined on the range of X.

10. **Zero Utility** premium (IP2.9, K.f): P solves $\mathsf{E}[u(P-X)] = 0$ where u is a continuous, nondecreasing, concave function with $u(0) = 0$ and $u'(0) = 1$ describing the utility of outcomes to the insurer. Utility is usually computed with respect to a wealth level, which complicates its application. The zero utility principle side-steps the wealth problem by equating the expected utility of the net position after collecting premium and paying losses to the utility of zero. The condition $u'(0) = 1$ means the insurer is approximately risk neutral for small risks.
11. **Swiss** premium (IP2.10): P solves $\mathsf{E}[f(X-\pi P)] = f((1-\pi)P)$ where f is a continuous, monotonic function. If f is increasing and concave and $\pi = 1$ the Swiss premium reduces to the zero utility premium. If f is increasing and $\pi = 0$ then it reduces to the mean value principle.
12. **Exponential** premium (K.e): is obtained as the zero utility premium for exponential utility $u(x) = (1-e^{-\pi x})/\pi$. A quick calculation shows $P = \log(\mathsf{E}[e^{\pi X}])/\pi$. The exponential premium is motivated by the Cramer-Lundberg formula; see Eq. (8.3). Gerber (1974) shows the zero utility premium is additive for independent risks iff utility is exponential.
13. **Esscher** premium (IP2.12, K.j): $P = \mathsf{E}[Xe^{\pi X}]/\mathsf{E}[e^{\pi X}]$ arises as the mean of the exponential tilt of X. The Esscher premium is discussed in Deprez and Gerber (1985) and Van Heerwaarden, Kaas, and Goovaerts (1989).
14. **Higher-order p deviation** premium: $P = \mathsf{E}[X] + \pi\mathsf{E}[|X - \mathsf{E}[X]|^p]^{1/p}$. When $p = 2$ the higher-order deviation is the standard deviation premium and when $p = \infty$ it is the maximum loss premium. It is coherent when $p = 1$ and $0 \le \pi \le 0.5$. It is not MON for any $p > 1$.
15. **Semideviation (Dutch)** premium: $P = \mathsf{E}[X] + \pi\mathsf{E}[(X-\mathsf{E}[X])^+]$, $0 \le \pi \le 1$. The Dutch premium is discussed at length in Heerwaarden and Kaas (1992).
16. **Higher-order p semideviation (Fischer)** premium: $P = \mathsf{E}[X]+\pi\mathsf{E}[((X-\mathsf{E}[X])^+)^p]^{1/p}$, $0 \le \pi \le 1$ and $1 \le p \le \infty$. The case $p = 1$ gives the Dutch principle. These risk measures are investigated in Fischer (2003).
17. **Higher-order p semideviation from target** premium: $P = \mathsf{E}[X]+\pi\mathsf{E}[((X-\tau)^+)^p]^{1/p}$, $1 \le p \le \infty$.

Further principles are possible based on the risk measures listed in Section 6.5. Classical PCPs are applied in Chapter 9.

8.4.2 Classical Risk Theory and the Pollaczeck-Khinchine Formula

The Pollaczeck-Khinchine formula determines the probability of eventual ruin in a portfolio where claims are driven by a compound Poisson process, in terms of starting surplus and the premium rate. The following notation is used only in this and the next subsection. Losses are generated by a Poisson process with λ annual expected claims and iid severity X. Losses up to time t are given by

$$A(t) = X_1 + \ldots + X_{N(t)},$$

where $N(t)$ is Poisson with mean λt. Expected loss per year equals $\lambda\mathsf{E}[X]$. Premium per year equals $(1+r)\lambda\mathsf{E}[X]$ where r is the ratio of profit to expected loss. The corresponding expected loss ratio is $1/(1+r)$. If $r \le 0$ then eventual ruin is certain, so assume $r > 0$.

Define the **integrated severity distribution** by

$$F_I(x) = \frac{1}{\mathsf{E}[X]}\int_0^x S(t)dt = 1 - \frac{\mathsf{E}[(X-x)^+]}{\mathsf{E}[X]}$$

where S is the survival function of X. F_I is a thicker tailed distribution than F. Let

$$U_{u,r}(t) = u + (1+r)\lambda\mathsf{E}[X]t - A(t)$$

denote accumulated surplus to time t given starting surplus u. U is called the **surplus process**. Finally, let

$$\psi(u,r) = \mathsf{Pr}(U_{u,r}(t) < 0 \text{ for some } t \geq 0) \tag{8.1}$$

be the probability of eventual ruin.

The **Pollaczeck-Khinchine formula** says that

$$\psi(u,r) = 1 - \frac{r}{1+r}\sum_{n\geq 0}(1+r)^{-n}F_I^{n*}(u) \tag{8.2}$$

where F_I^{n*} is distribution of the sum of n independent variables with distribution F_I. Note that

$$G(z) = \frac{r}{1+r}\sum_{n\geq 0}(1+r)^{-n}z^n = \frac{r}{1+r-z}$$

is the probability generating function of a geometric distribution M with mean $1/r$ and $\mathsf{Pr}(M=m) = \frac{r}{1+r}\frac{1}{(1+r)^m}$. Therefore $\psi(u) = \mathsf{Pr}(Y > u)$ where Y is an aggregate distribution with frequency M and severity F_I. A surprising consequence is that the probability of eventual ruin starting with no surplus, $\psi(0) = 1 - \mathsf{Pr}(Y=0) = 1 - \mathsf{Pr}(M=0) = \frac{1}{1+r}$, the expected loss ratio! Embrechts, Klüppelberg, and Mikosch (1997, Section 1.2) shows how to derive the Pollaczeck-Khinchine formula. The key step is to determine the distribution of $X - (1+r)T$ where T is the exponential waiting time between claims, and to observe that ruin can occur only at the moment of a claim. The distribution of Y can be computed using Fast Fourier transforms in the same way as any aggregate distribution, (Mildenhall, 2005), though some care is needed because the claim count is very large when the margin is very small.

The Pollaczeck-Khinchine formula gives combinations of u and r that are consistent with a top-down stability requirement expressed as a target probability of eventual ruin. Overlaying a cost of capital provides a link between r and u that determines a minimum viable market size. An example of this method is given in Section 9.3.2.

Because *eventual* is the same in days, weeks, or years, $\psi_{X,m}(u)$ is independent of the expected claim count λ. In unit of time $1/\lambda$ all portfolios have an expected claim count of one. Therefore $\psi^{-1}(p)$ gives a capital requirement (risk measure) that is a function of severity and not frequency, i.e. it is independent of portfolio size. Unlike most risk measures, it does not regard small portfolios as more risky than large ones.

The **Cramer-Lundberg formula** is an approximation to ψ that applies for thin-tailed severities. It says that

$$\psi(u, r) \le e^{-ku}$$

where $k > 0$ is a constant called the **adjustment coefficient** solving

$$e^{kP} = \mathsf{E}[e^{kA(1)}]$$

where $P = (1 + r)\lambda\mathsf{E}[X]$ is the premium. Given a top-down stability requirement, we can work backward from the Cramer-Lundberg formula to determine a premium.

Exercise 124. Show that if $k = -\log(p)/u$ and premium

$$P = \frac{1}{k}\log\mathsf{E}[e^{kA(1)}], \tag{8.3}$$

then the Cramer-Lundberg formula ensures the probability of eventual ruin is $\le p$. The properties of P given by Eq. (8.3) motivate the exponential premium. In turn, the approximation $P \approx \mathsf{E}[A(1)] + k\mathsf{Var}(A(1))/2$ motivates the variance principle. □

Both the Cramer-Lundberg and Pollaczeck-Khinchine formulas assume independent and identically distributed severity and Poisson frequency. These can be reasonable assumptions for the loss process of a small portfolio. The case of a mixed Poisson can be decomposed as a mixture of pure Poisson processes.

8.4.3 Premium Calculation from the Top Down

The Pollaczeck-Khinchine formula (Section 8.4.2) from classical risk theory gives a relationship between the probability of eventual ruin, the amount of starting assets, the risk loading, and properties of the loss process. This relationship leads to the idea of premium calculation from the **top down** (Bühlmann, 1985). The insurer establishes a **stability criterion**, which may be expressed as a ruin criterion or based on a regulatory or rating agency risk-based capital formula. Classical risk theory determines combinations of starting assets and risk loads consistent with the stability criterion. In a more modern approach, required assets and investor return requirements combine to determine the split of assets into premium and investor funding.

Bühlmann bemoans the existence of bottom-up pricing, which neglects to check whether total premium obtained by aggregating policy premiums satisfies a reasonable stability criterion. He says that

> [T]his bottom up philosophy is unreasonable. Premiums of individual risks are not exclusively determined by this individual risk but (at least in the choice of values of certain parameters) do depend on the portfolio to which they belong.

In this book we follow Bühlmann's top-down philosophy and start by pricing Ins Co.'s total portfolio. We assume an externally imposed stability criterion, expressed through a capital risk measure, determines the required level of assets. We then determine funding for the whole portfolio (Part II) and allocate it by unit (Part III).

8.5 Investment Income in Pricing

8.5.1 US Actuarial Practice

This section reviews how pricing evolved to include investment income, the differences between average timing, timing risk and amount risk, and the Ferrari decomposition of operating returns.

In the US, incorporating investment income into pricing proceeded in fits and starts over a number of decades, and was accompanied by considerable controversy.

The risk theoretic methods in Section 8.4 largely reflect European scholarship. In the US, practice was hijacked by the National Convention of Insurance Commissioners' 1921 Standard Profit Formula that stated, among other things (Solberg, 1957):

- Underwriting profit excludes "so-called banking profit," i.e, investment income.
- A reasonable underwriting profit is "six percent of premium rates consisting of five percent for profit and one percent for catastrophes (conflagrations)."

As a result, US thoughts about profit margins tended to be divorced from both insurance risk and return on capital. An endless debate about the inclusion of investment income ensued. Readers today likely don't know Plotkin. He caused considerable discombobulation among US actuaries by suggesting that investment income be accounted for in rates! Today we take that as self-evident, but it was not always the case.

> Since that fateful day in 1967 when Irving H. Plotkin burst upon the insurance scene, the insurance industry has been treated to an awesome swirl of new ideas, concepts and intellectual, as well as operational, challenges. Reactions have ranged from outrage that the hallowed truths of our forefathers should even be questioned, to prompt assimilation because "that's what I've been thinking all along". In between lie the group who struggled to understand, to evaluate, and to reach considered conclusions. Noting that about 50% of the current Fellows of the Casualty Actuarial Society reached their fellowship since 1967, we are passing into the era where we have educated our people as much on "Plotkin-theory" as we have on "1921-theory". I hope this is one of the last times that I will have to read about the evils of the 1921 NAIC profit formula. Resisting the temptation to rationalize or explain, I would only ask where economic theory was in 1921 compared to modern views and in the same breath ask where actuarial theory was as well. As the author says "The pre-tax underwriting profit allowance continues as a useful and even necessary regulatory tool for rate review" but let's not either idolize it as the only measure nor deprecate it as a useful measure. (Simon, 1979)

8.5.2 Investment Income in Ratemaking

The Commissioners' Standard Profit Formula explicitly excluded *banking* profits or losses, that is, investment income. Between 1923 and 1928, a minority opinion held that the overall allowance for profit, including investment income, was excessive.

AM Best's insurance reports from the 1930s discuss the analysis of insurance company accounts. They state that the usual method of computing underwriting results is incomplete because it excludes investment income on reserve funds insurers hold "solely because they transact an *insurance* business" and that are not contributions from stockholders. They go on, "It seems clear to us that at least a part of the interest earned by the companies upon the invested portion of these amounts should be considered, from the economic standpoint, to be part of the underwriting income, and adjusted with the underwriting profit or loss as usually computed." The question of *how much* of the interest earned should be credited depends on the details of each insurer's operations.

The 94% target survived the South East Underwriters Supreme Court case and was reiterated in 1955 by the Inter-Regional Insurance Conference (Magrath, 1958). A 5% provision for underwriting and contingencies in general liability is described as "constant for all liability insurance lines in most states" by Lange (1966). Kallop (1975) states that a 2.5% profit and contingency allowance for workers' compensation has been in use for "at least 25 years" and that it "contemplates additional profits from other sources to realize an adequate rate level." The higher load for property lines was justified by the possibility of catastrophic losses—meaning large conflagration losses, rather than today's meaning of hurricane, earthquake, or related catastrophes.

Regulators and actuaries focused more on investment income in the late 1960s. Bailey (1967) introduced actuaries to the idea of including investment income in profit. High interest rates through the 1970s and 1980s, which led to cash-flow underwriting, made the topic very relevant. During the 1970s actuaries developed techniques to include investment income in ratemaking, and financial economists began to consider how to determine a fair rate of return on insurance capital. The theoretical results they derived, summarized in Myers and Cohn (1987), focused on the use of discounted cash flow models, often using CAPM-derived discount rates for each cash flow, including taxes. Since CAPM prices only systematic risk, a side-effect of the financial work was to ignore idiosyncratic losses in setting profit provisions. The models also ignore the possibility of insurer default.

8.5.3 Timing, Timing Risk, and Amount Risk

The economic cost of insurance risk transfer depends on the timing of loss payments. Payments have timing risk and amount risk. These two may be dependent because larger claims often take longer to settle. Timing risk tends to be quite tame since payout patterns follow a predictable claim settlement process, regulated by the cadences of medicine and law.

There is a difference between a payment's *average* timing, its timing risk, and its amount risk. The economic impact of average timing (i.e. time value of money) always remains, even when timing and amount *risk* diversify away.

8.5.4 The Ferrari Decomposition of Operating Returns

Ferrari (1968) considered return on investor equity as well as margin on premium. He decomposes total return on equity into underwriting and investment income returns

$$
\begin{aligned}
TR &= \frac{\text{Income}}{\text{Equity}} \\
&= \frac{U+I}{Q} \\
&= \frac{U}{P}\frac{P}{Q} + \frac{I}{a}\frac{a}{Q} \\
&= (\text{Underwriting margin}) \times (\text{Underwriting leverage}) \\
&\qquad + (\text{Investment return}) \times (\text{Investment leverage})
\end{aligned}
$$

where U is underwriting income, P premium, I investment income, Q equity, and a assets. Today this formula seems straightforward and uncontroversial. At the time the idea of linking return to the amount of equity invested, rather than to the premium measure of insurance volume, was novel.

Assets $a = Q + R$ are funded by equity Q and policyholder funds R that, in turn, are comprised of loss reserves and some portion of unearned premium reserves. Thus $a/Q = 1 + R/Q$ and the total return can be decomposed as

$$
\begin{aligned}
TR &= \frac{U+I}{Q} \\
&= \frac{U}{Q} + \frac{I}{a}\frac{a}{Q} \\
&= \frac{U}{Q} + \frac{I}{a}\left(1 + \frac{R}{Q}\right) \\
&= \frac{I}{a} + \frac{U}{Q} + \frac{I}{a}\frac{R}{Q} \\
&= \frac{I}{a} + \frac{R}{Q}\left(\frac{I}{a} + \frac{U}{R}\right).
\end{aligned}
$$

The last expression shows policyholder-funded asset leverage of R/Q magnifies the net cost of policyholder provided funds $(I/a + U/R)$. Leverage is beneficial when $I/a + U/R > 0$, meaning the cost of the insurance *float* is negative, as Warren Buffett phrases it.

Given an allocation of capital, the same algebra can be applied by unit since the attribution of reserves by unit is known.

Ferrari describes reserves as leverage inducing non-equity capital. He states that an actuarial determination of the optimum capital structure must factor in underwriting and investment income variability. He concludes:

> According to financial theory, it is [total] return that management should be attempting to maximize. It appears, however, that management in general, and [US]actuaries in particular, have been overly zealous in addressing themselves to regulators rather than the shareholders. In order to remedy this imbalance, current techniques of ratemaking and rate regulation may have to undergo traumatic procedural and philosophical changes to properly accommodate the introduction of investment considerations into the ratemaking process.

These changes occurred over the next twenty years.

8.6 Financial Valuation and Perfect Market Models

Financial economists developed powerful asset valuation models such as CAPM and Black-Scholes in the 1960s and 1970s. We can apply these models to insurance by treating an insurance contract as a security. In this section, we cover the theory and assumptions underlying the CAPM and Black-Scholes asset valuations.

The most important assumptions in the academic literature are that financial markets are competitive, perfect, complete, and arbitrage-free with pricing determined in a general equilibrium framework. Here is what these terms mean.

Competitive has its standard microeconomics meaning: many small sellers and buyers and undifferentiated products.

Perfect means there are no information or transaction costs, and no bid-ask spread. There is the ability to borrow or lend at the same risk-free rate, and there are no restrictions on short sales. There are no taxes. Perfect markets are sometimes called frictionless.

A **security** is a set of cash flows. It is defined as a random variable on a sample space Ω. An individual sample point $\omega \in \Omega$ is interpreted as a possible *future state of the world* or *state of nature*. Throughout this section we assume Ω is finite. The value $X(\omega)$ gives the cash flow in state ω. In a **complete** market there are enough securities that it is possible to **replicate** any set of future period cash flows by securities trading. The specific securities used are called a **replicating portfolio.**

An **Arrow-Debreu security** pays ¤1 in a single future state ω and 0 in all other states. Its payout is given by the indicator function 1_ω. When Ω is finite, any security X can be built from Arrow-Debreu securities as

$$X \equiv \sum_{\omega} X(\omega) 1_\omega$$

since $X(\omega') = \sum_\omega X(\omega)1_\omega(\omega')$. (Remember $1_\omega(\omega') = 1$ if $\omega' = \omega$ and 0 if $\omega' \neq \omega$.)

Securities whose value can be determined from the value of other securities are called **redundant.** Options are redundant securities: they do not add to the set of cash flows an investor can generate. Securities that are not redundant are called **fundamental**. A company's common stock is a fundamental security. An **incomplete** market is one which is not complete. There are future cash flows that cannot be replicated by trading in securities.

An **arbitrage** is a money-making machine: it is an opportunity for a gain in some possible state of the world with no chance of a loss, for zero initial investment. No arbitrage implies that the pricing operator ρ is **linear**: $\rho(aX+bY) = a\rho(X)+b\rho(Y)$ for securities X, Y and constants a, b. If this were not the case there would be arbitrage opportunities from assembling or disassembling portfolios. In particular, linear implies **additive**, $\rho(X+Y) = \rho(X) + \rho(Y)$ and **homogeneous**, $\rho(aX) = a\rho(X)$. A positive homogeneous risk measure satisfies the same condition but only for $a \geq 0$.

Prices generated by a linear pricing rule have no **bid-ask spread**. The price $\rho(X)$ is understood as the price paid to the seller of X; it is the **ask price**. The **bid price**, the price to short X, is $-\rho(-X)$, since selling $-X$ is the same as buying X with the opposite flow of cash at purchase. Since an additive pricing functional is automatically normalized ($\rho(0) = \rho(0+0) = \rho(0)+\rho(0)$ implies $\rho(0) = 0$) it follows that $\rho(X-X) = \rho(X)+\rho(-X) = 0$ and so $\rho(X) = -\rho(-X)$, showing the ask price equals the bid price.

General equilibrium means the market clears and supply equals demand. No actor has an incentive to trade to improve their position and everyone agrees all products are fairly priced. General equilibrium prices are no arbitrage in a perfect market, because if there were arbitrage opportunities the prices would not be in equilibrium. Traders would take advantage of the arbitrage opportunity, and their trades would move prices. A set of prices is consistent with equilibrium provided there is at least one rational actor who prefers more to less and who is satisfied with their position, because the perfect market assumptions allow that actor to execute an arbitrage at arbitrary scale—and move market prices—if they are unsatisfied. In fact, the **Fundamental Theorem of Asset Pricing**, Dybvig and Ross (1992), says the following are equivalent:

1. Absence of arbitrage,
2. The existence of an optimal demand for some agent who prefers more to less, and
3. The existence of a positive linear pricing rule.

The Fundamental Theorem is best understood using Arrow-Debreu securities. The security 1_ω has actuarial value $\mathsf{P}(\omega)$, the probability that state ω occurs. Its market value equals $Z(\omega)\mathsf{P}(\omega)$ where Z, the **stochastic discount rate,** determines the market value *discount* relative to the actuarial value. $Z(\omega) > 0$ by no arbitrage. Stochastic discount rates are also called **state price densities, pricing kernels**, or **deflators.**

In an uncertain world, ¤1 is worth more in some future states than in others. In states of plenty it is worth less and $Z(\omega) < 1$ whereas in meager states it is worth more and $Z(\omega) > 1$. This follows from decreasing marginal utility.

By no arbitrage, the market value of a general security X must be

$$\sum_\omega X(\omega)Z(\omega)\mathsf{P}(\omega). \tag{8.4}$$

Eq. (8.4) is the linear (in X) pricing rule promised by part (3) of the Fundamental Theorem.

The present value of a certain 1 in *every* future state is $\sum_\omega Z(\omega)\mathsf{P}(\omega) = \mathsf{E}[Z]$, which, by definition, equals the risk-free discount rate $1/(1+r)$.

The stochastic discount rate and underlying probability function can be combined into an **risk-adjusted probability** function Q defined by

$$\mathsf{Q}(\omega) = Z(\omega)\mathsf{P}(\omega)(1+r) = \frac{Z(\omega)\mathsf{P}(\omega)}{\mathsf{E}[Z]}.$$

$\mathsf{Q}(\omega) \ge 0$ and Q is a probability because $\sum_\omega \mathsf{Q}(\omega) = \mathsf{E}[Z]/\mathsf{E}[Z] = 1$. Note that $(1+r)Z = \mathsf{Q}/\mathsf{P}$ is the **likelihood ratio** between Q and P, familiar from statistics. In a continuous model, it is the density of Q with respect to P, justifying state price *density*. It is a positive random variable with mean 1. The market value of X can now be rewritten as the risk-adjusted expected present value

$$\frac{1}{1+r}\sum_\omega X(\omega)\mathsf{Q}(\omega).$$

Q must be unique. If there were two such they have to agree on all securities by no arbitrage. Conversely if there is a risk-adjusted probability Q then it produces no arbitrage equilibrium prices with stochastic discount rate $Z(\omega) = \dfrac{1}{1+r}\dfrac{\mathsf{Q}(\omega)}{\mathsf{P}(\omega)}$ by considering its price for Arrow-Debreu securities.

The stochastic discount rate reflects aggregate supply and demand for securities across future states. From the properties of Z, we see that Q makes states of plenty less likely and meager states more likely. Since insurance contracts respond in states where things are going poorly, they tend to have a greater market value than their actuarial value: premium is greater than expected loss cost.

The nondiversifiable risk of a security X is quantified by covariance with the stochastic discount rate:

$$\begin{aligned}
\frac{1}{1+r}\mathsf{E}_{\mathsf{Q}}[X] &= \frac{1}{1+r}\sum_{\omega} X(\omega)\mathsf{Q}(\omega)\\
&= \sum_{\omega} X(\omega)Z(\omega)\mathsf{P}(\omega)\\
&= \mathsf{E}[XZ]\\
&= \mathsf{E}[X]\mathsf{E}[Z] + \mathsf{cov}(X, Z)\\
&= \frac{1}{1+r}\mathsf{E}[X] + \mathsf{cov}(X, Z).
\end{aligned}$$

The first term in the last line is the risk-free expected value of X and the second is a risk margin determined by the covariance of X with Z. This derivation is general and, unlike CAPM, does not assume normally distributed returns or quadratic utility or utility that is a function of mean and variance. It just reflects the fact that Z captures information about whether the world is in a good or bad state.

There are two broad classes of general equilibrium models distinguished by the securities they price.

1. **Classical** general equilibrium models price fundamental securities like stocks or insurance policies. Classical models price based on supply and demand and rely on diversification and pooling to manage risk. CAPM is the archetype. Early discounted cash flow models apply CAPM to insurance. We explore this further in Section 8.7.
2. **Derivative** general equilibrium models price redundant securities like stock options. They rely on the fact that a redundant security can be replicated by securities trading, and equate price with the cost of creating the replicating portfolio. Derivative general equilibrium models do not rely on diversification or pooling to manage risk. Black-Scholes is the archetype. We explore this further in Section 8.8.

Derivative general equilibrium models rely on replicating portfolios to hedge risk and do not use risk pooling. They have no need for insurers or capital. They price a security as the least cost of setting up a self-financing replicating portfolio. Risk bearing with a replicating portfolio is costly because replicating portfolios typically experience trading losses. For example, hedging a call uses a buy high, sell low strategy: at expiration the portfolio must own 1 stock if the price is *above* the strike but none if *below*. Replicating portfolios provide (theoretical) unlimited protection, unlike insurance solutions based on risk pooling with a capital back stop, which provide only probabilistic protection. To provide unlimited protection through pooling requires infinite capital for unbounded risks, which has infinite cost when capital is costly. Replication methods function as though backed by unlimited capital, a virtual *capital spigot*. It is important to remember that they do not rely on pooling and diversification to bear risk.

It is not enough to simply assert general equilibrium prices exist. We must specify the actors and restrictions and solve an optimization to prove it. A nice example of what is entailed to determine general equilibrium prices for catastrophe risk is provided in Meyers (1992) and Meyers (1996). The first paper also derives a CAPM-like model and draws out its connections with insurance. Dothan (1990) gives the same details for the Black-Scholes market.

Goldfarb (2006) provides a good introduction to the topics in this section, written for actuaries. Ingersoll (1987), Cochrane (2009), Duffie (2010), and Föllmer and Schied (2011) are finance-oriented treatments. Arrow-Debreu securities are introduced in Debreu (1959).

The discounted cash flow and internal rate of return models, described in Section 8.7 and the option pricing model, described in Section 8.8 are two of the earliest applications of finance to price insurance risk.

8.7 The Discounted Cash Flow Model

Discounted cash flow (DCF) models aimed to put insurance pricing on a solid financial foundation. DCF models discount each cash flow in a project, including the initial investment and recurring revenues and expenses, at an appropriate risk-adjusted interest rate. The early implementations used CAPM-determined rates. If the total DCF is positive, the project should be undertaken.

DCF analysis takes the insured's perspective. It focuses on premium and loss payments. Surplus appears indirectly. It is used only to compute the tax burden on investor-provided funds.

Several surveys describe the evolution of financial pricing for property-casualty insurance. D'Arcy and Doherty (1988) offer a summary of the CAPM and contingent claims approaches from a finance perspective, Robbin (1992) describes several actuarial techniques for incorporating investment income into the underwriting profit provision as well as a risk-adjusted DCF approach, D'Arcy and Dyer (1997) and Van Slyke (1999) take an actuarial viewpoint, and the survey Cummins and Phillips (2000) takes a finance view. Robbin (2007) treats detailed implementation of cash flow methods from an actuarial perspective. Goldfarb (2010a) applies DCF to insurance company valuation. Myers and Cohn (1987) present a definitive treatment of DCF pricing. Cummins (1990) provides a detailed explanation of both the DCF and internal rate of return models. This section follows the last two papers quite closely, and we refer to them here as Myers-Cohn and Cummins, respectively

DCF methods aim to be theoretically sound. They are prospective. Old business generates investment income but it is akin to a sunk cost. Pricing must be prospective and must anticipate discount rates that are expected to apply in future periods to the cash flows that new policies generate.

Early papers, such as Hill (1979) and Fairley (1979), used CAPM-based discount rates for each cash flow. In particular, CAPM rates were used to reflect nondiversifiable risk in insurance cash flows. The models did not compensate for idiosyncratic insurance risk in any way. From the beginning, the appropriate discount rates were debated, as was accounting for policyholder funds. Indications that the systematic risk of underwriting profits is very small led to what Biger and Kahane (1978) describe as the "intuitive solution" that underwriting profits should be proportional to the negative risk-free interest rate.

Quirin and Waters (1975) used fire data from Canadian companies between 1961 and 1971 to test Biger and Kahane's hypothesis. They found an average positive underwriting return. They ruled out a non-competitive market explanation. They prefer an explanation based on the risk of ruin and the fact that insurers can be rendered technically insolvent even when they have positive policyholders's surplus.

Quirin's findings, combined with substantial underwriting profits for property catastrophe reinsurance (which were substantially positive, especially in the post-Hurricane Andrew hard market), led to a crisis in the theory (Froot and O'Connell, 1999; Froot, 2001). Resolving the crisis requires the use of more realistic model assumptions discussed in Chapter 12. We now address the details of the DCF and the related internal rate of return (IRR) models.

8.7.1 Defining a Fair Rate of Return on Underwriting

The US literature in the 1970s and 1980s was very concerned with the problem of determining a fair rate of return for insurers in a regulated rate environment. Cummins and Harrington (1987) is a whole book of papers dedicated to that problem. Thus it can appear the proposed solutions are relevant only in a regulated environment and not a competitive market. This is not true. The successful methods are based on sound economic principles and can be used to model premiums that apply in a competitive market.

The **Myers-Cohn fair premium condition** states that a premium is fair if

> [W]henever a policy is issued, the resulting equity value equals the equity invested in support of that policy. (Myers and Cohn (1987))

It is unfair to policyholders if premium increases equity on issue because it implies a transfer of wealth from them to investors. Equally, decreasing equity indicates a transfer in the opposite direction. Myers-Cohn's definition is used throughout the book. Although born in the context of rate regulation, it is a statement about competitive market valuation. If rates are not fair as Myers-Cohn require, they cannot be equilibrium rates because investors have an incentive to write more or less insurance.

The Myers-Cohn fair premium condition is critical, so it is worth taking the time to spell out exactly what it means. Figure 8.5 shows economic and accounting balance sheets for Ins Co. at $t = 0$. Both views book assets at market value. The **accounting value of liabilities** equals the **objective expected present value**. The **market value of liabilities** equals the **risk-adjusted expected present value**, including a risk load, so $D > L$. Writing a new policy for premium P increases assets by P in both views: the market value of ¤1 is ¤1 (a dollar is a dollar). There is an increase in the accounting equity $Q^* > S$ when premium contains a

Market value balance sheet		Accounting balance sheet	
Assets a	Liabilities D	Assets a	Liabilities L
	Equity S		Equity Q^*

Figure 8.5 Market value and accounting value balance sheets. Assets booked at market value in both.

positive margin, creating an accounting *gain at issue*. The market value of liabilities increases by D and the equity value increases by $P - D$. Therefore premiums are fair, under Myers-Cohn's definition, if and only if $P = D$.

Myers-Cohn continues with the "very simple truth" that

> A fair system of regulation is one in which the stockholders get what they pay for, no more and no less. Fair compensation to equity capital implies that the company is indifferent to whether or not an insurance policy is written.

He concludes that fair rates are equal to the present value of losses plus expenses plus the present value of the tax burden on underwriting and investment income, all discounted at risk-adjusted rates. The policyholder must pay the tax on all investment income, even though some is the result of investing assets provided by investors, to avoid double taxation. An individual risk pricing actuary is well aware that competitive (walk-away) prices often leave everyone equally unhappy and the insurer indifferent to whether or not a deal gets done.

8.7.2 Discounted Cash Flow Pricing Formula

Three important principles of DCF analysis are value-additivity, the irrelevance of accounting, and the avoidance of double counting (Brealey and Myers, 1981).

- **Value additivity** requires that each policy is evaluated on a stand-alone basis. Premiums are prospective and not influenced by past actions, such as reserve levels or portfolio embedded yields. Ins Co. has no reserves because it exists only for one period.
- Cummins states accounting does not supersede financial principles. **Accounting** is relevant only to the extent it impacts cash flows. Past loss reserves are irrelevant. The analysis should focus on expected loss payout patterns for each policy.
- Cummins suggests that insurance is prone to **double counting** and recommends that a good way to avoid it is to take either the insured's or the insurer's perspective. All cash flows are from one to the other, so only one side needs to be considered.

Value additivity follows from the existence of a linear pricing rule, Section 8.6. It implies that prospective business can be evaluated separately from reserves. In Chapter 17 we see this may not the case when the pricing rule is not additive.

DCF considers an insurance policy as analogous to a project with an up-front investment. It starts with an investment or commitment of capital, and is followed by streams of premium, loss, and expense payments, often over many years, even though the policy is only on risk for one year. Policies are evaluated as though financed with equity. There is no debt or reinsurance in the model. The level and timing of capital commitments are the loosest parts of the analogy to a manufacturing project.

In the late 1980s, there were no stochastic catastrophe or capital models to compute economic capital. As a result, capital allocations were usually based on industry-wide premium to capital or reserve to capital ratios. A competitive insurance market finds an equilibrium level of capital, which is priced into the product. To the extent the market is competitive, industry averages should reflect this equilibrium level. Other insurance cash flows can be modeled reasonably accurately using standard actuarial techniques.

Premium, loss, expense, and tax cash flows are discounted to inception using appropriately risk-adjusted discount rates. Early DCF models used CAPM discount factors, though there is no reason to do so. Any defensible cost of capital model can be used, a fact that both Myers-Cohn and Cummins point out.

An offered premium rate is accepted and bound if it has a positive total DCF. Alternatively, the model can determine a premium with zero DCF, which can then be quoted. We take the latter approach.

The DCF premium equals the present value of loss plus tax on investment income, including that earned on capital to avoid double taxation, plus tax on underwriting income, all discounted at the appropriate rates. Thus for one-period Ins Co., with premium paid at $t = 0$ and losses and taxes at $t = 1$,

$$P = \frac{L}{1+R_L} + \frac{\tau R_f(P+Q)}{1+R_f} + \frac{\tau P}{1+R_f} - \frac{\tau L}{1+R_L}$$

where L is expected loss, P premium, Q capital invested to support the policy, $P+Q = a$, and τ is the tax rate. R_f is the risk-free rate and R_L is a risk-adjusted discount rate appropriate to losses. Risk-free cash flows are discounted at the risk-free rate. These are taxes on non-risky items, including premium, and risk-free earnings on capital. Risky items, including the tax deduction for loss expense, use a risk-adjusted discount rate. The year-end value of the firm is

$$V_1 = P(1+R_f) + Q(1+R_f) - L - \tau(P-L) - \tau R_f(P+Q).$$

Substituting for P and manipulating shows that P produces a return on equity of

$$R = \frac{V_1 - Q}{Q} = R_f + \frac{L}{Q}\frac{R_f - R_L}{1+R_L}(1-\tau). \tag{8.5}$$

The first term on the right pays the risk-free rate on equity. The second provides the return to underwriting as a leveraged after-tax spread. Normally, the risk adjustment for losses is negative meaning $R_f - R_L > 0$ and the spread term is positive.

What return on equity is required? Consider an economic balance sheet, where all items are booked at their market value, Figure 8.5. The market value of assets is always a. Let D be the market value of liabilities, S the market value of equity, and R_x return on $x = A, L, S$.

Since $a = D + S$ at the beginning of the period, equating expected end of period values gives

$$S(1 + R_S) = a(1 + R_A) - D(1 + R_L) \tag{8.6}$$
$$\implies \quad SR_S = aR_A - DR_L.$$

Therefore

$$\begin{aligned} R_S &= \frac{1}{S}(aR_A - DR_L) \\ &= \frac{1}{S}((S + D)R_A - DR_L) \\ &= R_A + \frac{D}{S}(R_A - R_L). \end{aligned} \tag{8.7}$$

Myers-Cohn's fair premium condition says that $P = D$ because adding the policy increases assets by P and the market value of liabilities by D and $Q = S$ for the same reason. Therefore equating Eq. (8.5) with Eq. (8.7) implies

$$R_f + \frac{L}{Q}\frac{R_f - R_L}{1 + R_L}(1 - \tau) = R_A + \frac{D}{S}(R_A - R_L). \tag{8.8}$$

Note the left-hand side uses accounting values, expected losses, and amount of equity investment, whereas the right-hand side uses market values. In the case assets are invested in the risk-free asset, so $R_A = R_f$, and premiums are fair, this equation reduces to

$$P = D = \frac{L}{1 + R_L}(1 - \tau), \tag{8.9}$$

showing the implied market value of liabilities is simply the risk-adjusted present value, adjusted for taxes. Eq. (8.9) assumes that losses generate a tax shield that can be immediately recovered at full value.

Let's apply Eq. (8.9) to a Bermuda-based Ins Co. with tax rate $\tau = 0$. It implies the fair market premium equals discounted losses: $P = D = L/(1 + R_L)$, and so $R_L = (L - P)/P$. Multiplying Eq. (8.7) by S and substituting for R_L gives

$$P = \frac{L + (R_S - R_A)S}{1 + R_A} \tag{8.10}$$

which says that premium equals discounted losses plus the risk spread over investment return paid to equity holders for bearing insurance risk. If assets are invested in the risk-free instrument, so $R_A = R_f$, this reduces to

$$P = \frac{L + (R_S - R_f)a}{1 + R_S} \tag{8.11}$$

because of the funding constraint $a = P + S$. Finally if $R_f = 0$, as we assume outside this chapter, we get

$$P = \frac{L + R_S a}{1 + R_S}. \tag{8.12}$$

Eq. (8.12) is used in Section 8.7.4 under the guise of constant cost of capital pricing.

Early applications used CAPM to estimate the fair rate of return on equity R_Q via

$$R_Q = -kR_f + \beta_L(R_M - R_f)$$

where k is the funds generating coefficient, β_L measures the correlation of underwriting returns with market returns, and R_M is the market return. The funds generating coefficient recognizes that a unit of premium can generate more than a unit of invested assets because of the build-up of loss reserves. It is defined by the relationship $a = kP + Q$. Since $QR_Q = aR_A + PR_L$, $\beta_Q = (a/Q)\beta_A + (P/Q)\beta_L$, a formula that can be used to infer underwriting beta. Therefore

$$\begin{aligned} QR_Q &= Q(R_f + \beta_Q(R_M - R_f)) \\ &= QR_f + (a\beta_A + P\beta_L)(R_M - R_f) \\ &= a(R_f + \beta_A(R_M - R_f)) + P(-kR_f + \beta_L(R_M - R_f)). \end{aligned}$$

If assets are priced using CAPM, $R_L = -kR_f + \beta_L(R_M - R_f)$, see Kahane (1979). Myers-Cohn's more natural presentation defines R_L as the discount rate for liabilities, giving $R_L = R_f + \beta_L(R_M - R_f)$. It avoids using k.

A cottage industry grew up trying to estimate so-called **underwriting betas**. Cummins and Harrington (1985) attempted to estimate them using quarterly accounting data but found the results were subject to "extreme instability." They suggested "extreme caution" be applied if using them in practice. The industry was unable to produce satisfactory estimates; it appears betas are "shadows of ghosts" in the title of Kozik (1994).

Fairley (1979) suggested the idea of switching from actual asset returns in Eq. (8.10) to risk-free returns in Eq. (8.11). He argued that premium profit margins should not depend on actual investment portfolios or outcomes, but only on the risk-free rate and systematic underwriting risk. Companies with riskier investment strategies are also required to compensate their investors with a higher return. Policyholders, on the other hand, receive the same loss payments and should pay the same premiums in either case. Fairley states, "Policyholders of stock companies, who do not share in the investment risks, pay exactly the same premiums for their insurance regardless of their company's investment policies." Policyholders who sought investment return could buy shares in insurers themselves if they chose. Cummins points out this argument is incorrect because adding investment risk increases the probability of default for policyholders and changes their expected loss recoveries. Therefore, he argues that **investment income credit should be at the insurer's anticipated market return**, not at the risk-free rate. The impact of asset risk on loss recoveries is modeled in the next section using option theoretic methods.

These formulas all deliver less than you hope. They ensure consistency but they do not give you the answer. To price you need to know either the cost of capital R_S or an appropriate loss discount rate R_L. As always in finance, there is no free lunch.

8.7.3 The Internal Rate of Return Model

The internal rate of return (IRR) model takes the investor's perspective. An IRR model estimates all cash flows to or from the investor and then computes the discount rate—the

IRR—required to produce a present value of zero. A project is acceptable if its IRR is greater than or equal to the investor's hurdle rate for similarly risky projects. The IRR model side-steps the tricky problem of determining a discount factor suitable for each cash flow, which is regarded as an advantage. However, it still requires the cost of capital to use as a decision hurdle rate at the last step.

Capital flows appear directly in the IRR model, in contrast to DCF. The investor's initial capital contribution, as well as the gradual return of capital as losses are paid, are both modeled explicitly. The National Council on Compensation Insurance (NCCI, the US worker's compensation ratemaking bureau) IRR model determines capital using a constant capital-to-reserves ratio, ϕ.

Given a cost of capital R_S the IRR model can be used to determine the premium that results in a net present value of zero—i.e. that gives an IRR of R_S. For Ins Co. the premium is

$$P = \frac{L}{1+R_f} + \phi D \frac{\tau R_f + (R_S - R_f)}{(1+R_f)(1-\tau)}. \tag{8.13}$$

DCF models discount cash flows and then add them. IRR models collapse all cash flows to create a net flow with investors and discount just that—in fact, they compute its implied return. Because of value additivity the two approaches should be the same, cf., Eq. (8.6). However, Cummins notes Eq. (8.13) does not generally give the same result as the DCF analysis. He also notes that ϕ needs to use the market value of liabilities, not the book value.

Cummins (1990) describes the NCCI IRR model, used for workers compensation ratemaking in the USA, and compares it to the DCF model. Feldblum (1992) treats the IRR model in great detail. Bingham's paper in Van Slyke (1999) reconciles the DCF and IRR models.

8.7.4 Portfolio Constant Cost of Capital Pricing

Portfolio CCoC pricing is based on a simplified discounted cash flow model with no taxes. It uses the fundamental relationships

$$\begin{aligned} \text{Premium} &= \text{Loss cost} + \text{Cost of capital} \\ \text{Cost of capital} &= \text{Target return on capital} \times \text{Amount of capital} \end{aligned} \tag{8.14}$$

justified by Myers-Cohn's fair premium condition, Section 8.7.1, and Eq. (8.12).

Eq. (8.14) opens a debate about how to risk-adjust the target return and fix the amount of capital. A firm-wide constant CoC assumption is realistic when all risk capital is common equity, as we saw in Section 8.2.4, Still, it becomes less so when capital is a blend of equity, debt, and reinsurance.

Insurers commonly use **economic capital** for the amount of capital in Eq. (8.14). Economic capital refers to an amount of capital that guarantees the payment of liabilities with a high degree of confidence. The guarantee is usually considered over one-year using mark-to-market accounting. Clearly, the definition is skewed towards VaR. Economic capital is also called **risk capital**. In practice, the target amount of (accounting) capital is largely exogenous, determined by a regulator, rating agency, or a market consensus capital standard.

Portfolio CCoC pricing relies on two parameters, a CoC equal to ι (since it is fixed $\bar{\iota} = \iota$) and required assets a. It applies Eq. (8.14) to define premium

$$\bar{P}(a) = \frac{\mathsf{E}[X] + \iota a}{1+\iota}. \tag{8.15}$$

Eq. (8.15) assumes zero taxes and risk-free rate. It is used widely in US regulatory ratemaking, Mahler (1985), and is buried in almost every rate filing.

Strictly speaking, Eq. (8.15) should use expected payments under limited liability $\mathsf{E}[X \wedge a]$ in place of $\mathsf{E}[X]$. To define a pricing *functional* acting on random variables we should also replace a with a capital risk measure. Combining these, the **Portfolio Constant Cost of Capital** premium calculation principle is

$$\bar{P}_a(X) = \frac{\mathsf{E}[X \wedge a(X)] + \iota a(X)}{1+\iota} = \nu E[X \wedge a(X)] + \delta a(X). \tag{8.16}$$

As TVaR_0, TVaR_1 are the mean and maximum respectively, we can express Eq. (8.16) as the weighted average

$$\bar{P}(a) = \nu \mathsf{TVaR}_0(X \wedge a) + \delta \mathsf{TVaR}_1(X \wedge a)$$

consistent with Example 174. CCoC pricing channels an underwriter who is risk-neutral a proportion ν of the time and expects the absolute worst the remaining proportion δ.

Despite its ubiquity in actuarial practice, it is hard to categorize portfolio CCoC pricing.

- It is not one of the classical PCPs listed in Section 8.4.1. Indeed, it is arguably opposite to classical PCPs: where they price the shape of risk on an unlimited basis and ignore capital, CCoC charges a constant rate for capital but ignores the shape of risk other than through its influence on the amount of capital.
- It is modern in our classification, taking a financial view that targets a return on capital rather than a margin to loss.
- It is an example of a compound risk measure, Section 5.2.20. In general, compound risk measures are not subadditive even when their components are because $\mathsf{E}[X \wedge a(X)]$ is not subadditive; see Exercise 100 and Remark 134 for an explicit example. Therefore it is not coherent, even when a is, and can't count as *that* modern.
- The special case when $a(X) \equiv a$ is fixed has the form

$$\bar{P}_a(X) = \nu \mathsf{E}[X \wedge a] + \delta\, a = \int_0^a (\nu S(x) + \delta)\, dx.$$

This formula reappears in Exercise 144 and gives a modern interpretation to CCoC pricing.

Classical PCP methods of the form $\mathsf{E}[X] + kR(X)$ can be *interpreted* as CCoC models by taking $R(X)$ to be capital. Sometimes this makes sense: standard deviation can be used to set a capital requirement based on a normal approximation, for example. However, there is no guarantee that k and R have the right order of magnitude to be interpreted as CoC and capital.

8.7.5 Concluding Observations on DCF and IRR Models

Cummins says that the DCF and IRR models represented a significant advance in pricing insurance risk as of 1990. They are both based on sound financial theory, using cash flow and market value inputs, rather than the accounting values and arbitrary profit loadings used previously. He identifies several lessons.

- Ratemaking is prospective, and prospective business should stand alone from legacy business and reserves.
- Investment returns should estimate yields expected during the policy term and not use embedded yields. They should reflect the insurer's actual investment strategy and not just apply the risk-free rate.
- Regulation and accounting are relevant only if they affect cash flows.
- It is difficult to determine the appropriate capital flows associated with writing a new policy, especially in a multiple-line insurer.
- Both models depend on a liability discount rate or, equivalently, the cost of capital. Available methodologies to estimate these factors "leave much to be desired." He suggests developing and testing multifactor models, as opposed to the single-factor CAPM and models that price nonsystemic risk, as alternatives to CAPM-based factors.
- He identifies that breaking a company-wide cost of capital into costs by unit is an important problem that "would be a fruitful topic for future research."

8.8 Insurance Option Pricing Models

In this section, we describe the application of option pricing models to insurance. After describing the models' development, we review Brownian motion, geometric Brownian motion, and Itô's Lemma in stochastic calculus. We explain why geometric Brownian motion has a unique risk adjustment but compound Poisson processes do not. We describe the famous Black-Scholes formula and compare its prices to a straw-person actuarial approach. We then build the Insurance Option Pricing Model and finish with a discussion its historical importance.

The reader familiar with financial option models can skip straight to Sections 8.8.9 and 8.8.10 for the insurance application and its contribution.

8.8.1 Development of Insurance Option Pricing Models

Before the mid-1980s, insurance pricing did not account for default risk, which Sommer (1996) calls a "significant deficiency" of the DCF and IRR models discussed in Section 8.7. Doherty and Garven (1986) and Cummins (1988) address these concerns using option and contingent claim theoretic methods, related to the Black-Scholes framework. They apply results from option pricing theory and use a geometric Brownian motion to model loss and asset outcomes. Option-based models have several advantages. First, they make pricing risk-sensitive, addressing a reservation about DCF models. They sidestep the difficulty of computing appropriate underwriting discount factors—the infamous underwriting beta problem. Finally, they can incorporate joint modeling of asset and underwriting risk.

Doherty and Garven (1986) provide a one-period model that includes taxes and incorporates investment income using a funds generating coefficient. The model addresses the insurer's probability of ruin as well as nonlinear tax effects and works in discrete time.

Cummins (1988) constructs a one-period continuous time model of the insurer's total liabilities. He adds a nonsystematic jump component for catastrophe to a geometric Brownian motion model. Cummins (1991) applies the option model to determine an appropriate discount rate for liabilities and shows that it is risk-sensitive and depends on the insurer's investment strategy. Cummins and Sommer (1996) use the option model to explore the relationship between insurer capital and risk. They show insurers have a target solvency level that balances capitalization and risk, and that this level is generally much greater than regulatory capital minimums. Capital levels are influenced by the desire to avoid regulatory and bankruptcy costs, managerial risk aversion, and to protect franchise value. Insurance demand is also inversely related to default risk, and better capitalized companies can charge a higher premium. The paper finds that closely held insurers have lower capital and higher risk than publicly traded ones, consistent with the fact that owner–manager incentives are more closely aligned.

The literature written in the 1980s and 1990s left many details to the reader. At the time, Black-Scholes was new and popular, and its techniques were well-known. Today, some of these derivations are less familiar, so we walk through the details in this section.

The theory gives solutions to problems that are hard to obtain with other methods. Our treatment follows Cummins (1988) and Cummins (1991) quite closely. The original paper Merton (1973) Section 6 is very readable and detailed. Other references on insurance pricing with options include Cummins and Danzon (1997) and Shimko (1992).

8.8.2 Brownian Motion

Brownian motion is a stochastic process W_t satisfying:

a. $W_0 = 0$.
b. Sample paths $t \mapsto W_t$ are continuous.
c. W_t has independent increments: the distribution of $W_{s+t} - W_s$ is independent of s.
d. The increment $W_{s+t} - W_s$ is normally distributed with mean zero and variance t.

It is nontrivial to construct such an object, although there are many different ways to do so. See Feller (1971), Karatzas and Shreve (1988), or Mörters and Peres (2011) for examples and more details. Brownian motion is extremely wiggly, and its paths are not differentiable at any point, despite being continuous.

8.8.3 Stochastic Calculus and Itô's Lemma

We can use an increasing function F to integrate, by defining the length of an interval $(a, b]$ to be $F(b) - F(a)$, $\int x dF$. Stochastic calculus is a way to extend this idea and integrate with respect to dW_t. Simple ways to do this run afoul of the fact that Brownian motion has infinite path length in any finite period of time. It is like a ruler that measures the distance between 0 and 1 as $\infty - \infty$, which is undefined. Therefore it is impossible to integrate with respect to "dW_t" in a naive sense.

Although W_t changes direction frenetically, it moves at a constant squared speed. The sum of the squares of changes in W_t over finer and finer deterministic partitions of the $[0, t]$ converges to t because the square of a standard normal is a chi-squared distribution with mean 1. (For a *given* path, you can always find a sequence of *particular* partitions for which the sum of squares diverges. But a random sequence will converge to t.)

Using this convergence property, the standard rules of calculus can be extended to include stochastic differentials. Itô's Lemma shows the **stochastic differential** dW_t satisfies

$$(dW_t)^2 = dt.$$

$dW_t \approx W_{t+dt} - W_t$, a normal with mean zero and variance dt, by properties (c) and (d).

Itô's Lemma can be used to extend the usual rules of calculus to include stochastic differentials. In deterministic calculus we often get a good approximation using a one-term Taylor's series. With stochastic calculus we need to include second-order differentials for stochastic terms because $(dW_t)^2 = dt$. For example, to approximate $f(W_t, t)$ we use

$$\begin{aligned} f(W_{t+dt}, t + dt) &= f(W_t, t) + \frac{\partial f}{\partial x} dW_t + \frac{\partial f}{\partial t} dt + \frac{1}{2}\frac{\partial^2 f}{\partial x^2}(dW_t)^2 + o(dt) \\ &= f(W_t, t) + \frac{\partial f}{\partial x} dW_t + \left(\frac{\partial f}{\partial t} + \frac{1}{2}\frac{\partial^2 f}{\partial x^2}\right) dt + o(dt) \end{aligned}$$

where $o(dt)$ indicates the omitted terms are all smaller than dt. The omitted second-order partials are of order $(dt)^{3/2}$ and dt^2. It is common to denote partials of $f(x, t)$ with respect to the first and second variables as f_x and f_t. With this notation **Itô's Lemma** is written as

$$df = (f_t + f_{xx}/2)dt + f_x dW_t.$$

8.8.4 Brownian Motion with Drift

A **Brownian motion with a drift** is a stochastic process $X_t = \mu t + \sigma W_t$. It evolves according to

$$dX_t = \mu dt + \sigma dW_t.$$

This notation means that $X_{t+dt} = X_t + \mu dt + \sigma dW_{dt}$. Itô's Lemma for X_t says

$$(dX_t)^2 = \mu^2 (dt)^2 + 2\mu\sigma(dt)(dW_t) + \sigma^2 (dW_t)^2 = \sigma^2 dt + o(dt).$$

Terms $(dX_t)^2$ cannot be ignored in the same way we ignore dt^2.

Example 125. We can apply Itô's Lemma to the function $f(x) = e^x$ to determine the dynamics of e^{X_t}. Since $df/dx = f$, $f = f_x = f_{xx}$, and we get

$$\begin{aligned} df &= f dX + \frac{\sigma^2}{2} f dt \\ &= (\mu + \frac{\sigma^2}{2}) f dt + \sigma f dW_t \end{aligned}$$

which is often written as

$$\frac{df}{f} = (\mu + \frac{\sigma^2}{2})dt + \sigma dW_t.$$

Notice that $\mathsf{E}[e^{X_t}] = e^{\mu t + \sigma^2 t/2}$ because X_t is normal with mean μt and variance $\sigma^2 t$. □

8.8.5 Geometric Brownian Motion

A **geometric Brownian motion** $S_t \geq 0$ has dynamics

$$\frac{dS}{S} = \mu dt + \sigma dW_t. \tag{8.17}$$

Without the stochastic component, if we integrate both sides we simply get $\log(S) = \mu t$ and $S = e^{\mu t}$, which leads us to suspect $S_t = \exp(\mu t + \sigma W_t)$. We can apply Itô's Lemma to $f(S_t) = \log(S_t)$ to check. Since $f_x = 1/S_t$ and $f_{xx} = -1/S_t^2$, it says

$$\begin{aligned} df &= f_x dS + (1/2) f_{xx} (dS)^2 \\ &= \frac{dS}{S} - \frac{1}{2}\left(\frac{dS}{S}\right)^2 \\ &= (\mu - \sigma^2/2)dt + \sigma dW_t \end{aligned}$$

ignoring terms smaller than dt. Thus geometric Brownian motion is **not** what we suspected: the drift is reduced by $\sigma^2/2$ and $\mathsf{E}[S_t] = e^{\mu t}$. The naive approximation assumes that $\log(1 + \mu t + \sigma dW_t) = \mu t + \sigma dW_t + o(dt)$, but because of the uncertainty in dW_t and the concavity of log it is actually equal to $\mu t + \sigma dW_t - \sigma^2 dt/2 + o(dt)$. Geometric Brownian motion is also called the Doléans-Dade exponential. The Black-Scholes model assumes stock prices follow a geometric Brownian motion.

The parameter μ in geometric Brownian motion is the average annualized return over short periods of time. The value $\mu - \sigma^2/2$ is the expected continuously compounded rate (a.k.a. force of interest or cumulative average growth rate, CAGR). It is computed as the geometric mean of returns over short periods. The adjustment $-\sigma^2/2$ reflects the fact that after a 20% decline and a 20% increase you are down 4% ($0.8 \times 1.2 = 24/25$). It is often a very good estimate.

Exercise 126. You are given annual returns 0.12, 0.10, 0.08, 0.20, 0.14, 0.10, 0.35, −0.15, 0.05, 0.08. What is the average annual return and compound average return? What is the sample standard deviation annual return? If you are parameterizing a geometric Brownian motion model to these returns what are μ and σ? What is the error in the approximation $\mu - \sigma^2/2$?

Solution. $\mu = 0.107$ is the average return, $\sigma = 0.1246$. The CAGR return is 0.1005 and $\mu - \sigma^2/2 = 0.0992$. Volatility in returns lowers the average return by 0.7 percentage points.

8.8.6 Unique Prices and Risk Adjustments

No-arbitrage prices exist if and only if there is a positive linear pricing rule. In turn, such a rule exists if and only if there is a risk-adjusted probability that removes any predictable trend in security prices, the Q from Section 8.6. Q must agree with the objective probability about which events are possible and impossible, that is, it must be equivalent to the objective probability P.

Stocks have a return above the risk-free rate, captured by the CAPM equity risk premium. As a result, the risk-free discounted value of a stock trends upwards under objective probabilities. However, under suitable Q, the discounted value has no trend. A probability function that achieves this reduction is called an **equivalent martingale probability** (measure, in finance texts). A martingale is the stochastic process equivalent of a constant, with no predictable trend. Expectations under Q then give arbitrage-free prices. However, they are not guaranteed to be unique.

Sometimes, the mathematics of the stochastic price process implies there is at most one equivalent martingale probability. In that case, if arbitrage-free prices exist, then they are unique and must be given by E_Q. The geometric Brownian motion model that underlies Black-Scholes has a unique equivalent martingale probability, and hence we obtain unique option prices. Unfortunately, the compound Poisson model used for insurance has multiple equivalent measures, resulting in a range of prices.

Why is there is just one equivalent martingale probability for geometric Brownian motion? Let S_t be a geometric Brownian motion, following Eq. (8.17). Observing S_t for a short time reveals enough information to know the parameter σ with *certainty* because S_t is moving so vigorously. The drift parameter μ, corresponding to the stock's annualized instantaneous return, is harder to determine, especially over short periods. A stock with $\mu = 0.1$ can experience a negative return for a year or more by chance. It is impossible to determine μ exactly by watching the process for a finite time, though the longer it is observed, the more certain we can become. These ideas are illustrated in Figure 8.6.

An equivalent martingale probability changes probabilities so the drift of S_t becomes the risk-free return. It must do so in such a way that an observer can believe the new model is possible—that's the *equivalent* part of the definition. The only way to achieve this is by altering μ and leaving σ unchanged. All market participants agree on σ and they would not deem a new model possible if it were changed. Since its drift and σ completely specify geometric Brownian motion, if such an adjustment is possible then it must be unique. Girsanov's Theorem shows it is possible to make the drift adjustment, leaving σ unchanged. As a result, Black-Scholes' prices are unique.

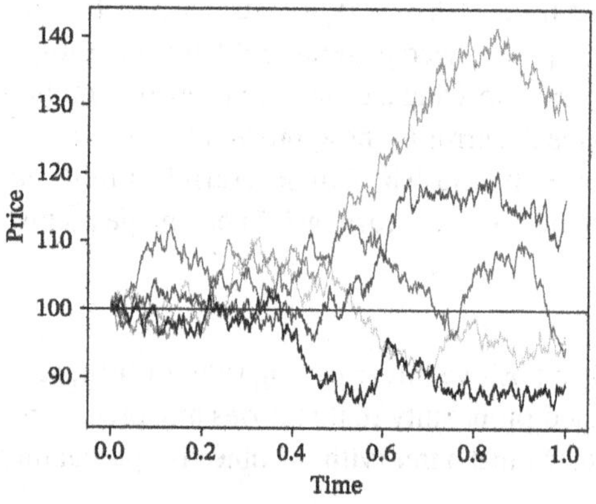

Figure 8.6 Sample geometric Brownian motion paths, characterized by $\mu = 0.1, \sigma = 0.15$. All market observers agree for certain that $\sigma = 0.15$ no matter how short a part of the process they observe. However, there is always potential disagreement about μ. Three of the five paths indicate $\mu < 0$.

Insurance losses are typically modeled using a compound Poisson frequency and severity process. The expected number of claims in time t is λt and each claim has severity sampled from a distribution F_X. If the premium is paid at a rate π per year, the surplus process, Section 8.4.2, has a drift of $\pi - \lambda \mathsf{E}[X]$ per year. To find an equivalent martingale probability, we need to adjust probabilities to reduce the discounted drift to zero. Is there a way to do this that all participants agree, an analog of the unique Black-Scholes adjustment? No! Why is that?

In a finite time, we can observe only finitely many events. From that limited information, it is impossible to determine λ for sure. In fact, over a short period dt the chances of seeing a claim are $\lambda dt \to 0$ as $dt \to 0$. Then there is no information. Over the same short time, Brownian motion reveals enough information to determine σ exactly. Observing the process for longer produces a better estimate of λ, but there is always some uncertainty about its value. For the same reasons, it is impossible to know the distribution of claim sizes F_X. Therefore flexibility exists about the choice of adjusted probabilities. Figure 8.7 illustrates these ideas for a compound Poisson. As a result, the arguments that lead to unique Black-Scholes prices *never* apply to insurance, even in an academic model. Mathematics is against us and there is no unique martingale measure. These facts are discussed in detail in Delbaen and Haezendonck (1989).

In some situations, the mathematics partially cooperates, but it does so grudgingly. There are plausible models for insurance losses, called infinite activity Lévy processes, with an infinite number of very small losses and a smaller number of larger losses. The gamma, Pareto, lognormal, inverse Gaussian, and many other common distributions are of this type. When there is infinite activity, there is an infinite amount of information available, forcing all market observers to come to the same conclusions about some model parameters. Therefore parameters related to the small losses can be known for sure. But in a finite time, there is only ever a finite number of losses above a given threshold, and market observers' opinions of parameters are always uncertain. Thus in an insurance world, we may price small jump processes uniquely but never obtain unanimity about large jumps. Since we are most concerned with large losses, this is poor consolation.

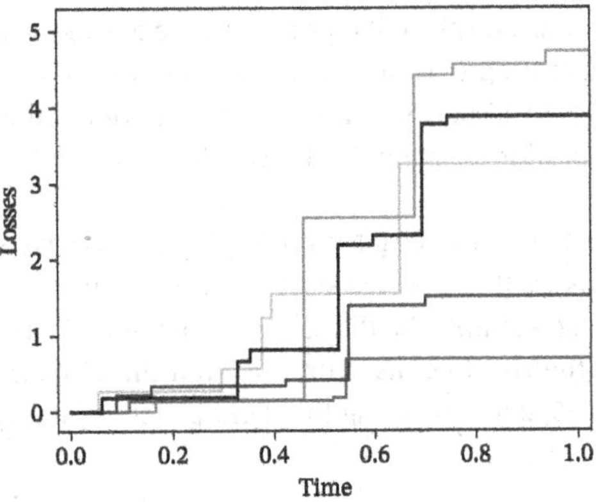

Figure 8.7 Sample compound Poisson paths, characterized by $\lambda = 5$ claims per year and lognormal severity with mean 1 and $\sigma = 0.15$. Market observers are unsure about both the frequency and severity distributions.

8.8.7 The Black-Scholes Model

We have mentioned Black-Scholes several times. It gives a price $C(S_0, a, t)$ for a call option with a strike a on a stock with current price S_0, with t years until expiration. The stock price is modeled by a geometric Brownian motion with parameters μ and σ, Eq. (8.17). Thus $S_t = S_0 X_t$ where X_t is a lognormal return variable with parameters $(\mu - \sigma^2/2)t$ and $\sigma\sqrt{t}$. The payoff is $(S_t - a)^+$. Let r denote the risk-free force of interest. Based on our general discussion, we should price the option by adjusting probabilities to lower the trend on the stock to the risk-free rate and then compute discounted expected values. Under adjusted probabilities Q, X_t has parameters $(r - \sigma^2/2)t$ and $\sigma\sqrt{t}$. By Section 8.8.6, the adjusted probabilities are unique. Hence,

$$\begin{aligned}
C(S_0, a, t) &:= e^{-rt}\mathsf{E}_Q[(S_t - a)^+] \\
&= e^{-rt} S_0 \mathsf{E}_Q[(X_t - a/S_0)^+] \\
&= e^{-rt} S_0 \left(e^{(r-\sigma^2/2)t + \sigma^2 t/2} \Phi(-d + \sigma\sqrt{t})) - a/S_0 \Phi(-d) \right) \\
&= S_0 \Phi(d^*) - a e^{-rt} \Phi(d^* - \sigma\sqrt{t}))
\end{aligned}$$

where $d = (\log(a/S_0) - (r - \sigma^2/2)t)/\sigma\sqrt{t}$ and

$$d^* = -d + \sigma\sqrt{t} = \left(\log(S_0/a) + (r + \sigma^2/2)t\right)/\sigma\sqrt{t}.$$

As above, $\Pr(S_t > a) = \Pr(X_t > a/S_0) = 1 - \Phi\left([\log(a/S_0) - (r - \sigma^2/2)t]/\sigma\sqrt{t}\right) = \Phi(d^* - \sigma\sqrt{t})$ is the probability the option expires in the money and the first term is the unconditional mean of S_t when the option expires in the money, i.e. $\mathsf{E}[(S_t - a)1_{\{S_t > a\}}$. Since the discounted value of S_t is a martingale, which has constant expectation, the first term involves S_0 rather than $e^{-rt}S_t$. Differentiating C with respect to S_0 gives the Δ of the option: the number of shares held in the replicating portfolio. After some cancellation $\Delta = \Phi(d^*)$. See Hull (1983) or Dothan (1990) for detailed accounts of Black-Scholes.

8.8.8 Actuarial vs. Black-Scholes Option Pricing

A call option has the same cash flows as an aggregate excess of loss with deductible a. How would an actuary price an option? They would project the stock price forward to the exercise date, estimate its distribution, compute the actuarial (objective probability) expected loss cost, discount back to inception, and then add a profit provision. The projection step requires knowing μ. It could be estimated based on historical performance, CAPM, or some other basis. Assuming a lognormal stock price distribution, Section 4.3.4 gives the expected loss cost.

Since μ is greater than the risk-free rate, the actuarial loss cost for a call option, i.e. excess of loss, is greater than the Black-Scholes price because the expected stock price at expiration is higher. How much higher? The actuarial loss cost is simply the Black-Scholes price replacing r in the definition of d^* with μ. The r equals the risk-free discount rate, and the discount factor e^{-rt}, is unchanged. Suppose that $\sigma = 0.25$, corresponding to a light general liability

Table 8.5 Actuarial vs. Black-Scholes pricing.

Strike	Black-Scholes	Actuarial	Intrinsic Value	Loss Ratio
500	500.1	551.7	500	1.103
600	401	456.9	400	1.14
700	305.5	363.9	300	1.191
800	219.2	276.2	200	1.26
900	147.6	198.7	100	1.347
1000	93.54	135.5	0	1.448
1100	56.14	87.76	0	1.563
1200	32.15	54.33	0	1.69
1300	17.72	32.33	0	1.825
1400	9.456	18.62	0	1.969
1500	4.921	10.43	0	2.12

book, $t = 1$ year period, and expected losses $1000e^{\mu}$. We can regard the current stock price $S_0 = 1000$ as a priori expected losses and S_1 as actual losses. We assume the risk-free rate is zero to keep the focus on the loss cost component. Table 8.5 summarizes the differences in pricing. Even though Black-Scholes gives a risk loaded price, it is lower than an actuarial approach.

Mildenhall (2000) gives a detailed comparison of actuarial and financial pricing of options, including a discussion of the replicating portfolio.

8.8.9 The Insurance Option Pricing Model

Consider a geometric Brownian motion model of assets and liabilities. Let A and L evolve according to

$$\frac{dA}{A} = \mu_A dt + \sigma_A dW_A \tag{8.18}$$

$$\frac{dL}{L} = \mu_L dt + \sigma_L dW_L. \tag{8.19}$$

Assets have an expected, objective probability, return of $e^{\mu_A} - 1$ per year. This could be the return estimated by CAPM, for example. The actuarial loss trend is $e^{\mu_L} - 1$. The instantaneous correlation between the two Brownian components is $dW_A dW_L = \rho\sigma_A\sigma_L$.

We are interested in the fair market value of contingent claims that depend on A and L, such as the insurance loss payment $A \wedge L$ (the minimum of A and L), the value of the owner's equity $(A - L)^+$, or the value of the default put $(L - A)^+$. Let $H(A, L, t)$ denote the value of one of these contingent claims at time t before expiration. All the expressions of interest are homogeneous in both A and L. Writing $H(A, L, t) = LH(A/L, 1, t)$ allows us to focus on $h(x) := H(x, 1, t)$, taking the current value of L out of the equation. It also collapses the dynamics of A and L into one new variable. This trick was introduced in Fischer (1978) and Margrabe (1978). Fischer concentrates on real returns and uses CAPM to derive the return on the hedge portfolio if it is not traded. Margrabe considers an option to swap two securities. If both are traded there is no net cost to holding the hedge portfolio because one security can be used as numeraire (currency) to replace money.

We need to know the dynamics of $x = x(A, L) = A/L$. Use subscripts to denote partial derivatives, $x_A = \partial x/\partial A$, etc. Then, applying Itô's Lemma gives

$$\begin{aligned} dx &= x_A dA + x_L dL + \frac{1}{2}(x_{AA}(dA)^2 + 2x_{AL}(dA)(dL) + x_{LL}(dL)^2) \\ &= \frac{1}{L}(A(\mu_A dt + \sigma_A dW_A)) - \frac{A}{L^2}(L(\mu_L dt + \sigma_L dW_L)) + R \\ &= x((\mu_A - \mu_L)dt + \sigma_A dW_A - \sigma_L dW_L) + R \end{aligned}$$

where R is the term involving second-order partials. R evaluates to

$$\begin{aligned} R &= \frac{1}{2}(x_{AA}(dA)^2 + 2x_{AL}(dA)(dL) + x_{LL}(dL)^2) \\ &= \frac{1}{2}\left(0 - 2\frac{1}{L^2}(AL\rho\sigma_A\sigma_L) + 2\frac{A}{L^3}(L^2\sigma_L^2)\right)dt \\ &= x(-\rho\sigma_A\sigma_L + \sigma_L^2)dt. \end{aligned}$$

Therefore the dynamics of x are a geometric Brownian motion

$$\frac{dx}{x} = (\mu_A - \mu_L - \rho\sigma_A\sigma_L + \sigma_L^2)dt + \sigma_A dW_A - \sigma_L dW_L. \tag{8.20}$$

Applying Itô's Lemma to h shows the dynamics of a general claim are

$$dh = h_x dx + h_t dt + (1/2)h_{xx}(dx)^2.$$

For h there is a time differential.

We value h using a **delta-hedging** argument, by explicitly constructing the replicating portfolio. Construct a portfolio Π long one unit of h and short h_x units of x. The Brownian (stochastic) component of Π is zero, so the portfolio is risk-free. But it is risk-free in units of $x = A/L$. There is no net cost to the asset component of the hedge portfolio, but in general there is no traded asset that can be used to hedge changes in L. If there were, then CAPM could be used to determine its expected return, r_h, (Fischer, 1978). The cost of the hedging portfolio is then the spread $r_h - \mu_L$. The return on the hedge portfolio can be written $r_h = r + \pi$ where r is the risk-free rate of interest and π is a risk load. Under CAPM $\mu_L = r_L + \pi$ and therefore $r_h - \mu_L = r - r_L$. If claim inflation equals general inflation then $r - r_L$ equals the real rate of interest, assuming the Fisher effect.

Returning to the hedging portfolio Π, its change in value over the short time dt is $d\Pi = (r_h - \mu_L)\Pi dt$, which implies $dh - h_x dx = (r_h - \mu_L)(h - h_x x)dt$. Substituting the expressions derived above, canceling dt, and pulling the h_{xx} term to the left gives the partial differential equation obeyed by h:

$$(r_h - \mu_L)h_x x + h_t + (1/2)h_{xx}x^2(\sigma_A^2 - 2\rho\sigma_A\sigma_L + \sigma_L^2) = (r_h - \mu_L)h.$$

Numerical methods can be used to solve this equation for general boundary conditions. Some explicit solutions are known.

The solution for the value of owners equity uses boundary condition $(A - L)^+$, which can be derived from Section 4.3.4. It is given by

$$C = A\Phi(d^*) - Le^{-(r_h-\mu_L)T}\Phi(d^* - \sigma\sqrt{t}) \tag{8.21}$$

where $d^* = (\log(A/L) + (r_h - \mu_L + \sigma^2/2))/\sigma\sqrt{t}$, t is time to the end of the period, and $\sigma^2 = \sigma_A^2 + \sigma_L^2 - 2\rho\sigma_A\sigma_L$. The fair market value of insurance liabilities, that is, the fair premium by Myers-Cohn's fair premium condition, is simply

$$D = A - C = A\Phi(-d^*) + Le^{-(r_h-\mu_L)t}\Phi(d^* - \sigma\sqrt{t}). \tag{8.22}$$

Note $A - A\Phi(d^*) = A\Phi(-d^*)$.

The yield to maturity on insurance liabilities can be defined as r_D solving

$$D = (Le^{\mu_L t})e^{-r_D t} = Le^{-t(r_D-\mu_L)}.$$

The bracketed term in the middle expression, expected monetary future value claims, is the objective, accounting for the rate of growth of liabilities, and $e^{-r_D t}$ is the risk-adjusted discount factor. The resulting discount rate is

$$r_D = \mu_L - \log(D/L)/t. \tag{8.23}$$

Thus the option model solves the problem of determining liability discount rates, at least if we ignore a possible risk premium on liability inflation.

8.8.10 The Historical Importance of Option Pricing Models

The option pricing model is tremendously important in the development of insurance pricing. It was the first pricing formula to exhibit three desirable properties.

1. Price depends on insurance risk.
2. Price depends on asset volatility.
3. Price depends on capitalization.

We have expended a lot of effort to arrive at such an "obvious" set of conclusions, but caution is in order: these results are not quite what they appear. Let's look at them in order.

First, the price of insurance depends on risk. The model charges riskier portfolios a *lower* premium because the insurer default put option becomes more valuable. This conclusion is likely the exact opposite of that expected. The model credits the insured for volatility to reflect possible insurer default. Older financial models, such as the DCF, failed to reflect the default haircut. *The model is not charging for diversifiable risk.* It charges for nondiversifiable risk through r_h.

Second, increasing asset volatility *lowers* the value of insurance because it increases the chance of default. This result is likely in-line with expectations, but for an unexpected reason.

We could argue that a riskier asset portfolio has a higher return, which allows for a higher discount rate and hence lower—more competitive—prices. The option model assumes an efficient asset market: all assets earn the same risk-adjusted return. Recall, Black-Scholes replaces the expected return on the stock with the risk-free rate. Similarly, here, the impact of higher volatility is to skew insurance results in favor of investors. Good asset returns increase the value of their residual interest. When returns are poor, they default. They capture the upside but do not pay the downside.

Before the option model, there was debate around the appropriate investment rate of return to apply in pricing when anticipating future investment income. This was an important question in rate regulation. Fairley (1979) held that actual returns and actual capital structure were irrelevant and claimed the policyholder should be credited at the risk-free rate. However, the options analysis shows this is not correct. Eq. (8.23) shows that r_D depends on asset and liability volatility.

The derivative of the fair value of insurance liabilities, i.e. the fair premium, with respect to total portfolio volatility σ is proportional to $-\phi(d^*) < 0$. Since σ accounts for asset risk, liability risk, and their correlation, this shows that an increase in insurance risk or asset risk or a *decrease* in the correlation between insurance and asset growth rates results in *lower* insurance premiums. Positive correlation ρ is good because it means asset growth and liability growth offset one another.

Third, a better capitalized insurer provides more valuable insurance, reflected in higher fair market prices. This result is expected. The derivative of liabilities with respect to assets is $\Phi(-d^*) > 0$

Cummins (1991) also shows that a Modigliani-Miller result holds for debt and equity: insurers have no financing arbitrages.

See Section 9.4 for an example using option insurance pricing.

8.9 Insurance Market Imperfections

The perfect market assumption is unrealistic because it ignores transaction costs and other market frictions. Insurers exist, in part, to ameliorate the effect of these imperfections.

8.9.1 Transaction Costs

Insureds do not purchase insurance directly from investors, as they would in a perfect market, because of underwriting expenses. Underwriting expenses are a market friction and transaction cost. Insurance intermediaries can lower underwriting expenses, providing a rationale for their existence.

It is costly for insureds and investors to search for and find each other. Even if they find a match, investors may lack the underwriting expertise to evaluate potential insureds, or find the cost of doing so prohibitive. Because underwriting is expensive investors often insist on a minimum deal size to lower their average costs, which precludes small individual risk transactions.

Unlike investors, intermediaries can develop underwriting expertise, systems, and data, and benefit from economies of scale in underwriting. Risk assessment is based on loss experience, creating another incentive to aggregate underwriting. As more business is underwritten and more data is gathered, more granular and accurate pricing becomes possible, creating a virtuous cycle. This effect is especially pronounced in the larger personal lines carriers, which use sophisticated predictive modeling and big data systems to underwrite.

In conclusion, as Froot and O'Connell (2008) point out, insurance intermediaries exist because they lower underwriting costs.

These arguments do not explain why insurers exist since underwriting service companies could disaggregate underwriting from risk bearing and serve as pure, non-risk-warehousing Pool Co., intermediaries between insureds and investors. Such entities do exist in some lines, where they are called managing general agents or managing underwriters. They access investors through fronted insurance arrangements. (A *front* is a licensed insurer that issues an insurance policy on behalf of another entity without retaining any of the risk.) However, they face information credibility and principal-agent problems because they advise on price without any *skin in the game*. Integrated insurance companies are preferred by investors because they solve management incentive problems by linking underwriting decisions with risk bearing.

Remark 127. Large homogeneous lines support investment in customized underwriting systems. The predominant personal lines carriers use a direct or captive agent model that integrates much of the customer acquisition and underwriting value chain. In contrast, specialty lines and program business favors a managing general agent model. Managing agents invest in a program meta-system designed to produce a series of related but differentiated program offerings across many sub specialties. As a result, specialty lines insurers have a greater separation between acquisition and underwriting (Customer and Pool Co.) versus risk bearing (Capital Co.). □

Remark 128. Catastrophe risk is an interesting special case. The catastrophe bond market separates underwriting and marketing from risk bearing. It relies on independent third-party models to provide an unbiased assessment of loss potential, helping to solve incentive problems. Catastrophe risk pricing is expertizable. The modeling fees for a catastrophe bond are, however, quite substantial, and bonds are written with substantial limits over multiple years in part to amortize them. More recently, property catastrophe reinsurers have disaggregated their underwriting expertise from risk bearing by sponsoring **sidecar** arrangements, where they underwrite on behalf of third-party capital. The binary nature and generally straightforward claims settlement (i.e. no claims!) of catastrophe risk facilitates the emergence of these markets. It is not clear whether parallel markets could emerge in other lines because of their greater information asymmetries and more complex claim adjusting. □

8.9.2 Frictional Costs of Capital

Cummins (2000) lists three important kinds of frictional costs:

1. **Agency** and **informational costs**, where managers behave opportunistically, or insurers fail to control adverse selection and moral hazard of insureds.

2. **Double taxation** of investment returns.
3. **Regulation** that allows insurer assets to be seized or temporarily controlled by a regulator if it fails minimum capital standards, that can restrict the possible investment opportunities, and that limit dividends and payments to investors.

Other frictions include the potential cost of financial distress, and lower liquidity of invested assets. Insurers allow market participants to balance benefits from lower underwriting expenses against the frictional cost of capital. Hitchcox *et al.* (2006), section 5, consider the impact of frictions on the cost of capital, including double taxation, agency, regulatory, and financial distress. Ibragimov, Jaffee, and Walden (2010) explicitly include frictional costs of holding capital within an insurance company, modeled as a cost τ per unit of capital per period.

Frictional costs imply a temporal element to risk bearing, over and above the cost of funding mentioned in Section 2.2. When frictional costs are present, we must allocate capital to correctly apportion them to units, as discussed in Part III.

The rate of frictional costs likely varies according to the type of regulation and institutional control on management opportunism under which Ins Co. operates. Management is controlled in part through financial disclosure and by the securities market. Therefore it is reasonable that τ varies with geography and corporate legal form, among other variables. It may also vary with level of capitalization, since a better capitalized company has greater scope for management frivolities.

It is hard (and generally unnecessary) to distinguish between frictional and risk costs. For example, costs related to certainty in capital budgeting, costly external capital for opaque intermediaries, contracting under asymmetric information, credit senstive customers, negatively skewed return distributions, and adverse selection are difficult to categorize. These issues are discussed in Froot, Scharfstein, and Stein (1993); Froot and Stein (1998); Cummins (2000); Merton and Perold (1993); Zanjani (2002); Perold (2005); and Froot (2007).

Exercise 129. In this exercise, we incorporate a frictional cost of capital into CCoC pricing, Section 8.7.4. We get a better understanding of the importance of time in risk pricing as a by-product.

Assume that the CCoC return r is for pure (non-intermediated) risk transfer to investors. A catastrophe bond is an example of pure risk transfer. In addition, assume investors incur constant frictional costs τ per period, incurred like a tax on capital. τ is the cost to investors of actually funding Ins Co. The capital risk measure a is unchanged. Finally, let $1 + \iota^* = (1 + \iota)(1 + \tau)$ be the combined cost of risk capital and frictions.

Show that under these assumptions the premium with frictions can be computed in two-steps, by grossing up a pure risk charge, or by assuming the CoC equals ι^*:

$$\frac{\bar{P}(a) + a\tau}{1+\tau} = \frac{\mathsf{E}[X \wedge a(X)] + \iota^* a(X)}{1+\iota^*}. \tag{8.24}$$

Kreps (2005) comments that "there is no sign of time dependence" in his riskiness leverage model. Frictional costs introduce a specific time dependence because they are a rate per unit time that investors incur to fund the insurer. ι is a return for risk bearing and has no direct connection to time. □

8.9.3 Market Frictions

The existence of **market frictions**, such as bid-ask spreads, are realities that cause other imperfections our models must account for. Bid-ask spreads can be driven by asymmetric and ambiguous information and correspond well with how underwriters think about risk. Underwriters always worry they are missing the buyer's motivation and the risk of adverse selection. They will price a positive load into two policies that combined have no risk, as we saw in the *Hot* and *Cold August* policies in Example 83. Perfect markets assumptions do not allow this behavior, but the modern approaches we develop do.

Technical Remark 130. Understanding market frictions caused by information asymmetries and ambiguity is an active area of research, but it is outside our scope. Here are some pointers to the relevant literature. Ambiguity is expressed using subjective (non-actuarial) probabilities, introduced in Anscombe and Aumann (1963). Insurance loss and underwriting data are ambiguous (claim development, "miscoded" data) and investors are ambiguity averse. Zhang (2002) and Klibanoff, Marinacci, and Mukerji (2005) describe ambiguity relevant to insurance pricing. The latter paper has been applied in an insurance context by Robert and Therond (2014), Dietz and Walker (2017), and Jiang, Escobar-Anel, and Ren (2020). Epstein and Schneider (2008) can be applied to underwriters who often weight bad news more heavily than good. Ambiguity is confounded with risk in the sense of Chapter 3 because more (process-)risky classes of business tend to rely on more ambiguous underwriting information, for example, high-excess Bermuda-form directors and officers liability insurance. □

8.9.4 Where We Go from Here

There are two fundamental flaws in the elegant theory presented in Section 8.6. To assume "complete and arbitrage-free markets where valuation is based on a general equilibrium framework" is not only unrealistic, but it says we are given prices: it assumes a solution to the hard part of the problem! It is equivalent to supposing the existence of a magic linear pricing functional that prices any security. Since prices are linear, there is no diversification benefit and insureds can transfer their risk directly into the securities market. There is no need for insurers at all; we should complain vociferously!

Modern Portfolio Pricing Theory, presented in Chapter 10, gives a pricing solution based on more realistic assumptions. We lose frictionless markets but gain a well-founded motivation for the existence of insurers. In Classical Portfolio Price Allocation Section 12.4 we show how the methods presented in this chapter evolved and adapted to encompass multiple line pricing.

8.10 Learning Objectives

1. Define and explain the terms perfect, complete, no arbitrage, general equilibrium, Arrow-Debreu security, replicating portfolio, and fundamental and derivative security.
2. Compare and contrast replication and pooling approaches to bearing risk.

3. List the three drivers of insurance demand, and discuss the most relevant for each major line of business.
4. List and describe desirable properties of an indemnity function.
5. List the five principle functions of an insurer. Describe different ways they are provided in the market.
6. Explain top-down insurance pricing. Give examples of capital constraints, referencing the risk measures in Part I.
7. Define and differentiate between capital, surplus, and equity.
8. Describe how accounting standards impact capital, giving examples of items with distinct treatments.
9. Describe and compare different forms of insurance capital. Discuss how to determine the cost of each.
10. List relevant considerations that influence the cost of equity capital and explain why it tends to be expensive for insurance companies.
11. Explain the process of liquidation and priority of claimants.
12. Given a priority waterfall, assets, and claims, compute the distribution of assets in liquidation.
13. Explain two market imperfections that motivate the existence of insurers.
14. Explain the importance and relevance of accounting conventions to insurance pricing.
15. Define and give examples of classical premium calculation principles.
16. Explain the phrase *pricing from the top-down*.
17. Describe Ferrari's model of total return.
18. Split total return into underwriting and investment return, based on data from a financial statement.
19. Price with DCF and IRR models given loss payout, premium collection, and surplus requirements.
20. Set up a simple spreadsheet model to implement DCF for a unit with a multiyear payout pattern.
21. Describe factors influencing appropriate interest rates for each cash flow in a DCF model.
22. Compare and contrast DCF and IRR, and explain when they give the same results.
23. Define a geometric Brownian motion and homogeneous Poisson process.
24. Explain why geometric Brownian motion has a unique martingale measure but a Poisson process does not, and the significance of this result for insurance pricing.
25. Explain the relationship between puts and calls and excess of loss insurance.
26. Compare financial non-arbitrage option pricing with actuarial pricing with reference to the Black-Scholes formula.
27. Describe how option pricing models react to changes in insurance and asset volatility, capital adequacy, and the correlation between insurance and asset returns.
28. Define and distinguish between short- and long-duration policies.
29. Define and explain the significance of the equivalence principle.

8.A Short- and Long-Duration Contracts

There are important economic and accounting differences between short- and long-duration contracts.

8.A.1 Short-Duration Contracts

Short-duration contracts typically have a six-month or twelve-month policy duration. They are characterized by a fixed premium and the lack of any predictable trend in expected losses. An insured may migrate between risk classes over time, but there is no expectation of a particular trend.

Ins Co. writes short-duration contracts. Almost all property-casualty insurance contracts are short-duration. Short-duration contracts can still have a long loss reserve *payout* tail, for example, workers' compensation.

8.A.2 Long-Duration Contracts

Long-duration contracts typically have a duration longer than one year and often last decades. They are characterized by premium uncertainty and a predictable, adverse trend in expected losses. Whole life insurance is the archetype: aging increases the probability of death each year in a predictable way. A level premium long-duration contract gives an insured inter-temporal smoothing, averaging the cost of low and high-risk states. The premium for a level premium whole life policy exceeds expected losses in the early years and is inadequate in the later ones.

The insurer must estimate the value of a long-duration policy periodically to evaluate profitability and ensure it sets aside sufficient reserves to pay future claims. Long-duration level premium contracts do not work when the risk is decreasing because the insured benefits from the lower premium in the early years, but the insurer has no way to force them to continue to pay when the premium becomes redundant in later years—the insured would lapse and start a new policy. When average risk increases, the insured has a financial interest in the policy, and a surrender charge can be used to encourage them not to lapse.

Premium risk in long-duration contracts can be more material than loss risk. For example, a whole life insurance policy has a known benefit amount, the face value of the policy. The present value of benefits varies with time of death. But the biggest risk to the insurer is the number of years for which the insured pays the premium.

Short-duration contracts typically have fixed premium that is collected at inception. Because there is no predictable drift in exposure, there is no need to use valuation reserves to smooth revenue over the policy term. The only risk is the timing and amount of any loss payments.

Struppeck (2015) applies life contingency long-duration contract concepts to property-casualty actuarial problems. He points out that property-casualty contracts tend to have decreasing hazard rates because the worst risks have accidents earlier and exit the cohort. Therefore fixed premium multiyear contacts do not work.

8.B The Equivalence Principle

The actuarial **equivalence principle** (Jewell, 1980) is used to determine fixed premium rates for long-duration contracts. The equivalence principles requires that at issue the expected present value of premiums equals the expected present value of benefits plus expenses.

An obvious objection to using the equivalence principle is the apparent absence of a risk load in *expected* present values. However, expected value does not imply actuarial, or objective, expected value. Instead, we can use a risk-adjusted expected value. Life actuaries regularly add implicit risk loads through the use of *margins*, via conservative mortality and interest crediting assumptions. Mildenhall (2021a) applies the equivalence principle with risk-adjusted probabilities to pricing catastrophe bonds.

9

Classical Portfolio Pricing Practice

In this chapter, we apply classical PCPs and the portfolio CCoC method from Chapter 8 to each Case, illustrate the use of the Pollaczeck-Khinchine formula from Section 8.4.2, and apply the option pricing formulas from Section 8.8.

Creating spreadsheet models to implement DCF or IRR models with a multiyear payout is relatively straightforward but does require careful attention to detail. These become especially intricate if the model incorporates taxes. The examples given in Cummins (1990) are a good introduction. Feldblum (1992) and Robbin (2007) provide more in-depth treatments. US rate filings using the IRR methodology are also available online.

All of the examples in the first two sections are easy to replicate in a spreadsheet or programming language. Again, we strongly recommend that you build your own implementation to check your understanding.

9.1 Stand-Alone Classical PCPs

We apply ten classical PCPs listed below to each Case Study. The Cases are described in Section 2.4, the PCPs in Section 8.4.1, pricing by unit in Table 7.2, and the reinsurance assumptions in Table 7.3.

Expected losses are computed on an unlimited basis. We apply each method to each unit on a stand-alone basis because this is a *portfolio* chapter. The Net and Expected Value methods always produce constant loss ratios by unit and obviously the Net method gives a 100% loss ratio.

The classical methods do not include an explicit capital assumption, so there are no leverage or return on capital statistics to report.

The ceded statistics report the difference between total gross and total net, rather than the result of applying the pricing method to the ceded loss distribution. This is the appropriate view for the cedent.

Pricing Insurance Risk: Theory and Practice, First Edition. Stephen J. Mildenhall and John A. Major.

9.1.1 Tame Case Study

Tables 9.2–9.4 show the parameters, pricing, and implied loss ratios by method. The two units are the same size and have similar, thin-tail, log-concave densities. The overall loss ratio is comparable to a stable personal auto portfolio (remember, there are no expenses). There is little differentiation across the methods, so it is hard to draw conclusions about their behavior. Unit B is more risky than unit A, which is reflected in the pricing and loss ratios across all methods, though the difference between the units is less than 2 loss ratio percentage points. Since the reinsurance attaches above the pricing VaR threshold, gross and net VaR pricing on unit B are the same. However, gross and net pricing in total are different.

Exercise 131. The reinsurance applied to unit B is an aggregate stop loss. Which of the following are true?

1. Net and gross losses are comonotonic, Section 5.2.10.
2. Net precedes gross in first-order stochastic dominance, Section 5.3.1.
3. Net precedes gross in second-order stochastic dominance, Section 5.3.2.
4. All monotone risk measures price net lower than gross, Section 5.2.3.
5. All coherent risk measures price net lower than gross, Section 5.2.14. □

Exercise 132. Does the difference between gross and net premium for unit B equal the ceded difference for total for any method? Explain your findings. □

9.1.2 Cat/Non-Cat Case Study

Tables 9.5 to 9.7 show the parameters, pricing, and implied loss ratios by method. The two units have quite distinct distributions and both are more volatile than the Tame Case. The overall portfolio loss ratio is lower and is comparable to a US or London market specialty portfolio. There is considerable loss ratio differentiation across the methods. Cat is more

Table 9.1 Classical PCPs applied to each Case Study.

No.	Name	Premium
1.	Net	$\mathsf{E}[X]$
2.	Expected value	$\mathsf{E}[X] + \pi\mathsf{E}[X]$
3.	Value at Risk	$\mathsf{VaR}_\pi(X)$
4.	Variance	$\mathsf{E}[X] + \pi\mathsf{Var}(X)$
5.	Standard deviation	$\mathsf{E}[X] + \pi\mathsf{SD}(X)$
6.	semivariance	$\mathsf{E}[X] + \pi\mathsf{Var}^+(X)$
7.	Exponential	$\log(\mathsf{E}[e^{\pi X}])/\pi$
8.	Esscher	$\mathsf{E}[Xe^{\pi X}]/\mathsf{E}[e^{\pi X}]$
9.	Dutch	$\mathsf{E}[X] + \pi\mathsf{E}[(X - \mathsf{E}[X])^+]$
10.	Fischer	$\mathsf{E}[X] + \pi\mathsf{E}[((X - \mathsf{E}[X])^+)^p]^{1/p}$

Table 9.2 Classical pricing by method for Tame Case Study. Pricing calibrated to total gross portfolio and applied to each line on a stand-alone basis. Sorted by gross premium for B.

		A	B		Total		
Method	**Parameter**	**Gross**	**Net**	**Gross**	**Net**	**Gross**	**Ceded**
Net		50.000	49.084	50.000	99.084	100.000	0.916
Expected value	0.034	51.712	50.765	51.712	102.476	103.423	0.947
Variance	0.042	51.053	50.620	52.370	101.673	103.423	1.750
Esscher	0.041	51.034	50.468	52.389	101.503	103.423	1.920
Exponential	0.080	51.028	50.420	52.395	101.447	103.423	1.976
semivariance	0.080	51.051	50.330	52.425	101.411	103.423	2.012
VaR	0.659	51.906	52.750	52.750	102.672	103.422	0.75
Dutch	0.953	51.899	51.498	52.846	102.096	103.423	1.327
Standard deviation	0.380	51.899	51.377	52.848	102.061	103.423	1.362
Fischer	0.523	51.897	51.149	52.881	101.907	103.423	1.516

Table 9.3 Sum of parts (SoP) stand-alone vs. diversified classical pricing by method for Tame Case Study. Delta columns show the difference.

	Total		SoP		Delta	
Method	**Gross**	**Net**	**Gross**	**Net**	**Gross**	**Net**
Net	100.000	99.084	100.000	99.084	0.000	0.000
Expected value	103.423	102.476	103.423	102.476	0.000	0.000
Variance	103.423	101.673	103.423	101.673	0.000	0.000
Esscher	103.423	101.503	103.423	101.503	0.000	0.000
Exponential	103.423	101.447	103.423	101.447	0.000	0.000
semivariance	103.423	101.411	103.477	101.382	0.054	−0.029
VaR	103.422	102.672	104.656	104.656	1.234	1.984
Dutch	103.423	102.096	104.745	103.397	1.322	1.301
Standard deviation	103.423	102.061	104.747	103.276	1.324	1.215
Fischer	103.423	101.907	104.778	103.047	1.355	1.140

risky than unit Non-Cat, with a substantially lower loss ratio in all methods except Net and Expected Value.

All methods except VaR price net unit B lower than gross and with a higher loss ratio. For VaR, the reinsurance attaches above the pricing VaR threshold so the gross and net premium

Table 9.4 Implied loss ratios from classical pricing by method for Tame Case Study. Pricing calibrated to total gross portfolio and applied to each line on a stand-alone basis.

	A	B		Total		
Method	**Gross**	**Net**	**Gross**	**Net**	**Gross**	**Ceded**
Net	1	1	1	1	1	1
Expected value	0.967	0.967	0.967	0.967	0.967	0.967
Variance	0.979	0.97	0.955	0.975	0.967	0.523
Esscher	0.98	0.973	0.954	0.976	0.967	0.477
Exponential	0.98	0.974	0.954	0.977	0.967	0.463
semivariance	0.979	0.975	0.954	0.977	0.967	0.455
VaR	0.963	0.931	0.948	0.965	0.967	1.22
Dutch	0.963	0.953	0.946	0.97	0.967	0.69
Standard deviation	0.963	0.955	0.946	0.971	0.967	0.672
Fischer	0.963	0.96	0.946	0.972	0.967	0.604

Table 9.5 Classical pricing by method for Cat/Non-Cat Case Study. Pricing calibrated to total gross portfolio and applied to each line on a stand-alone basis. Sorted by gross premium for Cat.

		Cat		Non-Cat	Total		
Method	**Parameter**	**Net**	**Gross**	**Gross**	**Net**	**Gross**	**Ceded**
Net		17.786	20.000	80.000	97.786	100.000	2.214
Expected value	0.152	20.480	23.030	92.121	112.601	115.151	2.550
VaR	0.818	30.109	30.109	90.734	113.391	115.141	1.750
Variance	0.028	22.573	31.141	84.013	106.585	115.151	8.566
Dutch	1.859	27.170	32.000	88.882	110.638	115.151	4.513
semivariance	0.040	22.513	32.785	83.092	105.194	115.151	9.957
Standard deviation	0.650	26.302	32.992	87.797	109.332	115.151	5.819
Fischer	0.776	26.249	33.918	86.844	108.380	115.151	6.771
Esscher	0.011	23.575	35.944	81.561	105.054	115.151	10.098
Exponential	0.014	24.760	39.697	81.059	105.619	115.151	9.532

for Cat are the same, and hence the net loss ratio is higher than the gross, again highlighting the undesirable behavior of VaR as a PCP.

Table 9.6 Sum of parts (SoP) stand-alone vs. diversified classical pricing by method for Cat/Non-Cat Case Study. Delta columns show the difference.

	Total		SoP		Delta	
Method	**Gross**	**Net**	**Gross**	**Net**	**Gross**	**Net**
Net	100.000	97.786	100.000	97.786	0.000	0.000
Expected value	115.151	112.601	115.151	112.601	0.000	0.000
VaR	115.141	113.391	120.844	120.844	5.703	7.453
Variance	115.151	106.585	115.154	106.585	0.002	0.000
Dutch	115.151	110.638	120.883	116.052	5.732	5.414
semivariance	115.151	105.194	115.877	105.605	0.726	0.410
Standard deviation	115.151	109.332	120.789	114.099	5.638	4.767
Fischer	115.151	108.380	120.762	113.093	5.611	4.712
Esscher	115.151	105.054	117.505	105.136	2.354	0.083
Exponential	115.151	105.619	120.756	105.819	5.604	0.200

Table 9.7 Implied loss ratios from classical pricing by method for Cat/Non-Cat Case Study. Pricing calibrated to total gross portfolio and applied to each line on a stand-alone basis.

	Cat		Non-Cat	Total		
Method	**Net**	**Gross**	**Gross**	**Net**	**Gross**	**Ceded**
Net	1	1	1	1	1	1
Expected value	0.868	0.868	0.868	0.868	0.868	0.868
VaR	0.591	0.664	0.882	0.862	0.869	1.27
Variance	0.788	0.642	0.952	0.917	0.868	0.258
Dutch	0.655	0.625	0.9	0.884	0.868	0.491
semivariance	0.79	0.61	0.963	0.93	0.868	0.222
Standard deviation	0.676	0.606	0.911	0.894	0.868	0.381
Fischer	0.678	0.59	0.921	0.902	0.868	0.327
Esscher	0.754	0.556	0.981	0.931	0.868	0.219
Exponential	0.718	0.504	0.987	0.926	0.868	0.232

9.1.3 Hu/SCS Case Study

9.8–9.10 show the parameters, pricing, and implied loss ratios by method. The two units are both thick-tailed. SCS has a similar CV to Cat in the second Case, but Hu is even more volatile. The total loss ratio is far lower, in line with a catastrophe reinsurance portfolio.

Table 9.8 Classical pricing by method for Hu/SCS Case Study. Pricing calibrated to total gross portfolio and applied to each line on a stand-alone basis. Sorted by gross premium for Hu.

		Hu		SCS	Total		
Method	**Parameter**	**Net**	**Gross**	**Gross**	**Net**	**Gross**	**Ceded**
Net		18.987	29.727	69.133	88.121	98.860	10.740
Expected value	2.250	61.713	96.619	224.695	286.408	321.314	34.906
Dutch	7.635	117.315	197.224	175.181	253.683	321.314	67.631
VaR	0.977	40.500	203.000	178.500	215.250	321.250	106.000
Variance	0.002	214.979	246.893	74.462	289.440	321.314	31.874
semivariance	0.002	217.084	248.496	73.705	290.285	321.314	31.029
Standard deviation	0.677	227.791	249.521	103.562	299.744	321.314	21.570
Fischer	0.681	228.909	250.331	101.024	300.187	321.314	21.127

Table 9.9 Sum of parts (SoP) stand-alone vs. diversified classical pricing by method for Hu/SCS Case Study. Delta columns show the difference.

	Total		SoP		Delta	
Method	**Gross**	**Net**	**Gross**	**Net**	**Gross**	**Net**
Net	98.860	88.121	98.860	88.121	0.000	0.000
Expected value	321.314	286.408	321.314	286.408	0.000	0.000
Dutch	321.314	253.683	372.405	292.496	51.091	38.813
VaR	321.250	215.250	381.500	219.000	60.250	3.750
Variance	321.314	289.440	321.354	289.441	0.040	0.000
semivariance	321.314	290.285	322.201	290.789	0.887	0.5038
Standard deviation	321.314	299.744	353.083	331.353	31.769	31.610
Fischer	321.314	300.187	351.355	329.933	30.041	29.746

There is less differentiation across the methods than the other Cases, but more between the two units. Neither the Exponential nor the Esscher methods can be readily applied because the loss distributions are too thick tailed (they require ad hoc scaling to compute $\mathsf{E}[e^{kX}]$).

The pricing illustrates how VaR is blind to large losses. The per occurrence reinsurance on Hu attaches below and detaches above the pricing VaR threshold and the VaR method is insensitive to any *over the top* loss exposure. As a result it prices net Hu far more cheaply than any other method. TVaR sees through this ruse, as we see in Chapter 11.

The last four methods listed in Table 9.10 are very tail sensitive, which is evident from their net Hu pricing. Net Hu has a higher CV, is more skewed, and has a higher kurtosis than gross. In the other two Cases, net is better behaved than gross (see tables in Section 2.4.)

Table 9.10 Implied loss ratios from classical pricing by method for Hu/SCS Case Study. Pricing calibrated to total gross portfolio and applied to each line on a stand-alone basis.

	Hu		SCS	Total		
Method	**Net**	**Gross**	**Gross**	**Net**	**Gross**	**Ceded**
Net	1	1	1	1	1	1
Expected value	0.308	0.308	0.308	0.308	0.308	0.308
Dutch	0.162	0.151	0.395	0.347	0.308	0.159
VaR	0.469	0.146	0.387	0.409	0.308	0.101
Variance	0.0883	0.12	0.928	0.304	0.308	0.337
semivariance	0.0875	0.12	0.938	0.304	0.308	0.346
Standard deviation	0.0834	0.119	0.668	0.294	0.308	0.498
Fischer	0.0829	0.119	0.684	0.294	0.308	0.508

Exercise 133. Complete Exercise 131 for the Hu/SCS Case. Remember, the reinsurance applied to unit Hu is an unlimited per occurrence cover, not an aggregate stop loss. In addition, is it true that using a coherent risk measure, the implied loss ratio for net will always be higher than for gross in this Case? □

9.2 Portfolio CCoC Pricing

We now apply portfolio CCoC, Section 8.7.4, pricing to the Case Studies. The difference between the Cases emphasizes the impact of tail thickness on indicated premium and on diversification benefit.

We fix the cost of capital at $\iota = 0.10$ and use a $p = 0.9999$ VaR capital standard for Tame and 0.999 for the other two. The results are shown in 9.12–9.14. Each exhibit shows all eight insurance statistics from the Insurance Pentagon, and all subsequent exhibits retain the same ordering and basic layout.

Although loss costs should account for the probability of default, that adjustment is often ignored in practice since policyholder deficits are usually very small. We price with and without default to illustrate the impact. In the first two Cases, the impact is indeed very small. But, in the Hu/SCS Case, default reduces recoveries to the very thick-tailed hurricane unit by 12.5% and for SCS by 0.4%. We apply per occurrence reinsurance to the hurricane unit. This actually *increases* the impact of default, to 19.6%, because the reinsurance reduces assets using a VaR risk measure. The calculation does not allow for possible reinsurer default.

Table 9.11 compares the sum of stand-alone premiums (SoP, or sum of parts) to the total (diversified). It confirms that thinner tailed distributions diversify more effectively: there is a greater diversification benefit for Tame than Cat/Non-Cat than Hu/SCS, and within each Case a greater benefit for the net portfolios than gross. Since premiums include expected

Table 9.11 Comparison of stand-alone and sum of parts (SoP) premium.

Case study	Metric	Gross SoP	Gross Total	Reduction	Net SoP	Net Total	Reduction
Tame	Premium	104.9	103.4	−1.4%	102.9	101.5	−1.4%
	Capital	48.69	34.23	-29.7%	37.79	24.64	-34.8%
Cat/Non–Cat	Premium	118.8	115.2	-3.0%	109.6	105.9	-3.4%
	Capital	188.7	152.1	-19.4%	118.3	81.68	-31.0%
Hu/SCS	Premium	361.5	321.3	-11.1%	318	278.9	-12.3%
	Capital	2,667	2,262	-15.2%	2,339	1,945	-16.8%

losses, which are close to additive at the capital levels used, there is a smaller diversification benefit for premium than capital within each Case.

Remark 134. Table 9.14 illustrates how CCoC can fail to be subadditive. Capital and assets are subadditive (SoP is greater than total) but expected loss is not. Total expected gross loss with default is 95.15 compared to SoP of 94.82. In this case, the diversification benefit between the two lines more than offsets the lower capital and higher leverage in the pool. □

9.3 Applications of Classical Risk Theory

9.3.1 The Pollaczeck-Khinchine Formula

The Pollaczeck-Khinchine formula, Section 8.4.2, determines the probability of eventual ruin in terms of starting surplus and the premium rate for a portfolio where claims are driven by a compound Poisson process. Figure 9.1 illustrates the theory using a lognormal severity with a mean of ¤50,000 and a CV of 10 ($\sigma = 2.15$) corresponding to a moderately risky liability line. It compares starting surplus levels for different eventual ruin probabilities assuming a margin $r = 0.1$ with a ¤1 million and ¤10 million occurrence limit. It also illustrates simulations of the surplus process in each case with starting surplus calibrated to a 0.05 probability of eventual ruin.

The simulations in Figure 9.1 show that the probability of eventual ruin is constrained by the buildup of surplus in most scenarios. Defaults occur early in the simulated history. This model could be appropriate for a mutual company—indeed some mutual companies have accumulated substantial amounts of capital. For a stock company, a more realistic approach adds dividends to manage capital; see Section 18.1.

9.3.2 Market Scale and Viability

Given severity X and ratio r of margin to expected loss, the Pollaczeck-Khinchine function ψ is monotone and hence invertible, allowing us to find $u_{X,r}(p) = \psi_{X,r}^{-1}(p)$, the starting capital necessary to guarantee probability p of eventual ruin.

Table 9.12 Constant CoC pricing by unit for Tame Case Study, with 0.1 cost of capital and $p = 0.9999$. The column SoP shows the sum by unit. ¤12.9 excess ¤56.2 aggregate reinsurance applied to B. All units produce the same rate of return, by construction.

		Gross				Net		
Method	**Statistic**	**A**	**B**	**SoP**	**Total**	**A**	**SoP**	**Total**
No default	Loss	50.00	50.00	100.00	100.00	50.00	99.08	99.08
	Margin	1.89	2.98	4.87	3.42	1.89	3.78	2.46
	Premium	51.89	52.98	104.9	103.4	51.89	102.9	101.5
	Loss ratio	0.964	0.944	0.954	0.967	0.964	0.963	0.976
	Capital	18.88	29.82	48.69	34.23	18.88	37.79	24.64
	Rate of return	0.1	0.1	0.1	0.1	0.1	0.1	0.1
	Leverage	2.75	1.78	2.15	3.02	2.75	2.72	4.12
	Assets	70.77	82.80	153.6	137.7	70.77	140.7	126.2
With default	Loss	50.00	50.00	100.00	100.00	50.00	99.08	99.08
	Margin	1.89	2.98	4.87	3.42	1.89	3.78	2.46
	Premium	51.89	52.98	104.9	103.4	51.89	102.9	101.5
	Loss ratio	0.964	0.944	0.954	0.967	0.964	0.963	0.976
	Capital	18.88	29.82	48.69	34.23	18.88	37.79	24.64
	Rate of return	0.1	0.1	0.1	0.1	0.1	0.1	0.1
	Leverage	2.75	1.78	2.15	3.02	2.75	2.72	4.12
	Assets	70.77	82.80	153.6	137.7	70.77	140.7	126.2

The amount of margin equals $r\lambda\mathsf{E}[X]$, where λ is the annual expected claim count. Since the expected margin must pay the cost of capital, we get a market viability constraint

$$r\lambda\mathsf{E}[X] \geq \iota\, u_{X,r}(p) \tag{9.1}$$

where ι is the cost of capital. Each element in Eq. (9.1) is influenced by different factors:

- the hazard and contract design determines X,
- the insurance product market determines r,
- the capital markets determine ι, and
- a regulator or rating agency determines (or strongly influences) p.

Eq. (9.1) can be applied in two ways.

First, consider a diversifying unit, such as motor liability, where insurers grow by adding new, independent insureds with the same severity. Here, Eq. (9.1) gives a **minimum size of market** constraint

$$\lambda \geq \iota \frac{u_{X,r}(p)}{r\mathsf{E}[X]}. \tag{9.2}$$

Eq. (9.2) is a function of four variables and λ is:

Table 9.13 Constant CoC pricing by unit for Cat/Non-Cat Case Study, with 0.1 cost of capital and $p = 0.999$. The column SoP shows the sum by unit. ¤79.6 excess ¤41.1 aggregate reinsurance applied to Cat. All units produce the same rate of return, by construction.

		Gross				Net		
Method	**Statistic**	**Cat**	**Non-Cat**	**SoP**	**Total**	**Cat**	**SoP**	**Total**
No default	Loss	20.00	80.00	100.00	100.00	17.79	97.79	97.79
	Margin	15.03	3.84	18.87	15.20	7.99	11.83	8.16
	Premium	35.03	83.84	118.9	115.2	25.77	109.6	105.9
	Loss ratio	0.571	0.954	0.841	0.868	0.69	0.892	0.923
	Capital	150.3	38.41	188.7	152.0	79.87	118.3	81.63
	Rate of return	0.1	0.1	0.1	0.1	0.1	0.1	0.1
	Leverage	0.233	2.18	0.63	0.758	0.323	0.927	1.3
	Assets	185.3	122.2	307.5	267.2	105.6	227.9	187.6
With default	Loss	19.95	80.00	99.94	99.95	17.73	97.73	97.73
	Margin	15.03	3.84	18.87	15.21	7.99	11.83	8.17
	Premium	34.98	83.84	118.8	115.2	25.72	109.6	105.9
	Loss ratio	0.57	0.954	0.841	0.868	0.689	0.892	0.923
	Capital	150.3	38.41	188.7	152.1	79.92	118.3	81.68
	Rate of return	0.1	0.1	0.1	0.1	0.1	0.1	0.1
	Leverage	0.233	2.18	0.63	0.757	0.322	0.926	1.3
	Assets	185.3	122.2	307.5	267.2	105.6	227.9	187.6

- Increasing and linear in ι: the market must be larger given more expensive capital.
- Decreasing in r: the market can be smaller with a higher margin.
- Decreasing in p: the market must be larger to support a stricter capital standard.
- Independent of expected severity (because ψ is homogeneous in $\mathsf{E}[X]$) but dependent on the shape of severity (which influences ψ).

Table 9.15 shows the natural scale using the lognormal example in Section 9.3.1. Size, measured by expected annual claim count, is shown for a range of margins, limits, and stability constraints. If claim frequency is 5%, the table shows that a market with ¤1M limits is reasonable for all p and r. For example, the strictest stability constraint $p = 0.01$ and lowest margin rate $r = 0.025$ needs 39,776 claims, or about 800,000 policies, to be viable. With a ¤10M limit and same r, the market size needs to be 128,843 claims, or about 2.5 million policies, which is less achievable. However, if the margin rate increases to $r = 0.1$, the market size reduces to 9,087 claims or about 180,000 policies.

Second, consider a nondiversifying unit, writing catastrophe exposed business, where insurers grow by covering a greater proportion of each event. Severity becomes market share times an industry severity X, and the number of events is fixed. US hurricane reinsurance

Table 9.14 Constant CoC pricing by unit for Hu/SCS Case Study, with 0.1 cost of capital and $p = 0.999$. The column SoP shows the sum by unit. ¤372.4 excess ¤40.3 per occurrence reinsurance applied to Hu. All units produce the same rate of return, by construction.

		Gross				Net		
Method	**Statistic**	**Hu**	**SCS**	**SoP**	**Total**	**Hu**	**SoP**	**Total**
No default	Loss	29.73	69.13	98.86	98.86	18.99	88.12	88.12
	Margin	223.4	42.92	266.4	225.8	190.6	233.5	194.1
	Premium	253.2	112.1	365.2	324.7	209.6	321.6	282.3
	Loss ratio	0.117	0.617	0.271	0.304	0.0906	0.274	0.312
	Capital	2,234	429.2	2,664	2,258	1,906	2,335	1,941
	Rate of return	0.1	0.1	0.1	0.1	0.1	0.1	0.1
	Leverage	0.113	0.261	0.137	0.144	0.11	0.138	0.145
	Assets	2,488	541.2	3,029	2,583	2,116	2,657	2,224
With default	Loss	26.01	68.82	94.82	95.15	15.27	84.08	84.41
	Margin	223.8	42.95	266.7	226.2	190.9	233.9	194.5
	Premium	249.8	111.8	361.5	321.3	206.2	318.0	278.9
	Loss ratio	0.104	0.616	0.262	0.296	0.074	0.264	0.303
	Capital	2,238	429.5	2,667	2,262	1,909	2,339	1,945
	Rate of return	0.1	0.1	0.1	0.1	0.1	0.1	0.1
	Leverage	0.112	0.26	0.136	0.142	0.108	0.136	0.143
	Assets	2,488	541.2	3,029	2,583	2,116	2,657	2,224

is an example. In this case, viability is independent of market share and is controlled by whether the inequality Eq. (9.1) has a solution that is acceptable to both the product market and the capital market. Viability is harder to achieve

- with smaller λ: rare events are more difficult to insure,
- with lower p: higher quality insurance is more expensive,
- with higher ι: more costly capital, and
- with lower r because u increases quickly.

9.4 Option Pricing Examples

We use the option pricing model to explore how price varies with insurance and asset volatility. The model and notation are described in Section 8.8.9. The example is similar to that shown in Cummins (1991).

To focus on the impact of different volatility assumptions, initially assume $r_h = \mu_L = 0$, meaning there is no trend in either losses or general prices, and that the risk-free rate is zero.

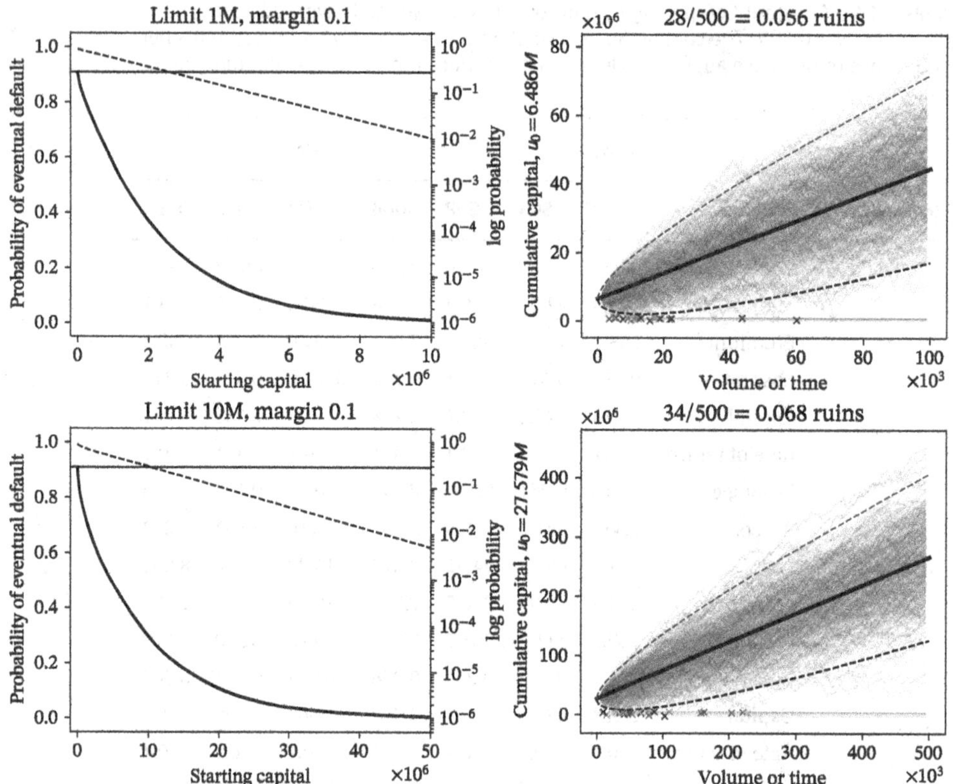

Figure 9.1 Left column: Pollaczeck-Khinchine formula starting surplus as a function of the eventual ruin probability with margin 0.1 on linear (solid) and log (dashed) scales. The Cramer-Lundberg formula says that the probability of eventual ruin is approximately exponential, which is a straight line on a log scale. Right column: 500 simulated surplus paths, with × indicating ruin scenarios. Capital calibrated to 0.05 eventual ruin probability. Time and volume are symmetric in the model, so volume can be regarded as time for a fixed size portfolio or a varying sized portfolio for a fixed time or a combination. Scale indicates cumulative exposure-years.

Work with a one-period model, $T = 1$. Finally, assume $\rho = 0$, there is no correlation between assets and liabilities.

Table 9.16 shows D/L, the market value of insurance claims as a percentage of unlimited *promised* expected insurance losses, the market value of equity per unit of loss, S/L, and the loss risk discount rate $r_D = 1 - D/L$ for various values of asset and liability volatility σ_A, σ_L at different asset to liability A/L ratios. Note that when $A/L < 1$ the company is technically insolvent. Limited liability implies that the market value of equity is always positive.

The table shows the expected behaviors. Premium increases with A/L: higher quality insurance is more valuable and has a lower policyholder deficit. The market value of equity S/L also increases, just as a call becomes worth more as it moves more in the money. Increasing asset or liability risk lowers premium and increases the market value of equity, just as a call becomes worth more with higher volatility. The market value of equity is always

Table 9.15 Natural scale of the market, expressed as expected annual claim count, for different margin rates r (by column), policy limits, eventual probabilities of default p, and fixed $\iota = 0.1$ according to Eq. (9.1).

Limit	p	r	0.025	0.05	0.075	0.1	0.15	0.2	0.25
1M	0.01		39,776	10,172	4,621	2,655	1,229	717.9	476.1
	0.05		25,784	6,572	2,975	1,704	783.6	455.2	300.2
	0.1		19,758	5,021	2,267	1,294	592.0	342.1	224.5
	0.25		11,792	2,971	1,330	752.9	338.6	192.4	123.9
5M	0.01		92,578	23,942	10,991	6,376	3,003	1,782	1,198
	0.05		59,901	15,411	7,038	4,063	1,896	1,115	744.0
	0.1		45,828	11,736	5,336	3,067	1,419	827.7	546.7
	0.25		27,224	6,879	3,086	1,750	787.9	452.8	290.4
10M	0.01		128,843	33,610	15,551	9,087	4,335	2,600	1,765
	0.05		83,243	21,570	9,915	5,758	2,714	1,610	1,079
	0.1		63,604	16,384	7,488	4,324	2,015	1,182	793.6
	0.25		37,642	9,530	4,279	2,427	1,101	613.6	382.0

greater than its *cash value*, $S/L \geq A/L - 1$, reflecting the option value. All effects are more pronounced at lower A/L ratios.

Notice that expected asset returns are not an input to the model. They would be required to compute an objective probability loss ratio. The model would show higher loss ratios with higher asset returns since insureds implicitly participate in asset risk.

To be clear, here is what the table is computing. Let L be lognormal with mean 1 and given σ_L. Let A be independent lognormal with mean equal to the value shown in the A/L column and given σ_A. The first, fourth, and fifth columns of the table all show $D/L = \mathsf{E}[A \wedge L]/\mathsf{E}[L]$, computed using Eq. (8.22). The second column shows $\mathsf{E}[(A - L)^+]/\mathsf{E}[L]$ computed using Eq. (8.21), and the third shows r_D using Eq. (8.23). The values in the table are easy to reproduce via simulation.

The table shows that insurance is priced at cost, $D = 1$ and $r_D = 0$, when $A/L = 1.5$ in the low volatility scenario, and below unlimited expected loss in all cases. There is no risk load. This is consistent with the assumption that $r_h = 0$, which means all underwriting risk is diversifiable.

The fourth column shows D/L when $\mu_L = 0.03$, corresponding to insurance trend above general inflation. The anticipated trend is incorporated into the value of insurance. Now $D/L > 1$ when A/L is reasonably large. A positive trend in the strike price of an option decreases the value of a call, such as owners equity, and increases the value of a put, such as insurance.

The final column shows the impact of nondiversifiable insurance risk on D/L. Computing underwriting betas has been the subject of much debate, and plausible arguments can

Table 9.16 Option values of insurance *D/L* and equity *S/L* for different levels of insurance volatility σ_L and asset volatility σ_A. Asset and liabilities are independent. In the first three columns there is no inflation and the risk-free rate is zero. The fourth column shows *D/L* when $\mu_L = 0.03$, corresponding to insurance trend above general inflation. The last column shows *D/L* when $\mu_L = 0.03$ and $r_h = -0.025$, indicating the excess claim inflation is not diversifiable.

σ_L	σ_A	A/L	D/L	S/L	r_D	$\mu_L = 0.03$	$\mu_L = 0.03$, $r_h = -0.025$
0.1	0.05	0.9	0.8902	0.009841	0.1164	0.8941	0.8963
	0.05	1	0.9554	0.04458	0.0456	0.9684	0.977
	0.05	1.1	0.9872	0.1128	0.01291	1.01	1.027
	0.05	1.2	0.9974	0.2026	0.002647	1.026	1.049
	0.05	1.3	0.9996	0.3004	0.0004063	1.03	1.055
	0.05	1.4	1	0.4	4.882e-05	1.03	1.056
	0.05	1.5	1	0.5	4.798e-06	1.03	1.057
0.25	0.05	0.9	0.8456	0.05442	0.1677	0.8539	0.8602
	0.05	1	0.8986	0.1014	0.107	0.9115	0.9216
	0.05	1.1	0.9362	0.1638	0.06595	0.9537	0.9675
	0.05	1.2	0.9613	0.2387	0.03948	0.9826	0.9999
	0.05	1.3	0.9772	0.3228	0.02305	1.002	1.022
	0.05	1.4	0.9869	0.4131	0.01318	1.013	1.036
	0.05	1.5	0.9926	0.5074	0.007407	1.021	1.044
0.1	0.15	0.9	0.8705	0.02952	0.1387	0.8773	0.882
	0.15	1	0.9282	0.07182	0.07453	0.9413	0.951
	0.15	1.1	0.9643	0.1357	0.03633	0.9838	0.9989
	0.15	1.2	0.9839	0.2161	0.01619	1.008	1.028
	0.15	1.3	0.9934	0.3066	0.006667	1.021	1.043
	0.15	1.4	0.9974	0.4026	0.002567	1.027	1.051
	0.15	1.5	0.9991	0.5009	0.0009347	1.029	1.054
0.25	0.15	0.9	0.8328	0.06716	0.1829	0.8416	0.8483
	0.15	1	0.8841	0.1159	0.1232	0.8969	0.907
	0.15	1.1	0.9219	0.1781	0.08131	0.9387	0.9521
	0.15	1.2	0.9486	0.2514	0.05275	0.9689	0.9853
	0.15	1.3	0.9668	0.3332	0.03374	0.9899	1.009
	0.15	1.4	0.9789	0.4211	0.02132	1.004	1.025
	0.15	1.5	0.9867	0.5133	0.01335	1.014	1.036

be made for positive or negative values for ρ. If the underwriting beta is negative then poor market returns are correlated with high underwriting losses, which results in a positive insurance loading because losses are discounted at a rate below risk-free. In the option model this translates into $r_h < 0$; claim inflation is negatively correlated with the market. The last column of the table shows the impact of taking $r_h = -0.025$, retaining the net trend $\mu_L = 0.03$. Again, the effect is to increase the value of insurance.

9.5 Learning Objectives

1. Compute premiums by applying classical PCPs to a given loss distribution.
2. Rank classical PCP prices for a given loss distribution based on its statistical properties.
3. Identify which classical PCPs are sensitive to volume, volatility, and tail risk.
4. Given a severity distribution, apply the Pollaczeck-Khinchine formula to determine the probability of eventual ruin.
5. Apply option pricing techniques to estimate premium, including asset risk.

10

Modern Portfolio Pricing Theory

In this chapter, we introduce a modern approach to pricing, where the risk and margin are compared to supporting capital rather than expected loss. A capital-centric view leads naturally to pricing by layer, a layer pricing distortion function, and finally, an associated spectral risk measure. We derive the distortion function's properties from its interpretation as a set of layer prices. We express total premium and loss as a function of supporting assets. We explain how to interpret a distortion function as a risk-adjusted probability and show how to use it to compute standard insurance statistics. We define the spectral risk measure (SRM) associated with a concave distortion function and relate the properties of the distortion and SRM. Finally, we show that an SRM can be represented as a weighted average of VaRs or TVaRs or using probability scenarios and provide a dictionary for translating between these.

We use the following notation and conventions.

- We call the distribution function value $F(x)$ the non-exceedance probability of x and the survival function $S(x)$ its exceedance probability.
- The five monetary variables are assets a, loss S, premium P, capital Q, and margin M. Survival, S, is used for loss because only losses $X > x$ attach the layer at x.
- Premium equals expected loss plus margin.
- Assets equal premium plus capital.
- Premium and related variables are expressed as functions of assets.
- These variables have a total form and a layer form—explained later. The total form is denoted with a bar: $\bar{S}$, $\bar{P}$, etc. The layer form is the derivative of the total form with respect to assets.
- The layer risk return, risk discount factor, and risk discount rate are ι, ν, and δ; see Appendix A.1. The average risk return over all layers equals $\bar{\iota}$, using the bar notation.
- Typically, s represents the probability of loss and $p = 1 - s$ the probability of no loss.

10.1 Classical vs. Modern Pricing and Layer Pricing

Classical actuarial pricing relates the margin to expected loss. Capital is either absent or obliquely present in the calculations. None of the actuarial PCPs in Section 8.4.1 explicitly

Pricing Insurance Risk: Theory and Practice, First Edition. Stephen J. Mildenhall and John A. Major.

reference capital. Modern or financial pricing explicitly relates margin to the cost of supporting capital—per the Adam Smith epigraph to Chapter 1. We start by exploring the implications of assuming that premium is a function of supporting assets.

We often tackle complex problems by breaking them into simpler ones. Financial economics values complex assets as the sum of their fundamental Arrow-Debreu components, Section 8.6. It is natural to consider a similar approach to premium calculation.

The first step is to determine the basic building block insurance contract. An Arrow-Debreu security that offers insurance against the occurrence of a particular event is the obvious choice. The Arrow-Debreu framework presupposes knowledge of all states of the world. It operates in an *exchange* economy with no need or place for a limited liability insurance intermediary. And it offers *relative*, rather than absolute, levels of indemnity, in the sense of sharing the realized output of the economy rather than guaranteeing a particular level. Its fundamental risk-sharing equilibrium is a quota share of aggregate output (Eeckhoudt, Gollier, and Schlesinger, 2011).

Insurers find it impossible to specify the objective state space of *all* future states of the world required by the Arrow-Debreu framework. Instead, outcomes are identified with their loss amounts, using implicit events, Section 3.4.2. An exception occurs with catastrophe models where events defining hurricanes, earthquakes, etc., are explicitly identified.

Insurance risk sharing is not bilateral but operates through **pooling** into **limited liability** insurance intermediaries. Insurers offer *absolute* levels of indemnity, with the caveat that they can default and take advantage of limited liability in certain situations. These differences between the Arrow-Debreu world and the real world are all noted in Arrow (1996). Because of them, we want to consider an alternative to Arrow-Debreu securities as a basic building block. Layers of portfolio losses are the natural choice.

Catastrophe bonds and reinsurance are marketed and priced by layer, an approach that mirrors the tranching of debt by seniority. Each individual layer is easier to understand than the entire risk. Market practitioners (Mango, 2005; Mango *et al.*, 2012), take it as a given that different layers are priced to different returns. Different reinsurers have appetites for risks at different probabilities of loss, often driven by their use of different forms of financing.

In a layered model, it appears that the price is varying by the layer's monetary attachment level. But it can equally be regarded as varying by each layer's probability of loss. This view allows risks to be compared easily. In insurance language, the investor's target return for a layer depends on its exceedance probability—casting it as a dual implicit event, Section 3.4.3. The fundamental question becomes: how does the investor's target return vary with exceedance probability? The investor does not *see* the attachment; they are only concerned with the default probability.

As a layer becomes thinner, it can be modeled by an all-or-nothing **Bernoulli layer** (defined in Section 10.4). Partial losses are not possible. A Bernoulli layer should be easy to price because it is entirely described by its probability of loss. Bernoulli layers are the appropriate insurance analog of Arrow-Debreu securities.

A Bernoulli layer pays ¤1 when $X > a$ and zero otherwise. It is a simple insurance contract but a complex, compound Arrow-Debreu security. It does not respond in just one state of the world; instead, it responds in all states that cause a loss greater than the attachment point. Its nature has profound implications for risk measurement and premium calculation.

This chapter develops the mathematics to price Bernoulli layers. Working by layer is consistent with the practice of underwriting. It is introduced in various papers including Venter (1991) and Wang (1996). Interest in the concept was reinvigorated by Bodoff (2007). The layering approach leads us to Spectral Risk Measures. With that background, we turn to the details of pricing by layer.

10.2 Pricing with Varying Assets

We analyze insurance pricing for Ins Co., the one period limited liability insurer introduced in Chapter 2. Ins Co. has assets a and writes total loss exposure given by a random variable X. X represents the total *promised* loss payments Ins Co. has made on a portfolio of policies. Required assets are assumed given; how they are determined is not relevant here.

The **total pricing problem** is to decide the split of asset funding between policyholder premium and investor capital.

In a one-period model with no franchise value and risk-free assets, there is no distinction between equity and its replacement by a most-junior tranche of debt. Therefore, the mix between debt and equity is irrelevant to Ins Co., and we can assume that all capital is debt. For example, 100% equity financing is equivalent to putting all debt capital at the same priority. However, we are left with the problem of **debt tranching** (or layering), that is, setting the debt priority schedule to define the capital structure. It is equivalent to specifying bond prices (risk return or CoC) in our model.

Debt holders within a tranche *quota share* the residual value to which they are entitled and all earn the same CoC. When more tranches (super senior, senior, junior, subordinated, mezzanine, etc.) are introduced, each has its own cost of capital, reflecting the credit yield curve. The most senior tranches have the lowest price, measured as a discount to par value, and the most subordinated tranches have the highest price. In this context, relating the bond's price to its estimated default rate is very natural—explaining why we label insurance risks by their probability of loss rather than their monetary attachment point. Our prices are set in a notional bond market, where investors evaluate default rates unaware of the monetary attachment bonds. The bond's performance is de-linked from the insurance attachment point; its default probability is all that matters. We allow a continuum of tranches, mirroring the decomposition of insurance pricing by Bernoulli layers described in Section 10.4.

The Myers-Cohn's fair premium condition says the **economically fair premium** equals expected losses plus the expected risk margin paid to capital providers for bearing insurance risk; see Eq. (8.12). To simplify the analysis, we assume the risk-free rate is zero or work with time discounted losses.

To compute expected losses we need to know the payments Ins Co. will make in each state of the world, allowing for the possibility it defaults. Although this seems obvious, it took until the mid-1980s before ex post default rules were incorporated into academic treatments of pricing.

Ins Co.'s loss payments are given by the random variable $X \wedge a$, the lesser of its promised payments X and its assets a. Ins Co. is *allowed* to default because of its limited liability legal structure. It is subject to the *possibility* of default because it uses diversification to leverage assets over multiple policies. Ins Co. usually has a slim chance of default, despite issuing aggregate limits that are many multiples of a. This safety despite leverage is the economic secret sauce of insurance.

Ins Co.'s expected losses are given by the limited expected value **total loss function**

$$\bar{S}(a) := \mathsf{E}[X \wedge a] = \int_0^a S(x)\,dx \tag{10.1}$$

derived in Eq. (3.7). The bar indicates the total—as opposed to layer—loss. The survival function (exceedance probability) $S(x) := \mathsf{P}(X > x)$ is integrable up to $a < \infty$ because it is decreasing and bounded by 1. $\bar{S}(a)$ is differentiable almost everywhere with derivative $S(x)$ because it is the integral of a non-negative, monotone function (Royden 1988). When $\bar{S}$ is not differentiable, it has a kink. It never has a jump.

Define $\bar{P}(a)$ to be the **total premium function**, giving the economically fair premium to insure X when Ins Co. holds assets a. Although the exact form of $\bar{P}$ is unknown—it is the function we are trying to determine—it must be an increasing function of a, otherwise it would be possible to find arbitrage opportunities. (If $\bar{P}(a)$ is decreasing in an interval $[a, a + da]$ then the layer between a and $a + da$ must sell for less than zero. The buyer has a guaranteed profit of at least its negative price, and possibly more if the layer has a loss. No rational seller would allow such pricing.) Because it is increasing, $\bar{P}$ is differentiable almost everywhere as a function of a.

Premium is the sum of expected losses and the **total margin function**

$$\bar{P}(a) = \bar{S}(a) + \bar{M}(a).$$

$\bar{M}$ is differentiable almost everywhere because it is the difference of two almost everywhere differentiable functions.

At the beginning of the period, Ins Co.'s only sources of assets are premium and capital. It faces a **portfolio funding constraint**

$$a = \bar{P}(a) + \bar{Q}(a). \tag{10.2}$$

$\bar{Q}(a)$ is the **total capital function**, giving the amount of capital provided by investors. It is differentiable with respect to a, again because it is a difference of two differentiable functions.

We have shown that total premium, margin, and capital are all differentiable functions of a. By symmetry, define $\bar{F}(a) = \int_0^a F(x)dx = a - \bar{S}(a) = \bar{Q}(a) + \bar{M}(a) = \mathsf{E}[(a - X)^+]$. $\bar{F}$ is the insurance savings or total residual value identified in Figure 3.10.

The capital markets determine the value $\bar{Q}$ and the expected return on capital. We call the return earned by investors for bearing risk the **risk return** or the **cost of capital** (CoC). We use the term CoC when taking the capital user's perspective, where it is an input variable, e.g. the required CoC. We use risk return when taking the capital provider's perspective, where it is an output, e.g. the expected risk return by unit. The average risk return function is denoted

$\bar{\iota}(a)$ and is defined by

$$\bar{\iota}(a) := \frac{\text{expected margin}}{\text{investment}} = \frac{\bar{M}(a)}{\bar{Q}(a)} = \frac{\bar{P}(a) - \bar{S}(a)}{a - \bar{P}(a)}. \tag{10.3}$$

Given expected losses and assets, any one of premium, capital, margin, loss ratio, or average risk return is sufficient to compute the other four—see Figure 10.7.

As Adam Smith points out, insureds must finance the expected—*common*—loss. Insureds and investors have a **shared liability** to fund the assets in excess of expected losses. It is convenient to introduce the **risk discount rate** that compares margin to the shared liability

$$\bar{\delta}(a) = \frac{\text{expected margin}}{\text{shared liability}} = \frac{\bar{M}(a)}{a - \bar{S}(a)} = \frac{\bar{P}(a) - \bar{S}(a)}{a - \bar{S}(a)} \tag{10.4}$$

and the corresponding **risk discount factor** comparing capital to the shared liability

$$\bar{v}(a) = \frac{\text{capital}}{\text{shared liability}} = \frac{\bar{Q}(a)}{a - \bar{S}(a)} = \frac{a - \bar{P}(a)}{a - \bar{S}(a)}. \tag{10.5}$$

When investors buy the insurer's residual value, they buy a bond with a face value equal to the assets subject to some degree of default. The expected amount of default equals the expected loss, so the bond's expected payout equals the shared liability. They apply the risk discount factor to the bond's expected payout to determine its fair, risk-adjusted value, i.e. the amount of capital they are willing to pay for it. This analogy explains our risk return, risk discount rate, and risk discount factor terminology. Exercise 135 explains the choice of notation.

Exercise 135.

1. Using Eqs. (10.3) and (10.4), show that $\bar{\delta} = \bar{\iota}/(1 + \bar{\iota})$.
2. Using Eqs. (10.3) and (10.5), show that $\bar{v} = 1/(1 + \bar{\iota})$.
3. Confirm that $1 = \bar{v} + \bar{\delta}$ and $\bar{\delta} = \bar{\iota}\bar{v}$. Recall, the same relations hold between the rate of interest, discount rate, and discount factor. i, d, and v.
4. If you split an amount a in proportion $\bar{\iota} : 1$ show the split is $\bar{\delta}a$ and $\bar{v}a$. □

The split of the shared liability into policyholder margin and capital is the nub of pricing. By the definition of $\bar{\delta}$ and $\bar{v}$, the split is simply

$$\bar{M}(a) = \bar{\delta}(a)(a - \bar{S}(a))$$
$$\bar{Q}(a) = \bar{v}(a)(a - \bar{S}(a)).$$

The next three equations give different expressions for the total premium function:

$$\bar{P}(a) = \bar{S}(a) + \bar{\delta}(a)(a - \bar{S}(a)) \tag{10.6}$$
$$= a - \bar{v}(a)(a - \bar{S}(a)) \tag{10.7}$$
$$= \bar{v}(a)\bar{S}(a) + \bar{\delta}(a)a. \tag{10.8}$$

Eq. (10.6) expresses premium as the loss cost plus the cost of capital, i.e. risk margin. Eq. (10.7) expresses it as that part of assets not funded by capital, a restatement of the funding constraint. Eq. (10.8) can be written in terms of the average cost of capital as

$$\bar{P}(a) = \frac{\bar{S}(a) + \bar{\iota}(a)a}{1 + \bar{\iota}(a)},$$

which is identical to Eq. (8.12) derived from the Myers-Cohn's fair premium condition with no taxes.

10.3 Pricing by Layer and the Layer Premium Density

We expended a lot of effort in Section 10.2 to check that the total expected loss and premium are differentiable functions of assets. In this section, we reap the dividends by showing their derivatives give the expected loss and premium of a Bernoulli layer all-or-nothing risk. We then figure the value of these Bernoulli layers to investors in Section 10.4. Bernoulli layers allow us to apply a divide and conquer approach to pricing, breaking the total price of a risk into a sum of prices for each layers. Throughout this section X is fixed, and S, P, etc., all depend on X.

Recall from our discussion of layer pricing, Section 3.5.3, that L_d^{d+l} denotes the layer l excess of d. It applies a limit l and deductible d. For a subject loss x, the layer pays $L_d^{d+l}(x) = (x - d)^+ \wedge l$. The notation L_d^{d+l} mimics integrals, with the attachment and detachment points as sub- and super scripts. When applied to a random loss X, $L_d^{d+l}(X)$ becomes a random variable. Ins Co. is providing a ground-up ($d = 0$), cover $L_0^a(X) = X \wedge a$ on X with limit $l = a$.

Using this notation, $\bar{P}(a)$ is the premium for $L_0^a(X)$. We want to argue that $\bar{P}(a+y) - \bar{P}(a)$ is the premium for $L_a^{a+y}(X)$. Since $L_0^{a+y} = L_0^a + L_a^{a+y}$, this follows by no arbitrage if $\bar{P}$ is linear, as it is in a perfect market. However, insurance pricing functionals are generally not linear. Instead, we rely on comonotonic additivity—the idea that price is additive for risks that do not diversify against one another. The two layers L_0^a and L_a^{a+y} *on the same* X are comonotonic because they are both increasing functions of the underlying loss. Therefore, assuming $\bar{P}$ is layer additive, $\bar{P}(a + y) - \bar{P}(a)$ equals the premium for $L_a^{a+y}(X)$.

It is natural to consider the impact of adding a small amount da to assets if we want to break the cover L_0^a into pieces, leading us to examine the derivative. Let's start by looking at the derivative of the total loss function $\bar{S}(a) := \mathsf{E}[L_0^a(X)] = \mathsf{E}[X \wedge a]$, Eq. (10.1). By the Fundamental Theorem of Calculus

$$\frac{d}{da}\bar{S}(a) = \frac{d}{da}\int_0^a S(x)dx = S(a). \tag{10.9}$$

We call $S(a)$ the **loss layer density function**. It provides an estimate $\bar{S}(a + da) - \bar{S}(a) \approx \bar{S}'(a)da = S(a)da$ of the rate of increase in Ins Co.'s expected loss cost when capital is increased by da, using Taylor's theorem.

Alternatively, we can evaluate Eq. (10.9) by differentiating through the expectation

$$\begin{aligned}
\frac{d}{da}\bar{S}(a) &= \frac{d}{da}\mathsf{E}[L_0^a(X)] \\
&= \mathsf{E}\left[\frac{d}{da}L_0^a(X)\right] \\
&= \mathsf{E}\left[\lim_{da\to 0}\frac{L_0^{a+da}(X) - L_0^a(X)}{da}\right] \\
&= \mathsf{E}\left[\lim_{da\to 0}\frac{(X-a)^+ \wedge da}{da}\right] \\
&= \mathsf{E}[1_{X>a}].
\end{aligned}$$

This derivation confirms that $S(a) = \mathsf{E}[1_{X>a}]$ (actually, true by definition Section 3.4.3) and shows that $1_{X>a}$ is the "layer" corresponding to the loss layer density $S(a)$. We call $1_{X>a}$ a **Bernoulli layer**. It is a random variable and whose payout is given by

$$1_{X>a}(\omega) = \begin{cases} 1 & X(\omega) > a \\ 0 & X(\omega) \le a. \end{cases}$$

Since $1_{X>a}$ has outcomes only 0 and 1, $\mathsf{E}[1_{X>a}] = \mathsf{P}(1_{X>a} = 1)$.

Similarly, we define the **premium**, **capital**, and **margin layer density functions** by

$$P(a) = \frac{d\bar{P}(a)}{da}, \quad Q(a) = \frac{d\bar{Q}(a)}{da}, \quad M(a) = \frac{d\bar{M}(a)}{da}.$$

Wang (1996) introduced the idea of loss and premium layer densities, inspired by the "insightful observations" in Venter (1991). By the remark at the end of Section 3.5.3, if $\bar{P}$ is additive for layers of X then $P(a)$ is the fair premium for $1_{X>a}$.

Finally, the **layer funding constraint**

$$1 = P(a) + Q(a) \tag{10.10}$$

is obtained by differentiating the portfolio funding constraint Eq. (10.2) with respect to a. It says that the only sources of assets for the Bernoulli layer are premium and capital.

10.4 The Layer Premium Density as a Distortion Function

We have built the left half of a bridge, having defined the layer density functions. In this section, we build the right half, by connecting layer densities to asset prices. Distortion functions emerge as the prices of Bernoulli layers.

Given an insurance risk X supported by assets a, payments to insureds and investors at $t = 1$ are split

$$a = (X \wedge a) + (a - X)^+. \tag{10.11}$$

Eq. (10.11) is an equality of random variables. It holds in every state ω. It is also quite complicated. When $0 < X < a$, which is typically the case, there are payments to the insured and the investors.

Let's simplify, and focus in on a single Bernoulli layer $1_{X>x}$ with supporting assets $a = 1$. There is no possibility of default because the assets equal the maximum possible loss. Eq. (10.11) becomes the simple split

$$1 = 1_{X>x} + 1_{X \le x} \tag{10.12}$$

into an insurance loss payment or a residual value payment but not both.

Suppose there is a capital market for securities. The market is not perfect: it has bid-ask spreads on risky assets. In other regards, it is close to perfect. In particular, we assume there is no arbitrage and that market participants can borrow or lend at the same risk-free rate, which we take to be 0.

Assume that prices in the market are determined by $A(X)$, the **ask** pricing functional. A is the market price asked to *pay* X. Let $B(X)$ be the **bid** pricing functional: the market price bid to *receive* X. (The A and B notation is used only in this chapter.) Remember, the price that applies in a particular transaction is that which *disadvantages the initiator* of the trade.

- If the buyer (who receives X) initiates the transaction, they pay the ask.
- If the seller (who pays X) initiates, they receive the bid.
- The bid-ask spread equals $A(X) - B(X)$.

In our model, there are two primary types of trade: insureds purchase from Ins Co. and pay the asking price, and Ins Co. sells its residual value to investors and receives their (lower) bid price. Bid-ask spreads are a feature of markets with dealers or market makers. We are assuming investors quote bid and ask prices themselves and do not assume the existence of market makers. Insurers usually only quote ask prices.

The bid and ask price functionals are related by

$$B(X) = -A(-X) \tag{10.13}$$

if there is no arbitrage. Selling both X and $-X$ creates a riskless portfolio with value zero. Ins Co. typically sells only one of the two, say X, at the customer's request, obtaining the asking price. It arranges to sell the other, at the bid price, as part of hedging. Since the value of $X + (-X) = 0$ must be zero, it follows that the proceeds $A(X) + B(-X) = 0$ as well. There are natural hedges where customers request both X and $-X$, such as life insurance and annuities. In such cases, Ins Co. can collect $A(X) + A(-X) > 0$ by subadditivity and make a profit. However, it is not necessarily a risk-free arbitrage profit because orders for X and $-X$ may not be equal. These cash flows are illustrated in Figure 10.1. In the lower row, A is used to price $-X$ on the lower left. Reversing the cash flows we get the lower right, which matches the cash flows for the bid price, upper left.

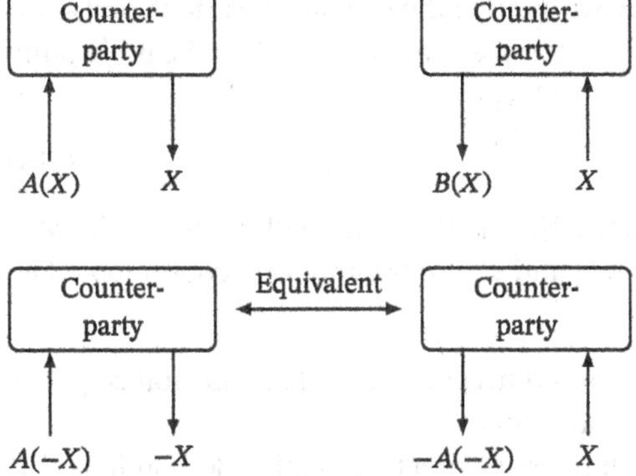

Figure 10.1 Cash flows corresponding to bid and ask prices, showing $B(X) = -A(-X)$.

A is not linear and not additive when $A(X) \neq B(X)$ because $A(-X) = -B(X) \neq -A(X)$—unlike the valuation functionals discussed in Section 8.6. (If A is additive, then $A(-X) = -A(X)$.) This critical difference addresses our concern at the end of Section 8.9.4, by providing a strong motivation for insurance pooling. It is a strength of the layer pricing model.

Furthermore, we assume that A is law invariant, comonotonic additive, and coherent, Section 5.2. We insist on law invariance to stay philosophically aligned with classical actuarial PCPs. We explain comonotonic additive later. Coherence assures us that A is well behaved: it is monotone, normalized $A(0) = 0$, translation invariant $A(X + c) = A(X) + c$ for constant c, subadditive $A(X + Y) \leq A(X) + A(Y)$, and positive homogeneous $A(\lambda X) = \lambda A(X)$ for $\lambda \geq 0$. It follows that $A(c) = c$ for risk-free cash flows. Subadditivity implies a bid-ask spread because

$$0 = A(0) = A(X - X) \leq A(X) + A(-X) = A(X) - B(X). \tag{10.14}$$

The price of an insurance policy paying $1_{X>x}$ in this market is simply the *ask* price given by $A(1_{X>x})$. What about B? Is it used at all? An arbitrageur can arrange to write $1_{X>x}$ by borrowing ¤1, to have the funds available to pay the claim and selling the residual value of the policy for $B(1_{X\leq x})$. By no arbitrage, we must have the relationship

$$A(1_{X>x}) = 1 - B(1_{X\leq x}). \tag{10.15}$$

If Eq. (10.15) did not hold, then the arbitrageur could make arbitrage profits.

The two halves of our bridge are now connected because A and B correspond to the premium and capital layer density functions P and Q defined in Section 10.3

$$P(a) = A(1_{X>a}) \text{ and } Q(a) = B(1_{X\leq a}). \tag{10.16}$$

Note that P and Q are functions of a real variable a, the layer attachment, defined for a fixed X, whereas A and B take random variable arguments. Substituting into Eq. (10.15) gives

$$P(a) = 1 - Q(a), \tag{10.17}$$

the layer funding equation.

Next, we consider the form of A and B. Since we assume they are law invariant, and since the distribution of a Bernoulli random variable is completely determined by the probability it equals 1, we can define functions $g, h : [0,1] \to [0,1]$ by

$$g(u) := A(1_{U<u}) \text{ and } h(u) := B(1_{U<u}) \tag{10.18}$$

where U is a standard uniform random variable. $1_{U<u}$ is Bernoulli with a probability u of loss. We can ignore the difference between $U < u$ and $U \le u$ because U is continuous. The interpretation of g and h is

- $g(s)$ is the premium (asked by the insurer or an arbitrageur) to write an insurance policy with Bernoulli payout having probability s of loss, and
- $h(p)$ is the value (bid by an investor or an arbitrageur) for a bond with a Bernoulli payout having probability p of full payment and $s = 1 - p$ of defaulting.

Applying Eq. (10.15) to U gives

$$\begin{aligned} A(1_{U>p}) &= 1 - B(1_{U\le p}) \\ \iff A(1_{U<1-p}) &= 1 - B(1_{U<p}) \\ \iff g(1-p) &= 1 - h(p) && (10.19) \\ \iff g(s) &= 1 - h(1-s). && (10.20) \end{aligned}$$

Pairs of functions related like Eqs. (10.19) and (10.20) are called **dual** functions. The graph of a dual pair is shown in Figure 10.2. The vertical distance between the two functions equals the bid-ask spread at each s, that is, the difference between the quoted insurance price for $1_{U>p}$ and the amount an investor would *pay* to receive the loss cash flows.

For general X,

$$P(a) = g(S(a)) \text{ and } Q(a) = h(F(a)),$$

and Eq. (10.20) translates into $g(S(x)) = 1 - h(F(x))$. Based on their meanings, what other properties should g and h possess?

- Insurance for impossible events (physically impossible, not merely very improbable) is free, $g(0) = 0$. (Good working hypothesis: it is not impossible if you are asked for a quote.)
- A bond certain to default is worthless $h(0) = 0$.
- Insurance for a certain loss has no risk and no markup: $g(1) = 1$.
- The value of a default-free bond has no haircut $h(1) = 1$ (remember, the risk-free rate is zero).
- Since higher layers respond in a subset of the events triggering lower layers, g must be increasing, because A is monotone and law invariant. The same is true for bonds.
- When investors are risk averse we expect they discount uncertain assets, so $h(p) \le p$ and therefore $g(s) \ge s$ by duality Eq. (10.19).

Functions obeying these rules are called **distortion functions** and are very important. Distortion functions price insurance; the dual of a distortion function prices assets.

Definition 6. *A* **distortion function** *is a function* $g : [0,1] \to [0,1]$ *satisfying*

1. $g(0) = 0$ *and* $g(1) = 1$.

2. *g is increasing.*
3. $g(s) \geq s$ *for all s.*

Table 10.1 summarizes and connects the three different price representations we have introduced.

Remark 136. The definition of a distortion is not standard. Some authors require that g is concave, and some require only that it is a function $g : [0,1] \to [0,1]$ with $g(0) = 0$ and $g(1) = 1$. □

Exercise 137. Which of the following are distortion functions? Which are dual functions of distortion functions? Which are neither?

1. $g(s) = \sqrt{s}$
2. $g(s) = s^{0.9}$
3. $g(s) = 3s$
4. $g(s) = 100s \wedge 1$
5. $g(s) = 1 - \sqrt{1-s}$
6. $g(s) = s(1-s)$

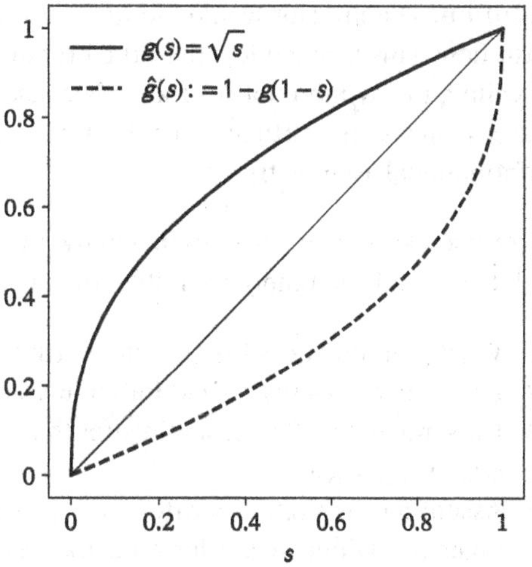

Figure 10.2 The function $g(s) = \sqrt{s}$ and its dual, $\hat{g}(s) = 1 - g(1-s)$. The dual can be obtained by reflecting in the plot horizontally ($s \leftrightarrow 1-s$) and vertically. The vertical distance $g(s) - \hat{g}(s)$ equals the bid ask spread.

Table 10.1 Summary of pricing functions and functionals, X a general risk random variable and U uniform. P, Q, and S depend on X.

Representation	Ask	Bid	Argument	Equivalences
Explicit	A	B	Random variable, X	$B(X) = -A(-X)$
Implicit, density	P	Q	Outcome, $x \in [0, \infty)$	$P(x) = A(1_{X>x}) = g(S(x))$
Implicit, total	$\bar{P}$	$\bar{Q}$	Same	$\bar{P}(x) = \int_0^x P(t)dt$
Dual implicit, density	g	h	Exceedance, $s \in [0,1]$	$g(s) = A(1_{U<s})$, $h(s) = 1 - g(1-s)$

Solution. Distortion: (1), (2), and (4); dual of a distortion: (5) is the dual of (1); neither: (3) takes values outside $[0, 1]$ and (6) is not increasing. □

Exercise 138. Compute and graph the dual of the distortion functions (a) $g(s) = s^{1/3}$ and (b) $g(s) = 1 - (1 - s)^3$. □

Solution. (a) $h(p) = 1 - g(1 - p) = 1 - (1 - p)^{1/3}$ satisfies $h(0) = 0$, $h(1) = 1$, and is increasing. However, $h(p) < p$. It is not a distortion function. (b) $h(p) = s^3$ is also $< p$ and not a distortion. In fact, the dual of a distortion is always $< p$ and not a distortion according to our definition. □

Exercise 139. Let $g(s) = \sqrt{s}$. What is the value of the residual and the premium for a Bernoulli layer with $s = 0.1$, $p = 0.9$ (i.e. 10% chance of having a loss)? What is the implied risk discount factor?

Solution. The value of the residual is $h(0.9) = 1 - \sqrt{0.1} = 0.684$ and the premium is $g(0.1) = \sqrt{0.1} = 0.316$. The risk discount factor is $h(0.9)/0.9 = 0.76$. □

Exercise 140. The roles of the insurance payment $1_{X>a}$ and residual value $1_{X\le a}$ are symmetric, they just swap p with $1 - p$. Thus we could *sell* insurance payments to investors (as the residual of the policy $1_{X\le a}$). How much would they offer to pay using $g(s) = \sqrt{s}$?

Solution. The investor would bid $h(1 - p) = 1 - g(p) = 1 - \sqrt{0.9} = 0.051$ to receive the cash flow. This is much less than the premium the insurer asks for the policy. The insured is willing to pay more for insurance because they hedge the insured's wealth. In addition, the cash flows are worth less to a third-party investor than to the insured in part because of informational asymmetry. □

Exercise 141. Ins Co. operates in a market where investors price using the distortion $g(s) = s^{0.4}$. U is a uniform random variable. Ins Co. currently writes no business.

1. What premium does Ins Co. quote (ask price) to write the Bernoulli layer $1_{U>0.95}$?
2. How much does Ins Co. bid for an investment paying $1_{U>0.95}$?
3. How much does Re Co., a reinsurer that currently writes no business, quote to Ins Co. to assume $1_{U>0.95}$?
4. Assuming Ins Co. has written $1_{U>0.95}$, which then comprises its entire portfolio, how much is it willing to pay for reinsurance to cede it? Compare your answer to (2).

Solution.

1. Ins Co. quotes $A(1_{U>0.95}) = A(1_{U\le 0.05}) = g(0.05) = 0.3017$.
2. Ins Co. bids $B(1_{U>0.95}) = B(1_{U\le 0.05}) = h(0.05) = 1 - g(1 - 0.95) = 0.0203$.
3. Re Co.'s ask price is the same as (1) in this market because prices only depend on the distribution of the outcome.
4. If Ins Co. buys the reinsurance, its net position will be zero. Thus it will be willing to pay any price up to an including 0.3107 for reinsurance. The cash flows Ins Co. receives from (2) and (3) are identical. But in (2) the other party is the transaction initiator, whereas in (3) it is Ins Co. The initiator always pays the price that disadvantages it.

In part, the spread reflects information asymmetries. In (2) Ins Co. values the payments it *receives* conservatively. In (3) the counter-party values the payments it *makes* conservatively. □

10.5 From Distortion Functions to the Insurance Market

This section summarizes basic insurance market statistics for Bernoulli layers and then analyzes the pricing of non-Bernoulli risks by showing how to integrate the premium layer density.

10.5.1 Insurance Market Statistics by Layer

Table 10.2 summarizes our notation and shows how to compute relevant insurance market statistics for Bernoulli layers. The distortion form uses Eq. (10.18) and $1_{U<s}$ defined by a uniform distribution. The premium density form uses Eq. (10.16) and $1_{X>x}$ for an arbitrary X. The difference $U < s$ versus $X > x$ in the first row reflects different sign conventions: actuaries take large positive, *right* tail events as bad whereas accountants and investors take large negative, *left* tail events as bad.

The distortion form is illustrated in Figure 10.3. The value of s on the horizontal axis is the probability of loss for the Bernoulli layer $1_{U<s}$. The dashed diagonal line shows its expected loss, which also equals s. The solid curve shows the $g(s)$, its premium, Eq. (10.18). The margin is the difference between the premium curve and the diagonal expected loss line, i.e. $g(s) - s$, and the capital equals $1 - g(s)$. The height of the graph corresponds to $a = 1$, the assets needed to write the risk. These amounts are all indicated on the right-hand plot.

Table 10.2 Insurance market statistics for a Bernoulli layer expressed in distortion notation and premium density notation.

Insurance Statistic	Distortion Form	Premium Density Form
Basic Bernoulli layer	$1_{U<s}$	$1_{X>x}$
Assets	1	1
Expected loss	s	$S(x)$
Premium, A(Bernoulli)	$g(s)$	$P(x)$
Margin	$g(s) - s$	$M(x) = P(x) - S(x)$
Loss ratio	$s/g(s)$	$S(x)/P(x)$
Capital	$1 - g(s)$	$Q(x) = 1 - P(x)$
Risk return, ι	$(g(s) - s)/(1 - g(s))$	$M(x)/Q(x)$
Risk discount rate, δ	$(g(s) - s)/(1 - s)$	$M(x)/(1 - S(x))$
Risk discount factor, ν	$(1 - g(s))/(1 - s)$	$Q(x)/(1 - S(x))$
Premium leverage	$g(s)/(1 - g(s))$	$P(x)/Q(x)$

It is clear from Figure 10.3 that the risk return (the ratio of margin to capital) varies with s unless g is a straight line through $(1, 1)$, in which case the ratio of margin to capital is constant—by similar triangles. See Exercise 144 for more.

Exercise 142. Compute the loss ratio, risk return, and premium leverage at $s = 0.01, 0.05, 0.1, 0.2$, and 0.5, for $g_1(s) = s^{0.4}$, $g_2(s) = s^{0.5}$, $g_3(s) = s^{0.7}$, and $g_4(s) = s^{0.9}$.

Solution. See Table 10.3. Note that for $g_2(s) = \sqrt{s}$ the loss ratio equals the premium. □

Remark 143. We have treated g—which prices outward cash flows—as fundamental. An investor might treat ι as fundamental, since it values the inward cash flows they buy. It corresponds to a credit yield curve, e.g. by bond rating. By no arbitrage, the two must contain the same information. They are linked by

$$g(s) = \frac{s + \iota(s)}{1 + \iota(s)} = s\nu(s) + \delta(s) \tag{10.21}$$

$$= s + \delta(s)(1 - s) \tag{10.22}$$

$$= 1 - \nu(s)(1 - s) \tag{10.23}$$

reproducing Eqs. (10.6) to (10.8). Eq. (10.21) is the standard Myers-Cohn fair premium condition. Eq. (10.22) says premium equals expected losses plus margin. It is the weighted average of a need for 1 with probability s when there is a loss and for δ with probability $1 - s$ when there is no loss. These correspond to the chances the capital is *consumed* or *rented* (Mango, 2005). Eq. (10.23) expresses the premium as the layer assets of 1 minus investor

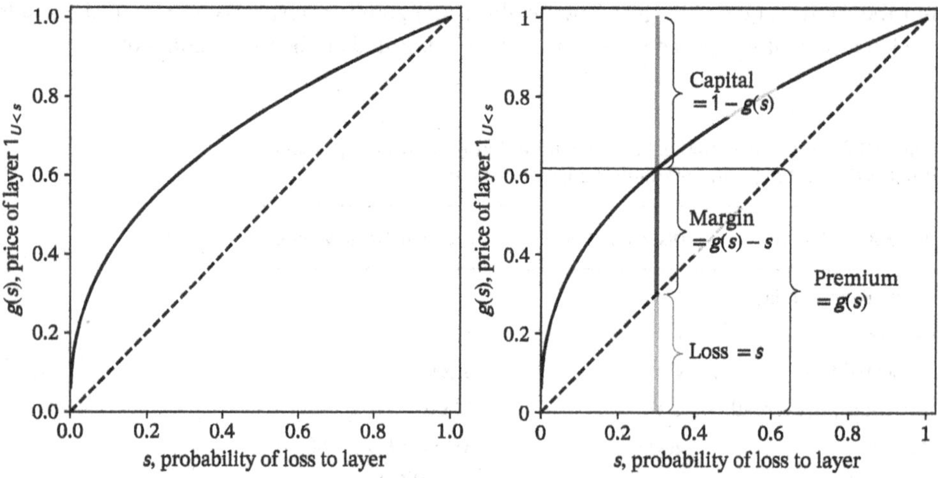

Figure 10.3 Left: graph of a distortion function g, giving the market price of a Bernoulli layer with probability s of a loss. Right: The important insurance market statistics for the layer can be read off from g. The expected loss equals the distance from the horizontal axis to the diagonal, the expected margin from the diagonal to the curve, and the capital from the curve to the top of the figure. The figure height equals 1, the outcome value of the Bernoulli layer in a loss state.

Table 10.3 Solution to Exercise 142.

Statistic	s	$g_1(s)=s^{0.4}$	$g_2(s)=s^{0.5}$	$g_3(s)=s^{0.7}$	$g_4(s)=s^{0.9}$
Loss ratio	0.01	0.0631	0.1000	0.2512	0.6310
	0.05	0.1657	0.2236	0.4071	0.7411
	0.1	0.2512	0.3162	0.5012	0.7943
	0.2	0.3807	0.4472	0.6170	0.8513
	0.5	0.6598	0.7071	0.8123	0.9330
Risk return, ι	0.01	0.1765	0.1000	0.0310	0.0059
	0.05	0.3605	0.2236	0.0830	0.0187
	0.1	0.4953	0.3162	0.1243	0.0296
	0.2	0.6853	0.4472	0.1837	0.0456
	0.5	1.0649	0.7071	0.3006	0.0773
Premium leverage	0.01	0.1883	0.1111	0.0415	0.0161
	0.05	0.4321	0.2880	0.1400	0.0723
	0.1	0.6614	0.4625	0.2493	0.1440
	0.2	1.1066	0.8090	0.4796	0.3071
	0.5	3.1298	2.4142	1.6013	1.1546

capital $\nu(1-s)$, showing how ν is the extra discount applied by investors to the actuarial expected payout $1-s$. □

Exercise 144. Define

$$g(s) = \begin{cases} \nu s + \delta & s > 0 \\ 0 & s = 0, \end{cases} \tag{10.24}$$

for constants $\nu > 0$, $\delta > 0$ and $\nu + \delta = 1$.

1. Confirm that g is a distortion function. Graph g and its dual. Is g continuous?
2. Compute the insurance market statistics for g. Confirm that all Bernoulli layers are priced to the same return $\iota = \delta/\nu$. This property justifies calling g the **Constant Cost of Capital** (CCoC) distortion. □

10.5.2 Insurance Market Statistics in Total

How do we combine Bernoulli layers to price a more realistic risk X? We rely on the critical observation that given X, as x varies **all Bernoulli layers $1_{X>x}$ are comonotonic.** In Section 10.4 we assumed the pricing functional A is coherent, law invariant, and comonotonic additive. Therefore we know that $A(1_{X>x_1} + 1_{X>x_2}) = A(1_{X>x_1}) + A(1_{X>x_2})$ for all x_1, x_2

and more generally, that

$$A\left(\sum_i w_i 1_{X>x_i}\right) = \sum_i w_i A(1_{X>x_i}) \tag{10.25}$$

for $w_i \geq 0$. In contrast, A is subadditive for Bernoulli layers defined by *different* X_i as they can diversify against one another: $A(1_{X_1>x_1} + 1_{X_2>x_2}) \leq A(1_{X_1>x_1}) + A(1_{X_2>x_2})$.

Using Eq. (10.25), we can show that total premium equals the *integral* of the layer premium density. Writing $0 = x_0 < x_1 < \cdots < x_n = 1$ with $x_i - x_{i-1} = dx$, we can use Riemann sums to obtain

$$\begin{aligned}\bar{P}(a) &:= \int_0^a P(x)dx \\ &\approx \sum P(x_i)dx = \sum A(1_{X>x_i})dx = \sum g(S(x_i))dx \\ &\approx \int_0^a g(S(x))dx.\end{aligned} \tag{10.26}$$

In the limit, we get

$$\bar{P}(a) = \int_0^a g(S(x))\,dx \tag{10.27}$$

and more generally

$$\bar{P}(a+y) - \bar{P}(a) = \int_a^{a+y} g(S(x))\,dx. \tag{10.28}$$

Figure 10.4 illustrates Eq. (10.27). The left plot shows the survival function $S(x)$ and the distorted version $g(S(x))$. Since $g(s) \geq s$, it acts to thicken the tail of the survival function, increasing the expected value of any excess layer. This plot is potentially misleading. Following the dotted arrow up suggests that the price of the outcome x equals $g(S(x))$. That is incorrect: $g(S(x))$ is the price of the cover $1_{X>x}$ which responds to all outcomes x or more, not just the single outcome.

The Lee diagram (right plot) keeps us honest. It is obtained by rotating the left plot counterclockwise by 90 degrees. After rotation, the horizontal axis shows s from 1 to 0, i.e. p from 0 to 1. The dashed line shows the quantile function $q(p)$—the inverse to F. Let $\hat{q}(p)$ be the equation of the solid line. It is the quantile function corresponding to the distorted survival function $g(S(x))$. $\hat{q}(p) = x$ means $g(S(x)) = 1 - p$ and therefore $\hat{q}(p) = q(1 - g^{-1}(1 - p))$. The argument variable $\hat{p} := 1 - g^{-1}(1 - p)$ equals the objective probability corresponding to distorted probability p, and we can write the risk-adjusted quantile as

$$\hat{q}(p) = q(\hat{p}). \tag{10.29}$$

The connections between points

$$(F(x), x) = (p, q(p)) \leftrightarrow (p, \hat{q}(p)) = (p, q(\hat{p})) \leftrightarrow (\hat{p}, q(\hat{p})) \tag{10.30}$$

are shown by the arrows on the right, and the solid arrows on the left.

The lower dot (right plot) is $(p, q(p))$, the objective loss event at objective p. The dot above it corresponds to the size of the risk-adjusted event at *distorted* p, i.e. objective $\hat{p}$. An agent who believes g sees the event at p as $q(\hat{p})$. Since $g(s) > s$, it follows that $\hat{p} > p$ and $\hat{q}(p) > q(p)$: the risk-adjusted loss is greater than the objective loss. An underwriter with a g-view of the world sees the objective $\hat{p}$ quantile as the p quantile. They might say, "The model says it is the 100 year event, but I think it is a 20 year event." (See the simulation interpretation of distortions, Section 10.10, for more.)

The Lee diagram shows clearly that all layers have a **positive risk load** because the dashed loss cost line is to the **right** of the solid risk-adjusted premium line. Thus, the layer premium $\int_a^{a+y} g(S(x))dx$ is always greater than expected loss $\int_a^{a+y} S(x)dx$.

It is tempting to look vertically and say all events also have a positive risk load because the solid risk-adjusted line lies above the dashed loss cost line, but this interpretation is incorrect. The two lines in the graph label events differently. The risk-adjusted p quantile loss is the $\hat{p}$ objective quantile. It does not make sense to compare events vertically.

We can now reconcile the layer view with a more traditional picture of insurer capital. The left plot in Figure 10.5 shows the Lee diagram from Figure 10.4. At each asset level, x on the vertical axis, the expected loss to the Bernoulli layer $1_{X>x}$ equals $S(x)$ and the premium equals $g(S(x))$. These quantities are measured from the right and are labeled on the horizontal line segment at height x. The graph shows that each layer of assets has a different exposure to loss as well as its funding between premium and capital. By integrating over asset layers from 0 to a, we obtain the total loss $\bar{S}(a) = \mathsf{E}[X \wedge a]$, margin $\bar{M}(a)$, and capital $\bar{Q}(a)$ shown in the shaded areas in the center plot.

At $t = 1$, the outcome becomes known. Each asset layer is paid to the insured or bondholder, resulting in the aggregate disposition shown on the right for the expected outcome. The right plot shows the traditional layer perspective. Loss, margin, and capital are stacked vertically and have an area equal to their expected values, the same as shown in the middle.

Figure 10.7 lays out our notation. It includes layer and total views.

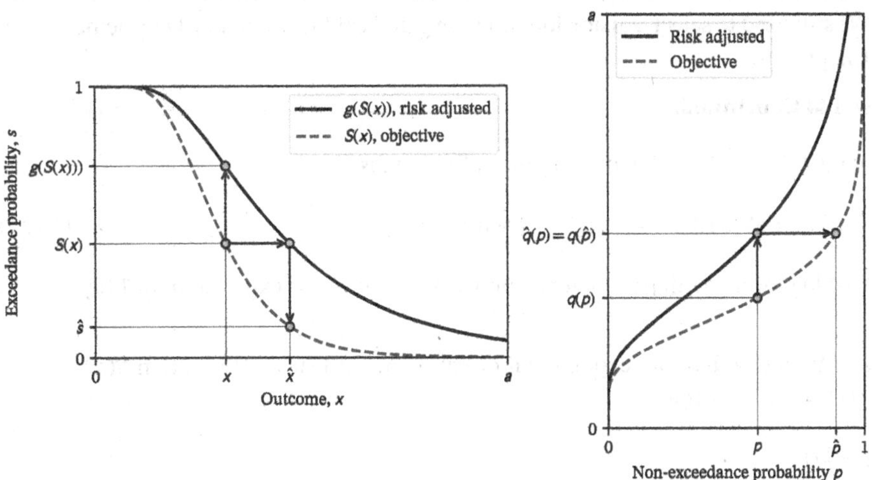

Figure 10.4 Left: Graph of the survival function $S(x)$ and distorted survival function $g(S(x))$ against x. Right: Lee diagram plot of the same quantities.

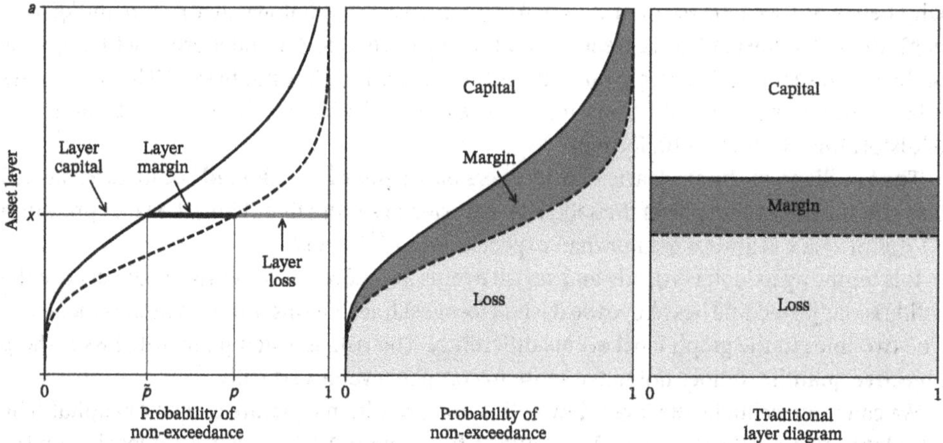

Figure 10.5 Continuum of risk sharing varying by layer of loss (dashed) and premium (solid): by layer (left), in total summed over layers (middle), and traditional (right). The total loss, margin, and capital areas are equal in the middle and right plots. Losses in the left and middle plots are Lee diagrams.

We have completed the divide and conquer program laid out at the beginning of the chapter. We have converted the total pricing problem—how to fund of a between premium and capital—into a series of layer pricing problems. Each Bernoulli layer is an insurance policy whose residual value mirrors a bond with a payoff complementary to the layer loss. Each *layer* must be fully funded. The layer-funding constraint implies the margin equals the expected investor risk return. Distortion functions arise naturally to price Bernoulli layers.

We have set up a flexible way of looking at the pricing problem, linked to market observables (e.g. credit yield curves and catastrophe bond prices) but have not determined any prices. We still need to select a distortion function g and calibrate it to market pricing. We do that in Chapter 11.

Exercise 144 Continued.

3. Using Eq. (10.27), show the total premium function is

$$\bar{P}(a) = \nu\bar{S}(a) + \delta a = \nu \mathsf{E}[X \wedge a] + \delta a. \tag{10.31}$$

4. Let X be lognormal with parameters μ and σ. Write down an expression for $\bar{P}(a)$. □

Exercise 145. Let X have an exponential distribution with survival function $S(x) = e^{-\beta x}$ and let $g(s) = s^{\alpha}$. Show that.

1. $\mathsf{E}[X] = 1/\beta$.
2. $\mathsf{E}[X \wedge a] = (1 - e^{-a\beta})/\beta$.
3. g is a distortion function when $0 \le \alpha \le 1$ but not when $\alpha > 1$.
4. $g(S(x))$ is the survival function of an exponential distribution with parameter $\alpha\beta$.

5. $\bar{P}(a) = (1 - e^{-a\alpha\beta})/(\alpha\beta)$. Since $\alpha < 1$, $\bar{P}(a) > \mathsf{E}[X \wedge a]$ showing the premium includes a positive margin. □

Solution. (2) follows by integration, e.g. $\mathsf{E}[X \wedge a] = \int_0^a S(x)\,dx = e^{-\beta x}/\beta|_a^0 = (1 - e^{-a\beta})/\beta$. □

Exercise 146. Let X have a Pareto distribution with survival function $S(x) = (k/(k+x))^\beta$ and let $g(s) = s^\alpha$. Show that.

1. $\mathsf{E}[X] = k/(k+\beta)$.
2. $\mathsf{E}[X \wedge a] = \dfrac{k}{\beta - 1}F(a) - \dfrac{a}{\beta - 1}S(a)$, provided $\beta > 1$.
3. Derive a formula for $\bar{P}(a)$ and state the condition required for it to hold. □

Remark 147. For monetary quantities (expected loss, premium, margin, and capital) the total and layer functions are integrals and differentials of one another. The same is not true for the average and layer functions of ratios (loss ratio, risk return, and leverage):

$$\frac{d\bar{\iota}(a)}{da} = \frac{d}{da}\frac{\bar{M}(a)}{\bar{Q}(a)} = \frac{M(a)\bar{Q}(a) - \bar{M}(a)Q(a)}{\bar{Q}(a)^2} \neq \iota(a).$$

The layer functions for the ratio variables are much easier to work with than their average versions. We use this fact to our advantage to create a natural capital allocation in Section 14.3.8. □

Remark 148. When the risk return varies across layers, its average also varies with assets a. This fact is striking and runs counter to the notion of a fixed and estimable cost of capital. A varying cost of capital may not seem consistent with the Modigliani-Miller theorem, which asserts the irrelevancy of capital structure to the firm's value. However, Modigliani-Miller is a statement about different ways of funding a fixed amount of assets. In contrast, we are making a statement about how the total cost of funding varies with the amount funded. □

Technical Remark 149. Figure 10.3 and the left and middle plots in Figure 10.5 seem very similar but are subtly different. Figure 10.6 walks between them. The left plot is the same as Figure 10.3. Each s on the horizontal corresponds to the Bernoulli layer $1_{U<s}$, for a uniform variable U. The values s and $g(s)$, shown vertically, equal the expected loss and price of $1_{U<s}$ respectively.

In Figure 10.5, the horizontal axis is used to show the probability of non-exceedance and the premium and capital split. The vertical axis shows the asset layer. Thus we need to reflect the left plot in the anti diagonal dotted line, yielding the middle plot, the Lee diagram for U. The point $(s, g(s))$ on the left is mapped to $(1 - g(s), 1 - s)$ on the middle. (If we rotated, as we do for the dual, $(s, g(s))$ maps to $(1 - s, 1 - g(s))$, which gives the bid price, not the ask price.) Thus the middle plot shows the graph of $(p, 1 - g^{-1}(1 - p)) = (p, \hat{p})$, in other words it shows the objective probability corresponding to a given distorted probability, in the notation of Eq. (10.30). Because of the reflection, the horizontal axis shows the probability of non-exceedance. The vertical axis shows the uniform outcome value that defines the Bernoulli layer.

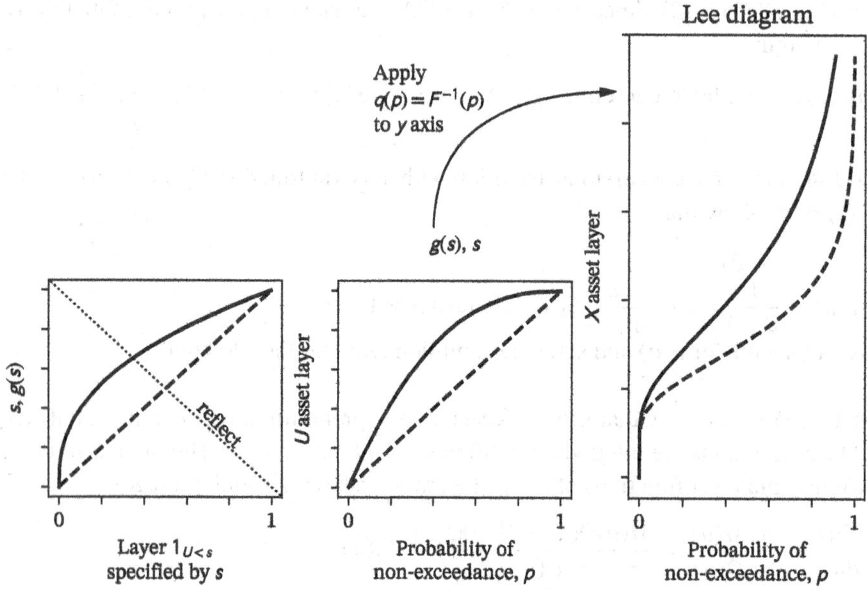

Figure 10.6 Reconciliation of Figure 10.3 and Figure 10.5.

The last step applies the quantile function of X to deform (stretch if X is continuous) the outcome axis to the values taken by X. The right-hand plot is identical to Figure 10.5. The solid line shows the graph of $(p, q(1 - g^{-1}(1 - p))) = (p, q(\hat{p})) = (p, \hat{q}(p))$, exactly as it should per Eq. (10.30).

It is confusing to think of *slicing* a uniform variable into height 1 layers. Remember, the slices define a density and not "thin" layers, and definitely not layers ¤1 wide! □

10.6 Concave Distortion Functions

Distortion functions that are also concave have particularly nice properties.

A function is **concave** if it is umbrella shaped: if we draw a straight line between any two points on the curve, the curve lies above the line.

Formally, for $s_1 < s_2$ and $0 \le w \le 1$, g being concave means

$$g(ws_1 + (1 - w)s_2) \ge wg(s_1) + (1 - w)g(s_2).$$

If g is concave then −g is **convex** meaning the curve lies below the line joining two points on it. Mathematically: $g(ws_1 + (1 - w)s_2) \le wg(s_1) + (1 - w)g(s_2)$.

For future reference, we note some useful properties of a concave distortion function g.

1. g is continuous everywhere except possibly at $s = 0$, where there can be a jump up to $g(0+) \ge 0$.

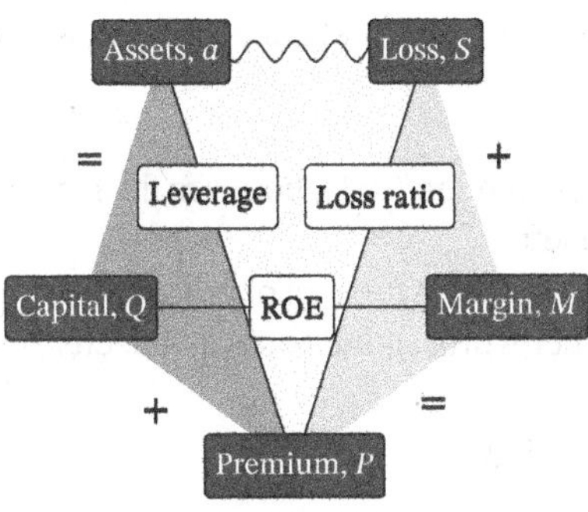

(a) The variables. Premium equals loss plus margin; assets equal premium plus capital.

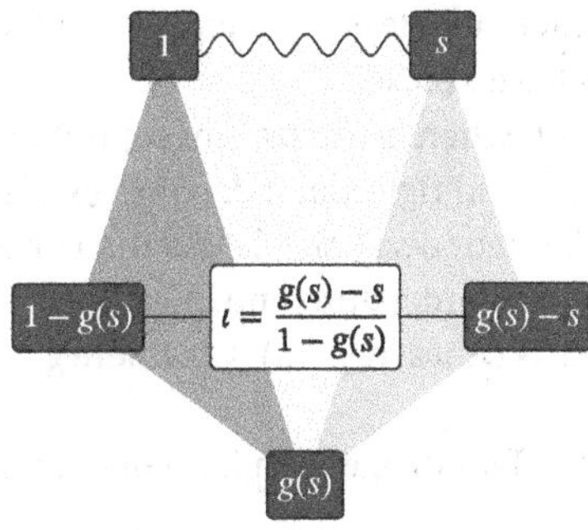

(b) Layer width 1, exceedance probability s.

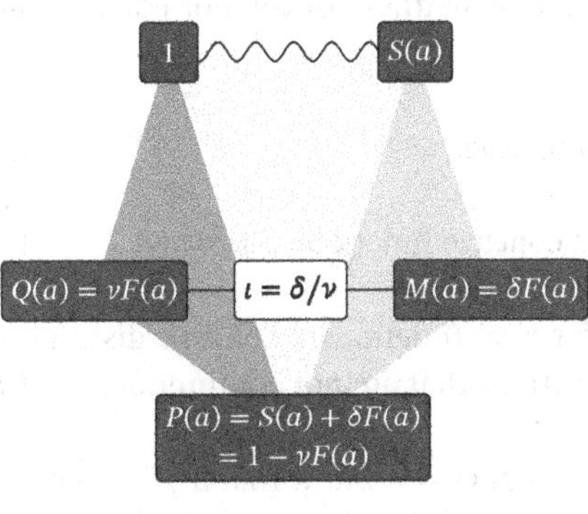

(c) Layer width 1 at a, $s = S(a)$.

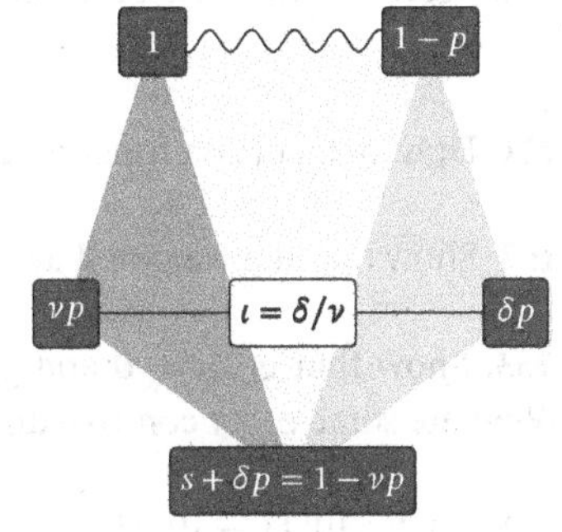

(d) Layer width 1 at a, $p = F(a) = 1 - s$.

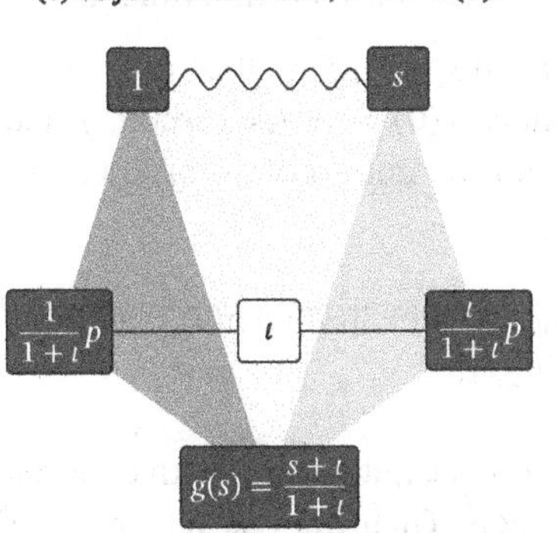

(e) Layer width 1 at a, exceedance probability s, calibrated to return ι.

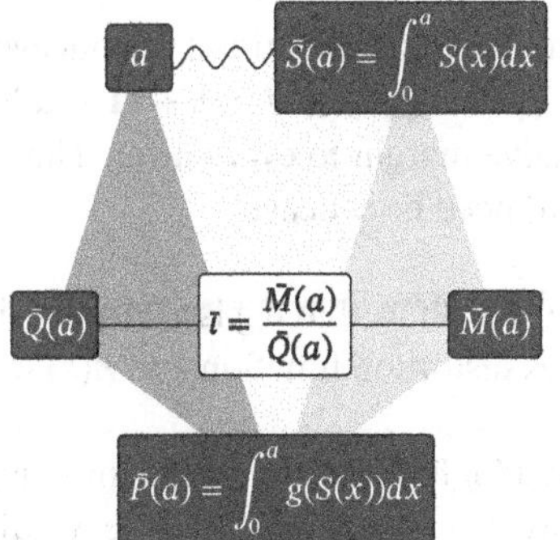

(f) Total, with assets a.

Figure 10.7 Relationships between the variables that control insurance pricing: (a) variable names; (b) in terms of distortion and exceedance probability; (c)–(e) by width 1 layer at a; and (f) in total with assets a. In (f), $\bar{Q} = a - \bar{P}$ and $\bar{M} = \bar{P} - \bar{S}$.

2. g is differentiable everywhere except for at most countably infinitely many points, where it can have kinks.
3. $g'(s) \ge 0$ where g' exists, since g is increasing.
4. The left- and right-hand derivatives of g exist everywhere on $(0, 1)$, both are decreasing, and the right derivative is less than or equal to the left.
5. g is second-order differentiable almost everywhere, i.e. except for a set of probability zero.
6. Since g is concave, $g''(s) \le 0$ where g'' exists, in other words, g increases at a decreasing rate.
7. If g is differentiable then it is concave iff g' is decreasing.

Exercise 150. Show that $\sqrt{x}$ and $\log(x)$ are concave functions of x. Show that x^2, $1/x$, and $\exp(x)$ are convex functions of x. Show that $\sin(x)$ is neither convex nor concave on $[-2\pi, 2\pi]$. □

Exercise 151. Draw a distortion function that is not concave. □

Exercise 152. Show that the weighted average of two concave functions is concave. □

Exercise 153. Show that $g(0) = 0$ and $g(s) - 1$ for $s > 0$ defines a concave distortion function. What are some other concave distortion functions that are not continuous? □

Exercise 154. Let $f : [0, 1] \to [0, 1]$ satisfy $f(0) = 0$ and $f(1) = 1$. Show that if f is concave then $f(s) \ge s$ for all $0 \le s \le 1$. Thus f is automatically a distortion function if it is concave. Show that if f is a convex then $f(s) \le s$ and that f is the dual of a distortion function.

Solution. Apply the definition of concave with $s_1 = 0$ and $s_2 = 1$. For all w, $w = wf(1) = wf(1) + (1 - w)f(0) \le f(w1 + (1 - w)0) = f(w)$, since $f(0) = 0$. As a result, f adds a non-negative margin to every layer. The converse is not true: not every distortion (per our definition) need be concave. □

Exercise 155. Show that if g is a concave distortion function then its dual $h(s) = 1 - g(1 - s)$ is a convex distortion function and $h(s) < s$ for all $0 \le s \le 1$. □

Example 156. In this example we investigate how the cost of capital varies with exceedance probability. Let g be a strictly concave distortion function. Then the risk return and risk discount rate functions both increase with s. This is easiest to see for the discount rate

$$\delta'(s) = \frac{g'(s)(1 - s) + g(s) - 1}{(1 - s)^2}.$$

When g is concave $g(s) + g'(s)(1 - s) \ge 1$, as is easily verified by drawing a picture—the line $x \mapsto g(s) + g'(s)(x - s)$ is the tangent to g at s and a concave function must always lie below its tangent line. Therefore the layer discount (and hence also return) increases with s and so decreases with increasing attachment point $q(1 - s)$. □

10.7 Spectral Risk Measures

Spectral Risk Measures are an important family of risk measures and are used throughout the rest of the book. They can be defined in several equivalent ways, for example, in Section 10.9 we show they are law invariant, comonotonic additive, and coherent. However, we start from the following more elementary definition, motivated by Eq. (10.27).

Definition 7. *Let* g *be a concave distortion function. The* **Spectral Risk Measure associated with** g *is the functional on loss random variables given by*

$$\rho_g(X) := \int_0^\infty g(S_X(x))\,dx. \tag{10.32}$$

The total premium function $\bar{P}(a)$, defined by Eq. (10.27), is an SRM. In fact, $\bar{P}(a) = \rho_g(L_0^a(X))$ because $L_0^a(X) = X \wedge a$, $S_{X\wedge a}(x) = S_X(x)$ for $0 \le x < a$, and therefore

$$\bar{P}(a) := \int_0^a g(S_X(x))\,dx = \int_0^\infty g(S_{X\wedge a}(x))\,dx =: \rho_g(X \wedge a). \tag{10.33}$$

Note that $\bar{P}$ is a function of the asset level x and only prices layers, whereas ρ_g is a functional and can be applied to any random variable.

We always use the notation ρ_g for the functional associated with g by Eq. (10.32). The formula still makes sense when g is not concave, but in that case, ρ_g is not an SRM. Remember $g(s) \ge s$ when g is concave, Exercise 154.

Remark 157. The motivation for our definition of an SRM is the layer pricing approach laid out in Section 10.4. However, in that section, we just assumed a market with the relevant pricing functionals. How do we know such a market exists? What are its properties? Is it as legitimate as CAPM, Black-Scholes, and related mainstays of finance? Rest assured. SRMs have a very long and distinguished academic pedigree and can be used with confidence. Here is some relevant background literature.

- SRMs are the simplest interesting non-additive pricing functional. They are well understood and tractable. The fact they are law invariant, comonotonic additive, and coherent is called Kusuoka's Theorem and has been derived multiple times in different contexts. Important early references include Huber (1981), Schmeidler (1986), Schmeidler (1989), Yaari (1987), Denneberg (1994), Kusuoka (2001), and Acerbi (2002).
- Yaari (1987) uses distortion functions as the basis for the dual theory of utility which, as an alternative to traditional utility, adjusts probabilities rather than outcomes in the same way as SRMs.
- Wang (1996), "Premium calculation by transforming the layer premium density," introduced the idea of a premium density that we use in Section 10.4. Wang, Young, and Panjer (1997) consider a pricing functional ρ that is law invariant, monotone, comonotonic additive, and continuous (in the sense that the price of $(X-d)^+$ (resp. $X \wedge d$) tends to that of X as $d \downarrow 0$ (resp. $d \to \infty$)). They show that ρ on a set of risks that includes all Bernoulli variables is proportional to ρ_g for an increasing $g : [0,1] \to [0,1]$ satisfying $g(0) = 0$

and $g(1) = 1$. If the functional is normalized then it equals ρ_g iff it satisfies the same conditions, and it has a non-negative loading iff $g(s) \geq s$, satisfies the no-ripoff condition, is subadditive if g is concave, and respects second-order stochastic dominance if g is concave. Wang and Young (1998) compare traditional and dual utility, and distortions and their duals. They show that second-order stochastic dominance, an ordering based on risk averse utility functions, and an ordering based on SRMs are all the same. Wang (1995) and (1998b) apply the SRM related to $g(s) = s^\alpha$ to excess ratemaking. Wang (2002) shows the similarities between pricing assets and insurance using SRMs.

- Castagnoli, Maccheroni, and Marinacci (2004) identify that nontrivial SRMs always have a bid-ask spread for all nonconstant risks.
- Results from Chateauneuf, Kast, and Lapied (1996), De Waegenaere (2000), and especially Castagnoli, Maccheroni, and Marinacci (2002) and De Waegenaere, Kast, and Lapied (2003) produce general equilibrium models that allow for non-additive prices, and show that SRM pricing—in the equivalent guise as a Choquet integral—is consistent with general equilibrium.

We conclude that it is legitimate to use SRMs to price risk transfer. They return a premium that charges for the shape of risk, even diversifiable risk. SRMs can be applied both to non-intermediated, direct-to-investor pricing, and insurer-intermediated pricing, where insurers sell the risk to investors. □

Remark 158. Although SRMs have a bid-ask spread their prices are arbitrage free. The existence of the spread lowers the effectiveness of no-arbitrage arguments because it greatly increases the cost of hedge trading. In Black-Scholes there is no spread and it is costless to re-balance the hedging portfolio. Earlier actuarial papers required additive pricing over *all* risks and not just comonotonic ones. Borch (1982) treated additivity as a constraint on PCPs. Remember, a fully additive solution leaves no role for insurers, Section 8.9.4. Venter (1991) considers constraints imposed by arbitrage and weaker notions of additivity, including additivity for independent risks, non-independent risks, and across layers (comonotonic). He shows that "the only premium calculation principles that preserve [layer] additivity are those generated by transformed distributions." SRM layer pricing is a development of Venter's ideas. □

10.7.1 SRMs and Adjusted Probabilities, Differentiable g

In this subsection we show how to rearrange Eq. (10.32) to connect it with adjusted probabilities. Throughout the subsection assume g is a differentiable, convex distortion and let ρ_g be the associated SRM. We make no restrictions on X because we use Riemann-Stieltjes integrals that allow for jumps. When X is continuous a standard Riemann integral suffices.

Using integration by parts, $\int u dv = uv - \int v du$, with substitutions $u = g(S(x))$, $du = -g'(S(x))dF(x)$ and $v = x$, shows that

$$\rho_g(X) = \int_0^\infty g(S(x))\, dx \tag{10.34}$$

$$= xg(S(x))\Big|_0^\infty + \int_0^\infty xg'(S(x))\,dF(x)$$

$$= \int_0^\infty xg'(S(x))\,dF(x) \tag{10.35}$$

$$= \mathsf{E}[Xg'(S(X))] \tag{10.36}$$

provided $xg(S(x)) \to 0$ as $x \to \infty$, which we assume. This expression shows $\rho_g(X)$ is a risk-adjusted mean, where the risk adjustment is $g'(S(x))$. We say that expressions like Eq. (10.34) take the **survival function** form whereas Eq. (10.35) takes the (implicit) **outcome-probability** form.

Next, define the **spectral weight function** $\phi(p) = g'(1-p) \geq 0$. The weight is positive because g is increasing. Starting from Eq. (10.35), substitute $p = F(x)$, $x = q(p)$, so $dF(x) = dp$, to get

$$\rho_g(X) = \int_0^1 q(p)g'(1-p)\,dp$$

$$= \int_0^1 q(p)\phi(p)\,dp. \tag{10.37}$$

The last integral shows that $\rho_g(X)$ is a weighted average of VaRs, since $q(p) = \mathsf{VaR}_p(X)$.

A third integral expression is possible, using the inverse to Eq. (10.29) to convert from objective p to distorted $\tilde{p}$ probabilities. The inverse transformation is $1 - \tilde{p} = g(1-p)$. Substituting into Eq. (10.37), and noting $d\tilde{p} = g'(1-p)dp = \phi(p)dp$, gives

$$\tilde{\rho}_g(X) = \int_0^1 q(1 - g^{-1}(1-\tilde{p}))\,d\tilde{p} = \int_0^1 \hat{q}(\tilde{p})\,d\tilde{p} \tag{10.38}$$

where $\hat{q}$ was defined in Section 10.5.2. The right-hand plot in Figure 10.4 from our previous discussion illustrates Eq. (10.38). It is the integral under the solid line.

Remark 159. The expression $q(p)\phi(p)\,dp$ in Eq. (10.37) should be interpreted as $q(p) \times \phi(p)dp$, the objective loss times a horizontally adjusted probability, and not $q(p)\phi(p) \times dp$, a vertically adjusted loss times objective probability. This difference is illustrated in Figure 10.8. While the areas under the two solid lines between $p = 0$ and $p = 1$ are equal, the correspondence for intermediate p does not hold in the manner the equation might suggest. □

Exercise 160. By applying integration by parts to Eq. (10.33), and following the logic in Eq. (10.37) and Eq. (10.38), show that $\bar{P}(a) = \rho_g(X \wedge a) = \mathsf{E}[(X \wedge a)g'(S(X))] = \int_0^a xg'(S(x))\,dF(x) + ag(S(a)) = \int_0^1 (q(p) \wedge a)\phi(p)\,dp = \int_0^1 \hat{q}(\tilde{p}) \wedge a\,d\tilde{p}$. □

Example 161. Dhaene *et al.* (2008) discuss a model that balances the cost of capital to the insurer against the societal costs of insurer default. They consider the total cost of capital

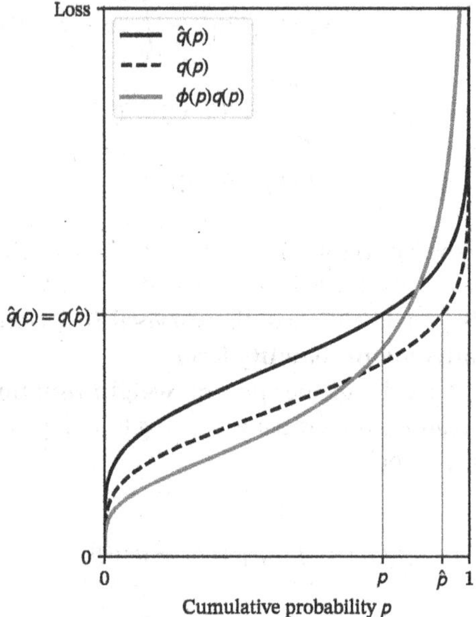

Figure 10.8 Plot of p against $q(p)$ (dashed black) and risk-adjusted $\hat{q}(p) = q(1 - g(1 - p))$ (solid black) compared to $q(p)\phi(p)$ (gray).

when assets equal a to be

$$C(a) = \mathsf{E}[(X - a)^+] + \tau a$$

where the first term is the expected value of losses in default and the second is the cost of assets assuming frictional costs τ. It is easy to see the lowest cost solution is $a = \mathsf{VaR}_{1-\tau}(X)$ (differentiating $C(a) = \int_a^\infty S(x)\,dx + \tau a$ with respect to a and setting equal to zero gives $-S(a) + \tau = 0$), providing an interesting motivation for using value at risk to set capital. More generally, if aggregate risk is priced with an SRM, then $a = \mathsf{VaR}_{1-g^{-1}(\tau)}(X)$. The first term in C is replaced with $\int_a^\infty g(S(x))\,dx$. □

10.7.2 SRMs and Adjusted Probabilities, General g

A general concave distortion g need not be continuous at 0. In fact, the widely used CCoC distortion (Exercise 144) that produces a constant CoC over all layers is not continuous at 0. A more general version of Eq. (10.37) allowing such behavior is

$$\rho_g(X) = \int_0^1 q(p)\phi(p)\,dp + g(0+)\sup(X) \tag{10.39}$$

where $g(0+) = \lim_{t\downarrow 0} g(t) \geq 0$ is the possible jump in g at 0 and $\phi(p) = g'(1 - p)$ as before. If X is unbounded then $\rho_g(X) = \infty$ when $g(0+) > 0$. Eq. (10.39) is derived in Section 10.A.1.

The value $\rho_g(X)$ as defined in Eq. (10.39) may be infinite, depending on $F(x)$ and $g(s)$, even when X has finite moments. In contrast, $\bar{P}(a)$ is never greater than a. Chapter 14 shows that the issue of unbounded X must be addressed when allocating $\bar{P}(a)$.

The name **spectral risk measure** was coined in Acerbi (2002) because of Eq. (10.39). The **spectral weight** function $\phi(p)$ describes how much you care about the event with cumulative probability p—remember $q^-(p) = \mathsf{VaR}_p(X)$. It describes your concern across the *spectrum* of loss return periods. Sample graphs of ϕ are shown in Figure 15.11.

The weights $\phi(p)$ in Eq. (10.39) are increasing because g is concave. Therefore they give more weight to higher losses. Any rational risk measure should have this property: the bad consequences of a higher loss include, at a minimum, all the bad consequences of smaller losses. Since $\phi(p)$ measures how much you care about the **exact** loss at p, the increasing condition is necessary to ensure economic consistency. It is possible that once losses cross a certain threshold—you are unemployed and all your deferred compensation worthless—you don't care *more* about *greater* losses. But you must care at least as much about the larger loss as you do about the triggering loss, because it has all the same bad consequences—plus more. Your *caring* spectrum must be increasing.

Example 162. The CCoC distortion, Exercise 144, is an example where the extra term $g(0+)$ is necessary. In that case, $g(0+) = \delta$, $g'(s) = \nu$, and $\int_0^s g'(t)\,dt = \nu s$. □

Example 163. We can write VaR in the form Eq. (10.39) using a Dirac delta function (point mass) weighting function. The corresponding g is a step function: zero up to the VaR threshold p and one above it. It is not concave when $p < 1$ and does not define an SRM. □

Exercise 164. Plot g and the associated $\phi(p) = g'(1-p)$ spectral weight function for (a) $g(s) = s^\alpha$ for a variety of $0 < \alpha \le 1$, (b) $g(s) = 1-(1-s)^m$ for a variety of $m \ge 1$, and (c) the CCoC distortion. □

Exercise 165. What are the differences between $\bar{P}(a)$ and ρ_g? □

Exercise 166. Why is $\bar{P}(a) \le a$ for all distributions? □

Exercise 167. Show that if X is Bernoulli with $\mathsf{Pr}(X=1) = s$ then $\rho_g(X) = g(s)$. This means the definition of ρ_g is consistent with the idea that g prices Bernoulli layers. □

Exercise 168. Show that if X is exponential with mean μ, $S(x) = e^{-x/\mu}$, and $g(s) = s^b$, $b < 1$, then $\rho_g(X) = \mu/b > \mu$. Compare Exercise 145. □

Exercise 169. Show that if X is Pareto with survival function $S(x) = (1+x)^{-\alpha}$ and $g(s) = s^b$, $b < 1$, then $\rho_g(X)$ is finite for $b < \alpha$. Give an example of a risk with a finite mean but infinite price using an SRM. Compare Exercise 146. □

Exercise 170. Verify all the change of variable formulas (Eqs. (10.27) and (10.35), and Eq. (10.37)) explicitly for X exponentially distributed, unlimited assets, and $g(s) = s^b$, $b < 1$ a proportional hazard transform. □

10.8 Properties of an SRM and Its Associated Distortion Function

In this section, we consider how properties of the functional ρ_g defined by Eq. (10.32) are related to properties of the function $g : [0,1] \to [0,1]$. We do not assume $g(0) = 0$, $g(1) = 1$, or g is increasing because we want to uncover which properties of ρ_g rely on these properties of g.

1. ρ_g is **law invariant** because it is expressed as a function of the survival function of X.
2. ρ_g is **positive homogeneous** because, for $\lambda > 0$ and continuous g,

$$\begin{aligned}\rho_g(\lambda X) &= \int_0^\infty g(\Pr(\lambda X > x))\,dx \\ &= \int_0^\infty g(S_X(x/\lambda))\,dx \\ &= \lambda \int_0^\infty g(S_X(y))\,dy \\ &= \lambda\rho_g(X)\end{aligned}$$

on substituting $\lambda y = x$. The same logic does not apply to $\lambda < 0$ because the limits of integration change. Since $\sup(\lambda X) = \lambda \sup(X)$ the result extends to general g.
3. ρ_g is **comonotonic additive**. If X_1, X_2 are comonotonic then $q_{X_1}(p) + q_{X_2}(p) = q_{X_1+X_2}(p)$ for all p and so Eq. (10.39) implies ρ_g is comonotonic additive.

Since SRMs are comonotonic additive, the SRM price of the excess layer $L_a^{a+y}(X)$ is

$$\rho_g(X \wedge a + y) - \rho_g(X \wedge a) = \int_a^{a+y} g(S_X(x))\,dx$$

consistent with Eq. (10.28). Any two layers on the same underlying risk are comonotonic.

4. For a constant $c \geq 0$, $q_{X+c}(p) = c + q_X(p)$ and therefore by Eq. (10.39), for continuous g

$$\rho_g(c + X) = \int_0^1 q_{X+c}(p)g'(1-p)\,dp = c(g(1) - g(0)) + \rho_g(X).$$

Thus ρ_g is **translation invariant** iff $g(1) - g(0) = 1$, which can occur iff $g(0) = 0$ and $g(1) = 1$. If g is not continuous, the requirement becomes $g(1) = 1$.
5. If $X \leq Y$ then $q_X(p) \leq q_Y(p)$. If g is increasing then $g'(1-s)$ is positive and therefore the representation in Eq. (10.39) implies

$$\rho_g(X) = \int_0^1 q_X(p)g'(1-p))\,dp \leq \int_0^1 q_Y(p)g'(1-p))\,dp = \rho_g(Y)$$

showing ρ_g is **monotone** for increasing continuous g. Since $\sup X \leq \sup Y$ the result also holds for increasing general g.
6. We shall see in Section 10.9 that ρ_g can be expressed as a weighted average of TVaRs with positive weights that sum to 1 iff g is increasing and concave. Since each TVaR is subadditive, it follows that ρ_g is too.

Property (6) is the reason we require g to be a *concave* distortion in Definition 7. Properties (1)–(5) show that an SRM is law invariant, comonotonic additive, and coherent. In Section 10.4 we assumed the (capital) pricing functional is law invariant and comonotonic additive when we derived the layer pricing formula. When g is not increasing (respectively, not concave), Acerbi (2002) shows how to construct explicit examples where the monotonic (resp. sub additive) property fails.

Four further properties of ρ_g are controlled by the behavior of g at $s = 0, 1$.

7. If the distortion function g is discontinuous at $s = 0$ then ρ_g has a minimum rate on line-like behavior, that applies when $S(x) > 0$. Unlike a true minimum rate on line, there is no charge for losses the model deems impossible. This is a feature, not a bug.
8. If g is continuous at $s = 0$ and $\lim_{s\downarrow 0} s/g(s) = \lim_{s\downarrow 0} 1/g'(s)$ exists (L'Hôpital's rule), then it equals the loss ratio as $s \downarrow 0$.
9. If g is continuous at $s = 0$ and there exist $c > 0$ and $\epsilon > 0$ so that $g(s) = cs$ for $0 \le s \le \epsilon$ then ρ_g is not *strictly risk averse for tail events*, Jouini, Schachermayer, and Touzi (2008). This means the risk measure ρ_g evaluates the tail events as being equivalent to their expected value. TVaR satisfies these conditions.
10. If $\lim_{s\uparrow 1} g'(s)$ exists and is > 0 then the rate of return is finite as $s \uparrow 1$, otherwise it is infinite.

Exercise 171. Given $g(s) = s^{0.8}$, compute the loss ratio and return on capital for s near 0 and near 1. Which applies to low layers and which to high? □

10.9 Six Representations of Spectral Risk Measures

The next theorem ties together SRMs, the axiomatic properties presented in Section 5.2, and the representation theorem presented in Section 5.4 . It says that every coherent, comonotonic additive, law invariant risk measure is a spectral risk measure, and shows the different ways they can be represented.

Theorem 3. *For a risk measure ρ the following are equivalent.*

1. *ρ is coherent, comonotonic additive, and law invariant.*
2. *ρ equals a spectral risk measure ρ_g for a concave distortion function g.*
3. *$\rho(X) = g(0+)\sup(X) + \int_0^1 \mathsf{VaR}_p(X)\phi(p)\,dp$ equals a weighted average of VaRs, where the weights $\phi(p) = g'(1-p)$ are positive, increasing, and sum to $1 - g(0+)$.*
4. *$\rho(X) = g(0+)\sup(X) + \int_0^1 \mathsf{TVaR}_p(X)(1-p)\phi'(p)\,dp + \sum_j \mathsf{TVaR}_{p_j}(X)(1-p_j)\Delta_j$ equals a weighted average of TVaRs, where ϕ' has a jump Δ_j at p_j, and the weights are positive and sum to $1 - g(0+)$.*

When these four conditions hold, ρ has two further representations:

5. *as the sup over a set of expectations*

$$\rho_g(X) = \sup\{\mathsf{E}[XZ] \mid Z \ge 0, \mathsf{E}[Z] = 1, \int_0^s q_Z(1-t)\,dt \le g(s)\, \textit{for all } s \in (0,1)\} \tag{10.40}$$

where q_Z is the quantile function of Z, and

6. *as the sup over a set of probability scenarios*

$$\rho_g(X) = \sup\{\mathsf{E}_{\mathsf{Q}}[X] \mid \mathsf{Q}(A) \le g(\mathsf{P}(A)) \textit{ for all events } A\}. \tag{10.41}$$

The equivalence of (1) with (4) is known as Kusuoka's Theorem, which we quoted as Theorem 1 part (d), and of (2) with (3) is Eq. (10.39). The rest of the proof, which is instructive but technical, is sketched in Section 10.A.2.

Remark 172.

1. When $g'(1) < 1$ the SRM ρ_g assigns weight $g'(1)$ to the mean. All such SRMs can be regarded as cost-plus.
2. Unlike the VaR representation, the weighted TVaR representation only requires that the weights are non-negative. There are no other restrictions because TVaR already reflects the fact an excess layer covers losses at or above the attachment. These properties justify taking an excess layer as the fundamental insurance contract, rather than an Arrow-Debreu-like security that pays on a single event.
3. Kusuoka's Theorem says the only value of X that can be singled out and given a probability mass is $\sup(X)$. Why? Since ρ is monotone the VaR weights must increase. Thus, if VaR_{p^*} is given atomic mass, the same must hold for all $p > p^*$. But this is impossible unless $p^* = 1$ because mass can only be applied to discrete points. As a result, g can only be discontinuous at 0, precisely where concave increasing g can have a discontinuity at 0.
4. In representations (5) and (6), the sup is achieved by a scenario function or probability iff g is continuous at zero, in which case g' defines a density and $g(0+) = 0$. □

Example 173. Tail Value at Risk. TVaR_p puts all its weight on the point mass at p, $\mu(\{p\}) = 1$. The corresponding VaR weight function is $\phi(s) = (1-p)^{-1}1_{[p,1]}(s)$. Therefore $g'(s) = (1-p)^{-1}1_{[0,1-p]}$ and $g(s) = \int_0^s g'(t)\,dt = (s/(1-p)) \wedge 1$ ramps up from $g = 0$ to $g = 1$ between $s = 0$ and $s = 1 - p$ and then stays constant. □

Example 174. Constant Cost of Capital Distortion (CCoC). Let g be given by the constant cost of capital distortion Eq. (10.24). The corresponding μ weights $p = 0$ with ν and $p = 1$ with δ. Applying Eq. (10.44) to μ shows that $g'(1-p) = \nu$ and Eq. (10.45) shows $g(s) = \nu s + \delta$, as expected. □

Example 175. Proportional Hazard. Let $g(s) = s^{\alpha}$ be a proportional hazard transform. Then $g'(s) = \alpha s^{\alpha-1}$ and $-g''(s) = \alpha(1-\alpha)s^{\alpha-2}$. Hence μ has density given by $f(s) = \alpha(1-\alpha)(1-s)^{\alpha-1}$. In this case $\int_0^1 f(s)ds = 1 - \alpha < 1$ and as expected, $g'(1) = \alpha$. Thus g gives weight α to the mean, TVaR_0. □

Example 176. Proportional Hazard and CCoC. Let

$$g(s) = \begin{cases} s^{1/2} & 0 \le s \le 1/4 \\ (2s+1)/3 & 1/4 < s \le 1 \end{cases}$$

be a proportional hazard $\alpha = 0.5$ transform up to $s = 1/4$ spliced together with the constant CoC distortion function $g_2(s) = 2s/3 + 1/3$ with return 0.5 for $1/4 \le s \le 1$. Note that the two distortion functions agree at $s = 1/4$ and that g is also the minimum of the two distortion functions. Then

$$g'(s) = \begin{cases} s^{-1/2}/2 & 0 \le s < 1/4 \\ \text{undefined} & x = 1/4 \\ 2/3 & 1/4 < s \le 1 \end{cases}$$

and $g''(s) = -s^{-3/2}/4$ for $0 < s < 1/4$ and $g''(s) = 0$ for $1/4 < s \le 1$. The slope of $s^{1/2}$ at $s = 1/4$ equals 1 and the slope of the constant CoC is 2/3. Thus the derivative g' jumps by $1 - 2/3 = 1/3$ at $s = 1/4$. In this case, the TVaR representation of g includes two masses, at $p = 0.75$ and $p = 0$. The weight on $\text{TVaR}_{0.75}$ is $(1/4)(1/3) = 1/12$. And at $s = 1$, $g' = 2/3$, so the weight on the mean is 2/3. The TVaR representation of g is a mixed density and equals

$$\mu(dp) = \begin{cases} (1-p)^{-1/2}/4 & \text{density for } 3/4 \le p < 1 \\ 1/12 & \text{mass at } p = 3/4 \\ 2/3 & \text{mass at } p = 0. \end{cases}$$

In comparison, the proportional hazard component has a mass 1/2 at $p = 0$ and weights all other TVaRs $p < 1$ by $(1-p)^{-1/2}/4$. □

Remark 177. The theory developed so far applies to a comonotonic additive, law invariant coherent risk measure. Theorem 1 shows that all law invariant coherent risk measures are simply the worst of a family of comonotonic measures. Thus many parts of the theory can be extended to more risk measures. □

10.10 Simulation Interpretation of Distortion Functions

Distortion functions act by changing the probability of events. The chance of a loss greater than x changes from $S(x)$ to $g(S(x))$. Up to now, the discussion has presented the pricing functional as a modified expectation. What if we sampled losses directly from the distorted distribution and used the unmodified expectation to calculate the price? How would that work?

We can use the inversion method. A uniform random $u \in [0, 1]$ generates the simulated loss x by solving $F(x) = u$. Since u is uniform we can equally solve $S(x) = u$.

The corresponding simulated loss from the distribution $g(S(x))$ solves $g(S(x)) = u$, giving $x = S^{-1}(g^{-1}(u))$.

We can interpret g as the distribution function of a random variable G on $[0, 1]$ taking values in $[0, 1]$. G has mean (cf., Gini coefficient) $\int_0^1 1 - g(s)ds = 1 - \int_0^1 g(s)ds < 0.5$, since $g(s) > s$. The value $g^{-1}(u)$ is a random sample from G. Thus the process of simulating from $g(S)$ can be understood as

1. simulate random uniform variables u_i,
2. transform to $g_i = g^{-1}(u_i)$, a random sample from $[0, 1]$ with distribution G, and
3. apply the inversion method to g_i to simulate $S^{-1}(g_i)$.

Example 178. Say g equals the p-TVaR distortion function $g(s) = 1 \wedge s/(1 - p)$. Random uniform u_i on $[0, 1]$ are transformed into random uniform g_i on $[0, 1 - p]$. Thus a sample from $g(S)$ is a uniform sample of the worst $1 - p$ proportion of outcomes—exactly what we expect from TVaR. □

Example 179. If g is the proportional hazard distortion function $g(s) = s^b$, $b < 1$, then u_i are transformed to $g_i = u_i^{1/b} < u_i$. The resulting sample from $g(S)$ is skewed toward worse outcomes. For example, if $b = 0.5$ then $u = 0.1$ is transformed to $g = u^2 = 0.01$; the risk-adjusted 90th percentile outcome is the objective 99th percentile outcome. □

The distortion function g affects how a decision maker thinks about random numbers. A TVaR agent only sees (adverse) $u \in [0, 1 - p]$. Their view of the world is not equivalent to the objective view because they disagree about the possible and impossible events. They see any loss less than the $\mathsf{VaR}_p(X)$ as impossible. A proportional hazard agent thinks $U^{1/b}$ is a uniform random sample. They agree about possible events with the objective probability. Finance theory only allows equivalent probability distributions to be used to price. Thus it would consider the proportional hazard distortion function to be a plausible pricing measure, but not the TVaR distortion function.

10.11 Learning Objectives

1. Define a distortion function and give examples.
2. Define a bid-ask spread and explain its relationship with distortion functions.
3. Describe the connection between a distortion function g and layer pricing in a one-period model via the layer density.
4. Describe how a positive margin for layer insurance occurs iff there is a discount for the layer residual and explain the connection with bid-ask spreads.
5. Compute loss ratio, leverage, and return on capital from a distortion function g, for a layer and in total.
6. Given a distortion, compute the dual distortion and explain how it can be used.
7. Explain the impact of a discontinuity in g at 0, the value $g'(0)$, and the value $g'(1)$ on the pricing functional associated with g.
8. Explain how a distortion function creates a law invariant pricing functional and use it to determine the price of excess layers.
9. Describe how properties of a distortion function correspond to properties of the associated pricing functional.
10. Convert a spectral risk measure between its distortion function, weighted VaR, and weighted TVaR representations.
11. Determine the set of scenario functions or probability scenarios corresponding to a distortion function.
12. Explain why VaR fails to be a spectral risk measure using the weighted VaR representation.

10.A Technical Details

10.A.1 Proof of Eq. (10.39)

This subsection derives Eq. (10.39)

$$\rho_g(X) = \int_0^1 q(p)\phi(p)\,dp + g(0+)\sup(X).$$

where $g(0+) = \lim_{t\downarrow 0} g(t) \geq 0$ is the possible jump in g at 0.

Recall from Section Section 4.1.1 that by definition $\mathsf{VaR}_p(X) = q_X^-(p) = \sup\{x \mid F_X(x) < p\}$ and that q^- is left continuous. Define a function of x and p by

$$I(F(x) < p) = \begin{cases} 1 & F(x) < p \\ 0 & F(x) \geq p \end{cases}.$$

Then, since q^- is left continuous,

$$q^-(p) = \int_0^\infty I(F(x) < p)\,dx.$$

Define $M = \sup(X) \leq \infty$. $S(M) = 0$ since S is continuous from the right (like F). Therefore $q^-(p) = \int_0^M I(F(x) < p)\,dx$. Substituting this expression, applying Fubini's theorem to swap the order of integration, and substituting for $t = 1 - p$ shows

$$\begin{aligned}\int_0^1 q^-(p)g'(1-p)\,dp &= \int_0^1 \int_0^M I(F(x) < p)\,dx\,g'(1-p)\,dp \\ &= \int_0^M \int_0^1 I(F(x) < p)\,g'(1-p)\,dp\,dx \\ &= \int_0^M \int_{F(x)}^1 g'(1-p)\,dp\,dx \\ &= \int_0^M \int_0^{S(x)} g'(t)\,dt\,dx \\ &= \int_0^M g(S(x)) - g(0+)\,dx \\ &= \int_0^\infty g(S(x))\,dx - g(0+)M \\ &= \rho_g(X) - g(0+)M\end{aligned}$$

Rearranging gives Eq. (10.39). The concave assumption is used to write g as the integral of its derivative, between the fourth and fifth steps. See Dhaene *et al.* (2012) for a more general and detailed treatment of Eq. (10.39).

10.A.2 Proof of Theorem 3

The equivalence of (1) with (4) is known as Kusuoka's Theorem, which we quoted as Theorem 1 part (d). We explain the connection to TVaR and VaR representations carefully, because of their intuitive appeal and because they give insight into the meaning of the associated SRM.

TVaR Representation (2) iff (4). Start with ρ_g. To illustrate the idea, assume first that the distortion function g is twice differentiable, with an absolutely continuous derivative. Then, $\phi(p) = g'(1-p)$ is an increasing, differentiable function that integrates to 1 that can be written as

$$\phi(p) = \phi(0) + \int_0^p \phi'(t)\,dt. \tag{10.42}$$

When g is continuous, $g(0+) = 0$. Recall $\mathsf{E}[X] = \mathsf{TVaR}_0(X)$. Using Eq. (10.39), Fubini's theorem, and the definition of TVaR gives

$$\begin{aligned}
\rho_g(X) &= \int_0^1 q^-(p)\phi(p)\,dp \\
&= \int_0^1 q^-(p)\left(\phi(0) + \int_0^p \phi'(t)\,dt\right)dp \\
&= \phi(0)\mathsf{TVaR}_0(X) + \int_0^1 q^-(p)\int_0^p \phi'(t)\,dt\,dp \\
&= \phi(0)\mathsf{TVaR}_0(X) + \int_0^1 \int_t^1 q^-(p)\,dp\,\phi'(t)\,dt \\
&= \phi(0)\mathsf{TVaR}_0(X) + \int_0^1 \frac{1}{1-t}\int_t^1 q^-(p)\,dp\,(1-t)\phi'(t)\,dt \\
&= \phi(0)\mathsf{TVaR}_0(X) + \int_0^1 \mathsf{TVaR}_t(X)\,(1-t)\phi'(t)\,dt.
\end{aligned}$$

Define a positive function $f(p) = (1-p)\phi'(p)$. Combining f with a mass of $g'(1) = \phi(0)$ at $p = 0$ defines a probability function because

$$\begin{aligned}
\phi(0) + \int_0^1 (1-p)\phi'(p)\,dp &= \phi(0) + (1-p)\phi(p)\big|_0^1 + \int_0^1 \phi(p)\,dp \\
&= \int_0^1 \phi(p)\,dp \\
&= \int_0^1 g'(1-p)\,dp \\
&= \int_0^1 g'(s)\,ds
\end{aligned}$$

$$= g(1) - g(0)$$
$$= 1.$$

Therefore the previous displayed equations show that ρ_g is a μ-weighted average of TVaRs where μ is the probability with density f on $(0, 1)$ and a mass $\mu(\{0\}) = \phi(0) = g'(1)$ at 0.

What adjustments are needed to this argument for general g? The situation when g is not continuous at 0 is already handled in Eq. (10.39) by adding the term involving M. When g is not differentiable on $(0, 1)$ it has a kink and ϕ has a jump that needs to be added to the integral in Eq. (10.42). By property (2) in Section 10.6 we can enumerate the discontinuities of g as s_j. Set $\Delta_j = g'(s_j-) - g'(s_j+) = \phi((1 - s_j)+) - \phi((1 - s_j)-)$ equal to the jump in g' at s_j (equivalently, in ϕ at $1 - s_j$). By construction, the function

$$C(p) = \phi(p) - \phi(0) - \sum_{s_j \le 1-p} \Delta_j$$

is a continuous, increasing function (Lebesgue decomposition). Even when C is not absolutely continuous, $\gamma([0, p]) = C(p)$ defines a probability γ and

$$\phi(p) = \phi(0) + C(p) + \sum_{s_j \le 1-p} \Delta_j. \tag{10.43}$$

Repeating the previous derivation of ρ_g using Eq. (10.43) replaces $\phi'(s)ds$ with $\gamma(ds)$ and adds a term

$$\sum_j \mathsf{TVaR}_{1-s_j}(X)\, s_j\, \Delta_j$$

to account for the jumps.

Therefore, we have shown ρ_g is a μ-weighted integral of TVaRs where μ is the mixed probability with continuous part $(1 - p)\gamma(dp)$ (or, if ϕ is absolutely continuous, with density $f(p) = (1 - p)\phi'(p) = -(1 - p)g''(1 - p)$ at $p \in (0, 1)$ where g is twice differentiable), plus point masses $s_j\Delta_j$ at $p = 1 - s_j$, $g(0+)$ at $p = 1$, and $g'(1)$ at $p = 0$.

Conversely, given *any* probability μ on $[0, 1]$, define the risk measure

$$\rho_\mu(X) = \int_{[0,1]} \mathsf{TVaR}_p(X)\mu(dp).$$

ρ_μ inherits the coherent, comonotonic additive, and law invariant properties from TVaR.

We must show how to obtain a distortion function g from μ. Decompose μ into its continuous part μ_c and masses $\mu(\{p_j\})$ at p_j. Then, set $\phi(0) = \mu(\{0\})$ and define

$$\phi(p) = \phi(0) + \int_0^p \frac{\mu_c(dt)}{1-t} + \sum_{p_j \le p} \frac{\mu(\{p_j\})}{1-p_j}. \tag{10.44}$$

(This expression can be written as $\displaystyle\int_{[0,p]} \frac{\mu(dt)}{1-t}$ using a Riemann-Stieltjes integral.) ϕ is an increasing positive function.

Next, define $g'(s) = \phi(1-s)$ and set $g(0) = 0$ and $g(0+) = \mu(\{1\})$. Integrating gives

$$\begin{aligned} g(s) &= g(0+) + \int_0^s g'(u)\,du = g(0+) + \int_0^s \phi(1-u)\,du \\ &= g(0+) + \int_{1-s}^1 \phi(p)\,dp. \end{aligned} \tag{10.45}$$

g is positive and increasing because ϕ is positive, and it is concave because g' is decreasing. To confirm g is a distortion function we need to check $g(1) = 1$:

$$\begin{aligned} g(1) &= g(0+) + \int_0^1 \phi(p)\,dp \\ &= \mu(\{1\}) + \int_0^1 \int_{[0,p]} \frac{\mu(dt)}{1-t}\,dp \\ &= \mu(\{1\}) + \int_{[0,1)} \int_t^1 dp\,\frac{\mu(dt)}{1-t} \\ &= \mu(\{1\}) + \int_{[0,1)} \mu(dt) \\ &= 1. \end{aligned}$$

VaR Representation (2) iff (3). Eq. (10.39) shows (2) implies (3). Remember that $\mathsf{VaR}_p(X) = q^-(p)$. VaR_p is weighted by $\phi(p) = g'(1-p)$ for $p < 1$ and $\mathsf{VaR}_1(X)$, interpreted as $\sup(X)$, is weighted by $g(0+)$ when g is not continuous at 0. We know from Section 10.6 that g is differentiable for all but countably many points in $(0,1)$ and so the discontinuities can be ignored without changing the value of the integral.

Since g is increasing, $g'(t) > 0$ and therefore ϕ is positive. (Note that ϕ is the derivative of g evaluated at $1-p$, not the derivative of $p \mapsto g(1-p)$, which equals $-g'(1-p) < 0$.)

Since g is concave, its derivative is decreasing by property 7 in Section 10.6 and therefore ϕ is increasing.

Finally

$$1 = g(1) = g(0+) + \int_0^1 g'(s)\,ds = g(0+) + \int_0^1 \phi(1-s)\,ds = g(0+) + \int_0^1 \phi(p)\,dp$$

showing the weights sum to 1.

Conversely, we start from representation (3). Given positive, increasing weights ϕ that integrate to $1-m \le 1$ we construct a distortion function g. Define $g(0) = 0$ and for $s > 0$ set

$$g(s) = m + \int_0^s \phi(1-t)\,dt.$$

Then $g'(s) = \phi(1-s) \ge 0$, showing g is increasing. $g(1) = 1$ by definition of m. It follows from property 7 in Section 10.6 that g is concave because it has a decreasing derivative.

Sup Representations (5) and (6). Representation (5) follows from Theorem 1, part (d). Z can be interpreted as a density because it is positive and integrates to 1. Therefore it defines a probability scenario Q giving the analogous representation (6). The probabilities in Eq. (10.41) define the **core** of g. Each Q defines an additive pricing functional dominated by ρ_g. This representation shows that ρ_g can be understood as taking the worst (highest) value produced by a set of probability scenarios defined by g.

The scenario function representation is law invariant because the constraints on Z are law invariant.

If g is continuous, then for any X there is a Z that achieves the sup in Eqs. (10.40) and (10.41). In general, any Z satisfying

$$\rho(X) = \mathsf{E}[XZ] \tag{10.46}$$

is called a **contact function** for X. By the Hardy-Littlewood inequality, a contact function is comonotonic with X. It is unique if X is one to one, (Marinacci and Montrucchio, 2004). It is unique iff q_X is strictly increasing, i.e. has no flat spots (Carlier and Dana, 2003) When q_X has flat spots there is flexibility about Z and it no longer needs to be comonotonic with X.

11

Modern Portfolio Pricing Practice

In this chapter, we show how to apply spectral risk measures to determine a technical price using discrete data. We start with a discrete implementation of the main formulas, illustrated by applying a distortion to the Simple Discrete Example. We explore properties of parametric and nonparametric families of distortions and apply a range of distortions to the three Case Studies. We offer guidance about selecting a distortion. We show how to calibrate SRMs to catastrophe bond pricing data. Finally, we resolve a potential pricing paradox, highlighting certain technical aspects of SRMs in the process.

11.1 Applying SRMs to Discrete Random Variables

11.1.1 Algorithm to Evaluate an SRM on a Discrete Random Variable

Algorithm input: X is a discrete random variable, taking values $X_j \geq 0$, and $p_j = \mathsf{P}(X = X_j)$, $j = 1, \dots, n$. ρ_g is a spectral risk measure.

Follow these steps to determine $\rho_g(X)$.

Algorithm steps

1. **Pad** the input by adding a zero outcome $X_0 = 0$ with probability 0.
2. **Sort** events by outcome X_j into ascending order.
3. **Group** by X_j and sum the corresponding p_j. Relabel events $X_0 < X_1 < \cdots < X_{n'}$ and probabilities $p_0, \dots, p_{n'}$. All X_j are distinct.
4. **Decumulate** probabilities to determine the survival function $S_j := S(X_j)$ using $S_0 = 1 - p_0$ and $S_j = S_{j-1} - p_j$, $j > 0$.
5. **Distort** the survival function, computing $g(S_j)$.
6. **Difference** $g(S_j)$ to compute risk-adjusted probabilities $\Delta g(S_0) = 1 - g(S_0)$, $\Delta g(S_j) = g(S_{j-1}) - g(S_j)$, $j > 0$.
7. **Sum-Product** to compute $\rho_g(X) = \sum_j X_j \, \Delta g(S_j)$.

Steps (4) and (6) are inverse to one another. The transition $p \to S \to gS \to \Delta gS$ from input probabilities to risk-adjusted probabilities is used in all SRM-related algorithms.

Pricing Insurance Risk: Theory and Practice, First Edition. Stephen J. Mildenhall and John A. Major.

The algorithm computes the outcome-probability formula

$$\rho_g(X) = \int_0^\infty x g'(S(x))\, dF(x) = \sum_{j>0} X_j \Delta g(S_j).$$

When X is discrete the Steiltjes integral becomes a sum—the joy of using dF. We can also use the survival function form with $\Delta X_j = X_{j+1} - X_j$

$$\rho_g(X) = \int_0^\infty g(S(x))\, dx = \sum_{j\geq 0} g(S_j)\Delta X_j.$$

Exercise 180. Explain why the data must be sorted by portfolio loss when applying a spectral risk measure. How does sorting relate to the six representations shown in Theorem 3? □

11.1.2 Application to the Simple Discrete Example

Recall that in the Simple Discrete Example, Section 2.4.1, Ins Co. writes two policies taking on loss values 0, 8, 10 and 0, 1, 90 respectively, with probabilities 1/2, 1/4, and 1/4. The policies are independent and sum to the portfolio loss X. The 9 possible outcomes, with associated probabilities, are presented in Table 2.2. We do not refer to the two policies in this chapter (we return to them in Chapter 15), so the subscript notation X_j now stands for the total portfolio loss in the jth outcome.

We apply the proportional hazard distortion $g(s) = \sqrt{s}$.

Step (1) makes no difference because $X = 0$ is already an event. The outcomes are all distinct, so Step (2) grouping does not change number of outcomes. The sorted data is shown in Table 11.1. The expected loss is 27.25 and $\rho_g(X) = 51.156$ is shown on the lower right.

Exercise 181. Add columns to Table 11.1 to compute $\rho_g(X)$ using the survival function form.

Table 11.1 Simple Discrete Example with nine possible outcomes, expected loss, and risk measure calculations.

j	X	p	S	Xp	$g(S)$	$\Delta g(S)$	$X\Delta g(S)$
1	0	0.2500	0.7500	0.000	0.866	0.134	0.000
2	1	0.1250	0.6250	0.125	0.791	0.075	0.075
3	8	0.1250	0.5000	1.000	0.707	0.083	0.668
4	9	0.0625	0.4375	0.563	0.661	0.046	0.411
5	10	0.1250	0.3125	1.250	0.559	0.102	1.024
6	11	0.0625	0.2500	0.688	0.500	0.059	0.649
7	90	0.1250	0.1250	11.250	0.354	0.146	13.180
8	98	0.0625	0.0625	6.125	0.250	0.104	10.148
9	100	0.0625	0.0000	6.250	0.000	0.250	25.000
Sum		1.0000		27.25		1.000	51.156

Solution. We need to add ΔX and related columns. The (same) answer is shown in Table 11.2. □

Figure 11.1 illustrates the effect of the distortion on S. The horizontal axis shows events and their cumulative objective probabilities $1-S$ in 1/16ths, as well as their distorted probabilities $1-g(S)$ as decimals. (Because all the outcomes are distinct there is a one-to-one mapping between events and outcomes.) The vertical axis shows the outcome loss amount by unit increment from 0 to 100. The pale shaded area shows the effect of the distortion $g(s)=\sqrt{s}$, which creates a leftward shift by increasing the exceedance probability of a given loss outcome.

We can also compute the asset-limited survival function form of Eq. (10.27) to obtain

$$\bar{P}(a)=\rho(X\wedge a)=\sum_{j=0}^{\mathrm{j}(a)-1} g(S_j)\Delta X_j+g(S_{\mathrm{j}(a)})(a-X_{\mathrm{j}(a)}) \tag{11.1}$$

where $\mathrm{j}(a)=\max\{j : X_j<a\}$ and $\mathrm{j}(0)=0$. $\mathrm{j}(a)$ equals the index of the last value of X below a. The right-hand term in Eq. (11.1) accounts for the fact that $X_{\mathrm{j}(a)+1}>a$.

The event-outcome forms, Eqs. (10.35) and (10.36), are

$$\bar{P}(a)=\sum_{j>0}(X_j\wedge a)\Delta g(S_j)=\sum_{j=1}^{\mathrm{j}(a)} X_j\Delta g(S_j)+ag(S_{\mathrm{j}(a)}). \tag{11.2}$$

The *outcome-probability form* may seem more familiar and natural then the *survival function form*. However, the latter is more useful in certain situations.

Suppose assets $a=80$. Table 11.3 shows the above calculations through the simple expedient of replacing X values with $X\wedge a$ and recomputing other columns that depend on X. Notice that columns involving S still use X's survival function. Numbers changed from Tables 11.1 and 11.2 are shown in bold.

Table 11.2 Simple Discrete Example with nine possible outcomes, expected loss, and risk measure calculations.

j	X	ΔX	p	S	$S\Delta X$	$g(S)$	$g(S)\Delta X$
1	0	1	0.2500	0.7500	0.750	0.866	0.866
2	1	7	0.1250	0.6250	4.375	0.791	5.534
3	8	1	0.1250	0.5000	0.500	0.707	0.707
4	9	1	0.0625	0.4375	0.438	0.661	0.661
5	10	1	0.1250	0.3125	0.313	0.559	0.559
6	11	79	0.0625	0.2500	19.750	0.500	39.500
7	90	8	0.1250	0.1250	1.000	0.354	2.828
8	98	2	0.0625	0.0625	0.125	0.250	0.500
9	100	0	0.0625	0.0000	0.000	0.000	0.000
Sum		100	1.000		27.25		51.156

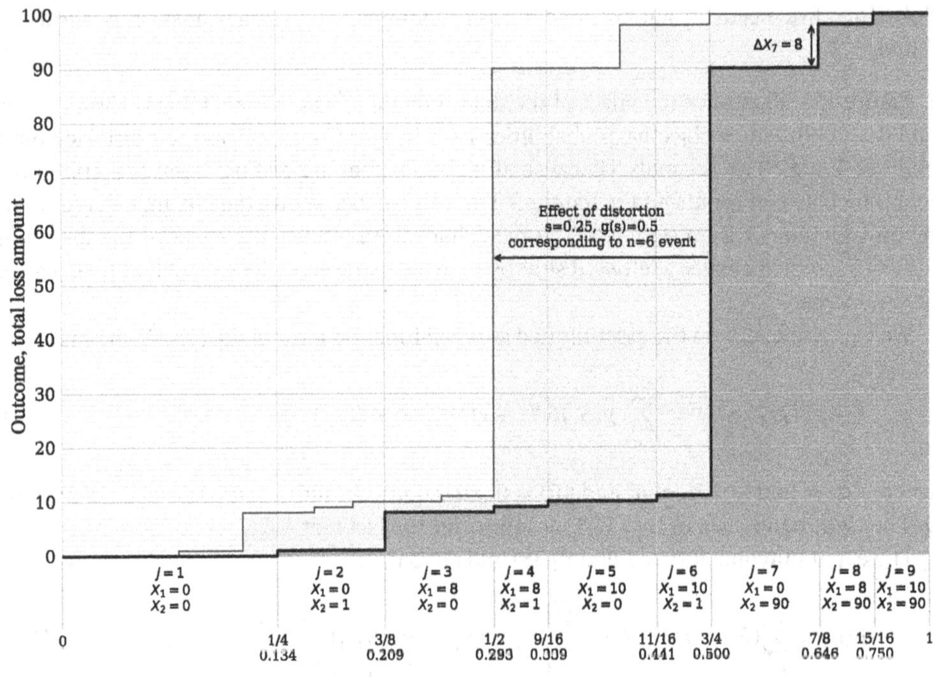

Figure 11.1 The Lee diagram illustrating objective and distorted probabilities.

Table 11.3 Simple Discrete Example with nine possible outcomes, expected loss, and risk measure calculations, assets limited to $a = 80$. X replaced by $X' = X \wedge a$ but values related to S are unchanged.

j	X'	$\Delta X'$	p	S	$X'p$	$S\Delta X'$	$g(S)$	$\Delta g(S)$	$X'\Delta g(S)$	$g(S)\Delta X'$
0	0	1	0.2500	0.7500	0.000	0.750	0.866	0.134	0.000	0.866
1	1	7	0.1250	0.6250	0.125	4.375	0.791	0.075	0.075	5.534
2	8	1	0.1250	0.5000	1.000	0.500	0.707	0.083	0.668	0.707
3	9	1	0.0625	0.4375	0.563	0.438	0.661	0.046	0.411	0.661
4	10	1	0.1250	0.3125	1.250	0.313	0.559	0.102	1.024	0.559
5	11	**69**	0.0625	0.2500	0.688	**17.250**	0.500	0.059	0.649	**34.500**
6	**80**	**0**	0.1250	0.1250	**10.000**	**0.000**	0.354	0.146	**11.716**	**0.000**
7	**80**	**0**	0.0625	0.0625	**5.000**	**0.000**	0.250	0.104	**8.284**	**0.000**
8	**80**	**0**	0.0625	0.0000	**5.000**	**0.000**	0.000	0.250	**20.000**	**0.000**
Sum			1.0000		**23.625**	**23.625**		1.000	**42.828**	**42.828**

Notice that $j(a) = 6$ and $g(S_{j(a)}) = 0.5$. The last term in Eq. (11.1) is $g(S_{j(a)})(a - X_{j(a)}) = (0.5)(80 - 11) = 34.5$ which is $g(S_6)\Delta X'_6$ in the table. The last term in Eq. (11.2) is $ag(S_{j(a)}) = (80)(0.5) = 40$ which is the sum of the $(X \wedge a)\Delta g$ entries for $j = 7, 8, 9$.

Exercise 182. Reproduce everything we've done in a spreadsheet! Change the parameters. Observe sensitivities. Get some cat model output and apply to a bigger example. Use a numerical solver to calibrate to market pricing. □

11.2 Building-Block Distortions and SRMs

We saw in Chapter 10 that any spectral risk measure can be represented as a convex combination of VaRs with decreasing weights or as a convex combination of TVaRs with arbitrary weights. Since VaR is not a coherent risk measure (and hence not an SRM), the TVaR family is the natural basic SRM building block. In this section we look at ways to build SRMs using two TVaRs. This is a stepping stone to general SRMs that are built from a continuum of TVaRs.

11.2.1 Tail Value at Risk

We know from Section 4.3 that

$$\mathsf{TVaR}_p(X) = \frac{1}{1-p}\int_p^1 q_X(s)ds, \tag{11.3}$$

where $0 \le p < 1$, is a single parameter SRM. Larger values of p correspond to greater risk aversion and larger values of $\mathsf{TVaR}_p(X)$. TVaR is defined by the distortion

$$g(s) = 1 \wedge \frac{s}{1-p}.$$

The distortion g is continuous and differentiable on $[0,1]$ except at $s = 1 - p$, where it has a kink.

The derivative $g'(s)$, equal to $1/(1-p)$ on $[0, 1-p)$ and 0 on $(1-p, 1]$, is the weight applied to VaR_{1-s} in the spectral representation. As the p parameter is increased, the weights increase and are applied to a narrower portion of the largest losses, and therefore TVaR_p is increasing in p. At one extreme, $p = 0$, $\mathsf{TVaR}_0(X) = \mathsf{E}[X]$ and at the other, $p = 1$, $\mathsf{TVaR}_1(X)$ is the maximum value of X.

$\mathsf{TVaR}_p(X)$ is continuous and differentiable in p because it is an integral. If we are given a target technical premium $\mathsf{E}[X] \le \bar{P} \le \sup X$, then we can use the intermediate value theorem to find a parameter $0 \le p^* \le 1$ so that $\mathsf{TVaR}_{p^*}(X) = \bar{P}$. Practically, we use Newton-Raphson or a one-dimensional search.

Exercise 183. Check that $p^* = 0.48732$ solves $\mathsf{TVaR}_p(X) = 51.156$ for p for the Simple Discrete Example. This value is the same technical premium as shown in Table 11.4.

Solution. Table 11.4 demonstrates p^* has the required properties. The value was estimated in a spreadsheet. The table shows both the outcome-probability and survival function forms. □

Table 11.4 Example risk measure calculations using TVaR_{p^*}.

j	X	ΔX	p	S	Xp	$S\Delta X$	$g(S)$	$\Delta g(S)$	$X\Delta g(S)$	$g(S)\Delta X$
0	0	1	0.2500	0.7500	0.000	0.750	1.000	0.000	0.000	1.000
1	1	7	0.1250	0.6250	0.125	4.375	1.000	0.000	0.000	7.000
2	8	1	0.1250	0.5000	1.000	0.500	0.975	0.025	0.198	0.975
3	9	1	0.0625	0.4375	0.563	0.438	0.853	0.122	1.097	0.853
4	10	1	0.1250	0.3125	1.250	0.313	0.610	0.244	2.438	0.610
5	11	79	0.0625	0.2500	0.688	19.750	0.488	0.122	1.341	38.523
6	90	8	0.1250	0.1250	11.250	1.000	0.244	0.244	21.944	1.951
7	98	2	0.0625	0.0625	6.125	0.125	0.122	0.122	11.947	0.244
8	100	0	0.0625	0.0000	6.250	0.000	0.000	0.122	12.191	0.000
Sum			1.000		27.25	27.25		1.000	51.156	51.156

11.2.2 Bi-TVaR

TVaRs are the simplest SRMs. A bi-TVaR, the weighted average of two TVaRs, is the next simplest. Bi-TVaRs are surprisingly useful. They turn out to be the extreme points (corners) of the set of SRMs that satisfy $\rho(X) = \bar{P}$, i.e., that price X at $\bar{P}$. Any SRM with this property can be written as a convex combination of bi-TVaRs with it. Therefore bi-TVaRs help us to understand how SRMs price risk and bound layer prices.

Let $\bar{P} = \mathsf{TVaR}_{p^*}(X)$ for some $0 \le p^* \le 1$. We know

$$\mathsf{E}[X] = \mathsf{TVaR}_0(X) \le \bar{P} \le \mathsf{TVaR}_1(X) = \sup X,$$

and so we can find a convex combination of TVaR_0 and TVaR_1 that equals $\bar{P}$. If $0 \le p_0 \le p^* \le p_1 \le 1$ we also know that

$$\mathsf{TVaR}_{p_0}(X) \le \bar{P} \le \mathsf{TVaR}_{p_1}(X)$$

because $\mathsf{TVaR}_p(X)$ is increasing in p. Therefore, we can also write $\bar{P}$ as a convex combination of $\mathsf{TVaR}_{p_0}(X)$ and $\mathsf{TVaR}_{p_1}(X)$. We formalize this in the following:

Definition 8. *Given* $0 \le p_0 \le p_1 \le 1$, *and* $0 \le w \le 1$ *define the* **bi-TVaR** *risk measure*

$$\mathsf{biTVaR}^{w}_{p_0,p_1}(Y) := (1-w)\mathsf{TVaR}_{p_0}(Y) + w\mathsf{TVaR}_{p_1}(Y). \tag{11.4}$$

When $p_0 \le p^* \le p_1$, $p_0 \ne p_1$, *and* w *is chosen so that* $\mathsf{biTVaR}^{w}_{p_0,p_1}(X) = \mathsf{TVaR}_{p^*}(X)$ *we call it the bi-TVaR* **associated** *with* p^**-TVaR.*

Exercise 184. A bi-TVaR corresponds to the discrete probability $\mu(\{p_0\}) = 1 - w$ and $\mu(\{p_1\}) = w$ in Theorem 3, Part IV. Let's work out the other representations.

1. Show the corresponding VaR weight function is $\phi(s) = g'(1-s) = \frac{1-w}{1-p_0}1_{[p_0,1)}(s) + \frac{w}{1-p_1}1_{[p_1,1)}(s)$.

2. Show $g'(s) = \frac{1-w}{1-p_0} 1_{[0,1-p_0)}(s) + \frac{w}{1-p_1} 1_{[0,1-p_1)}(s)$.
3. Integrate, to obtain the distortion function

$$g(s) = \begin{cases} \left(\dfrac{1-w}{1-p_0} + \dfrac{w}{1-p_1}\right)s & s < 1-p_1 \\ \dfrac{1-w}{1-p_0}s + w & 1-p_1 \le s < 1-p_0 \\ 1 & 1-p_0 \le s. \end{cases} \tag{11.5}$$

   If $p_1 = 1$ the first line is replaced by $g(0) = 0$.
4. Compute and graph the CoC function $\iota(s)$ and the discount function $\delta(s)$ for g.
5. What condition(s) on p_1, p_1 ensure that $\iota(s)$ is constant for a range of s? □

Exercise 185. Show that for an associated bi-TVaR, the weight w is unique except when $\mathsf{VaR}_{p_0}(X) = \sup X$, in which case we can take $w = 1$. Hint: first show that the derivative of TVaR_p with respect to p is $(\mathsf{TVaR}_p - q(p))/(1-p)$ where q is the quantile function of X. Deduce that TVaR_p is a strictly increasing function of p unless $\mathsf{TVaR}_p = q(p)$, which implies $q(p') = q(p)$ for all $p' \ge p$. □

Exercise 186. For TVaR_p with $p < 1$, what is the CoC for layers $s > 1-p$? How do you interpret this economically? Does it violate any premium constraints? What does it suggest for the construction of bi-TVaR pricing metrics used in practice?

Solution. If $s < 1$ and $g(s) = 1$ then $\iota(s) = (1-s)/(1-1) = \infty$. Policyholders in aggregate are paying 100% of the funding for those layers but are not expected to receive 100% in loss payments; some funds are likely be returned to investors. This violates the no-ripoff condition. Useable bi-TVaR pricing metrics should all be of the form $\mathsf{biTVaR}^w_{0,p}(X)$, including a term $\mathsf{TVaR}_0(X) = \mathsf{E}[X]$ with weight > 0. □

If $p_0 = p^* = p_1$, then take $w = 1$ (by definition) and $\mathsf{biTVaR}(Y) = \mathsf{TVaR}_{p^*}(Y)$. The set of all possible bi-TVaR coincides with the coherent subset of so-called GlueVaR risk measures proposed by Belles-Sampera, Guillén, and Santolino (2014).

Example 187. When $p_0 = 0$, $p_1 = 1$, $\mathsf{biTVaR}^w_{0,1}(X) = (1-w)\mathsf{E}[X] + w\sup(X)$. The corresponding distortion function is $g(0) = 0$, $g(s) = w + (1-w)s$, $s > 0$, recovering the CCoC distortion with return $w/(1-w)$ from Exercise 144. □

Exercise 188. Show that only bi-TVaRs of the form $\mathsf{biTVaR}^w_{p,1}$ exhibit a minimum rate on line. □

Exercise 189. The **capped linear** distortion is defined by a straight line with positive slope that lies above the diagonal on $(0,1)$ and that is clipped on the left at $s = 0$ and on the top at $g = 1$. Show every capped linear distortion is a bi-TVaR. □

11.2.3 The Distortion Envelope

The distortion envelope uses bi-TVaR distortions to determine the range of possible values of $g(s)$ for the set of distortions satisfying $\rho_g(X) = \bar{P}$ for a fixed X. It shows the range of layer pricing consistent with an overall price for X.

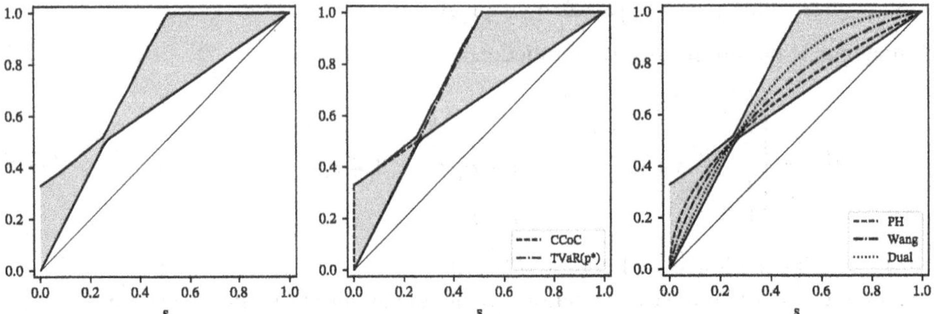

Figure 11.2 Distortion envelope for Discrete Example. Left plot shows the distortion envelope, middle overlays the CCoC and TVaR distortions, right overlays proportional hazard, Wang, and dual moment distortions.

The lower bound of the distortion envelope is swept out by the distortions corresponding to $\text{biTVaR}^w_{0,1}$ and TVaR_{p^*}. The former is the CCoC distortion. It gives the layer cost of capital when Ins Co. is funded entirely by equity (equivalently, funded by a single, equal priority tranche of debt.) At the other extreme, TVaR_{p^*} corresponds to funding by continuously tranched debt to the maximum extent possible consistent with $\bar{P}$. Low return period attritional "frequency" losses are funded entirely by premiums (dollar swapping in the aggregate).

Intuitively, a bi-TVaR with $0 < p_0 < p_1 < 1$ is intermediate between CCoC and TVaR. But, it turns out all the bi-TVaR are extreme cases in a specific mathematical sense. Mildenhall (2021b) shows that given an SRM ρ with $\rho(X) = \bar{P}$, and the set $\mathcal{E}$ consisting of all bi-TVaR pricing X to the same $\bar{P}$, the premium computed on another portfolio, $\rho(Y)$, is constrained to be between the minimum and maximum $\phi(Y)$ among $\phi \in \mathcal{E}$. In many cases the envelope is tight enough that this range conveys useful information.

In particular, given $\bar{P}$ and corresponding p^*, we can identify the set $\mathcal{E}$ by iterating over the pairs $(p_0 < p^* < p_1)$ and finding, for each, the associated w making $\text{biTVaR}^w_{p_0,p_1}(X) = \bar{P}$. By tracing the extreme high and low values of each associated bi-TVaR distortion function $g(s)$ we can identify the **distortion envelope** within which *all distortions pricing X at $\bar{P}$ must lie.* The lower bound of the pricing envelope is swept out by the CCoC and TVaR distortions, and is concave (because the minimum of concave functions is concave). The upper bound need not be concave (because the maximum of concave functions need not be concave.)

Example 190. Distortion envelopes for the Case Studies are shown in Figures 11.2–11.5. The left plot shows the envelope as the shaded area. The center plot highlights the CCoC and TVaR elements of $\mathcal{E}$. Notice that together they sweep out the lower edge of the envelope but not the upper extremes. The right plot shows three calibrated parametric distortions: proportional hazard and Wang, seen previously, and dual moment to be discussed later.

The pinched waist in the discrete example, Figure 11.2, occurs around the part of the distribution where X jumps from 11 to 90. As the profit margins increase in the three Cases, the envelopes become thicker and less useful. □

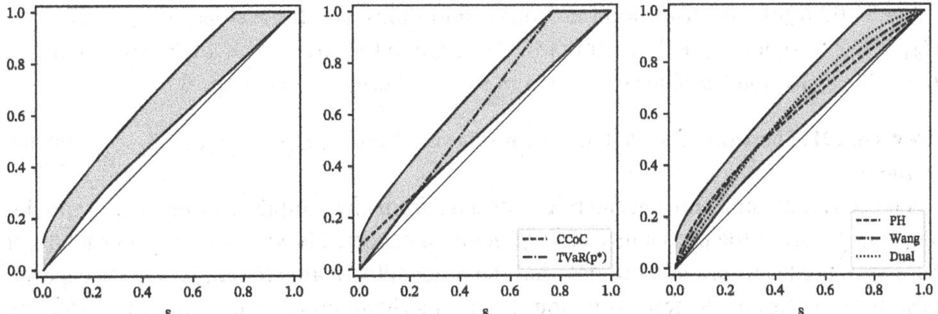

Figure 11.3 Distortion envelope for Tame Case Study, gross. Left plot shows the distortion envelope, middle overlays the CCoC and TVaR distortions, right overlays proportional hazard, Wang, and dual moment distortions.

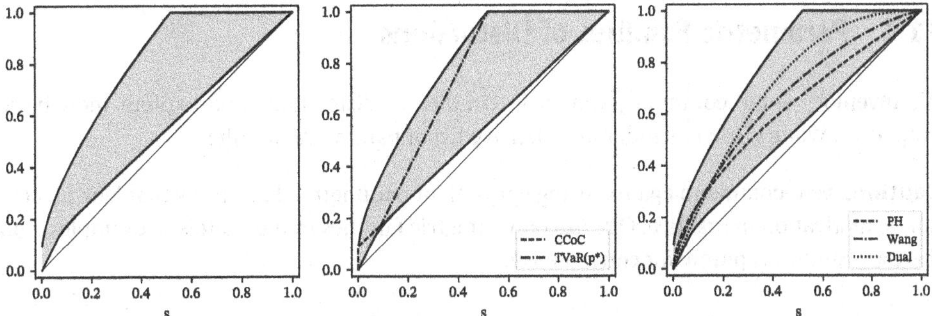

Figure 11.4 Distortion envelope for Cat/Non-Cat Case Study, gross. Left plot shows the distortion envelope, middle overlays the CCoC and TVaR distortions, right overlays proportional hazard, Wang, and dual moment distortions.

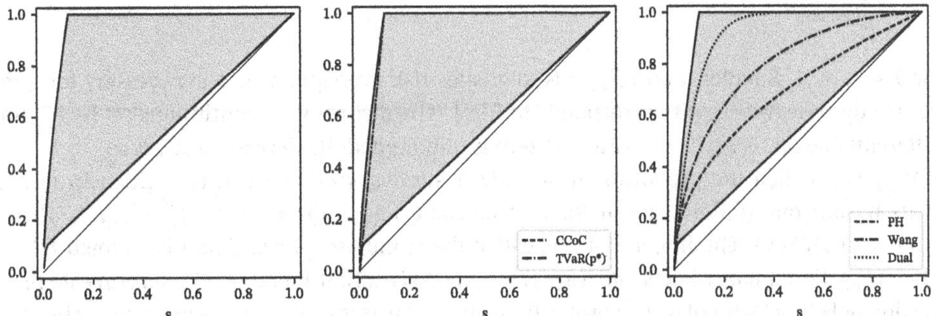

Figure 11.5 Distortion envelope for Hu/SCS Case Study, gross. Left plot shows the distortion envelope, middle overlays the CCoC and TVaR distortions, right overlays proportional hazard, Wang, and dual moment distortions.

11.2.4 Piecewise Linear Distortion

The **piecewise linear** (PWL) distortion is an empirical distortion defined as the concave envelope of a set of points $\{(s_j, g_j)\} \cup \{(0,0),(1,1)\}$, where all $s_j, g_j \in [0,1]$. If the smallest s_j

is greater than zero the distortion function is continuous with finite slope at $s = 0$. If there is a $(s_j = 0, g_j > 0)$ it is treated as a limit from the right. If the largest $s_j < 1$ with corresponding $g_j < 1$ the distortion has slope $0 < g' \le 1$ at $s = 1$; otherwise it has slope 0.

Exercise 191. Show that the PWL has a constant CoC equal to $(g_j - s_j)/(1 - g_j)$ over the last segment. □

A piecewise linear distortion can be constructed from any sample of observed layer pricing (taken as g_j) given the probability of attachment or expected loss (taken as s_j) in each layer. As long as the layers are thin enough that the probability of attachment is close to expected loss, this is a reasonable approximation. If an underlying loss distribution is available, the error can be computed by calculating the implied prices of each real (finite width) layer.

TVaR and bi-TVaR are special cases of PWL distortions.

11.3 Parametric Families of Distortions

We inventory some common parametric families of distortions, and explore their basic properties. Wang (1996) includes an extensive list of parametric families.

Caution: we recommend against using convenient parametric distortions that lack an economic motivation in practice. Our use of parametric families in the exercises, examples, and the Case Studies is purely for convenience.

11.3.1 Proportional Hazard

The **proportional hazard** (PH) transform is a single parameter transform given by

$$g(s) = s^\alpha,$$

for $0 < \alpha \le 1$. Smaller α corresponds to greater risk aversion. $\alpha < 1$ is necessary for g to be strictly concave; $\alpha = 1$ corresponds to $\mathsf{E}[X]$. The distortion is continuous on $[0, 1]$ and differentiable on $(0, 1]$. Its derivative at zero is unbounded. Its derivative at 1 is α.

Why is it called the proportional hazard? A survival function can be written in terms of its hazard rate (failure rate or force of mortality) as $S(x) = \exp(-\int_x^\infty h(t)dt)$, where $h(x) = f(x)/S(x)$. The integral of h is called the cumulative hazard and is denoted $H(x)$. The proportional hazard acts via $g(S(x)) = \exp(-\alpha H(x))$: it increases the hazard rate proportionately by a factor of α. The proportional hazard was introduced as a premium principle in Wang (1995).

11.3.2 Dual Moment

The **dual moment** distortion is given by

$$g(s) = 1 - (1 - s)^m$$

for $m \geq 1$. Larger m corresponds to greater risk aversion. It is continuous and everywhere differentiable. Its derivative at zero is m and at $s = 1$ is 0. Its properties mirror those of the proportional hazard.

Recall, the dual transform to g, is defined by Eq. (10.19)

$$h(s) = 1 - g(1 - s).$$

Thus, the dual moment transform is the dual of a proportional hazard-like transform $h(s) = s^m$. (It is not a proportional hazard transform because $m \geq 1$.) The graph of the dual transform is obtained by rotating that of g by 180 degrees about the point (0.5, 0.5).

The dual moment transform has an interpretation of applying powers to probabilities instead of outcomes (as moments do). Let X_i be independent, identically distributed random variables and let $Y_m = \max(X_1, \dots, X_m)$. Then $\Pr(Y_m > y) = 1 - (1 - \Pr(X > y))^n$. Therefore, for integer m, $g(S(x))$ is the probability $Y_m > x$ and

$$\rho_g(X) = \int_0^\infty g(S(x))\,dx = \mathsf{E}[\max(X_1, \dots, X_m)].$$

This interpretation explains why g is sometimes called the MAXVAR distortion.

11.3.3 Wang Transform

The **Wang transform** was introduced in Wang (2000). It is a single parameter transform given by

$$g(s) = \Phi(\Phi^{-1}(s) + \lambda),$$

for $\lambda > 0$. Φ is the cumulative distribution function of the standard normal. Larger λ corresponds to greater risk aversion. It is continuous and differentiable on [0, 1]. (Take $\Phi^{-1}(0) = -\infty$ and $-\infty + \lambda = -\infty$, etc.) Its derivative is unbounded at zero and greater than zero at $s = 1$.

Exercise 192.

1. Show

$$g'(s) = \frac{\phi(\Phi^{-1}(s) + \lambda)}{\phi(\Phi^{-1}(s))}$$

is a likelihood ratio.

2. Show that if X is normal with mean μ and standard deviation σ then the distorted distribution is normal with mean $\mu + \lambda\sigma$ and unchanged standard deviation σ.

Solution. Part (2): X has survival function $S(x) = 1 - \Phi((x - \mu)/\sigma) = \Phi(-(x - \mu)/\sigma)$. Therefore,

$$\begin{aligned} g'(S(x))\phi((x-\mu)/\sigma) &= \frac{\phi(-(x-\mu)/\sigma + \lambda)}{\phi((x-\mu)/\sigma)}\phi((x-\mu)/\sigma) \\ &= \phi((x - (\mu + \lambda\sigma))/\sigma). \end{aligned}$$

Remember ϕ is symmetric. We can also argue:

$$\begin{aligned} g(S(x)) &= g\left(\Phi\left(\frac{-x+\mu}{\sigma}\right)\right) \\ &= \Phi\left(\Phi^{-1}\left[\Phi\left(\frac{-x+\mu}{\sigma}\right)\right]+\lambda\right) \\ &= \Phi\left(\frac{-x+\mu}{\sigma}+\lambda\right) \\ &= \Phi\left(\frac{-x+\mu+\lambda\sigma}{\sigma}\right). \end{aligned}$$

□

Exercise 192 shows that the Wang transform operates on normal variables as an Esscher transform, a fact already noted in Wang (2003). Like the Esscher transform, the Wang alters the mean but leaves the standard deviation unchanged. In stochastic calculus, it gives the Girsanov transformation that adjusts the drift of a Brownian motion. Wang (2000) shows how to interpret λ as a measure of systematic risk and how to use the transform to recover the Black-Scholes formula.

Tsukahara (2009) discusses parametric families of distortions that compose in a natural way and shows they all arise in a Wang transform-like way using different increasing functions in place of Φ. For example, he shows the proportional hazard corresponds to using a Gumbel log-log distribution.

Samanthi and Sepanski (2019) show how to generate new distortion functions from distribution functions using a similar procedure. Junike (2019) shows that many families of distortions can be generated from distribution functions analogously to the Wang transform.

11.3.4 Linear Yield

The **linear yield**, invented by one of the authors, is a two parameter family of distortions defined by

$$g(s) = \begin{cases} 0 & s = 0 \\ \dfrac{s + r_f + rs}{1 + r_f + rs} & s > 0 \end{cases}$$

for $r_f \geq 0, r > 0$. Larger values of either parameter correspond to greater risk aversion. If $r_f > 0$ it is discontinuous at $s = 0$, with a mass $r_f/(1 + r_f)$. Its slope from the right at zero is bounded and its slope at 1 is > 0.

It is called the linear yield because the corresponding return on capital is a linear function of the probability of attaching the layer

$$\iota(s) = \frac{g(s) - s}{1 - g(s)} = r_f + rs.$$

It prices a layer to a return that is linear in its attachment probability, with a minimum of r_f for any layer with a nonzero probability of loss.

11.3.5 Leverage Equivalent Pricing

The **leverage equivalent pricing** distortion, invented by the other author, is a two parameter distortion defined by

$$g(s) = \begin{cases} 0 & s = 0 \\ 1 \wedge (d + (1-d)s + r\sqrt{s(1-s)}) & s > 0 \end{cases} \tag{11.6}$$

for $d, r > 0$. The parameter d is a cost of funding and r is a risk spread appropriate to a Bernoulli $s = 0.5$ layer.

The motivation is an investor who uses leverage to transform different layers into mean-variance equivalent layers, thereby pricing all layers with reference to a single unlevered layer. The natural reference layer is the one with highest variance, $s = 0.5$. Assume the investor has access to bank financing at an interest rate spread of i above the risk-free rate.

The investor takes a position in a layer with default probability s. Without leverage, this is an investment of $1-g$ for a gross return of $1_{X<q(1-s)}$ and profit $1_{X<q(1-s)} - (1-g)$. Suppose the investor takes out a loan in the amount λ with interest rate i for the period. Then the realized rate of return on own (out-of-pocket) funds is the random variable

$$\iota = \frac{1_{X<q(1-s)} - (1-g-\lambda) - (1+i)\lambda}{1-g-\lambda} = \frac{1_{X<q(1-s)} - (1-g) - i\lambda}{1-g-\lambda}.$$

The expected rate of return on own funds becomes

$$\mathsf{E}[\iota] = \frac{(1-s) - (1-g) - i\lambda}{1-g-\lambda}$$

and the variance of the rate of return is

$$\sigma_\iota^2 = \frac{(1-s)s}{(1-g-\lambda)^2}.$$

Taking $s^* = 1/2, \lambda^* = 0$ as the (unlevered) reference baseline,

$$\mathsf{E}[\iota^*] = \frac{1}{2(1-g^*)} - 1$$

and

$$\sigma_{\iota^*}^2 = \frac{1}{4(1-g^*)^2}.$$

To achieve the same variance rate of return for a layer at $s \neq s^*$,

$$\lambda(s) = (1 - g(s)) - 2(1-g^*)\sqrt{s(1-s)}.$$

Note that $g(s)$ is still unknown. Equating the expected rates of return results in a levered investment with the same return and variance, and substituting for λ we eventually arrive at

$$g(s) = \frac{i+s}{1+i} + \left(2g^* - 1 - \frac{i}{1+i}\right)\sqrt{s(1-s)}.$$

Setting $d = i/(1+i)$ we can rewrite this as

$$g(s) = d + (1-d)s + ((2g^* - 1) - d)\sqrt{s(1-s)}$$

and recalling the discount on a distortion is $d^* = 1 - (1-g^*)/(1-s^*)$ and that we have selected $s^* = 1/2$, we can see that $d^* = 2g^* - 1$. So a final rewrite gives

$$g(s) = d + (1-d)s + (d^* - d)\sqrt{s(1-s)}. \tag{11.7}$$

Eq. (11.7) is in the form of Eq. (11.6) with the additional insight that r is the spread between the discount on the reference layer $s^* = 1/2$ and the bank rate discount. Further enforcing $1 \wedge \cdot$ is required to ensure the expression results in a proper distortion function.

11.3.6 The Beta Transform

The **beta** transform is a two parameter distortion defined by

$$g(s) = \beta(s; a, b) = \int_0^s \frac{1}{\beta(a,b)} t^{a-1}(1-t)^{b-1}\, dt$$

where the integral defines the distribution function of a beta random variable with parameters a and b. g is automatically increasing from 0 to 1 and it is concave when $0 < a \le 1$ and $b \ge 1$; see Wirch and Hardy (1999).

The beta generalizes the proportional hazard ($b = 1$) and the dual moment distortion ($a = 1$).

The beta has two shape parameters, which makes it more difficult to parameterize than the other distortions we have listed. For the other two-parameter families the second parameter has a natural interpretation as a minimum rate on line or cost of funding, which enables it to be determined using external data, leaving a single parameter unknown. Both shape parameters for the beta need to be determined from the data.

Samanthi and Sepanski (2019) describe the Kumaraswamy distortion

$$g(s) = 1 - (1 - s^a)^b$$

which is also concave when $a \le 1$ and $b \ge 1$. When $a = 1$ it is the dual moment; when $b = 1$ the proportional hazard.

11.3.7 Altering g

Since an infinite variety of functions satisfy the constraints of distortion functions, the preceding examples are nowhere near exhaustive. However, they are representative of a wide range of behavior. Still, there are situations where they are not sufficient. One response is to start with known distortions and alter them. We consider two alterations: **mins** and **convex combinations**.

Exercise 193. Given two distortions g_1 and g_2 show that $g(s) = \min(g_1(s), g_2(s))$ is a distortion. □

Table 11.5 Parameters for the six SRMs and associated distortions that are applied in Section 11.4.

ID	Distortion	$g(s)$		Tame	Cat/Non-Cat	Hu/SCS
CCoC	CCoC	$(s+\iota)/(1+\iota)$	$\iota =$	0.10	0.10	0.10
PH	Proportional hazard	s^α	$\alpha =$	0.683	0.596	0.449
Wang	Wang	$\Phi(\Phi^{-1}(s)+\lambda)$	$\lambda =$	0.375	0.611	1.190
Dual	Dual moment	$1-(1-s)^m,\ m \ge 1$	$m =$	1.576	2.463	12.029
TVaR	TVaR	$s/(1-p)\wedge 1$	$p =$	0.227	0.482	0.899
Blend	PWL					

The minimum of a family of distortions has an important interpretation in terms of optimal risk sharing (Jouini, Schachermayer, and Touzi 2008).

Exercise 194. Show that any convex combination (weighted average with non-negative weights that sum to 1) of distortions is also a distortion. □

Example 195. All spectral risk measures are convex combinations of TVaRs. Convex combinations of TVaR_0 (mean) and TVaR_1 (maximum) yield all CCoC distortions. □

Example 196. You may have a distortion that fits your needs except that as $s \to 0$, $g(s)$ converges to 0 instead of a desired *minimum rate on line* (Flower and others, 2006). Taking a convex combination with TVaR_1 creates a distortion with a minimum rate on line. At the other extreme, as $s \to 1$, it may be that g climbs too rapidly, possibly causing the CoC to diverge. In that case, a mixture with $\text{TVaR}_0(\cdot) = \mathsf{E}[\cdot]$ moderates the CoC as $s \uparrow 1$. □

11.4 SRM Pricing

In Section 8.7.4 we fixed the cost of capital and VaR capital, and compared pricing by unit. In this section we consider six SRMs, compare the shapes of their associated distortions, and how they price different risks. The parameters are shown in Table 11.5.

All SRMs except Blend are parameterized to produce the same total gross premium. Blend is described in Exercise 197. It acts like a CCoC with a 0.1 return for $s > 0.2$, and proxies the use of debt or reinsurance to fund tail capital more cheaply. It produces lower premiums and higher loss ratios than CCoC and the other SRMs.

Exercise 197. Tabulate and plot the values of a PWL distortion that interpolates between the points shown in Table 11.6. Hint: start by completing the $g(s)$ row, using the formula from Section 10.5

$$g(s) = \frac{s+\iota}{1+\iota}$$

relating g to s given CoC ι. □

The first five SRMs are shown in order of the cost of tail capital. CCoC has the most expensive tail capital and cheapest body (of the distribution, or attritional) capital. TVaR has the cheapest tail capital and most expensive (infinitely expensive, in fact) body capital.

Table 11.6 Specification of a PWL distortion for Exercise 197.

s	Minimum	0.01	0.03	0.05	0.10	0.20
Layer CoC	0.02	0.03	0.04	0.06	0.08	0.10
g(s)	0.0196					

11.4.1 Distortion Function Properties

We illustrate the shapes of a selection of different distortions as well as the loss ratios and returns their associated SRMs imply. Although the distortions all have the same basic shape, bowed out from the diagonal, they produce different profiles for important insurance statistics.

Figures 11.6–11.8 show the relationship of premium, loss ratio, markup (premium to loss), margin, risk discount rate, and premium leverage (premium to equity ratio) against loss exceedance probability for each distortion function. The risk discount rate $\delta = \iota/(1+\iota)$ is shown rather than risk return ι, because discount always lies between 0 and 1. Discount increases monotonically with return. The parameters are shown in Table 11.5. The CCoC and Blend distortions do not change between Case. The other five are calibrated to the same gross total premium within each Case.

Note the loss ratio and markup behavior for the dual moment distortion compared to the others in the first group. Distortions with $g'(s) \to \infty$ as $s \downarrow 0$ have very high markup and very low loss ratio for high layers; all but the dual and TVaR exhibit this behavior. TVaR prices to a constant loss ratio for larger losses.

Figures 11.9–11.11 show the layer and total premium, assets, capital, and loss ratio and discount against *assets*. These plots illustrate how premium increases with assets. Again, the difference between the layer loss ratio for the dual moment and TVaR SRMs, which are asymptotically above 0, and the others, where it tends to zero, stands out. The second column shows that low layers are fully funded by premium (premium equals assets) and high layer premium is dominated by the cost of capital.

The impact of the minimum rate on line-like behavior for CCoC, which has a mass at zero, is evident in the first row. In the remaining rows there is no mass and the total premium line eventually becomes flat.

Distortions that do not have a mass at zero make it possible to price an unlimited cover on an unbounded risk—say, Worker's Compensation policies in the US—provided the integral $\int_0^\infty g(S(x))dx$ is finite. When there is a mass $g(0+)$ at zero, the integral $\int_0^a g(S(x))dx$ includes a term $ag(0+)$ and so the integral diverges as $a \to \infty$, no matter how thin the tail. If the risk is bounded then full cover is always possible at a finite price.

The discount rate at $s = 1$, the bottom asset layer, is $\lim_{s\to 1}(g(s) - s)/(1 - s) = \lim_{s\to 1} 1 - g'(s)$ by L'Hôpital's rule. Distortions with $g'(1) > 0$, such as the proportional hazard, have a finite return at $s = 1$ (second row) while those with $g'(1) = 0$, such as the dual moment and TVaR, have an infinite return (third row). A discount rate of 1 corresponds to an infinite return. The top row shows a constant marginal and total discount rate for the CCoC distortion, as expected.

At high asset layers, the loss ratio $s/g(s)$ tends to $1/g'(s)$ as $s \downarrow 0$. Distortions with an infinite slope at $s = 0$ have a zero loss ratio for the very highest layers. This is always the case when there is a minimum rate on line. However, it can also occur with distortions like a proportional hazard where $g'(0) = \infty$. In contrast, the dual distortion loss ratio tends to $1/m > 0$.

Remark 198. These plots help to develop an intuition for how an SRM prices a unit stand-alone, based on the behavior of its associated distortion.

- When g has a mass at zero (e.g., CCoC) there is a minimum rate on line and a capacity charge. Premium continues to increase with assets provided losses are possible, no matter how small the likelihood. These distortions have the most expensive tail capital.
- When $g'(s) \to \infty$ as $s \downarrow 0$ (e.g., PH and Wang) the layer loss ratio decreases to zero as the attachment increases. These distortions are expensive for tail risk.
- When $g'(s) < \infty$ as $s \downarrow 0$ (e.g., Dual, TVaR) the layer loss ratio decreases to $1/g'(0)$ as the attachment increases. These distortions are the most economical for tail risk.
- When $g'(1) < 1$ (e.g., CCoC, PH) the layer discount rate is always < 1, even for low layers. These distortions are cheaper for body risk.
- When $g(s) = 1$ for $s < 1$, or $g'(1) = 1$ (e.g., Dual, TVaR) the low layers are fully funded by premium and have a layer loss ratio of 100%. These distortions are more expensive for body risk. □

Exercise 199. Based on these properties, explain why SRM pricing is consistent with the idea that equity is the most economical way to bear well-diversified, thin-tailed risks whereas debt is most economical way to bear catastrophe exposed, thick-tailed risk. How is debt provided by alternative capital reinsurance arrangements? □

11.4.2 Pricing by Case Study

Tables 11.7–11.9 show the pricing implied by each SRM. As before, the SRMs are calibrated to equal total gross premium, producing a 10% gross return on VaR capital within each Case (Table 7.2), except for the Blend distortion, which is parameterized exogenously. Pricing is applied on a stand-alone and total basis. Expected losses account for default. The reinsurance assumption are described in Table 7.3.

The loss ratio is lower for the riskier unit, and the gross loss ratio is lower than the net in all Cases, in-line with actuarial expectations.

Loss ratios by SRM follow the rules of thumb laid out in Remark 198. In the first two Cases, loss ratios decrease from CCoC to TVaR. These Cases use a balance of body and tail capital. The net distributions are more body-heavy, by design, and become relatively more expensive as body capital costs increase. The third Case is tail driven. Reinsurance lowers the consumption of body capital, and so the order is reversed. The net CV, skewness, and kurtosis are all higher than gross, unlike the first two Cases; see the tables in Section 2.4.

The riskier unit has a *lower* CoC, except for the CCoC distortion where all returns are equal. The CCoC distortion shows that the same CoC can correspond to different loss ratios, depending on the risk. In general, CoC differences appear because the SRM picks up the

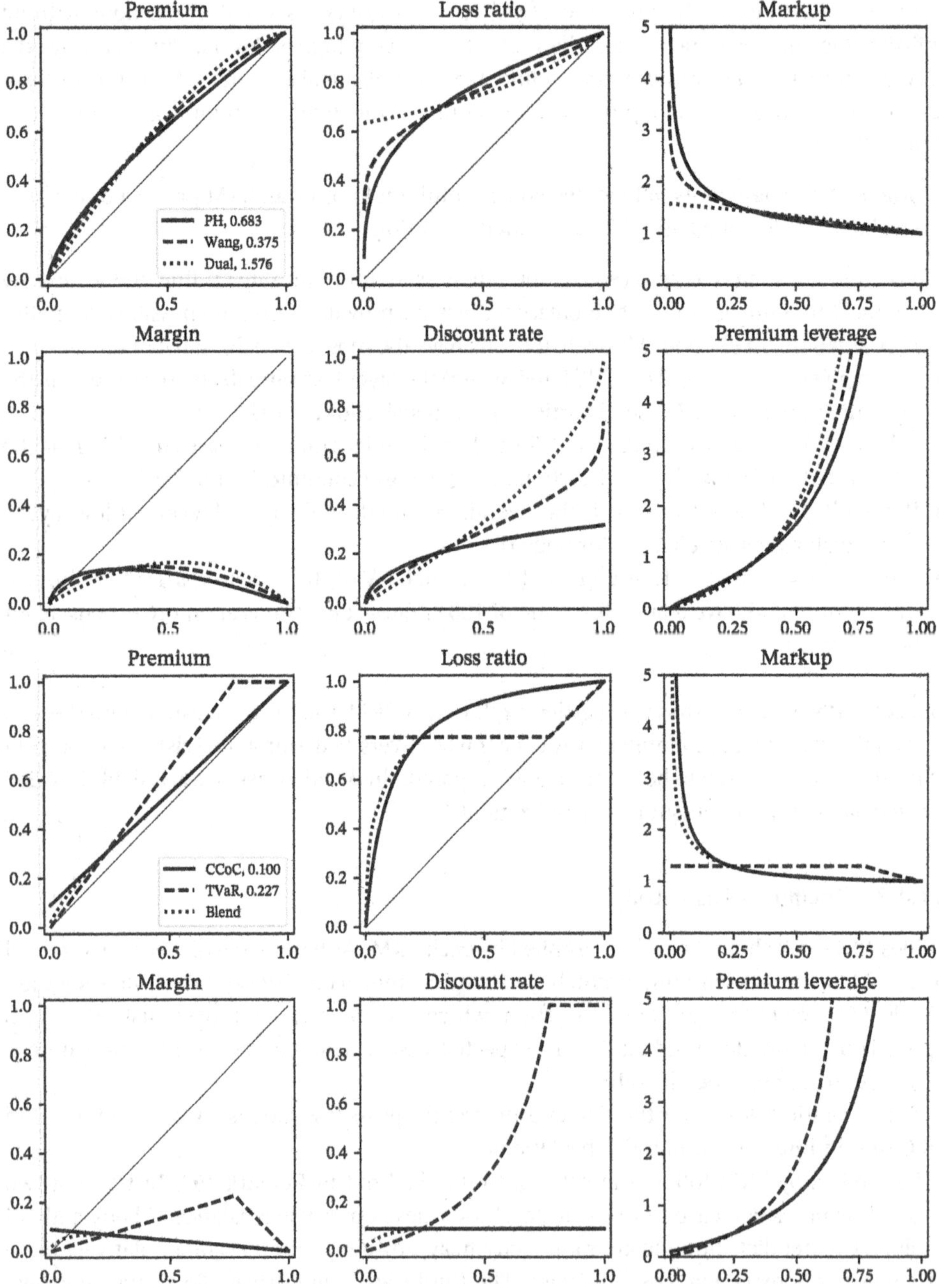

Figure 11.6 Tame Case: Variation in premium, loss ratio, markup (premium to loss), margin, discount rate, and premium to capital leverage for six distortions, shown in two groups of three. Top six plots show proportional hazard, Wang, and dual moment; lower six: CCoC, TVaR, and Blend.

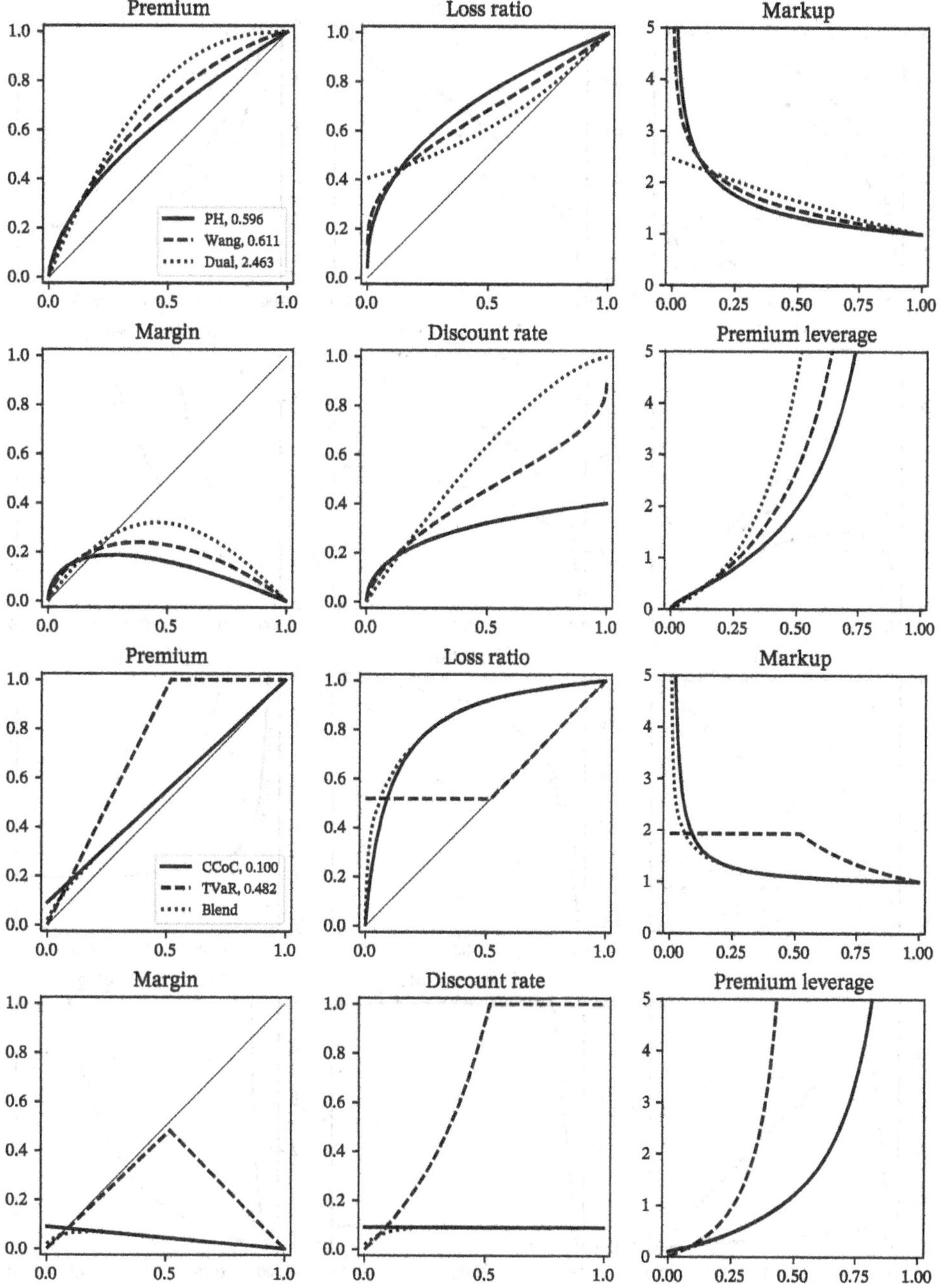

Figure 11.7 Cat/Non-Cat Case: Variation in premium, loss ratio, markup (premium to loss), margin, discount rate, and premium to capital leverage for six distortions, shown in two groups of three. Top six plots show proportional hazard, Wang, and dual moment; lower six: CCoC, TVaR, and Blend.

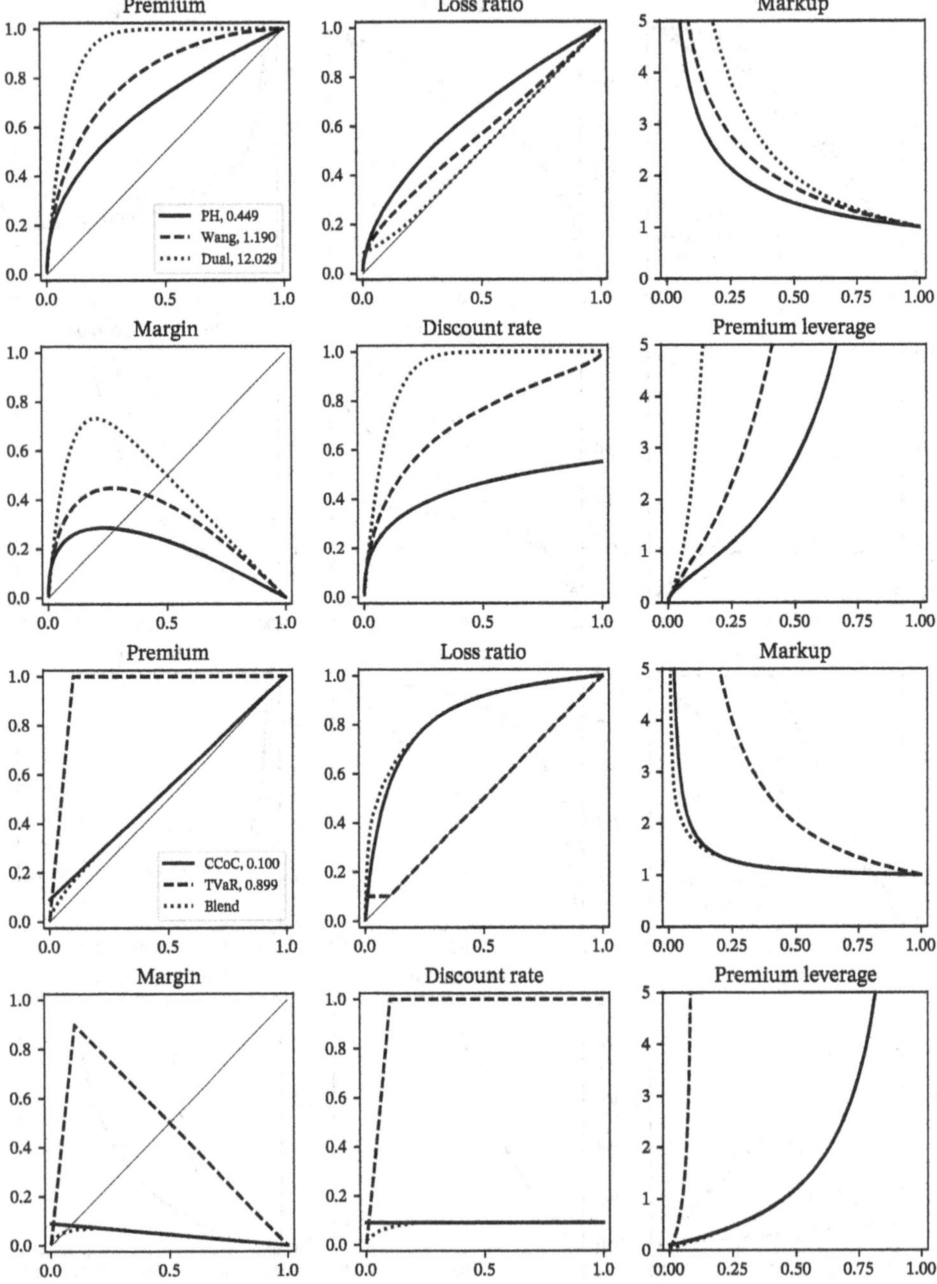

Figure 11.8 Hu/SCS Case: Variation in premium, loss ratio, markup (premium to loss), margin, discount rate, and premium to capital leverage for six distortions, shown in two groups of three. Top six plots show proportional hazard, Wang, and dual moment; lower six: CCoC, TVaR, and Blend.

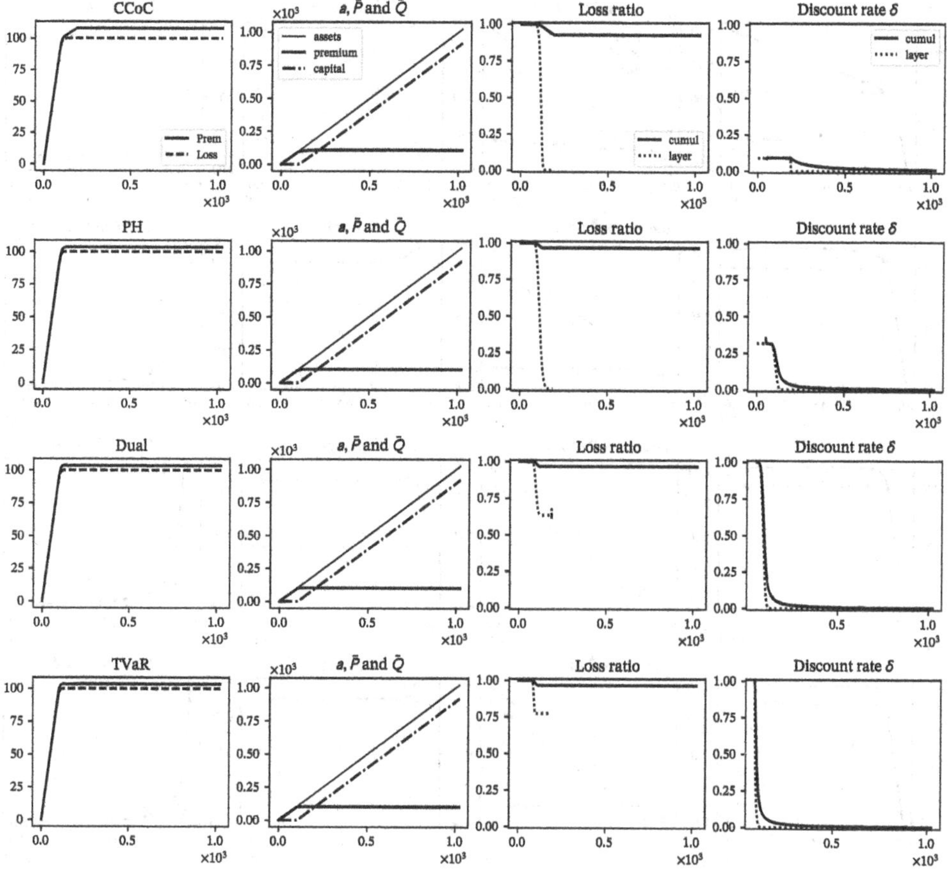

Figure 11.9 Tame Case: Variation in SRM properties as the asset limit (x-axis) is varied. Column 1: total premium and loss; 2: total assets, premium, and capital; 3; total and layer loss ratio; and 4: total and layer discount factor. By row CCoC, PH, Dual, and TVaR.

weighted consumption of capital by tranche and each tranche has its own cost. Thicker-tailed units consume relatively more high-margin cost but low CoC capital. At the top of a capital tower, capital can be provided by debt or alternative capital catastrophe bond instruments. These have a low single-digit CoC but a loss ratio of 50% or less; see the loss ratio and discount rate plots in Figures 11.6–11.8. While the loss ratio is easy to interpret, the average CoC is more difficult, as it reflects a risk-specific weighting of different layer costs. Of course, for the CCoC distortion all debt has the same cost because it all sits at the same priority—equivalent to 100% equity financing.

The leverage ratios are as expected. Even with a much stricter capital standard, the Tame Case can be written at a premium leverage of more than 3 to 1. Since rating agencies typically require lower leverage, stand-alone, low-risk companies search for ways to economize on capital.

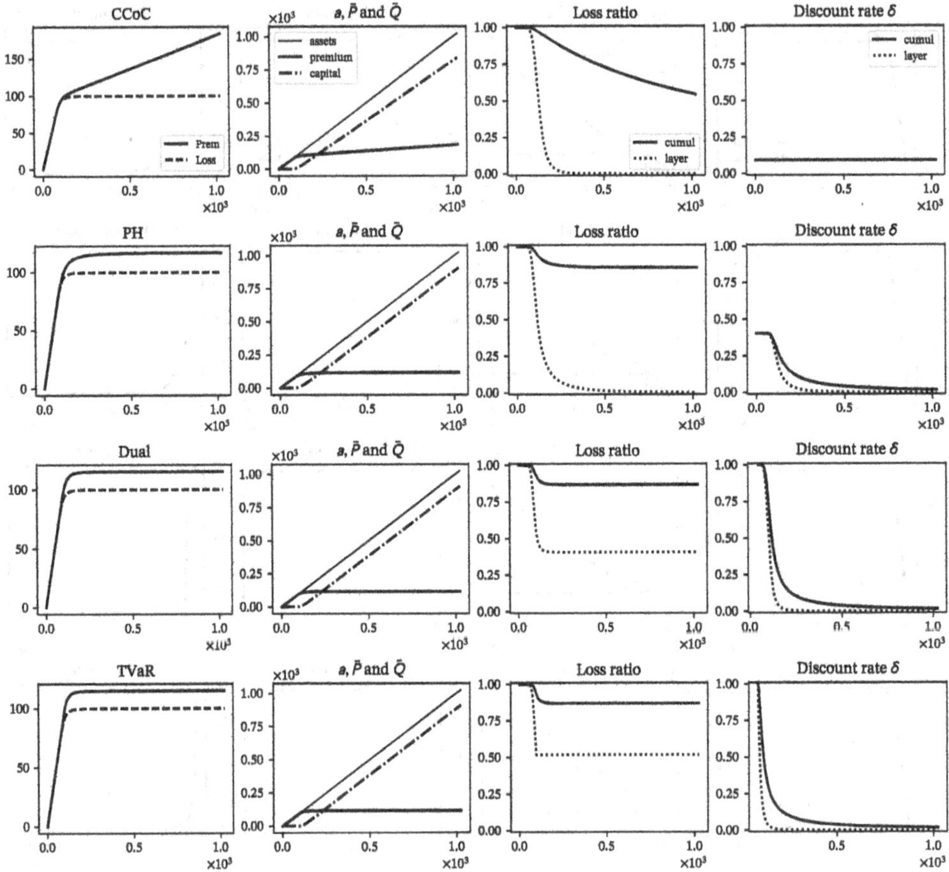

Figure 11.10 Cat/Non-Cat Case: Variation in SRM properties as the asset limit (x-axis) is varied. Column 1: total premium and loss; 2: total assets, premium, and capital; 3; total and layer loss ratio; and 4: total and layer discount factor. By row CCoC, PH, Dual, and TVaR.

Reinsurance affects the losses in each Case. Net premium is computed directly from the net loss distribution using the SRM. It is not gross premium minus a reinsurance premium. In this way, the model can be used to assess quoted reinsurance rates.

Exercise 200. What range of pricing for the reinsurance is attractive in each Case Study? □

11.5 Selecting a Distortion

Actuaries need to maintain professional conduct in this effort. We must review the relevant standards. In the US, the American Academy of Actuaries (AAA) sets standards through a Code of Professional Conduct and numerous Actuarial Standards of Practice (ASOP). In the UK, the Financial Reporting Council is tasked by the Institute and Faculty of Actuaries

Table 11.7 Pricing by unit and distortion for Tame Case Study, calibrated to CCoC pricing with 0.1 cost of capital and $p = 0.9999$. Losses and assets are the same for all distortions. The column SoP shows sum by unit, the different with total shows the impact of diversification. ¤12.9 excess ¤56.2 aggregate reinsurance applied to B.

		Gross				Net		
Statistic	**Distortion**	**A**	**B**	**SoP**	**Total**	**B**	**SoP**	**Total**
Loss	Blend	50.00	50.00	100.00	100.00	49.08	99.08	99.08
Margin	CCoC	1.89	2.98	4.87	3.42	1.89	3.78	2.46
	PH	1.9	2.89	4.79	3.42	1.82	3.72	2.76
	Wang	1.9	2.86	4.76	3.42	2.09	3.99	2.9
	Dual	1.9	2.84	4.73	3.42	2.36	4.26	3.03
	TVaR	1.9	2.81	4.71	3.42	2.54	4.44	3.15
	Blend	1.05	1.62	2.67	1.89	0.946	1.99	1.44
Premium	CCoC	51.89	52.98	104.9	103.4	50.98	102.9	101.5
	PH	51.90	52.89	104.8	103.4	50.91	102.8	101.8
	Wang	51.90	52.86	104.8	103.4	51.17	103.1	102.0
	Dual	51.90	52.83	104.7	103.4	51.44	103.3	102.1
	TVaR	51.90	52.81	104.7	103.4	51.63	103.5	102.2
	Blend	51.05	51.62	102.7	101.9	50.03	101.1	100.5
Loss ratio	CCoC	0.964	0.944	0.954	0.967	0.963	0.963	0.976
	PH	0.963	0.945	0.954	0.967	0.964	0.964	0.973
	Wang	0.963	0.946	0.955	0.967	0.959	0.961	0.972
	Dual	0.963	0.946	0.955	0.967	0.954	0.959	0.97
	TVaR	0.963	0.947	0.955	0.967	0.951	0.957	0.969
	Blend	0.979	0.969	0.974	0.981	0.981	0.98	0.986
Capital	CCoC	18.88	29.82	48.69	34.23	18.91	37.79	24.64
	PH	18.87	29.91	48.78	34.23	18.98	37.85	24.34
	Wang	18.87	29.94	48.80	34.23	18.72	37.58	24.20
	Dual	18.87	29.96	48.83	34.23	18.45	37.32	24.07
	TVaR	18.86	29.99	48.85	34.23	18.27	37.13	23.95
	Blend	19.72	31.18	50.89	35.76	19.86	39.58	25.66
Rate of return	CCoC	0.1	0.1	0.1	0.1	0.1	0.1	0.1
	PH	0.1	0.0967	0.0981	0.1	0.096	0.0982	0.114
	Wang	0.101	0.0956	0.0975	0.1	0.112	0.106	0.12
	Dual	0.101	0.0946	0.097	0.1	0.128	0.114	0.126
	TVaR	0.101	0.0937	0.0964	0.1	0.139	0.12	0.132
	Blend	0.0531	0.052	0.0524	0.0529	0.0476	0.0503	0.0563
Leverage	CCoC	2.75	1.78	2.15	3.02	2.69	2.72	4.12
	PH	2.75	1.77	2.15	3.02	2.68	2.72	4.18
	Wang	2.75	1.77	2.15	3.02	2.73	2.74	4.21
	Dual	2.75	1.76	2.14	3.02	2.79	2.77	4.24
	TVaR	2.75	1.76	2.14	3.02	2.83	2.79	4.27
	Blend	2.59	1.66	2.02	2.85	2.52	2.55	3.92
Assets	Blend	70.77	82.80	153.6	137.7	69.89	140.7	126.2

Table 11.8 Pricing by unit and distortion for Cat/Non-Cat Case Study, calibrated to CCoC pricing with 0.1 cost of capital and $p = 0.999$. Losses and assets are the same for all distortions. The column SoP shows sum by unit, the different with total shows the impact of diversification. ¤79.6 excess ¤41.1 aggregate reinsurance applied to Cat.

		Gross				Net		
Statistic	**Distortion**	**Cat**	**Non-Cat**	**SoP**	**Total**	**Cat**	**SoP**	**Total**
Loss	Blend	19.95	80.00	99.94	99.95	17.73	97.73	97.73
Margin	CCoC	15.03	3.84	18.87	15.21	7.99	11.83	8.17
	PH	13.81	6.37	20.17	15.21	7.38	13.75	9.82
	Wang	12.88	7.51	20.38	15.21	7.95	15.45	11.06
	Dual	11.88	8.6	20.48	15.21	8.83	17.43	12.40
	TVaR	11.21	9.17	20.38	15.21	9.15	18.32	13.15
	Blend	6.49	2.39	8.88	6.81	3.44	5.83	4.09
Premium	CCoC	34.98	83.84	118.8	115.2	25.72	109.6	105.9
	PH	33.75	86.36	120.1	115.2	25.11	111.5	107.6
	Wang	32.82	87.50	120.3	115.2	25.68	113.2	108.8
	Dual	31.83	88.59	120.4	115.2	26.57	115.2	110.1
	TVaR	31.15	89.17	120.3	115.2	26.88	116.0	110.9
	Blend	26.43	82.39	108.8	106.8	21.17	103.6	101.8
Loss ratio	CCoC	0.57	0.954	0.841	0.868	0.689	0.892	0.923
	PH	0.591	0.926	0.832	0.868	0.706	0.877	0.909
	Wang	0.608	0.914	0.831	0.868	0.691	0.863	0.898
	Dual	0.627	0.903	0.83	0.868	0.667	0.849	0.887
	TVaR	0.64	0.897	0.831	0.868	0.66	0.842	0.881
	Blend	0.755	0.971	0.918	0.936	0.838	0.944	0.96
Capital	CCoC	150.3	38.41	188.7	152.1	79.92	118.3	81.68
	PH	151.5	35.89	187.4	152.1	80.53	116.4	80.03
	Wang	152.5	34.75	187.2	152.1	79.96	114.7	78.79
	Dual	153.5	33.66	187.1	152.1	79.08	112.7	77.44
	TVaR	154.1	33.08	187.2	152.1	78.76	111.8	76.69
	Blend	158.9	39.86	198.7	160.4	84.47	124.3	85.76
Rate of return	CCoC	0.1	0.1	0.1	0.1	0.1	0.1	0.1
	PH	0.0911	0.177	0.108	0.1	0.0916	0.118	0.123
	Wang	0.0845	0.216	0.109	0.1	0.0994	0.135	0.14
	Dual	0.0774	0.255	0.109	0.1	0.112	0.155	0.16
	TVaR	0.0727	0.277	0.109	0.1	0.116	0.164	0.171
	Blend	0.0408	0.06	0.0447	0.0425	0.0407	0.0469	0.0477
Leverage	CCoC	0.233	2.18	0.63	0.757	0.322	0.926	1.3
	PH	0.223	2.41	0.641	0.757	0.312	0.958	1.34
	Wang	0.215	2.52	0.643	0.757	0.321	0.987	1.38
	Dual	0.207	2.63	0.644	0.757	0.336	1.02	1.42
	TVaR	0.202	2.7	0.643	0.757	0.341	1.04	1.45
	Blend	0.166	2.07	0.548	0.665	0.251	0.833	1.19
Assets	Blend	185.3	122.2	307.5	267.2	105.6	227.9	187.6

Table 11.9 Pricing by unit and distortion for Hu/SCS Case Study, calibrated to CCoC pricing with 0.1 cost of capital and $p = 0.999$. Losses and assets are the same for all distortions. The column SoP shows sum by unit, the different with total shows the impact of diversification. ¤372.4 excess ¤40.3 per occurrence reinsurance applied to Hu.

		Gross				Net		
Statistic	**Distortion**	**Hu**	**SCS**	**SoP**	**Total**	**Hu**	**SoP**	**Total**
Loss	Blend	26.01	68.82	94.82	95.15	15.27	84.08	84.41
Margin	CCoC	223.8	42.95	266.7	226.2	190.9	233.9	194.5
	PH	210.0	61.16	271.2	226.2	148.9	210.1	176.4
	Wang	199.8	72.46	272.2	226.2	126.9	199.3	168.6
	Dual	186.2	89.16	275.3	226.2	93.60	182.8	155.8
	TVaR	182.1	94.28	276.4	226.2	86.56	180.8	152.9
	Blend	63.72	16.28	80.01	67.20	49.05	65.34	54.64
Premium	CCoC	249.8	111.8	361.5	321.3	206.2	318.0	278.9
	PH	236.0	130.0	366.0	321.3	164.2	294.1	260.8
	Wang	225.8	141.3	367.0	321.3	142.1	283.4	253.0
	Dual	212.2	158.0	370.1	321.3	108.9	266.8	240.2
	TVaR	208.1	163.1	371.2	321.3	101.8	264.9	237.3
	Blend	89.73	85.10	174.8	162.3	64.32	149.4	139.1
Loss ratio	CCoC	0.104	0.616	0.262	0.296	0.074	0.264	0.303
	PH	0.11	0.529	0.259	0.296	0.093	0.286	0.324
	Wang	0.115	0.487	0.258	0.296	0.107	0.297	0.334
	Dual	0.123	0.436	0.256	0.296	0.14	0.315	0.351
	TVaR	0.125	0.422	0.255	0.296	0.15	0.317	0.356
	Blend	0.29	0.809	0.542	0.586	0.237	0.563	0.607
Capital	CCoC	2,238	429.5	2,667	2,262	1,909	2,339	1,945
	PH	2,251	411.3	2,663	2,262	1,951	2,363	1,963
	Wang	2,262	400.0	2,662	2,262	1,973	2,373	1,971
	Dual	2,275	383.3	2,659	2,262	2,007	2,390	1,984
	TVaR	2,279	378.2	2,658	2,262	2,014	2,392	1,986
	Blend	2,398	456.1	2,854	2,421	2,051	2,507	2,085
Rate of return	CCoC	0.1	0.1	0.1	0.1	0.1	0.1	0.1
	PH	0.0933	0.149	0.102	0.1	0.0763	0.0889	0.0898
	Wang	0.0883	0.181	0.102	0.1	0.0643	0.084	0.0855
	Dual	0.0818	0.233	0.104	0.1	0.0466	0.0765	0.0785
	TVaR	0.0799	0.249	0.104	0.1	0.043	0.0756	0.077
	Blend	0.0266	0.0357	0.028	0.0278	0.0239	0.0261	0.0262
Leverage	CCoC	0.112	0.26	0.136	0.142	0.108	0.136	0.143
	PH	0.105	0.316	0.137	0.142	0.0841	0.125	0.133
	Wang	0.0998	0.353	0.138	0.142	0.072	0.119	0.128
	Dual	0.0932	0.412	0.139	0.142	0.0543	0.112	0.121
	TVaR	0.0913	0.431	0.14	0.142	0.0506	0.111	0.119
	Blend	0.0374	0.187	0.0613	0.0671	0.0314	0.0596	0.0667
Assets	Blend	2,488	541.2	3,029	2,583	2,116	2,657	2,224

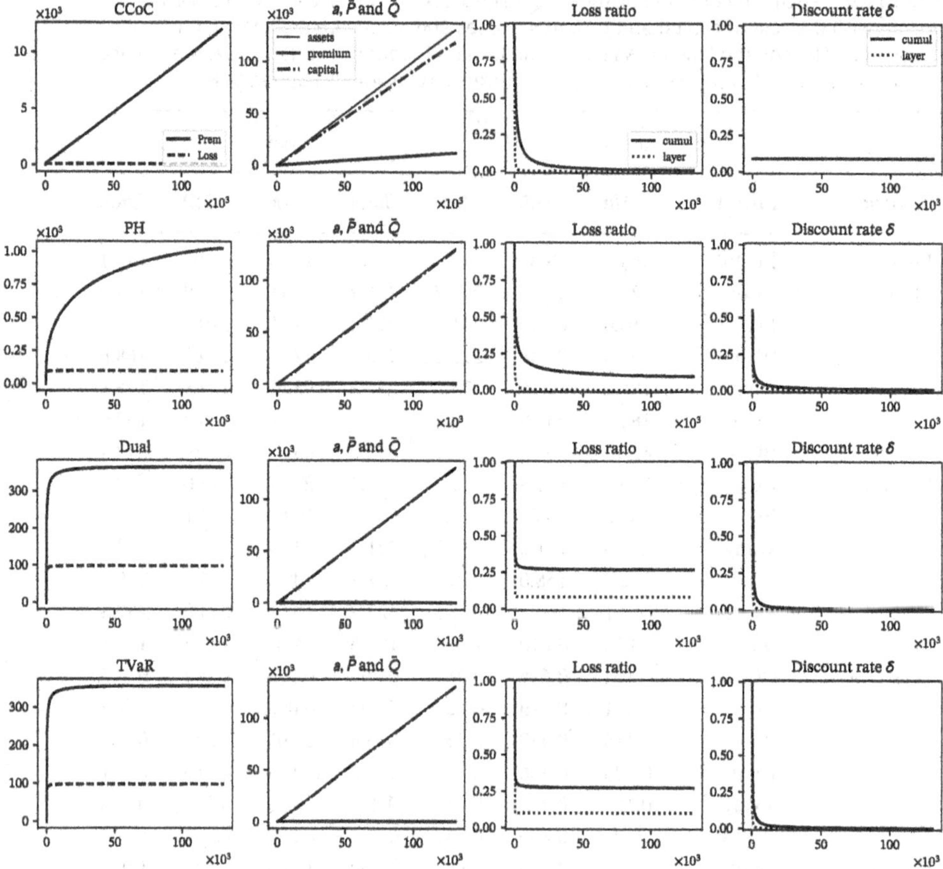

Figure 11.11 Hu/SCS Case: Variation in SRM properties as the asset limit (x-axis) is varied. Column 1: total premium and loss; 2: total assets, premium, and capital; 3; total and layer loss ratio; and 4: total and layer discount factor. By row CCoC, PH, Dual, and TVaR.

(IFoA) to create Technical Actuarial Standards. The Actuaries Institute Australia maintains a Code of Conduct as well as Professional Standards, Practice Guidelines, and Information Notes. The International Actuarial Association lists member organizations across 63 countries.

Whole company pricing models that include investment risk are not common. For pricing applications, we are more likely to be asked to model insurance risk only, and more likely not all the insurance risk, especially in larger companies. The typical application is examining a division and treating its cash flows as an arms-length transaction with the parent company (or larger unit) taking the role of investor. Pricing applications typically ignore carried reserves that are a sunk cost and instead consider expected prospective reserves.

The problem of choosing and calibrating a distortion function is just one part of a larger project. That project might be part of Enterprise Risk Management, or a performance review or goal-setting for lines of business, or an effort at re-underwriting or repricing existing business, or the development of a new underwriting or pricing system, etc. It is clear that within such a context, the team needs to *communicate* and *justify* their work to many stakeholders, including direct management, management of affected operating units, possibly the board of directors or board risk committee, and potentially outsiders such as regulators and rating agencies. The g designer needs an answer to "Why *this* pricing curve?"

The answer, ideally, is compelling. At a minimum, it must be defensible. Desirable attributes of the answer include: simplicity, transparency, evident fairness, objectivity (nonmanipulable, nonarbitrary), data-based (show a picture of the data!), and precedented. For example, a log-linear statistical model can show a parsimonious relationship revealed by (s, g) data and lead to a proportional hazard or capped log linear distortion. Or, if viewed in terms of (s, ι) perhaps a linear yield model would look compelling. The Wang transform, due to its connection with Black-Scholes option pricing, carries some weight of precedent. Similarly, Leverage Equivalent Pricing connects with a long tradition of mean-variance portfolio management.

The likely sequence is: constraints, data, analysis, judgment.

The overall weighted average cost of capital is either measured for the firm or part of the firm or it is simply declared by senior management. Previously, we saw that there is a one-to-one mapping between portfolio-level technical premium and several other financial metrics: required return, loss ratio, and margin. Any one of these, if specified exogenously, can be used to calibrate a one-parameter spectral risk measure. In the case of spectral risk measures with more than one parameter, other constraints need to be considered to develop the shape of the distortion function. Separate from the overall WACC, the cost of equity capital may be specified for the high-s layers. The low-s layer costs have outsize influence, so that is the place to start.

Look at the firm's capital structure. What is the default probability of its own bonds, and what is the spread being paid? Then look at the capital markets for what alternatives *could* be used to fund risk. Go out as far as possible (i.e., high s junk bonds) in understanding the risk/price profile of corporate bonds, bearing industry comparability in mind. Common equity is the last mile on the way to $s = 1$. As stated earlier, a straight-line constant-CoC segment represents the lowest priority asset layers. Insurance pricing data, principally catastrophe bond data, also has its place in the analysis. An example is provided in Section 11.6. The final distortion function cannot be wildly at odds with observed insurance risk pricing.

Unfortunately, the work does not end with, "Here's the answer." Communication and persuasion—in a word, sales—comes next. Prepare to address principal concerns of four types of audience:

1. What is it; how does it work?
2. Why is this the best?
3. Who else uses it?
4. What can it do for me?

Items 1 and 2 involve comparing the proposed approach to the existing way of doing things, and possibly alternatives that had been proposed. Item 3 includes some insurance industry pioneers as well as most of the investment banking world (especially if option pricing is construed to be a version of this technology). Item 4 needs to be focused on the particulars of the project.

11.6 Fitting Distortions to Cat Bond Data

Catastrophe bonds, first issued in the mid-1990s, provide protection for catastrophe perils such as hurricane, typhoons, earthquake, tornado-hail, severe convective storms, winter storms, wildfire, and flood, principally in the US, Japan, and Europe. Typically issued by insurance companies, they substitute for reinsurance. Bonds are usually fully collateralized and pay coupons with a fixed spread over the (floating) yield on the underlying assets, over a maturity of three to five years, but coupon payments and even principal repayment can be cancelled under specified conditions relating to the occurrence of a natural catastrophe, with cash flows then going to the issuer (the insurer) rather than the investors. The trigger for such an event can be parametric, index, or indemnity, meaning a geophysically specified event, a level crossing of an industry loss index or a modeled index, or the actual losses experienced by the issuer, respectively. Triggers requiring multiple conditions are also used. Losses can be measured on a per occurrence or aggregate basis. As of Fall 2021, the total catastrophe bond market had over USD 51 billion outstanding limit. More information can be found at artemis.bm.

Key metrics of a catastrophe bond include the expected loss EL, typically expressed as a percentage of limit. In reinsurance parlance, it is referred to as the loss on line (LOL). LOL measures the benefit from the issuer's perspective. It equals the probability of default times expected loss given default of a conventional bond. The ROL, or rate on line, is the premium expressed as a percentage of limit. It measures the cost from the issuer's perspective. ROL, also called the spread, is the additional coupon paid by the sponsor to the bond holder above and beyond investment income earned on the collateral. The bond expected loss ratio is EL/ROL.

The relationship between ROL and EL is influenced by numerous factors including: the size of the bond issue; the peril and geography; whether indemnity, index, or parametric trigger; the mix of personal and commercial and insurance or reinsurance business; and the management track record. Catastrophe bonds are typically analyzed by a third-party modeling firm to obtain an unbiased estimate of EL. However, the factors listed previously affect the confidence that investors put into such estimates.

There are several studies of catastrophe bond pricing in the literature, including Lane (2000); Lane and Mahul (2008); Gatumel and Guegan (2008); Galeotti, Gürtler, and Winkelvos (2013); Braun (2016); and the survey Major (2019).

To approach catastrophe bond pricing empirically, we make use of the Lane Financial LLC catastrophe bond database. We are grateful to Morton Lane and Roger Beckwith for making this data available to us. Figure 11.12 shows the US Wind portion of this data.

In the following, we fit distortion functions to observed catastrophe bond pricing in two ways. First, we fit a parametric statistical model centered on the Leverage Equivalent Pricing distortion, Section 11.3.5. This uses data from 454 US hurricane exposed catastrophe bonds issued since 2006. Prior to 2006 there were too few bonds to reliably fit a model. Various

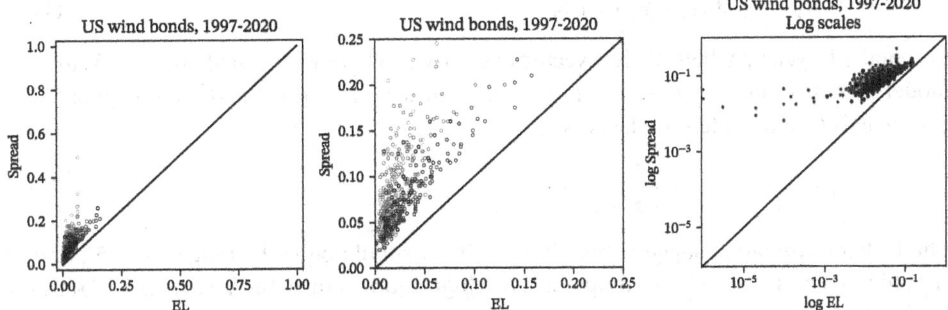

Figure 11.12 Spread (ROL) vs. EL on US wind (hurricane)-exposed catastrophe bonds since 1996. More recent years are shown darker black. The left and middle plots differ only in scale. Notice that catastrophe bond data includes observations for only $s < 0.20$. The right hand plot is on a log scale, emphasizing highly rated (low default probability) bonds, and illustrating the well-known minimum-rate-on line phenomenon of reinsurance pricing. Data: Lane Financial LLC.

features of the bonds are used as covariates in the regressions. Second, we develop a nonparametric distortion function based on bagged convex envelopes for all US hurricane exposed bonds since 1999.

11.6.1 Parametric Regression

We test whether a fit of leverage equivalent pricing (LEP) results in parameters that are statistically significant and of appropriate magnitude to comport with their LEP interpretation. We use the prior literature to inform the selection of specific control variables, see Table 11.10. The results show the fit parameters are indeed statistically significant and have the sign and magnitude suggested by LEP.

The distortion function for LEP was given in discount form by Eq. (11.7). For a general risk X supported by assets a the corresponding premium equals

$$\bar{P}(a) = \mathsf{E}[X \wedge a] + d_i\bar{F}(a) + (d^* - d)\int_0^a \sqrt{F(x)S(x)}dx$$

where $\bar{F}(a) := \int_0^a F(x)dx = a - \mathsf{E}[X \wedge a]$ is the insurance savings, $d_i = i/(1+i)$ is the rate of discount associated with a cost of bank financing i, and d^* is the reference discount on a Bernoulli(0.5) risk. Normalizing to the layer size, we treat a catastrophe bond as a Bernoulli contract that pays 1 with probability $p = 1 - s$. The *loss* random variable X takes on the value 1 with probability s. An asset amount $a = 1$ is needed to fully collateralize the contract, so we get

$$P(s) = s + d_i(1-s) + (d^* - d)\sqrt{s(1-s)}.$$

In order to test LEP we run an OLS regression of catastrophe bond risk margin $M = P - s$ against p and $r_{pq} := \sqrt{p(1-p)}$. M is estimated as premium rate on line minus expected loss on line $s = EL$ for each bond. The regression equation is

$$M_j = \alpha_y s_j + \beta_y r_{qp,j} + \gamma_j Y_j + \epsilon_{y,j} \tag{11.8}$$

for bond j in year y where Y_j is a vector of controls. There is no constant term. With this model specification $\alpha = d_i$, so $i = \alpha/(1-\alpha)$, and $\beta = d^* - d$ is the discount spread. The expected CoC of the reference layer is

$$\iota^* = \frac{1}{1-d^*} - 1 = \frac{1}{1-\alpha-\beta} - 1.$$

The LEP interpretation suggests two things. First, i should be in the range 1% to 5% and so should α. Second, ι^* should be comparable to a high equity return. Because $\alpha+\beta = \iota^*/(1+\iota^*)$, so should β.

Figure 11.13 shows historical issues, dollar issuance, and average expected loss ratio by year for US hurricane exposed bonds. Remember, a loss ratio of 25% corresponds to a premium multiple of 4—premium equals four times expected losses. (The magnitude of the risk margin for catastrophe risk underscores the importance of the topic of this book!) The clear pricing-year effect motivates estimating separate parameters by year.

A catastrophe bond pricing analysis typically includes a number of control variables. Table 11.10 shows common controls and their expected impact. IssueSize is a continuous variable measuring the total monetary volume of the bond issue. Indemnity is a binary variable indicating the default trigger is based on the issuer's own loss experience. Reinsurer and Retro are also binary variables indicating whether the sponsor is a reinsurer and whether the cover is a retrocession (reinsurance for reinsurers). Reinsurers can issue bonds as transformers for individual sponsors, which are not retros. We do not need controls for peril and geography since our analysis is based on US Hurricane exposed bonds.

Table 11.11 shows the results of various regressions. The first three models differ in treating α and β as constant or variable by year but do not use the controls. The fourth model uses the Retro Indemnity, and Reinsurer controls and varies α and β by year.

The coefficients of p and r_{pq} (α and β in Eq. (11.8)) have the signs and magnitudes predicted by LEP and they are all statistically significant. For the fixed parameter regressions, the cost of bank financing represented by the p coefficient is in the expected range and the

Table 11.10 Control variables with expected sign and rationale.

Control	Expected Sign	Rationale
IssueSize	Weakly negative	Lower expenses for larger issues, offset by potential marketing issues for larger offerings
Indemnity	Indeterminate	Indemnity triggers expose buyer to moral hazard from seller and command higher premium; in practice, only higher quality risks offered indemnity contracts
Reinsurer	Positive	Reinsurers are further removed from the original underwriter
Retro	Positive	Retro is further removed from the original underwriter
Geography	Varies	US hurricane (including wind) is the global peak peril and attracts the highest risk premium
Peril	Varies	Assessment of model quality varies by peril and geography

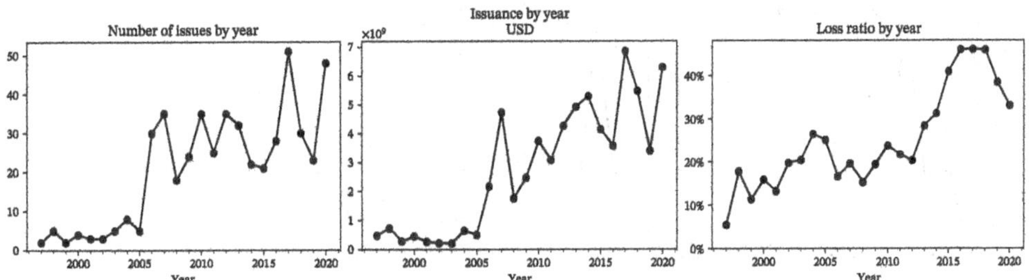

Figure 11.13 Number of issues, amount of issuance, and average loss ratio by year, US wind exposed bonds only. Data: Lane Financial LLC.

Table 11.11 Summary of regressions, with $p < 0.05$ and $p < 0.01$ significance.

Variable	(1)	(2)	(3)	(4)
p	0.032***	0.020***		
r_{pq}	0.184***			
Retro				-0.000***
Indemnity				0.006**
Reinsurer				-0.001
Year Effect	No	rpq	Both	Both
Observations	454	454	454	454
R^2	0.733	0.891	0.904	0.906
Adjusted R^2	0.732	0.887	0.897	0.899
Residual Std. Error	0.036	0.023	0.022	0.022
F Statistic	620.978***	223.941***	133.369***	127.258***

risk premium represented by the r_{pq} coefficient has a reasonable value. Figure 11.14 converts the year-dependent coefficients into the LEP bank rate i and benchmark return ι^* parameters. The bank rate is around 2%, except for a spike in 2009 after the Global Financial Crisis. The benchmark return shows a secular decline except for a spike in 2006 related to Hurricane Katrina (in 2005) and 2008. Between 2014 and 2018 it was below 20%, increasing more recently to around 30%. These values, in a maturing catastrophe bond market, are compatible with an equity risk return interpretation.

11.6.2 Bagged Convex Envelopes

In this section, we continue with the US hurricane exposed catastrophe bond data and present a non-parametric approach based on convex hulls. Unlike the previous regression analysis, we are not attempting to explain or predict catastrophe bond prices. Rather, we are using this data as an *example* of market data to be used as a guide to developing a reasonable

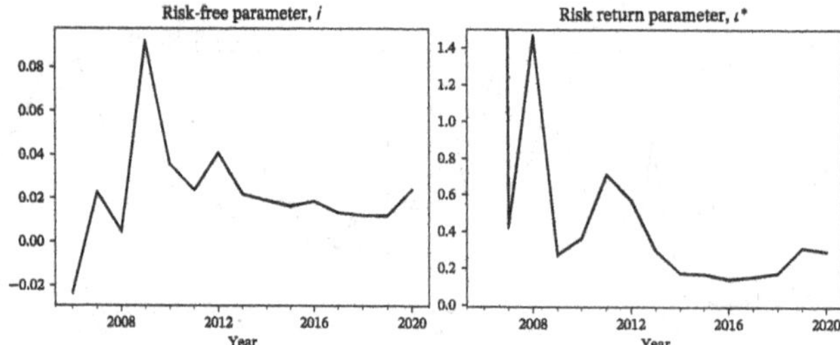

Figure 11.14 LEP parameters i and ι^* by year implied by model for US hurricane exposed bonds, 2006-2020, with issue year effect but no controls. Data Source: LaneFinancial LLC.

and realistic distortion function. We focus entirely on the observations (s_j, g_j) for the set of bonds, ignoring all ancillary information.

Nonparametric approaches tend to be more sensitive to the data than parametric ones. There are more effective degrees of freedom and more opportunity to capture nuances (overfit) in the shape of the data. Along with this, however, comes the problem of lack of data. The price data for catastrophe bonds (indeed, just about any insurance layers) is concentrated in the $s < 0.1$ region, with perhaps a few points $0.1 < s < 0.2$, and very few with $s > 0.2$. Since a distortion function must be defined out to $s = 1$, this requires considerable extrapolation beyond the range of the data.

We saw that various parametric distortions imply dramatically different CoC behavior in the $0.2 < s < 1$ range. Most have it rising: some rapidly (some even diverging) and some slowly. The CCoC has a constant CoC and the LEP has it rising and then going down again. Who can say what is correct? Jones and Rodes' Kropf (2004) and Cochrane (2005) examine the joint risk and return characteristics of venture capital funds; the former also includes buyout funds. By connecting tranche attachment probability s to volatility of return, we are able to map the findings of these two papers into the (s, ι) space. Unfortunately, the results are equivocal. Jones and Rhodes' Kropf suggest that returns plateau around 30% for default rates $0.3 < s < 0.4$ whereas Cochrane suggests they continue to rise more or less linearly to 80% at $s = 0.45$. Neither has anything to say for $s > 0.5$.

Our solution is a simple linear interpolation from the highest data-driven $(s^*, g(s^*))$ point to the $(1, 1)$ end point. This implies a constant CoC of $\iota^* = (g(s^*) - s^*)/(1 - g(s^*))$ over the range $s > s^*$. Besides simplicity (Occam's Razor) we might also appeal to the reality that there are no layers of equity; all equity is fungible and therefore must earn the same return. Because a layer with $s > 0.2$ is equity-like (greater than junk bond risk), we should expect to see the value of ι^* is also equity-like. For example, a last data point $(0.2, 0.304)$ corresponds to a CoC of $(0.304 - 0.2)/(1 - 0.304) = 15\%$. We call s^* the ROE point.

A **convex envelope distortion** (CED) defined by a set of (s, g) points in the unit square $[0, 1] \times [0, 1]$ that include (0,0) and (1,1) is the concave function greater than or equal to all of the points with minimum area under it. It is a piecewise linear distortion function, it is unique, and it forms the upper portion of the convex hull of the points in the plane.

Figure 11.15 shows a CED fitted to 40 price points in the data. An additional design point (the hexagon) at $(s, g(s)) = (0.2, 0.36)$ enforces a 25% CoC for $s > 0.2$; thin lines show what the CED and CoC are without the added design point.

The CED is not sensitive to the interior points. Being a type of max function, it is defined solely by the extreme upper points. To obtain a more realistic fit to the data, we employ a machine learning technique called bootstrap aggregation or *bagging*. Rather than fit one CED to all the data, we repeatedly take (bootstrap) samples of the data and fit a CED to each. The extreme points driving the original CED are not represented in all the samples, giving the subordinated data some opportunity to shape a CED. All the sample-driven CEDs are averaged for the final result. The average of a number of distortion functions is another distortion function.

Figure 11.16 shows a bagged CED formed from 1000 resamples of 10 % of the pricing data. Figure 11.17 displays the same on log scales.

In order to represent and use a bagged CED it must be stored as a numerical array since it is nonparametric.

Exercise 201. Describe two ways to enforce a minimum rate on line for a bagged CED. Do they always give the same result? □

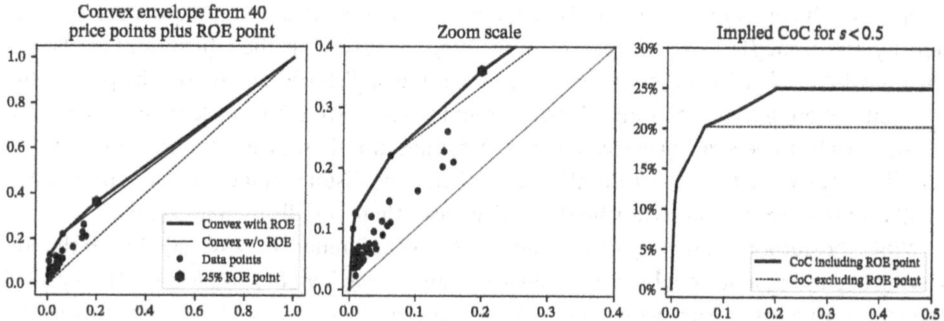

Figure 11.15 A convex envelope distortion defined by 40 observed pricing points plus a specified ROE point $(s, g(s)) = (0.2, 0.36)$ (left) and implied ROEs (right). The ROE is constant for $s > 0.2$ and sub linear from 0 to 0.2.

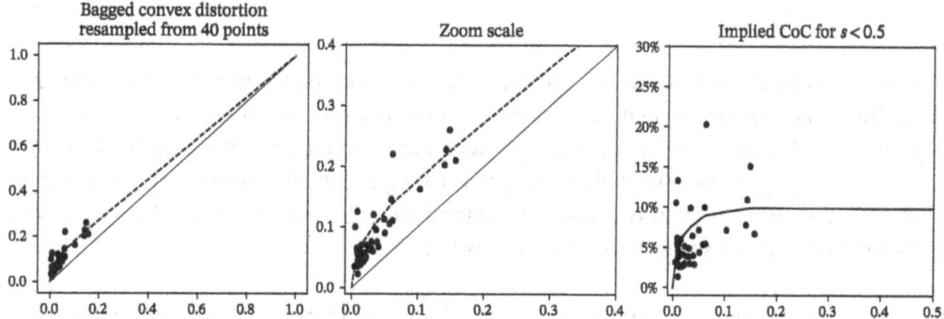

Figure 11.16 A bagged (bootstrap aggregated) convex envelope distortion defined as the average of 1000 resamples of 10% of 40 observed pricing points (left and middle, zoom) and implied CoCs (right).

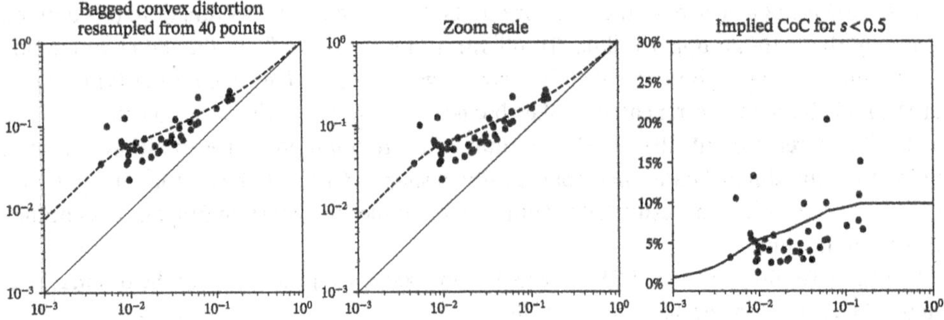

Figure 11.17 As Figure 11.16, on log scale.

11.7 Resolving an Apparent Pricing Paradox

A distortion function always increases the probability of a tail event $X > x$, but it can increase or decrease the probability of nontail events. When g and S are differentiable it changes the density at x from $f(x)$ to $g'(S(x))f(x)$, showing $g'(S(x))$ equals the adjustment applied to the probability (density) of the event $X = x$. Therefore a distortion increases the probability of events where $g'(S(x)) > 1$ and decrease them where $g'(S(x)) < 1$. Because a nontrivial distortion g has a decreasing derivative that integrates to 1, there is an x^* so that $g'(S(x)) \geq 1$ for all $x \geq x^*$ and $g'(S(x)) < 1$ for all $x < x^*$. Thus, the distortion increases the probability of all events above a certain threshold and decreases them for all smaller events.

While the authors were preparing materials for a conference, they wrestled with the following apparent paradox, which one colleague called a *big honking problem* (BHP) for SRM theory. Consider an insurance policy with indemnity function $V = 1_{X \leq x^*}$. Its outcome by state is

$$V(\omega) = \begin{cases} 1 & \text{if } X(\omega) \leq x^* \\ 0 & \text{if } X(\omega) > x^*. \end{cases}$$

V appears to create a policy which is priced below its expected value, which is a challenge to the theory because in the real world nobody would price a stand-alone contract below its expected loss. Using the TVaR distortion provides an extreme case of the BHP. All events below $x^* = \mathsf{VaR}_p(X)$ have adjusted probability zero, suggesting the market price of V is *zero*.

We can resolve the BHP in two ways: on a stand-alone basis or thinking of V as part of a portfolio. Before doing so, complete the next exercise.

Exercise 202. Assume the sample space is $\Omega = [0, 1]$ and that $X(\omega)$ is a lognormal variable with mean 10 and CV 0.5. Let $g(s) = s^{0.7}$ be a proportional hazard distortion. Plot X and V against ω. Separately plot the distribution function and quantile function of V. □

11.7.1 Stand-Alone Resolution

The stand-alone resolution highlights that SRMs do not define objective states and state prices. Instead, they are relative to the risk being priced. To compute $\rho_g(V)$ go back to the definition and use Eq. (10.39). For simplicity, assume g is continuous. Using Exercise 202, $q_V(p) = 0$ for $p \le S(x^*)$ and $= 1$ for $p > S(x^*)$. Then

$$\rho_g(V) = \int_0^1 q_V(p)g'(1-p)\,dp = \int_{S(x^*)}^1 g'(1-p)\,dp = \int_0^{F(x^*)} g'(s)\,ds = g(F(x^*))$$

and therefore $\rho_g(V) = g(F(x^*)) \ge F(x^*) = \mathsf{E}[V]$ by the properties of distortions. On a stand-alone basis, V defines its own ordering of events that is *different* from that determined by X.

SRM pricing mirrors the actions of a skeptical underwriter. A smart client (or their broker) creates V expecting a low price, by guessing how X is priced. The underwriter, ever conscious of adverse selection and fearful of being duped, appears to change the rules—or at least, changes the order of events—when asked to price V. As a result, ρ_g produces a positive margin for V. We saw the same bid-ask spread effect when considering the sale of residuals from Bernoulli layers in Section 10.4.

11.7.2 Portfolio Resolution

The portfolio resolution provides a good introduction to price allocation, the topic of Part III. Rather than price V stand-alone, we consider the fair price for V as part of the portfolio X.

We know, by Theorem 1, that there exists a probability Q with density $g'(S(X))$ so that $\rho_g(X) = \mathsf{E}_\mathsf{Q}[X]$. X's outcomes define implicit states that Q prices, reproducing a financial theory linear pricing rule. We shall see in Chapter 14 that it is natural to use E_Q to allocate premium. By construction, the allocated premium for V is less than its actuarial value. A change of perspective makes this appear rational.

A moments reflection is enough to see that a (fixed premium) direct insurance policy can be regarded as a (variable premium) ceded reinsurance policy by swapping the roles of premium and loss: direct loss becomes ceded premium and direct premium becomes ceded loss. Direct loss and ceded premium are cash outflows. Direct premium and ceded loss are cash inflows. Only the labels on the cash flows change, not their sign or amount.

The idea of *paying* for reinsurance is not a paradox. It is rational because reinsurance offers a hedge against adverse outcomes. *Adverse* is defined implicitly by X. But paying for reinsurance is exactly equivalent to writing a direct insurance policy at a loss: ceded premium (direct loss) is greater than ceded loss (direct premium). The policy V makes a reasonable reinsurance contract. It provides a ceded recovery (equal to the direct premium) in all states but only requires a ceded premium payment in good (low X loss) states.

One final objection could be raised: since the cedent pays variable ceded premiums, their risk-adjusted value should be greater than their actuarial expectation. This argument is precisely that of the stand-alone resolution. In the portfolio resolution, all risk aversion is collapsed into the X outcome and is priced by Q, the same way CAPM prices stocks relative to the market.

11.8 Learning Objectives

1. Use different expressions for calculating the mean $\mathsf{E}[X]$ and premium $\mathsf{E}_{\mathsf{Q}}[X]$, with and without asset limitation, associated with a spectral risk measure on discrete simulation output.
2. Calculate the margin, equity, loss ratio, leverage, and return on equity associated with an SRM based on the distortion function or on discrete simulation output.
3. Calibrate a one-parameter SRM to a margin or CoC target.
4. Describe how SRM pricing is influenced by the behavior of the underlying distortion at zero (mass, slope) and at 1 (slope).
5. Describe relative pricing of thick- and thin-tailed distributions given a distortion function.
6. Explain how to compute the envelope of possible distortions pricing a risk at a particular level. Identify and explain the significance of the TVaR and CCoC distortions that map out the lower bound of the envelope.
7. Modify a distortion to achieve a specific minimum rate on line.
8. Modify a distortion to achieve a specific CoC for high-frequency layers.
9. List considerations in the design or selection of an SRM.
10. Interpret the parameters of the leverage equivalent pricing SRM.
11. Explain how to develop a bagged convex envelope distortion, and the influence of each parameter on the result.
12. Explain why an SRM produces a positive margin for any realistic insurance product.

Part III

Price Allocation

12

Classical Price Allocation Theory

Determining prices for individual units written by a limited liability insurer is the technical heart of the book and the subject of Part III. It is a challenging problem because the investors' price for assuming risk is determined for the whole portfolio. Investors do not care about the constituent parts. The insurer needs to allocate the portfolio cost to individual insureds, who care greatly about their premium.

In this chapter, we introduce classical approaches to price allocation. These proceed via an allocation of capital, rather than allocating premium directly. We start by describing the allocation of CCoC pricing. We then examine a range of general allocation-based methods developed by actuaries in the 1990s and early 2000s. All are philosophically aligned with constant cost of capital pricing, and all ignore default. Next, we explain the equal priority rule for allocating assets in default. In practice, equal priority is always used. Finally, for the curious reader, we present a historical survey of academic price allocations that allow for default, laying out a forty-year journey to a realistic formula.

12.1 The Allocation of Portfolio Constant CoC Pricing

The widely used Portfolio CCoC pricing method, defined in Section 8.7.4, is based on the fundamental relationships

$$\begin{aligned} \text{Premium} &= \text{Loss cost} + \text{Cost of capital} \\ \text{Cost of capital} &= \text{Target return on capital} \times \text{Amount of capital} \end{aligned} \tag{12.1}$$

justified by Myers-Cohn's fair rate of return condition, Section 8.7.1 and Eq. (8.12).

The allocation of portfolio CCoC pricing involves four sets of variables: premium, expected loss, CoC target return, and assets, which are related by five equations:

$$P = l + \delta(a - l), \tag{12.2}$$

$$P_i = l_i + \delta_i(a_i - l_i), \tag{12.3}$$

$$P = \sum_i P_i, \quad l = \sum_i l_i, \quad a = \sum_i a_i. \tag{12.4}$$

Pricing Insurance Risk: Theory and Practice, First Edition. Stephen J. Mildenhall and John A. Major.

Ignoring default, expected loss payments by unit are all contractually determined. We have flexibility, however, for the other three variables: if we determine two of premium, discount rate, and assets then the equations determine the third. **Allocated CCoC pricing** *fixes* the target return and *allocates* assets, thus *determining* premium. Spectral risk measures allow an approach that *fixes* the target return by layer and *allocates* premium, thus *determining* assets and the average return by unit. In theory, we could allocate premium and assets, and determine discount, but that approach does not correspond to a mainstream PCP.

Eq. (12.1) opens a debate about how to risk-adjust the target return and fix the amount of capital. The two extreme approaches are

- Risk-adjusted return on capital **RAROC** methods that say return varies with risk.
- Return on risk-adjusted capital **RORAC** methods that say return is constant when capital reflects risk.

Banker's Trust developed RAROC in the late 1970s in response to regulatory pressure for better capital management (James, 1997).

Historically, there was a clear expectation that different units should be priced to different returns and that CoC should vary by unit (Cummins and Harrington, 1987). Cummins (2000) says "The risk-adjusted return should be compared with the cost of capital for business i, where the cost of capital is obtained using an appropriate asset pricing model." He goes on to say that estimating the cost of capital by unit is very difficult. One approach is to look at returns to monoline companies; another is to use CAPM. However, these methods are generally unsuccessful, suffering from a lack of monoline companies and the zero-beta catastrophe risk problem. Disheartened by these failures, users adopted a constant CoC assumption across units as a pragmatic solution. They looked to varying capital by unit as an easy and intuitively appealing way to reflect risk. The introduction of risk-based capital formulas in the 1990s further bolstered the adoption of RORAC.

As a result, the RORAC method, where a single **constant CoC (CCoC)** is combined with a **capital allocation** that normalizes for risk, has become mainstream. We call RORAC the **allocated CCoC** pricing method. The CoC used depends on the insurer's capital structure. It is estimated as the weighted average cost of capital. Debt and reinsurance have an explicitly quantifiable cost, leaving the cost of equity as the most important unknown input; see Section 8.2.6. Mango *et al.* (2013) describes CCoC as "the current industry standard approach (ISA)" in the context of assessing the effectiveness of reinsurance.

Allocated CCoC pricing is very popular. It is implicit in marginal return to marginal capital methods and motivates the use of marginal capital for performance measurement (Tasche, 1999). Marginal methods rely on a CCoC to be effective: increasing return to capital may not be an improvement if the target increases by more. Meyers (2003) applies it in an insurance context, comparing the marginal return on marginal capital to a fixed hurdle rate. The Solvency II CoC risk margin calculation statutorily requires a single CoC for the firm, Section 17.3.

How should capital be allocated to *normalize for risk*? Cummins (1990) wrote that deciding capital commitments is an issue with CCoC pricing and that "no widely-accepted theoretical rationale for surplus commitment in insurance presently exists." Today we still lack one, despite many developments in risk theory. This chapter takes a classical approach to allocation, proposing several recipes and applying a taste test to the results. We reference more theoretically motivated game theory allocations in Section 12.2.7, and in Chapter 14 we give modern, axiomatic characterizations.

Allocated capital is sometimes called **economic capital** or **risk capital,** mirroring the definition in Section 8.7.4. It is important to remember that while the firm has a free hand in allocating capital, its total amount of capital is largely exogenous, determined by a regulator, rating agency, or market consensus capital standard.

Allocated capital is only attributed by unit in a weak sense because, as Phillips, Cummins, and Allen (1998) points out, "The insurer's equity capital provides a cushion against unfavorable realized states of the world and is available to any line of business where it is needed." The allocation has no legal or accounting meaning and only impacts the real world through its influence on the insurer's decisions.

Spectral risk measures challenge the realism of a CCoC approach. In practice, insurers are financed using different types of capital, with varying cost characteristics, and each unit consumes a unique mix of capital. As a result, while all units should share proportionally in the cost *within* a layer, their weighted average CoC across all layers varies because they consume different mixes of capital. The spectral approach is developed in Chapter 14. It *allocates* premium, fixes a *layer* CoC for all units, and *determines* capital and average CoC by unit.

Exercise 203. You are given:

1. Ins Co. uses a 12% cost of capital for all lines.
2. Three units A, B, and C all have expected losses equal 100.
3. Total capital of 320 is allocated 40 to A, 80 to B, and 200 to C.
4. There are no expenses.

Compute the implied target loss ratio by unit using the allocated CCoC method.

Solution. See Table 12.1. □

Table 12.1 Solution to Exercise 203.

Item	A	B	C
EL	100	100	100
Capital	40	80	200
Cost of capital (rate)	0.12	0.12	0.12
Margin (¤)	4.80	9.60	24.00
Premium	104.80	109.60	124.00
Loss ratio	0.954	0.912	0.806

12.2 Allocation of Non-Additive Functionals

Allocated CCoC pricing relies on a capital allocation, and so in this section we consider different ways to do that. Since most popular allocations apply to all risk functionals, we start by describing at general methods that we can then use for any capital or pricing risk measure.

Example 204. Non-additive functionals we consider include:

1. Asset measures such as VaR_p and TVaR_p.
2. Capital measures such as regulatory minimum and solvency capital standards, rating agency capital adequacy formulas, and xVaR and xTVaR. For rating agency models, the safety level corresponds to a rating level.
3. Classical PCPs, Section 8.4.
4. A risk load functional computed from a PCP minus expected loss. □

Definition 9. *Given a functional* ρ *and a finite sum of random variables* $X = \sum_i X_i$, *an* **attribution** *of* ρ *is a functional taking the vector* $(X_i)_i$ *to a vector of real numbers* $(a_i)_i$. *The amount* a_i *is the attribution of* $\rho(X)$ *to unit* i *as part of* X, *which we write* $a(X_i;X)$. *If* $\sum_i a_i = \sum_i a(X_i;X) = \rho(X)$ *the attribution is* **additive** *("adds-up") and it is called an* **allocation** *of* ρ.

It is important that an attribution is a function of the vector $(X_i)_i$ in Definition 9. It does not act on each X_i stand-alone. An allocation is sometimes called a **contribution**, a **decomposition**, or an **assignment** of $\rho(X)$. The allocation problem is only interesting when ρ is not additive, i.e., $\rho(X) \neq \sum_i \rho(X_i)$.

By definition, an allocation is additive: the sum of allocations by unit equals the total being allocated. What other desirable properties should it have? Kreps (2005) lists three. An allocation

1. should work at any level of granularity, even down to the policy,
2. should be decomposable: the allocation to a sum of random variables equals the sum of their allocations, and
3. it should be computed using a single, consistent formula.

Property (2) is different from the case where an allocation to subsidiaries is further allocated to unit, as considered in Dhaene, Goovaerts, and Kaas (2003). In (2), it is implicit that all risks are in the same legal entity, and being decomposable is a management convenience.

Venter (2004) describes the allocation state of the art for US actuaries around 2000. Table 12.2 compares his taxonomy with Dhaene *et al.* (2012) and makes connections to other well-known methods. Our aim here is to give a representative sample of techniques, focusing on those best known to actuaries, rather than to provide a comprehensive list.

We use the term **endogenous** allocation when the same risk measure is used to determine the total and allocate it . In these applications, the risk measure is denoted $a(X, p)$ where p is a safety parameter. The choice of measure may or may not be under the control of the entity performing the allocation.

Table 12.2 Common allocation methods (Venter, 2004; Dhaene *et al.* 2012).

Venter	Dhaene	Other
Proportional spread	Proportional haircut	
Marginal business unit		Merton-Perold, Shapley
Marginal business		Euler or gradient
Game theory		Aumann-Shapley
Equal relative risk	Quantile	Equal risk
Co-measure	Aggregate portfolio driven	Riskiness leverage
		Weighted allocations

When the amount is stipulated by an external risk measure and allocated using a auxiliary measure, we call it an **exogenous** allocation (strictly speaking, it is an allocation of exogenous capital). Exogenous allocations occur when a regulator or rating agency determines the amount of capital, but an insurer determines its allocation. The external measure is still denoted a. The **auxiliary** risk measure is denoted ρ and it may also depend on a free safety-level parameter.

In both cases, we write a_i for the allocation to unit i. Note $a(X) = a(\sum_i X_i) = \sum_i a_i$.

Next, we discuss common allocation methods. For other general surveys, see Kaye (2005), Bauer and Zanjani (2013), and Tsanakas (2014). Considerations for selecting an appropriate method are discussed in Section 12.2.11.

12.2.1 Expected Value

The **expected value** allocation sets

$$a_i = a(X)\frac{\mathsf{E}[X_i]}{\mathsf{E}[X]}.$$

It allocates in proportion to expected loss. It is an exogenous allocation using expected value as the auxiliary measure. When applied to premium, it results in equal loss ratios across all units.

12.2.2 Proportional Allocation

The **proportional, proportional spread, stand-alone pro rata** or **scaled** allocation is an endogenous allocation with

$$a_i = a(X)\frac{a(X_i)}{\sum_i a(X_i)}.$$

Each unit is evaluated on a stand-alone basis and the total is pro rated to $a(X)$. As a result, the allocation is not influenced by the dependence between X_i.

12.2.3 Haircut Allocation

The **haircut allocation** is an exogenous version of the proportional allocation. It uses an auxiliary ρ and allocates

$$a_i = a(X)\frac{\rho(X_i)}{\sum_i \rho(X_i)}.$$

It is often applied with ρ given by VaR, TVaR, or EPD. Again, the allocation is not influenced by the dependence structure.

Exercise 205. Compute the haircut allocation of premium $P = 80$ to units 1 and 2 using the Simple Discrete Example, Section 2.4.1, and taking $\mathsf{TVaR}_{0.75}$ as the auxiliary risk measure. What are the loss ratios by unit?

Solution. The two TVaRs are 10 and 90. Therefore the allocations are 8 and 72 and the loss ratios are 56.3% and 31.6%, and 34.1% in total. □

12.2.4 Equal Risk Allocations

The endogenous **equal risk** or **quantile** allocation solves $\sum_i a(X_i, p^*) = a(X)$ for p^* and sets $a_i = a(X_i, p^*)$. The exogenous version solves $\sum_i \rho(X_i, p^*) = a$ for p^* and sets $a_i = \rho(X_i, p^*)$.

Equal risk allocations are discussed in Dhaene, Goovaerts, and Kaas (2003). When $\rho = \mathsf{VaR}_p$, each unit is capitalized to the same probability of default, which is regarded as treating units equitably. In the proportional and haircut allocations, the implied security level will vary by unit (though the actual security level is controlled by total losses). The solution is in effect replacing the actual dependence structure between units with comonotonic (worst-case) dependence.

Dhaene *et al.* (2012) show that equal risk VaR is the solution to the optimization problem:

$$\min_{a_1,\dots,a_n} \sum_{i=1}^{n} \mathsf{E}[(X_i - a_i)^+] \quad \text{such that} \quad \sum_{i=1}^{n} a_i = a.$$

The interpretation is straightforward: each unit, stand-alone, has an expected excess loss beyond its allocated capital. The objective is to allocate capital to minimize the sum of these expected excesses. The equal risk VaR allocation does this. The Lloyd's/London market often allocates capital this way.

Exercise 206. Compute the exogenous equal risk allocation of premium $P = 80$ to units 1 and 2 for the Simple Discrete Example, Section 2.4.1, and taking TVaR as the auxiliary risk measure. What are the loss ratios?

Solution. Refer to Table 2.2. We need to find p^* so that $\mathsf{TVaR}_{p^*}(X_1) + \mathsf{TVaR}_{p^*}(X_2) = 80$. The two TVaR values then give the allocation. Table 2.2 shows that $0.5 \le p^* \le 0.75$ because $\mathsf{TVaR}_{0.5}(X_1) = 9$, $\mathsf{TVaR}_{0.5}(X_2) = 45.5$ and $\mathsf{TVaR}_{0.75}(X_1) = 10$, $\mathsf{TVaR}_{0.75}(X_2) = 90$. For p in that range we have

$$\mathsf{TVaR}_p(X_1) = (1-p)^{-1}(8 \times (0.75-p) + 0.5 \times 10),$$
$$\mathsf{TVaR}_p(X_2) = (1-p)^{-1}(1 \times (0.75-p) + 0.5 \times 90).$$

Solving for the sum gives $p^* = 48.25/71 = 0.6796$ and the allocation $80 = 9.56 + 70.44$. The loss ratios are 47.1% and 32.3%, and 34.1% in total. □

12.2.5 Marginal Business Unit

The **marginal business unit** or **Merton-Perold** method attributes to each unit the reduction in capital from dropping it from the portfolio (Merton and Perold, 1993). This method is not additive: generally the sum of allocations is less than total capital. It mimics the actions of a corporate manager who optimizes atomically—keeping or dropping whole units.

12.2.6 Marginal Business Euler Gradient Allocation

A marginal business **Euler gradient** allocation is based on the marginal change in capital given a marginal change in the amount of unit i written. It is an endogenous allocation. It corresponds naturally to a marginal cost–marginal benefit optimization. If $X = X(x_1, \dots, x_n) = x_1X_1 + \cdots + x_nX_n$ for fixed X_i, and if the function $a(x_1, \dots, x_n) := a(X(x_1, \dots, x_n))$ is differentiable and positive homogeneous, then Euler's Theorem says

$$a(x_1, \dots, x_n) = \sum_i x_i \frac{\partial a}{\partial x_i}$$

and so $a_i = x_i(\partial a/\partial x_i)$ is an allocation. Euler's Theorem follows by differentiating $f(t) = a(tx_1, \dots, tx_n) = ta(x_1, \dots, x_n)$ with respect to t to get $\dot{f}(t) = a(x)$ and using the total derivative at $t = 1$, see Mildenhall (2004). Note that

$$x_i \frac{\partial a}{\partial x_i} = \lim_{t \to 0} \frac{a(x_1, \dots, x_i(1+t), \dots x_n) - a(x_1, \dots, x_n)}{t},$$

showing the allocation equals the directional derivative of a at X in the direction of unit i.

Tasche (2004) shows that the Euler allocation is the only one *suitable for performance measurement* in the sense that growing (shrinking) lines with a higher (lower) return to marginal capital always improves the average return. This assumes that the average return is sufficient for deciding whether a portfolio's pricing has improved; it does not allow for the possibility that a change in portfolio composition causes a change in the cost of capital. Myers and Read Jr. (2001) applies the Euler allocation to EPD capital.

Methods using homogeneous portfolios, where different participations apply to a fixed set of risks, are motivated by analysis of asset risk, where X_i is a return variable and x_i a position size. The homogeneous model does not reflect the realities of insurance portfolios, which grow by adding independent or partially independent risks. Non-additive pricing functionals are sensitive to the shape of risk and one must replace homogeneous derivatives with directional derivatives, where the direction may be independent of the evaluation point, as in Delbaen's Theorem 2.

Scaled distributions never change shape and the homogeneous assumption is violated when applied to the typical insurance product (Mildenhall, 2004; Mildenhall, 2017). However, Boonen, Tsanakas, and Wüthrich (2017) show how the Euler allocation, even when applied in such an ill-fitting context, still gives an allocation that is acceptable in the sense of satisfying certain fairness axioms.

Exercise 207. B. N. Wurtz rating agency uses a factor-based capital formula $\rho(P, R, a) = \sqrt{(0.4P)^2 + (0.25R)^2 + (0.1a)^2}$ where P denotes net written premium, R net reserves, and a invested assets.

a. Demonstrate that ρ is positive homogeneous, meaning $\rho(\lambda P, \lambda R, \lambda a) = \lambda\rho(P, R, a)$ for $\lambda \geq 0$.
b. Use the Euler allocation to allocate $\rho(1000, 3000, 3500)$ to premium, reserve, and asset risk.
c. Square root rules are sensitive to their largest components. How much does ρ decrease if the smallest charge is set to 0?

Solution. (a) Easy calculation. (b) Differentiating gives $\dfrac{\partial\rho}{\partial P} = \dfrac{0.4^2 P}{\rho(P, R, a)}$. The remaining calculations are laid out in Table 12.3. For part (c), the smallest charge is assets, 350. Computing ρ using just premium and reserves yields 850, or 92.5% of the total charge. □

Table 12.3 Solution to Exercise 207, part (b).

Item	P	R	a	$\rho(P, R, a)$
Factor	0.400	0.250	0.100	
Balance	1,000.0	3,000.0	3,500.0	
Charge	400.0	750.0	350.0	919.2
Derivative	0.174	0.204	0.038	
Allocation	174.1	611.9	133.3	919.2
% of total	18.9%	66.6%	14.5%	

12.2.7 Game Theory and the Aumann-Shapley Allocation

This section is somewhat technical and may be omitted with little adverse impact on understanding subsequent chapters.

Analyzing the fair allocation of undesirable quantities such as costs and risk measures has a long history. Various proposed sets of axioms of rationality and lines of argumentation have converged on the Aumann-Shapley allocation as being highly desirable. See in particular Billera, Heath, and Verrecchia (1981), Billera and Heath (1982), Tasche (2002), Denault (2001), Powers (2005), and Powers and Zanjani (2013).

To explain Aumann-Shapley, we first cast the problem as a cooperative multiplayer game. In such games, the participants work together to generate an outcome and bargain to share their costs. Here, they allocate the cost of capital.

Participants can decide whether to join together into one or more teams, or even to go it alone. In our context, unit i going alone is the equivalent of being burdened by $a(X_i)$. Clearly, all the units in aggregate can do better by joining together when a is subadditive. A minimal requirement then is to find an allocation such that no unit is allocated more than it would incur going it alone. If it were allocated too much, it would have an incentive to not join the coalition (portfolio). An allocation where no unit is allocated more than its stand-alone costs satisfies the **no-undercut** property. It gets more complicated if you consider that two units, say i and j could decide to opt out and form their own coalition (subportfolio) with $a(X_i + X_j) < a(X_i) + a(X_j)$ of course, but also less than what the proposed, unacceptable, allocations would give them together.

Formally, a **game** with n units (players) is a cost function c on subsets of $\{1, 2, \dots, n\}$ with $c(\emptyset) = 0$. c is monotone if $c(S) \le c(T)$ for all $S \subset T$. Game theory interprets $c(S)$ as the cost of operating the units in S together. The game is called **atomic** when each unit is in or out. When units can form fractional coalitions (quota share) it is called a **fractional** or **fuzzy** game. A game with a continuum of players is called **exact**. The set of allocations that works and keeps everyone happy, by satisfying the no-undercut property, is called the **core** of the game.

There are other axioms to be satisfied as well. Applications of game theory to insurance pricing are explored in Lemaire (1991); Mango (1998); Denault (2001); Powers (2005); Powers (2007); Tsanakas (2009); and Boonen, Tsanakas, and Wüthrich (2017).

Example 208. Insurance applications associate a game with a premium, capital, or asset functional ρ by $c(S) = \rho\left(\sum_{i\in S} X_i\right)$. □

Example 209. Let Pr be a probability defined on $\{1, 2, \dots, n\}$ and g a distortion. Then $c(S) = g(\mathsf{Pr}(S))$ defines game. When g is not linear, c is not additive and so allocation becomes difficult. □

The **Shapley** value or allocation is the solution to the allocation problem viewed as an atomic game. It extends Merton-Perold by considering a weighted contribution of marginal capital when unit i joins all other possible subportfolios. It is given by

$$c_i = \sum_{\substack{S\subset\{1,\dots,n\}\\ i\notin S}} \frac{|S|!\,(n-|S|-1)!}{n!}(c(S\cup\{i\}) - c(S)) \tag{12.5}$$

where the sum is over subsets of $\{1, \dots, n\}$ that do not contain i, $|S|$ denotes the number of elements in S, and $c(S)$ is shorthand for $c(\sum_{i\in S} X_i)$. The formula can be written as

$$c_i = \frac{1}{\text{number of units}} \sum_S \frac{\text{marginal contribution of } i \text{ to } S}{\text{number of coalitions of size } |S|}.$$

The Shapley value has several desirable properties.

- It is an allocation, i.e., it is additive. In game theory this is called the **efficiency** property.
- It is **symmetric**, in the sense that if two units i and j increase the cost of every S that contains neither i nor j by the same amount, $c(S\cup\{i\}) = c(S\cup\{j\})$, then $c_i = c_j$.
- It is decomposable in the sense of Kreps, called **linear** in game theory.
- It is homogeneous if c is.

- If c is subadditive then Shapley value satisfies the no-undercut property.
- It allocates no capital to a constant risk, called the **null player** or **riskless allocation** property.

It is possible to show the Shapley value is the only allocation that is additive, symmetric, linear, and allocates no capital to constant risks.

However, the Shapley value suffers from a severe practical drawback. To allocate to n units involves computing 2^n marginal impacts, which quickly becomes impractical. It also has a more serious conceptual problem: if a unit is subdivided further into two new units (with their aggregate being identical to the original) then the allocations assigned to the *other* units typically change (Powers, 2007). It is not decomposable.

Exercise 210. Write down the Shapley value for a two- and three-player game. How do you use these formulas to allocate capital?

Solution. Write $c(\{i\}) = c(i)$ and let c_i be the Shapley value. For a $n = 2$ player game $\Omega = \{1, 2\}$. Let's compute c_1. There are two subsets S with $1 \notin S$, $\emptyset$ and $\{2\}$. The corresponding incremental costs are $c(1) - c(\emptyset) = c(1)$ (explaining the requirement $c(\emptyset) = 0$) and $c(1,2) - c(2)$. The Shapley weights are both 0.5 (because $0! = 1$). Therefore $c_1 = (c(1)+c(1,2)-c(2))/2$ is the average of the stand-alone capital and the Merton-Perold marginal benefit of removing unit 1 from the total. The allocations add-up: $c_1 + c_2 = (c(1) + c(1,2) - c(2) + c(2) + c(1,2) - c(1))/2 = c(1,2)$.

Table 12.4 gives the weights for $n = 3$. Again, it is easy to see they add-up. To allocate using a capital risk measure ρ, figure $c(S) = \rho\left(\sum_{i\in S} X_i\right)$ for all seven non-empty subsets of $\{1, 2, 3\}$ and use the table weights and increments. □

Table 12.4 Solution to Exercise 210.

S	$\|S\|$	Weight	Increment
$\emptyset$	0	1/3	$c(1)$
$\{2\}$	1	1/6	$c(1,2) - c(2)$
$\{3\}$	1	1/6	$c(1,3) - c(3)$
$\{2,3\}$	2	1/3	$c(1,2,3) - c(2,3)$

Exercise 211. Compute the Shapley allocation using the cost function given by $\mathsf{TVaR}_{0.75}$ to units 1 and 2 for the Simple Discrete Example, Section 2.4.1. What are the loss ratios? Find p so that $\mathsf{TVaR}_p(X) = 80$ and compute its Shapley allocation.

Solution. Refer to Table 2.2 for the distribution of outcomes and Table 12.5 for the solution. □

Exercise 212. You are given:

1. Ins Co. writes three units A, B, and C. Losses from each unit are normally distributed with a mean of 1000, and with CVs of 10%, 20%, and 30%, respectively.
2. Units A and B are 50% correlated, A and C are 40% correlated, and B and C are 30% correlated.

Table 12.5 Solution to Exercise 211.

Item	Unit 1	Unit 2	Units 1 and 2
$\text{TVaR}_{0.75}$	10	90	94.5
Stand-alone	10	90	
Marginal = Merton Perold	4.5	84.5	
Shapley value	**7.25**	**87.25**	**94.5**
Loss ratio	62.1%	26.1%	28.8%
$\text{TVaR}_{0.6975}$	9.65	74.54	80.00
Stand-alone	9.65	74.54	
Marginal = Merton Perold	5.46	70.35	
Shapley value	**7.55**	**72.45**	**80.00**
Loss ratio	59.6%	31.4%	34.1%

3. Ins Co. prices using the standard deviation PCP, premium equals expected loss plus 50% of standard deviation.
4. There are no expenses.

Compute the following.

a. Ins Co.'s premium for each of the seven coalitions of A, B, and C.
b. What is the Shapley allocation of portfolio premium to each unit?

Solution. See Table 12.6 for part (a) and Table 12.7 for part (b). □

Table 12.6 Solution to Exercise 212 part (a).

Portfolio	EL	SD	Premium
A	1,000	100.00	1,050.00
B	1,000	200.00	1,100.00
C	1,000	300.00	1,150.00
AB	2,000	264.58	2,132.29
AC	2,000	352.14	2,176.07
BC	2,000	407.43	2,203.72
ABC	3,000	469.04	3,234.52

Fractional or **fuzzy** games extend atomic games by allowing fractional (quota share) combinations of units: $\sum_i x_i X_i$. They allow us to consider marginal allocations, using partial derivatives.

When the cost function a is differentiable, the **Aumann-Shapley** allocation generalizes both the Shapley allocation by allowing fractional participation and the Euler allocation

Table 12.7 Solution to Exercise 212 part (b).

Unit	Joins Coalition	Increment	Weight
A	Nothing	1,050.00	0.333
	B	1,032.29	0.167
	C	1,026.07	0.167
	BC	1,030.81	0.333
	Wtd. total	**1,036.66**	
B	Nothing	1,100.00	0.333
	A	1,082.29	0.167
	C	1,053.72	0.167
	AC	1,058.45	0.333
	Wtd. total	**1,075.48**	
C	Nothing	1,150.00	0.333
	A	1,126.07	0.167
	B	1,103.72	0.167
	AB	1,102.23	0.333
	Wtd. total	**1,122.38**	

by dropping the positive homogeneous assumption. It is based on the fact that $f(x) = \int_0^1 f'(tx)\,dt$ for any continuously differentiable function with $f(0) = 0$. The **Aumann-Shapley** allocation to unit i is defined as

$$a_i = \int_0^1 \frac{\partial a}{\partial x_i}(tx)\,dt. \tag{12.6}$$

Aumann-Shapley computes the average incremental capital as the portfolio grows from zero, uniformly across units. Since a is differentiable, it follows from a general theorem of calculus that the value of the *sum* of these integrals is independent of the path from the origin to $(x_1, \dots, x_n)$. That sum, of course, is the total asset a, and that makes the above an allocation. However, the individual allocations are path dependent, and so the reader may wonder, why does the integral use a straight line? Extrapolating from the Shapley logic in atomic games, one might expect to see some sort of averaging over all possible paths. The fact that only the diagonal matters is remarked upon in Aumann and Shapley (1974) (page 23):

> These formulas have an additional startling aspect: they show that the value is completely determined by the behavior of f near the *diagonal*.... Intuitively, the reason is that a coalition S chosen at "random"... will probably be a good "sample" of [the full coalition] I.

Billera, Heath, and Verrecchia (1981) show that the axiom of symmetry implies a symmetric path, which has to be the diagonal.

When a is positive homogeneous, the Aumann-Shapley allocation reduces to the Euler allocation as a special case. In particular, this applies if a is coherent.

The Aumann-Shapley solution is the unique allocation satisfying (1) linearity, (2) decomposable (aggregation invariance), and (3) either (a) continuity or (b) non-negativity when a is nondecreasing (Denault, 2001). In the presence of the first two, either of the third implies the other.

Exercise 213. Why does the Aumann-Shapley allocation for a positive homogeneous a equal the Euler allocation? Confirm for $a(x_1, x_2) = \sqrt{3x_1^2 + 4x_2^2}$.

Solution. The graph of a homogeneous function is a straight line along any line from the origin. By choosing coordinates appropriately, we can assume the ray is the x_1 axis and reduce to the one dimensional case. Then $a(x) = xa(1)$ has slope $a'(x) = a(1)$ and the Aumann-Shapley allocation equals the Euler allocation: $\int_0^1 a'(tx)\,dt = \int_0^1 a(1)\,dt = a(1) = a'(x)$. For the given a, $\partial a/\partial x_1 = 3x_1/a$. Therefore $(\partial a/\partial x_1)(tx_1, tx_2) = 3tx_1/a(tx_1, tx_2) = 3x_1/a(x_1, x_2) = \partial a/\partial x_1$ is independent of t. Then $a_1 = \int_0^1 (\partial a/\partial x_1)dt = \partial a/\partial x_1$. □

12.2.8 Co-Measure Allocations

If a risk measure ρ can be written in the form $\rho(X) = \mathsf{E}[h(X)L(X)]$ where h is an additive function, then we can use the **co-measure** $\mathsf{E}[h(X_i)L(X)]$ as an allocation to the ith unit. Venter, Major, and Kreps (2006) prefer the phrase decomposition to allocation. Kreps (2005) calls L the **riskiness leverage function**. Kreps footnotes that the term *co-measure* is used "in parallel with covariance and variance" and attributes it to Venter, though Venter (2004) attributes co-measures to Kreps. Co-*measure* refers to the *risk* measure and not a *probability* measure.

Example 214.

1. When $\rho(X) = k\mathsf{Var}(X)$, $k \ge 0$ constant, then $L(X) = k(X - \mathsf{E}X)$ and $h(X) = (X - \mathsf{E}X)$ define a co-measure $k\mathsf{E}[(X_i - \mathsf{E}X_i)(X - \mathsf{E}X)] = k\mathsf{cov}(X_i, X)$ called the **covariance** allocation. It is the capital allocation corresponding to the variance risk measure $\mathsf{E}[X] + k\mathsf{Var}(X)$. This is the prototypical example of a risk co-measure.
2. Let $x_p = \mathsf{VaR}_p(X)$. When $\rho(X) = \mathsf{TVaR}_p(X)$ then $L(X) = (1-p)^{-1}1_{X\ge x_p}(X)$ and $h(X) = X$ define a co-measure $(1-p)^{-1}\mathsf{E}[X_i 1_{X\ge x_p}(X)]$, which is the average of X_i over cases where $X \ge x_p$. It is called **coTVaR**. (To be correct, it requires $\mathsf{P}(X \ge x_p) = 1 - p$.)
3. Assume X is discrete at x_p with probability mass $f(x_p)$. When $\rho(X) = x_p$ then $L(X) = 1_{X=x_p}(X)/f(x_p)$ and $h(X) = X$ define a co-measure $\mathsf{E}[X_i \mid X = x_p]$ called **coVaR**.
4. Item (3) can be extended to co-measures defined relative to conditional expectations, where the condition is a function of X.
5. When $\rho(X) = \mathsf{SD}(X)$ then $L(X) = (X - \mathsf{E}X)/\mathsf{SD}(X)$ and $h(X) = (X - \mathsf{E}X)$ define a co-measure $\mathsf{E}[(X_i - \mathsf{E}X_i)(X - \mathsf{E}X)]/\mathsf{SD}(X) = \mathsf{cov}(X_i, X)/\mathsf{SD}(X)$. Venter, Major, and Kreps (2006) point out this is the Euler allocation of standard deviation. It is analogous

to a CAPM beta (with the portfolio representing the market portfolio) times the market standard deviation.

6. When $\rho(X) = \mathsf{E}[Xe^{kX}]/\mathsf{E}[e^{kX}]$ is the Esscher risk measure, $L(X) = e^{kX}/\mathsf{E}[e^{kX}]$ and $h(X) = X$ define a co-measure $\mathsf{E}[X_i e^{kX}]/\mathsf{E}[e^{kX}]$. □

Chapter 14 presents a systematic generalization of co-measures.

Exercise 215. Compute coTVaR allocation of $\mathsf{TVaR}_{0.75}$ to units 1 and 2 using the Simple Discrete Example, Section 2.4.1.

Solution. Refer to Tables 2.2 and 3.2. $\mathsf{VaR}_{0.75}(X) = 90$ and $\mathsf{TVaR}_{0.75} = 4\left(\frac{90}{8} + \frac{98}{16} + \frac{100}{16}\right) = 94.5$. Extracting the three largest outcomes we can compute the allocations: 4.5 to unit 1 and 90 to unit 2 (Table 12.8). □

Table 12.8 Solution to Exercise 215.

j	X_1	X_2	X	p	q
6	0	90	90	0.125	0.5
7	8	90	98	0.0625	0.25
8	10	90	100	0.0625	0.25
Sum				0.25	1
q-sum	4.5	90	94.5		

12.2.9 Exogenous Allocations

Exogenous allocations are helpful when a is determined by a risk measure that is difficult to allocate. For example, rating agency capital models often combine factor-based charges for noncatastrophe lines (which are not translation invariant) with VaR-based catastrophe charges (which are not subadditive). The AM Best, NAIC RBC, and Solvency II formulas also include a covariance adjustment.

In these cases, $a(X)$ can be allocated using a auxiliary measure ρ. The auxiliary measure can be calibrated so that $\rho(X, p^*) = a(X)$, and then allocated by applying one of the methods already mentioned to ρ.

Example 216. Kalkbrener (2005) proposes using the standard deviation or TVaR as an auxiliary risk measure to allocate VaR. For standard deviation, the allocation is implemented by solving $\mathsf{VaR}_p(X) = \mathsf{E}[X] + \pi(X)\mathsf{SD}(X)$ for a constant $\pi(X)$ and then using the scaled covariance allocation to unit i, $\mathsf{E}[X_i] + \pi(X)\mathsf{cov}(X_i, X)/\mathsf{SD}(X)$. □

Exercise 217. Use Kalkbrener's standard deviation auxiliary exogenous method to allocate total premium $P = 80$ to units 1 and 2 using for the Simple Discrete Example, Section 2.4.1. What are the loss ratios by unit?

Solution. Note, the data represents the population, not a sample. The solution is shown in Table 12.9. □

Table 12.9 Solution to Exercise 217.

j	X_1	X_2	X	p
1	0	0	0	0.250
2	0	1	1	0.125
3	0	90	90	0.125
4	8	0	8	0.125
5	8	1	9	0.0625
6	8	90	98	0.0625
7	10	0	10	0.125
8	10	1	11	0.0625
9	10	90	100	0.0625
E$[X]$	4.500	22.750	27.250	
E$[X^2]$	41.000	2,025.250	2,271.000	
Var(X)	20.750	1,507.688	1,528.438	
SD(X)	4.555	38.829	39.095	
E$[X_i X]$	143.375	2,127.625	2,271.000	
cov(X_i, X)	20.750	1,507.688	1,528.438	
$\pi(X)$			1.349	
Allocation	5.216	74.784	**80.000**	
Loss ratio	0.863	0.304	0.341	

12.2.10 The Pricing Implied by a Capital Allocation

How are premiums derived from these capital allocation methods? There are two common approaches: the allocated CCoC method and direct application to a PCP.

- **Allocated CCoC Pricing:** The capital allocation is converted into premium using CCoC pricing; see Section 13.1.
- **Direct Allocation of PCPs:** Classical PCPs are non-additive pricing functionals, and so the allocations described above can be applied to them directly. Premium can also be allocated via an auxiliary measure, such as TVaR. It is uncommon to see this approach used.

Determining premium by first allocating capital necessitates additional return assumptions, which are often arbitrary and at odds with the actual capital cost. The modern approach, Chapter 14, allocates premium directly, giving it a distinct advantage.

12.2.11 Selecting an Allocation Method

We hope that you read Chapter 14, and learn about the **natural allocation** of spectral risk measure premium, before choosing an allocation method from the ones we have covered in this chapter.

We also offer the following advice about selecting an allocation method.

Any allocation must be considered *fair*. This is quite a loaded term. In practice, it means the stakeholders consider the allocation reflective of reality and not unduly influenced by factors not germane to the problem the allocation is supposed to solve. We address mathematical characterizations of fairness further in Section 14.4.

Currently, Aumann-Shapley is considered the state-of-the-art cost allocation. Aumann-Shapley gives the Euler gradient method when it is applied to a positive homogeneous functional. However, it can produce an overly tail-focused answer. The body of the risk distribution also matters! An undue focus on the tail can be ameliorated by treating the capital measure as exogenous and applying a haircut allocation based on a more broad-based risk measure. For example, a capital metric of $\mathsf{VaR}_{0.995}$ might be the corporate mandate, but it can be allocated pro rata by a $\mathsf{TVaR}_{0.75}$. If the mandated metric is reasonably body-sensitive, then the marginal method could already be appropriate.

It is possible that the mandated metric is actually an SRM in disguise, e.g., a weighted average of TVaRs. In that case, the methods of Chapter 14 can be used, but the explanation couched in more familiar terms.

It should also be noted that much of the advice in Section 11.5 applies here. This includes:

- Being cognizant of professional actuarial standards.
- Recognizing the scope of the larger task within which allocation is a part.
- The value of simplicity, transparency, fairness, objectivity, and precedent.
- Sensitivity to stakeholder concerns.
- Communication and persuasion.

It might be tempting to take a hard principles-based approach and let the results be what they are, regardless of how the various stakeholders are affected. However, there is undoubtedly a material degree of ambiguity in the analysis and therefore uncertainty in the results. That is to say, the best estimate is only one number within a range. Therefore, it is not improper to see how an allocation plays out among the stakeholders and to let the implications for successful implementation guide where the final selection lands within that range.

Also, as we said above, please read on, and consider the contents of Chapter 14.

Exercise 218. Discuss the pros and cons of each of the allocations from Exercises 205, 206, 211, 215, and 217 with reference to the considerations listed in Section 12.2.11. □

12.3 Loss Payments in Default

The methods so far have ignored default and its impact on insured losses. In this section we explain the mechanics of loss payments in default, in preparation for presenting pricing models that do consider it.

The first step to price allocation is to determine the cash flows to each unit in each possible outcome. Recall the description of insolvency and the priority waterfall in Section 8.2.2. Assuming loss payments have the highest priority and the insurer has limited liability and assets a, losses are split between insurer payments and insurer default as

$$X = X \wedge a + (X - a)^+.$$

Next, actual aggregate payments $X \wedge a$ must be allocated to each unit, which requires specifying a default rule in the event of insolvency. By far the most common approach is to assume equal priority in default. At the unit level, equal priority implies the payments made to, and default borne by, unit i are split

$$\begin{aligned} X_i &= X_i \frac{X \wedge a}{X} + X_i \frac{(X - a)^+}{X} \\ &= (\text{payments to unit } i) + (\text{default borne by unit } i). \end{aligned}$$

Therefore payments to unit i are given by

$$X_i(a) := X_i \frac{X \wedge a}{X} \tag{12.7}$$

$$= \frac{X_i}{X}(X \wedge a) \tag{12.8}$$

$$= \begin{cases} X_i & X \le a \\ X_i \dfrac{a}{X} & X > a. \end{cases} \tag{12.9}$$

Eq. (12.7) expresses payments to unit i as a constant pro rata factor $(X \wedge a)/X$ of the contractually promised payment X_i. The factor is the same for all units, hence *equal* priority. The factor is a function of X alone, not losses by unit. As a result, we can further decompose payments within unit i all the way down to individual policies, in the case a unit contains more than one policy.

For unit i, Eq. (12.8) specifies the proportion X_i/X of *assets available to pay losses* it receives, where the latter is equal to $X \wedge a$. It is sometimes helpful to use this expression, but note the proportion depends on X_i and is not equal for all units.

Eq. (12.9) spells out the actual payments: unit i is paid in full when total losses are less than or equal to assets and payments are pro rated down by a/X in default states. The payments are contractual and are legally specified and determined. We call this ***ex post* equal priority**, to emphasize that shares in default are determined after claims are known. Below we also discuss ***ex ante* equal priority**, where shares are set at the beginning of the policy period, based on expected losses. Ex ante equal priority is not used in practice because it can result in a payment in default greater than the actual loss.

X_i is the amount promised to i by their insurance contract. Promised payments are limited by contractual provisions but not considered limited by insurer assets. The amount actually paid to unit i is $X_i(a)$, which depends on a, X and X_i. The dependence on X is critical. It is responsible for almost all the complexity of insurance pricing. In economics, the benefit of most products to the buyer is independent of who else purchases it. With insurance risk pools that is not the case: the value to one insurer is almost always changed in some way if the pool takes on other risks. In order to completely specify the product it is necessary to know about all the other units written by the insurer.

Doherty and Schlesinger (1990) consider optimal contract design in the face of possible default. There are alternatives to equal priority, at least in theory. Mahul (2003) discusses applying a deductible to all claims set at a level whereby total claims in excess of the deductible equals assets available. If the pain of a claim is proportional to its size, this approach could result in a welfare gain compared to an equal priority pro rata factor.

Exercise 219. You are given the following information about Ins Co.

1. It is a limited liability company operating under an equal priority in default law.
2. Total assets equals ¤1200.
3. It writes three lines of business, A, B, and C, with outstanding liabilities 800, 600, and 400, respectively.

Compute the recoveries to each line.

Solution. Outstanding liabilities $X = 1800$. The pro rata factor equals $1200/1800 = 0.667$. Recoveries are 533, 400, and 267, respectively. □

12.4 The Historical Development of Insurance Pricing Models

Practical [people] who believe themselves to be quite exempt from any intellectual influence, are usually the slaves of some defunct economist.

John Maynard Keynes

The epigraph applies to practical actuaries as well and explains why you should be interested in these academic models. Both authors have seen actuaries struggling to reconcile fat margins in zero-beta catastrophe risk with a misguided attachment to CAPM. Our recommendation: make the acquaintance of other relevant theories!

By the 1990s insurance pricing theory was in something of a pickle. Underwriting betas proved elusive, hard to compute, and close to zero Kozik (1994). More importantly, CAPM-based theories cannot explain why reinsurance contracts include substantial margins for zero beta catastrophe risk. Froot (2001) argued it is because of supply restrictions and capital market imperfections. Insurance markets are not complete, so a straightforward application of option theoretic methods is impossible. Each insurance risk is unique, so valuation by comparables is challenging. Insurance liabilities are not traded in liquid markets, subject to the forces of no-arbitrage. Insurance valuation is in a "predicament" Babbel, (1997).

In this section, we describe five models of the insurance market that show how academics tried to extricate theory from its predicament, which we call the Perfect Complete, Complete, Limited Liability Complete, Frictional Cost, and Realistic models. They show the evolution of pricing models to more accurately reflect contractual loss payments by unit. Special cases of our models include virtually all pricing techniques in use today. The models become gradually more realistic, with each differing from the previous in one key assumption. The names we use for the models are meant to be evocative but are not standard usage. Figure 12.1 summarizes the important assumptions each model makes.

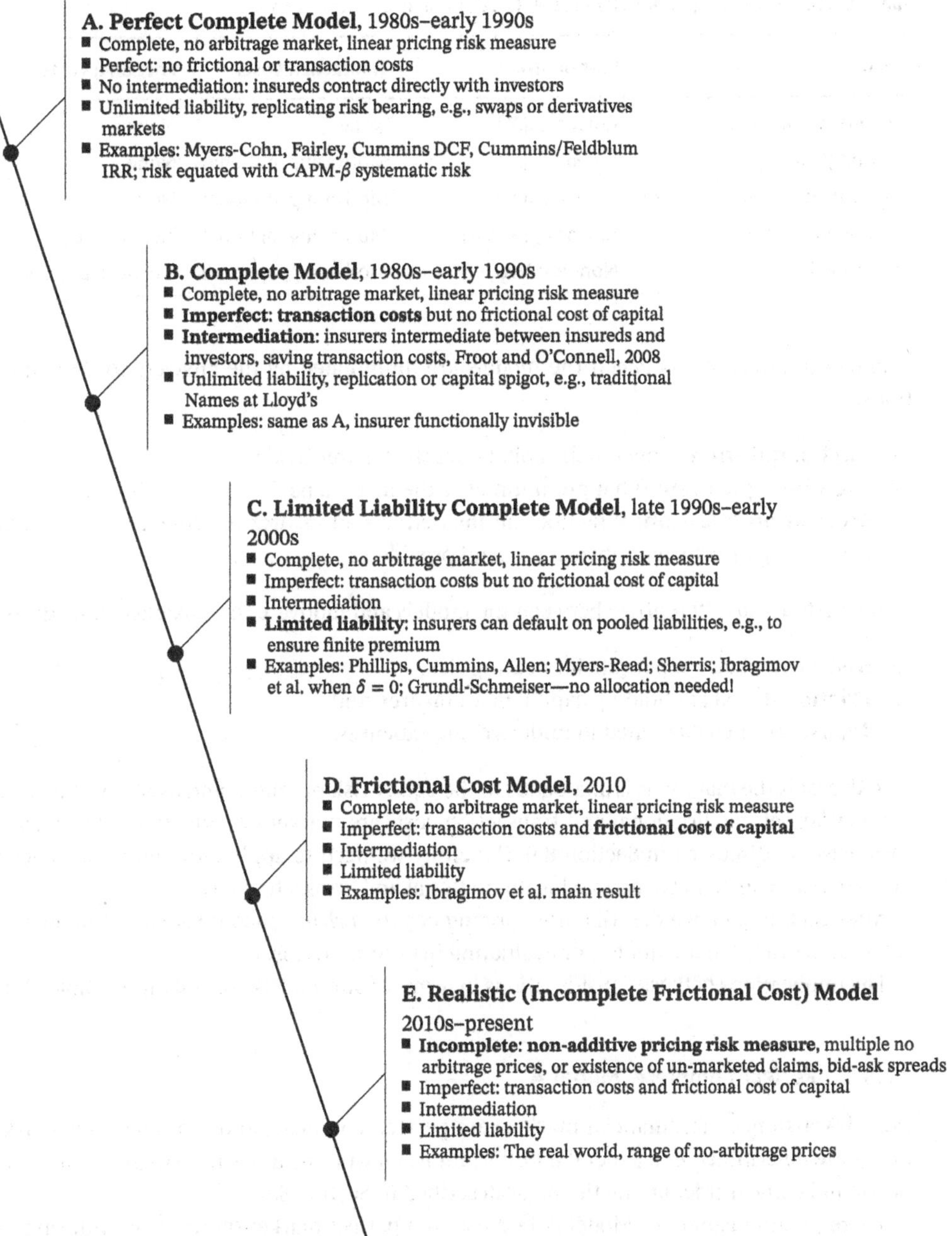

Figure 12.1 Development of insurance pricing financial model assumptions showing a path toward greater realism. Boldface highlights assumption changes.

Table 12.10 Cost components by Model. Cost of risk is always $\geq \mathsf{E}[X]$.

Model	Cost of Risk	Transaction Costs	Frictional Costs
A. Perfect complete	Linear $\mathsf{E}_{\mathsf{Q}}[X]$	None	None
B. Complete	Linear $\mathsf{E}_{\mathsf{Q}}[X]$	Motivating, optional	None
C. Limited liability complete	Linear $\mathsf{E}_{\mathsf{Q}}[\wedge a]$	Motivating, optional	None
D. Frictional cost	Linear $\mathsf{E}_{\mathsf{Q}}[X \wedge a]$	Motivating, optional	Tax on assets τa
E. Realistic	Non-additive $\rho(X \wedge a)$	Motivating, optional	Tax on assets τa

Practical differences between the models are illuminated by the answers to three questions.

1. **Capital question:** How much capital does the insurer hold?
2. **Premium question:** What premium does the insured pay?
3. **Motivation question:** Why does an insured use an insurer intermediary rather than contracting directly with investor capital providers?

Three costs act to differentiate between the models and motivate the existence of insurers:

a. **Risk costs** that compensate for bearing risk,
b. **Frictional costs** of holding capital in an insurer, and
c. **Transaction costs** related to underwriting expenses.

Risk cost is the margin. It is analogous to the equity risk premium and exists even in a perfect market setting. Frictional and transaction costs are market imperfections. The reasons they exist are discussed in Section 8.9. Generally we need to apply different approaches to allocate risk costs than we do to allocate frictional and transaction costs.

After each model, we describe how pricing occurs. *Pricing* encompasses setting manual rates, reservation prices, quotes, or evaluating firm-order terms.

The implications of these considerations in terms of our models are laid out in Table 12.10.

12.4.1 Perfect Complete, Model A

Model A assumes that financial markets are perfect, complete, and arbitrage-free. Market prices are determined in a general equilibrium framework by a positive stochastic discount factor and a linear pricing functional, as described in Section 8.6.

There are no insurers in Model A because in a perfect market there are no information costs and it is practical for insureds to contract directly with investors. Therefore the Capital and Motivation Questions are moot. Insureds pay the fair market value of their indemnity cash flows, answering the Premium Question. Contracts are priced stand-alone because the pricing functional is additive. Indemnity schedules are flexible, subject to standard assumptions to manage morale hazard and adverse selection.

The catastrophe bond securitization market is close to Model A. Large insureds (typically insurance companies) contract directly with investors to transfer risk. The derivatives and swaps markets also operate close to the Model A ideal, except that trades can be cleared through an exchange to ensure performance.

Decision making and pricing in Model A is very easy. The price is given by $\mathsf{E}_{\mathsf{Q}}[X_i]$ where Q is a risk-adjusted probability, Section 8.6. The pricing rule is additive and so pricing multiple units is trivial. There are no shared costs to allocate.

12.4.2 Complete, Model B

Model A has no insurers—not ideal, given most actuaries are employed by insurers. To motivate the introduction of insurers, Model B drops the perfect assumption by adding a transaction cost. Transaction costs are easy to explain: underwriting is resource and information intensive and expensive; see Section 8.9.

Insurers create economies of scale in risk assessment which allows them to underwrite insurance more cheaply than an individual could searching alone for a match in the investor markets; see Brennan (1993). We assume that underwriting costs are recouped through a separate fee that is not part of the premium.

The transparent insurer intermediary in Model B has **unlimited liability**. It sells the insured the same product they can purchase directly from investors. In Model B, the insurer does not hold any capital within its legal entity. It contracts with investors to provide financial resources as needed, an unlimited capital *spigot*. As a result there are no additional costs of risk transfer beyond the expected loss and risk margin paid to investors. The answers to the Three Questions are:

1. **Capital**: Insurers hold no capital. Risk is all passed through to investors. Insurers are a Pool Co., not an Ins Co., in the language of Section 8.1.2 and Figure 8.1. Capital Co. is provided by off-balance sheet investors.
2. **Premium**: The insured pays the same fair market value premium as in Model A plus an underwriting fee. We do not consider the underwriting fee—it is priced in a market for underwriting (pricing, structuring, contracting) services.
3. **Motivation**: Cost efficiencies in underwriting motivate the existence of insurer intermediaries.

An unlimited liability Lloyd's Name operates like Model B. Names are required to pledge assets to Lloyd's but retain control over them and how they are invested. Separately compensated underwriters work on their behalf. Names are subject to capital calls to cover adverse outcomes. This structure avoids double taxation of investment income and problems of sub-optimal investment strategies within regulated insurance entities. However, it is fragile precisely because the pledged assets are not directly under insurer control. It worked at a time and place in the UK, but is probably not scalable or exportable to other societies with different, more contentious legal systems—it is hard to imagine a US lawyer recommending a client sign an unlimited liability contract. Even Lloyd's has stepped back from the unlimited liability model and today only small minority of underwriting capacity is provided by unlimited liability Names.

Model B is implicit in many older pricing papers such as Myers and Cohn (1987) and Feldblum (1992). These papers discount cash flows between the insurer and an unlimited investor cash spigot. Some life insurance valuation models are similar.

Papers assuming Model A or B often use a CAPM pricing functional. The implication that zero beta risk, such as catastrophe risk, should be priced to a risk-free return was clearly at odds with market prices and resulted in an academic puzzle, (Froot and O'Connell, 1999). It is now recognized there are additional priced factors influencing insurance premiums and the puzzle has largely been resolved (Froot, 2007).

Practically, Model B is the same as Model A because the insurer is a transparent pass-through to investors, and underwriting expenses are charged separately. The insurer can be thought of as executing a 100% unlimited quota share with investor reinsurers. It makes no net margin on risk bearing, though it may make a margin (normal profits) on underwriting expenses.

12.4.3 Limited Liability Complete, Model C

Recognizing the contractual and enforcement problems with off-balance sheet capital, today almost every insurance company operates against on-balance sheet capital. In part, this is to ensure the effectiveness of mandatory insurance requirements (Cummins, 1988).

Model C assumes that the insurer has **limited liability**. The insurer has a finite risk bearing capacity, comprising capital on its balance sheet, reinsurance, and other contingent capital arrangements, and it is structured as a legal entity with limited liability.

Arrow (1996) identifies that the academic complete market ideal provides risk shifting that depends on the state of the world. The ideal is that everyone quota shares everything, eliminating all diversifiable risk. In contrast, insurance provides an **absolute** level of protection, irrespective of aggregate consumption. Absolute protection can be extremely expensive or even impossible to guarantee in adverse states. Guaranteed performance requires that aggregate insurance promises are no greater than the actual resources available in any state. In a decentralized, competitive market this restriction is almost impossible to arrange. Limited liability converts absolute insurance guarantees into contingent guarantees. The insurer legal entity is necessary to bind together otherwise unrelated insureds, so that limited liability can operate. Marshall (2018) makes the point that the California Earthquake Authority performs a similar function, capping industry losses from an earthquake. A limited liability legal entity allows the creation of unit cash flows that cannot be replicated by other means.

Model C assumes the insurer can hold capital on-balance sheet without the investor incurring any additional frictional costs. The answer to the Capital Question is determined by two factors. In practice, regulators mandate capital levels needed to ensure mandatory insurance laws operate effectively. In theory, the aggregated risk aversion determines an optimal allocation of resources to hold against adverse outcomes. Even though it is costless to hold capital within an insurer (remember the risk-premium is incorporated into the linear risk pricing functional) there is an opportunity cost of restricting when resources are available to meet other (non-insured) contingencies.

The Premium Question is answered in the same way as in Model B. The famous paper Grundl and Schmeiser (2007) asking "what good" is capital allocation points out that an allocation is not needed to price insurance contracts in Model C. It is worth quoting from their explanation at length (emphasis added):

> In this framework, the fair insurance price is determined by the claims payoff distribution, the arbitrage-free valuation function, and the contract's safety level (measured by the value of the default put option). Clearly, this method of calculating competitive insurance prices does not depend on the insurance company's preexisting portfolio, which in turn means that it makes no difference to the insurance price whether the company is a monoline or multiline insurer, everything else being held equal. Thus, **no allocation of equity capital to lines of business or to single insurance contracts is necessary in making the pricing decision**. To achieve a desired safety level, the insurance company must establish certain risk management measures. Equity capital is only one of these, and can be (partially) substituted by reinsurance, alternative risk transfer, and other measures. The necessary risk management costs are covered by the insurance premiums.

Insurers exist in Model C to ensure mandatory insurance laws are effective and to allow the operation of limited liability, answering the Motivation Question.

Model C is used in four landmark papers in the theory of insurance pricing.

- Phillips, Cummins, and Allen (1998) (herein after Phillips) considered pricing in a multiline insurance company from a complete-market option theoretic perspective, modeling losses with a geometric Brownian motion and without allocating capital. They famously state it is "not appropriate to allocate capital by line." They show it **is** necessary to allocate the insolvency put option to the different lines of business and they show how to do this assuming losses are paid based on an *ex ante* rule in default, where available assets are shared in proportion to expected losses at inception. They consider a Model B, unlimited liability insurer before moving on to "*assume* that equity holders have limited liability," i.e., to Model C with no frictional costs. They are concerned with the effect of firm-wide insolvency risk on individual policy pricing. Despite rejecting the idea of allocating capital, their work implied an allocation based on conditional expected values, which essentially develops into the natural allocation.
- Myers and Read Jr. (2001) also work in a complete market setting and use expected default value as a risk measure. They explicitly recognize the need for frictional costs to motivate allocation and include a term PV(surplus costs) in their formula for premium, but as a simplification it is omitted from further calculations. They determine surplus allocations by unit using expected policyholder deficit, and present a gradient vector, Euler theorem-based allocation that "adds-up" to total capital assuming losses scale homogeneously, but with no other distributional restrictions. They also assume *ex ante* equal priority.
- Sherris (2006) derives a result similar to Phillips, showing that there is a canonical allocation of the default put to lines of business. However, his treatment improves on Phillips by assuming assets in insolvency are allocated according to an *ex post* equal-priority rule. He recognizes that the conditional expected value approach to allocating the default put is not necessarily appropriate for allocating all assets, saying "[t]here is no unique way to do this

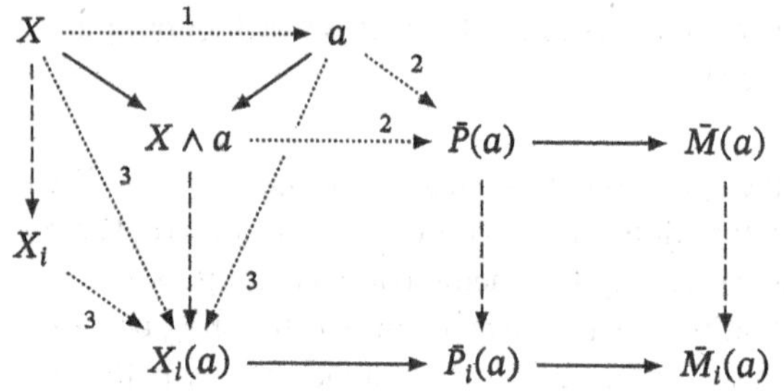

Figure 12.2 The order of decision making in an insurance market with default but no frictional capital costs, Model C.

since the allocation of assets to line of business is an internal insurer allocation that will have no economic impact on the payoffs or risks of the insurer since assets are available to meet the losses of all lines of business." There is no *economic impact* of allocating assets precisely because there are no *frictional costs* of holding them.

- Ibragimov, Jaffee, and Walden (2010) (Ibragimov) assume a base model without frictional costs that is the same as Sherris.

Phillips and Sherris give the same answer to the Pricing Question. The risk market still uses a linear pricing functional $\mathsf{E}_{\mathsf{Q}}[\cdot]$, which can be applied to indemnity payments. Phillips' ex ante equal priority results in a premium

$$\bar{P}_i^{pca}(a) = \mathsf{E}_{\mathsf{Q}}[X_i] - \frac{\mathsf{E}_{\mathsf{Q}}[X_i]}{\mathsf{E}_{\mathsf{Q}}[X]}\mathsf{E}_{\mathsf{Q}}[(X-a)^+] \tag{12.10}$$

whereas Sherris' ex post rule produces

$$\bar{P}_i^{s}(a) = \mathsf{E}_{\mathsf{Q}}[X_i] - \mathsf{E}_{\mathsf{Q}}\left[\frac{X_i}{X}(X-a)^+\right] = \mathsf{E}_{\mathsf{Q}}[X_i(a)] \tag{12.11}$$

where $X_i(a)$ is defined in 12.7. In both papers there is a time value of money adjustment we have set equal to one by assuming the risk-free rate is zero.

Figure 12.2 lays out decision making and accounting when the insurer can default but does not incur frictional costs holding capital. Again, any underwriting expenses are separate from the risk costs.

The top block of variables refers to the whole portfolio and the lower block to the ith unit. The vertical dashed arrows show the summing relationship $\sum_i$ between the two.

The nodes are random variables or constants. X represents the insurer's aggregate promise to pay, which is the sum of promised unit losses, $X = \sum_i X_i$. $\bar{P}$ represents premium and $\bar{M}$ expected margin in the premium. Both are functions of a, the insurer's assets that equal premium plus capital. Capital is not shown—reflecting our ability to price without a capital allocation. Since the insurer now has limited liability, the amount of assets on its balance sheet is an important decision variable.

The actual aggregate loss paid by the insurer equals $X \wedge a$. If $X \le a$ it pays X. If $X > a$ it pays a and defaults by $D = (X-a)^+$. In all cases, payments plus defaults sum to X. The actual losses paid to each unit, $X_i(a)$, are contractually agreed and satisfy $\sum_i X_i(a) = X \wedge a$, and $X_i = X_i(a)$ in no default states. In addition, $0 \le X_i(a) \le X_i$ is generally required. $X_i(a)$ can be fixed *ex ante* as in Phillips, although this is unusual (because $X_i(a)$ could lie outside the range 0 to X_i), or *ex post* as in Sherris or Ibragimov. Although other options are possible, such as an *ex post* variable deductible reducing losses to a (Mahul, 2003), in practice equal priority is always used.

The solid black arrows show accounting identities determining

- Actual losses $X \wedge a$,
- Expected insurer margin $\bar{M}(a) = \bar{P}(a) - \mathsf{E}[X \wedge a]$, and
- Expected unit i margin $\bar{M}_i(a) = \bar{P}_i(a) - \mathsf{E}[X_i(a)]$.

Decisions are indicated by the numbers above the dotted arrows. They can be thought of as occurring sequentially though, in reality, many occur simultaneously around common renewal dates.

1. The amount of assets a needed to support the risk X is determined. It can be specified by a regulator, rating agency, insured, or insurer management. The process to determine a is generally known by market participants before an insurer writes any business. Insureds know what they are buying.
2. Once a is known, the insurer knows its effective liability $X \wedge a$. Next, it has to finance assets a by issuing premium and investor capital liabilities. The split is effected by a linear pricing risk measure E_Q. The premium is $\bar{P}(a) = \mathsf{E}_\mathsf{Q}(X \wedge a)$ and $\bar{Q}(a) = a - \bar{P}(a)$ is capital paid-in. The insurer collects premium and capital at $t = 0$.
3. At $t = 1$, the insurer pays X_i to i if $X \le a$ and pays a contractually determined amount $X_i(a)$ if $X > a$.

Applying E_Q to all the variables in the diagram at $t = 0$ computes their market value. There is no need to allocate a, as Grundl and Schmeiser (2007) point out.

12.4.4 Frictional Cost, Model D

Model D adds frictional costs of capital to Model C. Section 8.9.2 discusses the reasons for these costs. Frictional costs erode but do not eliminate the advantages an insurer intermediary offers from lower transaction costs and access to different indemnity functions. Ibragimov, Jaffee, and Walden (2010) work in a Model D framework. They assume that insureds do not have direct access to the market for risk or that the costs of doing so exceed the insurer's frictional costs. They explicitly recognize this assumption is necessary to motivate the use of financial intermediaries compared to direct capital market access.

Froot and O'Connell (2008) discuss the pricing of intermediated risk in detail, particularly as it relates to catastrophe reinsurance. They point out insurers have competitive advantages in evaluating and monitoring risks, especially nonstandard, informationally opaque risks. The law of large numbers and central limit theorem help intermediaries communicate the quality of their portfolios to investors. Larger intermediaries can conserve on costly external finance because they are better able to diversify within their own portfolios. This is consistent with the market philosophy that the shape of risk influences the price of risk, even when the risk is idiosyncratic. The cost of risk is partially information and ambiguity driven.

To answer the Premium Question, premium in Model D reflects actual indemnity payments, allowing for default and allocating frictional capital costs to each unit. Capital must be allocated because it is a costly shared resource. An insurer can't determine whether a unit is earning the appropriate rate of return without an allocation of capital costs. Ibragimov comes up with a significant result. In Sherris's static version of Model C, allocating capital beyond the default put is economically meaningless and arbitrary. In contrast, Ibragimov finds a unique allocation that preserves fairness and equity between existing and new insureds as the portfolio grows incrementally, even without frictional costs. In the case of ex post equal priority in default, their fundamental pricing formula is

$$\begin{aligned} \bar{P}_i^{ijw}(a) &= \mathsf{E}_\mathsf{Q}[X_i] - \mathsf{E}_\mathsf{Q}\left[\frac{X_i}{X}(X-a)^+\right] + \tau a \mathsf{E}_\mathsf{Q}\left[\frac{X_i}{X}1_{X>a}(X)\right] \\ &= \mathsf{E}_\mathsf{Q}[X_i(a)] + \tau a \mathsf{E}_\mathsf{Q}\left[\frac{X_i}{X}1_{X>a}(X)\right] \end{aligned} \tag{12.12}$$

where τ is the frictional cost of capital. Eq. (12.12) says that the default put and assets are allocated according to expected payments in default. The middle quantity in the first row is the reduction in premium compared to the cost of a default-free cover owing to the insured's share of the default put. The right-hand term is an allocation of the total frictional costs τa. If $\tau = 0$ we recover Sherris' formula. Note it is obvious this expression adds-up and is a complete allocation of the total cost $\mathsf{E}_\mathsf{Q}[X \wedge a] + \tau a$. Chapter 20 presents Ibragimov's ideas more thoroughly.

The answer to the Motivation Question in Model D is similar to that in Model C.

Decision making in Model D requires the insurer allocate frictional costs by unit in order to determine unit margins $\bar{M}_i(a)$ that are then used to steer the company's decision making. The situation is shown in Figure 12.3. The new figure includes total capital $\bar{Q}(a) = a - \bar{P}(a)$. In addition to the three decisions at the end of Section 12.4.3, the insurer must determine

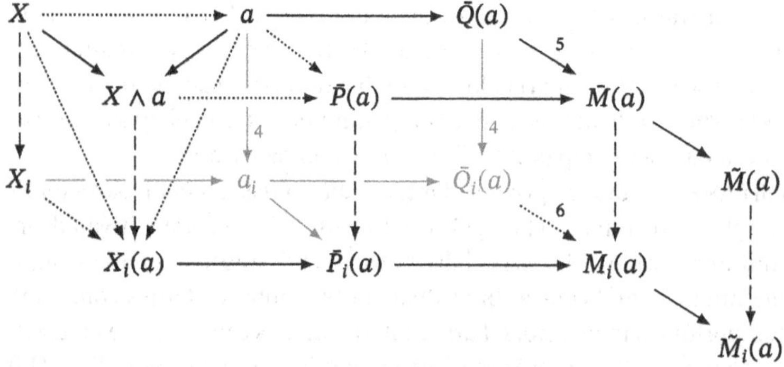

Figure 12.3 The order of decision making in an insurance market with frictional capital costs, Model D.

4. An asset allocation a_i and capital allocation $\bar{Q}_i(a) = a_i - \bar{P}_i(a)$ for each unit. These are shown and connected in gray because they are *purely notional*: they do not exist in reality or in any recognized accounting. Both allocations must add-up.

Finally the frictional costs are charged against each unit to determine its economic value to the insurer.

5. The overall frictional cost of holding assets τa is subtracted from the margin $\bar{M}(a) = \bar{P}(a) - \mathsf{E}[X \wedge a]$ to determine its economic return $\tilde{M}(a) = \bar{M}(a) - \tau a$.
6. The frictional cost of holding assets attributable to unit i, τa_i, is subtracted from the margin $\bar{M}_i(a) = \bar{P}_i(a) - \mathsf{E}[X_i(a)]$ to determine its economic value $\tilde{M}_i(a) = \bar{M}_i(a) - \tau_i a_i$. Ibragimov, Jaffee, and Walden (2010) show there is only one way to do this that is fair to existing and new insureds.

It is reasonable to assume the frictional costs are constant by unit $\tau_i = \tau$ in a one-period model.

Step (6) makes insurance pricing difficult: the cost of an entirely notional amount a_i must be incorporated into the return $\bar{M}_i(a)$. Without including the cost of a_i the insurer could make suboptimal decisions and not maximize its value. In Figure 12.2 this step is not necessary because there is no frictional cost of holding capital, $\tau = \tau_i = 0$, in Model C.

As the notation makes clear, there is *no direct connection* between a_i and $X_i(a)$—the latter is a function of a not a_i. Although total paid losses equal $X \wedge a$, in general $X_i(a) \neq X_i \wedge a_i$. $X_i(a)$ is determined by insurer total assets a, the individual losses X_i, and their sum X.

12.4.5 Realistic, Model E

The most realistic model works in an incomplete market, replacing the linear pricing functional with a non-additive functional we call ρ. If ρ is coherent it has the form $\rho(X) = \max_{\mathsf{Q}} \mathsf{E}_{\mathsf{Q}}[X]$; see Section 5.4. Each $\mathsf{E}_{\mathsf{Q}}[X]$ provides a possible no-arbitrage price. The range of prices depends on the set of possible Q.

The three questions have broadly the same answers as for Models C and D, with some important additional considerations. Because the price of risk depends on the shape of risk, insurers have an important role aggregating low risk-cost portfolios. The Pricing Question becomes much more complex, and we spend the rest of the book explaining different approaches to it.

Decision making in Model E is conceptually the same as Model D except the risk pricing functional is not additive. The risk premium can no longer be computed as $\mathsf{E}_{\mathsf{Q}}[X_i(a)]$ for a fixed Q that applies for all X. For a general coherent risk measure ρ, the risk-adjusted probability Q becomes a function of X. In many cases it is unique, but it need not be. The technicalities are discussed in Chapter 14 for SRM pricing measures.

Model	Paper(s)	Complete	Perfect	Default	Insurer	Capital	Multiline	Portfolio	Taxes	Inv Inc	Premium pricing formula
A	Myers-Cohn, Cummins	DCF/CAPM	n/a	n/a	No	n/a	No	Static	Yes	Yes	$PV_{r_X}(X) + PV_{r_f}(\text{UW profit tax}) + PV_{r_f}(\text{Inv Inc tax})$, where $r_X = r_f + \beta_X(r_m - r_f)$, r_m is the market return, r_f is the risk-free rate.
A	Feldblum, Cummins	IRR/CAPM	n/a	n/a	No	n/a	No	Static	Yes	Yes	No closed form; equivalent to DCF under certain conditions.
B	Phillips	Complete	Yes	n/a	Yes	n/a	Yes	Static, GBM	No	Yes	$v_f \mathsf{E}_\mathsf{Q}[X_i]$, where Q is the unique equivalent probability.
C		Complete	Yes	ex ante	Yes	Exogenous	Yes	Static, GBM	No	Yes	$v_f(\mathsf{E}_\mathsf{Q}[X_i] - \frac{\mathsf{E}_\mathsf{Q}[X_i]}{\mathsf{E}_\mathsf{Q}[X]}\mathsf{E}_\mathsf{Q}[(X-a)^+])$
C/D	Myers-Read	Complete	No	ex ante	Yes	EPD ratio	Yes	Dynamic, homog	No	Yes	Allocates all assets like default put.
C	Sherris	Complete	Yes	ex post equal priority	Yes	Solvency ratio	Yes	Static	No	Yes	$v_f(\mathsf{E}_\mathsf{Q}[X_i] - \mathsf{E}_\mathsf{Q}[X_i/X(X-a)^+]) = v_f \mathsf{E}_\mathsf{Q}\left[\frac{X_i}{X}(X \wedge a)\right]$. No unique allocation of surplus in excess of default put, but irrelevant as it has no economic meaning.
C	Froot	Complete	No	n/a	Yes	Choice	Yes	Two period, skew	No	Yes	Hedge all market risk, factor-based price for insurance risk.
C	Ibragimov et al.	Complete	Yes	Any	Yes	Fair	Yes	Dynamic, homog	No	$r_f = 0$	Same as Sherris, works with $\sum_i q_i X_i$
D		Complete	No	Any	Yes	Fair	Yes	Dynamic, homog	No	$r_f = 0$	$\mathsf{E}_\mathsf{Q}\left[\frac{X_i}{X}(X \wedge a)\right] + \tau a \mathsf{E}_\mathsf{Q}[X_i/X \mid X > a]$ where δ is the frictional capital cost.
E	Numerous	Incomplete	No	Any	Yes	Varies	Yes	Any	No		Varies with pricing functional; usually natural allocation based.

Figure 12.4 Assumptions from various important papers in the historical development of insurance pricing. Perfect implies no frictions. Model refers to Figure 12.1. Default column shows payments in default. "Any" indicates any reasonable rule can be used, but in practice only ex post equal priority is used.

12.4.6 Model Summary

Figure 12.4 summarizes the assumptions of some of the key papers mentioned in Figure 12.1. The references are Myers and Cohn (1987); Cummins (1990); Feldblum (1992); Phillips, Cummins, and Allen (1998); Myers and Read Jr. (2001); Sherris (2006); Froot (2007); and Ibragimov, Jaffee, and Walden (2010).

12.5 Learning Objectives

1. Describe common allocation methods.
2. Explain the difference between endogenous and exogenous allocation methods.
3. Explain the difference between atomic and fractional (fuzzy) game-theoretic allocation.
4. Define and compute the Shapley allocation in simple cases.
5. Define and apply the Euler gradient allocation given a differentiable cost function.
6. Define the general form of a Kreps-Venter co-measure.
7. Determine allocations using Kreps-Venter co-measures for TVaR, variance, and standard deviation risk margins.
8. Explain why capital allocation alone is insufficient for pricing.
9. Define the Constant Cost of Capital premium allocation method.
10. Explain the importance of limited liability in insurance.
11. Explain how equal priority in default functions.
12. Compute recoveries under equal priority given losses and available assets.
13. Define and differentiate between risk, frictional, and transaction costs.
14. Explain the importance of frictional and transaction costs for allocated pricing.
15. Define and differentiate between common pricing models (summarized as Models A–E).
16. Explain the importance of a nonlinear pricing rule to insurance.
17. Describe and implement common allocation procedures including pro rata, equal risk, marginal, and co-measures.

13

Classical Price Allocation Practice

In this chapter, we allocate the portfolio CCoC premium from Chapter 8 using the allocated CCoC method described in Section 12.2 for the three Case Studies.

13.1 Allocated CCoC Pricing

13.1.1 Description

To apply allocated CCoC pricing, we need a CoC and an asset allocation. We take the CoC as given. It is usually determined from a WACC analysis over Ins Co.'s capital structure combined with an assumption about the cost of equity, Section 8.2.7. A peer-valuation study usually informs the latter: what return is necessary to support a target price-to-book ratio? We apply the following asset allocation methods from Section 12.2.

1. **Expected value**: each line is priced to the same expected loss ratio as the total, Section 12.2.1.
2. **Scaled VaR, TVaR, and EPD**: each line is evaluated on a stand-alone basis and the total is pro rated. It is either a proportional, Section 12.2.2, or haircut, Section 12.2.3, allocation depending on the risk measures involved.
3. **Equal risk VaR, TVaR, and EPD**: solve $\sum_i a(X_i, p^*) = a$ for p^* and set $a_i = a(X_i, p^*)$ for $a =$ VaR, TVaR, and EPD, Section 12.2.4.
4. **Conditional TVaR:** solve $\mathsf{TVaR}_{p*}(X) = a$ for p^* and use a coTVaR allocation $a_i = \mathsf{E}[X_i \mid X \ge \mathsf{VaR}_{p^{*}*}(X)]$, Section 12.2.8. This is a exogenous allocation, Section 12.2.9.
5. **Covariance allocation:** solve $\mathsf{E}[X]+k\mathsf{Var}(X) = a(X)$ for k and allocate using covariance, $a_i = \mathsf{E}[X_i] + k\mathsf{cov}(X_i, X)$, another exogenous allocation.

The allocated CCoC pricing shown in Tables 13.2 to 13.4 computes expected losses as $\mathsf{E}[X_i(a)]$ whereas the portfolio method shown in Tables 11.7 to 11.9 uses $\mathsf{E}[X_i \wedge a_i]$. The difference between the two is generally slight, except for thick-tailed units. However, the dynamics between units can be subtle.

Table 13.1 compares $\mathsf{E}[X_i \wedge a_i]$ and $\mathsf{E}[X_i(a)]$ for Cat vs. Non-Cat and Hu vs. SCS in the second and third Cases. Total expected losses are the same under both methods, by definition.

Pricing Insurance Risk: Theory and Practice, First Edition. Stephen J. Mildenhall and John A. Major.

Table 13.1 Comparison of gross expected losses by Case, catastrophe-prone lines.

Unit	$\mathsf{E}[X_i \wedge a_i]$	$\mathsf{E}[X_i(a)]$
Cat	19.95	19.96
Non-Cat	80.00	79.99
Total	99.95	99.95
Hu	26.01	26.06
SCS	68.82	69.09
Total	95.15	95.15

Generally, a thicker-tailed unit benefits from pooling with a thinner-tailed one. Pooling makes more assets available to pay claims. In default, under equal priority, the thicker-tailed unit receives a greater than expected loss proportion of the assets—because it is more likely to *cause* the default with an enormous loss. Here, the ex post nature of equal priority comes into play. Both Cat and Hu benefit from pooling. Non-Cat loses from pooling: its expected recovery declines slightly. However, SCS also gains because Hu is associated with such a significant increase in available assets. Section 14.3.7 introduces some valuable tools to help visualize and explain these dynamics.

Capital is fixed at 0.9999 VaR for Tame Case and at 0.999 VaR for Cat/Non-Cat and Hu/SCS, computed separately for gross and net. The allocations use VaR as an endogenous measure and explore the impact of using TVaR and EPD as proxy measures for exogenous methods.

13.1.2 Application

Tables 13.2–13.4 show the results of applying the following allocations to each Case.

- Expected loss allocates capital (and hence assets) in proportion to expected loss.
- Scaled TVaR finds p^* so that TVaR_{p^*} applied to gross total equals the VaR-determined assets, and then scales stand-alone TVaR_{p^*} assets. It is an exogenous allocation. Scaled EPD works in the same way. Scaled VaR scales stand-alone VaR by unit to the total, which is already used to set assets.
- Equal risk TVaR finds p^* so that the sum of stand-alone TVaR_{p^*} assets equals VaR-determined assets, another exogenous method. Equal risk EPD and VaR work analogously.
- coTVaR finds p^* so that total TVaR_{p^*} equals VaR-determined assets and then applies a coTVaR allocation.
- Covariance finds k so that $\mathsf{E}[X] + k\mathsf{var}(X)$ equals VaR-determined assets and then uses a covariance allocation.

Both gross and net views are calibrated to overall CCoC of 0.1 pricing.

Table 13.2 Constant 0.10 ROE pricing for Tame Case Study, classical PCP methods.

		Gross			Net			Ceded
Statistic	**Method**	**A**	**B**	**Total**	**A**	**B**	**Total**	**Diff**
Loss	Expected loss	50.00	50.00	100.00	50.00	49.08	99.08	0.916
Margin	Expected loss	1.71	1.71	3.42	1.24	1.22	2.46	0.959
	Scaled EPD	1.17	2.25	3.42	1.16	1.3	2.46	0.959
	Scaled TVaR	1.22	2.2	3.42	1.23	1.24	2.46	0.959
	Scaled VaR	1.22	2.2	3.42	1.23	1.24	2.46	0.959
	Equal risk EPD	1.29	2.13	3.42	1.34	1.13	2.46	0.959
	Equal risk TVaR	1.34	2.08	3.42	1.39	1.07	2.46	0.959
	Equal risk VaR	1.34	2.08	3.42	1.39	1.07	2.46	0.959
	coTVaR	0.883	2.54	3.42	1.39	1.07	2.47	0.959
	Covar	1.05	2.37	3.42	1	1.46	2.46	0.959
Premium	Expected loss	51.71	51.71	103.4	51.24	50.30	101.5	1.87
	Scaled EPD	51.17	52.25	103.4	51.16	50.39	101.5	1.87
	Scaled TVaR	51.22	52.20	103.4	51.23	50.32	101.5	1.87
	Scaled VaR	51.22	52.20	103.4	51.23	50.32	101.5	1.87
	Equal risk EPD	51.29	52.13	103.4	51.34	50.21	101.5	1.87
	Equal risk TVaR	51.34	52.08	103.4	51.39	50.16	101.5	1.87
	Equal risk VaR	51.34	52.08	103.4	51.39	50.16	101.5	1.87
	coTVaR	50.88	52.54	103.4	51.39	50.16	101.5	1.87
	Covar	51.05	52.37	103.4	51.00	50.55	101.5	1.87
Loss ratio	Expected loss	0.967	0.967	0.967	0.976	0.976	0.976	0.488
	Scaled EPD	0.977	0.957	0.967	0.977	0.974	0.976	0.488
	Scaled TVaR	0.976	0.958	0.967	0.976	0.975	0.976	0.488
	Scaled VaR	0.976	0.958	0.967	0.976	0.975	0.976	0.488
	Equal risk EPD	0.975	0.959	0.967	0.974	0.978	0.976	0.488
	Equal risk TVaR	0.974	0.96	0.967	0.973	0.979	0.976	0.488
	Equal risk VaR	0.974	0.96	0.967	0.973	0.979	0.976	0.488
	coTVaR	0.983	0.952	0.967	0.973	0.979	0.976	0.488
	Covar	0.979	0.955	0.967	0.98	0.971	0.976	0.488
Capital	Expected loss	17.12	17.12	34.23	12.43	12.21	24.64	9.59
	Scaled EPD	11.71	22.52	34.23	11.60	13.04	24.64	9.59
	Scaled TVaR	12.21	22.02	34.23	12.27	12.37	24.64	9.59
	Scaled VaR	12.21	22.02	34.23	12.25	12.39	24.64	9.59

(Continued)

Table 13.2 (Continued)

		Gross			Net			Ceded
Statistic	**Method**	**A**	**B**	**Total**	**A**	**B**	**Total**	**Diff**
	Equal risk EPD	12.89	21.34	34.23	13.38	11.26	24.64	9.59
	Equal risk TVaR	13.40	20.84	34.23	13.89	10.75	24.64	9.59
	Equal risk VaR	13.39	20.84	34.23	13.89	10.75	24.64	9.59
	coTVaR	8.83	25.42	34.25	13.90	10.75	24.65	9.59
	Covar	10.53	23.70	34.23	10.03	14.61	24.64	9.59
Rate of return	Expected loss	0.1	0.1	0.1	0.1	0.1	0.1	0.1
	Scaled EPD	0.1	0.1	0.1	0.1	0.1	0.1	0.1
	Scaled TVaR	0.1	0.1	0.1	0.1	0.1	0.1	0.1
	Scaled VaR	0.1	0.1	0.1	0.1	0.1	0.1	0.1
	Equal risk EPD	0.1	0.1	0.1	0.1	0.1	0.1	0.1
	Equal risk TVaR	0.1	0.1	0.1	0.1	0.1	0.1	0.1
	Equal risk VaR	0.1	0.1	0.1	0.1	0.1	0.1	0.1
	coTVaR	0.1	0.1	0.1	0.1	0.1	0.1	0.1
	Covar	0.1	0.1	0.1	0.1	0.1	0.1	0.1
Leverage	Expected loss	3.02	3.02	3.02	4.12	4.12	4.12	0.195
	Scaled EPD	4.37	2.32	3.02	4.41	3.87	4.12	0.195
	Scaled TVaR	4.2	2.37	3.02	4.17	4.07	4.12	0.195
	Scaled VaR	4.2	2.37	3.02	4.18	4.06	4.12	0.195
	Equal risk EPD	3.98	2.44	3.02	3.84	4.46	4.12	0.195
	Equal risk TVaR	3.83	2.5	3.02	3.7	4.67	4.12	0.195
	Equal risk VaR	3.83	2.5	3.02	3.7	4.67	4.12	0.195
	coTVaR	5.76	2.07	3.02	3.7	4.67	4.12	0.195
	Covar	4.85	2.21	3.02	5.09	3.46	4.12	0.195
Assets	Expected loss	68.83	68.83	137.7	63.68	62.51	126.2	11.47
	Scaled EPD	62.88	74.78	137.7	62.76	63.42	126.2	11.47
	Scaled TVaR	63.43	74.23	137.7	63.50	62.69	126.2	11.47
	Scaled VaR	63.43	74.23	137.7	63.48	62.71	126.2	11.47
	Equal risk EPD	64.18	73.47	137.7	64.72	61.47	126.2	11.47
	Equal risk TVaR	64.74	72.92	137.7	65.28	60.90	126.2	11.47
	Equal risk VaR	64.73	72.92	137.7	65.28	60.91	126.2	11.47
	coTVaR	59.71	77.96	137.7	65.29	60.91	126.2	11.47
	Covar	61.59	76.07	137.7	61.03	65.16	126.2	11.47

Table 13.3 Constant 0.10 ROE pricing for Cat/Non-Cat Case Study, classical PCP methods.

		Gross			Net			Ceded
Statistic	**Method**	**Cat**	**Non-Cat**	**Total**	**Cat**	**Non-Cat**	**Total**	**Diff**
Loss	Expected loss	19.96	79.99	99.95	17.75	79.98	97.73	2.21
Margin	Expected loss	3.04	12.17	15.21	1.48	6.68	8.17	7.04
	Scaled EPD	15.68	−0.471	15.21	9.6	−1.43	8.17	7.04
	Scaled TVaR	12.85	2.36	15.21	6.17	2	8.17	7.04
	Scaled VaR	12.82	2.38	15.21	6.29	1.88	8.17	7.04
	Equal risk EPD	13.33	1.87	15.21	6.36	1.81	8.17	7.04
	Equal risk TVaR	11.78	3.42	15.21	5.29	2.87	8.17	7.04
	Equal risk VaR	11.74	3.47	15.21	4.7	3.47	8.17	7.04
	coTVaR	14.84	0.37	15.21	6.84	1.33	8.17	7.04
	Covar	11.18	4.03	15.21	4.44	3.72	8.17	7.04
Premium	Expected loss	22.99	92.16	115.2	19.23	86.67	105.9	9.25
	Scaled EPD	35.63	79.52	115.2	27.35	78.55	105.9	9.25
	Scaled TVaR	32.80	82.35	115.2	23.91	81.99	105.9	9.25
	Scaled VaR	32.78	82.37	115.2	24.04	81.86	105.9	9.25
	Equal risk EPD	33.29	81.86	115.2	24.10	81.80	105.9	9.25
	Equal risk TVaR	31.74	83.41	115.2	23.04	82.86	105.9	9.25
	Equal risk VaR	31.69	83.46	115.2	22.44	83.45	105.9	9.25
	coTVaR	34.80	80.36	115.2	24.59	81.31	105.9	9.25
	Covar	31.14	84.01	115.2	22.19	83.71	105.9	9.25
Loss ratio	Expected loss	0.868	0.868	0.868	0.923	0.923	0.923	0.239
	Scaled EPD	0.56	1.01	0.868	0.649	1.02	0.923	0.239
	Scaled TVaR	0.608	0.971	0.868	0.742	0.976	0.923	0.239
	Scaled VaR	0.609	0.971	0.868	0.738	0.977	0.923	0.239
	Equal risk EPD	0.599	0.977	0.868	0.736	0.978	0.923	0.239
	Equal risk TVaR	0.629	0.959	0.868	0.77	0.965	0.923	0.239
	Equal risk VaR	0.63	0.958	0.868	0.791	0.958	0.923	0.239
	coTVaR	0.574	0.995	0.868	0.722	0.984	0.923	0.239
	Covar	0.641	0.952	0.868	0.8	0.956	0.923	0.239
Capital	Expected loss	30.36	121.7	152.1	14.83	66.85	81.68	70.37
	Scaled EPD	156.8	−4.71	152.1	96.00	−14.32	81.68	70.37
	Scaled TVaR	128.5	23.60	152.1	61.66	20.02	81.68	70.37
	Scaled VaR	128.2	23.85	152.1	62.92	18.76	81.68	70.37

(Continued)

Table 13.3 (Continued)

		Gross			Net			Ceded
Statistic	**Method**	**Cat**	**Non-Cat**	**Total**	**Cat**	**Non-Cat**	**Total**	**Diff**
	Equal risk EPD	133.3	18.70	152.1	63.55	18.13	81.68	70.37
	Equal risk TVaR	117.8	34.20	152.1	52.94	28.74	81.68	70.37
	Equal risk VaR	117.4	34.70	152.1	46.98	34.70	81.68	70.37
	coTVaR	148.4	3.7	152.1	68.45	13.26	81.71	70.35
	Covar	111.8	40.27	152.1	44.43	37.25	81.68	70.37
Rate of return	Expected loss	0.1	0.1	0.1	0.1	0.1	0.1	0.1
	Scaled EPD	0.1	0.1	0.1	0.1	0.1	0.1	0.1
	Scaled TVaR	0.1	0.1	0.1	0.1	0.1	0.1	0.1
	Scaled VaR	0.1	0.1	0.1	0.1	0.1	0.1	0.1
	Equal risk EPD	0.1	0.1	0.1	0.1	0.1	0.1	0.1
	Equal risk TVaR	0.1	0.1	0.1	0.1	0.1	0.1	0.1
	Equal risk VaR	0.1	0.1	0.1	0.1	0.1	0.1	0.1
	coTVaR	0.1	0.1	0.1	0.1	0.1	0.1	0.1
	Covar	0.1	0.1	0.1	0.1	0.1	0.1	0.1
Leverage	Expected loss	0.757	0.757	0.757	1.3	1.3	1.3	0.131
	Scaled EPD	0.227	−16.88	0.757	0.285	−5.49	1.3	0.131
	Scaled TVaR	0.255	3.49	0.757	0.388	4.09	1.3	0.131
	Scaled VaR	0.256	3.45	0.757	0.382	4.36	1.3	0.131
	Equal risk EPD	0.25	4.38	0.757	0.379	4.51	1.3	0.131
	Equal risk TVaR	0.269	2.44	0.757	0.435	2.88	1.3	0.131
	Equal risk VaR	0.27	2.41	0.757	0.478	2.4	1.3	0.131
	coTVaR	0.234	21.71	0.757	0.359	6.13	1.3	0.131
	Covar	0.279	2.09	0.757	0.499	2.25	1.3	0.131
Assets	Expected loss	53.36	213.8	267.2	34.06	153.5	187.6	79.62
	Scaled EPD	192.4	74.81	267.2	123.3	64.23	187.6	79.62
	Scaled TVaR	161.3	105.9	267.2	85.57	102.0	187.6	79.62
	Scaled VaR	161.0	106.2	267.2	86.95	100.6	187.6	79.62
	Equal risk EPD	166.6	100.6	267.2	87.65	99.92	187.6	79.62
	Equal risk TVaR	149.6	117.6	267.2	75.98	111.6	187.6	79.62
	Equal risk VaR	149.0	118.2	267.2	69.42	118.2	187.6	79.62
	coTVaR	183.2	84.06	267.2	93.04	94.57	187.6	79.60
	Covar	142.9	124.3	267.2	66.62	121.0	187.6	79.62

Table 13.4 Constant 0.10 ROE pricing for Hu/SCS Case Study, classical PCP methods.

		Gross			Net			Ceded
Statistic	**Method**	**Hu**	**SCS**	**Total**	**Hu**	**SCS**	**Total**	**Diff**
Loss	Expected loss	26.06	69.09	95.15	15.33	69.08	84.41	10.73
Margin	Expected loss	61.94	164.2	226.2	35.33	159.2	194.5	31.68
	Scaled EPD	229.0	−2.84	226.2	198.7	−4.2	194.5	31.68
	Scaled TVaR	193.0	33.13	226.2	161.8	32.64	194.5	31.68
	Scaled VaR	190.5	35.68	226.2	159.6	34.91	194.5	31.68
	Equal risk EPD	224.4	1.81	226.2	194.4	0.128	194.5	31.68
	Equal risk TVaR	190.7	35.49	226.2	158.9	35.62	194.5	31.68
	Equal risk VaR	187.6	38.61	226.2	155.7	38.74	194.5	31.68
	coTVaR	219.2	7.01	226.2	181.8	12.68	194.5	31.66
	Covar	220.8	5.42	226.2	189.3	5.15	194.5	31.68
Premium	Expected loss	88.00	233.3	321.3	50.66	228.2	278.9	42.42
	Scaled EPD	255.1	66.25	321.3	214.0	64.88	278.9	42.42
	Scaled TVaR	219.1	102.2	321.3	177.2	101.7	278.9	42.42
	Scaled VaR	216.5	104.8	321.3	174.9	104.0	278.9	42.42
	Equal risk EPD	250.4	70.90	321.3	209.7	69.21	278.9	42.42
	Equal risk TVaR	216.7	104.6	321.3	174.2	104.7	278.9	42.42
	Equal risk VaR	213.6	107.7	321.3	171.1	107.8	278.9	42.42
	coTVaR	245.2	76.10	321.3	197.2	81.76	278.9	42.39
	Covar	246.9	74.50	321.3	204.7	74.23	278.9	42.42
Loss ratio	Expected loss	0.296	0.296	0.296	0.303	0.303	0.303	0.253
	Scaled EPD	0.102	1.04	0.296	0.0716	1.06	0.303	0.253
	Scaled TVaR	0.119	0.676	0.296	0.0865	0.679	0.303	0.253
	Scaled VaR	0.12	0.659	0.296	0.0877	0.664	0.303	0.253
	Equal risk EPD	0.104	0.974	0.296	0.0731	0.998	0.303	0.253
	Equal risk TVaR	0.12	0.661	0.296	0.088	0.66	0.303	0.253
	Equal risk VaR	0.122	0.642	0.296	0.0896	0.641	0.303	0.253
	coTVaR	0.106	0.908	0.296	0.0778	0.845	0.303	0.253
	Covar	0.106	0.927	0.296	0.0749	0.931	0.303	0.253
Capital	Expected loss	619.4	1,642	2,262	353.3	1,592	1,945	316.8
	Scaled EPD	2,290	−28.39	2,262	1,987	−41.99	1,945	316.8
	Scaled TVaR	1,930	331.3	2,262	1,618	326.4	1,945	316.8
	Scaled VaR	1,905	356.8	2,262	1,596	349.1	1,945	316.8
	Equal risk EPD	2,244	18.10	2,262	1,944	1.28	1,945	316.8

(Continued)

Table 13.4 (Continued)

		Gross			Net			Ceded
Statistic	**Method**	**Hu**	**SCS**	**Total**	**Hu**	**SCS**	**Total**	**Diff**
	Equal risk TVaR	1,907	354.9	2,262	1,589	356.2	1,945	316.8
	Equal risk VaR	1,876	386.1	2,262	1,557	387.4	1,945	316.8
	coTVaR	2,192	70.15	2,262	1,818	126.8	1,945	316.6
	Covar	2,208	54.17	2,262	1,893	51.48	1,945	316.8
Rate of return	Expected loss	0.1	0.1	0.1	0.1	0.1	0.1	0.1
	Scaled EPD	0.1	0.1	0.1	0.1	0.1	0.1	0.1
	Scaled TVaR	0.1	0.1	0.1	0.1	0.1	0.1	0.1
	Scaled VaR	0.1	0.1	0.1	0.1	0.1	0.1	0.1
	Equal risk EPD	0.1	0.1	0.1	0.1	0.1	0.1	0.1
	Equal risk TVaR	0.1	0.1	0.1	0.1	0.1	0.1	0.1
	Equal risk VaR	0.1	0.1	0.1	0.1	0.1	0.1	0.1
	coTVaR	0.1	0.1	0.1	0.1	0.1	0.1	0.1
	Covar	0.1	0.1	0.1	0.1	0.1	0.1	0.1
Leverage	Expected loss	0.142	0.142	0.142	0.143	0.143	0.143	0.134
	Scaled EPD	0.111	−2.33	0.142	0.108	−1.55	0.143	0.134
	Scaled TVaR	0.113	0.309	0.142	0.109	0.312	0.143	0.134
	Scaled VaR	0.114	0.294	0.142	0.11	0.298	0.143	0.134
	Equal risk EPD	0.112	3.92	0.142	0.108	53.96	0.143	0.134
	Equal risk TVaR	0.114	0.295	0.142	0.11	0.294	0.143	0.134
	Equal risk VaR	0.114	0.279	0.142	0.11	0.278	0.143	0.134
	coTVaR	0.112	1.08	0.142	0.108	0.645	0.143	0.134
	Covar	0.112	1.38	0.142	0.108	1.44	0.143	0.134
Assets	Expected loss	707.4	1,876	2,583	403.9	1,820	2,224	359.2
	Scaled EPD	2,545	37.86	2,583	2,201	22.89	2,224	359.2
	Scaled TVaR	2,149	433.5	2,583	1,796	428.1	2,224	359.2
	Scaled VaR	2,121	461.6	2,583	1,771	453.0	2,224	359.2
	Equal risk EPD	2,494	88.99	2,583	2,153	70.49	2,224	359.2
	Equal risk TVaR	2,123	459.5	2,583	1,763	460.9	2,224	359.2
	Equal risk VaR	2,089	493.8	2,583	1,728	495.2	2,224	359.2
	coTVaR	2,437	146.2	2,583	2,016	208.6	2,224	359.0
	Covar	2,455	128.7	2,583	2,098	125.7	2,224	359.2

All methods produce much lower loss ratios for thick-tailed Cat and Hurricane lines, driven by high capital allocations and corresponding low premium leverage, and the CCoC assumption.

13.1.3 Critique

Allocated CCoC pricing is often criticized for its extreme weighting of tail risk, which is evident in the Cat/Non-Cat and Hu/SCS Cases. The weighting is seen as a consequence of the choice of capital risk measure *and* of applying the same CoC to all capital layers.

Goldfarb (2010b) recognized the peculiar behavior of traditional CCoC pricing, and also the two uses for risk metrics:

> While this produces a "risk-based" allocation, it does so using a rather limited view of what drives the risk to the firm and tends to allocate capital primarily to those businesses with the most extreme levels of skewness, such as businesses exposed to property-catastrophe risks. This may make sense in the regulatory or rating agency applications where many of these risk capital models were first developed, but this is less appropriate when these models are used to manage the interests of the firm's shareholders.

He suggests that VaR or TVaR might still be appropriate if lower probability thresholds are used, instead of extreme thresholds of 0.99 or higher. A 0.95, 1 in 20-year return period, VaR typically corresponds well to the worst loss recalled by a roomful of insurance professionals!

Crouhy, Galai, and Mark (2010) characterize allocated CCoC pricing as we have described it as the "first-generation RAROC." They criticize the constant return assumption, rather than the capital allocation:

> The premise that underlies the first generation RAROC approach—keeping the probability of default constant—is inconsistent with a constant expected rate of return on equity for projects with different volatilities and correlations with the market portfolio.

Various alternatives for "second generation risk-adjusted performance measurement" are explored in Crouhy, Turnbull, and Wakeman (1999). They focus on determining a unit-specific hurdle rate.

Capital risk measures must be tail-centric because insurers must hold capital to protect policyholders from tail events. Regulators do not care about earnings volatility. Thus, the blame for allocated CCoC's tail-weighting must lie in the constant CoC assumption. CCoC pricing correctly says that it is expensive to bear catastrophe risk with equity capital—for the reasons laid out in Section 8.2.5. The market has developed mechanisms, such as catastrophe bonds, to deploy cheaper, non-equity capital that is better matched to the characteristics of such risks. We need an allocation method that sees through a WACC and allocates each unit the capital it actually consumes. SRM pricing techniques achieve this goal, as we describe in Section 14.3.8.

13.2 Allocation of Classical PCP Pricing

Classical PCPs are usually applied on a stand-alone basis and so do not need to be allocated. Should the need arise, most can be handled within the framework developed in Section 12.2. Table 13.5 gives a mapping from PCP to a reasonable allocation method that we have already

Table 13.5 Allocation of classical PCPs.

PCP	Coherent	Allocation
Expected value	Yes	Linear
Value at Risk	Not SA	CoVaR
Variance	Not MON or PH	Covariance
Standard deviation	Not MON	Euler
semivariance	Not PH or SA	
Exponential	Not PH or SA	Aumann-Shapley
Esscher	Not SA	Co-measure
Dutch	Yes	Natural
Fischer	Yes	Natural

described or that is discussed in Chapter 14. Section 14.5 discusses what makes an allocation *reasonable*. The second column notes whether the PCP is coherent, and where it is not, shows how it fails. If the PCP is positive homogeneous and differentiable we can apply the Euler gradient allocation, which we know is also a co-measure decomposition, by Delbaen's Theorem 2. All but variance, semivariance, and the exponential are positive homogeneous and can be allocated in this way. Tsanakas (2009) applies the Aumann-Shapley allocation to exponential and distorted exponential PCPs.

13.3 Learning Objectives

1. Allocate portfolio constant CoC premium to units.
2. Rank implied allocations based on statistical properties.
3. Identify the sensitivity of scaled, equal risk, and co-measure methods to volume, volatility, and tail risk.
4. Identify the impact of the choice of auxiliary exogenous measure on sensitivity to volume, volatility, and tail risk.
5. Describe ways to allocate classical PCP premium by unit.

14

Modern Price Allocation Theory

In this chapter, we show how to allocate premiums that are determined by coherent risk measures. Sections 14.1 and 14.2 present the natural allocation of a coherent risk measure and two specializations, the linear and lifted allocations. We explain when the natural allocation exists and its relationship to the marginal methods discussed in Chapter 12. We detail how to compute it, paying careful attention to the construction of the appropriate contact function. To the extent possible, we explain how the theory applies to an arbitrary coherent risk measure representing either capital or premium, but some of the specializations apply only to spectral risk measures.

In Section 14.3 we focus on the problem of allocating limited-liability premiums as specified by a spectral risk measure. We detail how funding by layer breaks out by unit. We introduce three functions that facilitate this analysis and that turn out to be helpful in visualizing and comparing risk. We apply them to explain a natural allocation of capital (as opposed to premium) and to clarify the differences between the natural allocation and Bodoff's Percentile Layer of Capital method.

In Sections 14.4 and 14.5 we present an axiomatic development and characterization of allocations.

The reader might want to read this chapter in parallel with Chapter 15.

14.1 The Natural Allocation of a Coherent Risk Measure

The natural allocation is an explicit allocation formula that applies to coherent risk measures. The allocation is natural because it entails no additional choices (no new probability threshold for example), it is consistent with financial, economic, and game theories, and it is additive. It follows the finance philosophy to *adjust the probabilities and act risk neutral.*

When the risk measure is differentiable the natural allocation is well known (Delbaen (2000), Tsanakas and Desli (2003), Follmer and Schied (2016)). We also present two specialized flavors just for SRMs: the linear and lifted natural allocations that address non-uniqueness problems. The linear was introduced in Cherny and Orlov (2011) and is discussed in Grechuk (2015).

Pricing Insurance Risk: Theory and Practice, First Edition. Stephen J. Mildenhall and John A. Major.

14.1.1 Lessons from Classical Allocations

Section 12.2 introduced nine different ways to allocate premium, margin, assets, or capital, many of which came in multiple flavors. Some, such as Shapley allocation, have a theoretical foundation. Others, like the proportional spread, are just pragmatic, practical solutions. Two emerged as particularly useful: the Euler gradient marginal and co-measure allocations.

Marginal methods are useful for performance management, meaning they give the right grow or shrink signal for portfolio optimization in a constant CoC world (Tasche 1999). Co-measures are intuitive, practical, and easy to apply. They can be interpreted as risk-adjusted probabilities, and this interpretation provides a philosophical alignment with finance. And they are closely related to the natural allocation.

Happily, in many cases marginal and co-measure allocations are the same (Venter, Major, and Kreps 2006). In general, Delbaen's Theorem 2 shows they are the same for every coherent risk measure, subject to a differentiability assumption, as we shall explain.

14.1.2 Definition of the Natural Allocation

The idea behind the natural allocation is very similar to that behind co-measures, such as coTVaR. Under a TVaR measure of risk, required assets are

$$a = \mathsf{TVaR}_p(X) = \mathsf{E}[X \mid X > \mathsf{VaR}_p(X)],$$

assuming $\mathsf{Pr}(X = \mathsf{VaR}_p(X)) = 0$ for simplicity. TVaR can be computed using a risk-adjusted probability that multiplies the chances of an outcome x by $1/(1-p)$ if $x > \mathsf{VaR}_p(X)$ and sets the probability of other outcomes equal to zero. Call this new probability scenario Q. Then, as Delbaen (2000, p. 33) observes, allocating $a_i = \mathsf{E}_{\mathsf{Q}}[X_i]$ to unit i is "**very natural**," explaining the name we have chosen. It is an allocation of ρ since expectation is linear

$$a = \mathsf{E}_{\mathsf{Q}}[X] = \mathsf{E}_{\mathsf{Q}}\left[\sum_i X_i\right] = \sum_i \mathsf{E}_{\mathsf{Q}}[X_i] = \sum_i a_i.$$

This process can be applied to any coherent or sublinear risk measure.

We now turn to the general case. Assume all random variables are defined on a probability space $(\Omega, \mathcal{F}, \mathsf{P})$. Let ρ be a coherent risk measure. By Theorem 1 we know that ρ has a representation

$$\rho(X) = \sup_{\mathsf{Q}\in\mathcal{Q}} \mathsf{E}_{\mathsf{Q}}[X] \tag{14.1}$$

as the worst expected value over a set of probability scenarios $\mathcal{Q}$.

Using Eq. 14.1 we would like to find one of those scenarios, Q_X, which of course depends on X, that satisfies the equality $\rho(X) = \mathsf{E}_{\mathsf{Q}_X}[X]$.

Recall, from Eq. 5.15, there is random variable Z associated with each scenario Q that gives us the identity $\mathsf{E}_{\mathsf{Q}}[Y] = \mathsf{E}[YZ]$ that holds for *all* Y. You can think of Z as the density of Q relative to P. In the case of Q_X, we call the corresponding $Z = Z_X$ a **contact function** for ρ at X. We often abuse the terminology and refer to Q_X as a contact function as well. The particular Z_X depends on X, because Q_X does.

Here is why Z is called a contact function. Consider the two real valued functions $t \mapsto \rho(X + tY)$ and $t \mapsto \rho(X) + t\mathsf{E}_{\mathsf{Q}_X}[Y]$. The first is convex, because ρ is. The second is a straight line that is tangent to, i.e. *makes contact with*, the first at $t = 0$. For all t the first function lies above the second:

$$\rho(X + tY) \geq \rho(X) + t\mathsf{E}_{\mathsf{Q}_X}[Y]. \tag{14.2}$$

This follows because $\rho(X + tY) \geq \mathsf{E}_{\mathsf{Q}_X}[X + tY] = \mathsf{E}_{\mathsf{Q}_X}[X] + \mathsf{E}_{\mathsf{Q}_X}[tY] = \rho(X) + t\mathsf{E}_{\mathsf{Q}_X}[Y]$. In the risk measure literature, such a Q_X is called a *subgradient* to ρ at X. The terminology comes from convex function theory and the recognition of its tangent-like behavior at $t = 0$. In that literature, the set of contact functions Q_X (subgradients) is called the *subdifferential*; see Section 5.5. We simply refer to it as the set of contact functions.

Exercise 220. In the derivation of Eq. 14.2, why is $\rho(X + tY) \geq \mathsf{E}_{\mathsf{Q}_X}[X + tY]$?

Solution. Because Q_X is one of the probability scenarios used to define ρ and $\rho(X + tY)$ is the largest value of $\mathsf{E}_{\mathsf{Q}}[X + tY]$ over *all* such scenarios. □

We would like to define the natural allocation of $\rho(X)$ to X_i as

$$D\rho_X(X_i) := \mathsf{E}_{\mathsf{Q}_X}[X_i], \tag{14.3}$$

but two problems can get in the way. First, Q_X might not be unique. Second, Q_X might not even exist.

Example 221. Let $\rho(X) = \mathsf{TVaR}_p(X)$ for $0 < p < 1$. We know from Section 4.3 that the corresponding $\mathcal{Q}$ contains all scenarios with densities given by $(1-p)^{-1}1_A$ for $A \subset \Omega$ satisfying $\mathsf{P}(A) = 1 - p$. To pick out the contact function, we take A as the worst $1 - p$ proportion of outcomes of X. So far, so good. Now, let $X = 1$ be the constant random variable. Then $\mathsf{TVaR}_p(X) = 1 = \mathsf{E}_{\mathsf{Q}}[X]$ for *any* $\mathsf{Q} \in \mathcal{Q}$. So Q_X is not unique. □

The case where Q_X is not unique is illustrated in Figure 5.8.

Example 222. Let $\rho(X) = \sup(X)$ be the worst-case risk measure. The scenarios $\mathcal{Q}$ defining ρ consist of *all* probability scenarios on Ω that are absolutely continuous with respect to P. Let $\Omega = [0, 1]$ and U be uniformly distributed, $U(\omega) = \omega$. Then $\rho(U) = 1$, but there is no $\mathsf{Q} \in \mathcal{Q}$ satisfying $\rho(U) = \mathsf{E}_{\mathsf{Q}}[U]$. The required Q puts all its mass at the point $\omega = 1$ (infinite density) and therefore is not absolutely continuous with respect to P. □

The first problem, uniqueness, is inescapable. We sidestep it by providing several definitions of the natural allocation. The most general is the *set* of expectations corresponding to the *set* of contact functions. To obtain a unique value allocation for an SRM, we introduce the linear natural allocation based on a privileged contact function.

The second problem, existence, can be assumed away. That is, our definition only holds if it exists. Kalkbrener (2005) works with random variables that are not necessarily bounded. On that space sup does not define a risk measure, because it may be infinite, giving one way to address the problem. Follmer and Schied (2016) work with bounded random variables and shows that Q_X exists when ρ is continuous from above, Theorem 1, part (b), giving another. We can now formally define the natural allocation set.

Definition 10. *Let ρ be a coherent risk measure and $\mathcal{Q}$ the corresponding set of probability scenarios. Let X be a random variable and $\mathcal{Q}(X) = \{\mathsf{Q} \in \mathcal{Q} \mid \rho(X) = \mathsf{E}_{\mathsf{Q}}[X]\}$ be its set of contact functions. The set $\{\mathsf{E}_{\mathsf{Q}}[X_i] \mid \mathsf{Q} \in \mathcal{Q}(X)\}$ is called the* **natural allocation set** *of $\rho(X)$ to X_i as part of X and is denoted $D\rho_X(X_i)$.*

The natural allocation set may be empty. See Example 222.

Remark 223. Associated with the selected probability scenarios $\mathcal{Q}(X)$ are the random variable contact functions $\{Z \mid \rho(X) = \mathsf{E}[XZ]\}$ so we could equivalently define the natural allocation set as $\{\mathsf{E}[X_i Z] \mid \rho(X) = \mathsf{E}[XZ]\}$. □

Delbaen's Theorem 2 shows that marginal risk calculated using directional derivatives is the same as the natural allocation if there is a *unique* contact function, and that this occurs if ρ is differentiable at X. Thus, the natural allocation provides a very general link between marginal methods and co-measure-like methods. ρ is differentiable at X in the direction X_i when the limit

$$\lim_{t\to 0} \frac{\rho(X + tX_i) - \rho(X)}{t} \tag{14.4}$$

exists. Generally, we think that $X = \sum_j X_j$ and X_i is a summand, but this is not necessary. The limit in Eq. 14.4 fails to exist when X takes on the same value at different events, see Marinacci and Montrucchio (2004), or when the quantile function q_X is not strictly increasing, Carlier and Dana (2003).

Example 224. What can we say about the largest and smallest elements of the natural allocation set? They must fall in the range

$$0 \le -\rho(-X_i) \le \mathsf{E}[X_i Z(X)] \le \rho(X_i), \tag{14.5}$$

This range is highly intuitive. Consider Ins Co. quoting X_i. Ins Co. evaluates how the new risk correlates with it's existing portfolio, X. It is best for Ins Co. if X_i is anti-comonotonic with X. In that case, Ins Co. quotes $-\rho(-X_i)$, below $\mathsf{E}[X_i]$ because of the value of X_i as a hedge against its portfolio. It is worst for Ins Co. if X_i is comonotonic with X, in which case $\rho(X+X_i) = \rho(X)+\rho(X_i)$ by comonotonic additivity, and Ins Co. quotes $\rho(X_i)$. In the first case, $-X_i$ is comonotonic with X and so comonotonic additivity applies again. Eq. 14.5 follows by the Hardy-Littlewood inequality, Eq. 5.17, and the representation of ρ. Note that $-\rho(-X) \le \mathsf{E}[X] \le \rho(X)$. We identify this range as the bid-ask spread in Section 5.2.9, and use it again in Section 10.4 when analyzing pricing by layer. The upper bound is achieved when X_i and X are comonotonic. The lower bound is achieved when they are anti-comonotonic. The allocation equals the mean when X_i and $Z(X)$ are independent, because $\mathsf{E}[Z(X)] = 1$. Proposition 14.1 shows the allocation is $\ge \mathsf{E}[X_i]$ if X_i are all independent. See Exercise 242 part (4) for an example. (To define $\rho(-X)$ assume $X \le b$. Then $b - X \ge 0$ is a loss random variable and $\rho(b - X) = b + \rho(-X)$ by translation invariance. Take $-\rho(-X) = b - \rho(b - X)$.) □

Example 225. Consider the joint distribution of $X_1 + X_2 = X$ given in Table 14.1. Each event has probability $1/10$. Let ρ be $\mathsf{TVaR}_{0.8}$.

Table 14.1 Joint distribution for Example 225.

Event	X_1	X_2	X
0	1	1	2
1	2	2	4
2	3	3	6
3	4	4	8
4	5	5	10
5	6	9	15
6	7	8	15
7	8	12	20
8	10	10	20
9	10	20	30

By definition, $\mathsf{TVaR}_{0.8}(X) = 25$. $\mathsf{TVaR}_{0.8}(X)$ can be computed as $(0.5)(20) + (0.5)(30) = 25$, but there is an ambiguity about which sample point with $X = 20$ to select. That ambiguity leads to nondifferentiability. Let us attempt to compute the derivative Eq. 14.4 with respect to X_1. To compute $\mathsf{TVaR}_{0.8}(X + tX_1)$, the X_1 column is scaled up by $1 + t$. For small $|t|$, the three largest values of $X + tX_1$ are $20 + 8t$, $20 + 10t$, and $30 + 10t$.

If t is a small *positive* number, the largest two outcomes are at event 9 and event 8, because $20 + 10t$ is larger than $20 + 8t$ (event 7). The numerator of Eq. 14.4 is then $(10t + 10t)/2$ and the limit equals 10. If t is a small *negative* number, the two largest outcomes are at event 9 and event 7, because $20 + 8t > 20 + 10t$ when $t < 0$. The numerator is then $(8t + 10t)/2$ and the limit equals 9. Since the limit from below is different than the limit from above, the limit does not exist and $\mathsf{TVaR}_{0.8}$ is not differentiable at X. □

Exercise 226. Compute the natural allocation sets for X_1 and X_2 as part of X for $\mathsf{TVaR}_{0.8}$ and $\mathsf{TVaR}_{0.9}$, using Example 225. Is $\mathsf{TVaR}_{0.9}$ differentiable at X? □

Example 227. Consider the more extreme example laid out in Table 14.2. Each event has probability $1/10$. Let ρ be $\mathsf{TVaR}_{0.8}$.

By definition $\mathsf{TVaR}_{0.8}(X) = 8.5$. What can we say about the contact functions? Four possible contact functions $Z_1, \dots, Z_4$ are shown. For any one of them, $\mathsf{E}[XZ_j] = (5)(1/10)(8) + (5)(1/10)(9) = 8.5 = \mathsf{TVaR}_{0.8}(X)$.

Any convex combination of these functions is also a contact function, so there are infinitely many. The first four are called **extreme** contact functions, in the sense that they are not convex linear combinations of two other contact functions. They are *corners* of the convex set of contact functions.

If some unit X_i took on different values among events 5 to 8, then the allocations $\mathsf{E}[X_iZ_j]$ would not be the same across all Z_j. □

Exercise 228. Let $\rho(X)$ be the CCoC SRM

$$\rho(X) = \nu\mathsf{TVaR}_0(X) + \delta\mathsf{TVaR}_1(X),$$

Table 14.2 Four extreme contact functions at X for $\mathsf{TVaR}_{0.8}$ and for the CCoC SRM.

Event	X	Z_1	Z_2	Z_3	Z_4	Z_5	Z_6	Z_7	Z_8
0	0	0	0	0	0	ν	ν	ν	ν
1	1	0	0	0	0	ν	ν	ν	ν
2	2	0	0	0	0	ν	ν	ν	ν
3	3	0	0	0	0	ν	ν	ν	ν
4	4	0	0	0	0	ν	ν	ν	ν
5	8	0	0	0	5	0	0	0	4ν
6	8	0	0	5	0	0	0	4ν	0
7	8	0	5	0	0	0	4ν	0	0
8	8	5	0	0	0	4ν	0	0	0
9	9	5	5	5	5	$\nu + 10\delta$	$\nu + 10\delta$	$\nu + 10\delta$	$\nu + 10\delta$

where $0 < \nu = 1 - \delta < 1$. Let X be the random variable appearing in Example 227. What are the extreme contact functions for ρ?

Solution. $(1, 1, \dots, 1, 1)$ is a contact function for TVaR_0, but it is not an extreme contact function at this particular X, which is not one-to-one. The (unique and extreme) contact function for TVaR_1 at X is $(0, 0, \dots, 0, 10)$. Mixing them in proportions (ν, δ) gives us a contact function $(\nu, \nu, \dots, \nu, \nu + 10\delta)$. However, because events 5 through 8 share the same $X = 8$ value, any four nonnegative values summing to 4ν work there. Four extreme contact functions $Z_5, \dots, Z_8$ are shown on the right in Table 14.2. □

Faced with multiple natural allocations, the obvious question to ask is whether one is privileged in some way.

14.1.3 The Linear Natural Allocation

To make progress, we need to constrain the coherent ρ in two ways.

First, it is productive to assume ρ is law invariant, Section 5.2.13. Classical PCPs and capital risk measures (except Lloyd's RDSs) are law invariant. Law invariance imposes strong constraints on the set $\mathcal{Q}$ of scenarios that defines ρ. In particular, $\mathcal{Q}$ is closed under conditional expectations, (Jouini, Schachermayer, and Touzi 2006). We apply this property as follows: if $\mathsf{Q} \in \mathcal{Q}$ has density Z then the scenario with density $\mathsf{E}[Z \mid X]$ is in $\mathcal{Q}$ too. If Z is a contact function for X then

$$\rho(X) = \mathsf{E}[XZ] = \mathsf{E}[\mathsf{E}[XZ \mid X]] = \mathsf{E}[X\mathsf{E}[Z \mid X]],$$

by the tower property of conditional expectations, and therefore $\mathsf{E}[Z \mid X]$ is also a contact function for X. Law invariance is critical for this replacement to be valid. Here is how it helps.

Example 227 (Continued). Each of $Z_1, \dots, Z_4$ Z_j in Table 14.2 has the *same* conditional expectation given X, viz:

$$\mathsf{E}[Z \mid X](\omega) = \begin{cases} 0 & \text{if } X(\omega) < 8 \\ 5/4 & \text{if } X(\omega) = 8 \\ 5 & \text{if } X(\omega) = 9. \end{cases}$$

Therefore the allocations with respect to $\mathsf{E}[Z_j \mid X]$ are all the same, regardless of which Z_j we start with. □

Notice that in Example 227, all four contact functions can be obtained from one another by applying a permutation to the underlying probability space—in a sense, they are the same. Since all events have equal probability, such a permutation is a probability preserving transformation (PPT) of the sample space. This permutation property does not hold for a general ρ, but it turns out to be important. The second constraint restricts attention to risk measures where it does hold. Theorem 1 parts (c) and (d) suggests that can be achieved by assuming ρ is comonotonic additive, which means **assuming ρ is an SRM.**

Example 229. This example shows what goes wrong if ρ is not an SRM. Let ρ_c be the CCoC measure from Exercise 228 with $\delta = 34/39, \nu = 5/39$. Let X be the same random variable in that example. Notice that $\rho_c(X) = \mathsf{TVaR}_{0.8}(X) = 8.5$. Define a risk measure $\rho(X) = \max\{\rho_c(X), \mathsf{TVaR}_{0.8}(X)\}$. This is a coherent risk measure but not an SRM, and not comonotonic additive. Z_1 through Z_4 of Example 227 are contact functions for ρ at X, and so are Z_5 through Z_8 of Exercise 228. However, the set of all eight are clearly not PPTs of one another. More to the point, $\mathsf{E}[Z_i \mid X] \neq \mathsf{E}[Z_j \mid X]$ if $i \in \{1, \dots, 4\}$ and $j \in \{5, \dots, 8\}$. □

Technical Remark 230. We look a little closer into the permutation property. Using the equivalent representations in Theorem 3, we can show that $\mathcal{Q}$ for an SRM—like TVaR in Example 227—is generated from a *single* extreme contact function Z by taking all (limits of) convex combinations of contact functions of the form $Z \circ T$ where T is an PPT of Ω. T acts like a shuffle on Ω.

A law invariant coherent risk measure is comonotonic additive if and only if all its extreme contact functions are PPTs of one another, (Shapiro, 2012, Theorem 2). In case (c) of Theorem 1, Shapiro proves in addition that

1. $\mathcal{Q}$ consists of all PPTs of a single Z iff ρ is an SRM, i.e. an m-weighting of TVaRs

$$\rho(X) = \int_0^1 \mathsf{TVaR}_p\, m(dp). \tag{14.6}$$

2. In case 1, m is unique.
3. ρ is comonotonic additive iff $\mathcal{Q}$ consists of convex combinations of $Z \circ T_i$ for some Z and PPTs T_i iff the extreme points of $\mathcal{Q}$ are $Z \circ T$ for some Z and any PPT T.

Shapiro's result explains that non-comonotonic risk measures appear as the maximum of a family of SRMs whose m-scenarios have different distributions.

The set $\{Z \circ T \mid T : \Omega \to \Omega \text{ PPT}\}$ consists of all random variables with the same distribution as Z and is the set of all extreme points in the set of all random variables dominated by Z in second-order dominance $\{Y \mid Y \preceq_2 Z\}$, Ryff (1967), Svindland (2014). Strassen's theorem says $Y \preceq Z$ iff $Y = \mathsf{E}[Z \mid \mathcal{G}]$ for some $\mathcal{G} \subset \mathcal{F}$, Strassen (1965). See also Cherny and Grigoriev (2007).

Thus, the behavior in Example 227 is typical for all SRMs: there is a single contact function Z that can be obtained as the contact function for a strictly increasing X and that Z *generates* all other extreme contact functions. For p-TVaR, $Z = (1-p)^{-1}1_A$ for a set A of probability $1-p$. *Any* contact function is a convex combination of Z and its shuffles, or equivalently is the conditional expectation of an extreme contact function. Example 229 shows the typical behavior of risk measures that are not comonotonic additive (and therefore are not SRMs). □

When ρ is an SRM we can always find a privileged contact function for X. It equals $\tilde{Z} = \mathsf{E}[Z \mid X]$ where Z is *any* contact function for X. Cherny and Orlov (2011) prove $\tilde{Z}$ is independent of the choice of Z, and calls the resulting allocation the linear risk contribution. In fact, $\tilde{Z}$ is uniquely defined by the two properties:

1. $\tilde{Z}$ is a contact function and
2. $\tilde{Z}$ is constant on sets $X = x$.

Therefore we can use $\tilde{Z}$ to define a version of the natural allocation that is unique, even when $\mathcal{Q}(X)$ contains multiple scenarios. We call it the linear natural allocation. The foregoing discussion allows us to make the following definition.

Definition 11. *Let ρ be a spectral risk measure. The* **linear contact function** *to ρ at X is the unique function given by $\tilde{Z}_X := \mathsf{E}[Z \mid X]$, where Z is any contact function for X. The* **linear (natural) allocation** *of $\rho(X)$ to X_i as part of X equals*

$$D^n\rho_X(X_i) := \mathsf{E}[X_i \tilde{Z}_X]. \tag{14.7}$$

Technical Remark 231. It is interesting to probe further into why $\mathsf{E}[Z \mid X]$ is unique. Initially, consider $\rho = \mathsf{TVaR}_p$, which has a contact function $Z_A = (1-p)^{-1}1_A$ for a set with $\mathsf{P}(A) = 1 - p$ and $X \geq \mathsf{VaR}_p(X)$ on A. By definition

$$\mathsf{E}[Z_A \mid X = x] = (1-p)^{-1}\mathsf{E}[1_A \mid X = x] = \begin{cases} 0 & x < \mathsf{VaR}_p(X) \\ z & x = \mathsf{VaR}_p(X) \\ (1-p)^{-1} & x > \mathsf{VaR}_p(X) \end{cases}$$

with the case $x = \mathsf{VaR}_p(X)$ only appearing when $\mathsf{P}(X = \mathsf{VaR}_p(X)) > 0$ and

$$z = \frac{1 - (1-p)^{-1}\mathsf{P}(X > \mathsf{VaR}_p(X))}{\mathsf{P}(X = \mathsf{VaR}_p(X))}.$$

The value of z is determined by the requirement $\mathsf{E}[Z_A] = 1$. Therefore $\mathsf{E}[Z_A \mid X]$ is independent of the choice of Z_A. By Fubini's theorem, the contact function of a mixture is the mixture of contact functions

$$\begin{aligned}\rho(X) &= \int_{[0,1]} \mathsf{TVaR}_p(X)\, m(dp) \\ &= \int_{[0,1]} \int_{\Omega} X(\omega) Z_A(\omega)\, \mathsf{P}(d\omega) m(dp) \\ &= \int_{\Omega} X(\omega) \int_{[0,1]} Z_A(\omega)\, m(dp) \mathsf{P}(d\omega).\end{aligned}$$

The inner integral defines Z. Applying Fubini's theorem again shows $\mathsf{E}[Z \mid X]$ is unique. This sketch proof ignores some technicalities that are addressed in Cherny and Orlov (2011). They characterize the privileged contact function as minimal in $\mathcal{Q}(X)$ with respect to second-order stochastic dominance. Their proof shows the resulting measure is constant on $X = x$. Since $Z \succeq_2 \mathsf{E}[Z \mid X]$ for any Z, the minimal measure must be $\mathsf{E}[Z \mid X]$. □

Remark 232. Cherny and Orlov (2011) also defines a directional risk contribution based on a one sided limit ($t \downarrow 0$ or $t \uparrow 0$) in the directional derivative Eq. 14.4. Because ρ is convex both these limits are guaranteed to exist, and the limit from above (resp. below) equals the largest (smallest) value $\mathsf{E}_{\mathsf{Q}}[X_i]$ for $\mathsf{Q} \in \mathcal{Q}(X)$, i.e. the extreme values of the natural allocation set. The linear natural allocation falls between the two. □

14.1.4 The Lifted Natural Allocation

Our motivating problem is to allocate premium or capital $\rho(X)$ for a limited liability Ins Co. operating under an equal priority default rule. Ins Co. promises to pay X in total and backs its promise with assets a. Limited liability means the total loss payment it actually makes equals $X \wedge a$ and we want an allocation of $\rho(X \wedge a)$ to $X_i(a)$, Section 12.3. We know that ρ is *never* differentiable at $X \wedge a$ if there is a positive probability of default and therefore the natural allocation is *never* unique. The linear natural allocation is one solution; it picks out a privileged member of the natural allocation set.

Exercise 233. It is possible for ρ to be differentiable at $X \wedge a$. Give an example where this is the case. It is the exception, not the rule. □

A situation similar to $X \wedge a$ can occur if $N = X - L_{r_a}^{r_a+r_l}(X)$ equals losses net of an aggregate excess of loss reinsurance contract attaching at r_a with limit r_l. Then, $N = r_a$ across all events where the gross loss X is between r_a and $r_a + r_l$. In both the $X \wedge a$ and N examples, while the allocation target is ill-behaved, there exists another, possibly well-behaved, random variable closely related to it. The idea behind the lifted allocation is to use a privileged random variable to obtain a privileged contact function.

Exercise 234. Let ρ be an SRM, $\tilde{X}$ and X be comonotonic random variables, and $\tilde{X}$ one-to-one. Show that the unique contact function Z for ρ at $\tilde{X}$ is also a contact function at X.

Solution. $\rho(\tilde{X} + X) = \rho(\tilde{X}) + \rho(X)$ from comonotonic additivity. Let W be a contact function for ρ at $\tilde{X} + X$. We then have

$$\rho(\tilde{X} + X) = \mathsf{E}[W(\tilde{X} + X)] = \mathsf{E}[W\tilde{X}] + \mathsf{E}[WX] \le \rho(\tilde{X}) + \rho(X) = \rho(\tilde{X} + X).$$

Individually, $\mathsf{E}[W\tilde{X}] \le \rho(\tilde{X})$ and $\mathsf{E}[WX] \le \rho(X)$, so equality must hold. Therefore W is a contact function at $\tilde{X}$, but there is only one at $\tilde{X}$, so $W = Z$ and Z is also a contact function at X. □

Therefore if the natural allocation of an SRM at $\tilde{X}$ is unique, it can be used to allocate the SRM at any comonotonic X. We formalize the following:

Definition 12. *Let ρ be a spectral risk measure and X a random variable. Let $\tilde{X}$ be one-to-one and comonotonic with X, with contact function $Z_{\tilde{X}}$. We call $\tilde{X}$ a* **lift** *of X. Let X_i be another random variable. The* **lifted (natural) allocation** *of $\rho(X)$ to X_i as part of X with respect to $\tilde{X}$ equals*

$$D^f \rho_{X,\tilde{X}}(X_i) := \mathsf{E}[X_i Z_{\tilde{X}}].$$

X plays no role in the right hand side of this definition! We include it on the left because it constrains what $\tilde{X}$ are acceptable. Also, in typical applications X_i and X are related through a summation $X = \sum X_i$ and we want to keep this context in mind.

The principal application of the lifted allocation is to allocate $\rho(X \wedge a)$ to $X_i(a)$. Each of the linear and lifted allocations is *one of* the natural allocations for $X \wedge a$. While we could use the linear allocation, lifting with the uncapped X gives economically useful information about the total cost of each default state. Regulators and society are concerned about the amount of default, encoded in X, even if management is only concerned with the event of default.

Example 235. Let X be defined on a sample space of ten equally likely outcomes and ρ = TVaR_p with $p = 0.8$. Suppose $a = 10$ and the values of X, X_1, X_2 are as shown in Table 14.3.

$X \wedge 10$ has $\binom{6}{2} = 15$ different extreme contact functions (picking two from scenarios 4-9). Their average equals the linear contact function Z_{lin}. The corresponding linear natural

Table 14.3 Assumptions and results for Example 235.

Event	X_1	X_2	X	$X \wedge a$	$X_1(a)$	$X_2(a)$	Z_{lin}	Z_{lift}
0	1	1	2	2	1	1	0	0
1	2	2	4	4	2	2	0	0
2	3	3	6	6	3	3	0	0
3	4	4	8	8	4	4	0	0
4	5	5	10	10	5	5	1.667	0
5	6	9	15	10	4	6	1.667	0
6	7	8	15	10	4.667	5.333	1.667	0
7	8	12	20	10	4	6	1.667	0
8	12	13	25	10	4.8	5.2	1.667	5
9	10	20	30	10	3.333	6.667	1.667	5
$D^n\rho_{X \wedge a}(\cdot)$				10	4.3	5.7		
$D^f\rho_{X \wedge a, X}(\cdot)$	11	16.5	27.5	10	4.067	5.933		

allocation is $D^n\rho_{X\wedge a}(X_i)$. In this case, X has a unique contact function given by Z_{lift}. The corresponding lifted allocation is $D^f\rho_{X\wedge a,X}(X_i)$ in the last row. The lifted allocation is sensitive to the more extreme nature of X_2 and allocates it 5.93 vs. only 5.7 for the linear allocation that treats all default states equally. Since Z_{lift} is a contact function for X it computes TVaR_p correctly and allocates it for X (bottom row, left columns). Z_{lin} is not a contact function for X; the relevant sum products are $8 + 11.1667 = 19.167$ (not shown). □

Exercise 236. Based on Example 235:

1. What is the range of natural allocations to $X_1(10)$ and $X_2(10)$ part of $X \wedge 10$. What contact functions correspond to the extremes?
2. What are the linear and lifted allocations for $X \wedge 20$? □

Example 227 (Continued). The lifted allocation does not apply to this example because there is no lift $\tilde{X}$ candidate. The non-uniqueness is not caused by a capping or other type of financial derivative operation. □

Example 237. This example shows how a risk measure that is law invariant and coherent but not comonotonic additive is not compatible with the lifted natural allocation. The absolute semideviation (Dutch) risk measure is defined as

$$\rho(X) = \mathsf{E}[X] + c\mathsf{E}[(X - \mathsf{E}[X])^+].$$

When $\{X = \mathsf{E}[X]\}$ has probability zero, the contact function Z is given by

$$Z(\omega) = \begin{cases} 1 - c\gamma & X(\omega) < \mathsf{E}[X] \\ 1 + c(1-\gamma) & X(\omega) > \mathsf{E}[X] \end{cases}$$

where $\gamma = \mathsf{Pr}(X > \mathsf{E}[X])$, see Shapiro (2012), Example 2.

(**Exercise:** Derive $Z(\omega)$.)

Let X be a one-to-one loss random variable with $a < \max(X)$. Say we want to allocate $X \wedge a$ to its units $X_i(a)$. Clearly, $X \wedge a$ is comonotonic with X. It is tempting to use the lifted natural allocations $D^f\rho_{X\wedge a,X}(X_i(a))$. In order to do this, we would find the unique contact function Z_X for X and compute

$$a_i := D^f\rho_{X\wedge a,X}(X_i(a)) = \mathsf{E}[X_i(a)Z_X].$$

Unfortunately, this is not (in general) an allocation of $\rho(X \wedge a)$ because

$$\sum_i a_i = \mathsf{E}[(X \wedge a)Z_X] \neq \rho(X \wedge a) = \mathsf{E}[(X \wedge a)Z_{X\wedge a}],$$

since the contact function $Z_{X\wedge a}$ for $X \wedge a$ is different from the contact function Z_X for X. See Figure 14.1 for an explicit example. □

14.1.5 Constructing the Linear Contact Function from a Distortion

In this section, we develop, in four stages with increasingly general assumptions, the full expression of the linear contact function Z at X for an SRM ρ with associated distortion function g. We assume that $\rho(X) < \infty$.

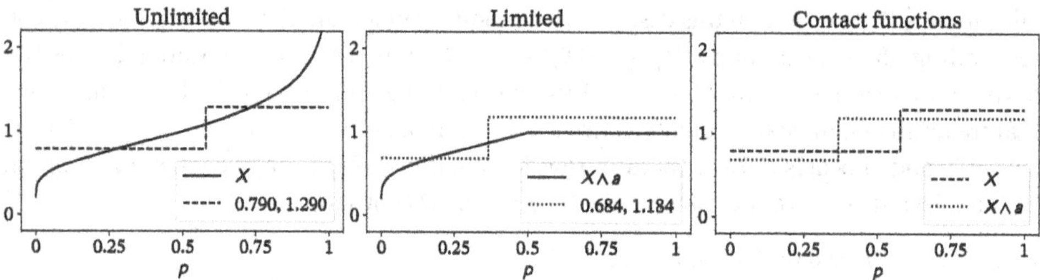

Figure 14.1 Computation of absolute semideviation with $c = 0.5$ where $a = 1$ and X is a lognormal distribution with $\mu = 0$, $\sigma = 0.4$. The Unlimited panel shows the contact function for X ($\gamma = 0.421$) and Limited for $X \wedge a$ ($\gamma = 0.633$). The final panel compares the contact functions showing the weights $w_l = 1 - c\gamma$ and $w_u = 1 + c(1-\gamma)$ for Z.

Stage 1. X has a density everywhere and g is continuous.
The only possible discontinuity for g is at $s = 0$, so this in particular means that $g(0+) = 0$ (no minimum rate on line). Applying integration by parts to Definition 7, we have

$$\begin{aligned}
\rho(X) &= \int_0^\infty g(S(x))\,dx \\
&= xg(S(x))\Big|_0^\infty + \int_{[0,\infty]} x\,d(gS(x)) \\
&= xg(S(x))\Big|_0^\infty + \int_0^\infty xg'(S(x))f(x)dx \\
&= \int_0^\infty xg'(S(x))f(x)dx
\end{aligned}$$

where we rely on several assumptions. First, because ρ is finite, $\lim_{x\to\infty} xg(S(x)) = 0$. Second, the continuity and concavity of g imply that it is differentiable except possibly at a finite or countably infinite number of points, where it has a kink. This, along with X having no mass points, means that $g'(S(x))$ exists almost everywhere, and so the kinks can be ignored in the integral.

Therefore, in this case,

$$Z(x) = g'(S(x)).$$

Remark 238. We are translating from the survival function form $\int g(S(x))\,dx$ to an event-outcome form $\mathsf{E}[XZ]$ to facilitate calculating the allocation $\mathsf{E}[X_iZ]$. In Section 14.2.1 Step 2 we give the outcome-probability form. □

Stage 2. X has mass points at $\{y_j\}$ and g is (still) continuous.
Now there are jumps $S(y_j-) - S(y_j) = \Pr(X = y_j)$ at a finite or countably infinite number of points. Integration by parts also applies to Riemann-Stieltjes integrals with jumps, Hewitt (1960):

$$\begin{aligned}\rho(X) &= \int_0^\infty g(S(x))\,dx \\ &= \int_0^\infty x g'(S(x)) f(x) dx \\ &\quad + \sum_j y_j \frac{g(S(y_j-)) - g(S(y_j))}{S(y_j-) - S(y_j)} \Pr(X = y_j)\end{aligned}$$

where we see a new summation term representing that part of the expectation contributed by the distorted jumps. We have written out the denominator $S(y_j-) - S(y_j)$ and the canceling factor $\Pr(X = y_j)$ explicitly in order to represent the ratio as $Z(y_j)$.

We now have

$$Z(x) = \begin{cases} g'(S(x)) & S \text{ is continuous at } x \\ \dfrac{g(S(x-)) - g(S(x))}{S(x-) - S(x)} & S \text{ has a jump at } x. \end{cases} \tag{14.8}$$

Stage 3. X **has mass points at** $\{y_j\}$ **including** $\max(X)$ **and** g **is discontinuous (at zero).** This adds nothing to the previous case! X having a jump at $M := \max(X)$ means $S(M-) > 0$ and so the summation in the previous case includes a last term

$$M\frac{g(S(M-)) - g(S(M))}{S(M-) - S(M)} \Pr(X = M) = Mg(\Pr(X = M)).$$

Note that the assumption $\rho(X) < \infty$ implies that $\max(X) < \infty$. If g is not continuous and X is unbounded then $\rho(X) > \max(X)g(0+) = \infty$. This applies in Stages 3 and 4.

Stage 4. X **has mass points at** $\{y_j\}$ **but not at** $\max(X)$ **and** g **is discontinuous (at zero).** In this case, the distorted probability P_g is not absolutely continuous with respect to the original P_X; they disagree on what events have probability zero. Specifically, the original $P_X\{X = M\} = 0$ but $P_g\{X = M\} = g(0+) > 0$. Symbolically, $P_g \not\ll P_X$. This calls for one last term to be added to the expression for $\rho(X)$:

$$\begin{aligned}\rho(X) &= \int_0^\infty g(S(x))\,dx \\ &= \int_0^\infty x g'(S(x)) f(x) dx \\ &\quad + \sum_j y_j \frac{g(S(y_j-)) - g(S(y_j))}{S(y_j-) - S(y_j)} \Pr(X = y_j) \\ &\quad + 1_{P_g \not\ll P_X} g(0+) M.\end{aligned} \tag{14.9}$$

Stage 4 does not change the definition of Z. What is different is the definition of $\rho(X)$:

$$\rho(X) = \begin{cases} \mathsf{E}[XZ(X)] & P_g \ll P_X \\ \mathsf{E}[XZ(X)] + g(0+)\max(X) & \text{otherwise} \end{cases} \tag{14.10}$$

with Z defined by Eq. 14.8.

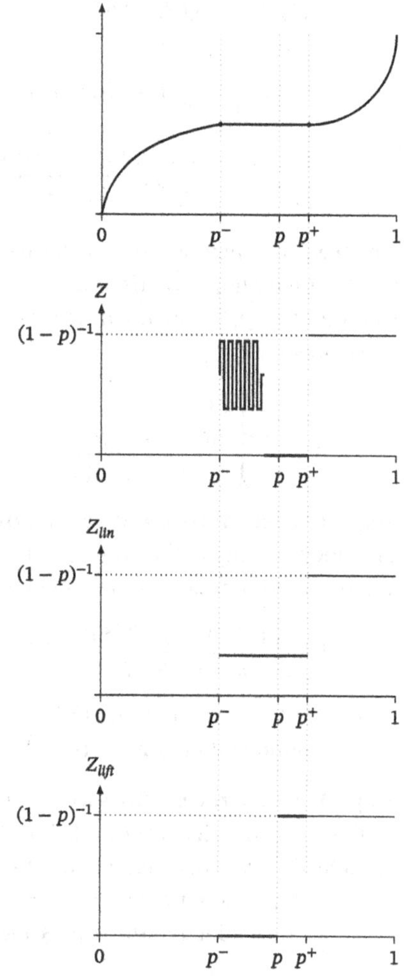

Figure 14.2 Contact functions for TVaR, illustrating the problems caused by flat spots in q_X. Top graph shows $q_X(p)$ plotted against p. The points $p^+ = \mathsf{P}(X \le q_X(p))$ and $p^- = \mathsf{P}(X < q_X(p))$ are shown on the horizontal axis. Three smaller plots show a sample (wiggly) contact function for the natural allocation and the unique linear and lifted natural allocation contact functions. The choices are shown by the thicker lines.

Since Z is a contact function and is constant on sets $X = x$ it must be the linear contact function, by the two properties listed before Definition 11.

Example 239. Consider X depicted in Figure 14.2. The top panel shows the quantile function q_X. It has a flat spot where $\mathsf{P}(X = q_X(p)) > 0$, resulting in

$$\mathsf{P}(X < q_X(p)) < p < \mathsf{P}(X \le q_X(p)).$$

A natural allocation contact function for TVaR_p at X is any non-negative Z, bounded by $(1 - p)^{-1}$, that integrates to 1 and equals $(1-p)^{-1}$ on $\{X > q_X(p)\}$. This leaves a lot of flexibility on $\{X = q_X(p)\}$, and therein lie all our problems! The second panel shows a possible natural allocation Z. The linear natural allocation fixes Z_{lin} by requiring it is constant on $\{X = q_X(p)\}$. It is now fully determined: its value z on $\{X = q_X(p)\}$ solves $z(p^+ - p^-) + (1-p^+)/(1-p) = 1$. It is plotted in the third panel. Finally, the lifted allocation presumes an ordering within

$\{X = q_X(p)\}$ and we select the right hand most part of it. This is the set we would have selected had q_X been increasing. A possible Z_{lift} is plotted on the bottom panel. In all three cases $Z(\omega) = 0$ for $\omega < p^-$. □

Exercise 240. Draw some other possible Z_{lift} functions for Example 239. How are they characterized? □

Having allocated TVaR, we can extend to SRMs by observing that a contact function for a weighted average is the weighted average of the individual contact functions. Many SRMs weight all TVaRs (e.g. see Example 175 for the proportional hazard) and so the problems caused by flat spots in q_X cannot be ignored. But they can be solved using either the linear or lifted approaches.

Example 241. Let's work out the natural allocation for the CCoC SRM from Exercise 228,

$$\rho(X) = \nu \mathsf{E}[X] + \delta \mathsf{TVaR}_1(X)$$

Allocating the mean is easy: the linear contact function is the identity. Allocating $\mathsf{TVaR}_1 = \sup$, the maximum value is trickier. First note that $\rho(X) < \infty$ iff $\sup(X) < \infty$, so we can assume X is bounded. Two cases can occur.

1. If $\mathsf{P}(X = \sup(X)) > 0$ then ρ does not have a unique contact function at X and we must use the linear allocation. The linear contact function is $\tilde{Z} = \mathsf{P}(X = \sup(X))^{-1} 1_{X=\sup(X)}$ since

$$\mathsf{E}[\tilde{Z}X] = \mathsf{P}(X = \sup(X))^{-1}\mathsf{E}[X 1_{X=\sup(X)}] = \mathsf{E}[X \mid X = \sup(X)] = \sup(X).$$

   Therefore the linear natural allocation is

$$D^n \sup{}_X(X_i) = \mathsf{E}[X_i \mid X = \sup(X)]. \tag{14.11}$$

2. If $\mathsf{P}(X = \sup(X)) = 0$ then we are in Stage 4. The associated distortion is not continuous and there is no contact function. There is no robust way to allocate the mass term because it depends on an event with probability zero. But, don't worry: that means it never occurs in a simulation.

The CCoC SRM is usually applied to $X \wedge a$. Case 1 holds provided $\mathsf{P}(X > a) > 0$, in which case $\sup(X \wedge a) = a$. Combining Eq. 14.11 with the mean term shows the linear natural allocation to $X_i(a)$ part of $X \wedge a$ is

$$\begin{aligned} D^n \rho_{X \wedge a}(X_i(a)) &= \nu \mathsf{E}[X_i(a)] + \delta \mathsf{E}[X_i(a) \mid X \wedge a = \sup(X \wedge a)] \\ &= \nu \mathsf{E}[X_i(a)] + \delta a \mathsf{E}[X_i / X \mid X > a]. \end{aligned} \tag{14.12}$$

To apply the lifted natural allocation using X as the lift of $X \wedge a$ also requires $\sup(X) < \infty$ and $\mathsf{P}(X = \sup(X)) > 0$. □

Exercise 242. Continuing Exercise 19. This exercise finds the natural allocation set and linear natural allocation for $\rho = \mathsf{TVaR}_{0.95}$ when applied to the two-unit model in Exercise 19. (Since there is no obvious lift, we do not compute a lifted natural allocation.)

1. There are 252 contact functions to $\mathsf{TVaR}_{0.95}$ at X whose densities take only the values 0 and 20 (the extreme contact functions). What are they?

2. What are the allocations given by each contact function in (1)? Do any produce a 50/50 allocation?
3. Describe the set of *all* contact functions.
4. Using the results of (3), describe the natural allocation *set* for each unit.
5. Pick one of the contact functions Z from (1). Show that

$$\tilde{Z}(\omega) := \mathsf{E}[Z \mid X](\omega) = \mathsf{E}[Z \mid X = X(\omega)] = \begin{cases} 0 & \omega < 90 \\ 10 & 90 \le \omega < 100. \end{cases}$$

6. Confirm $\tilde{Z}$ is consistent with Eq. 14.8 at $x = 200$ and $x = 1000$.
7. Confirm that the linear natural allocation, computed using the contact function $\tilde{Z}$, results in a 50/50 allocation, i.e. check $\mathsf{E}[X_1\tilde{Z}] = \mathsf{E}[X_2\tilde{Z}] = 500$.
8. Explain why

$$\lim_{t\downarrow 0} \frac{\rho(X + tX_1) - \rho(X)}{t} = 1000$$

and

$$\lim_{t\uparrow 0} \frac{\rho(X + tX_1) - \rho(X)}{t} = 0.$$

What is the significance of these two limits being different?
9. Let $g(s) = 0.9s + 0.1$ if $s > 0$ and $g(0) = 0$ be the CCoC distortion with cost of capital $1/9 = 0.1\dot{1}$. Show that $\rho_g(X) = 352$. Mirroring the notation from (5), show that

$$\tilde{Z}(x) = \begin{cases} 0.9 & x = 200 \\ 1.9 & x = 1000 \\ 0 & \text{otherwise,} \end{cases}$$

and confirm that $\mathsf{E}[X_i\tilde{Z}] = \rho_g(X)/2$.
10. Let $g(s) = \sqrt{s}$. Show that $\rho_g(X) = 452.98$,

$$\tilde{Z}(x) = \begin{cases} \frac{1-\sqrt{0.1}}{1-0.1} = 0.7597 & x = 200 \\ \frac{\sqrt{0.1}}{0.1} = 3.1623 & x = 1000 \\ S(x)^{-1/2}/2 & \text{otherwise,} \end{cases}$$

and confirm that $\mathsf{E}[X_i\tilde{Z}] = \rho_g(X)/2$.
11. Is the failure of $\mathsf{TVaR}_{0.95}$ to be differentiable at X a property of X or of the risk measure $\mathsf{TVaR}_{0.95}$?

Solutions.

1. Any function of the form $Z = 20 \cdot 1_A$, where A is a subset of five elements from $\{90, \dots, 99\}$. There are $\binom{10}{5} = 252$ ways of picking a set of five elements from a set of ten.

2. Depending on which A we select, we can produce an allocation of 1000/0, 800/200, 600/400, 400/600, 200/800, or 0/1000. Alas, none of these equals the desired 500/500.
3. The set of all contact functions can be obtained as convex combinations of the functions in (1). There are a *lot* of contact functions.
4. The set of natural allocations equals the set of convex combinations of the allocations in (2) since $\mathsf{E}[X_i \sum_j w_j Z_j] = \sum_i w_j \mathsf{E}[X_i Z_j]$. *Either unit can be allocated anywhere between zero and 1000*, with the complement allocated to the other! This highlights the value of a privileged contact function such as $\tilde{Z}$ used in the linear natural allocation.
5. $\tilde{Z}$ is constant on $X = X(\omega)$ and has the same integral (sum product) as Z over such sets.
6. For $\mathsf{TVaR}_{0.95}$, $g(s) = 20s \wedge 1$. When $x = 200$, $S(x) = 0.1$, $S(x-) = 1$, and therefore $g(S(x)) = g(S(x-)) = 1$ showing $Z(200) = 0$. When $x = 1000$, $S(x) = 0$, $S(x-) = 0.1$, and therefore $g(S(x)) = 0$, $g(S(x-)) = 1$ showing $Z(1000) = (1-0)/(0.1-0) = 10$.
7. Easy calculation.
8. When $t > 0$, the five largest values of $X + tX_1$ are equal to $1000(1+t)$, they occur when $X_1 = 1000$, and the limit equals 1000. When $t < 0$, the five largest values are equal to 1000, but they occur when $X_2 = 1000$, and the limit equals 0. Since the limits from above and below are different, the limit $t \to 0$ does not exist, and we cannot hope for an allocation with a marginal interpretation. Delbaen's Theorem 2 implies that the contact function is not unique—as we saw in (1). ρ is balanced on a knife edge at X—like the kink in $|x|$ at 0—and a slight perturbation either way causes a discontinuous shift in our view of the more risky unit. Unfortunately, this behavior is common. Even if ρ is differentiable at X, there are nearby X' where ρ is not differentiable.
9. Easy calculation. X has a mass at 1000 and the jump at $g(0+)$ is included in Z.
10. Only the two probability masses of X are used to compute the expectation.
11. It is a property of X and not TVaR. The same logic shows that neither the SRM defined by the proportional hazard nor the CCoC distortion is differentiable at X. □

Remark 243. nondifferentiable points are, alas, very common, and we are often forced to use the linear allocation.

1. For any coherent risk measure ρ, any continuous random variable X is arbitrarily close to a variable X' at which ρ is not differentiable. Simply take a small $A \subset \Omega$ and let $X' = \mathsf{E}[X \mid A]$ on A and $X' = X$ otherwise. Thus, ρ has a lot of kinks.
2. It gets even worse. It is possible to find risk measures that are nowhere differentiable! See Phelps (1993), Example 1.21. □

14.2 Computing the Natural Allocations

In this section, we give a detailed explanation showing how to compute the linear and lifted natural allocations for continuous random variables. The reader who wants to apply the methods to a discrete probability space might skim this section and concentrate on the examples in Chapter 15.

The decision path for the allocations we have discussed is laid out in Figure 14.3.

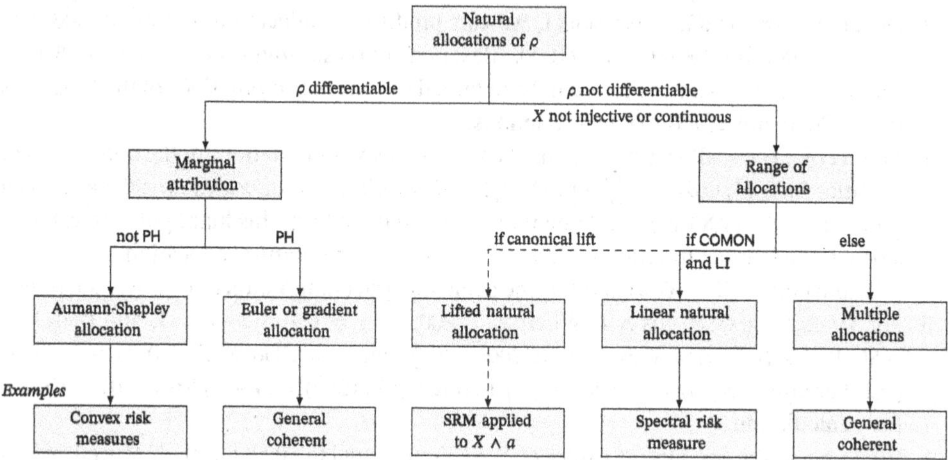

Figure 14.3 Conditions and properties for allocations of coherent risk measures, with example risk measure types.

14.2.1 Algorithm to Compute the Linear Natural Allocation

Step 1. Setup. Given an SRM ρ associated with a distortion function g and a loss random variable $X = \sum_{i=1}^{n} X_i$, with X, X_i defined on a probability space Ω, we want to allocate $\rho(X)$ to each unit using a unique contact function to ρ at X.

Step 2: Move X to sample space $\mathbb{R}$. X defines a random variable $X(x) = x$ on $\mathbb{R}$ with distribution function $F(x) := \mathsf{P}(X \le x)$. (Since X is a loss random variable, it is actually defined on $[0, \infty) \subset \mathbb{R}$.) The expectation of X can be computed using the outcome-probability form

$$\mathsf{E}[X] = \int_{\mathbb{R}} x dF_X(x).$$

The integral is a Riemann-Stieltjes integral. It can handle jumps (probability masses) in F.

Step 3: Extend to units X_i. The next step is similarly to turn each X_i into a function on $[0, \infty)$ so that we can integrate it with respect to $F(x)$. This is accomplished by replacing X_i with

$$\kappa_i(x) := \mathsf{E}[X_i \mid X = x]. \tag{14.13}$$

(The κ_i function is covered in depth in Section 14.3.1.) X_i is replaced by its average value over X outcomes, consistent with the grouping in step 2.

A result of steps 2 and 3 is that for each value of $X = x$ the set of states $\{\omega \mid X(\omega) = x\}$ is effectively collapsed to a single point. The collapsing emerges as a group-and-summarize process in discrete applications, Chapter 15. If X is one-to-one, then there is no collapsing, each state $X = x$ is identified with a unique ω and unit value list $X_1, \dots, X_n$, and the contact function is unique.

Technical Remark 244. The situation is more complicated for continuous variables. For example, let $X = X_1 + X_2$, where X_i are independent, continuous loss random variables. In that case, X is not one-to-one but still has a strictly increasing quantile function and a unique contact function. Although each set $X = x$ has probability zero, we still need to use Eq. 14.13. □

Step 4. Apply the probability distortion. We know how g acts on survival and distribution functions: it changes $S(x)$ into $g(S(x))$ and F into F_g defined by

$$F_g(x) := 1 - g(1 - F(x)).$$

Step 5: Apply properties of g to identify Z, the density and jumps of $F_g(x)$. The idea is to write gS as the integral of its derivative, with an adjustment for the jumps, as described in Section 14.1.5.

Step 6. Compute allocations. The linear natural allocation is computed using Z from Eq. 14.8 in parallel with Eq. 14.9, and including a *co-max* allocation of the mass if needed:

$$\begin{aligned} D^n\rho_X(X_i) &= \mathsf{E}[X_i Z(X)] + 1_{\mathsf{P}_g \not\ll \mathsf{P}_X} g(0+)\mathsf{E}[X_i \mid X = \max(X)] \\ &= \int_0^\infty \kappa_i(x) g'(S(x)) f(x) dx \\ &\quad + \sum_j \kappa_i(y_j)(g(S(y_j-)) - g(S(y_j))) \\ &\quad + 1_{\mathsf{P}_g \not\ll \mathsf{P}_X} g(0+)\kappa_i(M). \end{aligned} \tag{14.14}$$

The last term is only needed when $\mathsf{P}(X = \max(X)) = 0$ and only meaningful when $\max(X) < \infty$. When it is needed, we interpret it as

$$\lim_{t \uparrow \max(X)} \mathsf{E}[X_i \mid X > t]. \tag{14.15}$$

These steps are illustrated in Chapter 15. They are easy to carry out in a simulation spreadsheet.

It is possible to construct perverse examples where the limit Eq. 14.15 does not exist.

Exercise 245. Let $X(\omega) = 1 - \omega$ be uniform on $\Omega = [0, 1]$. We construct $X = X_1 + X_2$ so that the limit Eq. 14.15 does not exist. $\max(X) = 1$, achieved at $\omega = 0$. Define

$$X_1(\omega) = \begin{cases} \omega & 2^{-2n-1} < \omega < 2^{-2n} \\ 0 & 2^{-2n-2} < \omega < 2^{-2n-1} \end{cases}$$

and $X_2 = X - X_1$. Compute $\mathsf{E}[X_1 \mid X < 2^{-m}]$ as a function of m and hence show Eq. 14.15 does not exist. □

Remark 246. Theory, presented in De Waegenaere, Kast, and Lapied (2003), assures us that pricing with a law invariant, coherent risk measure is consistent with a general equilibrium model. Working with a non-additive measure like ρ is consistent with no-arbitrage and modern finance. □

Remark 247. Our concern throughout with the case $g(0+) > 0$ may seem excessive. However, the CCoC distortion, which is very common in application, has this property, meaning it is an important case in practice. □

14.2.2 Algorithm to Compute the Lifted Natural Allocation

In this section, we describe how to compute the lifted natural allocation for X using a comonotonic and one-to-one lift $\tilde{X}$. Typically, X is a function of $\tilde{X}$, e.g. $\tilde{X} \wedge a$. The objective is to allocate $\rho(X)$ to X_i. Typically, $X = \sum_i X_i$.

The lifted natural allocation relies on $\tilde{X}$ having a unique contact function Z. Z is given by Eq. 14.8 applied to $\tilde{X}$. Then we use Eq. 14.14 to compute

$$D^f \rho_{X,\tilde{X}}(X_i) = \mathsf{E}[X_i Z] + 1_{\mathsf{P}_g \not\ll \mathsf{P}_X} g(0+) \mathsf{E}[X_i \mid \tilde{X} = \max(\tilde{X})].$$

Again, the second term is only needed when $\mathsf{P}(X = \max(X)) = 0$ and $g(0+) > 0$, which is possible, but very unusual in practice. When $g(0+) > 0$ and $\tilde{X}$ is unbounded, $\rho(\tilde{X})$ is infinite, but $\rho(X)$ may be finite. In particular, $\rho(\tilde{X} \wedge a) \le a$ is always finite.

The algorithm proceeds along the lines of the linear natural allocation.

Remark 248. When X is not one-to-one, and so does not define a lift of $X \wedge a$, it can still contain useful information about the set $X > a$. We can apply that information to allocate $\rho(X \wedge a)$ by using the linear contact function for X. The linear allocation for $X \wedge a$ computes

$$\mathsf{E}[\mathsf{E}[X_i(a) \mid X \wedge a]\mathsf{E}[Z_a \mid X \wedge a]]$$

where Z_a is any contact function for $X \wedge a$. A quasi-lifted version computes

$$\mathsf{E}[\mathsf{E}[X_i(a) \mid X]\mathsf{E}[Z \mid X]]$$

where Z is any contact function for X. The two expressions differ only on $X > a$ where the linear allocation gives

$$a\mathsf{E}\left[\frac{X_i}{X} 1_{X \ge a}\right]$$

versus

$$a\mathsf{E}\left[\frac{X_i}{X} 1_{X \ge a} \mathsf{E}[Z \mid X]\right]$$

incorporating information in X. The second expression allocates more to thick-tailed units. Notice that the outcome $X = a$ gets merged into $X > a$ by $X \wedge a$ if we only know $X_i(a)$. That is, we cannot tell whether we are given a scenario where losses equal a or exceed a. □

14.2.3 Dependence on Assumptions

The lifted natural allocation of $X \wedge a$ depends on a remarkable confluence of circumstances, depending on all of the assumptions implied by ρ being an SRM and equal priority in default.

1. ρ is an SRM yields the representation by a concave increasing associated distortion, and ensures it is coherent, law invariant, and comonotonic additive.
2. Convex analysis implies an increasing concave function is continuous on $(0, 1]$.
3. The continuity of the associated distortion ensures the adjusted probability function is absolutely continuous with respect to the original probabilities.
4. As a result, we can compute a unique linear contact function Z, using Eq. 14.8.
5. Law invariance lets us replace X, defined on an arbitrary probability space, with a simpler random variable defined on $[0, \infty)$ combined with probabilities defined by the distribution of X.
6. Law invariance and equal priority in default are needed for us to replace X_i with $\mathsf{E}[X_i \mid X]$:
   a. Law invariance ensures the value of X is all that matters to ρ, not the specific state or split of loss by unit, and
   b. Equal priority guarantees that the expected recovery to X_i given X equals the recovery afforded to $\mathsf{E}[X_i \mid X]$, since the pro rata factor $X \wedge a / X$ is a function of X. We make this replacement so we can use the contact function in (4) and probability in (5).
7. Finally, we can allocate to $X_i(a)$ as part of $X \wedge a$ using the (lifted or linear) contact function defined by X because ρ is comonotonic additive and X and $X \wedge a$ are comonotonic.

Remark 249. For equal priority, circumstance (6b) means we can work with X_i or $\mathsf{E}[X_i \mid X]$ and get the same expected recovery:

$$\mathsf{E}[X_i(a)] = \mathsf{E}\left[\mathsf{E}\left[X_i \frac{X \wedge a}{X} \mid X\right]\right] = \mathsf{E}\left[\mathsf{E}[X_i \mid X] \frac{X \wedge a}{X}\right].$$

This substitution can fail for some priority rules. Section 12.3 introduces a common deductible rule: find $d = d(X_1, \dots, X_n)$ so that

$$\sum_i (X_i - d)^+ = X \wedge a$$

and pay $X_i^{(d)}(a) := (X_i - d)^+$ to unit i. Now

$$\mathsf{E}[X_i^{(d)}(a)] = \mathsf{E}[\mathsf{E}[(X_i - d(X_1, \dots, X_n))^+ \mid X] \neq \mathsf{E}[(\mathsf{E}[X_i \mid X] - d(X_1, \dots, X_n))^+].$$

For example, if $X_1 = X_2 = 10$ and $a = 10$, then both units receive 5. But if $X_1 = 18$ and $X_2 = 2$, then unit 1 receives 10 and unit 2 nothing. In both cases $X = 20$. If the two outcomes are equally likely then $\mathsf{E}[X_1 \mid X = 20] = 14$ and $\mathsf{E}[X_2 \mid X = 20] = 6$, which is allocated as 9 and 1, not the average of the actual allocations. In practice, equal priority is near universal. □

14.3 A Closer Look at Unit Funding

So far in this chapter, we have presented the allocation of a coherent (possibly spectral) risk measure ρ with no commitment as to whether it represented capital, premium, or something else. In this section, we commit to interpreting ρ as a pricing SRM in the context of allocating $\rho(X \wedge a)$ to units $X_i(a)$. We study the intricacies of the funding equation as it operates within and across layers and units. While this section might have been titled "unit capital structure", we want to emphasize it is more about margin than capital.

We introduce three functions, κ, α, and β, to facilitate this analysis by way of nicely symmetric and easy to use formulas for the lifted natural allocation. We also show how they can be used to create helpful visualizations that make properties of the natural allocation more intuitive and accessible.

Throughout the section we assume equal priority in default, Section 12.3, assets a are exogenous, and the pricing risk measure is given by a spectral risk measure ρ associated with the distortion g. We also assume total unlimited losses X have a strictly increasing quantile function, so ρ is differentiable at X and X defines a lift of $X \wedge a$. We assume that default is possible $\mathsf{P}(X > a) > 0$ where necessary to avoid complications when $g(0+) > 0$. Finally, all integrals are interpreted as Riemann-Stieltjes integrals, allowing for jumps, including possible jumps at the upper and lower limits of integration.

14.3.1 Conditional Expected Loss: κ

The conditional expectation of loss by unit given the total loss is important in Step 5 of Section 14.2.1. It is the first of our three functions:

$$\kappa_i(x) := \mathsf{E}[X_i \mid X = x]. \tag{14.16}$$

In any expression of the form $\mathsf{E}[X_i h(X)]$ (compare co-measures), X_i can be replaced by $\kappa_i(X)$ since $\mathsf{E}[X_i h(X)] = \mathsf{E}[\mathsf{E}[X_i h(X) \mid X]] = \mathsf{E}[\mathsf{E}[X_i \mid X]h(X)] = \mathsf{E}[\kappa_i(X)h(X)]$ by the tower property. This simple trick often pays big dividends. In general, evaluating an expression like $\mathsf{E}[X_1 h(X)]$ requires knowing the full bivariate distribution of X_1, X. But using κ_i reduces it to a one dimensional problem. In spreadsheet terms, we can compute $\mathsf{E}[X_i h(X)]$ from three columns, containing X, $\kappa_i(X)$, and the probability of each row. We do not need an array of X_1, X pair probabilities. This is even true if X_i are correlated.

Examples 250. Here are several examples of κ_i functions.

1. If Y_i are independent and identically distributed and $X_n = Y_1 + \cdots + Y_n$ then

$$\mathsf{E}[X_m \mid X_{m+n} = x] = mx/(m+n)$$

   for $m \geq 1, n \geq 0$. This is obvious when $m = 1$ because $\mathsf{E}[Y_i \mid X_n]$ are independent of $i = 1, \dots, n$ and sum to x. The result follows because conditional expectations are linear. In this case $\kappa_i(x) = mx/(m+n)$ is a line through the origin.
2. If X_i are multivariate normal then κ_i are straight lines, given by the usual least-squares fits

$$\kappa_i(x) = \mathsf{E}[X_i] + \frac{\mathsf{cov}(X_i, X)}{\mathsf{var}(X)}(x - \mathsf{E}[X]).$$

   This example is familiar from the securities market line and the β-CAPM analysis of stock returns. If X_i are iid it reduces to example (1) because the slope is $1/n$.

3. If X_i, $i = 1, 2$, are compound Poisson with the same severity distribution then κ_i are again lines through the origin. Suppose X_i has random claim count N_i. Conditional on $N_1 = m, N_2 = n$, we have the same situation as item 1 above: $\mathsf{E}[X_1 \mid X_1 + X_2 = x] = mx/(m+n)$. Unconditionally, we have a linear combination of such linear functions, namely $\kappa_1(x) = \mathsf{E}[N_1/(N_1+N_2)]x$. The common severity is essential. The result means that if a unit is defined to be a group of policies that shares the same severity distribution, then premiums for policies within the unit have rates proportional to their expected ratios of claim counts.
4. A theorem of Efron says that if X_i are independent and have log-concave densities then all κ_i are nondecreasing (Saumard and Wellner 2014). The multivariate normal example is a special case of Efron's theorem.
5. For two units X_1, X_2 with unit 1 having thinner tail, the archetypal behavior is κ_1 looks like $X \wedge a$ and κ_2 looks like $(X - a)^+$. See Hu/SCS Case in Section 15.4.1.
6. Combining thick-tailed distributions, which do not have log-concave densities, can produce humped, non-monotone κ. See the Cat/Non-Cat Case in Section 15.4.1.
7. In general it is easy to make examples where κ_i has bizarre behavior. For example take X_i compound Poisson with claim count 1, and severities Y_1 a 1000 xs 0 layer from a distribution with a large mean and Y_2 a 1100 xs 0 layer. The likelihood of a full limit loss from unit 1 when losses are between 1000 and 1100 produces discontinuous behavior in κ. □

Exercise 251. Assume X consists of n independent units, each distributed normally with mean μ_i and variance σ_i^2. Let pricing be given by a Wang transform distortion with parameter λ and assume assets a are large enough that the probability of portfolio insolvency is negligible (i.e. treat it as zero). What is the total margin on the portfolio? What is the natural allocation of margin to each component?

Solution. Let $\mu = \sum \mu_i$ and $\sigma^2 = \sum \sigma_i^2$. Applying Exercise 192 shows the total margin is $\lambda\sigma$. Now derive the natural allocations. Example 250, item 2

$$\kappa_i(x) = \mu_i + \frac{\sigma_i^2}{\sigma^2}(x - \mu)$$

$$\implies \mathsf{E}_\mathsf{Q}[\kappa_i(X)] = \mu_i + \frac{\sigma_i^2}{\sigma^2}(\mathsf{E}_\mathsf{Q}[X] - \mu)$$

$$= \mu_i + \lambda\frac{\sigma_i^2}{\sigma}$$

showing margin is allocated in proportion to the component variances. Remember $\rho(X) = \mathsf{E}_\mathsf{Q}[X]$. □

Exercise 252. Denuit and Dhaene (2012) consider an interesting risk sharing mechanism where each pool member pays $\kappa_i(X)$ and receives X_i. Would you subscribe to such a pool (a) if your loss is relatively thin-tailed compared to the other risks? (b) relatively thick-tailed? Why? □

14.3.2 Expected Loss by Asset Level

By Eq. 3.7, under limited liability, expected total losses are a function of assets

$$\bar{S}(a) := \mathsf{E}[X \wedge a] = \int_0^a S(x)\,dx \tag{14.17}$$

and therefore the loss density in the layer at a is $d\bar{S}(a)/da = S(a)$.

Expected losses for unit i are denoted $\bar{S}_i(a) := \mathsf{E}[X_i(a)]$. They can be computed by conditioning on X, to give

$$\bar{S}_i(a) = \mathsf{E}[\mathsf{E}[X_i(a) \mid X]] = \mathsf{E}[X_i \mid X \le a]F(a) + a\mathsf{E}\left[\frac{X_i}{X} \mid X > a\right]S(a) \tag{14.18}$$

$$= \int_0^a \kappa_i(x)\,dF(x) + a\alpha_i(a)S(a) \tag{14.19}$$

where we introduce the new function α_i defined by

$$\alpha_i(a)S(a) = \mathsf{E}\left[\frac{X_i}{X}1_{X>a}\right] = \int_a^\infty \frac{\kappa_i(x)}{x}\,dF(x). \tag{14.20}$$

The two substitutions of κ_i in Eq. 14.19 and 14.20 follow by conditioning X_i (resp. X_i/X) on X and using the tower property. The function α_i appears in Eq. 14.12, the natural allocation of the CCoC SRM.

The value $\alpha_i(x)$ is the expected proportion of recoveries by unit i in $1_{X>x}$, the layer at x. Since total assets available to pay losses are 1, and the chance the layer attaches is $S(x)$, it is intuitively clear $\alpha_i(x)S(x)$ is the derivative of $\bar{S}_i(x)$ with respect to x. We now show this, in two ways.

Differentiate Eq. 14.19 with respect to a, term-by-term. Apply the product rule to the second term as a times the rest, substituting the integral expression in Eq. 14.20 for $\alpha_i(a)S(a)$. Assuming $F(x)$ is continuous with density $f(x)$ we obtain

$$\begin{aligned}\frac{d}{da}\bar{S}(a) &= \kappa_i(a)f(a) + \alpha_i(a)S(a) - a\frac{\kappa_i(a)}{a}f(a)\\ &= \alpha_i(a)S(a).\end{aligned}$$

We could also integrate $\alpha_i(x)S(x)$ using integration by parts $\int u dv = uv - \int v du$ with substitutions $u = \alpha_i(x)S(x)$ and $v = x$, to compute

$$\begin{aligned}\int_0^a \alpha_i(x)S(x)\,dx &= x\alpha_i(x)S(x)\Big|_0^a + \int_0^a x\,\frac{\kappa_i(x)}{x}f(x)\,dx\\ &= a\alpha_i(a)S(a) + \int_0^a \kappa_i(x)\,dF(x)\\ &= \bar{S}_i(a).\end{aligned}$$

Either way, we conclude that unit i loss density in the asset layer at a, i.e. the derivative of Eq. 14.18 with respect to a, is

$$S_i(a) = \alpha_i(a)S(a).$$

To recap, we have a wonderful survival function form relationship

$$\bar{S}_i(a) = \mathsf{E}[X_i(a)] = \int_0^a \alpha_i(x)S(x)dx \tag{14.21}$$

giving a direct analog to Eq. 14.17 for unit i losses.

14.3.3 Premium by Asset Level

We denote the lifted natural allocation of premium to $X_i(a)$ as part of X by $\bar{P}_i(a)$. By definition of the lifted natural allocation and equal priority and using Z from Eq. 14.8 we obtain the following formula for unit i premium:

$$\begin{aligned}\bar{P}_i(a) :=& D^f \rho_{X\wedge a,X}(X_i(a)) \\ =& \mathsf{E}[X_i(a)Z(X)] \\ =& \mathsf{E}[\kappa_i(X)Z(X) \mid X \le a](1 - S(a)) + \\ & \qquad a\mathsf{E}[(X_i/X)Z(X) \mid X > a]S(a),\end{aligned} \tag{14.22}$$

which is a direct analog of Eq. 14.18.

Our third useful function is the expectation in the second term of Eq. 14.22

$$\beta_i(a)g(S(a)) := \mathsf{E}\left[\frac{X_i}{X}Z(X)1_{X>a}\right] = \int_a^\infty \frac{\kappa_i(x)}{x}Z(x)\,dF(x). \tag{14.23}$$

The value $\beta_i(x)$ is the *risk-adjusted* expected proportion of recoveries by unit i in $1_{X>x}$. Notice its similarity to α_i, Eq. 14.20. In finance $\beta_i(x)$ would be called the fair market value of the recoveries to unit i of 1 paid in total in default, i.e. $1_{X>a}$.

Just as with α and losses, $\beta_i(x)g(S(x))$ is the derivative of $\bar{P}_i(x)$ with respect to x. This can be seen as follows. From Eq. 14.23 and the fundamental theorem of calculus,

$$\frac{d}{dx}(\beta_i(x)g(S(x))) = -\frac{\kappa_i(x)}{x}Z(x). \tag{14.24}$$

Now use integration by parts $\int u dv = uv - \int v du$ with substitutions $u = \beta_i(x)S(x)$ and $v = x$, to compute

$$\begin{aligned}\int_0^a \beta_i(x)g(S(x))\,dx &= x\beta_i(x)g(S(x))\Big|_0^a + \int_0^a x\,\frac{\kappa_i(x)}{x}Z(x)\,dF(x) \\ &= a\beta_i(a)g(S(a)) + \mathsf{E}[\kappa_i(X)Z(X) \mid X \le a](1 - g(S(a))) \\ &= \bar{P}_i(a)\end{aligned}$$

by Eq. 14.22. Therefore the unit i premium density in the asset layer at a, i.e. the derivative of Eq. 14.22 with respect to a, is

$$P_i(a) = \beta_i(a)g(S(a)).$$

We get the premium analog of the survival function form Eq. 14.21

$$\bar{P}_i(a) = \mathsf{E}_\mathsf{Q}[X_i(a)] = \int_0^a \beta_i(x)g(S(x))dx \tag{14.25}$$

and a direct analog to Eq. 14.21 for unit i premium. The analog in outcome-probability form Eq. 14.19 is

$$\bar{P}_i(a) = \int_0^a \kappa_i(x)g'(S(x))dF(x) + a\beta_i(a)g(S(a)). \tag{14.26}$$

We can also write β using E_Q where Q is the probability scenario with density Z. By (Follmer and Schied, 2016, Proposition A.16)

$$\mathsf{E}_\mathsf{Q}[X \mid A] = \frac{\mathsf{E}[XZ \mid A]}{\mathsf{E}[Z \mid A]}. \tag{14.27}$$

In our situation, $\mathsf{E}[Z \mid X > a] = g(S(a))/S(a)$. Therefore, starting with Eq. 14.23 and dividing top and bottom by $S(a)$ in the second line,

$$\begin{aligned}\beta_i(a) :=& \frac{\mathsf{E}[(X_i/X)Z1_{X>a}]}{g(S(a))} \\ =& \frac{\mathsf{E}[(X_i/X)Z \mid X > a]}{\mathsf{E}[Z \mid X > a]} \\ =& \mathsf{E}_\mathsf{Q}[X_i/X \mid X > a].\end{aligned}$$

As a result, the lifted natural allocation premium for unit i at part of X under equal priority and when total losses are supported by assets a, is given by any of the following three expressions

$$\begin{aligned}D^f\rho_{X\wedge a,X}(X_i(a)) &= \mathsf{E}_\mathsf{Q}[X_i \mid X \le a](1 - g(S(a))) + a\mathsf{E}_\mathsf{Q}\left[\frac{X_i}{X} \mid X > a\right]g(S(a)) \\ &= \mathsf{E}[X_iZ \mid X \le a](1 - S(a)) + a\mathsf{E}\left[\frac{X_i}{X}Z \mid X > a\right]S(a) \\ &= \int_0^a \beta_i(x)g(S(x))\,dx.\end{aligned}$$

Notice the use of $g(S(a))$ in the first line and $S(a)$ in the second, explained by Eq. 14.27.

14.3.4 The Case with No Default

It is instructive to work out the special case with no default, to gain more insight into how premiums are determined by unit while avoiding the extra complication caused by default. If X is unbounded and premium is finite, no default implies $a = \infty$ and that g is continuous. If X is bounded it implies $a \ge \sup(X)$.

From a practical perspective assuming no default is not unreasonable. Most insurance companies have a very low annual probability of default. Indeed, Schlesinger (2012) says insolvency is "always present for an insurable risk, but almost universally ignored in insurance theory." Premiums are dominated by what happens in solvent scenarios, despite much of the allocation literature being focused on default. It is a rare and unusual circumstance to see default explicitly factored into a practical pricing problem, although most ERM programs haircut catastrophe reinsurance recoveries for potential default.

In the spirit of simplicity, we also assume X and g are both continuous, so $Z(x) = g'(S(x))$. Assuming no default means we are *almost* in the situation of Model A-D from Chapter 12. However, unlike traditional finance theories, where the pricing operator is linear, ρ is not linear. It is only sublinear, Section 5.2.9. Linearity fails because the risk adjustment varies with X and so in general X, Y and $X + Y$ all have different risk-adjusted probabilities.

Assuming no default simplifies the analysis because the default term vanishes in all applications of integration by parts:

$$\begin{aligned}\int_0^\infty S(x)\,dx &= xS(x)\Big|_0^\infty + \int_0^\infty xf(x)\,dx \\ &= \int_0^\infty xf(x)\,dx.\end{aligned}$$

The formulas for loss and premium density are unchanged: $S_i(x) = \alpha_i(x)S(x)$ and $P_i(x) = \beta_i(x)g(S(x))$ and they still depend on the asset layer x. The formulas for total premium and loss are no longer functions of a. We can assume $a = \infty$ and drop a as an argument. The loss and premium formulas become

$$\bar{S} = \mathsf{E}[X] = \int_0^\infty S(x)\,dx \tag{14.28}$$

$$\bar{S}_i = \mathsf{E}[X_i] = \int_0^\infty \kappa_i(x)f(x)\,dx \tag{14.29}$$

$$\bar{P} = \int_0^\infty g(S(x))\,dx \tag{14.30}$$

$$\bar{P}_i = \int_0^\infty \kappa_i(x)g'(S(x))f(x)\,dx, \tag{14.31}$$

compare Eq. 14.18 and 14.22.

When X is defined on sample space $\Omega = [0, 1]$, we can change variables to express Eqs. (14.29) and (14.31) in terms of $p \in [0, 1]$, see Section 10.4. The unit-specific expected losses and premiums simply replace x by $\kappa_i(x)$. For losses we substitute $1-p = S(x)$, $dp = f(x)dx$, $x = q(p)$, to get

$$\bar{S}_i = \int_0^1 \kappa_i(q(p))\,dp. \tag{14.32}$$

For premium we substitute $1 - \tilde{p} = g(S(x))$, $d\tilde{p} = g'(S(x))f(x)dx$, $x = q(1 - g^{-1}(1 - \tilde{p}))$, to get

$$\bar{P}_i = \int_0^1 \kappa_i(q(1 - g^{-1}(1 - \tilde{p})))\, d\tilde{p}. \tag{14.33}$$

The right hand plot in Figure 10.4 illustrates the last integral. It is tempting to scale the allocation given by $\kappa_i(q(1 - g^{-1}(1 - \tilde{p})))$ up along the vertical arrow, that is, to scale premium like loss. Such a "proportional spread" scaling is a common actuarial practice, Venter (2004), but as Sherris (2006) points out it is an arbitrary and economically unmotivated choice. The vertical shift is like a dis-utility, increasing the loss in bad outcomes, but it does not correspond to a single utility function because the transformation depends on the distribution of X.

Remark 253. The assumption g is continuous is not innocuous. When g is not continuous, premium can be heavily influenced by the maximum value taken by X, even in the absence of default. □

14.3.5 Summary of Allocation Formulas

The allocation formulas we have derived are laid out in Table 14.4.

To recap: the formulas Eq. 14.22 and 14.25—labeled Conditioning expectation and Survival integral expectation in Table 14.4—give the lifted natural allocations as part of X. They have been derived assuming q_X is strictly increasing, capital is priced using a distortion function g, and there is equal priority in default. They are computationally tractable and require *no other assumptions*. There is no need to assume the X_i are independent.

Eq. 14.22 is a direct premium analog of Eq. 14.18. Eq. 14.22 is the same as Tsanakas and Barnett (2003) Eq. (19), although their derivation is in the context of a homogeneous portfolio whereas our portfolio is static. Eq. 14.25 identifies the premium density, giving an allocation of premium and a premium analog of Eq. 14.21. It provides a clear and illuminating way to visualize risk by collapsing a multidimensional problem to one dimension, see the examples in Chapter 15.

The allocation reflects the value of payments to insureds implicit in the cost of capital distortion function. It is not necessary—indeed, it is economically incorrect—to select another allocation. We have an entirely general, canonical determination of premium in the presence of shared costly capital. Grundl and Schmeiser (2007) pointed out that with an additive pricing functional, Model A, B, or C there is no need to allocate capital in order to price. Here we have extended that result to the situation of a non-additive pricing functional.

In Eq. 14.22, the action of equal priority allocation only has an effect when $X > a$. For outcomes $X < a$, the vast majority of the time, the actual loss X_i is used unchanged. So far, our analysis has assumed a static portfolio with an exogenous, and fixed, a. If one adopts a marginal cost allocation for insolvency scenarios (Chapter 20), the $a\mathsf{E}_{\mathsf{Q}}[...]$ term is replaced by a different allocation of a, but the first summand remains the same. Therefore, using

Table 14.4 All the different ways of computing expected losses and the lifted natural allocation.

Quantity	Loss	Premium
Cash flow	$X_i(a) = X_i \dfrac{X \wedge a}{X}$	N/a
Probability	Objective, $S(x)$, $f(x)$	Risk adjusted, Q, $g(S(x))$, $g'(S(x))f(x)$
Expectation	$\bar{S}_i(a) = \mathsf{E}[X_i(a)]$	$\bar{P}_i(a) = \mathsf{E}_{\mathsf{Q}}[X_i(a)] = \mathsf{E}[X_i(a)g'(S(X))]$
Conditional layer expectation	$\kappa_i(x) = \mathsf{E}[X_i \mid X = x]$	also $= \mathsf{E}_{\mathsf{Q}}[X_i \mid X = x]$
Conditioning expectation	$\mathsf{E}[X_i \mid X \le a]F(a) + a\mathsf{E}[X_i/X \mid X > a]S(a)$	$\mathsf{E}_{\mathsf{Q}}[X_i \mid X \le a](1 - g(S(a))) + a\mathsf{E}_{\mathsf{Q}}[X_i/X \mid X > a]g(S(a))$
Share function	$\alpha_i(x) = \mathsf{E}[X_i/X \mid X > x]$	$\beta_i(x) = \mathsf{E}_{\mathsf{Q}}[X_i/X \mid X > x] = \mathsf{E}[(X_i/X)g'S(X)) \mid X > x]$
Derivative of share function	$(\alpha S)'(x) = -\kappa_i(x)f(x)/x$	$(\beta g(S))'(x) = -\kappa_i(x)g'(S(x))f(x)/x$
Survival integral expectation	$\int_0^a \alpha_i(x)S(x)\,dx$	$\int_0^a \beta_i(x)g(S(x))\,dx$
Outcome integral expectation	$\int_0^a \kappa_i(x)f(x)\,dx + a\alpha_i(a)S(a)$	$\int_0^a \kappa_i(x)g'(S(x))f(x)\,dx + a\beta_i(a)g(S(a))$
Scenario integral expectation	$\int_0^{F(a)} \kappa_i(q(p))\,dp + a\alpha_i(a)S(a)$	$\int_0^{1-g(S(a))} \kappa_i(q(1 - g^{-1}(1 - p)))\,dp + a\beta_i(a)g(S(a))$

an asset *rule* that focuses solely on the insolvency tail, we do not expect large differences between the equal priority solution and a marginal cost solution. However, some capital formulas—for example RBC and the Solvency II standard formula—are sensitive to more than tail behavior. For those, we might expect a materially different result from a marginal capital calculation.

14.3.6 Properties of Margin by Unit

In this section, we explore properties of κ, α, and β and show they interact to determine premiums and margin by unit.

By definition, we immediately get the following identities. Prime indicates derivative with respect to x.

$$\sum_i \kappa_i(x) = x, \qquad \sum_i \alpha_i(x) = 1, \qquad \sum_i \beta_i(x) = 1;$$

$$\sum_i \kappa_i'(x) = 1, \qquad \sum_i \alpha_i'(x) = 0, \qquad \sum_i \beta_i'(x) = 0.$$

Consider margin by unit. Using Eqs. 14.21 and 14.25 we can compute the margin $\bar{M}_i(a)$ in $\bar{P}_i(a)$ as

$$\begin{aligned} \bar{M}_i(a) &:= \bar{P}_i(a) - \bar{L}_i(a) \\ &= \int_0^a \beta_i(x)g(S(x)) - \alpha_i(x)S(x)\,dx. \end{aligned} \tag{14.34}$$

Differentiating we get the margin density for unit i at a expressed in terms of α_i and β_i

$$M_i(a) = \beta_i(x)g(S(x)) - \alpha_i(x)S(x). \tag{14.35}$$

What does Eq. 14.35 say about by unit margins? First, we know from the required properties of g that $P(a) = g(S(a)) \ge S(a)$ for all $a \ge 0$. Thus all **asset layers contain a non-negative total margin**. It is a different situation by unit where we can see

$$M_i(a) \ge 0 \iff \beta_i(a)g(S(a)) - \alpha_i(a)S(a) \ge 0 \iff \frac{\beta_i(a)}{\alpha_i(a)} \ge \frac{S(a)}{g(S(a))}.$$

The unit layer margin is positive when β_i/α_i is greater than the average layer loss ratio. Since the loss ratio is ≤ 1 there must be a positive layer margin whenever $\beta_i(a)/\alpha_i(a) > 1$. But when $\beta_i(a)/\alpha_i(a) < 1$ it is possible the unit has a negative margin.

In general, the natural allocation applies a positive loading to all independent risks (see Proposition 14.1) but that does not apply because equal priority payments are no longer independent. With finite capital there are potential transfers between units caused by their behavior in default that overwhelm the positive margin implied by the Proposition.

How can a negative unit margin occur and why does it make sense? To explore this we look at the shape of these functions in more detail.

By definition $\alpha_i(x)$ is the average proportion of losses from unit i in the layer $1_{X>a}$, when total losses are above x, and $\beta_i(x)$ is the risk-adjusted proportion. They are average proportions not proportions of the averages: $\alpha_i(x) = \mathsf{E}[X_i/X \mid X > t] \neq \mathsf{E}[X_i \mid X > t]/\mathsf{E}[X \mid X > t]$ because of Jensen's inequality applied to the convex function $x \mapsto 1/x$.

To better understand the shape of α_i and β_i we can compute their derivatives. Let us look at α_i in particular. Differentiating

$$\alpha_i(x)S(x) = \mathsf{E}[(X_i/X)1_{X>x}] = \int_x^\infty \frac{\kappa_i(t)}{t} f(t)dt$$

we get

$$\frac{d}{dx}(\alpha_i(x)S(x)) = -\frac{\kappa_i(x)}{x} f(x).$$

By the product rule we also get

$$\frac{d}{dx}(\alpha_i(x)S(x)) = \alpha_i'(x)S(x) + \alpha_i(x)\frac{d}{dx}S(x) = \alpha_i'(x)S(x) - \alpha_i(x)f(x)$$

Combining and re-arranging, gives

$$\alpha_i'(x) = \left(\alpha_i(x) - \frac{\kappa_i(x)}{x}\right)\frac{f(x)}{S(x)}. \tag{14.36}$$

The results for β_i are analogous. The term $h(x) := f(x)/S(x)$ is called the hazard rate function, see Section 11.3.1.

Eq. 14.36 shows that $\alpha_i'(x) \to 0$ if $f(x) \to 0$ and $S(x) \gg 0$, which occurs in the extreme left tail when X includes some level of near certain losses. Then α_i is flat for small x, while $f(x) \approx 0$. Flat behavior can also occur if $\alpha_i(x) - \kappa_i(x)/x = 0$, but that is an exceptional circumstance.

For thick-tailed insurance distributions $f(x)/S(x)$ is eventually decreasing but remains strictly positive. If $\kappa_i(x)/x$ is decreasing then $\alpha_i'(x) < 0$ because $\alpha_i(x)$ is the probability weighted integral of $\kappa_i(t)/t$ over $t > x$, and so $\alpha_i(x) < \kappa_i(x)/x$. Conversely if $\kappa_i(x)/x$ is increasing $\alpha_i'(x) > 0$.

As previously noted, $\sum_i \kappa_i'(x) = 1$. It is typical for the thickest tail distribution, i say, to behave like $\kappa_i(x) \approx x - \sum_{j\neq i} \mathsf{E}[X_j]$ for large x. Then $\kappa_i'(x) = 1$ and the remaining $\kappa_j(x) \approx \mathsf{E}[X_j]$ are almost constant for large x. In that case $\kappa_j(x)/x > \alpha_j(x)$ and so $\alpha_j'(x) < 0$ and $\alpha_i'(x) > 0$. To have two units with α_i increasing requires a very delicate balancing of the thickness of their tails with $\kappa_i(x)$, growing with order x. Compound Poisson distributions with the same severity is an example, as seen in the Example 250.

In general we can make two observations about margins.

Observation 1: Units where $\alpha_i(x)$ or $\kappa_i(x)/x$ increase with x always have a positive margin.

Observation 2: A thin-tailed unit aggregated with a thick tailed unit can have a negative margin for lower asset layers.

thin-tailed means a log-concave density, such as a normal or gamma distribution. Lognormal and Pareto are thick-tailed. The exponential distribution is the boundary between thin and thick.

Observation 1 follows because the action of risk adjustment puts more weight on X_i/X for larger X and so $\beta_i(x)/\alpha_i(x) > 1 > g(S(x))/S(x)$. Recall the risk adjustment is proportional to total losses X.

Conversely, a thin-tailed unit aggregated with thick-tailed units has a decreasing $\alpha_i(x)$ with asset layer x. Now the risk adjustment produces $\beta_i(x) < \alpha_i(x)$ and it is possible that $\beta_i(x)/\alpha_i(x) < g(S(x))/S(x)$. In most cases, $\alpha_i(x)$ eventually becomes constant and so $\beta_i(x)/\alpha_i(x)$ increases with x, while the layer loss ratio decreases—and margin increases—and the thin unit gets a positive margin. Whether or not the thin unit has a positive total margin $\bar{M}_i(a) > 0$ depends on the particulars of the units and the level of assets a. Generally a negative overall margin it is more likely for less well capitalized insurers, which makes sense because they have a lower overall dollar cost of capital.

We should find these results comforting. The thick-tailed unit benefits from pooling with the thin one because pooling increases the assets available to pay losses in default. Economically, equal priority transfers wealth from thin to thick units in default states, which are dominated by outcomes where the thick unit has a bad loss. Thin risks are very moderate and very rarely cause the portfolio to default. Looking solely within the portfolio, the thin risk is idiosyncratic and the thick risk systematic.

Another interesting situation occurs for asset levels within attritional losses. Most realistic insured loss portfolios are quite skewed and are almost certain to generate losses above a high proportion of expected. Said another way, it is unusual for a balanced, low volatility insured portfolio to have an extremely low loss ratio. If the expected loss ratio is 65 percent, for example, it almost never happens that losses are less than 45–50%. For these low loss layers, $S(x) \approx 1$ and they are funded entirely with premiums. The margin and capital components are zero. Now, since the sum of the margins over component units equals the total margin, when the total margin is zero it necessarily follows that either all unit margins are also zero or that some are positive and some are negative. Negative unit margins that occur when $S(x)$ is close to 1 reflect inter-insured payments ("dollar swapping"); the total margin paid to investors is always positive. Again, for the reasons noted above, it is the thin-tailed units that get the negative margin as thick-tailed units compensate them for the improved cover they obtain by pooling.

Table 14.4 shows that $\bar{S}_i(a)$ and $\bar{P}_i(a)$ can both be computed in three different ways, based on a Lee diagram integral, a loss outcome integral or a scenario integral. The Lee integral expression is much easier to visualize than the last two. The latter are confusing because there is a change in perspective. In the solvent states recoveries are driven by κ_i. In the insolvent states they are driven by α_i. At asset level a, it is true that $a = \sum_i a\alpha_i(a) = \sum_i \kappa_i(a)$. But it is not true that $a\alpha_i(a) = \kappa_i(a)$ and this difference is important in determining margins by unit. However, for the Lee expression there is no split between solvent and insolvent states: the same integrand is used throughout.

14.3.7 Alpha, Beta, and Kappa as Portfolio Diagnostics

Negative margins occur as a *side payment* between units. There is never negative margin paid to the investor, because at the portfolio level, all layers have nonnegative margin. These side payments, if large, indicate that the portfolio is not well balanced, and would benefit from coverage changes or reinsurance. The metrics α, κ, and to a lesser extent β can be used as portfolio diagnostics to identify such unbalanced situations.

An area chart where $\kappa_i(x)/x$ is on the vertical axis shows how the conditional expected losses are shared among the units at any given portfolio loss level x. Suitable choices of the horizontal axis—such as x, $\log(x)$, cumulative probability $F(x)$, return period $1/S(x)$, or log return period—emphasizes different parts of the loss distribution. A picture that shows one or more units dominating the larger losses suggests that the portfolio is not balanced and not being diversified effectively.

The vertical axis can also show $\alpha_i(x)$ or $\beta_i(x)$. Since α is the forward expectation of κ/x, it emphasizes imbalances in the upper tail. Even more emphasis is added by β, because it uses distorted expectations. The advantage of κ/x and α as diagnostics is that they can be computed without committing to a distortion. See Chapter 15 for examples of these diagnostics.

14.3.8 The Natural Allocation of Capital

Eq. 14.35 allows us to compute economic value added by unit and to assess static portfolio performance by unit—one of the motivations for performing capital allocation in the first place—when we are using an SRM and have equal priority. In many ways it is also a good place to stop. However, if desired, the ideas behind the natural premium allocation can be extended to give a capital allocation.

By definition, the average portfolio risk return equals

$$\bar{\iota}(a) := \frac{\bar{M}(a)}{\bar{Q}(a)}. \tag{14.37}$$

Eq. 14.37 has important implications. The question of so-called excess capital often comes up when performing capital allocation. The balance sheet contains more capital than is required by regulators, rating agencies or even prudence. Under the standard approach there is a single cost of (equity) capital that holds regardless of the overall asset level, $\bar{\iota}(a) = \bar{\iota}$. CAPM or Fama-French is often used to estimate $\bar{\iota}$, with a range of 7–20% common, Cummins and Phillips (2005). Eq. 14.37 tells us the implied CoC varies with the level of assets. Recall from Chapter 10 that if g is nontrivially concave then its CoC increases with increasing s, implying decreasing CoC with increasing a. The more well-capitalized a company is, the lower its average cost of capital. In fact, if insured losses were capped then any assets above the maximum loss would not require a *risk* return at all, because $g(0) = 0$. Recall, we are assuming the risk-free rate is zero; there would still be a cost of funding charge driven by the risk-free rate.

We may also object that just because the model says there is no chance of a loss, actually there is. At the moment we are working in an academic model with perfect information, so that is not possible. We are assuming the model is correct. The SRM approach answers the excess capital problem: the target CoC varies with the capital level and it is lower for more well-capitalized companies.

Although we have margin by unit, from Eq. 14.35 we cannot compute an average CoC by unit because we still lack a capital allocation, a problem we now address.

Assume pricing is governed by the SRM ρ associated with distortion g. Recall from Section 10.5.1 that the layer CoC at a is

$$\iota(a) := \frac{M(a)}{Q(a)} = \frac{P(a) - S(a)}{1 - P(a)} = \frac{g(S(a)) - S(a)}{1 - g(S(a))}.$$

We claim that for a law invariant pricing approach the layer CoC **must be the same for all units.** Law invariance implies the risk measure is only concerned with the attachment probability of the layer and not with the cause of loss within the layer. If CoC *within a layer* varied by unit then the allocation could not be law invariant. This crucial observation underlies the natural allocation of capital by unit.

The path forward is clear. Since risk return equals margin over capital, and since both margin and risk return are known by layer and by unit, with the latter constant across units, we can compute unit capital by layer $Q_i(a)$ via

$$\iota(a) := \frac{M(a)}{Q(a)} = \frac{M_i(a)}{Q_i(a)} \implies Q_i(a) = \frac{M_i(a)}{\iota(a)}. \tag{14.38}$$

Substituting for M and ι justifies the following definition.

Definition 13. *The* **natural allocation of capital** *to unit i is given by*

$$Q_i(a) = \frac{\beta_i(a)g(S(a)) - \alpha_i(a)S(a)}{g(S(a)) - S(a)} \times (1 - g(S(a))). \tag{14.39}$$

Since $1 - g(S(a))$ is the proportion of capital in the layer at a, Eq. 14.39 says the allocation to unit i is given by the nicely symmetric expression

$$\frac{\beta_i(a)g(S(a)) - \alpha_i(x)S(a)}{g(S(a)) - S(a)}. \tag{14.40}$$

To determine total capital by unit we integrate Q_i

$$\bar{Q}_i(a) := \int_0^a Q_i(x)dx.$$

And finally we can determine the average CoC for unit i at asset level a

$$\bar{\iota}_i(a) = \frac{\bar{M}_i(a)}{\bar{Q}_i(a)}. \tag{14.41}$$

Although the CoC within each layer is the same for all units, the margin, the proportion of capital, and the proportion attributable to each unit, all vary by a. Therefore, average CoC generally *varies by unit* and *varies by asset level* a. For a typical, strictly concave distortion with decreasing CoC by layer we find:

- Lower layers of assets, around the expected losses, have a high CoC but, offsetting this, they are mostly funded by premium and require little supporting investor capital.
- Higher layers of assets have a lower CoC but higher capital content: they are mostly funded by capital.

- Low volatility units tend to have losses close to their expected value, regardless of the value of total losses, and so consume relatively more of the expensive lower layer capital and a smaller proportion of cheaper, higher asset layers. Offsetting this there is more capital in higher layers than lower ones.
- High volatility units tend to be a larger proportion of total losses when the total is large, and so they consume a greater proportion cheaper, higher layer capital.

Eq. 14.41 shows the average CoC by unit is an M_i-weighted harmonic mean of the layer returns given by the distortion g, viz.

$$\frac{1}{\bar{\iota}_i(a)} = \int_0^a \frac{1}{\iota(x)} \frac{M_i(x)}{\bar{M}_i(a)} dx.$$

This view solves the problem that lower layers of asset potentially have an infinite CoC. The infinities don't matter. At lower asset layers there is little or no capital: the layer is fully funded by the loss component of premium. When so funded, there is no margin and so the infinite CoC gets zero weight. In this instance, the sense of the problem dictates that $0 \times \infty = 0$: with no initial capital there is no final capital regardless of the return. Since margin also tends to zero, unless g has a mass at zero, this is the continuous choice.

We have identified a natural capital allocation, but we also recommend against using it. It gives CoCs that vary by unit and are hard to interpret. With price, quantity, and proportion all variable it is clear the overall effect of the natural allocation of capital is hard to predict. Since price, amount, and use are all correlated it is never adequate to assume that the average cost of capital is the average CoC times the average amount. $\mathsf{E}[\iota Q] = \mathsf{E}[\iota]\mathsf{E}[Q]$ only when ι and Q are uncorrelated—for example when ι is constant. This is the fundamental flaw in the CCoC approach, which uses the same CoC for all capital layers. Academic approaches emphasized the possibility that CoCs vary by unit, but struggled with parameterization (Myers and Cohn 1987). Our methods produce varying CoCs by unit in a defensible manner, tied to the actual cost of the capital structure.

14.3.9 The Percentile Layer of Capital Approach

Bodoff (2007) describes the percentile layer of capital (PLC) approach to capital allocation. It is similar to the natural allocation and this section explains the connection.

Bodoff's work has been quite influential among US actuaries. It is worth quoting his abstract (emphasis added).

> This paper describes a new approach to capital allocation; the catalyst for this new approach is a new formulation of the meaning of holding Value at Risk (VaR) capital. This new formulation expresses the firm's total capital as the sum of many granular pieces of capital, or "percentile layers of capital." As a result, one must allocate capital separately on each layer and perform the capital allocation across all layers. The resulting capital allocation procedure, "capital allocation by percentile layer," exhibits several salient features. First, **it allocates capital to all losses, rather than allocating capital only to extreme losses** in the tail of the distribution. Second, despite allocating capital to this broad range of loss events, the proposed procedure does not

allocate in proportion to average loss; rather, it allocates disproportionate capital to severe losses. Third, it allocates capital by relying neither upon esoteric parameters nor upon elusive risk preferences. Ultimately, on the practical plane, capital allocation by percentile layer produces allocations that are different from many other methods.

Bodoff proposes a layered approach, similar to Section 10.3. However, he allocates only the shared liability and requires another step to determine premium, rather than computing premium directly as we do. His insights that layers of capital respond to a range of loss events and not just tail events and that they aggregate nonlinearly with expected loss are important contributions to capital allocation and actuarial science.

While Bodoff refers to layers of capital, in our terminology his subject is layers of assets. Any layer x is subject to being consumed in events whose portfolio loss exceeds the layer's attachment, i.e. $X > x$. The key assumption for PLC is that assets in $1_{X>x}$ should be allocated to unit i in proportion to its share of the portfolio losses, $\mathsf{E}[X_i/X \mid X > x]$, which equals our $\alpha_i(x)$. Since the asset density is 1, the total assets across all layers allocated to unit i should be:

$$a_i = \int_0^a \alpha_i(x)dx, \tag{14.42}$$

which is exactly the PLC allocation.

The asset allocation is not proportional to expected loss, because the expected loss payment to unit i, given by Eq. 14.21, is the integral of $\alpha_i(x)S(x)$ and α_i and S are not independent. For relatively thick-tailed units they are negatively correlated and thin, positively.

PLC allocates the shared liability as

$$\bar{M}_i(a) + \bar{Q}_i(a) = a_i - \int_0^a \alpha_i(x)S(x)dx = \int_0^a \alpha_i(x)F(x)dx. \tag{14.43}$$

Without a pricing principle added to it, however, PLC cannot separate margin and capital, even when the portfolio premium is given exogenously. Bodoff (2007), section 8, assumes a constant CoC.

Within a layer, the problem is separating $M_i(x) + Q_i(x) = \alpha_i(x)F(x)$. Having settled on a pricing distortion $g(s)$, the layer margin $M(x) = g(S(x)) - S(x)$ and capital $1 - g(S(x))$, and therefore layer CoC are all known. The sum $M_i(x)+Q_i(x)$ can then be decomposed assuming all units have the same CoC, as in Eq. 14.38. Since expected loss and the shared liability are both proportional to $\alpha_i(x)$, the premium, margin, and capital components must be as well. Integrating over layers recovers total margin, premium, and capital.

Under PLC, the unit i premium density is given by a modification of Eq. 14.25 where $\beta_i(a)$ is replaced by $\alpha_i(a)$. The implied capital allocation is given by a modification of Eq. 14.39 where again $\beta_i(a)$ is replaced by $\alpha_i(a)$. Such a modified equation simplifies to:

$$Q_i(a) = \alpha_i(a)(1 - g(S(a))). \tag{14.44}$$

Bodoff's approach is internally consistent, giving allocations that add up to the required totals. However, because of Eq. 14.25 we know that this modification does not express the distorted expectation of the unit's losses under equal priority, $X_i(a)$. In general, the PLC allocations and the natural allocations are not the same. These observations are confirmed in Section 15.4.4.

Exercise 254.

1. Under PLC, how does the choice of g affect the proportions of margin within a layer that are allocated between units?
2. How does it affect the proportions of total portfolio margin allocated between units? □

14.4 An Axiomatic Approach to Allocation

The influential paper Artzner *et al.* (1999) proposes desirable properties of a risk measure, casts them as axioms, and then finds all risk measures with those properties. Section 5.2 lists the axioms defining a coherent risk measure as well as others that have proven useful. In this section, we apply the same approach to allocations to identify potential coherent allocations. Once we have identified relevant properties, we consider which combinations characterize particular allocation methods.

Denault (2001) gives the first axiomatic approach to allocation for risk measures, inspired by game theory axioms. Kalkbrener (2005) considers alternative axioms and provides a characterization of the natural allocation. Buch and Dorfleitner (2008) extend Denault by showing that the symmetric axiom is too strong in an insurance context. They also prove equivalences between properties of risk measures and the Euler gradient allocation.

Figure 14.4 lays out the some important definitions and relationships between game theory (Section 12.2.7), capital allocation, and risk measures.

The subsequent subsections consider a decomposition $X = \sum_i X_i$ into units, a risk measure ρ, and a potential attribution $a_i = a(X_i; X)$ of $a := \rho(X)$ to each unit. If needed, we write a^ρ to emphasize the connection. Properties asserted for the natural allocation assume ρ is coherent and hold for any element of the natural allocation set. When ρ is coherent, it is defined by the scenario set $\mathcal{Q}$. In the homogeneous model, $X(x) = \sum_i x_i X_i$ for a fixed basis X_i.

Remark 255. Figure 14.4 relies on the following nomenclature. Atomic (resp. fractional, non-atomic) games are also called coalitional (fuzzy, exact). A **value** in game theory is a recipe taking a cost function (risk measure) to an attribution by unit. Allocations determine costs for players (units) directly in atomic and fractional games. In a non-atomic game, a player represents a state of the world and the cost allocation determines a state price density used to impute a cost allocation to units. The continuous, aggregation invariance, and monotonic (non-negativity) properties for game theory are defined in Denault (2001). Continuous and decomposable properties for allocations are defined in Kalkbrener (2009). He calls the no-undercut property diversifying. The symmetric allocation property is defined in Buch and Dorfleitner (2008). □

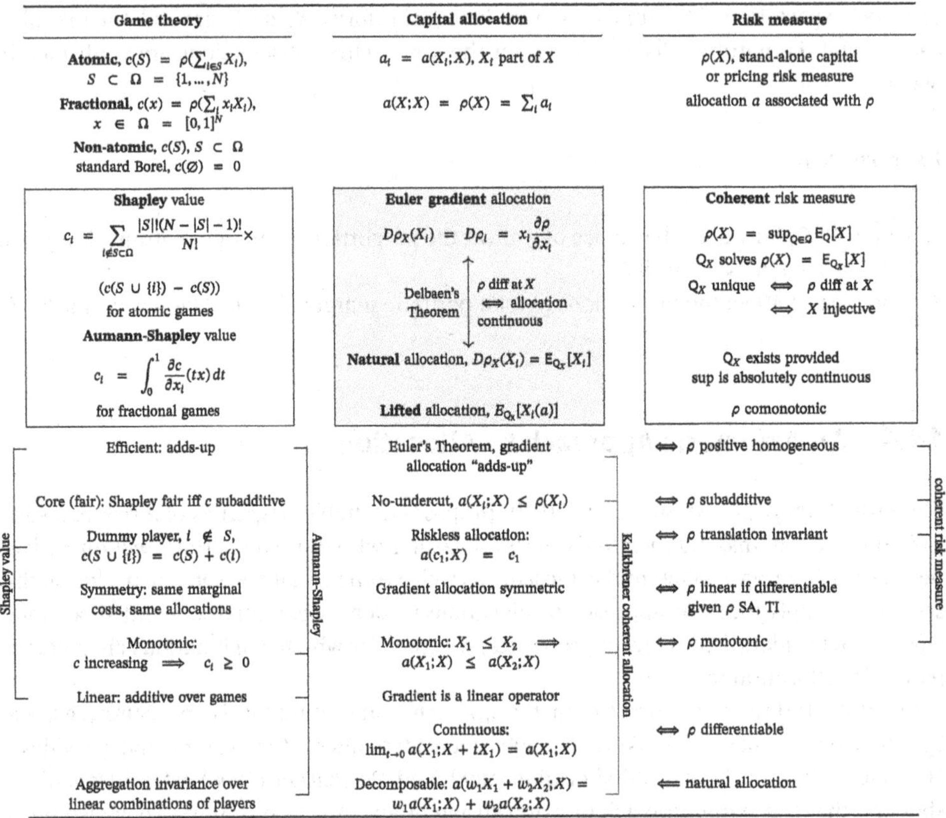

Figure 14.4 Relationship between game theory, allocations, and risk measures.

14.4.1 Additive

An attribution is **additive** if $a = \sum_i a_i$. It is then called an **allocation**. Myers and Read Jr. (2001) coin the phrase, "adds-up."

By Euler's theorem, the gradient allocation is additive if and only if ρ is differentiable and positive homogeneous (Mildenhall 2004). The natural allocation is additive because it is a risk-adjusted expected value. The Merton-Perold marginal business unit attribution is not additive.

14.4.2 No-Undercut

The **no-undercut** condition requires that the attribution to each unit is less than or equal to its stand-alone cost

$$a(X_i;X) \le \rho(X_i).$$

No-undercut is necessary for stability: when it fails, it is cheaper for units to operate stand-alone. No-undercut is also known as the **fairness** or the **diversifying property**.

Table 14.5 Example showing the coVaR allocation does not satisfy no-undercut.

Statistic	X_1	X_2	X
Simulation 99	0	12	12
Simulation 100	1	10	11
$\mathsf{VaR}_{0.98}$	0	10	11
coVaR allocation	1	10	11

The natural allocation always satisfies no-undercut because $\mathsf{Q}_X \in \mathcal{Q}$ and so

$$D\rho_X(X_i) = \mathsf{E}_{\mathsf{Q}_X}[X_i] \le \sup_{\mathsf{Q}\in\mathcal{Q}} E_{\mathsf{Q}}[X_i] = \rho(X_i).$$

When ρ is additive and differentiable, then the gradient allocation satisfies no-undercut iff ρ is subadditive, Buch and Dorfleitner (2008).

Example 256. The coVaR allocation does not satisfy no-undercut. By Eq. 4.20, the marginal allocation in the homogeneous model is also coVaR, $\mathsf{E}[X_i \mid X(x) = q_x(p)]$. Table 14.5 gives an explicit example. It shows the worst two outcomes by unit and in total from a simulation with 100 equally likely events. $\mathsf{VaR}_{0.98}$ is the second highest outcome. Stand-alone VaR for X_1 is zero, but the coVaR allocation is 1. The total VaR event is simulation 100, which gives the coVaR allocation, whereas stand-alone for unit 1 it is simulation 99. VaR is not subadditive. □

14.4.3 Riskless Allocation

The **riskless allocation** property determines the attribution to a constant

$$a(c; X) = c.$$

In game theory it is called the *dummy player* property. A constant cost does not diversify or provide any economies of pooling, it is a "non-player character".

The natural allocation satisfies the riskless allocation property because $\mathsf{E}[cZ] = c\mathsf{E}[Z] = c$.

Denault (2001) calls it translation invariance, which we use for a different property described next.

When ρ is additive and differentiable, then the gradient allocation satisfies the riskless allocation property iff ρ is translation invariant (Buch and Dorfleitner 2008).

Standard deviation does not satisfy the riskless allocation property.

14.4.4 Translation Invariant

The **translation invariant** property requires that

$$a(X_i + c_i; X_i + c) = a(X_i; X_i) + c_i$$

for constants c_i, c. It pairs with ρ being translation invariant since

$$a(X + c; X + c) = \rho(X + c) = \rho(X) + c = a(X; X) + c.$$

It was introduced by Kalkbrener (2009), who also considers a stronger property

$$a(X_i + c_i; X + c) = a(X_i; X) + c_i$$

The natural allocation has the translation invariant property because X and $X + c$ have the same contact functions and

$$a(X_i + c_i; X + c) = \mathsf{E}[(X_i + c_i)Z_X] = \mathsf{E}[X_i Z_X] + c_i = a(X_i; X) + c_i.$$

The equality is interpreted as an equality of sets when the natural allocation is not unique. Kalkbrener gives an example of a decomposable allocation with the no-undercut property that is translation invariant but that does not satisfy the stronger form.

14.4.5 Monotone

Coherent risk measures are positive homogeneous, subadditive, translation invariant, and monotone. The first three correspond to the additivity, no-undercut, and translation invariance properties for an attribution. Monotone is not needed to derive a reasonable attribution. For example, the covariance allocation of standard deviation is well behaved but standard deviation is not monotone—though it has the other three properties. Buch and Dorfleitner (2008) do not define a property paired with monotone.

Kalkbrener (2009) makes the following definition and uses it to characterize a coherent allocation, Section 14.5.4. The **monotone** property requires that if $X_1 \le X_2$ then

$$a(X_1; X) \le a(X_2; X)$$

for all X.

The natural allocation is monotone. The covariance allocation is not.

14.4.6 Symmetry

The **symmetry** property requires that when two subportfolios make the same marginal contributions to every other portfolio, then their allocation must be the same. In the homogeneous model with n units, symmetry requires that when

$$\rho(\sum_{k\in M} X_k + X_i) - \rho(\sum_{k\in M} X_k) = \rho(\sum_{k\in M} X_k + X_j) - \rho(\sum_{k\in M} X_k)$$

for all $M \subset \{1, \dots, n\} \setminus \{i, j\}$ (a coalition excluding i and j), then

$$a(X_i; X) = a(X_j; X),$$

Buch and Dorfleitner (2008). In game theory, units i and j are called **interchangeable.**

Symmetry is motivated by game theory. It is used to characterize the Shapley allocation. It becomes problematic in an insurance context and Buch and Dorfleitner (2008) show that when ρ is differentiable, symmetry holds iff ρ is linear, which is undesirable (no diversification). As a result, the symmetry property does not appear in characterizations of coherent allocations.

Example 257. Here is the example Buch and Dorfleitner (2008) use to prove the equivalence between linearity and symmetry for differentiable ρ. When $n = 2$, $M = \emptyset$ is the only subset of $\{1, 2\}$ that need be considered to test the symmetry property. Symmetry then requires that when $\rho(X_1) = \rho(X_2)$, the allocations to X_1, X_2 part of $X = X_1 + X_2$ are the same. Therefore, the gradient allocation is symmetric if the directional derivatives at X in each direction are the same. This is a strong condition because the dependence between X and X_i can be quite different. For example, let Y be a positive, bounded random variable and set $X_1 = c_1 - Y/2$ and $X_2 = c_2 + 2Y$ where c_i are selected so that $\rho(X_1) = \rho(X_2)$. The impact of adding X_1 or X_2 to X is different because X_1 is negatively correlated to the total whereas X_2 is positively correlated. The paper shows that equal impact occurs iff $\rho(-X) = -\rho(X)$ (no bid-ask spread) iff ρ is linear. □

14.4.7 Linear

An attribution can be regarded as a function applied to a risk measure (or cost function) to obtain an allocation, $\rho \mapsto a^\rho(\,\cdot\,;\,\cdot\,)$. The gradient allocation applied to a positive homogeneous risk measure is a good example. The gradient operator is linear in its argument since the derivative of a sum is the sum of the derivatives. In general, an attribution is called **linear** if it is a linear function of the risk measure

$$a^{\rho_1+\rho_2}(X_i;X) = a^{\rho_1}(X_i;X) + a^{\rho_2}(X_i;X).$$

The linear property means we can allocate costs by kind to division and then add them up, or add them first and then allocate the total. It is less applicable in the insurance context where we focus only on the cost of capital.

14.4.8 Decomposable

Whereas the linear property is concerned with additivity across types of cost, decomposability involves the units to which costs are allocated. If insurance risks are categorized by line of business and business unit, we want the same allocation at the line and business unit level regardless of whether we allocate to them directly, or first allocate to line and then business unit, or vice versa. Mathematically, let $(X_1, \dots, X_n)'$ denote an $n \times 1$ column vector of loss random variables at the most detailed decomposition of aggregation and let G be a $r \times n$ matrix of weights between 0 and 1, whose rows sum to 1. Usually $r < n$ and we think of $G(X_1, \dots, X_n)' = (Y_1, \dots, Y_r)'$ as the $r \times 1$ vector of loss random variables by line or by business unit. An attribution is called **decomposable** if

$$a(Y_i;X) = G(a(X_1;X), \dots, a(X_1;X))'.$$

Decomposability is one of three desirable properties listed by Kreps (2005). Denault (2001) and Billera and Heath (1982) call it **aggregation invariance**. Kalkbrener (2005) calls the decomposable property *linear aggregation*, which is distinct from the linear property (Section 14.4.7).

If a is a decomposable allocation of ρ then

$$\rho(X) = \sum_i a(X_i;X) = a(\sum_i X_i;X) = a(X;X) \tag{14.45}$$

and a is **associated** with ρ.

14.4.9 Continuous

The allocation a is **continuous** at X if for all X_1

$$\lim_{t\to 0} a(X_1;X + tX_1) = a(X_1;X). \tag{14.46}$$

That is, the allocation to X_1 part of $X + tX_1$ gets closer and closer to the allocation part of X as $t \to 0$.

Kalkbrener (2005) proves that when a has the no-undercut and decomposable properties then continuity implies a equals the directional derivative of ρ, Eq. 14.4. In the context of Delbaen's Theorem 2, continuity corresponds to ρ being differentiable. (The contact functions for $X + tX_1$ converge to a limit in the subdifferential at X. If the subdifferential only contains one element then the limit is unique.) When ρ is not differentiable at X it is because q_X has a flat spot and the limits $t \uparrow 0$ and $t \downarrow 0$ in Eq. 14.46 are different, which implies the limit does not exist and the allocation is not continuous. See Example 225.

14.4.10 Continuous in Direction

The allocation a is **continuous in direction** at X if for all sequences Y_n with $|Y_n| \le 1$ and $Y_n \to Y$ in probability,

$$\lim_{n\to\infty} a(Y_n;X) = a(Y;X). \tag{14.47}$$

Compared to Section 14.4.9 the direction is varying and X is fixed rather than the direction being fixed and X varying. Continuity in direction is used by Cherny and Orlov (2011) to characterize the linear natural allocation in Section 14.5.5.

14.4.11 Law Invariant Allocation

The allocation $a(X_i;X)$ is **law invariant** if it only depends on the joint distribution of (X_i, X). If ρ is law invariant then the natural allocation is too.

14.4.12 Positive Loading

An attribution is called **positive** if $a(X_i;X) \ge 0$ for all X_i. An allocation has the **positive loading** property if $a(X_i;X) \ge \mathsf{E}[X_i]$. Actuaries become very animated debating the merits of the positive loading property. When ρ is a premium risk measure, $\rho(X)$ is the total premium paid to assume the risk X. All PCPs insist it contains a positive loading. The allocation gives the premium just for unit i. Since reinsurance can be regarded as insurance with re-labeled premium and loss (Section 11.7.2), and since it is generally accepted that reinsurance has a cost, it is not reasonable to insist on a positive loading for all units.

The natural allocation is not positive in general, though it is when X_i are independent and ρ is law invariant, as the next result shows. This result does not apply to $X \wedge a = \sum_i X_i(a)$ because the summands are not independent. The action of equal priority, which re-allocates assets between insureds in default, can create negative margins by unit.

Proposition 14.1. *Let $X = \sum_{i=1}^n X_i$, X_i non-negative and independent, and let ρ be a law invariant, coherent risk measure. Then the natural allocation premium to X_i contains a positive loading, i.e. $D\rho_X(X_i) \ge \mathsf{E}[X_i]$.*

Proof. It is enough to prove for $n = 2$ by considering X_1 and $X_2' = X_2 + \cdots + X_n$.

Let $\tilde{X}_1 = X_1 + \mathsf{E}[X_2]$ and $\tilde{X}_2 = X_2 - \mathsf{E}[X_2]$. Then by Rothschild and Stiglitz (1970) $\tilde{X}_1 + \tilde{X}_2 \succeq^2 \tilde{X}_1$, where $\succeq^2$ denotes second-order stochastic dominance. Svindland (2014) shows that ρ respects second-order stochastic dominance (in fact, it is law invariant iff it does so). Therefore

$$\rho(\tilde{X}_1 + \tilde{X}_2) \ge \rho(\tilde{X}_1).$$

By translation invariance $\rho(\tilde{X}_1) = \rho(X_1) + \mathsf{E}[X_2]$. Since $\tilde{X}_1 + \tilde{X}_2 = X_1 + X_2$ we conclude

$$\rho(X_1 + X_2) \ge \rho(X_1) + \mathsf{E}[X_2].$$

Combining these results we get

$$\begin{aligned} D\rho_X(X_1) + D\rho_X(X_2) &= \rho(X_1 + X_2) \\ &\ge \rho(X_1) + \mathsf{E}[X_2] \\ \implies D\rho_X(X_2) &\ge \rho(X_1) - D\rho_X(X_1) + \mathsf{E}[X_2] \\ &\ge \mathsf{E}[X_2] \end{aligned}$$

because $\rho(X_1) \ge D\rho_X(X_1)$ by no-undercut. □

The proof leverages ρ's translation invariance. If we add constant c to X_1 then its natural allocation is c. In a sense, this is the *best case*. Any non-constant independent variable, no matter how low its variance, must slightly increase risk. It does not make sense to grant the new variable a credit off expected loss, when we would not do so for a constant. A credit is possible for dependent variables, however.

14.5 Axiomatic Characterizations of Allocations

We turn next to axiomatic characterizations of allocations. We present five:

1. the Shapley value,
2. the Aumann-Shapley value,
3. a characterization for decomposable allocations with the no-undercut property, Kalkbrener (2005),
4. a coherent allocation, Kalkbrener (2009), and
5. the linear natural allocation, Cherny and Orlov (2011).

The linear natural allocation only applies to SRMs; the remaining four apply to all coherent risk measures.

14.5.1 The Shapley Value

The Shapley value, Eq. 12.5, is the only attribution that is additive (efficient), symmetric, linear, and has the riskless allocation (null-player) property. This characterization was originally shown in Shapley (1953). Denault (2001) presents it in an allocation setting. If the cost function is subadditive then the Shapley value also has the no-undercut property.

14.5.2 The Aumann-Shapley Value

The Aumann-Shapley value, Eq. 12.6, is the only allocation that is linear, decomposable, and monotonic. This formulation appears in Billera and Heath (1982) in the context of cost allocations. It was originally proved in Aumann and Shapley (1974).

14.5.3 Kalkbrener's Decomposable and No-Undercut Allocation

Kalkbrener (2005) shows that ρ has a decomposable allocation with the no-undercut property iff it is positive homogeneous and subadditive (sublinear), in which case it is the natural allocation. It also equals the directional derivative when ρ is differentiable. Specifically, he shows:

1. Let a be a decomposable allocation of ρ with the no-undercut property. If a is continuous at X for all directions X_i, then $a(X_i;X) = \lim_{t\to 0}(\rho(X + tX_i) - \rho(X))/t$ equals the directional derivative.
2. If ρ is positive homogeneous and subadditive, then it has a natural allocation; see Section 5.2.9.
3. If ρ has a decomposable allocation with the no-undercut property, then ρ is positive homogeneous and subadditive.
4. If ρ is positive homogeneous and subadditive, then its natural allocation is decomposable and has the no-undercut property.
5. If ρ is positive homogeneous and subadditive, then the following are equivalent:
   a. The natural allocation has the continuity property at X (Section 14.4.9).

   b. The directional derivative of ρ at X exists in all directions.
   c. The natural allocation of X exists and is unique.
6. When the conditions in 5 hold, the natural allocation is the directional derivative.

In particular, these results all apply when ρ is coherent. There is one subtle point: the linear space V on which ρ is defined. If every element of V is absolutely integrable, $\mathsf{E}|X| < \infty$, then ρ has a representation on continuous functionals. This is usually the case—since we are rarely concerned with random variables with an infinite mean.

Buch and Dorfleitner (2008) restates the same connections for the gradient allocation.

14.5.4 Kalkbrener's Coherent Allocation

In a paper titled "Coherent allocation of risk capital," Denault (2001) called an allocation principle coherent if it has the no-undercut, symmetry, and riskless allocation properties. He says these three axioms are "necessary conditions of the fairness, and thus credibility, of allocation principles." No-undercut and riskless allocation seem unassailable. He continues, "The symmetry property ensures that a portfolio's allocation depends only on its contribution to risk within the firm, and nothing else." His definition adds no-undercut to the characterization of the Shapley value. It holds if ρ is subadditive. However, Buch and Dorfleitner (2008) show that symmetry is too strong to be useful in the insurance context, precisely because it isn't sensitive to interactions between unit risk within the firm.

Kalkbrener (2009) defines a **coherent allocation** to be one that is decomposable and has the no-undercut, translation invariance, and monotone properties. He proves that if there exists a coherent allocation associated with the risk measure ρ, then ρ is coherent and, conversely, that the natural allocation associated with a coherent risk measure is a coherent allocation. He also shows that for an allocation a associated with the risk measure ρ

1. a is translation invariant iff ρ is translation invariant.
2. If a is decomposable and has the no-undercut and translation invariance properties then the following are equivalent:
   a. $a(X_i;X) \le \sup(X_i)$ for all bounded X_i and all X
   b. a has the monotone property
   c. ρ is monotonic.

Covariance is an example of an allocation that is not monotone.

14.5.5 Cherny and Orlov's Linear Natural Allocation

The linear natural allocation of ρ, Eq. 14.7, is characterized by being a law invariant, decomposable allocation of ρ with the no-undercut property that is continuous in direction for all X. It was introduced in Cherny and Orlov (2011).

The linear natural allocation is very similar to Kalkbrener's decomposable and no-undercut allocation, Section 14.5.3. Kalkbrener assumes a is continuous, rather than continuous in direction. As a result, his allocation does not exist when ρ is not differentiable. This is exactly the problem the linear natural allocation overcomes.

14.5.6 Selecting an Allocation Method, Revisited

What properties should we require of an allocation? Four emerge as paramount: an allocation

1. Must add-up,
2. Should have the no-undercut property so that units don't have an incentive to leave,
3. Should be translation invariant for convenience, and
4. Should respect monotone order to be explainable and defensible.

The natural allocation has all four properties. When it is unique, it equals the directional derivative of ρ, giving it an intuitive rationale. Moreover, it does not rely on any additional assumptions—it is truly *natural*. We arrive where we hoped: with a marginal allocation, bringing the investigations of Venter, Major, and Kreps (2006) to a very satisfactory conclusion.

When ρ is not differentiable but is law invariant and comonotonic additive, the linear natural allocation gives a unique allocation that averages over the non-uniqueness, again with no additional assumptions. And when there is a lifting, the lifted natural allocation is a unique allocation that takes advantage of the information in the lift. Both allocations are illustrated in Chapter 15. The class of law invariant, comonotonic additive coherent risk measures, i.e. SRMs, is quite broad. Cherny and Orlov (2011) says, "This class is very wide and, in our opinion, is sufficient for any practical application of coherent risks." It is certainly adequate for capital regulation, and *local* pricing applications where macro-risk considerations are irrelevant.

Before we declare victory, however, remember the controversial role of positive homogeneity in the definition of a coherent risk measure. Long-Term Capital Management and similar more recent debacles show that risk is not scale invariant. Risk theory has moved on from coherent risk measures to convex risk measures over the last twenty years. Convex risk measures stipulate a different approach to diversification that is not positive homogeneous. The natural allocation does not work for convex measures because of the penalty term (handicapping scenarios, Eq. 5.11) in their representation, and more advanced allocation methods are required. These topics are beyond our scope. See Tsanakas (2009), Boonen, Tsanakas, and Wüthrich (2017) for an introduction using the Aumann-Shapley value.

The four properties listed above are Kalkbrener's definition of a **coherent allocation**, which we discuss further in Sections 14.4 and 14.5.

Figures 14.3 and 14.4 provides a schematic representation of the various dependencies we have outlined.

14.6 Learning Objectives

1. Define and compute the natural, linear natural, and lifted natural allocation, given appropriate loss distributions.
2. Explain the assumptions needed for each kind of allocation, and give examples to show why each is needed.
3. Explain when each kind of allocation should be used.

4. Define and give examples of a lifting.
5. What properties define a coherent allocation? Why is each regarded as reasonable?
6. Given a portfolio of losses explain the properties you expect of the natural, linear natural, and lifted natural allocations such as ordering by unit.
7. Define and compute alpha, beta, kappa given loss data.
8. Recognize thick and thin-tailed units from graphs of alpha, beta, kappa.
9. Compute the natural allocations of premium, margin, and capital given a distortion.
10. Explain how limited assets can cause certain lines to be priced under cost; why does this make sense? Under what assumptions does it commonly occur?
11. Explain why returns to natural allocated capital vary with the stochastic characteristics of the portfolio.
12. Compare the natural allocation with the percentile layer of capital allocation.

15

Modern Price Allocation Practice

In this chapter, we show how to apply the natural allocations and unit funding analysis developed in Chapter 14 to discrete data. We apply the formulas to an adjusted version of Simple Discrete Example introduced in Section 2.4.1. We illustrate how the auxiliary functions κ, α, and β can be used to diagnose risk characteristics of the three Case Studies. We compute the lifted natural allocations for each Case Study. As always, the reader is encouraged to replicate all the calculations.

15.1 Applying the Natural Allocations to Discrete Random Variables

In this section, we show how to compute the various natural allocations of $\rho(X)$ to X_i as part of X by extending the algorithm in Chapter 11 that computes $\rho(X)$. We work with a multivariate discrete distribution as produced by a simulation or catastrophe model.

15.1.1 Algorithm to Compute the Linear Natural Allocation for Discrete Random Variables

Algorithm Inputs:

i. The outcome values $(X_{1,j}, \dots, X_{m,j})$, $j = 1, \dots, n$, of a discrete m-dimensional multivariate loss random variable. Outcome j occurs with probability p_j. $X_j = \sum_i X_{i,j}$ denotes the total loss for outcome j.
ii. A spectral risk measure ρ associated with the distortion function g.

Follow these steps to determine $D^n\rho_X(X_{i,\cdot})$, the natural allocation of $\rho(X)$ to unit i.

Algorithm Steps

1. **Pad** the input by adding a zero outcome $X_{1,0} = \cdots = X_{m,0} = X_0 = 0$ with probability $p_0 = 0$.
2. **Sort** events by total outcome X_j into ascending order.

Pricing Insurance Risk: Theory and Practice, First Edition. Stephen J. Mildenhall and John A. Major.

3. **Group** by X_j and take p-weighted averages of the $X_{i,j}$ within each i and $X_j = x$ group. Sum the corresponding p_j. Relabel events using $j = 0, 1, \dots, n'$ as $X_{i,j}$ and probabilities $p_0, \dots, p_{n'}$.
4. **Decumulate** probabilities to determine the survival function $S_j := S(X_j)$ using $S_0 = 1 - p_0$ and $S_j = S_{j-1} - p_j$, $j > 0$.
5. **Distort** the survival function, computing $g(S_j)$.
6. **Difference** $g(S_j)$ to compute risk-adjusted probabilities $\Delta g(S_0) = 1 - g(S_0)$ and $\Delta g(S_j) = g(S_{j-1}) - g(S_j)$, $j > 0$.
7. **Sum-Product** to compute $\rho_g(X) = \sum_j X_j \, \Delta g(S_j)$ and

$$D^n \rho_X(X_i) = \mathsf{E}[X_i Z] = \sum_j X_{i,j} \, Z_j \, p_j = \sum_j X_{i,j} \frac{\Delta g(S_j)}{p_j} p_j = \sum_j X_{i,j} \, \Delta g(S_j). \tag{15.1}$$

Comments.

a. When the data is produced by a simulation model, n equals the number of simulations and m the number of units. With realistic data n is in the range thousands to millions and m ranges from a handful up to the hundreds for a full corporate model.
b. The algorithm follows the steps described in Section 14.2.1.
c. Step (1) only results in a new outcome row when the smallest X_j observation is > 0.
d. The averages in Step 3 are implemented as

$$\mathsf{E}[X_i \mid X = x] = \frac{\sum_{j:X_j=x} p_j \, X_{i,j}}{\sum_{j:X_j=x} p_j}. \tag{15.2}$$

e. After Step (3), the X_j are distinct, they are in ascending order, $X_0 = 0$, and $p_j = \mathsf{P}(X = X_j)$.
f. The backward difference $\Delta g(S_j)$ computed in Step (6) replaces $g'(S)dF(x)$ in various formulas.
g. Eq. (15.1) is an exact equation for a discrete distribution. Approximation occurs if it is applied to the empirical distribution of a discrete sample representing a different underlying distribution, possibly one with density.
h. The multivariate data array $X_{i,j}$ is oriented with units by row and simulation by column. This orientation is opposite to that shown in the tables and typically shown in a spreadsheet. The row-major orientation is preferred in programming applications that iterate down units. A column-major orientation is preferred when iterating across units within a simulation.

15.1.2 Application to the Adjusted Simple Discrete Example

Recall that in the Simple Discrete Example, Section 2.4.1, Ins Co., writes two policies taking on loss values $0, 8, 10$, and $0, 1, 90$ respectively, with probabilities $1/2, 1/4$, and $1/4$. In this subsection, we consider an adjusted version of the same example where the losses for unit 1 take on values 0, 9, or 10. As a result, there are two ways the portfolio loss can equal 10:

$9 + 1 = 10 + 0$, making it a better illustration of the Natural Allocation. We re-frame the example as follows.

Example 258. Inputs: you are given a multivariate distribution defined by Table 15.1. It is generated by a simulation model of Ins Co.'s portfolio. Ins Co. has calibrated its pricing risk measure to be a proportional hazard transform, $g(s) = s^{1/2}$.

Steps (1) and (2) add a zero outcome and sort by portfolio loss, yielding Table 15.2.

Events 0 and 1 have the same portfolio loss $X_0 = X_1 = 0$. Events 4 and 5 have the same portfolio loss $X_4 = X_5 = 10$. Step (3) groups events with the same X value together and relabels them. Events 0 and 1 group to an equivalent of event 1, since event 0 has probability 0. Combining events 4 and 5, using Eq. (15.2) we get

$$X_{1,3} = (9 \times (1/16) + 10 \times (1/8))/(1/16 + 1/8) = (29/16)/(3/16) = 9.6667$$

Table 15.1 Simulation output.

Event Description	X_1	X_2	X	p
Nothing happening	0	0	0	1/4
Tropical storm	9	0	9	1/8
Hurricane	10	0	10	1/8
Wildfires	0	1	1	1/8
Tropical storm and wildfires	9	1	10	1/16
Hurricane and wildfires	10	1	11	1/16
Earthquake	0	90	90	1/8
Tropical storm and earthquake	9	90	99	1/16
Hurricane and earthquake	10	90	100	1/16

Table 15.2 Sorted events.

j	X_1	X_2	X	p
0	0	0	0	0
1	0	0	0	1/4
2	0	1	1	1/8
3	9	0	9	1/8
4	9	1	10	1/16
5	10	0	10	1/8
6	10	1	11	1/16
7	0	90	90	1/8
8	9	90	99	1/16
9	10	90	100	1/16

and

$$X_{2,3} = (1 \times (1/16) + 0 \times (1/8))/(1/16 + 1/8) = (1/16)/(3/16) = 0.3333.$$

The sum equals 10, as it must. The result of Step (3) is shown in Table 15.3, with $n' = 7$.

Step (4) generates the survival function and Step (5) applies the distortion. Step (6) differences the distorted survival function to obtain the distorted event probabilities.

Expected losses are computed as

$$\mathsf{E}[X_i] = \sum_{j=0}^{7} X_{i,j}\, p_j \tag{15.3}$$

resulting in $\mathsf{E}[X_1] = 4.75$, $\mathsf{E}[X_2] = 22.75$, and $\mathsf{E}[X] = 27.5$ (Table 15.4).

Table 15.3 Grouped events.

j	X_1	X_2	X	p
0	0	0	0	0.2500
1	0	1	1	0.1250
2	9	0	9	0.1250
3	9.6667	0.3333	10	0.1875
4	10	1	11	0.0625
5	0	90	90	0.1250
6	9	90	99	0.0625
7	10	90	100	0.0625

Table 15.4 Grouped events with distorted event probabilities.

j	X_1	X_2	X	p	S	$g(S)$	$\Delta g(S)$
0	0	0	0	0.2500	0.7500	0.8660	0.1340
1	0	1	1	0.1250	0.6250	0.7906	0.0755
2	9	0	9	0.1250	0.5000	0.7071	0.0835
3	9.6667	0.3333	10	0.1875	0.3125	0.5590	0.1481
4	10	1	11	0.0625	0.2500	0.5000	0.0590
5	0	90	90	0.1250	0.1250	0.3536	0.1464
6	9	90	99	0.0625	0.0625	0.2500	0.1036
7	10	90	100	0.0625	0.0000	0.0000	0.2500
$\mathsf{E}[\cdot]$	4.75	22.75	27.5				
$D^n\rho(\cdot)$	6.2048	45.1838	51.3887				

Premium allocations are computed as distorted expected losses per Eq. (15.1):

$$D^n\rho_X(X_i) := \mathsf{E}_g[X_i] = \sum_{j=0}^{7} X_{i,j}\, \Delta g(S_j)$$

resulting in $D^n\rho_X(X_1) = 6.2048$, $D^n\rho_X(X_2) = 45.1838$, and $\rho(X) = 51.3887$, as shown in Table 15.4. □

15.1.3 Computing the Natural Allocation Set

In the construction of the linear allocation, Step (3) groups and collapses events that have the same portfolio loss X, resulting in a one-to-one correspondence between events and loss outcomes. That, in turn, guarantees a unique contact function and unique allocation. To develop the natural allocation set, we embrace the multiplicity of X values. If the original data includes a $X = 0$ member, the extra row added in Step (1) will have no impact because $p_0 = 0$.

Following the linear allocation procedure without Step (3) computes *one* of the natural allocations. Equally valid allocations arise from convex combinations of extreme contact functions. These all arise from permuting the order of the multiple events within each $X = x$ group.

Example 259. Applying the linear natural allocation procedure of the previous section without implementing the Step (3) grouping gives us Table 15.5.

This particular assignment of distorted probabilities results in $D\rho_X(X_1) = 6.2085$, $D\rho_X(X_2) = 45.1801$. The portfolio $\rho(X) = 51.3887$ is the same as before.

If there are k rows with the same $X = x$, there will be $k!$ permutations, each corresponding to one extreme contact function. In this example, with $k = 2$, there are only two alternatives.

Table 15.5 Ungrouped events with distorted event probabilities. Original event numbers from Table 15.2 are retained for clarity. Duplicate $X = 10$ events are shown in bold face.

j	X_1	X_2	X	p	S	$g(S)$	$\Delta g(S)$
1	0	0	0	0.2500	0.7500	0.8660	0.1340
2	0	1	1	0.1250	0.6250	0.7906	0.0755
3	9	0	9	0.1250	0.5000	0.7071	0.0835
4	**9**	**1**	**10**	**0.0625**	**0.4375**	**0.6614**	**0.0457**
5	**10**	**0**	**10**	**0.1250**	**0.3125**	**0.5590**	**0.1024**
6	10	1	11	0.0625	0.2500	0.5000	0.0590
7	0	90	90	0.1250	0.1250	0.3536	0.1464
8	9	90	99	0.0625	0.0625	0.2500	0.1036
9	10	90	100	0.0625	0.0000	0.0000	0.2500
$D\rho(\cdot)$	6.2085	45.1801	51.3887				

Table 15.6 Alternative order of ungrouped events with distorted event probabilities. Duplicate $X = 10$ events, swapped from Table 15.5, are shown in bold face, with changed numbers italicized.

j	X_1	X_2	X	p	S	$g(S)$	$\Delta g(S)$
1	0	0	0	0.2500	0.7500	0.8660	0.1340
2	0	1	1	0.1250	0.6250	0.7906	0.0755
3	9	0	9	0.1250	0.5000	0.7071	0.0835
5	**10**	**0**	**10**	**0.1250**	*0.3750*	*0.6124*	*0.0947*
4	**9**	**1**	**10**	**0.0625**	*0.3125*	*0.5590*	*0.0534*
6	10	1	11	0.0625	0.2500	0.5000	0.0590
7	0	90	90	0.1250	0.1250	0.3536	0.1464
8	9	90	99	0.0625	0.0625	0.2500	0.1036
9	10	90	100	0.0625	0.0000	0.0000	0.2500
$D\rho(\cdot)$	6.2009	45.1878	51.3887				

The first appears in Table 15.5. The second is shown in Table 15.6. In general, if there are multiple ties with k_1, k_2, etc. equal rows, there will be $(k_1!)(k_2!)\dots$ different alternatives.

The ordering in Table 15.5 gives the maximum for X_1 and minimum for X_2; the ordering in Table 15.6 gives the opposite.

In this case the two different natural allocations are very similar: 6.2085 or 6.2009 for X_1 and 45.1801 or 45.1878 for X_2. However, as we saw in Example 224 the natural allocations can lie anywhere between $-\rho(-X_i)$ and $\rho(X_i)$, where X_i denotes the marginal for unit i on a stand-alone basis. □

Exercise 260. Using the data in Table 15.5, generate the extreme allocations with the $\mathsf{TVaR}_{0.65}$ distortion $g(s) = 1 \wedge (s/0.35)$.

Solution. $D\rho_X(X_1)$ equals 6.1429 or 6.2500 and $D\rho_X(X_2)$ equals 64.5714 or 64.4643. □

Exercise 261. In Example 260, the lowest allocation for one unit and the highest allocation for the other unit result from the same reordering. Does this always happen when the portfolio consists of two units and $k > 2$? What about three or more units? Explain.

Table 15.7 Solution to Exercise 261.

X_1	X_2	X_3	X
1	3	2	6
2	4	0	6
3	0	3	6
4	1	1	6

Solution. With two units, because $X_1 + X_2 = X = x$ within groups, they are necessarily anticomonotonic (within groups) and so this will always happen. With three or more units, any unit will always be anticomonotonic with the sum of the other units, but it is possible for its minimum (resp., maximum) not to occur with the maximum (resp., minimum) of any of the others. In Table 15.7, the min of X_1 does not occur with the min of X_2 or of X_3, nor does the max of X_1 occur with the min of X_2 or of X_3. □

Remark 262. The natural allocation set defines the extreme possible allocations given a particular SRM. Section 11.2.3 described the distortion envelope of all SRMs that price the portfolio to a given value. The extreme SRMs defining this envelope could be iteratively applied in the natural allocation set procedure to calculate the extreme possible allocations consistent with a given portfolio price, without committing to a particular SRM. □

15.1.4 Computing the Lifted Natural Allocation

The typical application of the lifted allocation is to $X \wedge a = \sum X_i(a)$ using the lift X, i.e. $D^f \rho_{X\wedge a, X}(X_i(a))$. However, we can use any variable as the lift, provided it takes on unique values and defines a unique ordering of events. We can also use a variable with fewer ties than X to implement a quasi-lift in the manner of Remark 248. For example, if each unit purchased reinsurance separately, the sum of gross losses might be a lift.

In preparation for the typical application, we first note the computation of $X_i(a)$ via Eq. (12.9) is unchanged in a discrete setting; loss amounts are simply pro-rated:

$$X_{i,j}(a) = X_{i,j}\frac{X_j \wedge a}{X_j} = \begin{cases} X_{i,j} & X_j \le a \\ X_{i,j}\dfrac{a}{X_j} & X_j > a. \end{cases} \tag{15.4}$$

The Algorithm in Section 15.1.1 is adapted as follow to compute the lifted or quasi-lifted allocation:

- In Step (2), sort by $\tilde{X}_j$ rather than X_j.
- Step (3)
  - If $\tilde{X}$ is a one-to-one lift: Step (3) is superfluous.
  - Else, implementing a quasi-lift: group by values of $\tilde{X}_j$ rather than X_j.
- Steps (4)-(7): no change.

The lifted allocation is always a member of the natural allocation set, which only had two elements in our example (one tie). Thus, there are only two possible lifted allocations, which we have already computed.

Example 263. From Table 15.4 we compute $D^f \rho_{X\wedge a, X}(X_i(a))$ taking $a = 80$. First, we prepare the additional columns $X \wedge a$ and $X_i(a)$. Note that for simulations $j = 5, 6$, and 7 the loss is limited at 80. Then we can add the relevant expectations and distorted expectations, computed as sum-products. The results are shown in Table 15.10. The adjusted probabilities, $\Delta\, g(S)$, are unchanged because we use the lift to *see through* the capped loss. The events above the cap are ordered according to their impact, as measured by X. □

Table 15.10 Simple example with assets limited to $a = 80$.

j	X_1	X_2	X	$X \wedge a$	$X_1(a)$	$X_2(a)$	p	S	$g(S)$	$\Delta g(S)$
0	0	0	0	0	0	0	0.2500	0.7500	0.8660	0.1340
1	0	1	1	1	0	1	0.1250	0.6250	0.7906	0.0755
2	9	0	9	9	9	0	0.1250	0.5000	0.7071	0.0835
3	9.67	0.33	10	10	9.6667	0.3333	0.1875	0.3125	0.5590	0.1481
4	10	1	11	11	10	1	0.0625	0.2500	0.5000	0.0590
5	0	90	90	80	0	80	0.1250	0.1250	0.3536	0.1464
6	9	90	99	80	7.2727	72.7273	0.0625	0.0625	0.2500	0.1036
7	10	90	100	80	8	72	0.0625	0.0000	0.0000	0.2500
$\mathsf{E}[\cdot]$	4.7500	22.7500	27.5000	23.8125	4.5170	19.2955				
$D\rho_X(\cdot)$	6.2048	45.1838	51.3887	42.9567	5.5260	37.4307				

15.2 Unit Funding Analysis

In this section, we implement the auxiliary functions κ, α, and β and detail the alternative approaches to computing natural allocations. We also implement the computation of margin and equity by unit. We continue to work with the Adjusted Simple Discrete Example.

15.2.1 Computing κ

There are several possible discrete implementations of κ. The definition is

$$\kappa_i(x) := \mathsf{E}[X_i \mid X = x] \tag{15.5}$$

and the simplest implementation is Eq. (15.2).

While technically correct for a discrete distribution, this formula overlooks the fact that a discrete simulation is merely a *sample* of a larger conceptual population. In that context, a particular $\kappa_i(x)$ is an estimator of the true κ, and, if based on a small number of realizations, a potentially high-variance estimator. Eq. (15.2) may be adequate, however, in applications where $\kappa_i(x)$ values over multiple x values are being summed together in the computation of the quantity of interest. There, the law of large numbers could guarantee convergence to the correct value. Any particular application of Eq. (15.2) needs to be examined in this light.

Crafting a more stable estimator involves regression modeling, using kernel smoothing, local regression (loess, Cleveland (1979)), splines, or other techniques to borrow strength from neighboring x values.

Example 264. A *kernel estimate* of the expectation of a random variable Y conditional on $X = x$ is defined as

$$\hat{Y} = \frac{\sum_j Y_j \, p_j \, K(\frac{X_j - x}{h})}{\sum_j p_j \, K(\frac{X_j - x}{h})}$$

where K is called the *kernel* and h the *bandwidth*.

The popular *Epanechnikov kernel*, also known as the *parabolic kernel*, is defined as

$$K(u) = (1 - u^2)^+.$$

The estimate of $\varkappa_1(10) = \mathsf{E}[X_1 \mid X = 10]$ from Table 15.2 using the Epanechnikov kernel with bandwidth $h = 2$ is 9.5238, as tabulated in Table 15.11. The actual value is 9.6667. □

15.2.2 Computing α

The discrete analog to Eq. (14.20) is

$$\alpha_i(a) := \frac{\sum_{j:X_j>a} p_j X_{i,j}/X_j}{\sum_{j:X_j>a} p_j}. \tag{15.6}$$

Recall from Chapter 11, $\mathrm{j}(a) = \max\{j : X_j < a\}$.

The analog to Eq. (14.19) is

$$\bar{S}_i(a) = \mathsf{E}[X_i(a)] = \sum_{j \le \mathrm{j}(a)} X_{i,j}\Delta S_j + a\alpha_i(X_{\mathrm{j}(a)})S_{\mathrm{j}(a)}. \tag{15.7}$$

The analog to Eq. (14.21) is

$$\bar{S}_i(a) = \mathsf{E}[X_i(a)] = \sum_{j < \mathrm{j}(a)} \alpha_i(X_j)S_j\Delta X_j + (a - X_{\mathrm{j}(a)})\alpha_i(X_{\mathrm{j}(a)})S_{\mathrm{j}(a)}. \tag{15.8}$$

Example 265. Referring to Table 15.12, we can see in row 6 that $\alpha_1(99) = 0.1$ and $\alpha_2(99) = 0.9$ because the only outcome in the conditional event $X > a$ is row 7. In row 5, there are two outcomes in the condition so the calculation is $\alpha_1(90) = (0.0909 \times 0.0625 + 0.1 \times$

Table 15.11 Computation of kernel smoothed estimate of $\varkappa_{1(10)}$.

j	X_1	X_2	X	p	K	pK	X_1pK
1	0	0	0	0.2500	0	0	0
2	0	1	1	0.1250	0	0	0
3	9	0	9	0.1250	0.75	0.0938	0.8438
4	9	1	10	0.0625	1	0.0625	0.5625
5	10	0	10	0.1250	1	0.1250	1.25
6	10	1	11	0.0625	0.75	0.0469	0.4688
7	0	90	90	0.1250	0	0	0
8	9	90	99	0.0625	0	0	0
9	10	90	100	0.0625	0	0	0
Sum						0.3281	3.1250
Ratio							9.5238

0.0625)/(0.0625+0.0625) = 0.0955. Calculations for lower numbered outcomes include progressively more terms in the numerator and denominator per Eq. (15.6). The two policies are fairly well balanced in the lower layers but then X_2 dominates for $a \geq 10$.

Note that the expected losses of the two policies are 4.75 and 22.75, respectively, which equal the row totals for the $\alpha_i S \Delta X$ columns. □

Exercise 266. using the data in Table 15.12, compute $\bar{S}_i(a)$ for $a = 80$.

Solution. Limiting to $a = 80$ sets $\mathrm{j}(a) = 4$. The sum of $\alpha_i S \Delta X$ in rows 0 to 3 is 3.6938 for X_1 and 2.8688 for X_2. The final term multiplies $(80 - 11) \times 0.25$ by α of 0.0477 and 0.9523, respectively. The $\bar{S}_i(a)$ are 4.5170 and 19.2955, respectively, totaling 23.8125. □

Remark 267. Notice that the simpler Eq. (15.3) gets the same answers. The utility of α will become evident later on. □

15.2.3 Computing β

The discrete analog to Eq. (14.23) is exactly parallel to Eq. (15.6):

$$\beta_i(a) := \frac{\sum_{j:X_j>a} \Delta g(S_j) X_{i,j}/X_j}{\sum_{j:X_j>a} \Delta g(S_j)}. \tag{15.9}$$

The analog to Eq. (14.22) is

$$\bar{P}_i(a) = \mathsf{E}_{\mathsf{Q}}[X_i(a)] = \sum_{j \leq \mathrm{j}(a)} X_{i,j} \Delta g(S_j) + a\beta_i(X_{\mathrm{j}(a)}) g(S_{\mathrm{j}(a)}). \tag{15.10}$$

The analog to Eq. (14.25) is

$$\bar{P}_i(a) = \mathsf{E}_{\mathsf{Q}}[X_i(a)] = \sum_{j < \mathrm{j}(a)} \beta_i(X_j) g(S_j) \Delta X_j + (a - X_{\mathrm{j}(a)}) \beta_i(X_{\mathrm{j}(a)}) g(S_{\mathrm{j}(a)}). \tag{15.11}$$

These are the distorted equivalents to Eqs. (15.7) and (15.8).

Example 268. Table 15.13 shows the computation of $\beta_i(X)$ for the simple example. This closely parallels Table 15.12. □

Exercise 269. Limiting assets to $a = 80$, apply Eq. (15.10) to the data in Table 15.13.

Solution. The sum of $X_i \Delta g(S)$ in rows 0 through $\mathrm{j}(a) = 4$ is 2.7729 for X_1 and 0.1838 for X_2. The end term is $a = 80$ times $g(S_4) = 0.5$ times $\beta_i(X_4)$ of 0.0688 and 0.9312, respectively. The totals $\bar{P}_i(a)$ are 5.5260 and 37.4307, respectively, for a total of 42.9567. □

15.2.4 Computing Margin

Margin is the difference between premium and expected loss. Compare Eqs. (15.8) and (15.11):

Table 15.12 Simple example showing $\alpha_i(a)$ and $\bar{S}_i$. Entries for X_i/X in row 1 and α_i in row 7 are meaningless, because there is no possibility of a loss >100.

j	X_1	X_2	X	ΔX	p	S	$S\Delta X$	X_1/X	X_2/X	α_1	α_2	$\alpha_1 S\Delta X$	$\alpha_2 S\Delta X$
0	0	0	0	1	0.2500	0.7500	0.7500			0.5000	0.5000	0.3750	0.3750
1	0	1	1	8	0.1250	0.6250	5.0000	0.0000	1.0000	0.6000	0.4000	3.0000	2.0000
2	9	0	9	1	0.1250	0.5000	0.5000	1.0000	0.0000	0.5000	0.5000	0.2500	0.2500
3	9.67	0.33	10	1	0.1875	0.3125	0.3125	0.9667	0.0333	0.2200	0.7800	0.0688	0.2438
4	10	1	11	79	0.0625	0.2500	19.7500	0.9091	0.0909	0.0477	0.9523	0.9426	18.8074
5	0	90	90	9	0.1250	0.1250	1.1250	0.0000	1.0000	0.0955	0.9045	0.1074	1.0176
6	9	90	99	1	0.0625	0.0625	0.0625	0.0909	0.9091	0.1000	0.9000	0.0063	0.0563
7	10	90	100	0	0.0625	0.0000	0.0000	0.1000	0.9000				
Sum			100	1			27.5					4.75	22.75

Table 15.13 Simple example showing $\beta_i(a)$. Entries for X_i/X in row 1 and β in row 7 are undefined.

j	X_1	X_2	X	ΔX	$g(S)$	$\Delta g(S)$	$g(S)\Delta X$	X_1/X	X_2/X	β_1	β_2	$\beta_1 g(S)\Delta X$	$\beta_2 g(S)\Delta X$
0	0	0	0	1	0.8660	0.1340	0.8660			0.3634	0.6366	0.3147	0.5513
1	0	1	1	8	0.7906	0.0755	6.3246	0.0000	1.0000	0.3980	0.6020	2.5175	3.8071
2	9	0	9	1	0.7071	0.0835	0.7071	1.0000	0.0000	0.3270	0.6730	0.2312	0.4759
3	9.67	0.33	10	1	0.5590	0.1481	0.5590	0.9667	0.0333	0.1575	0.8425	0.0881	0.4710
4	10	1	11	79	0.5000	0.0590	39.5000	0.9091	0.0909	0.0688	0.9312	2.7187	36.7813
5	0	90	90	9	0.3536	0.1464	3.1820	0.0000	1.0000	0.0973	0.9027	0.3097	2.8723
6	9	90	99	1	0.2500	0.1036	0.2500	0.0909	0.9091	0.1000	0.9000	0.0250	0.2250
7	10	90	100	0	0.0000	0.2500	0.0000	0.1000	0.9000				
Sum				100		1.0000	51.3887					6.2048	45.1838

$$\bar{S}_i(a) = \sum_{j<j(a)} \alpha_i(X_j)S_j\Delta X_j + (a - X_{j(a)})\alpha_i(X_{j(a)})S_j(a)$$

$$\bar{P}_i(a) = \sum_{j<j(a)} \beta_i(X_j)g(S_j)\Delta X_j + (a - X_{j(a)})\beta_i(X_{j(a)})g(S_{j(a)}).$$

Layer margin by unit equals the difference between premium density and expected loss density:

$$M_{i,j} = \beta_{i,j}g(S_j) - \alpha_{i,j}S_j \tag{15.12}$$

times the layer width, ΔX or $a - X$, whichever applies.

Example 270. Table 15.14 illustrates the calculation of margin by layer by unit for the simple example. It combines the results of Tables 15.12 and 15.13. The sums of the margin columns ($M_i = \beta_i g - \alpha_i S$) times the layer widths yield the total margin for each unit.

In the presence of limited assets, only a partial sum is used. For example, if $a = 11$ then only rows 0 through 3 are summed. Rows 0 through 2 are in the $j < j(a)$ summation and row 3 is in the $(a - X_{j(a)})$ term, where that difference equals ΔX in this example. In such a case, the margins are -0.5423 for unit 1 and 2.4365 for unit 2. Unit 1 has a negative margin! This is because the assets are so small, and the insolvency probability so high, that unit 2 takes payments away from unit 1 too often. Unit 1 needs to be compensated for sharing its claim payments with unit 2.

To compute the margins when $a = 80$, we sum rows 0 through 4, but the row 4 ΔX value of 79 is replaced by $80 - 11 = 69$. The reader can verify, by either the partial sums of the survival function form, or the $X_{i,j}\Delta g(S_j)$ haircut sum products of the outcome-probability form, that the two margins in that case are 1.0089 and 18.1353, respectively, for a total of 19.1442. □

15.2.5 Computing Capital and CoC

Layer capital density is asset density (unity) less premium density: $Q_j = 1 - g(S_j)$. At the unit level,

$$Q_{i,j} = \frac{\beta_{i,j}g(S_j) - \alpha_{i,j}S_j}{g(S_j) - S_j} \times (1 - g(S_j)) \tag{15.13}$$

$$= \frac{M_{i,j}}{M_j} \times Q_j. \tag{15.14}$$

As with margin, total capital equals capital density times ΔX or $(a-X)$ as appropriate. Return on capital is simply margin divided by capital.

Example 271. Table 15.15 shows the capital allocation, using margin allocations previously calculated from Table 15.14. When unit 1 has a negative margin in a layer, it is allocated negative capital. In total, unit 1 has a margin of 1.4548 and a 3.5274 capital allocation, for a weighted CoC of 41.24%. For unit 2, the weighted CoC is 49.76%. If assets are limited to $a =$

Table 15.14 Simple example with by-unit margin calculation. Entries for $\beta - \alpha$ in row 7 are undefined. $M = g(S) - S$, $M_i = \beta_{ig}(S) - \alpha_{iS}$.

j	X	ΔX	S	$g(S)$	M	$M\Delta X$	M_1	M_2	$M_1\Delta X$	$M_2\Delta X$
0	0	1	0.7500	0.8660	0.1160	0.1160	−0.0603	0.1763	−0.0603	0.1763
1	1	8	0.6250	0.7906	0.1656	1.3246	−0.0603	0.2259	−0.4825	1.8071
2	9	1	0.5000	0.7071	0.2071	0.2071	−0.0188	0.2259	−0.0188	0.2259
3	10	1	0.3125	0.5590	0.2465	0.2465	0.0193	0.2272	0.0193	0.2272
4	11	79	0.2500	0.5000	0.2500	19.7500	0.0225	0.2275	1.7761	17.9739
5	90	9	0.1250	0.3536	0.2286	2.0570	0.0225	0.2061	0.2023	1.8546
6	99	1	0.0625	0.2500	0.1875	0.1875	0.0188	0.1688	0.0188	0.1688
7	100	0	0.0000	0.0000	0.0000	0.0000				
Sum		100				23.8887			1.4548	22.4338

Table 15.15 Simple example with capital by layer by unit calculation. $Q_j = 1 - g(S_j)$ and $Q_{i,j} = M_{i,j}/\iota_j$.

j	X	ΔX	M	Q	$\iota = M/Q$	$M_1\Delta X$	$M_2\Delta X$	$Q_1\Delta X$	$Q_2\Delta X$
0	0	1	0.1160	0.1340	0.8660	−0.0603	0.1763	−0.0696	0.2036
1	1	8	0.1656	0.2094	0.7906	−0.4825	1.8071	−0.6104	2.2858
2	9	1	0.2071	0.2929	0.7071	−0.0188	0.2259	−0.0266	0.3195
3	10	1	0.2465	0.4410	0.5590	0.0193	0.2272	0.0346	0.4064
4	11	79	0.2500	0.5000	0.5000	1.7761	17.9739	3.5522	35.9478
5	90	9	0.2286	0.6464	0.3536	0.2023	1.8546	0.5723	5.2457
6	99	1	0.1875	0.7500	0.2500	0.0188	0.1688	0.0750	0.6750
7	100	0	0.0000	1.0000	0.0000				
Sum		100				1.4548	22.4338	3.5274	45.0839

80, the sums of margin and capital only go through row 4, with the same $\Delta X = 80 - 11 = 69$ replacement in row 4 as in the previous section. The reader can verify that the returns become 41.51% and 52.39%, respectively. □

15.2.6 Computing the Lifted and Linear Natural Allocations

The formulas for $\bar{P}_i(a)$, Equations (14.25), (14.26), (15.10), and (15.11), are all lifted versions of the natural allocation, since $\bar{P}_i$ is defined as the lifted allocation in Eq. (14.22). For the record, the non-lifted versions in outcome-probability form simply replace β_i with α_i, viz.:

$$\bar{P}_i(a) = \int_0^a \kappa_i(x) g'(S(x)) dF(x) + a\alpha_i(a) g(S(a)) \tag{15.15}$$

Table 15.16 Joint outcomes and probabilities.

Event	ID	X_1	X_2	X	p
Nothing	1	0	0	0	0.2500
Storm	2	0	10	10	0.1250
Fire	3	10	0	10	0.1250
Fire and storm	4	10	10	20	0.0625
Fires	5	20	0	20	0.1250
Fires and storm	6	20	10	30	0.0625
Bad storm	7	0	40	40	0.1250
Fire and bad storm	8	10	40	50	0.0625
Fires and bad storm	9	20	40	60	0.0625
Sum					1

$$= \sum_{j \le j(a)} X_{i,j} \Delta g(S_j) + a\alpha_i(X_{j(a)}) g(S_{j(a)}). \tag{15.16}$$

The survival function form equations do not admit of such a simple replacement because β_i appears in all the terms. In practical applications should use the formulas based on the haircut data $X_i(a)$, Eq. (15.4).

Example 272. Consider the two independent units X_1, X_2 laid out in Table 15.16. The first has losses $0, 10, 20$ with respective probabilities $1/2, 1/4, 1/4$. The second has losses $0, 10, 40$ with respective probabilities $1/2, 1/4, 1/4$. Assume premium is determined by the proportional hazard SRM ρ with exponent 0.87. Compute:

1. The lifted premium allocations when assets are limited to 30.
2. The linear premium allocations when assets are limited to 30.
3. *Extra credit.* The linear and lifted allocations for $a = 10, 20, 40, 50, 60$.
4. *Extra credit.* Compute the natural allocation set for $X \wedge 30$, i.e. ignoring values of X, find the range of potential allocations to X_1, X_2.

Solution. For part (1), first we assemble the joint outcomes and probabilities. We follow the steps in Section 11.1.1. Since $X = 0$ is already an outcome, Step (1) has no effect. Steps (2) and (3), sort and group, combine outcomes 2–3 (resp., 4–5) that have the same value $X = 10$ (resp., $X = 20$), resulting in Table 15.17. Decumulating, distorting, and differencing, Steps (4)-(6), produces Table 15.18, which we can use to compute the lifted allocations. The sum-product, Step (7), of $X_1(a)$ and q in Table 15.18 is 6.8419; the corresponding figure for X_2 is 10.0505. The total premium is 16.8924.

For (2), to calculate the linear premium allocation, we further collapse the table rows that have $X \wedge a = 30$. The sum-product of $X_1(a)$ and q in Table 15.19 is 6.8350; the corresponding figure for X_2 is 10.0574. For (3), the allocations for various values of a are set out in Table 15.20. The solution for part (4) is omitted. □

Table 15.17 Joint outcomes with unique X values.

j	IDs	$\varkappa_1$	$\varkappa_2$	X	p
0	1	0	0	0	0.2500
1	{2,3}	5	5	10	0.2500
2	{4,5}	16.6667	3.3333	20	0.1875
3	6	20	10	30	0.0625
4	7	0	40	40	0.1250
5	8	10	40	50	0.0625
6	9	20	40	60	0.0625

Table 15.18 Calculation of premium and lifted allocations. p- and q-sum rows show $\sum p_j X_j$, $\sum \Delta g(S)_j X_j$ respectively.

j	$X_1(a)$	$X_2(a)$	$X(a)$	p	S	$g(S)$	$\Delta g(S)$
0	0	0	0	0.2500	0.7500	0.779	0.221
1	5	5	10	0.2500	0.5000	0.547	0.231
2	16.6667	3.3333	20	0.1875	0.3125	0.364	0.184
3	20	10	30	0.0625	0.2500	0.299	0.064
4	0	30	30	0.1250	0.1250	0.164	0.136
5	6	24	30	0.0625	0.0625	0.090	0.074
6	10	20	30	0.0625	0.0000	0.000	0.090
p-sum	6.6250	9.0000	15.6250				
q-sum	6.8419	10.0505	16.8924				

Table 15.19 Calculation of premium and non-lifted allocations.

IDs	$X_1(a)$	$X_2(a)$	$X(a)$	p	S	$g(S)$	$\Delta g(S)$
1	0	0	0	0.2500	0.75	0.7786	0.2214
{2,3}	5	5	10	0.2500	0.5	0.5471	0.2314
{4,5}	16.6667	3.3333	20	0.1875	0.3125	0.3635	0.1836
{6,7,8,9}	7.2	22.8	30	0.3125	0	0	0.3635
p-sum	6.6250	9.0000	15.6250				
q-sum	6.8350	10.0574	16.8924				

Table 15.20 Comparison of lifted and non-lifted allocations.

a	$D^l\rho_{X\wedge 30,X}(X_1)$	$D^l\rho_{X\wedge 30,X}(X_2)$	$D^n\rho_{X\wedge 30}(X_1)$	$D^n\rho_{X\wedge 30}(X_2)$	$\rho(X\wedge a)$
10	3.5622	4.2236	3.6983	4.0875	7.7858
20	5.9672	7.2901	6.2183	7.0390	13.2573
30	6.8419	10.0505	6.8350	10.0574	16.8924
40	7.2890	12.5971	7.0972	12.7889	19.8861
50	7.7361	13.7880	7.6846	13.8395	21.5241
60	8.0348	14.3855	8.0348	14.3855	22.4203

15.2.7 Summary of Formulas

The formulas we have derived are laid out in Table 15.21. In general, to convert from the integral notation used in 14 to summations, apply these substitutions:

$$
\begin{aligned}
\Delta X &\longleftrightarrow dx \\
p &\longleftrightarrow f(x)dx,\ dF(x) \\
\Delta g(S) &\longleftrightarrow g'(S(x))f(x)dx,\ g'(S(x))dF(x) \\
\mathit{function}(x_i) &\longleftrightarrow \mathit{function}(x) \\
\sum_{n}^{n=j(a)} &\longleftrightarrow \int_0^a .
\end{aligned}
$$

In addition, it is always helpful to draw a picture.

15.3 Bodoff's Percentile Layer of Capital Method

In this section, we reproduce and analyze *Thought Experiment 1* from Bodoff (2007), translating it into our framework and comparing it to the natural allocation.

There are two independent events: X_1 hurricane with loss 99 at probability 0.20, and X_2 earthquake with loss 100 at probability 0.05. We set available assets at $a = 100$. There is equal priority in default. The basic elements are laid out in Table 15.21. In this and subsequent tables, the Sum row shows either the sum or the probability weighted average expectation, as appropriate to each column.

Exercise 273. Reproduce Table 15.21 in a spreadsheet. □

Expected losses in total are computed using either $\sum(X \wedge a)p$ in event-outcome form, or $\sum S\Delta(X \wedge a)$ in survival function form. In both cases, the sum is over the outcomes j, i.e. the sum-product of the columns. By unit, we can use either $\sum X_i(a)p$ or $\sum \alpha_i S\Delta(X \wedge a)$ (not shown).

The shared liability a', equal to assets less expected loss or equivalently margin plus capital, is easiest to compute in the survival function form, and equals $\sum(1-S)\Delta(X \wedge a)$ in total. The

Table 15.21 Various ways of computing expected losses and the linear and lifted $(X \wedge a)$ natural allocations.

Quantity	Loss	Premium
Cash flow	$X_{i,j}(a) = X_{i,j}\dfrac{X_j \wedge a}{X_j}$	same
Probability	Objective, S_j, $p_j = \Delta S_j$	risk-adjusted, $g(S_j)$, $\Delta g(S_j)$
Conditional layer expectation	$\kappa_i(x) = \dfrac{\sum_{j:X_j=x} X_{i,j}p_j}{\sum_{j:X_j=x} p_j}$	same (= linear)
Expectation (after grouping and $X_{i,j} \leftarrow \kappa_i(X_j)$)	$\bar{S}_i = \sum_j X_{i,j}p_j$	$\bar{P}_i = \sum_j X_{i,j}\Delta g(S_j)$
Threshold index	$j(a) = \max\{j : X_j < a\}$	same
Share function	$\alpha_i(a) = \dfrac{\sum_{j:X_j>a}(X_{i,j}/X_j)p_j}{\sum_{j:X_j>a} p_j}$	$\beta_i(a) = \dfrac{\sum_{j:X_j>a}(X_{i,j}/X_j)\Delta g(S_j)}{\sum_{j:X_j>a} \Delta g(S_j)}$
Lifted allocation, outcome-probability form	$\bar{S}_i(a) = \sum_{j\le j(a)} X_{i,j}p_j + a\alpha_i(X_{j(a)})S_{j(a)}$	$\bar{P}_i^f(a) = \sum_{j\le j(a)} \kappa_{i,j}\Delta g(S_j) + a\beta_i(X_{j(a)})g(S_{j(a)})$
Lifted allocation, survival function form	$\bar{S}_i(a) = \sum_{j<j(a)} \alpha_i(X_j)S_j dX_j + (a - X_j(a))\alpha_i(X_{j(a)})S_j(a)$	$\bar{P}_i^f(a) = \sum_{j<j(a)} \beta_i(X_j)g(S_j)dX_j$ $+(a - X_j(a))\beta_i(X_{j(a)})g(S_j(a))$
Linear allocation, outcome-probability form	$\bar{S}_i(a)$ same as above	$\bar{P}_i^n(a) = \sum_{j\le j(a)} \kappa_{i,j}\Delta g(S_j) + a\alpha_i(X_{j(a)})g(S_{j(a)})$
Linear allocation, survival function form	$\bar{S}_i(a)$ same as above	$\bar{P}_i^n(a) = \bar{P}_i^f(a) + a\left(\alpha_i(X_{j(a)}) - \beta_i(X_{j(a)})\right) g(S_{j(a)})$

Table 15.21 Bodoff's *Thought Experiment 1* basic elements, assets $a = 100$.

j	X_1	X_2	X	p	S	$X \wedge a$	$\Delta(X \wedge a)$	$X_1(a)$	$X_2(a)$
1	0	0	0	0.76	0.24	0	99	0	0
2	99	0	99	0.19	0.05	99	1	99	0
3	0	100	100	0.04	0.01	100	0	0	100
4	99	100	199	0.01	0	100	0	49.7487	50.2513
Sum	19.8	5	24.8	1		23.81		19.3075	4.5025

Table 15.22 Bodoff's *Thought Experiment 1*, PLC allocation of the shared liability when $a = 100$.

j	$\Delta(X \wedge a)$	S	α_1	α_2	a_1'	a_2'
1	99	0.2400	0.8124	0.1876	61.1246	14.1154
2	1	0.0500	0.0995	0.9005	0.0945	0.8555
3	0	0.0100	0.4975	0.5025	0.0000	0.0000
4	0	0.0000				
Sum	100				61.2191	14.9709

PLC method says the shared liability is allocated to units *within each layer* in proportion to α_i. Therefore the total allocation to unit i is $a_i' := \sum \alpha_i(1-S)\Delta(X \wedge a)$. The latter equation is the discrete manifestation of Eq. (14.43). Allocating the shared liability in this way is Bodoff's principal innovation. Table 15.22 shows the results.

Exercise 274. The outcome-probability form of a' is less tractable. To see why, deduce it, using integration by parts. Illustrate the two terms involved on a Lee diagram. □

If we assume a *portfolio* cost of capital of $\iota = 0.1$, we have enough information to begin filling in the funding table, Table 15.23. In total, the shared liability is shared between margin and capital in proportions $\iota : 1$, i.e. $M = \delta a'$, $Q = \nu a'$. We can then compute total premium as the sum of expected loss plus margin.

At this stage, we cannot allocate the total margin by unit without making an explicit pricing assumption. The PLC method, on its own, does not address pricing, as we observed in Section 14.3.9. Assuming the same ι CoC applies to each unit individually, we can again separate each a_i' in the proportions $\iota : 1$, complete the funding table. The order of calculation is: EL, shared liability by unit using PLC, margin split from shared liability using CCoC, and premium equals EL plus margin. Table 15.24 shows the completed calculation.

More generally, we can introduce a pricing SRM that allows for the possibility that each unit does not have the same *total* CoC but only the same CoC *within each layer*. In line with previous assumptions, let us examine how the CCoC SRM ($g(s) = \nu s + \delta, s > 0$) plays out. Obviously, the total must be the same. But what about by unit? Table 15.25 shows the computations.

Table 15.23 Bodoff's *Thought Experiment 1* funding, assets $a = 100$, portfolio $\iota = 0.1$, funding table. Rows shown in order of calculation.

Item	Unit 1	Unit 2	Portfolio
EL	19.3075	4.5025	23.8100
Shared liability	61.2191	14.9709	76.1900
Margin			6.9264
Capital			69.2636
Premium			30.7364
Return			0.1000

Table 15.24 Bodoff's *Thought Experiment 1*, full PLC allocation, assets $a = 100$, each unit cost of capital $\iota = 0.1$.

Item	Unit 1	Unit 2	Portfolio
EL	19.3075	4.5025	23.8100
Premium	24.8729	5.8635	30.7364
Margin	5.5654	1.3610	6.9264
Capital	55.6538	13.6099	69.2636
Return	0.1000	0.1000	0.1000

There is no surprise that with this SRM, the CoC is constant across layers. We now apply the $\iota : 1$ split of the shared liability a_i' into margin and capital in Table 15.26. Again, the same results already seen in Table 15.24 are obtained. However, it is evident that if ι is different across layers, different results are to be expected.

How does Bodoff's pricing compare to the natural allocation premium? Since we know unlimited losses, and all outcomes are distinct, we compute the lifted allocation premium. To be consistent, continue with the CCoC SRM with $\iota = 0.1$ calculated in Table 15.25. With distorted probabilities $\Delta g(S)$ available from Table 15.25, and equal-priority capped losses $X_i(a)$ available from Table 15.21, we can compute distorted expectations (premiums) at the unit level $\sum_j X_{i,j}(a)\Delta g(S_j)$, and then subtract expected losses to obtain unit margins. The results are in Table 15.27.

To allocate capital to units, we need β by layer by unit. Then, margin density $M = \beta g(S) - \alpha S$ and capital density $Q = M/\iota$.

Table 15.29 is the completed funding table. Notice that the $\sum M_i \Delta X$ in Table 15.28 match the unit margins already posted in Table 15.27.

The linear natural allocation groups and collapses all rows with $X \geq a$ into one event row. If we only know $X \wedge a$, then the two events $X = a$ and $X > a$ are indistinguishable and must be combined into one, which has a profound impact on pricing in this example. Unit

Table 15.25 Bodoff's *Thought Experiment 1*, pricing with the CCoC SRM, portfolio $\iota = 0.1$.

j	p	S	$g(S)$	$\Delta g(S)$	$M = g(S) - S$	$Q = 1 - g(S)$	$\iota = M/Q$
1	0.76	0.24	0.3091	0.6909	0.0691	0.6909	0.1
2	0.19	0.05	0.1364	0.1727	0.0864	0.8636	0.1
3	0.04	0.01	0.1	0.0364	0.09	0.9	0.1
4	0.01	0	0	0.1	0	1	0
Sum	1			1			

Table 15.26 Bodoff's *Thought Experiment 1*, CCoC $\iota = 0.1$ assumption applied to layers, separate margin and capital allocations from PLC results. M and Q are the margin and capital layer densities, respectively.

j	a_1'	a_2'	$M_1\Delta X$	$M_2\Delta X$	$Q_1\Delta X$	$Q_2\Delta X$
1	61.1246	14.1154	5.5568	1.2832	55.5678	12.8322
2	0.0945	0.8555	0.0086	0.0778	0.0859	0.7777
3	0.0000	0.0000	0.0000	0.0000	0.0000	0.0000
4						
Sum	61.2191	14.9709	5.5654	1.3610	55.6538	13.6099

Table 15.27 Bodoff's *Thought Experiment 1*, CCoC $\iota = 0.1$ SRM pricing, assets $a = 100$, lifted natural allocation of premium.

Item	Unit 1	Unit 2	Portfolio
EL	19.3075	4.5025	23.8100
Premium	22.0749	8.6615	30.7364
Margin	2.7674	4.1590	6.9264
Capital			69.2636
Return			0.1000

2 now dominates the event $X \wedge a = a$: 80% of the time it accounts for 100% of the loss, and the remaining 20% it accounts for about 50%. Since the CCoC distortion assigns a relatively large distorted probability, $g(0.05) = 0.05\nu + \delta = 0.1364$, to that single largest event, the unit 2 margin becomes much larger than with the lifted allocation. When lifted, the largest event still gets outsized probability ($g(0.01) = 0.1$), but it is split about 50/50 so the units share the cost more evenly. Table 15.30 shows the funding table.

Table 15.28 Bodoff's *Thought Experiment 1*, CCoC $\iota = 0.1$ SRM, assets $a = 100$, lifted natural allocation of margin and capital.

j	$\Delta(X \wedge a)$	β_1	β_2	M_1	M_2	$M_1 \Delta X$	$M_2 \Delta X$	$Q_1 \Delta X$	$Q_2 \Delta X$
1	99	0.7198	0.2802	0.0275	0.0416	2.7226	4.1174	27.2261	41.1739
2	1	0.3648	0.6352	0.0448	0.0416	0.0448	0.0416	0.4477	0.4159
3	0	0.4975	0.5025	0.0448	0.0452	0	0	0	0
4	0								
Sum						2.7674	4.1590	27.6739	41.5898

Table 15.29 Bodoff's *Thought Experiment 1*, lifted natural allocation funding, CCoC $\iota = 0.1$ SRM, assets $a = 100$.

Item	Unit 1	Unit 2	Portfolio
EL	19.3075	4.5025	23.8100
Premium	22.0749	8.6615	30.7364
Margin	2.7674	4.1590	6.9264
Capital	27.6739	41.5898	69.2636
Return	0.1000	0.1000	0.1000

Table 15.30 Bodoff's *Thought Experiment 1*, linear natural allocation, CCoC $\iota = 0.1$ SRM, assets $a = 100$.

Item	Unit 1	Unit 2	Portfolio
EL	19.3075	4.5025	23.8100
Premium	18.4568	12.2796	30.7364
Margin	−0.8507	7.7771	6.9264
Capital	−8.5070	77.7707	69.2636
Return	0.1	0.1	0.1

Let's take stock and compare the pricing implied by these various methods. Before we do that, spend a few minutes completing the next exercise.

Exercise 275. (Important!) You are the chief pricing actuary for Ins Co. Keeping our assumptions, equal priority, $a = 100$, and $\iota = 0.1$, what allocation of the total needed premium 30.7363 to each unit do you recommend? Create an Executive Summary with a few bullets to justify and explain your answer. □

Table 15.31 Bodoff's *Thought Experiment 1*, summary of pricing and implied loss ratios by method, CCoC $\iota = 0.10$, assets $a = 100$.

Item	Unit 1	Unit 2	Total
Unlimited loss, $\mathsf{E}[X_i]$	19.8000	5.0000	24.8000
Limited loss, $\mathsf{E}[X_i(a)]$	19.3075	4.5025	23.8100
CV	2.0000	4.3589	1.8226
Correlation to Total	0.8761	0.4822	1.0000
EPD	0.0249	0.0995	0.0399
Expected value premium	24.9241	5.8123	30.7364
Loss ratio, unlimited	0.7944	0.8602	0.8069
Loss ratio, limited	0.7747	0.7747	0.7747
Var/covariance premium	24.6236	6.1128	30.7364
Loss ratio, unlimited	0.8041	0.8180	0.8069
Loss ratio, limited	0.7841	0.7366	0.7747
Bodoff PLC premium	24.8729	5.8635	30.7364
Loss ratio, unlimited	0.7960	0.8527	0.8069
Loss ratio, limited	0.7762	0.7679	0.7747
Lifted natural premium	22.0749	8.6615	30.7364
Loss ratio, unlimited	0.8969	0.5773	0.8069
Loss ratio, limited	0.8746	0.5198	0.7747
Linear natural premium	18.4568	12.2796	30.7364
Loss ratio, unlimited	1.0728	0.4072	0.8069
Loss ratio, limited	1.0461	0.3667	0.7747

Table 15.31 summarizes the indicated unit pricing by method. The top block presents the expected loss by unit on a capped and uncapped basis, CV, expected policyholder deficit, and correlation of each unit with the total. These show that unit 2 is more volatile than unit 1. Its CV is 4.4 vs. 2.0 for unit 1, and it has a far higher EPD. (EPD is computed based on equal priority; it does not depend on a capital allocation.) In addition, unit 2's lower expected frequency, 0.05 vs. 0.20, makes it subject to greater parameter estimation risk.

The subsequent blocks of the table lay out pricing from five methods: expected value (proportional to expected loss), variance/covariance premium, Bodoff's PLC premium, the lifted, and the linear premiums. Each block shows the loss ratio on a limited and unlimited basis—insureds and underwriters who ignore default may mistake the loss ratio for the unlimited value—however, all pricing is based on the limited loss. The total premium and loss ratios are the same for each method by construction.

The pricing falls into three groups:

- The expected value, variance/covariance, and PLC methods are very similar. They do not differentiate between the two units.
- The lifted natural allocation reflects the greater risk of unit 2.
- The linear natural allocation illustrates the problems PLC is designed to solve.

There is no "right" answer. We like the lifted allocation and understand why the linear allocation is tricked. Ultimately, the market sets the price, and we decide whether to participate. The market can support prices that leave all insurers unhappy—for reasons that we explore in Chapter 20.

Exercise 276. Using the data from Table 15.21 and applying a proportional hazard SRM with exponent 0.82156, calculate the funding summary tables for the PLC and lifted natural methods.

Solution. The PLC allocation splits the shared liability into margin and capital using the return generated in each layer separately. The results are shown in Table 15.32. □

Exercise 277. Using the data from Table 15.21 and applying a Wang Transform SRM with parameter 0.209615, calculate the funding summary tables for the PLC and lifted natural methods.

Solution. The Wang Transform PLC and lifted natural allocations are shown in Table 15.33. □

Exercise 278. Compute the linear natural allocations applying the same two transforms.

Solution. Table 15.34 shows the linear natural allocations of premium, by distortion, with CCoC shown for comparison. □

Table 15.32 Proportional hazard PLC and lifted natural allocations.

Item	Unit 1	Unit 2	Portfolio	Unit 1	Unit 2	Portfolio
Method	**PLC**			**Lifted**		
EL	19.3075	4.5025	23.8100	19.3075	4.5025	23.8100
Premium	24.9090	5.8271	30.7361	23.3342	7.4020	30.7361
Margin	5.6016	1.3246	6.9261	4.0267	2.8994	6.9261
Capital	55.6176	13.6463	69.2639	40.0416	29.2223	69.2639
Return	0.1007	0.0971	0.1000	0.1006	0.0992	0.1000

Table 15.33 Wang Transform PLC and lifted natural allocations.

Item	Unit 1	Unit 2	Portfolio	Unit 1	Unit 2	Portfolio
Method	PLC			Lifted		
EL	19.3075	4.5025	23.8100	19.3075	4.5025	23.8100
Premium	24.9162	5.8202	30.7364	24.0282	6.7082	30.7364
Margin	5.6087	1.3177	6.9264	4.7207	2.2057	6.9264
Capital	55.6104	13.6532	69.2636	46.8427	22.4209	69.2636
Return	0.1009	0.0965	0.1000	0.1008	0.0984	0.1000

Table 15.34 The linear natural allocations of premium, by distortion, with CCoC shown for comparison for Exercise 278.

Method	Unit 1	Unit 2	Portfolio
CCoC	18.4568	12.2796	30.7364
PH	23.0517	7.6844	30.7361
Wang	23.9277	6.8087	30.7364

15.4 Case Study Exhibits

15.4.1 Visualizing Risk for Case Studies

Figures 15.2–15.7 illustrate the visualizations developed in Section 14.3. The first row repeats graphics shown in Section 2.4 for easy reference. There are twelve plots in each display and we refer to the plot in row $r = 1, 2, 3, 4$, and column $c = 1, 2, 3$ matrix-style, as (r, c), starting at the top left. The horizontal axis shows the asset level in all plots except $(3, 3)$ and $(4, 3)$, where it shows probability, and $(1, 3)$ where it shows loss.

- $(1, 1)$ shows density for each unit (dotted and dashed) and the total (solid). The two units are independent.
- $(1, 2)$: log density, for comparing tail thickness.
- $(1, 3)$: the bivariate log-density. This plot illustrates the support of the losses, or where they *live*. The diagonal lines show contours of total loss. Where the diagonals intersect the cloud shows how a given level of loss is likely to be split between the two units.
- $(2, 1)$: the form of κ_i becomes clear from looking at $(1, 3)$. The two unit kappas sum to the diagonal, $\mathsf{E}[X \mid X = x] \equiv x$.
- $(2, 2)$: The α_i functions. The two functions sum to 1. For small x the expected proportion of losses is approximately given by the means. For large x it is driven by tail thickness. These plots vary materially across the three Cases.
- $(2, 3)$: The thicker lines are β_i and the thinner lines α_i from $(2, 2)$. When α decreases $\beta(x) \le \alpha(x)$. This can lead to a negative margin in low asset layers.

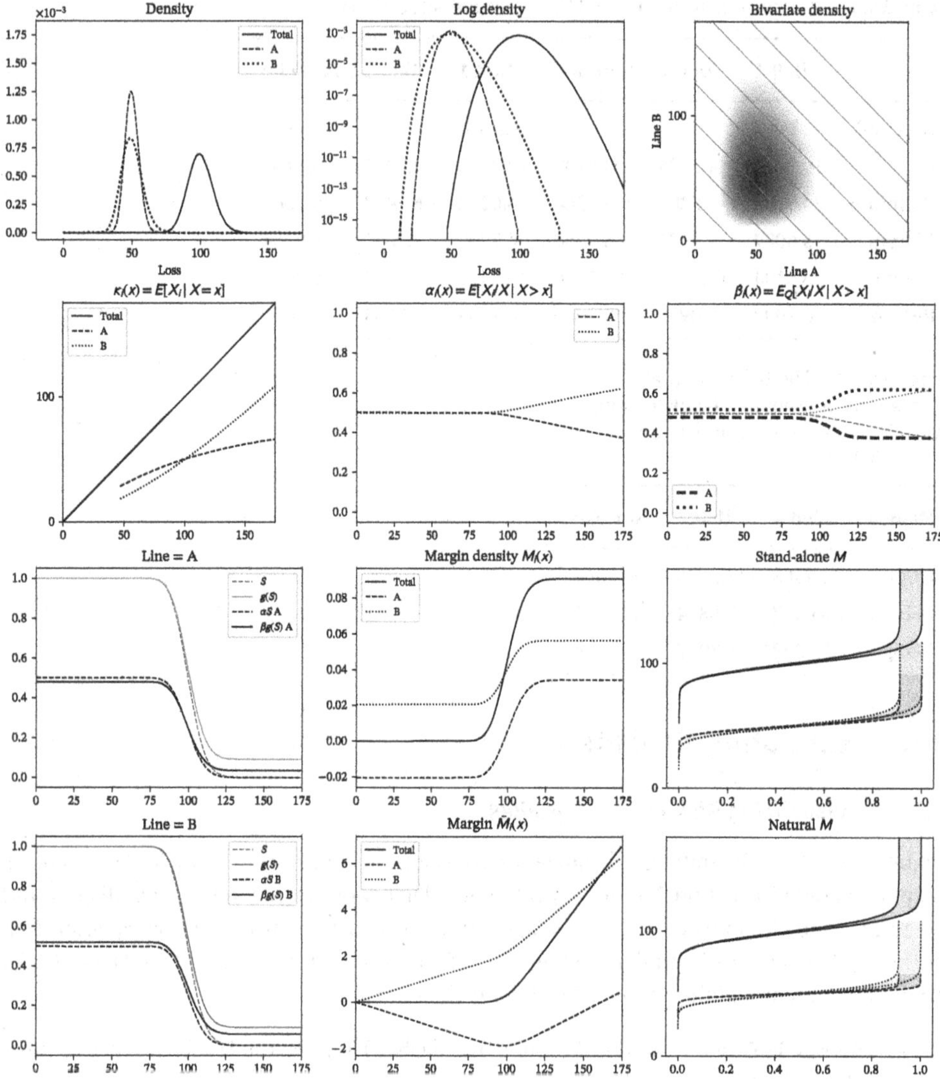

Figure 15.2 Gross Tame Case Study, CCoC distortion.

- (3, 1): illustrates premium and margin determination by asset layer for the first unit using Eq. (14.21) and Eq. (14.25). The top two grey lines show S (dashed) and $g(S)$ (solid). The difference between these lines is the total portfolio margin density. The lower two black lines show premium density $\beta g(S)$ (solid) and loss density αS (dashed). For low asset layers, if $\alpha(x)S(x) > \beta(x)g(S(x))$ (dashed above solid) then there is a negative layer margin. Eventually layer margins are positive for all units because with unlimited coverage the total margin is positive; see Section 5.2.4.
- (4, 1): shows the same thing as (3, 1) for the second unit.
- (3, 2): shows the layer margin densities $\beta g(S) - \alpha S$. For low asset layers, total premium (solid) is fully funded by loss with zero overall margin. If one unit has a positive margin the

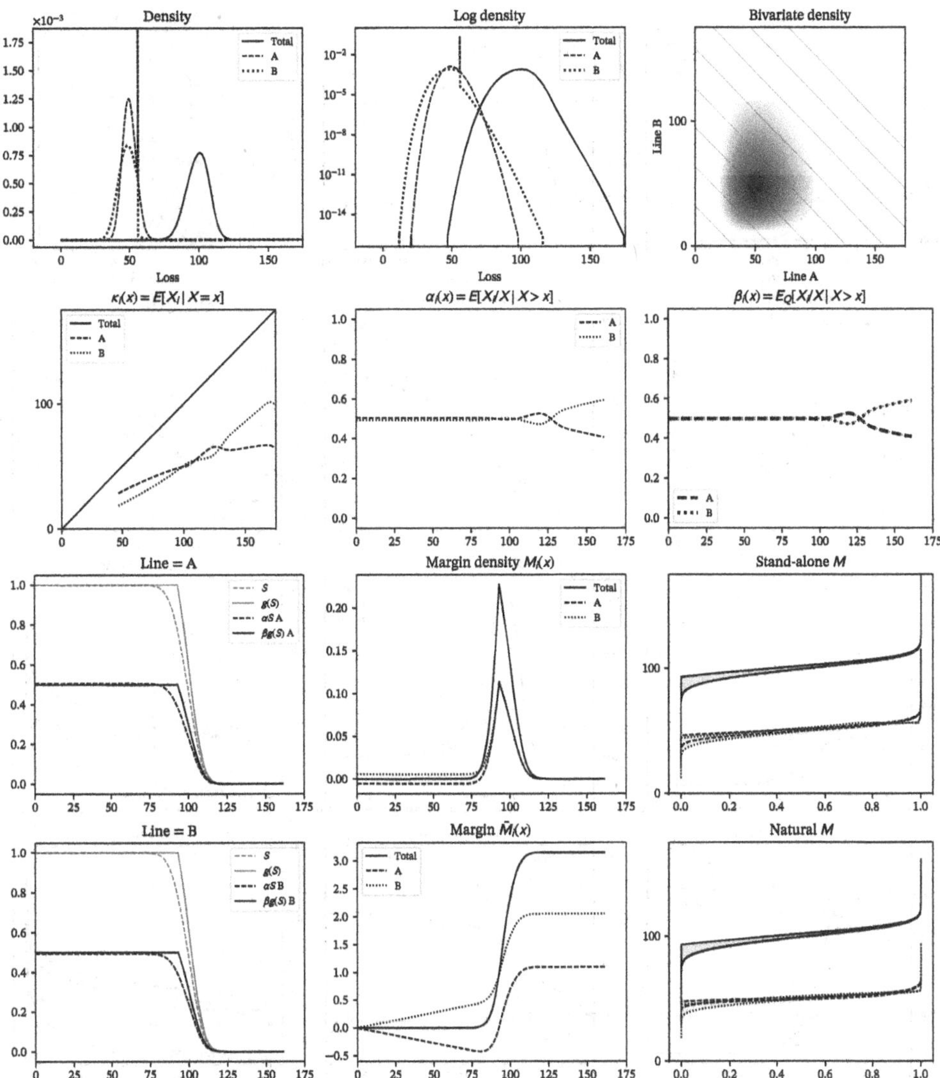

Figure 15.3 Net Tame Case Study, TVaR distortion.

other must have a negative one because the two sum to zero. The thick-tailed unit pays the positive margin, reflecting the benefit it receives from pooling in low layers. Again, the overall margin is always non-negative and eventually both units pay a positive layer margin.

- $(4, 2)$: shows the cumulative margin component of premium by asset level. Total margin (solid) is zero in low layers and then increases, and is always non-negative. The curves in this plot are the integrals of those in $(3, 2)$ from 0 to x.
- $(3, 3)$: shows *stand-alone* loss $(1 - S(x), x) = (p, q(p))$ and premium $(1 - g(S(x)), x) = (p, q(1 - g^{-1}(1 - p))$ (shifted left) for each unit and total. The margin is the shaded

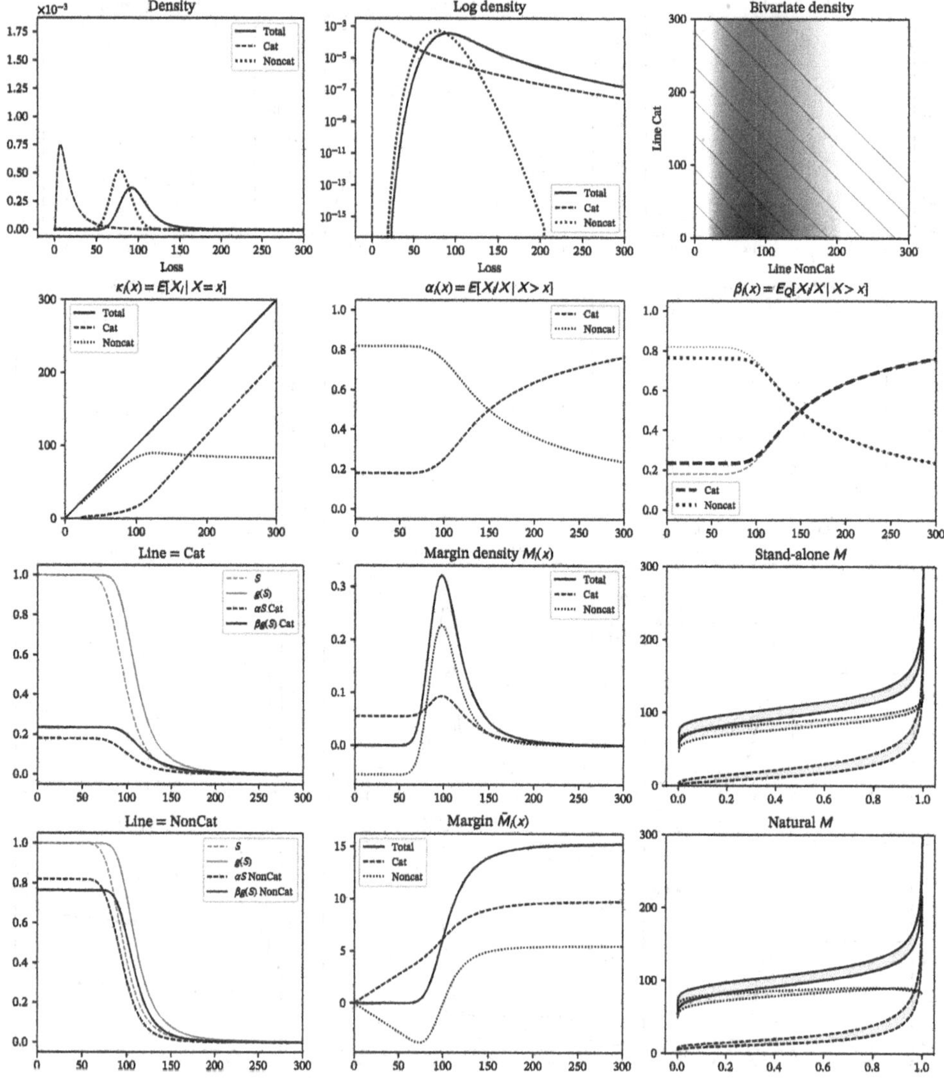

Figure 15.4 Gross Cat/Non-Cat Case Study, dual moment distortion.

area between the two. Each set of three lines does not add-up vertically because of diversification. The same distortion g is applied to each unit's stand-alone S_{X_i}.

- (4, 3): shows the natural allocation of loss and premium to each line. The total is the same as (3, 3). For each unit, the shape shows the range between $(p, \mathsf{E}[X_i \mid X = q(p)])$, i.e. the expected loss conditioned on total losses $X = q(p)$, and $(p, \mathsf{E}[X_i \mid X = q(1 - g^{-1}(1 - p))])$, i.e. the natural premium allocation, which may be negative. Here shapes *add up* vertically: they are allocations of the total. Looking vertically above p, the shaded areas show how the

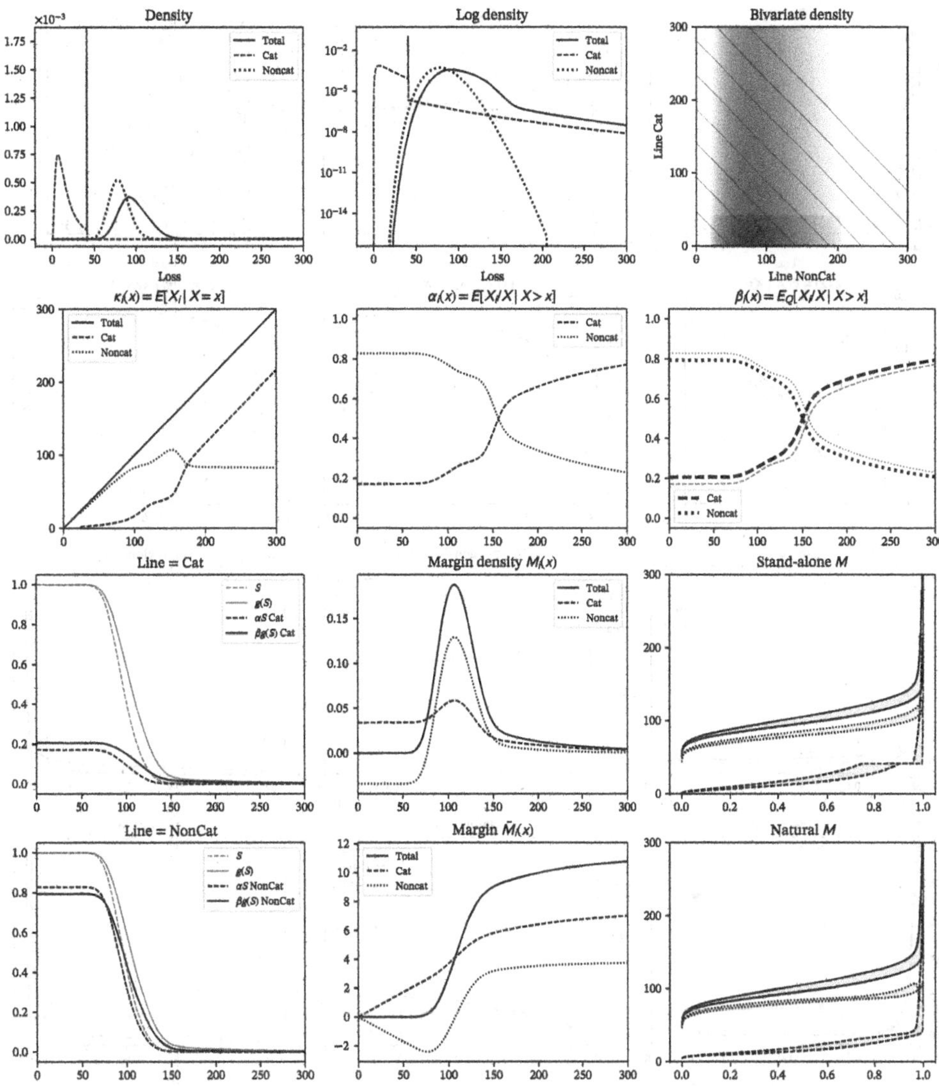

Figure 15.5 Net Cat/Non-Cat Case Study, proportional hazard distortion

total margin at that loss level is allocated between lines. A change in shape of the shaded margin area shows that the unit benefits from pooling and requires a lower overall margin.

There may appear to be a contradiction between figures (3, 2) and (4, 3) but it should be noted that a particular p value in (4, 3) refers to different events on the premium (generally top) and loss (generally bottom) lines.

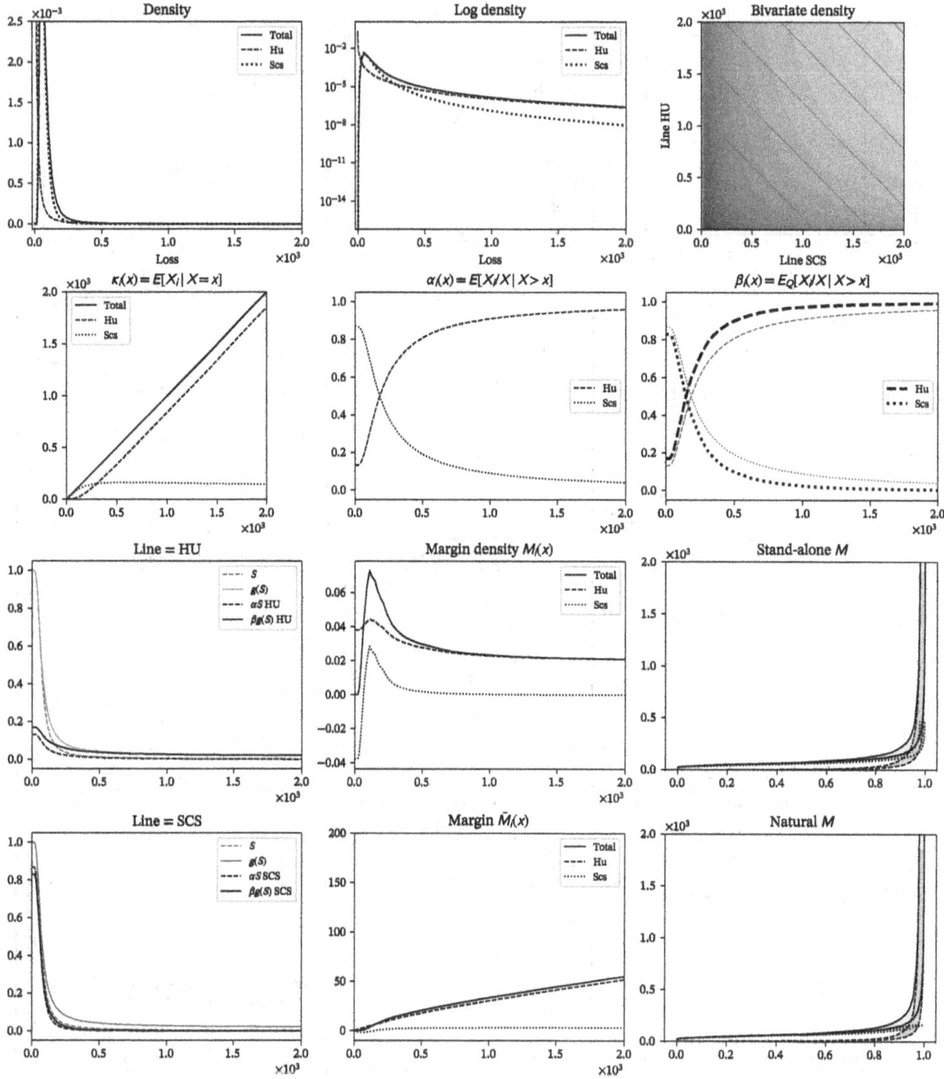

Figure 15.6 Gross Hu/SCS Case Study, blended distortion.

Plots (3, 3) and (4, 3) explain why a thick-tailed unit requires relatively more margin. The margin shape for a thick-tailed unit does not change when it is pooled with the thin-tailed unit. In Figure 15.4, (3, 3) the total shaded area for the cat unit is essentially an upward shift of stand-alone (upper and lower shaded areas), and the corresponding areas in (3, 3) and (3, 4) are the same shape. This means that adding the noncat unit has virtually no impact on the shape of cat; it is like adding a constant. Since coherent risk measures are translation invariant, constants are allocated no capital.

For the Hu/SCS Case, it comes as no surprise that SCS dominates layer premiums for lower layers whereas hurricane dominates for the higher layers. This is illustrated in Figure 15.6 (gross), where (2, 1) shows κ is completely dominated by hurricane, (2, 2) shows that α for SCS decreases while hurricane increases, and (2, 3) shows the impact of the risk adjustment, β is above α for the riskier line. Plot (3, 2) illustrates the margins by layer. SCS has negative margins (its α is decreasing and so $\beta < \alpha$) for small portfolio losses. Hurricane has positive margins across all layers (its α is increasing and so $\beta > \alpha$).

Each set of plots uses a different distortion function (for variety):

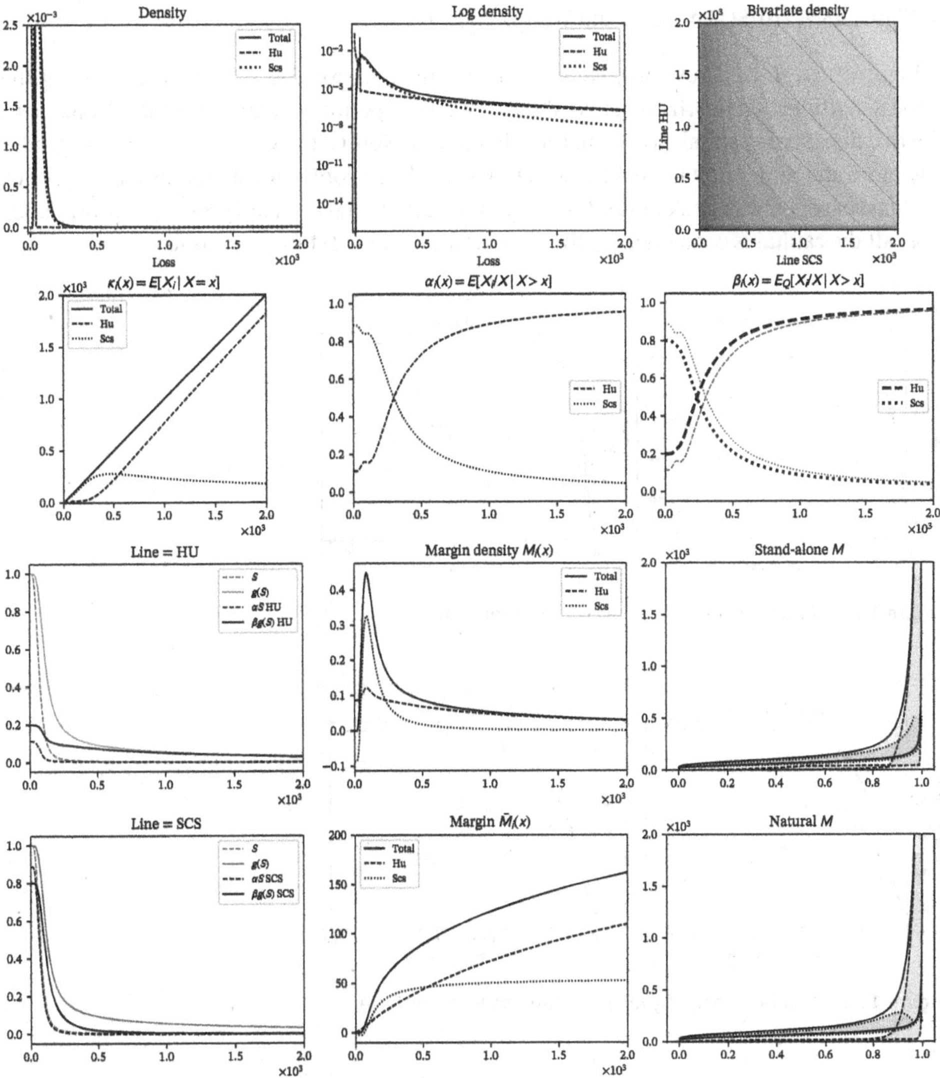

Figure 15.7 Net Hu/SCS Case Study, Wang transform.

- Figure 15.2, Tame gross uses CCoC. Note the effect of the mass at $s = 0$ in (3, 3) and (4, 3). The CCoC distortion includes a minimum rate on line, causing the fat tails to gS in (3, 1) and (4, 1), and margins in (3, 3) and (4, 3).
- Figure 15.3, Tame net uses TVaR. Note angular shifts in S and gS, and margin in (4, 1) and (3, 2)). The TVaR distortion causes the sudden drop off in gS in (3, 1) and (4, 1) and spiked margin in (3, 2).
- Figure 15.4, Cat/Non-Cat gross uses dual moment.
- Figure 15.5, Cat/Non-Cat net uses proportional hazard.
- Figure 15.6, Hu/SCS gross uses the blended distortion. Note magnitude of total margin (4, 2).
- Figure 15.7, Hu/SCS net uses the Wang transform.

Figures 15.8–15.10 show how capital is distributed across layers in each case, using the same distortions. The horizontal axis shows the return period of total loss. In the Tame Case, the two lines share capital equally in the tail. For Cat/Non-Cat, the cat unit consumes gradually more and more capital. For Hu/SCS, hurricane has a continuously rising capital profile. Capital shares for SCS peak around the 10 year return period then fall steadily. For very large loss, all the capital is consumed by the (much thicker-tailed) hurricane line.

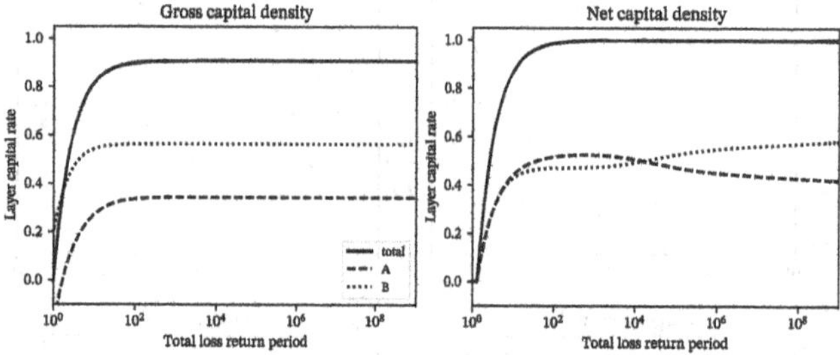

Figure 15.8 Capital density by layer for the Tame Case.

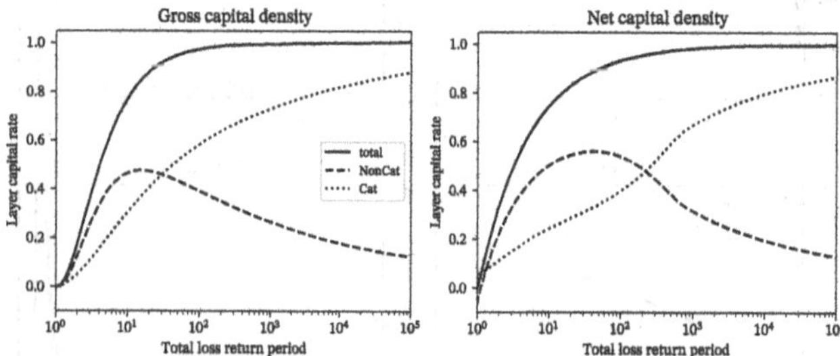

Figure 15.9 Capital density by layer for the Cat/Non-Cat Case.

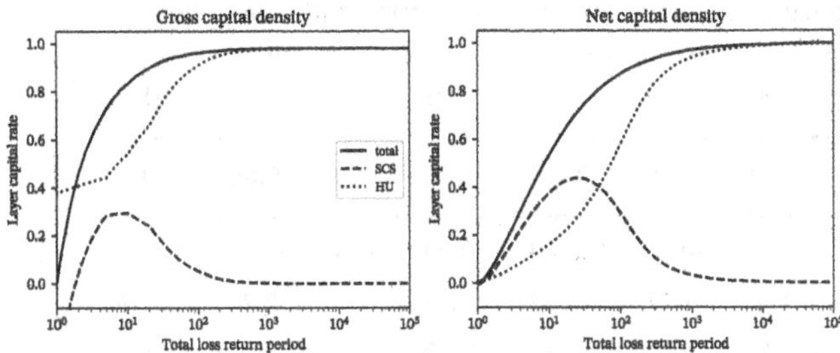

Figure 15.10 Capital density by layer for the Hu/SCS Case.

15.4.2 Applying the Natural Allocation to the Case Studies

Tables 15.35–15.37 show the lifted natural allocation pricing across the six distortions introduced in Section 11.4. Recall, the CCoC, proportional hazard, Wang, dual moment and TVaR distortions are calibrated to achieve a 0.1 CoC at 0.9999 VaR capital for the Tame Case and 0.999 for the other two Cases. The blend distortion *shaves the edge off* CCoC, proxying the impact of using debt or reinsurance to finance higher layers of capital. It produces lower overall pricing. The parameters are shown in Table 11.5.

Observe the following:

1. The CCoC distortion prices total and each line to a 0.1 return. The corresponding loss ratios vary gross to net and by unit. Net loss ratios are higher than gross, as expected.
2. The totals are the same as shown in Section 11.4, as expected. By unit, this section shows the natural allocation, vs. applying the distortions stand-alone previously. The same heavy-handedness of CCoC noted in Section 13.1.3 is evident here. Unit A and Non-Cat are priced to a loss (117% loss ratio for Non-Cat) for Tame and Cat/Non-Cat Cases, and the dispersion between thick- and thin-tailed line loss ratios is more marked for CCoC than the other distortions in the two other Cases. The expected ordering of pricing by distortion remains consistent.
3. Negative margins beget negative capital allocation.
4. The average rate of return (i.e. priced CoC) varies by unit for the non-constant return distortions. Note that the opposite to what we noted stand-alone in Section 11.4.2 applies. Stand-alone, the thinner-tailed line was priced to a *higher* loss ratio and *higher* average return, because it consumes more expensive *body* capital. Now, the thinner-tailed line is priced to a *higher* loss ratio but *lower* average return for Tame and Cat/Non-Cat, whereas Hu/SCS it is a higher loss ratio and higher return. This applies between the units in each Case, as well as between gross and net. Recall that net hurricane is perversely *thicker-tailed* according to moment measures.
5. The last column shows the difference between gross and net. It gives a hurdle that reinsurance must beat in order to be economically attractive.

Table 15.35 Constant 0.10 ROE pricing for Tame Case Study, distortion, SRM methods.

		Gross			Net			Ceded
Statistic	Method	A	B	Total	A	B	Total	Diff
Loss	Expected Loss	50.00	50.00	100.00	50.00	49.08	99.08	0.916
Margin	Expected Loss	1.71	1.71	3.42	1.4	1.37	2.76	0.659
	Dist ROE	−0.792	4.21	3.42	−0.62	3.08	2.46	0.959
	Dist PH	1	2.42	3.42	1.37	1.39	2.76	0.659
	Dist Wang	1.04	2.39	3.42	1.28	1.63	2.9	0.52
	Dist Dual	1.07	2.36	3.42	1.18	1.85	3.03	0.393
	Dist TVar	1.1	2.33	3.42	1.1	2.05	3.15	0.269
	Dist Blend	0.462	1.43	1.89	0.622	0.821	1.44	0.45
Premium	Expected Loss	51.71	51.71	103.4	51.39	50.45	101.8	1.57
	Dist ROE	49.21	54.21	103.4	49.38	52.17	101.5	1.87
	Dist PH	51.00	52.42	103.4	51.37	50.48	101.8	1.57
	Dist Wang	51.04	52.39	103.4	51.28	50.71	102.0	1.44
	Dist Dual	51.07	52.35	103.4	51.18	50.93	102.1	1.31
	Dist TVar	51.10	52.33	103.4	51.10	51.14	102.2	1.18
	Dist Blend	50.46	51.43	101.9	50.62	49.91	100.5	1.37
Loss Ratio	Expected Loss	0.967	0.967	0.967	0.973	0.973	0.973	0.582
	Dist ROE	1.02	0.922	0.967	1.01	0.941	0.976	0.488
	Dist PH	0.98	0.954	0.967	0.973	0.972	0.973	0.582
	Dist Wang	0.98	0.954	0.967	0.975	0.968	0.972	0.638
	Dist Dual	0.979	0.955	0.967	0.977	0.964	0.97	0.699
	Dist TVar	0.979	0.956	0.967	0.978	0.96	0.969	0.773
	Dist Blend	0.991	0.972	0.981	0.988	0.984	0.986	0.671
Capital	Expected Loss	17.12	17.12	34.23	12.28	12.06	24.34	9.89
	Dist ROE	−7.91	42.12	34.23	−6.19	30.81	24.64	9.59
	Dist PH	14.19	20.04	34.23	12.46	11.88	24.34	9.89
	Dist Wang	15.46	18.78	34.23	12.43	11.77	24.20	10.03
	Dist Dual	15.63	18.60	34.23	12.37	11.70	24.07	10.16
	Dist TVar	15.66	18.57	34.23	12.31	11.64	23.95	10.28
	Dist Blend	11.70	24.06	35.76	11.45	14.21	25.66	10.10
Rate of Return	Expected Loss	0.1	0.1	0.1	0.114	0.114	0.114	0.0666
	Dist ROE	0.1	0.1	0.1	0.1	0.1	0.1	0.1

(Continued)

Table 15.35 (Continued)

Statistic	Method	Gross A	Gross B	Gross Total	Net A	Net B	Net Total	Ceded Diff
	Dist PH	0.0705	0.121	0.1	0.11	0.117	0.114	0.0666
	Dist Wang	0.0671	0.127	0.1	0.103	0.138	0.12	0.0518
	Dist Dual	0.0683	0.127	0.1	0.0954	0.158	0.126	0.0387
	Dist TVar	0.07	0.125	0.1	0.0895	0.176	0.132	0.0261
	Dist Blend	0.0395	0.0595	0.0529	0.0543	0.0578	0.0563	0.0445
Leverage	Expected Loss	3.02	3.02	3.02	4.18	4.18	4.18	0.159
	Dist ROE	−6.22	1.29	3.02	−7.98	1.69	4.12	0.195
	Dist PH	3.59	2.62	3.02	4.12	4.25	4.18	0.159
	Dist Wang	3.3	2.79	3.02	4.12	4.31	4.21	0.143
	Dist Dual	3.27	2.81	3.02	4.14	4.35	4.24	0.129
	Dist TVar	3.26	2.82	3.02	4.15	4.39	4.27	0.115
	Dist Blend	4.31	2.14	2.85	4.42	3.51	3.92	0.135
Assets	Expected Loss	68.83	68.83	137.7	63.68	62.51	126.2	11.47
	Dist ROE	41.30	96.33	137.7	43.19	82.98	126.2	11.47
	Dist PH	65.19	72.46	137.7	63.83	62.35	126.2	11.47
	Dist Wang	66.49	71.16	137.7	63.71	62.48	126.2	11.47
	Dist Dual	66.70	70.96	137.7	63.55	62.63	126.2	11.47
	Dist TVar	66.76	70.90	137.7	63.41	62.77	126.2	11.47
	Dist Blend	62.16	75.49	137.7	62.07	64.12	126.2	11.47

Point (4) is especially important. It shows that the average return to allocated capital is hard to interpret and is not a reliable metric for performance evaluation. When Ins Co. uses different types of capital, with costs by layer, we must understand how much capital each unit consumes by layer to determine its benchmark return. The natural allocation margin accomplishes this automatically and is the appropriate metric for performance management. Overlaying allocated capital and return by unit obfuscates the answer.

15.4.3 Visualizing *Spectral* Risk Measures

Spectral risk measures are so named because they are determined by *how much we care* about losses at each point across the spectrum of return periods. We know from Theorem 3 that an SRM is a weighted average of VaR_p values, where the weights are positive, increasing with

Table 15.36 Constant 0.10 ROE pricing for Cat/Non-Cat Case Study, distortion, SRM methods.

		Gross			Net			Ceded
Statistic	**Method**	**Cat**	**Non-Cat**	**Total**	**Cat**	**Non-Cat**	**Total**	**Diff**
Loss	Expected loss	19.96	79.99	99.95	17.75	79.98	97.73	2.21
Margin	Expected loss	3.04	12.17	15.21	1.78	8.04	9.82	5.38
	Dist ROE	27.08	−11.88	15.21	20.25	−12.08	8.17	7.04
	Dist PH	12.94	2.27	15.21	6.32	3.51	9.82	5.38
	Dist Wang	11.31	3.9	15.21	6.15	4.91	11.06	4.15
	Dist dual	9.72	5.49	15.21	6.47	5.94	12.40	2.8
	Dist TVaR	8.74	6.47	15.21	6.65	6.5	13.15	2.05
	Dist blend	7.32	−0.507	6.81	4.31	−0.217	4.09	2.73
Premium	Expected loss	22.99	92.16	115.2	19.53	88.02	107.6	7.6
	Dist ROE	47.04	68.11	115.2	38.00	67.90	105.9	9.25
	Dist PH	32.89	82.26	115.2	24.06	83.49	107.6	7.6
	Dist Wang	31.26	83.89	115.2	23.89	84.89	108.8	6.36
	Dist dual	29.68	85.48	115.2	24.21	85.92	110.1	5.02
	Dist TVaR	28.69	86.46	115.2	24.39	86.49	110.9	4.27
	Dist blend	27.28	79.48	106.8	22.05	79.77	101.8	4.94
Loss ratio	Expected loss	0.868	0.868	0.868	0.909	0.909	0.909	0.291
	Dist ROE	0.424	1.17	0.868	0.467	1.18	0.923	0.239
	Dist PH	0.607	0.972	0.868	0.738	0.958	0.909	0.291
	Dist Wang	0.638	0.954	0.868	0.743	0.942	0.898	0.348
	Dist dual	0.673	0.936	0.868	0.733	0.931	0.887	0.441
	Dist TVaR	0.696	0.925	0.868	0.728	0.925	0.881	0.519
	Dist blend	0.732	1.01	0.936	0.805	1	0.96	0.448
Capital	Expected loss	30.36	121.7	152.1	14.53	65.49	80.03	72.03
	Dist ROE	270.8	−118.7	152.1	202.4	−120.8	81.68	70.37
	Dist PH	103.2	48.80	152.1	42.98	37.04	80.03	72.03
	Dist Wang	92.20	59.85	152.1	35.79	43.00	78.79	73.26
	Dist dual	89.01	63.04	152.1	33.53	43.92	77.44	74.61
	Dist TVaR	88.87	63.19	152.1	33.27	43.43	76.69	75.36
	Dist blend	149.5	10.90	160.4	78.74	7.02	85.76	74.68

(Continued)

Table 15.36 (Continued)

		Gross			Net			Ceded
Statistic	**Method**	**Cat**	**Non-Cat**	**Total**	**Cat**	**Non-Cat**	**Total**	**Diff**
Rate of return	Expected loss	0.1	0.1	0.1	0.123	0.123	0.123	0.0747
	Dist ROE	0.1	0.1	0.1	0.1	0.1	0.1	0.1
	Dist PH	0.125	0.0465	0.1	0.147	0.0946	0.123	0.0747
	Dist Wang	0.123	0.0651	0.1	0.172	0.114	0.14	0.0566
	Dist dual	0.109	0.087	0.1	0.193	0.135	0.16	0.0376
	Dist TVaR	0.0983	0.102	0.1	0.2	0.15	0.171	0.0272
	Dist blend	0.049	−0.0465	0.0425	0.0547	−0.0309	0.0477	0.0365
Leverage	Expected loss	0.757	0.757	0.757	1.34	1.34	1.34	0.105
	Dist ROE	0.174	−0.574	0.757	0.188	−0.562	1.3	0.131
	Dist PH	0.319	1.69	0.757	0.56	2.25	1.34	0.105
	Dist Wang	0.339	1.4	0.757	0.668	1.97	1.38	0.0868
	Dist dual	0.333	1.36	0.757	0.722	1.96	1.42	0.0673
	Dist TVaR	0.323	1.37	0.757	0.733	1.99	1.45	0.0566
	Dist blend	0.182	7.29	0.665	0.28	11.36	1.19	0.0661
Assets	Expected loss	53.36	213.8	267.2	34.06	153.5	187.6	79.62
	Dist ROE	317.8	−50.62	267.2	240.4	−52.86	187.6	79.62
	Dist PH	136.1	131.1	267.2	67.05	120.5	187.6	79.62
	Dist Wang	123.5	143.7	267.2	59.68	127.9	187.6	79.62
	Dist dual	118.7	148.5	267.2	57.74	129.8	187.6	79.62
	Dist TVaR	117.6	149.6	267.2	57.66	129.9	187.6	79.62
	Dist blend	176.8	90.38	267.2	100.8	86.79	187.6	79.62

p, and sum to 1. We interpret the weights as a measure of our concern. By Eq. (10.37), they equal the derivative of the distortion function.

Remark 279. The authors have heard the argument that management doesn't care about *really large* losses because their company is "dead already". As a result, decreasing spectral weights can be appropriate. This argument is incoherent: every bad outcome associated with a given level of loss occurs for all greater losses. You must, therefore, care at least as much. This is the monotonic property of risk preferences, Section 5.3.1. □

The top row of Figure 15.11 shows gross loss by return period (on a log scale). κ for the lower volatility unit is the dashed line, and the area between the two lines is κ for the higher. The upper line is therefore total loss at each return period. These graphs illustrate expected

Table 15.37 Constant 0.10 ROE pricing for Hu/SCS Case Study, distortion, SRM methods.

		Gross			Net			Ceded
Statistic	**Method**	**Hu**	**SCS**	**Total**	**Hu**	**SCS**	**Total**	**Diff**
Loss	Expected loss	26.06	69.09	95.15	15.33	69.08	84.41	10.73
Margin	Expected loss	61.94	164.2	226.2	32.03	144.3	176.4	49.81
	Dist ROE	241.1	−14.95	226.2	209.3	−14.86	194.5	31.68
	Dist PH	203.6	22.53	226.2	143.0	33.32	176.4	49.81
	Dist Wang	188.3	37.92	226.2	115.9	52.70	168.6	57.59
	Dist dual	166.5	59.68	226.2	74.75	81.01	155.8	70.41
	Dist TVaR	159.5	66.67	226.2	63.90	89.00	152.9	73.27
	Dist blend	64.00	3.2	67.20	49.66	4.98	54.64	12.56
Premium	Expected loss	88.00	233.3	321.3	47.37	213.4	260.8	60.55
	Dist ROE	267.2	54.14	321.3	224.7	54.22	278.9	42.42
	Dist PH	229.7	91.61	321.3	158.4	102.4	260.8	60.55
	Dist Wang	214.3	107.0	321.3	131.2	121.8	253.0	68.33
	Dist dual	192.5	128.8	321.3	90.08	150.1	240.2	81.15
	Dist TVaR	185.6	135.8	321.3	79.23	158.1	237.3	84.01
	Dist blend	90.06	72.29	162.3	64.99	74.06	139.1	23.30
Loss ratio	Expected loss	0.296	0.296	0.296	0.324	0.324	0.324	0.177
	Dist ROE	0.0975	1.28	0.296	0.0682	1.27	0.303	0.253
	Dist PH	0.113	0.754	0.296	0.0968	0.675	0.324	0.177
	Dist Wang	0.122	0.646	0.296	0.117	0.567	0.334	0.157
	Dist dual	0.135	0.537	0.296	0.17	0.46	0.351	0.132
	Dist TVaR	0.14	0.509	0.296	0.194	0.437	0.356	0.128
	Dist blend	0.289	0.956	0.586	0.236	0.933	0.607	0.461
Capital	Expected loss	619.4	1,642	2,262	356.6	1,606	1,963	298.7
	Dist ROE	2,411	−149.1	2,262	2,093	−148.2	1,945	316.8
	Dist PH	2,111	150.4	2,262	1,758	205.0	1,963	298.7
	Dist Wang	2,075	186.9	2,262	1,716	254.3	1,971	290.9
	Dist dual	2,050	211.9	2,262	1,682	301.6	1,984	278.1
	Dist TVaR	2,052	210.0	2,262	1,685	301.6	1,986	275.2
	Dist blend	2,344	76.32	2,421	1,977	107.6	2,085	336.0
Rate of return	Expected loss	0.1	0.1	0.1	0.0898	0.0898	0.0898	0.167
	Dist ROE	0.1	0.1	0.1	0.1	0.1	0.1	0.1

(Continued)

Table 15.37 (Continued)

		Gross			Net			Ceded
Statistic	Method	Hu	SCS	Total	Hu	SCS	Total	Diff
	Dist PH	0.0965	0.15	0.1	0.0814	0.163	0.0898	0.167
	Dist Wang	0.0907	0.203	0.1	0.0675	0.207	0.0855	0.198
	Dist dual	0.0812	0.282	0.1	0.0444	0.269	0.0785	0.253
	Dist TVaR	0.0777	0.317	0.1	0.0379	0.295	0.077	0.266
	Dist blend	0.0273	0.042	0.0278	0.0251	0.0463	0.0262	0.0374
Leverage	Expected loss	0.142	0.142	0.142	0.133	0.133	0.133	0.203
	Dist ROE	0.111	−0.363	0.142	0.107	−0.366	0.143	0.134
	Dist PH	0.109	0.609	0.142	0.0901	0.5	0.133	0.203
	Dist Wang	0.103	0.573	0.142	0.0764	0.479	0.128	0.235
	Dist dual	0.0939	0.608	0.142	0.0536	0.498	0.121	0.292
	Dist TVaR	0.0904	0.646	0.142	0.047	0.524	0.119	0.305
	Dist blend	0.0384	0.947	0.0671	0.0329	0.688	0.0667	0.0693
Assets	Expected loss	707.4	1,876	2,583	403.9	1,820	2,224	359.2
	Dist ROE	2,678	−94.96	2,583	2,318	−94.02	2,224	359.2
	Dist PH	2,341	242.0	2,583	1,916	307.4	2,224	359.2
	Dist Wang	2,289	293.9	2,583	1,848	376.1	2,224	359.2
	Dist dual	2,242	340.7	2,583	1,772	451.7	2,224	359.2
	Dist TVaR	2,237	345.8	2,583	1,764	459.7	2,224	359.2
	Dist blend	2,434	148.6	2,583	2,042	181.6	2,224	359.2

losses by unit as a function of the return period of total loss. They provide a useful and informative way of visualizing and communicating which units *cause* or *contribute* to large losses.

- Tame Case: the split of losses is close to equal across the entire spectrum, slightly favoring the more volatile unit B. Both κ functions are increasing, as implied by Efron's theorem in the log-concave density case.
- Cat/Non-Cat Case: extreme losses are dominated by Cat losses. In a bad scenario, Non-Cat losses are about average (flat dotted line). For higher return periods, the expected contribution of Non-Cat losses actually decreases (dotted line is humped and peaks around a 10 year return period).
- Hu/SCS Case: exaggerates the Cat/Non-Cat Case. Expected SCS losses are humped and extreme tails are dominated by Hu losses.

Rows 2 to 4 show *how much we care* about each return period, that is, the spectra weights implied by each distortion. The distortion parameters are shown in Section 11.4.

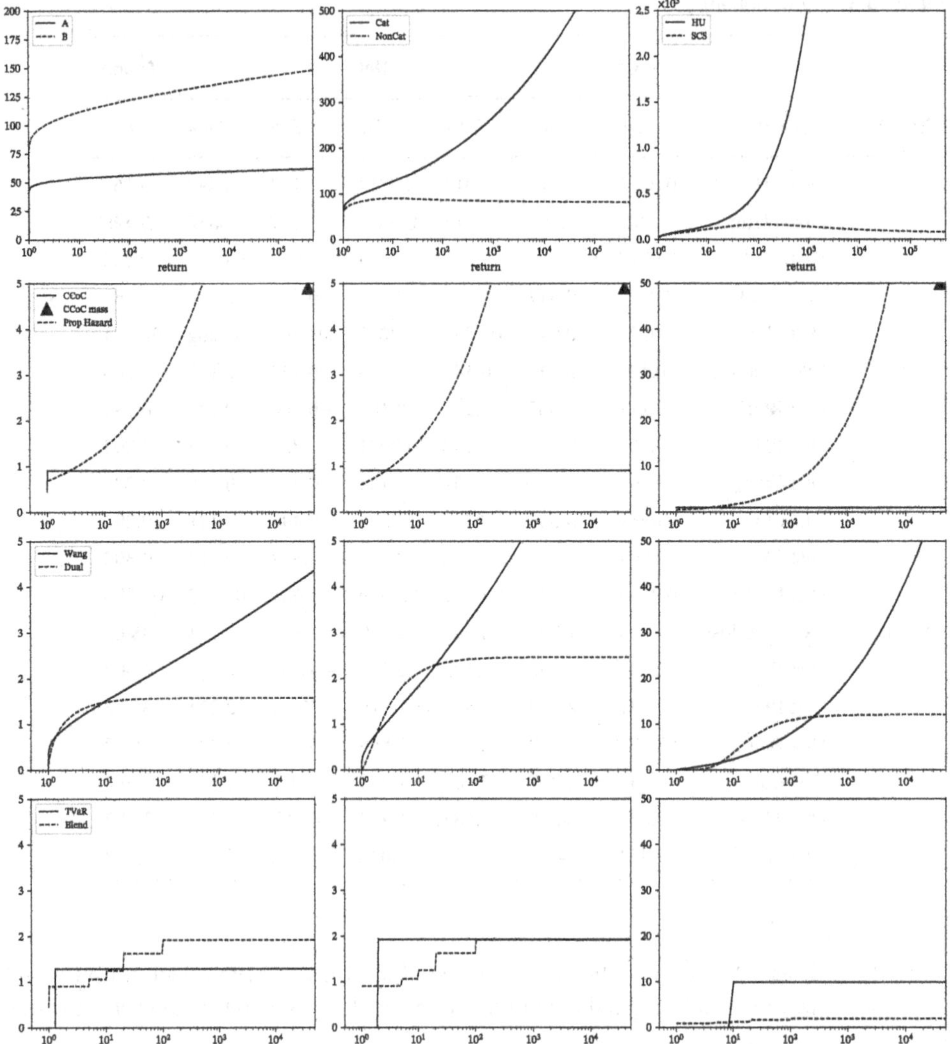

Figure 15.11 Loss spectrums by Case (top row). Rows 2 to 4 show VaR weights by distortion. In the second row, the CCoC distortion includes a mass putting weight $d = 0.1/1.1$ at the maximum loss, corresponding to an infinite density.

The distortions appear two per plot. The third, Hu/SCS column uses a different vertical scale. The distortions are in the same order as the other exhibits: CCoC, proportional hazard, Wang, dual moment, TVaR, and blend. The plots explain their relative tail sensitivity. For CCoC, although the weighting is $v = 1/1.1 < 1$ across the entire spectrum $0 \leq p < 1$, it is augmented by the weight d given to the maximum, $p = 1$ loss (schematic triangle).

15.4.4 Percentile Layer of Capital Examples

Figures 15.12–15.14 show the PLC allocation of assets by total asset level. PLC emerges as even less tail-sensitive than the TVaR distortion. To convert PLC into premium requires a CoC assumption.

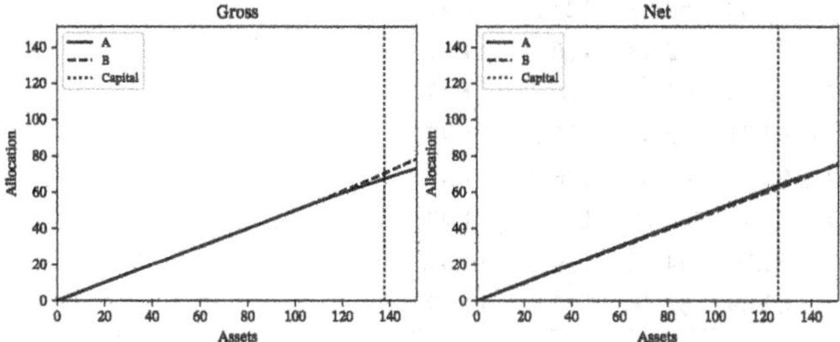

Figure 15.12 Tame Case Study percentile layer of capital allocations by asset level, showing 0.999 capital.

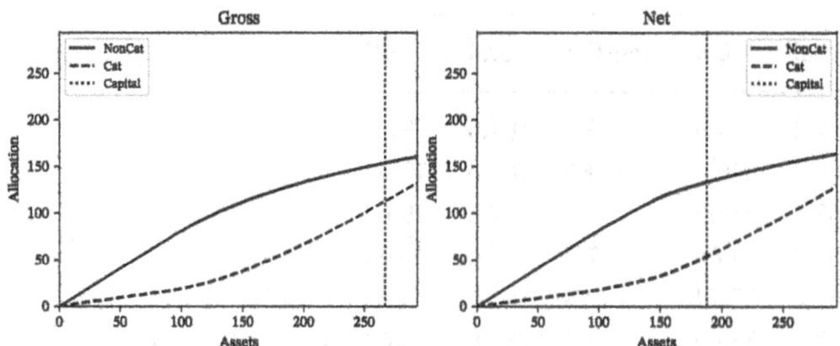

Figure 15.13 Cat/Non-Cat Case Study percentile layer of capital allocations by asset level, showing 0.999 capital.

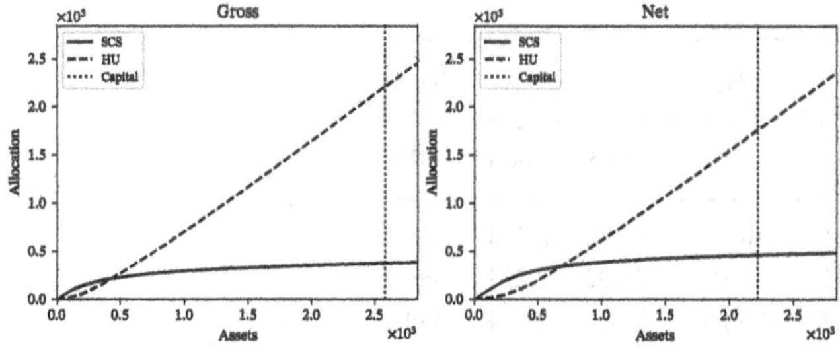

Figure 15.14 Hu/SCS Case Study percentile layer of capital allocations by asset level, showing 0.999 capital.

Table 15.38 Tame Case Study percentile layer of capital allocations compared to distortion allocations.

	Gross			Net			Ceded
Method	**A**	**B**	**Total**	**A**	**B**	**Total**	**Diff**
EL	68.83	68.83	137.7	63.68	62.51	126.2	11.47
Dist ROE	41.30	96.33	137.7	43.19	82.98	126.2	11.47
Dist PH	65.19	72.46	137.7	63.83	62.35	126.2	11.47
Dist Wang	66.49	71.16	137.7	63.71	62.48	126.2	11.47
Dist dual	66.70	70.96	137.7	63.55	62.63	126.2	11.47
Dist TVaR	66.76	70.90	137.7	63.41	62.77	126.2	11.47
Dist blend	62.16	75.49	137.7	62.07	64.12	126.2	11.47
PLC	67.34	70.32	137.7	63.89	62.30	126.2	11.47

Table 15.39 Cat/Non-Cat Case Study percentile layer of capital allocations compared to distortion allocations.

	Gross			Net			Ceded
Method	**Cat**	**Non-Cat**	**Total**	**Cat**	**Non-Cat**	**Total**	**Diff**
EL	53.36	213.8	267.2	34.06	153.5	187.6	79.62
Dist ROE	317.8	−50.62	267.2	240.4	−52.86	187.6	79.62
Dist PH	136.1	131.1	267.2	67.05	120.5	187.6	79.62
Dist Wang	123.5	143.7	267.2	59.68	127.9	187.6	79.62
Dist dual	118.7	148.5	267.2	57.74	129.8	187.6	79.62
Dist TVaR	117.6	149.6	267.2	57.66	129.9	187.6	79.62
Dist blend	176.8	90.38	267.2	100.8	86.79	187.6	79.62
PLC	113.2	154.0	267.2	54.00	133.6	187.6	79.62

Table 15.40 Hu/SCS Case Study percentile layer of capital allocations compared to distortion allocations.

	Gross			Net			Ceded
Method	**Hu**	**SCS**	**Total**	**Hu**	**SCS**	**Total**	**Diff**
EL	707.4	1,876	2,583	403.9	1,820	2,224	359.2
Dist ROE	2,678	−94.96	2,583	2,318	−94.02	2,224	359.2
Dist PH	2,341	242.0	2,583	1,916	307.4	2,224	359.2
Dist Wang	2,289	293.9	2,583	1,848	376.1	2,224	359.2
Dist dual	2,242	340.7	2,583	1,772	451.7	2,224	359.2
Dist TVaR	2,237	345.8	2,583	1,764	459.7	2,224	359.2
Dist blend	2,434	148.6	2,583	2,042	181.6	2,224	359.2
PLC	2,209	373.8	2,583	1,761	462.7	2,224	359.2

15.5 Learning Objectives

1. Implement calculations for the lifted and non-lifted natural allocation of premium in a discrete simulation setting.
2. Implement calculations for α, β, and κ in a discrete simulation setting.
3. Explain when and why κ is necessary.
4. Give examples of situations producing linear κ functions.
5. Give examples of canonical κ behavior.
6. Compute margin, capital allocation, and CoC.
7. Explain and compare typical CoC results between the natural allocation of a general SRM and classical capital allocation methods.
8. Recognize examples of effective and ineffective diversification.

Part IV

Advanced Topics

16

Asset Risk

In this chapter, we briefly look at the other side of the balance sheet and consider asset risk. Our focus is still on insurance operations, however. The main question is: How does asset risk affect the funding balance between policyholders and investors? We conclude that it reduces the fair value of loss payments.

16.1 Background

Assets are generally priced in the capital markets so that they all have the same *risk-adjusted* return. Beware of any method that appears to create value or capacity by disregarding market prices.

Bookshelves, nay book *stores*, worth of writings exist on the subject of asset risk. We will add only a few comments. We are of the opinion that insurance operations and investment operations are separate and should be separate—except where there are specific insurance product needs to be met by investments. For most property-casualty lines of business, the correlation between insurance risk and asset risk is tenuous to nonexistent, so any hedging benefit is second-order at best. When liabilities extend out into the future, e.g. with worker's compensation lines, the question of making provision for future payments (asset–liability management) is something the investment group should consider after obtaining the reserve actuaries' best understanding of the likely emergence of those payments. The pricing actuary should leave it in their hands and assume it will get done.

Risky assets affect insurance liabilities in at least two ways. First, when it comes to discounting extended-time liabilities, the actuary should defer to Cummins (1990) and use a yield curve representing the firm's own investment portfolio. Because risky assets tend to have higher expected yields, this will tend to produce a lower present value of expected loss and therefore a lower premium. Second, as will be shown below, even for short tail lines, investing in a risky asset typically *lowers* the fair price of insurance being sold, because it adds to the probability that full payments will not be made.

The basic pricing formula assumes that assets are held in a safe instrument with no possibility of default. Now allow a risky asset which pays 1 in a good asset return state at $t = 1$ with probability p and 0 otherwise. Assume asset returns are independent of loss outcomes

Pricing Insurance Risk: Theory and Practice, First Edition. Stephen J. Mildenhall and John A. Major.

and suppose the market price of the risky asset at $t = 0$ is q. By risk aversion $q < p$. An investment in the risky asset of ¤ 1 at $t = 0$ becomes worth, at $t = 1$, either ¤ $1/q$, with objective probability p (risk-adjusted probability q), or zero with probability $1 - p$ (resp. $1 - q$). The expected return on the asset is therefore $p/q - 1 = (p - q)/q > 0$.

16.2 Adding Asset Risk to Ins Co.

We now investigate three questions for Ins Co. writing a single binary risk with limit 1. As usual suppose the probability of loss is s and the layer price is $g(s)$ for a distortion g.

- What level of initial assets $a = a(s)$ is required to support the policy?
- What proportion $f = f(s)$ of assets should Ins Co. hold in the safe asset?
- What is the new fair price of insurance?

The insurance risk is unchanged. The price q of the risky asset is exogenous and assumed independent of the insurance outcome. Ins Co. can select an investment strategy f. It can also select its funding level a. However, they are jointly subject to two product market constraints.

First, it has a **face capital** constraint: assets in the good state at $t = 1$ must be at least 1, otherwise the promise to pay is not credible. If initial assets af are invested in the safe asset and $a(1-f)$ in the risky asset, then at time $t = 1$ they are worth $af + a(1-f)/q$ in the good return state. Therefore the face capital constraint requires

$$a(f + (1-f)/q) \geq 1 \iff a \geq \frac{1}{f + (1-f)/q} = \frac{q}{1 - f(1-q)}. \tag{16.1}$$

This is a **lower** bound on a which increases with f, assuming risk aversion $q < 1$.

Second, there is a **utilization** constraint: insureds will not pay for assets in excess of the maximum amount of their loss. In the bad asset scenario ending assets are af and maximum losses are 1, therefore

$$af \leq 1 \iff a \leq \frac{1}{f}. \tag{16.2}$$

The utilization constraint is an **upper** bound on assets which decreases with f. When the utilization constraint holds loss payments in the bad asset return state equal $af \leq 1$.

Within the ranges jointly determined by the face capital and utilization constraints, Ins Co. is free to select values of a and f. *There is no unique solution.* We shall now show that any of these values are fair to insureds and investors. First we compute the fair insurance premium given by the risk-adjusted expected value of loss payments. The risk-adjusted probability of a loss is $g(s)$. The risk adjusted probability of the good asset return state is q. Asset and insurance results are independent. Table 16.1 lays out the possible outcomes assuming the constraints given by Eq. (16.1) and Eq. (16.2) both hold.

Based on Table 16.1 the fair market value of insurance payments is

$$P = 1 \cdot g(s)q + af \cdot g(s)(1-q) = g(s)(q + af(1-q)) < g(s). \tag{16.3}$$

Therefore, investing in a risky asset lowers the fair price of the insurance by an amount corresponding to the haircut on payments in the bad asset return scenario. Rather than paying 1

Table 16.1 Probabilities and outcomes with risky assets. Insurance and asset returns are independent, giving the probabilities in the top block. The residual value in the bad asset return-loss state is zero by Eq. (16.2).

Variable	Outcome	Good asset return	Bad asset return
risk-adjusted probability			
	No loss	$(1-g(s))q$	$(1-g(s))(1-q)$
	Loss	$g(s)q$	$g(s)(1-q)$
Loss payments			
	No loss	0	0
	Loss	1	af
Residual value			
	No loss	$a(f+(1-f)/q)$	af
	Loss	$a(f+(1-f)/q)-1$	0

in that scenario Ins Co. now only pays $af \le 1$. Note that it is possible to obtain $af = 1$ with $f < 1$ by setting $a > 1$, i.e. over-collateralizing the layer with a risky asset. Over-collateralizing this way can produce an ending asset of 1 even in the bad asset return scenario. In the good asset return scenario it will result in a positive residual value even when there is a loss; as usual the residual value is passed back to the investor. By the funding constraint, the market value of the residual cash flows, i.e. equity paid in by the investor, is $a - P$.

Exercise 280. Show the $t = 0$ residual value conditional on no loss equals a. □

We can now compute the market value of investor cash flows (unconditional residual value). It is given by

$$
\begin{aligned}
(1-g(s))a + g(s)q[a(f+(1-f)/q)-1] &= a - g(s)a + g(s)a(qf+1-f) - g(s)q \\
&= a + g(s)(a(qf-f)-q) \\
&= a - g(s)(q + af(1-q)) \\
&= a - P
\end{aligned}
$$

showing that the indicated pricing results in fair market returns for both investors and insureds. This equation also shows there is no unique level of asset risk.

Example 281. Table 16.2 shows the fair market value of losses for different values of f (rows) and a (columns). The value $f = 1$ in the bottom row corresponds to a risk-free asset portfolio; the top row corresponds to a 100 percent risky asset. The max and min a columns show the utilization and face capital bounds on a. The void on the left indicates combinations where the assets are insufficient to meet the face capital requirement. The void on the right indicates that assets are in excess of the utilization constraint. In the bottom row, with only the risk-free

Table 16.2 The fair market value of loss payments for different proportions f of investment in the safe asset and starting asset levels a.

f	max a	min a	a = 0.93	0.94	0.95	0.96	0.97	0.98	0.99	1
0.0	∞	0.9	0.1839	0.1839	0.1839	0.1839	0.1839	0.1839	0.1839	0.1839
0.1	10.0	0.9	0.1853	0.1853	0.1854	0.1854	0.1854	0.1854	0.1854	0.1854
0.2	5.0	0.9		0.1868	0.1868	0.1869	0.1869	0.1869	0.1870	0.1870
0.3	3.3	0.9			0.1883	0.1884	0.1884	0.1885	0.1885	0.1886
0.4	2.5	1.0				0.1899	0.1899	0.1900	0.1901	0.1901
0.5	2.0	1.0				0.1914	0.1915	0.1915	0.1916	0.1917
0.6	1.7	1.0					0.1930	0.1931	0.1932	0.1933
0.7	1.4	1.0		*face*				0.1946	0.1947	0.1948
0.8	1.3	1.0							0.1963	0.1964
0.9	1.1	1.0								0.1980
1.0	1.0	1.0								0.1995

f	max a	min a	a = 1	1.1	1.5	2	10
0.0	∞	0.9	0.1839	0.1839	0.1839	0.1839	0.1839
0.1	10.0	0.9	0.1854	0.1856	0.1862	0.1870	0.1995
0.2	5.0	0.9	0.1870	0.1873	0.1886	0.1901	
0.3	3.3	0.9	0.1886	0.1890	0.1909	0.1933	
0.4	2.5	1.0	0.1901	0.1908	0.1933	0.1964	
0.5	2.0	1.0	0.1917	0.1925	0.1956	0.1995	
0.6	1.7	1.0	0.1933	0.1942	0.1980		
0.7	1.4	1.0	0.1948	0.1959			*utiliz-*
0.8	1.3	1.0	0.1964	0.1976			*ation*
0.9	1.1	1.0	0.1980	0.1994			
1.0	1.0	1.0	0.1995				

asset, there is only one asset amount that satisfies both constraints. Premiums increase to the right and down the columns, as expected. The example assumes the risk-adjusted probability of loss $g(s) = 0.1995$, which is then the price when $a = f = 1$. The exogenous risky asset discount factor $q = 0.9215$.

When $f = 0$ the market value is independent of assets a because the only loss payment occurs in the good asset return scenario when there is no default and the insured is paid 1. There is no payment in the bad asset scenario because the asset portfolio is worthless. Thus payments to the insured are independent of assets provided the face capital constraint holds, which we are assuming. In this case the premium is $g(s)q = 0.1839$, which is the lowest possible premium consistent with the utilization and face capital constraints. □

To summarize: with risky assets, the fair market value (price) of a layer of insurance is a function of two new decision variables: funding a for the layer and the proportion f of the layer assets invested in the risk-free asset. Previously we took both of these variables to be 1. When they are 1 we recover $P = g(s)$ because $af = 1$. Notice the original solution also satisfies Eqs. 16.1 and 16.2.

16.3 Learning Objectives

1. Describe the lower and upper bounds for investment in a risky asset.
2. Describe the impact of risky investments on the fair value of insurance to the insured.
3. Compute the fair value of insurance payments when Ins Co. partially invests in a risky asset.

Learning Objectives

17

Reserves

In this chapter, we extend the one period Ins Co. model, first incorporating reserves for a single accident year, then allowing for multiple accident years. We discuss modeling with ultimate losses and then consider the Solvency II approach.

17.1 Time Periods and Notation

Our one-period model includes time in a rudimentary fashion: policies are written at time 0, liabilities are incurred between time 0 and 1, and they are paid in full at time 1. There are no reserves. To add reserves, we need to define three standard actuarial reserving time measures. For each paid loss transaction, which occurs on the **transaction date**, define:

- The **accident year** (AY) is the year in which the *accident* (loss) triggering the transaction occurs.
- The **calendar year** (CY) is the year in which the *transaction* occurs.
- The **development lag** (DY) is the elapsed time from the beginning of the transaction's accident year to the end of its calendar year.

Reserving systems also use an **evaluation date**. Only transactions with a transaction date before the evaluation date are counted in any claims tabulation. We assume all claims activity occurs at integer times. Year 1 extends from $t = 0$ to $t = 1$, year 2 from $t = 1$ to $t = 2$, and so forth. Policies are written, and claims are paid at $t = 0, 1, 2, \dots$. The evaluation dates are at the end of each year. Development lag is denoted $d = 1, 2, \dots$. A payment on an accident year t transaction with development lag d occurs at time $t + d$ because the AY starts at $t - 1$.

We can arrange **incremental paid claims** in a two-dimensional array of random variables, where $X_{t,d}$ equals the sum of all payment transactions from accident year t with development lag d. These payments occur at time $t + d$. (The one-period model has only $t = 0$ and $d = 1$ and the single paid loss random variable $X_{0,1}$.) Our development model is very simple and does not include case reserves. All information about claims is captured by paid losses.

Pricing Insurance Risk: Theory and Practice, First Edition. Stephen J. Mildenhall and John A. Major.

Table 17.1 Array of incremental claim payments. Rows show the accident year t in which claim liabilities are incurred; columns show the calendar year $t+d$ in which claim payments are made.

AY\CY	t-1	t	t+1	t+2	t+3
$t-2$	$X_{t-2,1}$	$X_{t-2,2}$	$X_{t-2,3}$	…	
$t-1$		$X_{t-1,1}$	$X_{t-1,2}$	$X_{t-1,3}$	…
t			$X_{t,1}$	$X_{t,2}$	$X_{t,3}$
$t+1$				$X_{t+1,1}$	$X_{t+1,2}$
$t+2$					$X_{t+2,1}$

The distribution of $X_{t,d}$ varies with the evaluation date τ. When $\tau < t+d$, it is *estimated* as a conditional expectation on the basis of information known at τ. When $\tau \geq t+d$ the payment is *known* with certainty. We use the notation $\mathsf{E}[X \mid \mathcal{F}_\tau]$ to mean the expected value of X based on the information available up to time τ. Graphically, we can arrange incremental claim payments as in Table 17.1.

Technical Remark 282. Formally, $X_{t,d}$ is defined on a probability space $(\Omega, \mathcal{F}, \mathsf{P})$. The σ-algebra $\mathcal{F}$ describes events that can (eventually) be observed. A family $\mathcal{F}_0 \subset \mathcal{F}_1 \subset \cdots \subset \mathcal{F}_N$ of sub-algebras, increasing to $\mathcal{F}$, describes the flow of information. $\mathcal{F}_\tau$ includes everything known at time τ. At $\tau = 0$ we know nothing about the loss outcome and $\mathcal{F}_0 = \{\emptyset, \Omega\}$ is the trivial σ-algebra and $\mathsf{E}[X_{t,d} \mid \mathcal{F}_0] = \mathsf{E}[X_{t_d}]$. $\mathsf{E}[X_{t,d} \mid \mathcal{F}_\tau]$ equals the expected value of $X_{t,d}$ conditional on information available at time τ. We take it to be the best estimate. □

17.2 Liability for Ultimate Losses

In a multi-period model, there are two ways to evaluate risk. One focuses on sufficient capital to cover the ultimate losses, which we consider here. The other, oriented toward one year of risk at a time and used in Solvency II, is discussed in Section 17.3. In a steady state book, these two should be approximately equal—they are just different ways of cutting the cake.

Assume that the ultimate distribution of losses at each point in time is used to evaluate risk and set capital standards. This view is consistent with the option (the default put) that Ins Co. holds at each regulatory evaluation not to re-capitalize to the required standard—a feature we will explore later. It also reflects the inherent difficulties in modeling a future distribution of market values. Concern that the ultimate view overstates risk can be offset by selecting a lower probability threshold in the capital risk measure.

We assume all policies written in the accident year have the same effective date and a one period policy term. There is no unearned premium reserve at the end of the period. The only liability carried forward is an unpaid loss reserve.

First, we formalize the distinction between cash flows and liabilities. Define the claim liability as the sum of outstanding payment random variables:

$$Y_{t,d} = \sum_{s>d} X_{t,s}, \tag{17.1}$$

where $d = 0$ denotes the initial incurred liablity when the business is written at accident year t. Notice that because the cash flows $X_{t,d}$ are random variables, so are the liabilities $Y_{t,d}$.

We then have the recursive relation

$$Y_{t,d} = X_{t,d+1} + Y_{t,d+1}, \tag{17.2}$$

which states that at time $t + d$ there is a total liability $Y_{t,d}$ consisting of a portion $X_{t,d+1}$ to be paid in the next period plus a residual liability $Y_{t,d+1}$ outstanding in the next period. One may want to modify Eq. (17.1) to incorporate discounting; we prefer to stay with the zero interest rate assumption for expository simplicity.

The simplest approach to multiperiod pricing is to use $Y_{0,0}$ in place of portfolio X in all previous pricing formulas and treat the end of first period liability as if it is paid off. While certainly manageable, this is perhaps too simplistic. Section 17.2.1 presents a more elaborate approach.

17.2.1 The Single Stand Alone Accident Year

Consider we have only accident year $t = 0$, with no prior business having been written and no subsequent business contemplated. Dropping the t subscript, we denote claim payouts as X_d with $d = 1, \dots, N$. Since Ins Co. has promised to pay Y_0, clearly that is the appropriate argument to the capital risk measure. Thus, at time 0, we have required assets

$$a_0 = a(Y_0).$$

At time 1, X_1 is paid out in claims, leaving assets $a_1' = a_0 - X_1$ on the balance sheet. The new liability is Y_1. The regulatory authority, however, wants $a_1 = a(Y_1)$ available. The difference, $\Delta_1 = a_1' - a_1$, if positive, can be given back to the investors as a dividend. If negative, it is a capital call that needs to be met if the firm is to avoid regulatory supervision where investor appointed managers are replaced with regulator appointees. Investors want to avoid supervision because it is not likely to put the investors' best interests first. These considerations are outside our model for now, and we assume that such calls are always met.

Assume we have an SRM ρ for pricing and denote $\bar{P}_t = \rho(Y_t)$. We will call $\bar{P}_0$ the *premium* but subsequent $\bar{P}_t$ the *market value of liabilities* (MVL). The MVL is what the premium would be if Ins Co. were taking on that liability as a new policy (in the absence of any others on the books). It equals the reserve plus a risk margin. The margin is $\bar{M}_t = \bar{P}_t - \mathsf{E}[Y_t]$.

The timing and evolution of balance sheet calculations is set out in Table 17.2. At inception, $d = 0$:

Table 17.2 Timeline of random variables and financial quantities from a single accident year starting at $t = 0$.

Variable	$d=0$	$d=1$	$d=2$
Time	0	1	2
Paid loss		X_1	X_2
Unpaid loss	Y_0	Y_1	Y_2
Assets	a_0	a_1	a_2
Premium or MVL	$\bar{P}_0$	$\bar{P}_1$	$\bar{P}_2$
Capital	$\bar{Q}_0$	$\bar{Q}_1$	$\bar{Q}_2$
Dividend		Δ_1	Δ_2

- Policies are written.
- $Y_0 = \sum_{d>0} X_d$ is the newly acquired liability for future payments X.
- Assets $a_0 = a(Y_0)$ must be funded.
- Premium $\bar{P}_0 = \rho(Y_0)$ is collected from policyholders. It equals the market value of the liabilities on the balance sheet.
- Capital $\bar{Q}_0 = a_0 - \bar{P}_0$ is collected from investors. It equals the investors' equity on the balance sheet.
- Actual assets a_0 are thereby funded on the balance sheet.

At a future time $d > 0$:

- Losses X_d are paid to the policyholders.
- Assets on the balance sheet are reduced to $a'_d = a_{d-1} - X_d$.
- $Y_d = \sum_{s>d} X_s$ is the new liability.
- $a_d = a(Y_d)$ is the new required asset amount.
- $\Delta_d = a'_d - a_d$, if positive, is a dividend paid to the investors. If it is negative, it is a capital injection asked of the investors.
- Assets on the balance sheet become a_d.
- $\bar{P}_d = \rho(Y_d)$ is the market value of liabilities on the balance sheet.
- $\bar{Q}_d = a_d - \bar{P}_d$ is the investors' equity on the balance sheet.

The *income statement* values, such as earned premium, loss, margin, and profit, that are booked at time d reflect activities that occur between $d - 1$ and d, whereas *balance sheet* values, such as assets, unearned premium, unpaid loss reserve liabilities, unearned margin, and capital, are their respective evaluations at time d. In Table 17.2, paid loss and dividends are income statement values, and the rest are balance sheet values—premium is unearned premium reserve and MVL is unpaid loss reserve plus a risk margin. All quantities involving expectations or distorted expectations are taken conditional on the information available at time $\tau = 0 + d$.

The dividend paid or capital call at $d > 0$ can be decomposed as follows:

$$\begin{aligned}
\Delta_d &= \text{Release of Capital} \\
&\quad + \text{Release of Margin} \\
&\quad\quad - \text{Incurred Losses} \\
&= (a_{d-1} - \bar{P}_{d-1}) - (a_d - \bar{P}_d) \\
&\quad + (\bar{P}_{d-1} - \mathsf{E}[Y_{d-1} \mid \mathcal{F}_{d-1}]) - (\bar{P}_d - \mathsf{E}[Y_d \mid \mathcal{F}_d]) \\
&\quad\quad + \mathsf{E}[Y_{d-1} \mid \mathcal{F}_{d-1}] - (X_d + \mathsf{E}[Y_d \mid \mathcal{F}_d]) \\
&= a_{d-1} - X_d - a_d \\
&= a'_d - a_d.
\end{aligned} \tag{17.3}$$

Incurred loss is incremental and specific to year d. It consists of realized deviations from the expected trajectory of losses and reserves caused by new information revealed during year d.

Example 283. Recall the Wang transform exercise Exercise 192. Assume the incremental paid losses X_d are independent and normally distributed with means μ_d and variances σ_d^2. More concretely, let us assume $N = 5$, $\mu_d = (6-d)^2$ and $\sigma_d = \mu_d/5$. The expected payout pattern is given in Table 17.3.

Let pricing be given by a Wang transform distortion with parameter $\lambda = 0.5$ and assume the capital risk measure $a = \mathsf{VaR}_p$ where $p = \Phi^{-1}(4) = 3.17 \times 10^{-5}$. For normal X, this means $a(X) = \mu + 4\sigma$. Treat the probability of portfolio insolvency as zero. Assume there are no information updates other than X_d being realized.

These assumptions imply $\mathsf{E}[Y_d] = \sum_{s>d} \mu_s$, $\mathsf{var}(Y_d) = \sum_{s>d} \sigma_s^2$, and $a_d = \mathsf{E}[Y_d] + 4\sigma(Y_d)$, where we use the notation $\sigma(Z) = \sqrt{\mathsf{var}(Z)}$ for convenience. Furthermore, $\bar{P}_d = \mathsf{E}[Y_d] + \lambda\sigma(Y_d)$.

The expected pattern of earnings is shown in Table 17.4. The total margin is 3.129 of which nearly 40 percent is earned in the first development period with diminishing shares thereafter. **Profit** is defined as the margin released minus incremental incurred loss, which is

Table 17.3 Expected incremental and cumulative payout pattern for the Wang transform example.

d	Incremental	Cumulative	Percent Paid
1	25	25	45.5
2	16	41	74.5
3	9	50	90.9
4	4	54	98.2
5	1	55	100.0

Table 17.4 Expected evolution for the Wang transform example, single accident year. Paid losses assumed equal to expected values, so profit equals released margin. Total shown for only income statement values.

Item	$d=0$	1	2	3	4	5	Total
Expected liability, $\mathsf{E}[Y_d]$	55	30	14	5	1		
SD liability	6.258	3.763	1.980	0.825	0.200		
Expected incr. paid, $\mathsf{E}[X_d]$		25	16	9	4	1	55
Required assets, a	80.031	45.052	21.920	8.298	1.800	0	
Realized assets, a'		55.031	29.052	12.920	4.298	0.800	
Assets released, $\Delta = a' - a$		9.979	7.132	4.621	2.498	0.800	25.031
Premium or MVL, $\bar{P}$	58.129	31.881	14.990	5.412	1.100	0	
Margin, $\bar{M}$	3.129	1.881	0.990	0.412	0.100	0	
Margin released		1.247	0.892	0.578	0.312	0.100	3.129
Equity, $\bar{Q}$	21.902	13.170	6.930	2.886	0.700	0	45.589
Equity released		8.732	6.241	4.043	2.186	0.700	21.902
Profit		1.247	0.892	0.578	0.312	0.100	3.129
Return (%)		5.70	6.77	8.34	10.82	14.29	6.86

assumed zero (runoff at plan) in this table. The overall rate of return to total capital consumed (3.129/45.589) is 6.86 percent.

Table 17.5 shows an example where X_d is higher than expectations in every year, so incremental incurred losses are consistently positive. Profits are earned in some years, but not all. The overall return is −5.91%. There is no capital call—it is unlikely for losses to be so high as to require that—but there is less than a full return of capital. □

17.2.2 The Steady State Portfolio

Up to this point, Ins Co. has been a single accident year entity, created *do novo* at the beginning of the period and extinguished at the end when all liabilities are paid. Now extend this concept by allowing Ins Co. to write new business while carrying forward reserve liabilities and supporting assets resulting from business written in prior periods. As a matter of terminology, **new business** refers to policies that are written and become effective during a period. It encompasses both renewals of existing policies and new–new policies. The model is not addressing whether new–new business performs differently than renewal business.

In the single stand alone accident year model, premium must be sufficient to fund losses and provide an additional margin so that the residual value of the portfolio is attractive enough for investors to provide an adequate capital cushion. With multiple accident years and existing liabilities, each item brought onto the balance sheet—new premium, existing premium or existing loss reserves—must similarly contain an adequate risk margin to attract investor interest for the coming period. Apart from new business, these margins must be provided from the prior period assets.

Table 17.5 One sample path evolution for the Wang transform example, single accident year. Paid losses (bolded) are higher than expected in every year, so profit is less than released margin by the amount of incremental incurred loss.

Item	$d=0$	1	2	3	4	5	Total
Expected liability, $\mathsf{E}[Y_d]$		55	30	14	5	1	
SD liability		6.258	3.763	1.980	0.825	0.200	
Expected incr. paid, $\mathsf{E}[X_d]$		25	16	9	4	1	55
Actual incr. paid, X_d		**26.138**	**18.794**	**9.436**	**5.446**	**1.011**	**60.825**
Incr. incurred loss		1.138	2.794	0.436	1.446	0.011	5.825
Required assets, a	80.031	45.052	21.920	8.298	1.800	0	
Realized assets, a'		53.893	26.258	12.484	2.852	0.789	
Assets released, $\Delta = a' - a$		8.841	4.338	4.186	1.052	0.789	19.206
Premium or MVL, $\bar{P}$	58.129	31.881	14.990	5.412	1.100	0	
Margin, $\bar{M}$	3.129	1.881	0.990	0.412	0.100	0	
Margin released		1.247	0.892	0.578	0.312	0.100	3.129
Equity, $\bar{Q}$	21.902	13.170	6.930	2.886	0.700	0	45.589
Equity released		8.732	6.241	4.043	2.186	0.700	21.902
Profit		0.109	−1.902	0.142	−1.134	0.089	-2.696
Return (%)		0.498	−14.44	2.05	−39.29	12.70	-5.91

At time t, Ins Co. writes new business incurring the ultimate liability $Y_{t,0}$. At the end of the first year, $d = 1$, Ins Co. must pay losses $X_{t,1}$ and book a reserve reflecting the liability $Y_{t,1}$. New business is written as part of the total portfolio liability (the new business plus existing reserves), which is the sum

$$W_t = \sum_{d\ge 0} Y_{t-d,d}.$$

We take the premium for the *new business* to be its natural allocation with respect to the total market value of liabilities $\bar{P}_{t,0} = D\rho_{W_t}(Y_{t,0})$. If the natural allocation is not unique we take the linear allocation or the lifted allocation if there is a suitable lift.

In Table 17.6, calendar year 2 liabilities include new business written in accident year 2 as well as runoff carried forward from accident years 0 and 1. The total liability is $W_2 = \sum_{t+d=2} Y_{t,d}$. The market value of each $Y_{t,d}$ is its natural allocation of $\rho(W_2)$. The fair premium of the new liability, being an natural allocation of $\rho(W_2)$, will be no more than the stand alone $\rho(Y_{2,0})$.

For clarity of illustration, assume the business is in steady state—similar but more complex results can be obtained assuming constant growth. Steady state means that for each d, $Y_{t,d}$ and $Y_{t',d}$ have the same distribution for all t, t'. That is, the outstanding liability depends only on the development year, not the accident year. This implies that all W_t have the same distribution and therefore the same market value as evaluated by ρ. The premium for the new business is therefore also the same in each accident year.

Table 17.6 Timeline of liability random variables in steady state, showing three development periods per accident year and three accident years. New business written in accident year 2 creates liability $Y_{2,0}$ which is contemporaneous with prior accident year developed liabilities $Y_{0,2}$ and $Y_{1,1}$.

AY\CY	0	1	2	3	4
0	$Y_{0,0}$	$Y_{0,1}$	$Y_{0,2}$		
1		$Y_{1,0}$	$Y_{1,1}$	$Y_{1,2}$	
2			$Y_{2,0}$	$Y_{2,1}$	$Y_{2,2}$

Going forward one step in time from $t-1$ to t, the realized assets increase by the new premium $\bar{P}_{t,0}$ and decrease by the paid claims from previous accident years' business:

$$a'_t = a_{t-1} + \bar{P}_{t,0} - \sum_{d>0} X_{t-d,d}.$$

There is no net change to the liabilities nor their expected loss, margin, nor capital components due to the steady state assumption. The asset requirement is the same, $a_t = a_{t-1}$. Therefore, the dividend to the shareholders is expected to be

$$\begin{aligned}\Delta_t &= a'_t - a_t \\ &= \bar{P}_{t,0} - \sum_{d>0} \mathsf{E}[X_{t-d,d}] \\ &= \bar{P}_{t,0} - \sum_{d>0} \mathsf{E}[X_{t,d}].\end{aligned}$$

The last line follows because $X_{t-d,d}$ has the same distribution as $X_{t,d}$. The last expression equals the total margin $\bar{M}_{t,0}$ embedded in the premium $\bar{P}_{t,0}$.

Similarly, the equality of distributions across accident years shows that the margin expected to be released from each reserve update sums to the margin written in the new business:

$$\sum_{s\geq 0} (\bar{M}_{t-s,s} - \bar{M}_{t-s,s+1}) = \sum_{s\geq 0} (\bar{M}_{t,s} - \bar{M}_{t,s+1}) = \bar{M}_{t,0},$$

which is the margin released to the investors. And so the total margin on the balance sheet stays constant.

Example 283, continued. Additionally, we assume the reserves and new business are independent for computational convenience. Assume calendar year $t=0$. We obtain $\mathsf{E}[W] = \sum_{d\geq 0} \mathsf{E}[Y_{-d,d}]$, $\mathsf{var}(W) = \sum_{d\geq 0} \mathsf{var}(Y_{-d,d})$, and $a = a(W) = \mathsf{E}[W] + 4\sigma(W)$. Finally, $\bar{P} = \mathsf{E}[W] + \lambda\sigma(W)$.

Table 17.7 sets out the key figures. The total liability and SD can be computed from rows 1 and 2 of Table 17.4. Assets and premium are $a(W) = \mathsf{E}[W] + 4\sigma(W)$ and $\rho(W) = \mathsf{E}[W] + \lambda\sigma(W)$ respectively.

Table 17.7 steady state financials for the Wang transform example.

Item	Value
Expected Liability, $\mathsf{E}[W]$	105.000
SDLiability, $\sigma(W)$	7.613
Assets, a	135.453
Premium, $\bar{P}$	108.807
Margin, $\bar{M}$	3.807
Equity, $\bar{Q}$	26.646

The *new business* premium is computed from the natural allocation:

$$\begin{aligned}\bar{P}_{0,0} &= \mathsf{E}[Y_{0,0}] + \frac{\sigma^2(Y_{0,0})}{\sigma^2(W_{0,0})}(\lambda\sigma(W_{0,0})) \\ &= \mathsf{E}[Y_{0,0}] + \frac{\sigma(Y_{0,0})}{\sigma(W_{0,0})}(\lambda\sigma(Y_{0,0})).\end{aligned}$$

The stand alone new business premium equals $\mathsf{E}[Y_{0,0}] + \lambda\sigma(Y_{0,0}) = 58.129$, consisting of expected loss 55 and margin $3.129 = \lambda\sigma(Y_{0,0})$. Folding in the reserves, the new margin is $3.807 = \lambda\sigma(W_{0,0})$, of which the new business gets a $0.675 = (6.258/7.613)^2$ share for a premium of $55 + 0.675 \times 3.807 = 57.572$. Therefore pooling new business with existing reserves lowers the fair premium for new business by 0.557, or about 1%. Similarly, the reserve run-off benefits from pooling with new business. The MVL as part of a steady state portfolio equals 51.235, whereas the stand alone MVL for the reserves equals 52.168. □

Exercise 284. Verify the previous paragraph. □

Table 17.8 compares the stand alone and allocated premiums for new business $Y_{t,d=0}$ and reserves $Y_{t,d>0}$.

Table 17.8 Premiums (for $d = 0$, market value of liabilities for $d > 0$), and margins for the Wang transform example, comparing stand alone (SA) versions to the steady state natural allocation (NA).

d	Expected loss	SA margin $\bar{M}$	SA premium $\bar{P}$	Loss ratio	NA margin $\bar{M}$	NA premium $\bar{M}$	Loss ratio
0	55	3.129	58.129	0.946	2.572	57.572	0.955
1	30	1.881	31.881	0.941	0.930	30.930	0.970
2	14	0.990	14.990	0.934	0.257	14.257	0.982
3	5	0.412	5.412	0.924	0.045	5.045	0.991
4	1	0.100	1.100	0.909	0.003	1.003	0.997
sum	105	6.513	111.513	0.942	3.807	108.807	0.965

17.2.3 Problems in Steady State and the Runoff Decision

In steady state, if losses exceed expectations by more than the expected margin release, investors get a capital call. In the Wang transform example, the margin is 3.807, only 3.6% of the expected loss of 105. In the single accident year runoff, there was ample cushion from the release of equity. In steady state, there is no *net* release of equity; new business requires equity equal to what is released from old business.

There are several alternatives. The surplus strain of writing new business can be ameliorated by writing less business. At the extreme, the firm goes into runoff. Runoff is depicted for the Wang transform example in Table 17.9, which is the multi-AY counterpart to Table 17.4. The total equity $\bar{Q} = 53.031$ represents the cumulative ¤-years amount consumed over the life of the liabilities. It is not booked in any one year—the maximum held is 26.646 in year 1. However total equity, or discounted total equity, is the appropriate denominator in a return calculation.

In the first year of runoff, only 1.639 of margin is released, but relieved of having to fund a new accident year of business, an additional 11.470 of equity is released. An incoming loss of 12.5% over expected, or 1.7 standard deviations, could be sustained without the need for a capital call.

A second possibility is that the investors walk away from the business and put it to the insurance regulators. This would make sense only if the incoming loss were so great that a capital call was necessary even in runoff. There is likely to be a zone where a small capital call is acceptable. As discussed in the single-accident year case, if the regulatory authority were to replace management with a new team, their approach to runoff would likely be more favorable to the claimants and less favorable to the investors. The original management team

Table 17.9 Expected evolution for the Wang transform example, going concern and runoff.

Item	$d=0$	1	2	3	4	5	Total
Expected liability, $\mathsf{E}[W]$	105.000	50.000	20.000	6.000	1.000	0	
SD liability, $\sigma(W)$	7.613	4.336	2.154	0.849	0.200	0	
Expected incr. paid, $\mathsf{E}[Y]$		55.000	30.000	14.000	5.000	1.000	
Required assets, a	135.453	67.344	28.616	9.394	1.800	0	
Realized assets, a'		80.453	37.344	14.616	4.394	0.800	
Assets released, Δ		13.109	8.727	5.222	2.594	0.800	30.453
Premium, $\bar{P}$	108.807	52.168	21.077	6.424	1.100	0	
Margin, $\bar{M}$	3.807	2.168	1.077	0.424	0.100	0	
Margin released		1.639	1.091	0.653	0.324	0.100	3.807
Equity, $\bar{Q}$	26.646	15.176	7.539	2.970	0.700	0	53.031
Equity released		11.470	7.636	4.569	2.270	0.700	26.646
Profit		1.639	1.091	0.653	0.324	0.100	3.807
Return (%)		6.15	7.19	8.66	10.92	14.29	7.18

might even be able to negotiate partial payments on the claims, lessening the ultimate loss payments. Nonetheless, there is a loss level so great that the investors will simply walk away.

A third possibility—one that avoids runoff—is to ask the new insureds to pay for prior losses. Depending on the market dynamics, and supply of capital in the industry as a whole, buyers may or may not be willing to do this. Generally, periods where they are essentially forced to overpay are called hard markets. Conversely, periods where accumulated risk margins in reserves are excessive and allow insurers to charge inadequate premiums to new policies (which, recall, include renewals) are called soft markets. Whenever the premium for a risk depends on factors other than the specifics of the risk being priced there is a market imperfection, see Winter (1994).

A fourth possibility is to change the rules governing the required asset amount. While regulatory authorities or rating agencies may stipulate a required asset $a(X)$, it could be that Ins Co. had been using a more stringent rule $a^*(X)$, leaving a cushion $a^*(X) - a(X)$. To fully appreciate the economic impact of making such a change, we must consider the possibility of default.

Recall, while X represents the *promised* payments, the *actual* payments are given by $X \wedge a$. The **market value** of Ins Co. is defined as the market value of assets less the market value of liabilities. Since assets are held at market value, $MV(X, a) = a - \rho(X \wedge a)$. The **economic gain or loss** for investors from a change to Ins Co. assets or liabilities is defined as the change in market value minus the change in assets invested. If there is a change X to X^* and a to a^* then it is given by

$$\begin{aligned} EGL &= \Delta MV - \text{Investment} \\ &= (a^* - \rho(X^* \wedge a^*)) - (a - \rho(X \wedge a)) - (a^* - a) \\ &= \rho(X \wedge a) - \rho(X^* \wedge a^*), \end{aligned} \tag{17.4}$$

showing that changes in economics are driven solely by their impact on insured claim liabilities. An economic gain or loss for investors is exactly offset by an economic loss or gain for insureds. This is consistent with the Myers and Cohn (1987) definition of fair premium cited in Section 8.7.1.

The simple form of Eq. (17.4) relies on the fact assets are booked at market value and invested in a risk-free instrument, so a does not change from its initial value. It also relies on there being no frictional costs to investors of holding assets within Ins Co. With frictional costs there could be a loss of value immediately on investment. Practitioners speak of regulated insurers as capital traps: it is easy to add capital but hard to get it back out. We are assuming an efficient capital market without such frictions.

The market value impact of a small change da in assets with no change in liabilities, i.e. an increase in capital, is

$$\begin{aligned} MV(X, a + da) - MV(X, a) &= (a + da - \rho(X \wedge (a + da))) - (a - \rho(X \wedge a)) \\ &= da + (\rho(X \wedge a) - \rho(X \wedge (a + da))) \\ &= da - \frac{d\rho(X \wedge a)}{da} da \\ &= (1 - g(S(a)))da \end{aligned}$$

which has an economic gain

$$EGL = -g(S(a))da < 0. \tag{17.5}$$

Investors will *never* voluntarily add assets to Ins Co. with no change in X because it is a gift to insureds. On the other hand they will *always* benefit from decreasing assets, but insureds will never voluntarily submit to such a reduction. Here there is a critical distinction between new business and reserves: new business has a choice of insurer in a competitive market whereas *claimants* (liability holders) are locked into Ins Co. In a transparent market it is not possible to extract excess profits, beyond the fair market cost of capital, from new business because insureds would not purchase at a price above the fair market value. However, it is possible to do so from claimants because they are unable to unilaterally move their claim to another insurer. The insurer has latitude to change capitalization for claimants provided it complies with regulation. In particular, it has the right to dividend excess capital, above the regulator standard, to owners resulting in a transfer of market value from claimants to shareholder owners. Extracting this value creates an incentive for Ins Co. to continue as a going-concern.

Example 285. Let's analyze the investor's decision at renewal in the steady state example.

At $t = 0$, Ins Co. has a total liability $W_0 = Y_0 + W_1$, where Y_0 equals the ultimate loss liability from new business written at 0, and W_1 is the reserve liability from all older accident years. The capital requirement is a_0. The cost to bear W_0 with assets a_0 equals $\rho(W_0 \wedge a_0)$. $\bar{P}_0$ equals the lifted natural allocation $D^f \rho_{W_t \wedge a, W_t}(Y_0)$ to new business, i.e. the fair premium for new business. The remaining premium, $\bar{P}'$, is the MVL, computed as the lifted natural allocation to reserves (point estimate plus risk margin). $\bar{P}'$ is funded from reserves carried forward, as the risk margin is earned over time. Note $\rho(W_0 \wedge a_0) = \bar{P}_0 + \bar{P}'$. The premium contains a positive margin, $\bar{P}_0 > \mathsf{E}[Y_0]$, provided Y_0 is positively correlated with W_0, which is always true in practice.

At $t = 1$, the paid loss amount X_1 (from new business and reserves) becomes known, and assets are reduced to $a_1' = a_0 - X_1$. The steady state assumption implies $\mathsf{E}[X_1] = \mathsf{E}[Y_0]$. Our simple, steady state emergence model assumes future paid losses are independent of X_1. To simplify the analysis further, assume the investors take the best **economic** course of action in an economy where

a. there are no frictional costs of holding capital in Ins Co.,
b. there are no costs of financial distress, e.g. caused by operating under regulatory supervision, and
c. all contracts are enforceable.

These assumptions make liability values independent of whether the investor funds Ins Co. and imply that the investor's decision can be made by considering only its impact on the fair value of liabilities. Investors have two choices: they can stop writing new business and enter run-off or continue as a going concern.

1. **Run-off.** In run-off, the fair value of liabilities is $\rho(W_1 \wedge a_1 \wedge a_1')$, by steady state law invariance, $a_1 = a(W_1)$ equals the required assets to hold W_1 (the assets held in

Ins Co. to avoid regulatory supervision), and a'_1 equals actual assets. As we have seen, investors never add assets to Ins Co. without an offsetting gain. Therefore, in run-off, they extract a dividend $(a'_1 - a_1)^+$ but never contribute more capital. This conclusion relies on the assumption (b). It is here that regulation allows Ins Co. to lower the claimant's security. We do not need to consider the value of the dividend separately, by assumption (a).

2. **Going concern.** If Ins Co. continues as a going concern and writes new business, it collects premiums $\bar{P}_0$ and holds a liability with value $\rho(W_1 \wedge a_0)$, again by steady state and law invariance. Thus, the fair value of liabilities as a going concern equals $\rho(W_1 \wedge a_0) - \bar{P}_0$.

Ins Co. continues as a going concern provided that results in lower liabilities, which occurs when

$$\rho(W_1 \wedge a_0) - \bar{P}_0 \leq \rho(W_1 \wedge a_1 \wedge a'_1) \tag{17.6}$$

$$\iff \bar{P}_0 \geq \rho(W_0 \wedge a_0) - \rho(W_1 \wedge a_1 \wedge (a_0 - X_1)). \tag{17.7}$$

$$\iff \bar{P}' \leq \rho(W_1 \wedge a_1 \wedge (a_0 - X_1)). \tag{17.8}$$

Here, we have written $a'_1 = a_0 - X_1$ to show the decision depends on the losses paid, i.e. that emerge, during the year. The result makes perfect sense: Ins Co. writes new business provided the premium exceeds the amount by which its liabilities increase in value, Eq. (17.7). Equivalently, Eq. (17.8) says Ins Co. continues as a going concern when the cost of bearing reserve risk as part of a going concern is lower than the stand-alone cost. Since the right hand side of Eq. (17.8) is monotonically decreasing in X_1, there exists a unique x_1 so that Ins Co. enters runoff when $X_1 > x_1$. Investors are willing to contribute up to the difference between the left and right sides of Eq. (17.7) to keep Ins Co. a going-concern.

What do we expect to occur? Under normal circumstances $a_1 < a_0 - X_1$. Thus $\rho(W_1 \wedge a_1 \wedge (a_0 - X_1)) = \rho(W_1 \wedge a_1)$. We expect $P' < \rho(W_1 \wedge a_1)$ because of diversification efficiencies within the going concern portfolio. Ins Co. enters run off only when X_1 is exceptionally large, again, in line with our intuitions. □

17.3 The Solvency II Risk Margin

The European Solvency II directive, European Commission (2009), prescribes a risk margin calculation for technical provisions (loss reserves). It extends a one-period cost of capital model to a multi-period model and establishes a risk load that depends on how uncertainty is resolved over time. The resulting **Cost of Capital Risk Margin** (CoCRM) is described in many places, including Risk Margin Working Group of the International Actuarial Association (2009), Floreani (2011), and Meyers (2019b), chapter 11. This section provides a brief introduction.

The technical provision combines the best estimate reserve, computed as the expected present value of payments, discounted using a risk-free term structure, and the risk margin. Article 77, paragraph 5 of the statute requires

> The risk margin shall be calculated by determining the cost of providing an amount of eligible own funds equal to the Solvency Capital Requirement necessary to support the insurance obligations over the lifetime thereof.
>
> The rate used in the determination of the cost of providing that amount of eligible own funds (Cost-of-Capital rate) shall be the same for all insurance and reinsurance undertakings and shall be reviewed periodically.
>
> The Cost-of-Capital rate used shall be equal to the additional rate, above the relevant risk-free interest rate, that an insurance or reinsurance undertaking would incur holding an amount of eligible own funds, as set out in Section 3, equal to the Solvency Capital Requirement necessary to support insurance and reinsurance obligations over the lifetime of those obligations.

Let i be the risk-free rate of interest, r the cost of capital, and X be a random variable describing ultimate losses for a homogeneous risk group. Denote the best estimate of X at time t as $X_t := \mathsf{E}[X \mid \mathcal{F}_t]$. X_t is random before t and fixed and known at or after t. By definition, $X_0 = \mathsf{E}[X]$ is the unconditional expected value because $\mathcal{F}_0$ is trivial. Underwriting information known up to $t = 0$ is used to specify X. Define V_t as the random variable X_{t+1} specified at time t. It reflects what we know at time t about what our next-period best-estimate X_{t+1} will be.

The **Solvency Capital Requirement** defines time-t required capital

$$Q_t := \rho(V_t) = \mathsf{VaR}_{0.995}(V_t) - \mathsf{E}[V_t] = \mathsf{xVaR}_{0.995}(V_t).$$

This particular risk measure is known as **excess VaR** or **xVaR**. As used, the measure defines capital, not assets.

Remark 286. Excess VaR it is susceptible to disaggregation regulatory arbitrage, where each yearly change falls below the VaR threshold, similar to problems discussed in Wang (2016). □

For example, at the time X is priced, i.e. $t = 0$, the best estimate of X is $X_0 = \mathsf{E}[X]$. At the end of the first year, Ins Co. will hold a liability booked at $X_1 = \mathsf{E}[X \mid \mathcal{F}_1]$. This liability is a random variable from the time $t = 0$ perspective. Over the first year, the *risk* is $X_1 - X_0$. To cover the variability during the year, Ins Co. must hold capital equal to $Q_0 = \rho(V_0) = \rho(X_1)$. The risk that will emerge during the second year is $X_2 - X_1$. Capital held during the second year (booked at $t = 1$) is $Q_1 = \rho(V_1)$. This process continues, determining capital Q_t from t to $t + 1$, until losses reach ultimate.

We could dispense with the enigmatic V_t and even X_t if we were willing to write out in full

$$Q_t := \mathsf{VaR}_{0.995}(\mathsf{E}[X \mid \mathcal{F}_{t+1}] \mid \mathcal{F}_t) - \mathsf{E}[\mathsf{E}[X \mid \mathcal{F}_{t+1}] \mid \mathcal{F}_t] \tag{17.9}$$

where the semantics of $\mathsf{VaR}_p(\cdot \mid \mathcal{F}_t)$ are obvious.

Paid losses are irrelevant for capital because they are part of X_t at time t, and capital is held only for prospective risk. In insurance terms, the risk is change in reserve, not paid loss. (As a matter of accounting, all loss is reserved before it is paid.) Paid loss is relevant to determining the expected present value of X, and the final underwriting outcome, but not the required capital.

If no new information about the risk becomes known during year t, then $X_t = X_{t+1}$ and there is no capital held *for year t*.

The margin associated with required capital Q_t is $(r-\iota)Q_t$ where $r-\iota$ is the spread between the cost of capital and the risk-free rate. To emphasize, the Solvency II cost of capital rate, 6%, is a *spread* over the risk-free rate. The pricing measure defines margin (not premium!) as a required rate of return times capital.

In our notational conventions:

$$\begin{aligned}\bar{Q} &= \mathsf{VaR}_{0.995}(V) - \mathsf{E}[V] \\ \bar{M} &= (r-\iota)\bar{Q} = (r-\iota)(\mathsf{VaR}_{0.995}(V) - \mathsf{E}[V]) \\ \bar{P} &= E[V] + \bar{M} = (r-\iota)\mathsf{VaR}_{0.995}(V) + (1-r+\iota)\mathsf{E}[V] \\ a &= \bar{P} + \bar{Q} = (1+r-\iota)\mathsf{VaR}_{0.995}(X) - (r-\iota)\mathsf{E}[V].\end{aligned}$$

The total capital needed over time is $\sum_t Q_t$ in ¤-year units, resulting in a nominal cost of capital charge of $(r-\iota)\sum_t Q_t$. Since this amount is paid over a number of years, it should be discounted. Solvency II discounts using the risk-free rate, and so we arrive at our interpretation/approximation of the Solvency II Cost of Capital Risk Margin

$$R_C = (r-\iota)\sum_{t\ge 0}\frac{Q_t}{(1+\iota)^t}. \tag{17.10}$$

Remark 287. Meyers (2019b) advocates a slightly different approach that assumes invested capital earns the risk-free rate but that cash flows with investors are discounted at the risk-adjusted rate, giving

$$R_C^* = (r-\iota)\sum_{t\ge 0}\frac{Q_t}{(1+r)^{t+1}}.$$

Meyers (2020), Section 6, includes a comparison of the two formulas. □

Margin $\bar{M}_t$ is thus accumulated from the end period back to the current period. Premium $\bar{P}_t$ is the sum of margin and similarly accumulated expected paid losses. Capital Q_t, however is the capital needed in the *current* period. Rate of return uses released premium less paid claims as the numerator (which is expected to be released margin) and capital as the denominator. If information comes in to cause $\mathsf{E}[X \mid \mathcal{F}_{t+1}]$ to differ from $\mathsf{E}[X \mid \mathcal{F}_t]$, this will be reflected in updated capital, margin, and premium figures and therefore in the releases as well.

Remark 288. The astute reader will notice that even Eq. (17.10) is not quite accurate. At time $t = 0$, Q_0 is known but Q_t for $t > 0$ are still random variables! Hewing to formalities,

Table 17.10 Solution to Exercise 290.

Outcome	Bad	Good	Expected
Probability	0.5	0.5	
Expected loss at $t = 0$	7,500	7,500	
$t = 1$ VaR at $t = 0$	10,000	10,000	
Capital	2,500	2,500	2,500
Cost of capital	150	150	150
Expected loss at $t = 1$	10,000	5,000	
$t = 2$ VaR at $t = 1$	79,712	39,856	
Capital	69,712	34,856	52,284
Cost of capital	4,183	2,091	3,137
Risk margin			**3,287**

and more generally expressing the remaining margin at arbitrary future valuation dates s, the proper expression for the CoCRM is

$$R_C(s) = (r - i)Q_s + (r - i)\sum_{t>s} \frac{\mathsf{E}[Q_t \mid \mathcal{F}_s]}{(1 + i)^{t-s}}. \tag{17.11}$$

□

Exercise 289. Substitute Eq. (17.9) into Eq. (17.11). Frame the resulting expression, mount it on a wall and stare at it. Contemplate the fact that it was originally specified using no mathematical notation. □

Exercise 290. Ins Co. writes insurance which pays out at $t = 2$. At the end of year 1, Ins Co. learns if the experience is bad or good. At the end of year 2, the actual losses become known and are paid. Bad losses have a lognormal distribution with an expected value of 10,000 and $\sigma = 1$ whereas for good losses it is 5,000 and the same σ. Each state is equally likely to occur. Compute the Solvency II risk margin using $r = 0.06$ cost of capital and $i = 0$ risk-free rate. What is $\mathsf{VaR}_{0.995}$ of ultimate loss? What is the risk margin if all the risk is resolved in one year? What if no information is revealed at $t = 1$? Comment on the results.

Solution. The lognormal μ parameters are 8.7103 and 8.0172. At $t = 0$ the expected loss equals 7500. At $t = 1$ the reserve will equal 10,000 or 5,000, with equal chances. Therefore, the 99.5% VaR of year-end reserves at $t = 0$ equals 10,000. At $t = 1$ the reserve equals $\mathsf{VaR}_{0.995}$ of the good or bad lognormal, i.e. $79{,}712 = \exp(8.7103 + \Phi^{-1}(0.995) \times 1))$ or 39,856. Applying Eq. (17.10) gives a risk margin 3,287.

When risk is resolved all in one year, the loss distribution is a mixture of two lognormals. Solving numerically gives $\mathsf{VaR}_{0.995} = 64,861$ and the risk margin equals $0.06 \times (64,861 - 7,500) = 3,442$. Capital in this case is higher than the expected amount in year 2, resulting in a higher risk margin.

Table 17.11 Solution to Exercise 291.

Outcome	No information	Discounted
Expected loss at $t = 0$	7,500	
$t = 1$ VaR at $t = 0$	7,500	
Capital	0	0
Cost of capital	0	0
Expected loss at $t = 1$	7,500	
$t = 2$ VaR at $t = 1$	64,861	
Capital	57,361	57,361
Cost of capital	3,442	3,442
Risk margin		**3,442**

If nothing is revealed at $t = 1$ there is no variability in the reserve booked then and the risk margin is still 3,442. (If $i > 0$ is would be lower by the amount of discount.) □

Exercise 291. Repeat Exercise 290 assuming both outcomes are normally distributed with $\sigma = 13,108$. Comment on the differences.

Solution. Risk margins are 2,176 and 2,062. The mixture's VaR equals 41,860. In this case the same capital is held at $t = 1$ in either state. Resolving over two years adds the expense of holding capital to resolve uncertainty at $t = 1$, with no offsetting savings through lower capital in the Good state. □

The relationship between R_C and the to-ultimate risk charge if losses emerge in one year is affected by offsetting factors. We can decompose ultimate losses into the pricing best estimate and a series of yearly changes:

$$X = \mathsf{E}[X] + (\mathsf{E}[X \mid \mathcal{F}_1] - \mathsf{E}[X]) + (\mathsf{E}[X \mid \mathcal{F}_2] - \mathsf{E}[X \mid \mathcal{F}_1]) + \cdots.$$

(Recall $\mathsf{E}[X \mid \mathcal{F}_0] = \mathsf{E}[X]$.) If the capital risk measure is subadditive, translation invariant, and normalized, then

$$\rho(X) \le \mathsf{E}[X] + \sum_{t\ge 0} \rho(\mathsf{E}[X \mid \mathcal{F}_{t+1}] - \mathsf{E}[X \mid \mathcal{F}_t]). \tag{17.12}$$

This inequality reflects the fact that yearly evaluations represent a stricter standard than losses being revealed in one year with no interim evaluations—it is analogous to the difference between the stock market being above a threshold at the end of 5 years vs. above a threshold at the end of *each* year. Thus, the cumulative, undiscounted capital requirement from the one-year-ahead risks is greater than the to-ultimate risk. However, time value discounting offsets the inequality Eq. (17.12). The net result is indeterminate.

Example 292. Continue with the one-accident-year normal example from Section 17.2.1 with $N = 5$, $\mu_d = (6 - d)^2$ and $\sigma_d = \mu_d/5$. Regardless of when claims are paid, the ultimate

Table 17.12 Expected evolution for the Wang transform example, single accident year, Cost of Capital Risk Margin method. Paid losses assumed equal to expected losses, so profit equals released margin.

Item	$d=0$	1	2	3	4	5	Total
Expected incr. paid, $\mathsf{E}[X_d]$		25	16	9	4	1	55
SD incr. paid, $\sigma(X_d)$		5	3.2	1.8	0.8	0.2	11.000
Required assets, a	69.824	39.303	19.131	7.237	1.551	0	
Realized assets, a'		44.824	23.303	10.131	3.237	0.551	
Assets released		5.521	4.172	2.894	1.687	0.551	14.825
Incremental premium, P	25.884	16.566	9.318	4.141	1.035	0	56.945
Cumulative premium, $\bar{P}$	56.945	31.061	14.495	5.177	1.035	0	
Incremental margin, M	0.884	0.566	0.318	0.141	0.035	0	1.945
Cumulative margin, $\bar{M}$	1.945	1.061	0.495	0.177	0.035	0	
Margin released		0.884	0.566	0.318	0.141	0.035	1.945
Equity, $\bar{Q}$	12.879	8.243	4.636	2.061	0.515	0	28.334
Equity released		4.637	3.606	2.576	1.546	0.515	12.880
Profit		0.884	0.566	0.318	0.141	0.035	1.945
Return		6.86%	6.86%	6.86%	6.86%	6.86%	6.86%

loss is $Y_{t,0}$. At time 0 this has a normal distribution with mean 55 and standard deviation 6.258 Table 17.4.

All incremental expected values are known ahead of time, so the risk between year $d-1$ and d is defined by a normal with mean zero and variance σ_d^2. The Solvency II capital requirement is $2.576\sigma_d$, since $\Phi^{-1}(0.995) = 2.576$. The sum of the capital requirements is 2.576×11 which is quite a bit more than the 2.576×6.258 it would be if the ultimate loss were revealed in one year, Table 17.4. But the loss is not revealed in one year; it takes several years to develop. Investors have their capital exposed for a prolonged period of time.

Table 17.12 shows how the CoCRM approach assigns capital and risk margin. We assume the risk-free rate is zero and the cost of capital is 6.86%, the same overall return shown in Table 17.4. (Solvency II prescribes 6% cost of capital.) While the two tables are laid out with essentially the same row structure, the computation in Table 17.12 proceeds in a different order. First Q is obtained from the distribution of subsequent paid losses using 2.576 times the volatility. Then the *one-year* margin M is obtained by multiplying Q by the 6.86% target rate of return. One-year premium P is margin plus expected loss. Cumulative margin $\bar{M}$ and premium $\bar{P}$ are forward sums. Finally, required asset a is cumulative premium plus current capital. Assets, capital, and margin are released as losses unfold. Expected profit equals released margin and return is profit divided by outstanding capital. In every year, the (expected) return is exactly the same 6.86%. □

Remark 293. In general, the distribution of X_t will depend on the realized value of previous X_s by more than just a mean shift. In such a case, computing R_C involves simulating over *paths* of loss emergence. Meyers (2019b) shows how to this using Markov Chain Monte Carlo (MCMC) methods. □

Remark 294. Although Solvency II mandates a constant-cost-of-capital approach, we could nonetheless substitute different asset (or capital) and premium (or margin) risk measures. □

Advanced Exercise 295. Consider a model of loss emergence over three years. Ultimate losses are a mixed compound Poisson with iid severity. The mixing distribution has a gamma distribution with mean 1 and CV $m = 0.25$. The unconditional claim count is 10. Severity is lognormal with mean 1000 and $\sigma = 1$. Information is revealed over three years:

1. At the end of year 1 the gamma mixing variable G is revealed.
2. At the end of year 2 the number of claims is revealed, sampled from a Poisson $100G$ distribution.
3. At the end of year 3 each individual claim amount is known.

Set up a simulation model to compute Q_i and R_C. Test the sensitivity to r and i. Test the sensitivity to the expected claim count, m, and σ. Which variable is most important? Add a variable that adjusts the severity in each simulated year, multiplying expected severity by a gamma variable with mean 1 (what Heckman and Meyers (1983) call a mixing variable), creating a fourth uncertainty, resolved at the end of year 3, with losses ultimately known at the end of year 4. Repeat each step. □

Advanced Exercise 296. Let B_t be an iid sequence of Bernoulli(0.5) random variables, modeling an infinite sequence of coin tosses. We can define B_t on $\Omega = [0, 1]$ by using a binary expansion $\omega = 0.\omega_1\omega_2 \ldots$ and setting $B_t(\omega) = \omega_t$. Let $X = \sum_t B_t/2^i$. X is a uniform random variable. Let $\mathcal{F}_t$ be the σ-algebra generated by the outcome of the first t tosses. It includes subsets of $[0, 1]$ that are defined by their first t digits.

At time t the risk emerging the coming year is a Bernoulli(0.5) random variable multiplied by 2^{-t}. The full tail risk is a uniform variable, multiplied by 2^{-t+1}. These outcomes are easily visualized using a binary tree and evolve as follows.

At $t = 1$ you will learn from ω_1 whether X will be distributed as $U/2$ ($\omega_1 = 0$) or $0.5 + U/2$ ($\omega_1 = 1$), where U is uniform. Thus, at $t = 0$, the amount you will be required to book at $t = 1$ is either 0.25 or 0.75, with equal probability. At $t = 0$ you book the best estimate 0.5 and hold excess 99.5-VaR capital on a 0.25/0.75 risk, $Q_0 = 0.25$.

At $t = 2$ you will learn from ω_2 if the loss will be $U/4$ or $0.25 + U/4$ (if $\omega_1 = 0$), or $0.5 + U/4$ or $0.75 + U/4$ (if $\omega_1 = 1$). Thus, at $t = 1$, the amount you will be required to book at $t = 2$ is a random draw from either a 1/8 or 3/8 distribution, or from a 5/8 or 7/8 distribution, both have excess VaR of 0.125. At $t = 1$ you book the best estimate (either 0.25 or 0.75) and hold $Q_1 = 0.125$.

a. What is $\mathsf{E}[X \mid \mathcal{F}_t](\omega)$?
b. If the ultimate risk is resolved in one year instead, what are the required capital and risk margin? (Keep r and i as free parameters.)
c. Use Eq. (17.10) to develop an expression for the Solvency II margin.

Solution.

a. $\mathsf{E}[X \mid \mathcal{F}_t](\omega) = \sum_{i \le t} \omega_i/2^i + 2^{-(t+1)}$. This is the value ω truncated at the tth binary digit, plus the expectation of the remaining digits.

b. $\mathsf{VaR}_{0.995}(U) - 0.5 = 0.495$ and the cost of capital risk margin equals $0.495(r - i)$.
c. Using Eq. (17.10),

$$R_C = 0.25(r - i)\sum_{t\geq 0} \frac{0.5^t}{(1+i)^t} = \frac{r-i}{2}\frac{1+i}{1+2i}.$$

□

17.4 Learning Objectives

1. Differentiate between evaluating multiyear risk on a to-ultimate and one-year basis, and the factors affecting their relative magnitudes.
2. Name the three components of shareholder dividend for a runoff portfolio.
3. Explain why new business in a steady state portfolio demands lower premium than that of a stand alone accident year.
4. Describe and analyze possible responses to a capital call when there are no frictional costs of capital.
5. Explain why the market value impact (economic gain) of a small increase in assets with no change in liabilities is always negative. Describe the impact on investor behavior.
6. Describe and compare the two formulas for the Cost of Capital Risk Margin.

18

Going Concern Franchise Value

In Parts I, II, and III, we modeled Ins Co. as writing business for one year and then closing the books and distributing any remaining funds to the shareholders. In Chapter 17 we relaxed this to consider multiyear runoff of liabilities and how the firm would look as a stacked succession of one-year deals with overlapping reserves. In this chapter, we look at Ins Co. as a **going concern**. From this perspective, the investors own a business that they expect to continue, year after year, and their valuation of that investment reflects this expectation. We first look at valuation via optimal dividends in some generality. Then we look at a particularly tractable simplification, the firm life annuity model.

18.1 Optimal Dividends

Theorizing about insurance valuation has been dominated by ruin theory, inaugurated by Lundberg (1903) and amplified by Harald Cramér in the 1930s (Cramér, 1994). We saw in Section 8.4.2 how classical ruin theory based on the compound Poisson process led to the famous Pollaczeck-Khinchine formula for the probability of eventual ruin. (The Cramer-Lundberg formula is an approximation that holds for thinner tailed risks.) Solvency was the focus: firms should make a profit, of course, but subject to controlling the risk of ruin.

Bruno de Finetti challenged this paradigm with an "alternative approach to collective risk theory," (de Finetti, 1957). He combined the profit and ruin criteria into one principle: the firm should maximize the present value of the dividend stream going to the investors. Despite the primacy of the ruin perspective—a natural one for regulators—work on *optimal dividends* problems continues into the twenty-first century. Literature reviews are provided in Gerber and Shiu (2004), Major (2009), and Lindensjö and Lindskog (2020).

Dividends add one more term to the **surplus process** Eq. (8.1):

$$U(t) = u + (1 + r)\mu t - \sum_{i=1}^{N(t)} X_i - \int_0^t D(s)ds.$$

$U(t)$ is the level of surplus at time t, u is the starting surplus, $(1 + r)\mu$ is the premium rate per unit time, $N(t)$ is the number of claims up to time t, and X_i are the iid claim amounts.

Pricing Insurance Risk: Theory and Practice, First Edition. Stephen J. Mildenhall and John A. Major.

The new term is the accumulated dividends where $D(t)$ is the rate of dividends at time t. The differential form of this equation is known as a **stochastic differential equation** Øksendal and Sulem (2007).

Let the stopping time $T = \min\{t : U(t) \le 0\}$. Then the optimal dividends objective is to choose $D(t)$ to maximize the expected value of cumulative discounted dividends

$$V(T) = \mathsf{E}\left[\int_0^T e^{-rt} D(t) dt\right]$$

where r is a discount rate. In discrete time, this **value equation** can be rewritten in recursive form as a **Bellman equation**

$$V(T) = D(0) + e^{-r}\mathsf{E}\left[V(T-1)\right].$$

The continuous version of this is known as the **Hamilton-Jacobi-Bellman equation**.

Various formulations of the problem put different constraints on the allowable choices for $D(t)$. Typically, $D(t)$ is a function of $U(t)$, making U a Markov process, and it is usually constrained to lie between 0 and $(1+r)\mu$.

With no further constraints, the typical solution is a **barrier strategy**

$$D(t) = \begin{cases} 0 & U(t) < h \\ (1+r)\mu & U(t) \ge h \end{cases}$$

for some barrier value h. It pays a dividend at the same rate as premium once surplus exceeds h, and nothing otherwise. Figure 18.1 shows a sample path for U with no dividends; Figure 18.2 the path with the same realized losses but a dividend barrier $h = 1$.

Exercise 297. Here is the version of de Finetti's original model from Major (2008). You have a magic coin box that can hold $W = 0, 1$, or 2 one-dollar coins. Every fixed time interval, one coin randomly appears (with probability p) or disappears (with probability $1-p$). If the box already holds two coins and a third one appears, the new coin is ejected and you keep it. But once the box runs out of coins, it vanishes in a puff of smoke. The interest rate per unit time

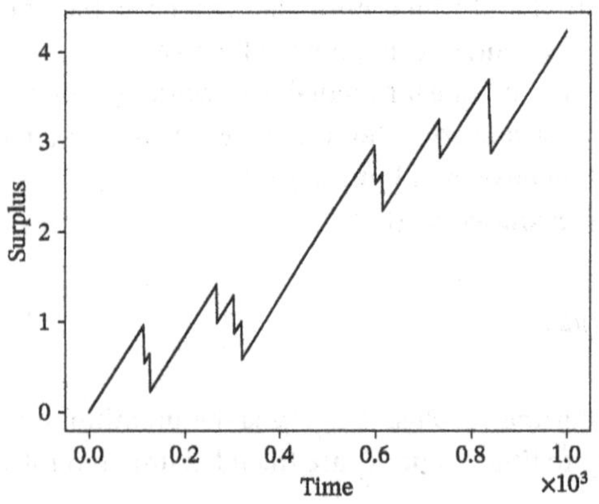

Figure 18.1 Sample path for surplus process with unit Poisson losses, no dividends.

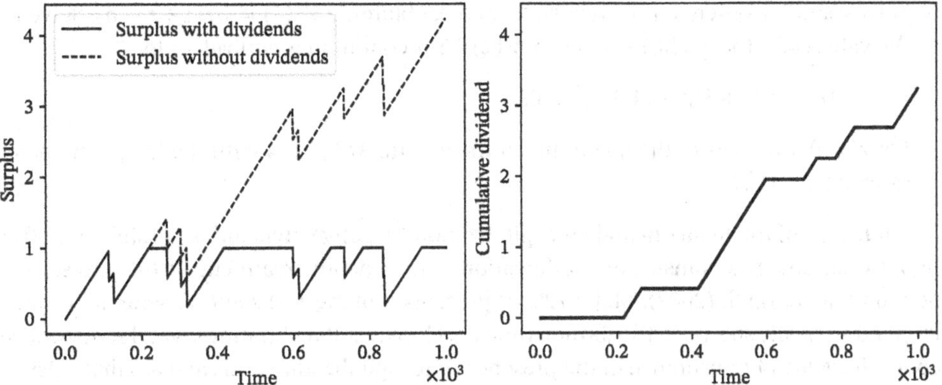

Figure 18.2 Left: sample path for surplus process with unit Poisson losses and dividend barrier at $h = 1$. Dashed line indicates surplus without dividends. Right: cumulative dividends paid.

interval is r. Currently, the box has two coins in it and will transition at the end of the next time interval.

a. What is the discounted present value of the income stream from this device?
b. At the start, you can flip a switch to get one of the coins immediately, but thereafter the limit the box can hold is 1 coin, not 2. If your time value is $r = 0$, for what values of p would it be advantageous to flip the switch?

Solution.

a. Draw a lattice of state transitions for this Markov process. At time 0, the state is $U(0) = 2$. At time 1 with probability p it will be $U(1) = 2$ with a payoff of 1, or with probability $1 - p$ it will be $U(1) = 1$ with no payoff. At time 2 there are three possible states, of which $U(2) = 0$ ends the process. Using backward induction, write the value $V(U)$ of the three states as follows:

$$V(0) = 0$$
$$V(1) = \frac{pV(2) + (1-p)V(0)}{1+r}$$
$$V(2) = \frac{p(V(2)+1) + (1-p)V(1)}{1+r}.$$

Then solve algebraically for $V(1)$ and $V(2)$, $V(2)$ being the answer:

$$V(1) = \frac{p^2}{(1+r)(1+r-p) - p(1-p)}$$
$$V(2) = \frac{(1+r)p}{(1+r)(1+r-p) - p(1-p)}.$$

b. Solve a similar system for the two-state model, obtaining $V^*(1) = p/(1+r-p)$. Solve for the values of p that yield $1 + V^*(1) > V(2)$. This condition is equivalent to

$$2p^2 - (2r+3)p + (1+r)^2 > 0.$$

For $r = 0$, the roots of the quadratic on the left are $3/4 \pm 1/4$ with the inequality being satisfied if $p < 1/2$. □

Extensions of the model include recapitalization (negative dividends), possibly with frictional cost, and risk transfer or modification. An in-depth treatment of the subject can be found at Schmidli (2007). Major (2009) presents a numerical solution scheme for arbitrary, numerically specified distributions and develops results exhibiting several stylized facts about the value of reinsurance in the presence of recapitalization costs and auxiliary risk.

The choice of discount rate r is seldom discussed in this literature but needs to be addressed to integrate an optimal dividends framework with the SRM approach. The natural choice is to use distorted probabilities for the losses and a risk-free rate for discounting. Otherwise, we have to recalibrate the discount rate if any risk transformations (e.g. reinsurance) are analyzed. Under fair premiums, however, premium equals distorted expected losses and so the surplus process has zero (distorted) expectation of growth! We turn to a potential solution next.

18.2 The Firm Life Annuity

This section presents a version of the firm life annuity valuation model from Major (2011). It consists of a simplified, discrete time optimal dividends model allowing for immediate recapitalization. A similar model is detailed in Panning (2013).

We have considered Ins Co. as operating on a one year cycle, with the investors closing the books at time 1 (the end of the cycle) and walking away with whatever residual assets are left. The time 0 (beginning of cycle) value of those residual assets is given by

$$\bar{Q} = \frac{a - \bar{S}}{1 + \bar{\iota}} = \frac{a - \rho(X)}{1 + r_f}.$$

Assuming fair premiums, the investors contribute those funds $\bar{Q}$, the policyholders contribute the balance $\bar{P} = a - \bar{Q}$, and the one-period net present value to the investors is $NPV_1 = \bar{Q} - \bar{Q} = 0$. Once again, we recover the Myers-Cohn's fair premium condition.

In subsequent periods, the investors have the option to participate in the deal once more, but with $NPV_1 = 0$ each period stands alone. We now alter the model to accommodate abnormal earnings and consequent implications for the investors.

First, assume that at time 0 policyholders pay actual premiums $\bar{P}_{act} = \bar{P} + F_0 > \bar{P}$. They may be willing to do so because of perceived superiority of service or security, or because they are paying for a competitive level of expenses that Ins Co. has managed to beat, or for myriad other reasons. Investors need only supply funds $\bar{Q}_{act} = \bar{Q} - F_0$ to achieve the required assets a. The net present value of the deal to the investors is now $NPV_1 = \bar{Q} - \bar{Q}_{act} = F_0$. F_0 goes by various names such as economic profit, abnormal earnings, residual income, and economic value added. A direct connection between NPV_1 and economic value added can be seen by rewriting $\bar{P} = \bar{S} + \bar{M}$ and defining $R := \bar{P}_{act} - \bar{S}$ as the *profit*. Then $F_0 = \bar{P}_{act} - \bar{P} = R - \bar{M}$

is the excess of profit over the capital charge (margin), which is exactly how economic value added is defined.

Assume that at time 1, the investors have the *real option* to reinvest $\bar{Q}$ in the next cycle of operations. We assume that all parameters—the required assets, the probability distribution of losses, etc.—are the same in the second cycle as they were in the first.

At time 1, say there are two possibilities for premiums. Either the policyholders will again pay $\bar{P}_{act}$ or they will pay only $\bar{P}$. In the first case, upon exercising the option the investors will collect at time 1^+ a rebate on their investment of $NPV_1 = F_0$, the same as they did at time 0. Call this the *in the money* outcome. The alternative *out of the money* outcome leaves the investor with $NPV_1 = 0$ regardless of the exercise decision. Let us assume that once policyholders revert to paying $\bar{P}$, they will not go back to paying $\bar{P}_{act}$ in the foreseeable future.

Assume that the time 0 *risk neutral* probability of the real option expiring out of the money is given by λ. A possible approach to computing such a number is discussed below.

It is evident that the time 0 net present value of this arrangement is

$$NPV_2 = F_0 + (1-\lambda)\frac{F_0}{1+r_f}.$$

To extend this logic further in time, encompassing optionality at times $t = 2, 3, \ldots$ it is necessary to hypothesize a forward curve of risk-neutral out-of-the-money probabilities. To keep it simple, assume the year-on-year risk-neutral probabilities are all the same λ. A simple recursive argument gives

$$NPV_\infty = F_0 + (1-\lambda)\frac{NPV_\infty}{1+r_f} \tag{18.1}$$

which in turn can be solved to yield

$$NPV_\infty = \frac{1+r_f}{r_f+\lambda}F_0 =: a_x F_0 \tag{18.2}$$

where a_x is the value of a unit (whole life) annuity that terminates when the firm's ability to earn excess profits F_0 fails. NPV_∞ is known as **franchise value**. In applications, franchise value is defined as the difference between the stock market value of the firm (shares outstanding times share price in the capital markets) and its financial statement book value. In terms of our model, $MV = \bar{Q} + NPV_\infty$.

Next, let us consider growth. Assume Ins Co.'s scale of operations grows by the factor $1+\gamma$ each year. Then the NPV_1 is either 0 or $(1+\gamma)F_0$, and our recursion again gives us $NPV_\infty = a_x F_0$, however now

$$a_x = \frac{1+r_f}{r_f - \tilde{\gamma}} \tag{18.3}$$

where

$$\tilde{\gamma} = (1-\lambda)(1+\gamma) - 1. \tag{18.4}$$

Exercise 298. Verify Eqs. (18.3) and (18.4) □

The safest assumption for growth rate γ is an industry-wide figure which should reflect the growth rate of the national economy (or economies) in which the firm operates. A higher growth rate assumption may on occasion be justified—for example a smaller firm succeeding in gaining market share—but the longevity of that growth needs to be considered as well. A particularly useful assumption is to set $\gamma = r_f$. There is some economic justification for this, see Damodaran (2016). This assumption results in a wonderful simplification:

$$a_x = \frac{1}{\lambda}. \tag{18.5}$$

Exercise 299. Verify Eq. (18.5). □

The preceding logic and mathematics is similar to the Gordon (1962) Growth Model, which is a DCF model, c.f. Section 8.7.2.

Above, we hypothesized that the mortality of franchise value depended on the behavior of the customers. It could also be a result of investors refusing to recapitalize, say, after a very large loss. If losing franchise value turned on a specific, modeled financial outcome, an objective probability λ_{obj} could be calculated. If investor risk aversion is encoded in a distortion function g, then we submit that the appropriate risk-neutral probability to use in Eq. (18.5) is $\lambda = g(\lambda_{obj})$. This follows from treating the non-monetary but economically valuable NPV_∞ in Eq. (18.1) the same as any other contingent cash flow the investors may value.

One plausible trigger is having a loss X big enough that post-loss assets $a - X$ fall below a critical threshold. The news of an incipient ratings downgrade or watch, along with the suspicion that the firm would not soon or easily recapitalize, could be enough for sophisticated commercial customers to reconsider their attitude toward insuring with Ins Co.

Example 300. Table 18.1 is built on the Simple Discrete Example from Section 2.4.1. The square root distortion is used for valuation. There is the possibility of buying a 10 excess 80 aggregate reinsurance contract on X_2. The ceded cash flows are shown as X_{2c}. Expected ceded loss equals 2.5, with a 25% objective and 50% distorted probability of a full recovery. Suppose the reinsurance premium is 5.5. Is it a good deal?

Since net losses are comonotonic with gross, there is no reordering problem and we can use the risk-adjusted probabilities ΔgS to determine the natural allocation. The ceded flows' allocated premium of 5.0 is less than the reinsurance premium of 5.5, so on a one-year basis, this is not a good deal. Net premium and reinsurance premium sum to $46.156 + 5.5 = 51.656$ which is greater than the gross premium of 51.156 by exactly that 0.5 by which reinsurance premium is greater than ceded allocated premium.

Now suppose that the firm is collecting *actual* premiums of 53.656, corresponding to abnormal profits of $F_0 = 2.5$. Suppose further that assets $a = 100$ are being held and that a loss sufficient to bring those assets down to 10 or less will trigger loss of franchise value.

Using Eq. (18.5) we can compute franchise value with or without reinsurance.

With the gross book, assets will fall from 100 to 10 or below in outcomes 6, 7, and 8. These occur with objective probability 0.25 and distorted probability $\lambda = 0.5$. Therefore the annuity factor $a_x = 2$ and franchise value $NPV_\infty = 2 \times 2.5 = 5$.

With the net book, only outcome 8 will trigger loss of franchise value, with $\lambda = 0.25$ and $a_x = 4$. However, due to the reinsurance premium being higher than its allocated value by 0.5, the excess profits going to investors will only be $F_0 = 2$. Franchise value is therefore 8, or 3 higher than without reinsurance.

Table 18.1 Outcomes and financials for simple example with XOL reinsurance on unit 2.

j	X_1	X_2	X_g	X_{2c}	X_n	p	ΔgS
0	0	0	0	0	0	0.2500	0.1340
1	0	1	1	0	1	0.1250	0.0755
2	8	0	8	0	8	0.1250	0.0835
3	8	1	9	0	9	0.0625	0.0457
4	10	0	10	0	10	0.1250	0.1024
5	10	1	11	0	11	0.0625	0.0590
6	0	90	90	10	80	0.1250	0.1464
7	8	90	98	10	88	0.0625	0.1036
8	10	90	100	10	90	0.0625	0.2500
EL	4.500	22.750	27.250	2.5	24.750		
Margin	1.476	22.430	23.906	2.5	21.406		
Premium	5.976	45.180	51.156	5.0	46.156		

Table 18.2 Alternatives affecting franchise value, simple example with XOL reinsurance on line 2.

Situation	Baseline	G-1	G-9	N-0	N-4
Portfolio	Gross	Gross	Gross	Net	Net
Capital position change $\Delta\bar{Q}$	0	1	9	0	-4
Starting assets	100	101	109	100	96
Franchise collapse events	6,7,8	7,8	8	8	7,8
Prob. franchise collapse $\Pr\{a - X \leq 10\}$	0.25	0.1250	0.0625	0.0625	0.1250
Distorted probability λ	0.50	0.3536	0.25	0.25	0.3536
Annuity factor $a_x = 1/\lambda$	2.00	2.8284	4.00	4.00	2.8284
Abnormal earnings F_0	2.50	2.5000	2.50	2.00	2.0000
Franchise value $NPV_\infty = a_x F_0$	5.00	7.0711	10.00	8.00	5.6569
Change from baseline	0	2.0711	5.00	3.00	0.6569

While reinsurance does not look like a good deal on a one year basis, by doubling the longevity of excess profits, it increases franchise value by 60 percent. □

Example 301. There are other possibilities beyond the reinsurance purchase for affecting franchise value. Some examples are spelled out in Table 18.2. The first column represents the baseline with no changes. For the gross portfolio, the next two columns (situations G-1, G-9) show the impact of adding 1 or 9 to invested capital. This changes which loss outcomes bring total assets below the threshold, thus increasing franchise value relative to the baseline. Abnormal earnings for the gross portfolio are assumed 2.5, but under net this is reduced to

2.0 to pay for the reinsurance. For the net portfolio, Ins Co. can *dividend back* 4 from capital and still have no possibility of insolvency as well as an increase in franchise value relative to baseline. □

18.3 Learning Objectives

1. Write down the surplus process equations with dividends and explain the meaning of each term.
2. Explain the term optimal dividends.
3. Define and apply a barrier option dividend strategy. Compute the present value of dividends given premium and loss assumptions.
4. Compare formulas for the Gordon Growth model and a life annuity and explain how they can be combined into a valuation of a risky business.
5. Describe a situation where buying a reinsurance policy does not look economically viable over one year but does look advantageous over multiple years.

19

Reinsurance Optimization

Ceded reinsurance, i.e. buying reinsurance to protect the portfolio from losses, is an important ingredient of risk managment. In this chapter, we analyze ceded reinsurance using a spectral risk measure framework and offer advice about evaluating proposed programs and optimizing parameters thereof.

19.1 Background

Analyzing assumed reinsurance—i.e. selling reinsurance as a line of business—is in principle no different than the analysis of selling other insurance products, though there is a wrinkle. Commitments made to reinsureds stand at **lower priority** than insurance claimants in most US states. The NAIC Model Act, quoted in Section 8.2.2, puts insurance claims in Class 3, behind only administrative expenses and Guarantee Association expenses. Reinsurance is in Class 7. This standing means that if an insurer writes assumed reinsurance and becomes insolvent because of reinsurance claims (i.e. would be solvent excluding reinsurance), then the insurance liabilities will be paid in full.

Ceded reinsurance—i.e. buying reinsurance to protect the portfolio—is another matter. In Section 8.2 we stated that reinsurance is a form of capital and that, as such, it should inform the choice of distortion function. In what follows we analyze reinsurance in terms of contingent cash flows where it is *almost* treated as a negative line of business. The main difference is that when portfolio losses put the firm into insolvency, reinsurance payments are still due in full, they are not pro-rated by a/X. For ease of exposition, we assume in the remainder of this section that insolvency is impossible.

19.2 Evaluating Ceded Reinsurance

Say Ins Co. has portfolio losses X_g and the opportunity to buy reinsurance promising cash flows X_c with annual premium π. After reinsurance, it is responsible for losses $X_n = X_g - X_c$. However, the reinsurance premium must also be funded. The notation is suggestive; the initial position is the *gross* portfolio and the final position is the *net* portfolio. It does not

Pricing Insurance Risk: Theory and Practice, First Edition. Stephen J. Mildenhall and John A. Major.

mean that there is no other reinsurance involved with X_g, simply that X_g is gross of this particular reinsurance contract. Inuring details (how different contracts interact in terms of payments and priorities) are assumed already worked out in the definition of the X_c cash flows. Finally, if there are reinstatement premiums (additional premiums due after collecting on a reinsured loss), they are treated as decrements to the X_c payouts.

Suppose Ins Co. prices with an SRM ρ. The technical premiums are

$$\begin{aligned}\bar{P}_g &:= \rho(X_g)\\ \bar{P}_n &:= \rho(X_n + \pi) = \rho(X_n) + \pi = \rho(X_g - X_c) + \pi,\end{aligned}$$

since SRMs are normalized and translation invariant. Ins Co. treats the reinsurance cost as a pass-through.

Should Ins Co. enter into this contract? There are three approaches to making this decision.

1. **A/B method.** Compare SRM premiums $\bar{P}_g$ and $\bar{P}_n$. Whichever is lower points to the more desirable situation.
2. **Allocate gross.** Evaluate the SRM premium allocated to the ceded cash flows from the gross perspective $D\rho_{X_g}(X_c)$. If this is greater than the premium π then buy the reinsurance.
3. **Allocate net.** Evaluate the SRM premium allocated to the ceded cash flows from the net perspective $D\rho_{X_n}(X_c)$. If this is greater than the premium π then buy the reinsurance.

We might expect the three approaches to yield the same decision most of the time. However, if used to set reservation prices for the contracts—e.g. before market prices are known—they will generally produce slightly different answers.

The A/B method is the gold-standard answer because it directly compares the SRM premiums. The two allocation methods are first-order Taylor approximations to the A/B method

$$\begin{aligned}\rho(X_n) &= \rho(X_g - X_c) \approx \rho(X_g) - D\rho_{X_g}(X_c)\\ \rho(X_g) &= \rho(X_n + X_c) \approx \rho(X_n) + D\rho_{X_n}(X_c).\end{aligned}$$

We cannot expect them to produce exactly the same answer. Recall, Delbaen's Theorem 2 says that the natural allocation can be interpreted as a directional derivative provided ρ is differentiable. Directional derivatives are linear.

Example 302. We return to the Simple Discrete Example from Section 2.4.1. Table 19.1 shows the outcomes and financials. Valuation is with respect to the gross portfolio, with gross technical premium of 51.156. A simple aggregate excess of loss contract on X_1 of 2.5 xs 7 is available, with its cash flows shown as X_{1c}. Its allocated premium is 1.2613.

Table 19.2 shows that the results are slightly different when the valuation is taken with respect to the net loss. Outcomes 3 and 4 trade places in the sort order. The net technical premium is 49.8986 with the allocation to ceded cash flows being 1.2497.

The A/B method concludes that the reinsurance is a good deal as long as its premium less than $\rho(X_g) - \rho(X_n) = 51.1560 - 49.8986 = 1.2574$. The allocating gross method sets the reservation price at 1.2613 and allocating net sets it at 1.2497. The range of these figures is 0.0115 or roughly 3% of ceded margin.

Table 19.1 Outcomes and financials for the Simple Discrete Example with XOL reinsurance on unit 1. Valuation is with respect to the gross loss (X_g) sort order.

j	X_1	X_2	X_g	X_{1c}	p	ΔgS
0	0	0	0	0.0	0.2500	0.1340
1	0	1	1	0.0	0.1250	0.0755
2	8	0	8	1.0	0.1250	0.0835
3	8	1	9	1.0	0.0625	0.0457
4	10	0	10	2.5	0.1250	0.1024
5	10	1	11	2.5	0.0625	0.0590
6	0	90	90	0.0	0.1250	0.1464
7	8	90	98	1.0	0.0625	0.1036
8	10	90	100	2.5	0.0625	0.2500
EL	4.5000	22.7500	27.2500	0.8750		
Margin	1.4759	22.4301	23.9060	0.3863		
Premium	5.9759	45.1801	51.1560	1.2613		

Table 19.2 Outcomes and financials for simple example with XOL reinsurance on unit 1. Valuation is with respect to the net loss (X_n) sort order.

j	X_1	X_2	X_g	X_{1c}	X_n	p	S	gS	ΔgS
0	0	0	0	0.0	0.0	0.2500	0.7500	0.8660	0.1340
1	0	1	1	0.0	1.0	0.1250	0.6250	0.7906	0.0755
2	8	0	8	1.0	7.0	0.1250	0.5000	0.7071	0.0835
4	10	0	10	2.5	7.5	0.1250	0.3750	0.6124	0.0947
3	8	1	9	1.0	8.0	0.0625	0.3125	0.5590	0.0534
5	10	1	11	2.5	8.5	0.0625	0.2500	0.5000	0.0590
6	0	90	90	0.0	90.0	0.1250	0.1250	0.3536	0.1464
7	8	90	98	1.0	97.0	0.0625	0.0625	0.2500	0.1036
8	10	90	100	2.5	97.5	0.0625	0.0000	0.0000	0.2500
EL	4.5000	22.7500	27.2500	0.8750	26.3750				
Margin	1.4605	22.4378	23.8983	0.3747	23.5236				
Premium	5.9605	45.1878	51.1483	1.2497	49.8986				

A better understanding of what these figures mean may be obtained by widening the scope to net results with a fractional participation (percentage placed, in reinsurance terminology)

$$\bar{P}_n := \rho(X_n(t)) + t\pi := \rho(X_g - tX_c) + t\pi$$

where $0 \leq t \leq 1$. We assume that the reinsurance premium scales with the participation. With this definition, $\rho(X_n(t))$ uses the gross sort order for $t < 2/3$ and the net sort order for $t > 2/3$. At $t = 2/3$, outcomes 4 and 5 collapse, but for evaluating $X_n(2/3)$, either of the original sort orders can be used to obtain the same result. □

Exercise 303. Add reinsurance to your spreadsheet implementation of the Simple Discrete Model and reproduce our conclusions. □

Figure 19.1 shows two possible traces for $\rho(X_n(t)) + t\pi$, the lower with $\pi = 1.2497$ and the upper with $\pi = 1.2613$. For lower values of the reinsurance premium, 100% participation provides the minimum net premium. For higher values, the gross portfolio has the lowest premium. For intermediate values, the lowest premium is found at $t = 2/3$.

Despite the superiority of the A/B method in correctly identifying the lowest cost solution, there may be situations where it is difficult to use. Imagine that instead of one contract, Ins Co. was considering 20 contracts and sought to determine which combination would provide the lowest total cost of risk. Without some sort of initial pruning, there would be $2^{20} \approx 1$M combinations to evaluate, which is impractical.

In such situations, a combination of the A/B and allocation methods is useful. Starting at the gross portfolio, allocation provides gradients for each contract i as

$$D\rho_{X_g}(-tX_{ci} + t_i\pi_i) = -tD\rho_{X_g}(X_{ci}) + t_i\pi_i$$

which can be used to implement a steepest-descent search for a minimum premium set of participations.

More complex reinsurance questions revolve around attributing the cost and benefit of reinsurance units. If it is possible to split the reinsurance cash flows into unit-specific ceded losses, the application is straightforward. However, it may be the case that multiple units' gross losses are combined and that ceded losses are a function of the summed losses. Then, there may be no obviously correct way to allocate the ceded losses back to the components (although there will be a contractually agreed approach if the units fall into different accounting segments). This problem is treated in Major (2018). There are additional complicating issues that are beyond the scope of this book.

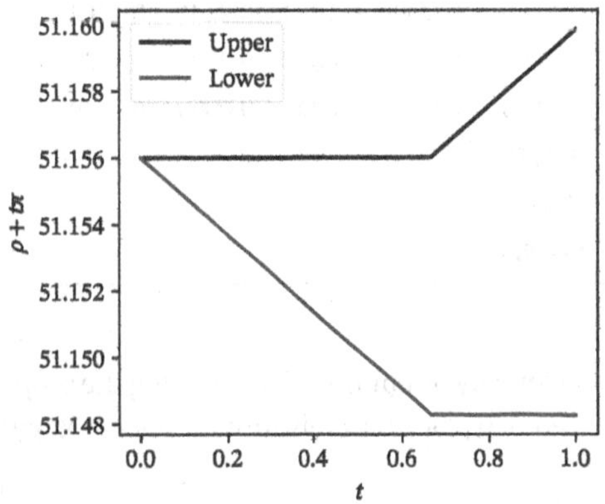

Figure 19.1 Technical premium for net portfolio at t participation in ceded reinsurance, two values of reinsurance premium.

19.3 Learning Objectives

1. Describe the A/B and natural allocation methods of reinsurance optimization.
2. Explain why the different methods might not produce the same reservation prices.
3. Explain the circumstances under which one method may be preferable to another.
4. Apply the A/B and allocation methods to simple discrete examples to determine optimal placement percentages.

20

Portfolio Optimization

In this chapter, we extend our analysis out of a static framework to address decision making with regards to the composition of the insured portfolio. This requires exploring the complex interaction of cost allocation, benefit allocation, and premium regulation. In the end, we will find some unavoidable market distortions.

20.1 Strategic Framework

We have already solved the pricing problem in a static model with a pricing spectral risk measure. There, assets are specified exogenously and there is no need for a capital risk measure. Prices are computed as fair premiums and give the most an insured will pay. They determine marginal revenue.

We need a dynamic model to evaluate marginal costs. To specify it, we need a capital risk measure and a portfolio model in addition to the pricing risk measure. The capital risk measure is usually given by a regulatory or rating agency.

Ins Co. can then use a dynamic model for portfolio optimization, by equating marginal cost and marginal revenue for each unit.

In the static model, $X = \sum_i X_i$, risk is backed with assets a, and paid losses are $X \wedge a$ in total and $X_i(a)$ by unit. In the dynamic model, we replace each unit with a stochastic process $X_i(v_i)$, where v_i denotes the volume of business written. Volume is parameterized so that $\mathsf{E}[X_i(v_i)] = v_i\mathsf{E}[X(1)]$. Portfolio volume is controlled by the vector $\mathbf{v} = (v_1, \dots, v_n)$. Total losses are $X(\mathbf{v}) = \sum_i X_i(v_i)$. We continue to assume ρ is a spectral risk measure determined by distortion g and that loss payments in default are made according to equal priority. There is a clash of notation between $X_i(a)$ and $X_i(v_i)$; we use only the latter in this chapter, losses from unit i with volume v_i.

There are two flavors of dynamic model: a homogeneous model where $X_i(v_i) = v_iX_i(1)$ and an inhomogeneous one where $X_i(v_i)$ is a stochastic process, such as a compound Poisson or Lévy process (Sato, 1999). The shape of an inhomogeneous model changes with volume, so $v_1X_1(1)$ and $X_1(v_1)$ have different distributions. Most of the results apply to both models and we highlight when that is not the case.

Pricing Insurance Risk: Theory and Practice, First Edition. Stephen J. Mildenhall and John A. Major.

Note that $X_i(v_i)$, unlimited losses to unit i, is a function of v_i alone. They are the amounts promised to unit i by their insurance contract(s). The amount actually paid to unit i is $X_i(\mathbf{v}, a)$, a function of volumes in *each unit*, $\mathbf{v} = (v_1, \dots, v_n)$, and total assets a. This distinction remains critical.

Any functions introduced earlier in the book that depend on X or X_i now depend on $\mathbf{v}$. For example, the survival function for $X(\mathbf{v})$ is denoted $S_{\mathbf{v}}(a)$. Formulas for expected total losses, loss density, total premiums, premium density, and premium allocation functions are all obvious extensions of the formulas in previous chapters.

Call the capital risk measure $a = a(\mathbf{v}) = a(X(\mathbf{v}))$. It is assumed translation invariant, so it can be used to determine assets or capital

We work with both VaR and TVaR capital standards. Solvency II is 99.5% VaR, AM Best, Standard & Poor's, and NAIC Risk Based Capital formulas are all implicitly VaR based, especially for catastrophe losses. The Swiss stand out, using coherent TVaR. Recently Basel III adopted TVaR (Wang and Zitikis, 2019).

20.2 Market Regulation

We consider dynamic performance management within a regulated market. Almost all jurisdictions regulate insurance to ensure its solvency. Regulation attempts to balance four conflicting constraints:

1. To ensure **effective** insurance, assets must be appropriate relative to *potential* loss (as opposed to expected loss). Regulation and market discipline manage effectiveness, and imply an upper bound on premium leverage.
2. To provide **efficient** insurance, the amount of assets should bear a reasonable relationship to the amount of loss transferred, implying a lower bound on leverage.
3. To provide **affordable** insurance, the price must be attractive to the insured, implying a lower bound loss ratio.
4. To ensure **available** insurance, the return on capital must be attractive to investors, implying an upper bound loss ratio.

Efficiency is usually satisfied as a consequence of affordability and availability. Section 9.3.2 investigated how to identify features conducive to a functioning insurance market.

Morale hazard and adverse selection can cause insurance market failures. But failures can also be caused by risk, especially catastrophe risk. Regulation may demand capital be so high that premiums become unattractive to insureds. Risk-driven failures have occurred in the Florida property market after Hurricane Andrew, the California earthquake and homeowners markets after the Northridge Earthquake, and in the terrorism market after 9/11. These events speak to the importance of correctly measuring, managing, and pricing insurance risk.

Most US states also have strict rules about premium that regulate the variables used in underwriting and often insist rating plans are mutually exclusive and exhaustive. Each insured must fall into one cell, and all insureds in a cell must get the same rate. As a result of these rate regulations, it is typically the case that

1. adding business in one unit cannot change the premium in another unit, and
2. new and existing policies in a unit must get the same rate. (Renewal discounts exist in practice. They reflect information asymmetries. We assume perfect information in this section.)

Let $\bar{P}_i(\mathbf{v}, a)$ equal i's premium for insurance when Ins Co. writes mix $\mathbf{v}$ and is supported by assets a. If either the mix or the assets change then the cash flows to unit i change and hence the premium can also change. We assume that all insureds in unit i get the same *rate* (premium per unit of exposure), which is therefore P_i/v_i. And if Ins Co. were to grow unit i, the assumption that new and renewal policies all get the same rate implies that P_i/v_i is the resulting **marginal revenue**. Later, we shall see the consequences of this pricing constraint.

20.3 Dynamic Capital Allocation and Marginal Cost

By assuming a functional relationship between assets $a = a(\mathbf{v})$ and portfolio volumes $\mathbf{v}$ we can reduce the portfolio premium function $\bar{P}(\mathbf{v}, a)$ to a function of $\mathbf{v}$ alone. In order to make this clear, and to stress dependence on the function a, write

$$\bar{P}^a(\mathbf{v}) : = \bar{P}(\mathbf{v}, a(\mathbf{v})).$$

To understand portfolio dynamics we must compute derivatives of $\bar{P}^a$ with respect to portfolio loss volumes, i.e. compute the marginal cost to the insurer of a small change in each unit's volume. (Previously a was a free variable and we computed derivatives with respect to a to obtain loss, premium, and margin densities by unit.) The rule of the total derivative gives

$$\frac{\partial \bar{P}^a}{\partial v_i} = \frac{\partial \bar{P}}{\partial v_i} + \frac{\partial \bar{P}}{\partial a}\frac{\partial a}{\partial v_i}. \tag{20.1}$$

The first term represents the incremental cost caused by any change in the shape of the loss distribution $X(\mathbf{v})$. The second term represents the cost of the change in capital caused by the change in volume. It is computed as the amount of additional capital needed times the per unit cost capital: $\partial a/\partial v_i$ is the rate of change in assets caused by a change in volume v_i and $\partial \bar{P}/\partial a$ is the cost of that change. These calculations are all performed from the perspective of the insurance pool and do not account for the risk preferences of the insureds.

How does this calculation play out for an SRM? By definition

$$\bar{P}(\mathbf{v}, a) = \int_0^{a(\mathbf{v})} g(S_{\mathbf{v}}(x))dx.$$

Assume that X grows homogeneously so that Eq. (4.19) for the derivative of $S_{\mathbf{v}}$ applies. Then, differentiating through the integral, we get

$$
\begin{aligned}
\frac{\partial \bar{p}^a}{\partial v_i} &= \int_0^{a(\mathbf{v})} \frac{\partial}{\partial v_i} g(S_{\mathbf{v}}(x))\,dx + g(S_{\mathbf{v}}(a(\mathbf{v})))\frac{\partial a(\mathbf{v})}{\partial v_i} \\
&= \int_0^{a(\mathbf{v})} \mathsf{E}[X_i \mid X(\mathbf{v}) = x] g'(S_{\mathbf{v}}(x)) f_{\mathbf{v}}(x)\,dx + g(S_{\mathbf{v}}(a))\frac{\partial a(\mathbf{v})}{\partial v_i} \\
&= \mathsf{E}[X_i g'(S_{\mathbf{v}}(X(\mathbf{v}))) \mid X(\mathbf{v}) \le a(\mathbf{v})](1 - S_{\mathbf{v}}(a(\mathbf{v})) + \\
&\qquad g(S_{\mathbf{v}}(a(\mathbf{v}))\frac{\partial a(\mathbf{v})}{\partial v_i} \\
&=: \mathscr{E}_i + \frac{\partial a(\mathbf{v})}{\partial v_i} g(S(a)).
\end{aligned} \tag{20.2}
$$

Compare Eq. (20.2) to the natural allocation formula Eq. (14.22), which we can write as:

$$
\bar{P}_i(a) = \mathscr{E}_i + a\mathsf{E}\left[\frac{X_i}{X} g'(S(X)) \mid X > a\right] S(a).
$$

It is astonishing these two equations have the same first term, given the completely different ways they have been computed. The equality reflects Delbaen's Theorem 2: the Gâteaux derivatives of a spectral risk measure equal the natural allocation when ρ is differentiable. The possibility of default means that ρ is not differentiable at $X \wedge a(X)$ and so Delbaen's Theorem does not apply—but in a sense, it does in the part of Eq. (20.2) captured by $\mathscr{E}$. It applies fully and implies that the marginal allocation equals the natural when there is no chance of default and q_X increases. For the remainder of this section, we focus on the potential difference between the second terms.

To recap, Eq. (20.2)

1. assumes a **homogeneous** loss model, interpreting $X(\mathbf{v})$ as $\sum v_i X_i$ in order to use Eq. (4.19) for the derivative of the survival function, and
2. is independent of how losses are allocated to the units in default states, i.e. does not assume the equal priority default rule.

Neither the insurer nor the investor cares how losses are allocated in default. Allocation does not impact the amount of capital needed, which is a function of $X(\mathbf{v})$ alone. Regulation may restrict priorities—most do; see Section 8.2.2. Allocations do not impact total cost in any way, however. Investors do not care about how capital is notionally allocated to insureds, nor about how premiums are actually allocated to policyholders. They care only about earning their cost of capital.

Next we apply Eq. (20.2) to two standard capital risk measures: VaR and TVaR. It is clear from the formula that only the $\partial a/\partial v_i$ term on the right will vary.

Example 304. Value at Risk Capital Risk Measure. Assume $a(\mathbf{v}) = \mathsf{VaR}_p(X(\mathbf{v})) = q_{\mathbf{v}}(p)$. By Eq. (4.20), the derivative of the quantile function for a homogeneous family is

$$
\frac{\partial q_{\mathbf{v}}(p)}{\partial v_i} = \mathsf{E}[X_i(1) \mid X(\mathbf{v}) = q_{\mathbf{v}}(p)]
$$

and so Eq. (20.2) becomes

$$\frac{\partial \bar{P}^a}{\partial v_i} = \mathscr{E}_i + \mathsf{E}[X_i(1) \mid X(\mathbf{v}) = q_{\mathbf{v}}(p)]\, g(S(a)). \tag{20.3}$$

$\mathsf{E}[X_i(1) \mid X(\mathbf{v}) = q_{\mathbf{v}}(p)]$ can equally be regarded as risk-adjusted because the SRM is law invariant and so doesn't *see inside* the scenario set $\{X(\mathbf{v}) = q_{\mathbf{v}}(p)\}$. □

Example 305. Tail Value at Risk Capital Risk Measure. Assume $a(\mathbf{v}) = \mathsf{TVaR}_p(X(\mathbf{v})) = (1-p)^{-1}\int_p^1 q_{\mathbf{v}}(s)ds$ and that the distribution of X has a density. By Eqs. (4.20) and (4.21), for the derivative of the quantile function and of TVaR of a homogeneous family, and by substituting $x = q_{\mathbf{v}}(s)$, $F_{\mathbf{v}}(x) = s$, we get

$$\begin{aligned}
\frac{\partial a}{\partial v_i} &= \frac{1}{1-p}\int_p^1 \frac{\partial}{\partial v_i} q_{\mathbf{v}}(s)\, ds \\
&= \frac{1}{1-p}\int_p^1 \mathsf{E}[X_i(1) \mid X(\mathbf{v}) = q_{\mathbf{v}}(s)]\, ds \\
&= \frac{1}{1-p}\int_{q(p)}^\infty \mathsf{E}[X_i(1) \mid X(\mathbf{v}) = x] f_{\mathbf{v}}(x)\, dx \\
&= \mathsf{E}[X_i(1) \mid X(\mathbf{v}) > q(p)].
\end{aligned}$$

The last expectation uses objective probabilities and it usually differs from its risk-adjusted value. Substituting it into Eq. (20.2) gives

$$\frac{\partial \bar{P}^a}{\partial v_i} = \mathscr{E}_i + \mathsf{E}[X_i(1) \mid X(\mathbf{v}) > q_{\mathbf{v}}(p)]\, g(S(a)).$$

□

20.4 Marginal Cost and Marginal Revenue

Eq. (14.22) for the marginal revenue assumes SRM pricing, and equal priority but not a homogeneous loss model. Eq. (20.2) for the marginal cost to Ins Co. assumes SRM pricing and homogeneous losses, but nothing about equal priority. The two expressions differ only in one term, corresponding to what happens in default scenarios. The default focus makes sense: in solvent scenarios everyone is paid in full.

Marginal revenue takes the insured's perspective. It considers the fair market value of insurance recoveries in default, which equal

$$a\mathsf{E}\left[\frac{X_i}{X} g'(S(X)) \mid X > a\right].$$

Marginal cost considers only the amount of additional capital required by an increase in unit i, $\partial a/\partial v_i$, and specializes to

$$\mathsf{E}\left[X_i(1) \mid X(\mathbf{v}) = a\right]$$

under VaR capital and to

$$\mathsf{E}\left[X_i(1) \mid X(\mathbf{v}) > q(p)\right]$$

under TVaR capital. The VaR and TVaR expectations are not risk adjusted. Under TVaR the conditioning set is not the same as the default set because assets are $a = \mathsf{E}[X \mid X > q(p)]$, which is greater than or equal to $q(p)$.

Since we are assuming X has a density (no masses), $\mathsf{Pr}(X > q_{\mathbf{v}}(p)) = 1 - p$ and so $a(\mathbf{v}) = \mathsf{TVaR}_p(\mathbf{v}) = \mathsf{E}[X \mid X > q_{\mathbf{v}}(p)]$. Thus, the two default terms for TVaR capital can be re-arranged (multiplying and dividing by a on the right) as

$$\mathsf{E}\left[\frac{X_i(v_i)}{X(\mathbf{v})} g'(S_{\mathbf{v}}(X(\mathbf{v}))) \mid X(\mathbf{v}) > a(\mathbf{v})\right] \quad \text{versus} \quad \frac{\mathsf{E}[X_i(v_i) \mid X(\mathbf{v}) > q_{\mathbf{v}}(p)]}{\mathsf{E}[X(\mathbf{v}) \mid X(\mathbf{v}) > q_{\mathbf{v}}(p)]}$$

to draw out their similarities. The marginal revenue insured value expression, left, uses risk-adjusted probabilities defined by unlimited loss and looks at ex post recoveries state by state. The marginal cost expression, right, uses objective probabilities, is only concerned with marginal capital requirements, and is agnostic to priority in default. The fact the left depends on the default rule but the right doesn't is an easy way to see they cannot be identical. The expression on the right appears in Phillips, Cummins, and Allen (1998).

Finally, remember the differences in this section all appear because ρ is not differentiable and Delbaen's Theorem does not apply.

20.5 Performance Management and Regulatory Rigidities

We know in Model C, Section 12.4.3, there is no need to allocate assets. The default put must be allocated, but that follows directly from the default priority rule: we know exactly how much each unit recovers in every state of the world. Thus it appears there is no need to allocate capital, which is precisely what Grundl and Schmeiser (2007) pointed out. Sherris (2006) stops here; not only is there no need to allocate capital, there is not even a canonical way to do it.

It was left to the ground-breaking work of Ibragimov, Jaffee, and Walden (2010) to show how to combine the ingredients we have into a cohesive picture. They realized that the fairness constraints, encapsulated in marginal revenue and premium rates, actually imply the rate of change of assets with changes to the underlying portfolio. But if a regulator imposes a particular capital risk measure it is highly unlikely to produce the same changes. Thus, the most likely outcome is what we call **regulatory rigidity**: Ins Co. might want to increase volume in a certain unit to improve overall return, but the well-informed insureds will balk. Ins Co. would try to increase volume in a unit where marginal revenue is greater than marginal cost. The difference exists because the capital risk measure does not increase capital enough to offset the increased risk of the new business. The change would result in a wealth transfer between insureds. In a competitive market, insureds would leave the pool, leaving Ins Co. (or any other insurers) unable to effect their desired portfolio change. These facts have profound implications for portfolio construction and insurer management.

We now work out the form of the capital risk measure consistent with marginal revenue pricing. We want to find the amount by which assets must grow to compensate existing insureds for a change in volume while keeping the rates and economics unchanged for all participants. The derivation will show that the answer is unique.

To ease the notation, assume there are just two units so $\mathbf{v} = (v_1, v_2)$. Consider a change to unit 1. We need to compute the incremental assets da corresponding to an ϵ proportion increase in unit 1 volume from v_1 to $(1+\epsilon)v_1$. The incremental premium is

$$\bar{P}((1+\epsilon)v_1, v_2, a+da) - \bar{P}(v_1, v_2, a). \tag{20.4}$$

We can look at this in two ways, the first corresponding to marginal revenue and being fair to insureds, and the second to marginal cost and being fair to investors.

First, the insured view. We know how $\bar{P} = \bar{P}_1 + \bar{P}_2$ splits between the two units. Our product market and regulatory assumptions come into play and require that new and existing insureds in unit 1 pay the same rate. A transparent market requires that the fair value is unchanged for insureds in unit 2 as well, otherwise they would seek coverage elsewhere. The rate for unit i is $\bar{P}_i(v_1, v_2, a)/v_i$. Therefore the same-rate conditions imply

$$\bar{P}_1((1+\epsilon)v_1, v_2, a+da) = (1+\epsilon)\bar{P}_1(v_1, v_2, a) \tag{20.5}$$

and

$$\bar{P}_2((1+\epsilon)v_1, v_2, a+da) = \bar{P}_2(v_1, v_2, a). \tag{20.6}$$

Combining the last three equations shows the incremental premium is simply

$$\bar{P}((1+\epsilon)v_1, v_2, a+da) - \bar{P}(v_1, v_2, a) = \epsilon\bar{P}_1(v_1, v_2, a). \tag{20.7}$$

Dividing by ϵv_1 and taking a limit gives

$$\lim_{\epsilon v_1 \to 0} \frac{\bar{P}((1+\epsilon)v_1, v_2, a+da) - \bar{P}(v_1, v_2, a)}{\epsilon v_1} = \frac{\partial \bar{P}^a(v_1, v_2)}{\partial v_1} = \frac{\bar{P}_1(v_1, v_2, a)}{v_1}. \tag{20.8}$$

Note that da is defined so that $a(v_1(1+\epsilon), v_2) = a(v_1, v_2) + da$ and so $P((1+\epsilon)v_1, v_2, a+da) = P^a((1+\epsilon)v_1, v_2)$.

Next, we look at the marginal cost of capital to Ins Co. We use Eq. (20.1); to a first order

$$\bar{P}((1+\epsilon)v_1, v_2, a+da) - \bar{P}(v_1, v_2, a) = \left(\frac{\partial \bar{P}}{\partial v_1} + \frac{\partial \bar{P}}{\partial a}\frac{\partial a}{\partial v_1}\right)\epsilon v_1. \tag{20.9}$$

Applying the same formula to $\bar{P}_2$, the premium for unit 2, shows the condition for its rate to remain constant is

$$\frac{\partial \bar{P}_2^a}{\partial v_1} = \frac{\partial \bar{P}_2}{\partial v_1} + \frac{\partial \bar{P}_2}{\partial a}\frac{\partial a}{\partial v_1} = 0. \tag{20.10}$$

This equation determines a by determining $\partial a/\partial v_1$:

$$\frac{\partial a}{\partial v_1} = -\frac{\partial \bar{P}_2}{\partial v_1}\bigg/\frac{\partial \bar{P}_2}{\partial a} \tag{20.11}$$

which follows from the implicit function theorem. It can also be derived from Eq. (20.7) and Eq. (20.9) as

$$\frac{\partial a}{\partial v_1} = \left(\frac{\bar{P}_1(v_1, v_2, a)}{v_1} - \frac{\partial \bar{P}_1}{\partial v_1} \right) \Big/ \frac{\partial \bar{P}_1}{\partial a}.$$

In this case the implicit function theorem does not apply because $\bar{P}_1$ is not constant.

Happily, this asset increment is exactly what is required for the rate for unit 1 to stay constant because it implies

$$\begin{aligned} \frac{\partial \bar{P}^a}{\partial v_1} &= \frac{\partial \bar{P}_1^a}{\partial v_1} + \frac{\partial \bar{P}_2^a}{\partial v_1} \\ &= \frac{\partial \bar{P}_1^a}{\partial v_1} \\ &= \frac{\bar{P}_1(v_1, v_2, a)}{v_1} \end{aligned}$$

using Eq. (20.8) in the last step.

Thus, Eq. (20.11) determines the unique amount by which assets must grow to compensate existing insureds for a change in volume while keeping the rates and economics unchanged for all participants.

Now, there is an obvious problem: generally the regulator-determined capital risk measure a will not replicate the required asset increment. And what is the difference? It is precisely the difference between marginal revenue (fair to insureds) and marginal cost (fair to investors given regulation) that we discussed in the previous section.

Bauer and Zanjani (2014) take the insured's view one step further, and determine a risk measure whose marginals are consistent with their own utility maximizing insurance purchases. In a complete market, their results agree with Ibragimov, Jaffee, and Walden (2010), but in general they are different. They derive a risk measure

$$\rho(X) = \exp \mathsf{E}_{\mathsf{Q}}[\log(X)]$$

where Q reflects the insureds' average risk aversion and is supported only in default states. The authors argue it is appropriate for the adjusted probability to be supported in default states because those are the only ones where the insurer's risk is relevant to insureds. Their risk measure is positive homogeneous, and hence its gradient allocation is additive by Euler's Theorem. It is also monotonic. However, it is generally not subadditive, and therefore neither coherent nor convex. The roles of exp and log are reversed relative to the exponential risk measure. They argue that using $\log(X)$ inside the expectation is appropriate because equal priority uses a recovery factor proportional to $1/X$, which averages to $\log(X)$.

20.6 Practical Implications

The practitioner may have encountered the phenomena of this chapter in the context of expansion into a new catastrophe-prone territory. When new business is an insignificant portion of the whole it appears cheap to write, as it does not contribute to tail events and requires very little marginal capital. However, as it grows, it quickly comes to dominate the tail and becomes woefully under-priced. Regulatory rigidities can then prevent the insurer from correcting these inadequate rates for many years. Practitioners today are aware of these traps, and model relative to an anticipated end-state notional portfolio. Reinsurers also plan relative to notional portfolios to avoid the ordering-problem in pricing.

The history of Florida homeowners since Hurricane Andrew in 1992 shows how regulatory rigidities played out for the US industry. In very short order, Andrew and catastrophe models reset insurer expectations about tail exposure. Companies were left with portfolios they deemed extremely under-priced. The ensuing history is well known.

Another mechanism for market infeasibility occurs when a regulator or rating agency stipulates a very high capital requirement through a conservative risk measure. As a result, insurers must hold substantial capital, which drives a high cost of insurance that insureds are unwilling to pay. Multi-peril homeowners in Florida, and the California personal lines earthquake market are examples. In Florida, rating agency arbitrage has led to Demotech, Inc. replacing AM Best. Demotech allows companies to write at lower, but still reasonable, capital standards, resulting in cheaper insurance. The AM Best capital formula required insurers to survive through a catastrophe event—a much stricter standard than being able to pay their claims. In the terrorism market post-9/11, insurers' uncertainty about loss potential led to extremely high, self-enforced capital requirements and uneconomic covers (Cummins and Lewis, 2003).

In conclusion, market failure and recovery can occur in the following steps:

- Insurers optimize their portfolios to produce balanced, low-volatility portfolios that are cheap to transfer to investors.
- A new risk enters the system, e.g. through a radical revision of loss propensity, as happened after Andrew, Northridge, 9/11, and to some extent Katrina.
- With no portfolio changes, insurers now hold a more volatile risk with a more *expensive* tail.
- The expensive tail is clearly attributable to a small number of insureds (in Florida, California, New York City, etc.) and these insureds are unwilling to pay for the extra capital attributable to their risk.
- Rather than raise capital, which insurers could do in theory, they recognize that insureds will be unwilling to buy and instead cut their exposures, leading to growth in residual market providers such as Florida Citizens, or an outright market freeze such as in California homeowners post-Northridge, or the terrorism market post-9/11.
- The regulatory and consumer reaction paints insurers as proposing unwarranted, unfair, and unreasonable rate increases. Regulators act to curtail non-renewals and attempt to force insurers to remain in the market.
- Over time, insurer portfolios adjust, and alternative capital that is better suited to tail risk replaces some equity capital.

20.7 Learning Objectives

1. Differentiate between marginal cost and marginal revenue in portfolio optimization.
2. Explain regulatory rigidity, with reference to the impact of a portfolio change on existing and new insureds, and capital providers.
3. Explain how an ill-chosen capital standard can cause conflict between different groups of insureds, and insureds and investors.

Appendix A

Background Material

A.1 Interest Rate, Discount Rate, and Discount Factor

The symbol ¤ denotes a generic monetary unit; ¤1 is calibrated to roughly \$1, €1, £1, or (Japanese) ¥100.
The following standard time value of money notation is a convenient shorthand.

- **Interest** earned at a rate i per year pays i per ¤1 at the end of the year.
- The **discount factor** $v = 1/(1 + i)$ gives the value today of a payment of ¤1 in one year.
- The corresponding **discount rate** $d = i/(1 + i)$ gives the value of the interest at the start of the year.
- The basic relationships

  $$d + v = 1, \qquad d = iv$$

  are used frequently.

By analogy with the time value of money, define the **risk return** ι, **risk discount rate** $\delta = \iota/(1 + \iota)$, and **risk discount factor** $\nu = 1/(1 + \iota)$. They are also linked via $\nu + \delta = 1$. If ¤1 is shared in proportion $\iota : 1$ it is shared as $\delta + \nu$. The analogy is explained in Section 10.2. The risk return is called the **Cost of Capital** (CoC) when it is used as an input by the capital user rather than as an output by the capital provider.

The phraseology emphasizes the relationships $1 = \delta + \nu$ and $\delta = \iota\nu$. It is not perfect because the realized risk margin is always paid to the investor at the end of the period, when the residual is distributed, and never at the beginning.

A.2 Actuarial vs. Accounting Sign Conventions

In this section of the appendix we cover the difference between the actuarial and accounting sign conventions. We always use the actuarial sign convention, but the finance literature on risk uses the accounting. Many trivial issues are caused by the different conventions.

Actuaries model losses as positive. Smaller values are preferred to—are less risky than—bigger ones. Accountants model income and revenue as positive and so losses are negative.

Table A.1 Dictionary between the accounting and actuarial sign conventions.

Relationship type	Signs	$X \succeq Y$ means	Numerical representation
Preference	Accounting	X preferred to Y	$X \succeq Y$ iff $U(X) \geq U(Y)$
Risk preference	Actuarial	X is less risk than Y	$X \succeq Y$ iff $\rho(X) \leq \rho(Y)$

When analyzing investments, positive values are assets or gains and negative ones liabilities or losses. The **actuarial sign convention is used throughout the book** unless explicitly stated otherwise. A loss random variable models losses as positive. The difference between considering large positive or large negative values as bad causes many superficial complications in the literature. Most papers take the accounting view: the left tail (e.g. 1st percentile) is bad. In the actuarial view the right tail (e.g. 99th percentile) is bad.

Given a **preference** $\succeq$ with a numerical representation U, taking the accounting view. U treats big positive values as good and X is preferred to Y if $U(X) \geq U(Y)$. We can create a ***risk* preference** represented by ρ by defining

$$\rho(X) = -U(-X).$$

If X is less risky than Y then $-X$ is preferred to $-Y$ (prefer to assume X over Y) so $U(-X) \geq U(-Y)$ and therefore

$$\rho(X) = -U(-X) \leq -U(-Y) = \rho(Y).$$

Changing X to $-X$ swaps the actuarial to accounting sign convention. Changing U to $-U$ swaps measuring pleasure to measuring pain. If U is increasing then $\rho'(x) = U'(-x)$ is also increasing. If U is concave, $U''(x) < 0$, then $\rho''(x) = -U''(x) > 0$ is convex.

A.3 Probability Theory

We use several concepts from probability theory. Sample spaces are fundamental:

- A **sample space** is a set representing all possible results from an experiment or observation. The sample space is conventionally denoted Ω.
- In *theory* we can always assume Ω equals $[0, 1]$, the set of all real numbers between 0 and 1, and in *practice* we can always assume Ω is finite. We focus on the practical case, but include some Technical Remarks about the theoretical one.
- The elements of Ω are called **sample points.**
- An **event** E is a subset of the sample space corresponding to the result of an experiment or observation.
- The collection of events is usually denoted $\mathcal{F}$. It is required to be an **algebra**, meaning

(A) it contains the empty set, $\emptyset$,
(B) it contains Ω,
(C) it is closed under unions (given two events you can determine if one or other has occurred), intersections (if both have occurred), and complements (not observing an event).

When Ω is finite we usually assume that all subsets of Ω are events.

- If $\mathcal{F}$ is closed under countable unions it is called a **σ-algebra**.
- A **probability** or **probability function** is a set function Pr defined on a σ-algebra of events that assigns a number $0 \le \Pr(E) \le 1$ to each $E \in \mathcal{F}$ that satisfies

(a) $\Pr(\emptyset) = 0$
(b) $\Pr(\Omega) = 1$
(c) Pr is additive: if $E_i \in \mathcal{F}, i = 1, 2, \dots$ is a countable collection of pairwise disjoint events ($E_i \cap E_j = \emptyset$ for all $i \ne j$) then $\Pr(\cup_i E_i) = \sum_i \Pr(E_i)$.

$\Pr(E)$ quantifies the likelihood of observing event E. If Ω is discrete, Pr is also called a **probability mass function**..

- The triple $(\Omega, \mathcal{F}, \Pr)$ is called a **probability space**.

Example 306. The sample space for the toss of a coin could be based on outcome $\{H, T\}$, since this is generally all we need and want to know. But it could quantify the upward velocity of the coin, its height at toss, and its rotation speed, yielding a point in $\mathbb{R}^3$. Mechanics maps this more complex labeling to $\{H, T\}$. The coin toss is random because slight perturbations in initial parameters change the outcome. Thus, a coin toss, regarded as selecting a point at random from within a region of $\mathbb{R}^3$ maps randomly to a head or tail outcome. □

Example 307. If $E \in \mathcal{F}$ then $E' = \Omega \setminus E \in \mathcal{F}$, and E and E' are disjoint and have union Ω. Therefore, applying (b) and (c) shows $\Pr(E') + \Pr(E) = \Pr(\Omega) = 1$ and so $\Pr(E') = 1 - \Pr(E)$. □

Technical Remark 308. Sample points are also called **elementary events**. Probability functions are also called **probability measures**. Events in a probability space are also called **measurable sets**. □

Random variables are used to model risky outcomes:

- A **random variable** is a function $X : \Omega \to \mathbb{R}$ associating a numerical outcome to each sample point, with the property that for each $x \in \mathbb{R}$, $\{\omega \in \Omega \mid X(\omega) \le x\}$ is an event, i.e. is in $\mathcal{F}$. Whether or not a function is a random variable depends on $\mathcal{F}$.
- The event $\{\omega \in \Omega \mid X(\omega) \le x\}$ is typically written as $\{X \le x\}$ or just $X \le x$. Similarly for $X = x, X > x$, and so forth.
- An **outcome** is the value of a random variable.
- In German, the sample space is the *Merkmalraum* or *label space*, which better conveys the arbitrary nature of the connection between ω and the outcome $X(\omega)$.
- A **loss** random variable is one taking nonnegative values. Actuaries take losses to be positive.
- A **loss outcome** is the value of a loss random variable. Loss outcomes are also referred to simply as **losses**.
- Random variables are denoted by uppercase Roman letters, notably X for losses and N for claim counts.
- The **expectation** $\mathsf{E}[X]$ of a random variable X is the probability weighted average of its outcomes. It equals the mean or average value of X.

We expect the reader to be familiar with common parametric families of random variables:

- Continuous: beta, gamma, normal, lognormal, Pareto, power law stable, uniform, Weibull.
- The standard normal distribution has mean 0 and standard deviation $\sigma = 1$. It has pdf $\phi(x) := (2\pi)^{-1/2}\exp(-x^2/2)$ and cdf $\Phi(x) := \int_{-\infty}^{x}\phi(t)dt$.
- Discrete: Bernoulli, binomial, Poisson, negative binomial.
- The **uniform distribution** is assumed uniformly distributed on $[0, 1]$. It is usually denoted U.
- The **Bernoulli distribution** is used frequently. Bernoulli variables assume outcome values only 0 and 1, and have a mean equal to the probability they equal 1.
- See Klugman, Panjer, and Willmot (2012) for more details about families of distributions.

Example 309. Let Ω be the sample space of employees at a firm. A random variable $X(\omega)$ could represent a particular employee ω's age, sex, height, weight, salary, shoe size, etc. $\Omega = \{\omega_1, \dots, \omega_n\} = \{\text{Ada, Bernhard}, \dots, \text{Zeno}\}$. The labeling and associations are essentially arbitrary: they could be determined by name, social security number, etc. The exact association is irrelevant for one random variable. But when several variables are applied to the same sample space, the label is critical in order to understand correlations and dependencies between them. □

Distribution functions capture much, but not all, of the useful information in a random variable:

- The **distribution function** of X maps $x \in \mathbb{R}$ to $F(x) := \mathsf{Pr}(X \le x)$. Remember, $X \le x$ is shorthand for the event $\{\omega \in \Omega \mid X(\omega) \le x\} \in \mathcal{F}$.
- The **survival function** of X is $S(x) = \mathsf{Pr}(X > x) = 1 - F(x)$.
- In general, a distribution function is any nondecreasing function on $\mathbb{R}$ satisfying $\lim_{x\to-\infty} F(x) = 0$, $\lim_{x\to\infty} F(x) = 1$, and that is continuous from the right, meaning $\lim_{x\downarrow x_0} F(x) = F(x_0)$. The continuity requirement is why $F(x) = \mathsf{Pr}(X \le x)$ rather than $\mathsf{Pr}(X < x)$.
- A random variable has a **continuous distribution** if its distribution function is continuous. It has a **discrete distribution** if the set of outcomes is discrete, in which case its distribution is a step function. A **mixed distribution** function has both continuous and discrete portions. A lognormal variable is continuous, a Poisson is discrete, and a Tweedie is mixed.
- The **probability density function** (pdf) associated with $F(x)$ is $f(x) = \dfrac{dF}{dx}$ where the derivative exists. The **probability mass function** is $p(x) = \mathsf{Pr}(\{\omega \mid X(\omega) = x\}) = \mathsf{Pr}(X = x)$ where that probability is greater than zero.

We can create a new probability function from a distribution function:

- Ordinarily, we think of the length of an interval $(a, b]$ in the real line as $b - a$. This is known as **Lebesgue length** (or measure). Lebesgue length on $\Omega = [0, 1]$ is denoted P, so $\mathsf{P}((a, b]) = b - a$. Note $\mathsf{P}(\{x\}) = 0$: points have zero length.
- Given a distribution function F, we can redefine the length of $(a, b]$ as $F(b) - F(a)$. If $\{\omega \mid X(\omega) = x_1\}$ has probability $h > 0$, then F has a jump at x_1 of height h. This means

the redefined length of $(x_1 - \epsilon, x_1]$ is greater than or equal to h for all ϵ. The point at b is *stretched* to length h.

- A probability function Q is **absolutely continuous** with respect to another P, written $\mathsf{Q} \ll \mathsf{P}$, if $\mathsf{P}(A) = 0$ implies $\mathsf{Q}(A) = 0$. When $\mathsf{Q} \ll \mathsf{P}$, Q has a density with respect to P, meaning there is a function f on Ω with $f(\omega) \geq 0$ and $\mathsf{Q}(A) = \int_A f(\omega)\mathsf{P}(d\omega)$ for all events A. The function f is written $d\mathsf{Q}/d\mathsf{P}$.

Some properties hold **almost everywhere**, meaning they hold except for a set of probability zero. When the sample space is finite and the probability function assigns a nonzero probability to every sample point, almost everywhere is the same as everywhere. However, almost everywhere is an important concept on infinite sample spaces.

Technical Remark 310. The Borel σ-algebra $\mathcal{B}$ on $[0,1]$ is the smallest σ-algebra generated by all open sets. In almost all practical situations it is possible to assume the probability space is $(I, \mathcal{B}, \mathsf{P})$. If X is defined on another probability space $(\Omega, \mathcal{F}, \mathsf{Pr})$, this means there is a map $f : [0,1] \to \Omega$ with $f^{-1}(A) \in \mathcal{B}$ for all $A \in \mathcal{F}$ and $\mathsf{P}(f^{-1}(A)) = \mathsf{Pr}(A)$. For example, suppose X models the throw of a dice and is defined on $\Omega = \{1,2,3,4,5,6\}$ with $\mathsf{Pr}(\omega) = 1/6$. X can be modeled as $X \circ f$ where $f : I \to \Omega$ equals $f(x) = 1$ for $0 \leq x < 1/6$, $f(x) = 2$ for $1/6 \leq x < 2/6$, and so on. It can be hard to see how to define f. For example, Brownian motion and compound Poisson distributions can be defined on I, even though it seems a larger sample space should be required to specify a whole path. □

Conditional probabilities (Bayes' Theorem) and conditional expectations relate risk and information:

- The **conditional expectation** $\mathsf{E}[X \mid A]$ given an event $A \subset \Omega$ is the expectation of X under the **conditional probability** defined by $\mathsf{Pr}(E \mid A) = \mathsf{Pr}(E \cap A)/\mathsf{Pr}(A)$.
- The conditional expectation of one random variable with respect to another $\mathsf{E}[X_i \mid X]$ is a function on Ω taking ω to $\mathsf{E}[X_i \mid \{X = X(\omega)\}]$.
- The **tower property** of conditional expectations says $\mathsf{E}[\mathsf{E}[Z \mid X]] = \mathsf{E}[Z]$.
- If X is a random variable on the probability space $(\Omega, \mathcal{F}, \mathsf{P})$ and $\mathcal{F}' \subset \mathcal{F}$ is sub σ-algebra then we can form $\mathsf{E}[X \mid \mathcal{F}']$, the conditional expectation of X given $\mathcal{F}'$. It is another random variable with the property that

$$\int_A X \, d\mathsf{P} = \int_A \mathsf{E}[X \mid \mathcal{F}'] \, d\mathsf{P} \tag{A.1}$$

  for all $A \in \mathcal{F}'$. In the finite case, $\mathsf{E}[X \mid \mathcal{F}'](\omega)$ is the average value of X over the smallest set in $\mathcal{F}'$ containing ω.
- It is possible to extend these concepts to cases of infinite Ω and to condition on sets of measure zero, see Billingsley (1986) or Shiryaev (1996).

Indicator functions are very useful:

- An **indicator function** for the event $A \subset \Omega$ is the function $1_A : \Omega \to \{0,1\}$, given by

$$1_A(\omega) = \begin{cases} 1 & \omega \in A \\ 0 & \omega \notin A. \end{cases}$$

- If X is a random variable, we denote the indicator function on $A = \{X(\omega) > x\}$ by $1_{X>x}$. It takes values

$$1_{X>x}(\omega) = \begin{cases} 1 & X(\omega) > x \\ 0 & X(\omega) \le x. \end{cases}$$

$1_{X>x}$ determines the payoff for an all-or-nothing excess layer attaching at x.

Scenarios are an important way to define risk measures:

- A **scenario** is a probability function defined on a σ-algebra of events in Ω.
- The **objective** or **actuarial** scenario is privileged yet hard to define. It is the "real world" probability that defined **objective probabilities.** In some cases, it can be defined canonically by symmetry, e.g. probabilities associated with the toss of a fair coin, roll of a fair dice, or choice of a random number between 0 and 1 (which is just a sequence of coin tosses). In insurance it is estimated from loss experience. In other contexts, it may not exist despite being referenced frequently.
- The **objective value** or **actuarial value** of a random variable is its expected value using objective probabilities. It is similar to the *best estimate,* although accountants often go out of their way *not* to define the best estimate explicitly. The objective scenario is usually denoted P and is called the P probability.
- Scenarios allow for future uncertainty that varies from objective probabilities.

In the Oxford English Dictionary, scenario is defined as an outline plot or storyline; it lays out a possible future. In Artzner *et al.* (1999), a scenario is called a **generalized scenario.** Scenario planning selects one possible *event* and gives it probability 1; the associated probability function is conditional probability given that event. It says: this is a future that could unfold; if it does, how should we act?

Scenarios lead to **risk adjustments**:

- A **risk-adjusted** probability reflects the preferences of risk averse individuals. It weights bad outcomes more and good ones less than the objective scenario. Bad and good are relative to the individual: good for the buyer or a long position is bad for the seller or a short position.
- The **risk-adjusted value** of a random variable is its expected value using any probability scenario other than the objective one. It includes a risk margin above (or sometimes below) the objective value. Typically there is a unique objective scenario but a plethora of risk-adjusted ones.
- When a risk-adjusted scenario reflects the risk preferences of market participants its values give the **market price, market value,** or **fair price.** If it reflects a regulator's risk preferences its values give **required capital** levels. A risk adjusted scenario is usually denoted Q and is called a Q-probability.
- Two central problems of finance are to find a risk-adjusted scenario whose values reproduce market prices and to identify situations in which such a scenario is unique.
- Reading P and Q should trigger *loss cost* and *premium* (net of expenses) or *required capital,* depending on the context.

Events can be identified in different ways, with different levels of specificity:

- The labeling of an **explicit** event $\omega \in \Omega$ provides the most resolution but, alas, often depends on an arbitrary parameterization.
- An event can be identified with its outcome $X(\omega)$, with ω unknown, which we call an **implicit** event. Typically many different explicit events ω can define the same implicit event.
- An event can be identified with a **non-exceedance probability** $F(X(\omega))$, **exceedance probability** $S(X(\omega))$, or **rank**, which we call a **dual implicit** event. Again ω is typically unknown.
- See Section 3.4 for more details.

It is important to conceptualize the relationships between events and outcomes:

- An **event-outcome diagram** is the graph of a random variable with Ω on the horizontal axis and the outcome value on the vertical. It corresponds to an explicit labeling of events.
- A **distribution** (resp. **density**) **plot** shows outcome on the horizontal axis and probability distribution (density) on the vertical. It corresponds to the implicit labeling of events.
- A **Lee diagram** is a plot with probability distribution on the horizontal axis and the outcome on the vertical. It is the reflection of the distribution function in a 45 degree line. Lee diagrams plot a *sorted* version of the event-outcome diagram.

The concept of an atom in a probability space is used when we discuss TVaR:

- An **atom** is an event $A \subset \Omega$ with $\mathsf{Pr}(A) > 0$ such that for all events $B \subset A$, either $\mathsf{Pr}(B) = 0$ or $\mathsf{Pr}(B) = \mathsf{Pr}(A)$. Atoms are events that have no nontrivial sub-events.
- A probability space is **atomless** if it contains no atoms.
- Equivalently, a probability space is atomless if and only if it supports a random variable with a continuous distribution, (Follmer and Schied, 2016, Proposition A.27). Thus, when we assume X is continuous we automatically know that Ω is atomless.
- Discrete probability spaces always contain atoms: all sample points with positive probability are atoms.

Probability preserving transformations are important.

- A **probability preserving transformation** (PPT) is a mapping $T : \Omega \to \Omega$ such that, for all events A, $T^{-1}(A)$ is an event and $\mathsf{P}(T^{-1}(A)) = \mathsf{P}(A)$.
- A PPT shuffles Ω: we can define a PPT by splitting Ω into equal probability events and then reordering them.
- If X is a continuous random variable then $F(X(\omega))$ is an PPT, see Ryff (1970).
- PPTs are also known as measure preserving transformations.

We call risk measures **functionals** rather than functions because their arguments are random variables.

A.4 Additional Mathematical Terminology

A function is described as **increasing** if it is nondecreasing, that is if $x \le y$ implies $f(x) \le f(y)$. We say **strictly** increasing if $x < y$ implies $f(x) < f(y)$. Similarly, **decreasing** means nonincreasing.

A **convex combination** means a weighted average with weights $0 \le \lambda \le 1$ that sum (or integrate) to 1.

A **convex function** on a suitable domain satisfies

$$f(\lambda x + (1-\lambda)y) \le \lambda f(x) + (1-\lambda)f(y)$$

for all x and y in the domain and $0 \le \lambda \le 1$, and a **concave function** satisfies

$$f(\lambda x + (1-\lambda)y) \ge \lambda f(x) + (1-\lambda)f(y).$$

A **convex set** C in a vector space is closed under convex combinations. If $x, y \in C$ and $0 \le w \le 1$ then $wx+(1-w)y \in C$, i.e. the line joining x and y is in C. An **extreme point** in a convex set is one that cannot be written as a convex combination of two other points in the set: if $x = wy + (1-w)z$, $y \ne z$, then either $w = 0$ and $z = x$ or $w = 1$ and $y = x$. Extreme points are the *corners* of a convex set. The Krein-Milman theorem says that all points in a convex sets are convex combinations of extreme points of the set, Borwein and Vanderwerff (2010).

The **convex hull** of a set of points is the set of all convex combinations of the points. For example, the convex hull of the four points $(0,0)$, $(1,0)$, $(1,1)$, and $(0,1)$ is the unit square at the origin. The four corners are the extreme points of the set.

A function $F(x)$ is **left (resp. right) continuous** (or continuous from the left or right) at $x = a$ if the limit of F as x approaches a from below (resp. above) equals $F(a)$. The limit from the left is designated $F(a-) = \lim_{x\uparrow a} F(x)$ and the limit from the right $F(a+) = \lim_{x\downarrow a} F(x)$. Distribution functions are right continuous. They also have limits from the left because they are increasing functions.

The **left (resp. right) derivative** of a function f at a is given by $\lim_{\epsilon\downarrow 0}(f(x-\epsilon)-f(x))/\epsilon$ (resp. $\lim_{\epsilon\downarrow 0}(f(x+\epsilon)-f(x))/\epsilon$). If f is differentiable the left and right derivatives both equal $f'(a)$. The absolute value function has left derivative -1 and right derivative $+1$ at $x = 0$.

The **supremum (sup)** of a set S of real numbers is the smallest number greater than or equal to all elements of S. The **infimum (inf)** is the largest number less than or equal to all the elements.

The supremum (resp. infimum) of a function is the supremum (infimum) of the values it takes. A function may not achieve its supremum. For example $f : (0,1) \to (0,1)$, $f(x) = x$ has $\sup f = 1$, but 1 is not in the domain of f.

Technical Remark 311. The **essential supremum (ess sup)** and **essential infimum (ess inf)** are related concepts that apply in probability theory where we ignore sets of probability zero. The essential supremum is the least value greater than or equal to all values achieved by X with positive probability

$$\text{ess sup}(X) = \inf\{k \mid \Pr(X > k) = 0\}. \tag{A.2}$$

It allows for the following behavior. Suppose X is defined on $\Omega = (0, 1)$ and $X(\omega) = \omega$ for irrational ω but $X(\omega) = 1/\omega$ for rational ω. Then $\sup X = \inf$ because there are arbitrarily small rational $\omega > 0$. Behavior at rational numbers is deemed irrelevant because they have probability zero, and so we want to ignore them. The ess sup accomplishes the task with $\text{ess sup}(X) = 1$. There are some situations in Chapters 5, 10, and 14 where we should use essential supremum, but we ignore these and use sup.

We use a generalized version of the Riemann integral called the **Riemann-Stieltjes** integral. It allows for points to have a mass (positive width), which is impossible for Riemann integrals. It can be thought of as splicing in a width in place of a point and extending the function across the point. It is essential when working with mixed distributions.

For a continuous distribution with density $f(x)$, ordinary Riemann integrals such as

$$\int_a^b h(x)f(x)dx$$

suffice to take the expected value of $h(X)$. For a discrete or mixed distribution, with masses at x_i, $i = 1 \ldots N$ (N possibly infinite), we need the Riemann-Stieltjes integral:

$$\int_a^b h(x)dF(x) = \int_a^b h(x)f(x)dx + \sum_{i=1}^{N} h(x_i)p(x_i)$$

where in the first term, $f(x_i)$ are treated as zero. The end points a or b may be masses and must be accounted for in the integral. To emphasize this, the Riemann-Stieltjes integral is sometimes written $\int_{[a,b]} h(x)dF(x)$.

Fubini's Theorem tells us we can change the order of integration in a multiple integral:

$$\int_X \int_Y f(x, y)\, dy\, dx = \int_Y \int_X f(x, y)\, dx\, dy$$

when $|f|$ has a finite integral.

Integration by parts is a method of transforming an integral expression into another, typically easier, expression. It is a consequence of the **product rule** of calculus:

$$\frac{d}{dx}(f(x)g(x)) = g(x)f'(x) + f(x)g'(x)$$

where the prime notation signifies first derivative. The integration by parts formula for Riemann integrals is:

$$\int_a^b f(x)g'(x)\, dx = f(x)g(x)\Big|_a^b - \int_a^b f'(x)g(x)\, dx$$

and for Riemann-Stieltjes integrals it is:

$$\int_a^b f(x)dg(x) = f(x)g(x)\Big|_a^b - \int_a^b g(x)df(x).$$

Appendix B

Notation

Table B.1 Standard notation and abbreviations. The link column provides a reference to their derivation where terms are derived or nonstandard.

Notation	Link	Meaning
Mathematical		
$f(x+), f(x-)$	Appendix A.4	$\lim_{y\downarrow x} f(y)$, $\lim_{y\uparrow x} f(y)$ for function f
$\log(x)$		The natural logarithm of x, `=ln(A1)` in a spreadsheet
x^+		$\max(x, 0)$
$\lfloor x \rfloor$		Integer part of x
$x_1 \wedge x_2$		$\min(x_1, x_2)$, $\wedge$ has lower priority than arithmetic operations, e.g. $x + y \wedge aX = \min(x + y, aX)$
$[x_1, x_2], (x_1, x_2], (x_1, x_2)$		Closed, half-open, and open intervals of real numbers between x_1 and x_2
$A \setminus B$		Set difference, elements in A that are not in B
Probability		
1_Z	Appendix A.3	Indicator function on the set Z
E_Q		Expectation with respect to probability Q
F		Distribution function of X, $\Pr(X \le x)$
f		Density function of X
Ω	Appendix A.3	Sample space for all random variables, often taken to be $[0, 1]$
P	Appendix A.3	Lebesgue probability (length), $P(dx)$ abbreviated dx, dt, ds, etc.
Pr	Appendix A.3	Probability function
ϕ, Φ		Density and distribution of standard normal
Q	Appendix A.3	risk-adjusted probability

(Continued)

Pricing Insurance Risk: Theory and Practice, First Edition. Stephen J. Mildenhall and John A. Major.

Table B.1 (Continued)

Notation	Link	Meaning
$q = q(p)$	Section 4.1.1	Quantile function of X, the left inverse of F
q^-, q^+	Section 4.1.1	Lower and upper quantile functions
S		Survival function of X, $\Pr(X > x)$, loss density in layer at x
$\mathsf{TVaR}_p(X)$	Section 4.3	p-Tail Value at Risk of random variable X
$\mathsf{VaR}_p(X)$	Section 4.2	p-Value at Risk of random variable X
$\mathsf{Var}^+(X)$		Positive semivariance, $\int_{\mathsf{E}[X]}^{\infty}(x - \mathsf{E}[X])^2 f(x)dx$
Risk Modeling		
$\mathcal{A}$	Section 5.2.19	An acceptance set for a risk measure
a		Asset level
$a(\cdot), a(\cdot, p)$	Section 20.3	Regulatory risk measure, used to determine total assets, with safety level p
$a_i = a(X_i; X)$	Section 12.2	Allocation to unit X_i part of X
$\alpha_i(x), \alpha_i(\mathbf{v}, x)$	Section 14.3	$\mathsf{E}[X_i/X \mid X > x]$
$\beta_i(x), \beta_i(t\mathbf{v}, x)$	Section 14.3	$\mathsf{E}[(X_i/X)g'(S(x)) \mid X > x]$
$\delta(x), \bar{\delta}(x)$	Chapter 10	Layer and total risk discount rate, $\delta = \iota/(1+\iota)$
$D\rho_X(X_i)$	Definition 10	Natural allocation of $\rho(X)$ to X_i as part of X
$D^n\rho_X(X_i)$	Definition 11	Linear (natural) allocation of $\rho(X)$ to X_i as part of X
$D^f\rho_{X;\tilde{X}}(X_i)$	Definition 12	Lifted (natural) allocation of $\rho(X)$ to X_i as part of $\tilde{X}$
$\bar{F}(a)$	Section 11.6.1	$\int_0^a F(t)\,dt$
g	Section 10.4	Distortion function
$\iota, \iota(p)$	Section 10.4	Beginning of period expected return on capital in layer at $q(p)$
$\bar{\iota}(a)$	Section 10.2	Beginning of period expected average return on capital with assets a
$\kappa_i(x), \kappa_i(\mathbf{v}, x)$	Section 14.3	$\mathsf{E}[X_i \mid X = x]$
$L_d^l(x)$	Section 3.5.3	Layer l excess of d on x, pays $(x-d)^+ \wedge l$
$M(x), \bar{M}(x)$	Section 10.3	Margin density in layer at x; total margin with assets x
$\nu(x), \bar{\nu}(x)$	Chapter 10	Layer and total risk discount factor, $\nu = 1/(1+\iota)$
$P(x), \bar{P}(x)$	Section 10.3	Premium density in layer at x; total premium with assets x
$\bar{P}^a(\mathbf{v})$	Section 20.3	Total premium when assets are determined by a
$\phi(p)$	Section 10.9	Spectral weight applied to p-VaR
$Q(x), \bar{Q}(x)$	Section 10.3	Equity density in layer at x; total equity with assets x
Ω	Section 5.4	

(*Continued*)

Table B.1 (Continued)

Notation	Link	Meaning
Set of scenarios or risk-adjusted probabilities		
ρ	Section 3.6	Risk measure functional
ρ_g	Section 10.7	Spectral risk measure associated with distortion g
$S(x), \bar{S}(x)$	Section 10.3	Survival function, equal to loss density in layer at x; total expected loss with assets x
$S_i(x), \bar{S}_i(x)$	Section 14.3.2	Expected loss for unit i under equal priority, and similarly P_i, M_i, Q_i
s, p		Usually probability level or variable in $[0,1]$, s generally $1-p$
t		Usually variable for integration when x is in use, time in Part IV
$v, \mathbf{v} = (v_1, \dots, v_n)$	Section 4.4	Volume, by unit, mostly Part IV
$X, X(\mathbf{v})$		Random variable of total portfolio losses, $X = \sum_i X_i$, $X(\mathbf{v}) = \sum_i X_i(v_i)$
$X_i, X_i(v_i)$		Random variable of loss from unit i, with volume v_i, Part IV
$\{X = x\}$ or $X = x$		$\{\omega \in \Omega \mid X(\omega) = x\}$
x		Usually asset or loss level
$\ll$	Appendix A.3	Absolute continuity
$\preceq$	Section 3.6.1	Precede in a risk preference
$\preceq_2$	Section 5.3.2	Precede in second-order stochastic dominance order
Model A-E	Section 12.4	Cascade of increasingly general market models
Abbreviations		
¤1		one unit of a generic currency
iid		independent and identically distributed
AY, CY, DY	Chapter 17	Accident, calendar, and development year
CED	Section 11.6.2	Convex envelope distortion
CoC	Section 8.2	Cost of capital
CCoC	Section 8.7.4, Section 13.1	Constant cost of capital
CCoCRM	Section 17.3	Constant cost of capital risk margin
CV		Coefficient of variation
EL	Section 3.5.2	Expected loss
EP	Section 3.4.3	Exceedance probability
EPD	Section 3.5.4	Expected policyholder deficit
FSD	Section 5.3.1	First-order stochastic dominance

(*Continued*)

Table B.1 (Continued)

Notation	Link	Meaning
GAAP		Generally accepted accounting principles
GFC		The global financial crisis of 2008–09
LOL	Section 3.5.3	Loss on line, i.e. expected loss to limit
MFL	Section 4.2.4	Maximum foreseeable loss
PCP	Section 8.4	Premium calculation principle
pdf		probability density function
PML	Section 4.2.4	Probable maximal loss
PPT	Section 5.4.3	Probability preserving transformation
RBC	Section 3.6.2	Risk based capital
ROE	Section 8.2.6	Return on equity
ROL	Section 3.5.3	Rate on line, i.e. premium to limit
SRM	Section 10.7	Spectral risk measure
SD		Standard deviation
SSD	Section 5.3.2	Second-order stochastic dominance
CTE	Section 4.3	Conditional tail expectation
TVaR	Section 4.3	Tail Value at Risk
VaR	Section 4.2	Value at Risk
Var		Variance
WACC	Section 8.2.7	Weighted average cost of capital
WCE	Section 4.3	Worst conditional expectation
Risk Properties		
COH	Section 5.2.14	Coherent
COM	Section 3.6.1	Complete risk preference
COMON	Section 5.2.11	Comonotonic additive risk measure
CONVEX	Section 5.2.18	Convex risk measure
CX	Section 5.2.16	Convexity property of risk measures
LI	Section 5.2.13	Law invariant risk measure
MON	Section 5.2.3	Monotone risk measure
MONO	Section 3.6.1	Monotonic risk preference
MRM	Section 5.2.5	Monetary risk measure
NORM	Section 5.2.2	Normalized risk measure
PH	Section 5.2.6	Positive homogeneous risk measure
QCX	Section 5.2.17	Quasi-convexity risk measure
SA	Section 5.2.8	Subadditive risk measure
TI	Section 5.2.1	Translation invariant risk measure
TR	Section 3.6.1	Transitive risk preference

References

Acerbi, C. (2002) Spectral measures of risk: A coherent representation of subjective risk aversion, *Journal of Banking & Finance*, 26(7), pp. 1505–1518. doi: 10.1016/S0378-4266(02)00281-9.

Acerbi, C. and Tasche, D. (2002a) Expected shortfall: A natural coherent alternative to value at risk, *Economic Notes*, pp. 1–9. Available at: http://onlinelibrary.wiley.com/doi/10.1111/1468-0300.00091/full.

Acerbi, C. and Tasche, D. (2002b) On the coherence of expected shortfall, *Journal of Banking & Finance*, 26(7), pp. 1487–1503. doi: 10.1016/S0378-4266(02)00283-2.

Actuarial Standards Board (2011) *Treatment of Profit and Contingency Provisions and the Cost of Capital in Property / Casualty Insurance Ratemaking*. 30.

Anscombe, F. J. and Aumann, R. J. (1963) A definition of subjective probability, *The Annals of Mathematical Statistics*, 34(1), pp. 199–205.

Aon Benfield (2015) Insurance Risk Study, 10th edition, 2015, Aon Benfield Inc. *Cyber opportunity and future growth*.

Arrow, K. J. (1996) The theory of risk-bearing: Small and great risks, *Journal of Risk and Uncertainty*, 12(2-3), pp. 103–111. doi: 10.1007/BF00055788.

Artzner, P. *et al.* (1997) Thinking coherently, *RISK*, 10(11), pp. 68–70.

Artzner, P. *et al.* (1999) Coherent measures of risk, *Mathematical Finance*, 9(3), pp. 203–228. Available at: http://onlinelibrary.wiley.com/doi/10.1111/1467-9965.00068/abstract.

Aumann, R. J. and Shapley, L. S. (1974) *Values of non-atomic games*. Princeton, NJ, USA. doi: 10.1515/9781400867080.

Babbel, D. F. (1997) Review of two paradigms for the market value of liabilities by Reitano, *North American Actuarial Journal*, 1(4), pp. 122–123.

Bailey, R. A. (1967) Underwriting profits from investments, *Proceedings of the Casualty Actuarial Society*, LIV, pp. 1–8.

Barinov, A., Xu, J. and Pottier, S. W. (2020) Estimating the cost of equity capital for insurance firms with multiperiod asset pricing models, *Journal of Risk and Insurance*, 87(1), pp. 213–245. doi: 10.1111/jori.12267.

Bauer, D. and Zanjani, G. (2013) Capital allocation and its discontents, in *Handbook of insurance*. New York, NY:Springer, pp. 863–880.

Bauer, D. and Zanjani, G. (2014) The marginal cost of risk, risk measures, and capital allocation, *Management Science*. 62.5 (2016): 1431–1457.

Pricing Insurance Risk: Theory and Practice, First Edition. Stephen J. Mildenhall and John A. Major.

Bäuerle, N. and Müller, A. (2006) Stochastic orders and risk measures: Consistency and bounds, *Insurance: Mathematics and Economics*, 38(1), pp. 132–148. doi: 10.1016/j.insmatheco.2005.08.003.

Belles-Sampera, J., Guillén, M. and Santolino, M. (2014) GlueVaR risk measures in capital allocation applications, *Insurance: Mathematics and Economics*, 58(1), pp. 132–137. doi: 10.1016/j.insmatheco.2014.06.014.

Bernstein, P. L. (1996) *Against the gods: The remarkable story of risk*. New York:Wiley.

Biger, N. and Kahane, Y. (1978) Risk considerations in insurance ratemaking, *The Journal of Risk and Insurance*, 45(1), p. 121. doi: 10.2307/251812.

Billera, L. J. and Heath, D. C. (1982) Allocation of shared costs: a set of axioms yielding a unique procedure, *Mathematics of Operations Research*, 7(1), pp. 32–39. Available at: http://www.jstor.org/stable/3689357.

Billera, L. J., Heath, D. C. and Verrecchia, R. E. (1981) A unique procedure for allocating common costs from a production process, 19(1), pp. 185–196.

Billingsley, P. (1986) *Probability and measure*. Second. J. Wiley; Sons.

Bodoff, N. M. (2007) Capital allocation by percentile layer, *Variance*, 3(1), pp. 13–30.

Boonen, T. J., Tsanakas, A. and Wüthrich, M. V. (2017) Capital allocation for portfolios with non-linear risk aggregation, *Insurance: Mathematics and Economics*, 72, pp. 95–106. doi: 10.1016/j.insmatheco.2016.11.003.

Borch, K. (1962) Equilibrium in a reinsurance market, *Econometrica*, 30(3), pp. 424–444.

Borch, K. (1982) Additive insurance premiums: a note, *The Journal of Finance*, 37(5), pp. 1295–1298. doi: 10.1111/j.1540-6261.1982.tb03619.x.

Borwein, J. M. and Vanderwerff, J. D. (2010) *Convex functions—construction, characterizations and counterexamples*. Cambridge University Press.

Braun, A. (2016) Pricing in the primary market for cat bonds: new empirical evidence, *Journal of Risk and Insurance*, 83(4), pp. 811–847. doi: 10.1111/jori.12067.

Brealey, R. A. and Myers, S. C. (1981) *Principles of corporate finance*. Fourth. McGraw-Hill.

Brennan, M. J. (1993) Aspects of insurance, intermediation and finance, *The GENEVA Papers on Risk and Insurance Theory*, 18(1), pp. 7–30. doi: 10.1007/BF01125816.

Brunnermeier, M. K. and Oehmke, M. (2013) Bubbles, Financial Crises, and Systemic Risk, in Constantinides, George M., Milton Harris, and René M. Stulz, eds. Handbook of the Economics of Finance: Corporate Finance. North Holland, 2013. pp. 1221–1288. doi: 10.1080/01932691.2016.1147360.

Buch, A. and Dorfleitner, G. (2008) Coherent risk measures, coherent capital allocations and the gradient allocation principle, *Insurance: Mathematics and Economics*, 42(1), pp. 235–242. doi: 10.1016/j.insmatheco.2007.02.006.

Butsic, R. P. (1994) Solvency measurement for property-liability risk-based capital applications, *The Journal of Risk and Insurance*, 61(4), pp. 656–690. Available at: http://www.jstor.org/stable/253643.

Bühlmann, H. (1970) *Mathematical methods in risk theory*. Berlin Heidelberg: Springer Verlag.

Bühlmann, H. (1980) An economic premium principle, *ASTIN Bulletin*, 11(1), pp. 52–60.

Bühlmann, H. (1985) Premium calculation from top down, *ASTIN Bulletin*, 15(2), pp. 89–101. doi: 10.2143/ast.15.2.2015021.

Carlier, G. and Dana, R. A. (2003) Core of convex distortions of a probability, *Journal of Economic Theory*, 113(2), pp. 199–222. doi: 10.1016/S0022-0531(03)00122-4.

Castagnoli, E. *et al.* (2021) Star-shaped Risk Measures, (March), pp. 1–28. Available at: http://arxiv.org/abs/2103.15790.

Castagnoli, E., Maccheroni, F. and Marinacci, M. (2002) Insurance premia consistent with the market, *Insurance: Mathematics and Economics*, 31(2), pp. 267–284. doi: 10.1016/S0167-6687(02)00155-5.

Castagnoli, E., Maccheroni, F. and Marinacci, M. (2004) Choquet insurance pricing: A caveat, *Mathematical Finance*, 14(3), pp. 481–485. doi: 10.1111/j.0960-1627.2004.00201.x.

Chang, C. L. *et al.* (2019) Choosing expected shortfall over VaR in Basel III using stochastic dominance, *International Review of Economics and Finance*, 60(Icefs), pp. 95–113. doi: 10.1016/j.iref.2018.12.016.

Chateauneuf, A., Kast, R. and Lapied, A. (1996) Choquet pricing for financial markets with frictions, *Mathematical Finance*, 6(3), pp. 323–330. doi: 10.1111/j.1467-9965.1996.tb00119.x.

Chen, H. *et al.* (2013) Systemic risk and the interconnectedness between banks and insurers: an econometric analysis, *Journal of Risk and Insurance*, 81(3), pp. 623–652. doi: 10.1111/j.1539-6975.2012.01503.x.

Cherny, A. and Orlov, D. (2011) On two approaches to coherent risk contribution, *Mathematical Finance*, 21(3), pp. 557–571. doi: 10.1111/j.1467-9965.2010.00441.x.

Cherny, A. S. (2008) Pricing with coherent risk, *Theory of Probability & Its Applications*, 52(3), pp. 389–415. doi: 10.1137/S0040585X97983158.

Cherny, A. S. and Grigoriev, P. G. (2007) Dilatation monotone risk measures are law invariant, *Finance and Stochastics*, 11(2), pp. 291–298. doi: 10.1007/s00780-007-0034-8.

Cleveland, W. S. (1979) Robust locally weighted regression and smoothing scatterplots, *Journal of the American Statistical Association*, 74(368), pp. 829–836. doi: 10.1080/01621459.1979.10481038.

Cochrane, J. H. (2005) The risk and return of venture capital, *Journal of Financial Economics*, 75(1), pp. 3–52. doi: 10.1016/j.jfineco.2004.03.006.

Cochrane, J. H. (2009) *Asset pricing (Revised Edition)*. Princeton, NJ: Princeton University Press.

Cramér, H. (1994) *Collected works, vol. II*. Springer.

Crouhy, M., Galai, D. and Mark, R. (2010) Risk exposures, *Encyclopedia of Quantitative Finance*. Rama Cont, ed., Wiley.

Crouhy, M., Turnbull, S. and Wakeman, L. (1999) Measuring risk-adjusted performance, *The Journal of Risk*, 2(1), pp. 5–35. doi: 10.21314/jor.1999.018.

Cummins, J. D. (1988) Risk-based premiums for insurance guaranty funds, *Journal of Finance*, 43(4), pp. 823–839.

Cummins, J. D. *et al.* (1990) Applications of the GB2 family of distributions in modeling insurance loss processes, *Insurance: Mathematics and Economics*, 9(4), pp. 257–272. doi: 10.1016/0167-6687(90)90003-V.

Cummins, J. D. (1990) Multi-period discounted cash flow rate-making models in property-liability insurance, *Journal of Risk and Insurance*, 57(1), pp. 79–109.

Cummins, J. D. (1991) Capital structure and fair profits in property-liability insurance, in *Managing the insolvency risk of insurance companies*. Springer, pp. 295–308.

Cummins, J. D. (2000) Allocation of capital in the insurance industry, *Risk Management and Insurance Review* (October 1998), pp. 7–28. Available at: http://onlinelibrary.wiley.com/doi/10.1111/j.1540-6296.2000.tb00013.x/full.

Cummins, J. D. *et al.* (2010) Economies of scope in financial services: A DEA efficiency analysis of the US insurance industry, *Journal of Banking and Finance*, 34(7), pp. 1525–1539. doi: 10.1016/j.jbankfin.2010.02.025.

Cummins, J. D. and Danzon, P. M. (1997) Price, financial quality, and capital flows in insurance markets, *Journal of Financial Intermediation*, 6(1), pp. 3–38. doi: 10.1006/jfin.1996.0205.

Cummins, J. D., Dionne, G. and Gagne, R. (2008) The Costs and Benefits of Reinsurance. Available at: http://ssrn.com/abstract=1142954.

Cummins, J. D. and Doherty, N. A. (2002) Capitalization of the property-liability insurance industry: Overview, *Journal of Financial Services Research*, 21(1-2), pp. 5–14. doi: 10.1023/A:1014366800354.

Cummins, J. D. and Harrington, S. (1985) Property-liability insurance rate regulation: estimation of underwriting betas using quarterly profit data, *The Journal of Risk and Insurance*, 52(1), p. 16. doi: 10.2307/252614.

Cummins, J. D. and Harrington, S. E. (1987) *Fair rate of return in property-liability insurance*. Boston: Kluwer-Nijhoff.

Cummins, J. D. and Lewis, C. (2003) Catastrophic events, parameter uncertainty and the breakdown of implicit long-term contracting: the case of terrorism insurance, *The Risks of Terrorism*. W. Kip Viscusi, ed. Springer, Boston, MA, 2003. 55-80.

Cummins, J. D. and Phillips, R. D. (2009) Capital adequacy and insurance risk-based capital systems, *Journal of Insurance Regulation*, 28(1), pp. 25–72.

Cummins, J. D. and Phillips, R. D. (2000) Applications of financial pricing models in property-liability insurance, in Dionne, G. (ed.) *Handbook of insurance*. Boston: Kluwer Academic Publishers.

Cummins, J. D. and Phillips, R. D. (2005) Estimating the Cost of Equity Capital for Property-Liability Insurers, *Journal of Risk and Insurance*, 72(3), pp. 441–478. Available at: http://onlinelibrary.wiley.com/doi/10.1111/j.1539-6975.2005.00132.x/full.

Cummins, J. D. and Sommer, D. W. (1996) Capital and risk in property-liability insurance markets, *Journal of Banking and Finance*, 20(6), pp. 1069–1092. doi: 10.1016/0378-4266(95)00044-5.

Cummins, J. D. and Weiss, M. A. (2013) Analyzing firm performance in the insurance industry using frontier efficiency and productivity methods, in Georges Dionne *Handbook of insurance*. New York: Springer.

D'Arcy, S. P. and Dyer, M. A. (1997) Ratemaking: A Financial Economics Approach, *Proceedings of the Casualty Actuarial Society*, LXXXIV, pp. 301–390.

D'Arcy, S. P. and Doherty, N. A. (1988) *The Financial Theory of Pricing Property Liability Insurance Contracts*. Huebner Foundation-Irwin, Homewood IL.

Damodaran, A. (2016) Myth 5.2: As g → *r* ... To Infinity and Beyond!.

Daníelsson, J. and Jorgensen, B. (2013) Fat tails, VaR and subadditivity, *Journal of Financial Econometrics*, pp. 1–30. Available at: http://www.sciencedirect.com/science/article/pii/S0304407612001959.

De Finetti, B. (1957) Su un'impostazione alternativa della teoria collettiva del rischio, in *Transactions of the XVth international congress of Actuaries*. New York, pp. 433–443.

De Waegenaere, A. (2000) Arbitrage and Viability in Insurance Markets, *GENEVA Papers on Risk and Insurance Theory*, 25(1), pp. 81–99. doi: 10.1023/A:1008701608588.

De Waegenaere, A., Kast, R. and Lapied, A. (2003) Choquet pricing and equilibrium, *Insurance: Mathematics and Economics*, 32, pp. 359–370. doi: 10.1016/S0167-6687(03)00116-1.

Debreu, Gerard. (1959) *Theory of value; an axiomatic analysis of economic equilibrium.* Yale University Press, p. 114.

Delbaen, F. (2000) Coherent risk measures (Pisa Notes), *Pisa Notes*, 24(4), pp. 733–739. doi: 10.1007/BF02809088.

Delbaen, F. (2002) Coherent risk measures on general probability spaces, *Advances in finance and stochastics: essays in honour of dieter sondermann*, pp. 1–37. doi: 10.1007/978-3-662-04790-3.

Delbaen, F. (2009) Risk measures for non-integrable random variables, *Mathematical Finance*, 19(2), pp. 329–333. doi: 10.1111/j.1467-9965.2009.00370.x.

Delbaen, F. and Haezendonck, J. (1989) A martingale approach to premium calculation principles in an arbitrage free market, *Insurance: Mathematics and Economics*, 8, pp. 269–277. Available at: http://www.sciencedirect.com/science/article/pii/0167668789900024.

Delbaen, F. and Schachermayer, W. (1994) A general version of the fundamental theorem of asset pricing, *Mathematische Annalen*, 300(1), pp. 463–520. doi: 10.1007/BF01450498.

Denault, M. (2001) Coherent allocation of risk capital, *The Journal of Risk*, 4(1), pp. 1–34. doi: 10.21314/jor.2001.053.

Denneberg, D. (1990) Premium calculation: why standard deviation should be replaced by absolute deviation, *ASTIN Bulletin*, 20(2), pp. 181–190. doi: 10.2143/ast.20.2.2005441.

Denneberg, D. (1994) *Non-additive measure and integral.* Dordrecht: Kluwer Academic.

Denuit, M. and Dhaene, J. (2012) Convex order and comonotonic conditional mean risk sharing, *Insurance: Mathematics and Economics*, 51(2), pp. 265–270. doi: 10.1016/j.insmatheco.2012.04.005.

Deprez, O. and Gerber, H. U. (1985) On convex principles of premium calculation, *Insurance: Mathematics and Economics*, 4(3), pp. 179–189. doi: 10.1016/0167-6687(85)90014-9.

Dhaene, J. *et al.* (2008) Can a coherent risk measure be too subadditive?, *Journal of Risk and Insurance*, 75(2), pp. 365–386. doi: 10.1111/j.1539-6975.2008.00264.x.

Dhaene, J., Tsanakas, A., *et al.* (2012) Optimal capital allocation principles, *Journal of Risk and Insurance*, 79(1), pp. 1–28. doi: 10.1111/j.1539-6975.2011.01408.x.

Dhaene, J., Kukush, A., *et al.* (2012) Remarks on quantiles and distortion risk measures, *European Actuarial Journal*, 2(2), pp. 319–328.

Dhaene, J. *et al.* (2017) Is the capital structure logic of corporate finance applicable to insurers? review and analysis, *Journal of Economic Surveys*, 31(1), pp. 169–189. doi: 10.1111/joes.12129.

Dhaene, J., Goovaerts, M. J. M. and Kaas, R. (2003) Economic capital allocation derived from risk measures, *North American Actuarial Journal*, 7(2), pp. 44–56. doi: 10.1080/10920277.2003.10596084.

Diaconis, P. and Skyrms, B. (2018) *Ten great ideas about chance.* Princeton; Oxford: Princeton, NJ, USA. doi: 10.1090/noti1888.

Diamond, P. A. and Stiglitz, J. E. (1973) *Increases in risk and risk aversion.* Cambridge: MIT.

Dietz, S. and Walker, O. (2017) Ambiguity and insurance: capital requirements and premiums, *Journal of Risk and Insurance*, 86(1), pp. 213–235. doi: 10.1111/jori.12208.

Doherty, N. A. and Garven, J. R. (1986) Price regulation in property-liability insurance: a contingent-claims approach, *Journal of Finance*, 41(5), pp. 1031–1050.

Doherty, N. A. and Schlesinger, H. (1990) Rational insurance purchasing: consideration of contract nonperformance, *The Quarterly Journal of Economics*, 105(1), p. 243. doi: 10.2307/2937829.

Dothan, M. U. (1990) *Prices in financial markets*. Oxford, England: Oxford University Press.

Duffie, D. (2010) *Dynamic asset pricing theory*. Princeton, NJ: Princeton University Press.

Dybvig, P. H. and Ross, S. A. (1992) Arbitrage, in *The new Palgrave dictionary of money and finance*. London: Palgrave Macmillan, pp. 44–49.

Eeckhoudt, L., Gollier, C. and Schlesinger, H. (2011) *Economic and financial decisions under risk*. Princeton, NJ: Princeton University Press.

EIOPA, E. I. and Authority, O. P. (2014) The underlying assumptions in the standard formula for the Solvency Capital Requirement calculation (25 July), pp. 1–74. Available at: https://eiopa.europa.eu.

Embrechts, P., Klüppelberg, C. and Mikosch, T. (1997) *Modelling extremal events*. Berlin Heidelberg: Springer Verlag. doi: 10.1007/978-3-642-33483-2.

Embrechts, P., Puccetti, G. and Ruschendorf, L. (2013) Model uncertainty and VaR aggregation, *Journal of Banking and Finance*, 37(8), pp. 2750–2764. doi: 10.1016/j.jbankfin.2013.03.014.

Embrechts, P. and Wang, R. (2015) Seven proofs for the subadditivity of expected shortfall, *Dependence Modeling*, 3(1), pp. 126–140. doi: 10.1515/demo-2015-0009.

Emmer, S., Kratz, M. and Tasche, D. (2015) What is the best risk measure in practice? A comparison of standard measures, *Journal of Risk*, 18(2), pp. 31–60. doi: 10.21314/JOR.2015.318.

Epstein, L. G. and Schneider, M. (2008) Ambiguity, information quality, and asset pricing, *Journal of Finance*, LXIII(1), pp. 197–228.

Erel, I., Myers, S. C. and Read, J. A. (2013) A Theory of Risk Capital. *Journal of Applied Corporate Finance*, 33(1), pp. 8–21.

European Commission (2009) DIRECTIVE 2009/138/EC OF THE EUROPEAN PARLIAMENT AND OF THE COUNCIL of 25 November 2009 on the taking-up and pursuit of the business of Insurance and Reinsurance (Solvency II) (recast). doi: 10.1093/acprof:oso/9780195388138.003.0029.

Exley, C. Jon and Smith, Andrew. D. (2006) The cost of capital for financial firms, *British Actuarial Journal*, 12(I), pp. 229–301.

Fairley, W. B. (1979) Investment income and profit margins in property-liability insurance: theory and empirical results, *The Bell Journal of Economics*, 10(1), p. 192. doi: 10.2307/3003326.

Feldblum, Sholom (1992). Pricing insurance policies: The internal rate of return model. Casualty Actuarial Society Part 10A Examination Study Note. (May).

Feller, W. (1971) *An Introduction to Probability Theory and Its Applications, Volume 2*. Second. J. Wiley and Sons, p. 669.

Ferrari, R. (1968) The relationship of underwriting, investment, leverage, and exposure to total return on owner's equity, *Proceedings of the Casualty Actuarial Society*, pp. 295–303. Available at: http://www.casact.com/pubs/proceed/proceed68/68295.pdf.

Fischer, S. (1978) Call option pricing when the exercise price is uncertain, and the valuation of index bonds, *The Journal of Finance*, 33(1), pp. 169–176. doi: 10.1111/j.1540-6261.1978.tb03396.x.

Fischer, T. (2003) Risk capital allocation by coherent risk measures based on one-sided moments, *Insurance: Mathematics and Economics*, 32(1), pp. 135–146. doi: 10.1016/S0167-6687(02)00209-3.

Floreani, A. (2011) Risk margin estimation through the cost of capital approach: Some conceptual issues, *Geneva Papers on Risk and Insurance: Issues and Practice*, 36(2), pp. 226–253. doi: 10.1057/gpp.2011.2.

Flower, M. and Others (2006) *Reinsurance pricing: practical issues & considerations*. Report. Institute; Faculty of Actuaries, General Insurance Research Organising (GIRO) Committee.

Föllmer, H. and Schied, A. (2016) *Stochastic Finance: An Introduction in Discrete Time*. Fourth. Berlin, Boston: Walter de Gruyter. doi: 10.1017/CBO9781107415324.004.

Föllmer, H. and Schied, A. (2011) *Stochastic finance: an introduction in discrete time*. Third Walter de Gruyter.

Froot, K. A. (2001) The Market for Catastrophe Risk: a clinical examination, *Journal of Financial Economics*, 60, pp. 529–571.

Froot, K. A. (2007) Risk management, capital budgeting, and capital structure policy for insurers and reinsurers, *Journal of Risk and Insurance*, 74(2), pp. 273–299. Available at: http://onlinelibrary.wiley.com/doi/10.1111/j.1539-6975.2007.00213.x/full.

Froot, K. A. and O'Connell, P. G. J. (1999) *The pricing of US catastrophe reinsurance*. (January), pp. 195–232. doi: 10.3386/w6043.

Froot, K. A. and O'Connell, P. G. J. (2008) On the pricing of intermediated risks: Theory and application to catastrophe reinsurance, *Journal of Banking and Finance*, 32(1), pp. 69–85. doi: 10.1016/j.jbankfin.2007.09.008.

Froot, Kenneth A., David S. Scharfstein, and Jeremy C. Stein (1993). Risk management: Coordinating corporate investment and financing policies. *The Journal of Finance* 48.5: 1629-1658.

Froot, K. A. and Stein, J. C. (1998) Risk management, capital budgeting, and capital structure policy for financial institutions: An integrated approach, *Journal of Financial Economics*, 47(1), pp. 55–82. doi: 10.1016/S0304-405X(97)00037-8.

Froot, K. A., Venter, G. G. and Major, J. A. (2004) Capital and Value of Risk Transfer, in *14th annual international AFIR colloquium*, pp. 181—-195.

Galeotti, M., Gürtler, M. and Winkelvos, C. (2013) Accuracy of Premium Calculation Models for CAT Bonds — An Empirical Analysis, *Journal of Risk and Insurance*, 80(2), pp. 401–421. doi: 10.1111/j.1539-6975.2012.01482.x.

Gatumel, M. and Guegan, D. (2008) Towards an understanding approach of the Insurance Linked Securities Market, *HAL archives-ouvertes*, pp. 106–112.

Gerber, H. and Shiu, E. (1994) Option pricing by Esscher transforms, *Transactions of the Society of Actuaries*, 4.

Gerber, H. U. (1974) On Additive Premium Calculation Principles, *ASTIN Bulletin*, 7(3), pp. 215–222. doi: 10.1017/S0515036100006061.

Gerber, H. U. and Shiu, E. S. W. (2004) Optimal Dividends: Analysis with Brownian Motion, *North American Actuarial Journal*, 8(1), pp. 1–20. doi: 10.1080/10920277.2004.10596125.

Gilboa, I. and Schmeidler, D. (1989) Maxmin expected utility with non-unique prior, *Journal of Mathematical Economics*, 18(2), pp. 141–153. doi: 10.1016/0304-4068(89)90018-9.

Goldfarb, R. (2006) The Evolution of Insurance Pricing. Available at SSRN: https://ssrn.com/abstract=3995597.

Goldfarb, R. (2010a) P&C Insurance Company Valuation, *Casualty Actuarial Society Part 8 Examination Study Note.*

Goldfarb, R. (2010b) *Risk-Adjusted Performance Measurement for P&C Insurers.* CAS, p. 55. Available at: http://www.casact.org/library/studynotes/goldfarb8.2.pdf.

Goovaerts, M., De Vylder, F. E. and Haezendonck, J. (1984) *Insurance premiums.* North-Holland, pp. 1–398.

Gordon, M. J. (1962) *The investment, financing, and valuation of the corporation.* RD Irwin Homewood, IL.

Grechuk, B. (2015) The center of a convex set and capital allocation, *European Journal of Operational Research*, 243(2), pp. 628–636. doi: 10.1016/j.ejor.2014.12.004.

Grundl, H. and Schmeiser, H. (2007) Capital allocation for insurance companies—What Good Is It?, *Journal of Risk and Insurance*, 74(2). Available at: http://www.jstor.org/stable/2691539.

Heckman, P. E. and Meyers, G. G. (1983) The calculation of aggregate loss distributions from claim severity and claim count distributions, *Proceedings of the Casualty Actuarial Society*, pp. 49–66.

Heerwaarden, A. E. van and Kaas, R. (1992) The Dutch premium principle, *Insurance: Mathematics and Economics*, 11(2), pp. 129–133. doi: 10.1016/0167-6687(92)90049-H.

Hewitt, E. (1960) Integration by Parts for Stieltjes Integrals, *The American Mathematical Monthly*, 67(5), p. 419. doi: 10.2307/2309287.

Heyde, C. C., Kou, S. G. and Peng, X. H. (2007) What Is a Good External Risk Measure: Bridging the Gaps between Robustness, Subadditivity, and Insurance Risk Measures, *Preprint*, pp. 1–31.

Hill, R. D. (1979) Profit regulation in property-liability insurance, *The Bell Journal of Economics*, 10(1), pp. 172–191.

Hitchcox, B. A. N. *et al.* (2006) Assessment of target capital for general insurance firms, *British Actuarial Journal*, 44(November), pp. 81–183.

Huber, P. J. (1981) *Robust statistics.* John Wiley & Sons, Inc. doi: 10.1016/0001-8708(86)90016-2.

Huberman, G., Mayers, D. and Smith, C. W. (1983) Optimal Insurance Policy Indemnity Schedules, *The Bell Journal of Economics*, 14(2), p. 415. doi: 10.2307/3003643.

Hull, J. C. (1983) *Options futures and other derivative securities.* Second. Hoboken, NJ: Prentice-Hall.

Ibragimov, R., Jaffee, D. and Walden, J. (2010) Pricing and Capital Allocation for Multiline Insurance Firms, *Journal of Risk and Insurance*, 77(3), pp. 551–578. doi: 10.1111/j.1539-6975.2010.01353.x.

Ingersoll, J. E. (1987) *Theory of financial decision making.* Lanham, MD: Rowman & Littlefield.

James, C. M. (1997) *RAROC Based Capital Budgeting and Performance Evaluation: A Case Study of Bank Capital Allocation.* Risk Management in Banking Conference, Wharton Financial Institutions Center. doi: 10.2139/ssrn.1000.

Jewell, W. S. (1980) *Models in Insurance: Paradigms, Puzzles, Communications and Revolutions.* Berkeley: University of California.

Jiang, W., Escobar-Anel, M. and Ren, J. (2020) Optimal insurance contracts under distortion risk measures with ambiguity aversion, *ASTIN Bulletin*, 50(Dm), pp. 1–28. doi: 10.1017/asb.2020.12.

Jones, C. M. and Rodes' Kropf, M. (2004) *The price of diversifiable risk in venture capital and private equity.* Columbia Working Paper.

Jouini, E., Schachermayer, W. and Touzi, N. (2006) Law invariant risk measures have the Fatou property, *Advances in Mathematical Economics*, 9, pp. 49–71. doi: 10.1007/4-431-34342-3.

Jouini, E., Schachermayer, W. and Touzi, N. (2008) Optimal risk sharing for law invariant monetary utility functions, *Mathematical Finance*, 18(2) pp. 269–292. doi: 10.1111/j.1467-9965.2007.00332.x.

Junike, G. (2019) Representation of concave distortions and applications, *Scandinavian Actuarial Journal*, 2019(9), pp. 768–783. doi: 10.1080/03461238.2019.1615543.

Kaas, R. *et al.* (2008) *Modern Actuarial Risk Theory*. Springer. doi: 10.1007/978-3-540-70998-5.

Kahane, Y. (1979) The theory of insurance risk premiums—a re-examination in the light of recent developments in capital market theory, *ASTIN Bulletin*, 10(2), pp. 223–239. doi: 10.1017/S051503610000653X.

Kahneman, D. (2011) *Thinking, fast and slow*. Farrar, Straus; Giroux.

Kahneman, Daniel, and Amos Tversky. Prospect theory: An analysis of decision under risk. Handbook of the fundamentals of financial decision making: Part I. eds Leonard C MacLean and William T Ziemba Singapore: World Scientific Publishers (2013). pp. 99-127. doi: 10.1142/9789814417358_0006.

Kalkbrener, M. (2005) An axiomatic approach to capital allocation, *Mathematical Finance*, 15(3), pp. 425–437. Available at: http://onlinelibrary.wiley.com/doi/10.1111/j.1467-9965.00227.x/full.

Kalkbrener, M. (2009) An axiomatic characterization of capital allocations of coherent risk measures, *Quantitative Finance*, 9(8), pp. 961–965. doi: 10.1080/14697680902814266.

Kallop, R. H. (1975) A current look at Workers' Compensation ratemaking, *Proceedings of the Casualty Actuarial Society*, LXII, pp. 62–81.

Karatzas, I. and Shreve, S. (1988) *Brownian Motion and Stochastic Calculus*. New York: Springer-Verlag.

Kaye, P. (2005) Risk measurement in insurance a guide to risk measurement, capital allocation and related decision support issues, *Casualty Actuarial Society Discussion Paper*, pp. 1–34. Available at: http://www.casact.com/pubs/dpp/dpp05/05dpp1.pdf%5Cnpapers2://publication/uuid/57D8A742-2DA8-4D53-8DD2-169135E7850A.

Kieso, D. E., Weygandt, J. J. and Warfield, T. D. (2010) *Intermediate accounting: IFRS edition*. John Wiley & Sons, Inc.

Klibanoff, P., Marinacci, M. and Mukerji, S. (2005) A smooth model of decision making under ambiguity, *Econometrica*, 73(6), pp. 1849–1892. doi: 10.1111/j.1468-0262.2005.00640.x.

Klugman, S. A., Panjer, H. H. and Willmot, G. E. (2012) *Loss Models: from data to decisions*. Fourth. John Wiley & Sons, Inc.

Klugman, S. A., Panjer, H. H. and Willmot, G. E. (2018) Loss models, from data to decisions,, *SOA Study Note*.

Kozik, T. J. (1994) Underwriting betas-the shadows of ghosts, *Proceedings of the Casualty Actuarial Society*, 81(154, 155), pp. 303–329.

Kreps, R. (2005) Riskiness leverage models, *Proceedings of the Casualty Actuarial Society*, 92, pp. 31–60.

Kunreuther, H. C., Pauly, M. V. and McMorrow, S. (2013) *Insurance and behavioral economics: Improving decisions in the most misunderstood industry*. Cambridge University Press.

Kusuoka, S. (2001) On law invariant coherent risk measures, *Advances in Mathematical Economics*, 3, pp. 83–95. Available at: http://link.springer.com/chapter/10.1007/978-4-431-67891-5_4.

Laeven, R. J. A. and Goovaerts, M. J. (2008) Premium Calculation and Insurance Pricing, *Encyclopedia of Quantitative Risk Analysis*, Brian S. Everitt and Edward L. Melnick, eds.; John Wiley & Sons, Ltd., pp. 1–22. doi: 10.1002/97804700 61596.risk0364.

Landsman, Z. and Valdez, E. A. (2005) Tail conditional expectations for exponential dispersion models, *ASTIN Bulletin*, 35(1), pp. 189–209. doi: 10.1017/S0515036100014124.

Lane, M. N. (2000) Pricing Risk Transfer Transactions, *ASTIN Bulletin*, 30(02), pp. 259–293. doi: 10.2143/ast.30.2.504635.

Lane, M. N. and Mahul, O. (2008) Catastrophe risk pricing: an empirical analysis, *Working Paper, The World Bank*, 4765(November), pp. 1–26. Available at: http://ideas.repec.org/p/wbk/wbrwps/4765.html.

Lange, J. T. (1966) General liability insurance ratemaking, *Proceedings of the Casualty Actuarial Society*, pp. 26–53.

Lee, Y. (1988) The mathematics of excess of loss coverages and retrospective rating—a graphical approach, *PCAS*, LXXV. Available at: http://casact.net/pubs/proceed/proceed88/88049.pdf.

Lemaire, J. (1991) Cooperative game theory and its insurance applications, *ASTIN Bulletin*, 21(1), pp. 17–40. doi: 10.2143/ast.21.1.2005399.

Li, H. and Wang, R. (2019) *PELVE: Probability Equivalent Level of VaR and ES*. doi: 10.2139/ssrn.3489566.

Lindensjö, K. and Lindskog, F. (2020) Optimal dividends and capital injection under dividend restrictions, *Mathematical Methods of Operations Research*, 92(3), pp. 461–487. doi: 10.1007/s00186-020-00720-y.

Lloyd's (2021) Realistic Disaster Scenarios - Scenario Specification (January). Available at: https://www.lloyds.com/market-resources/underwriting/realistic-disaster-scenarios-rds.

Lowenstein, R. (2000) *When genius failed: the rise and fall of long-term capital management*. Random House trade paperbacks.

Lundberg, F. (1903) *I. Approximerad framstallning af sannolikhetsfunktionen: II. Aterforsakring af kollektivrisker*. Almqvist & Wiksell.

Machina, M. J. and Pratt, J. W. (1997) Increasing Risk: Some Direct Constructions, *Journal of Risk and Uncertainty*, 14(2), pp. 103–127. doi: 10.1023/A:1007719626543.

Machina, M. J., Teugels, J. L. and Sundt, B. (2004) Nonexpected utility theory, *In Encyclopedia of Actuarial Science*, 2, pp. 1173–1179.

Magrath, J. J. (1958) Ratemaking for fire insurance, *Proceedings of the Casualty Actuarial Society*, XLV, pp. 176–195.

Mahler, H. C. (1985) An introduction to underwriting profit models, *Proceedings of the Casualty Actuarial Society*, LXII, pp. 239–277. doi: 10.2307/253527.

Mahul, O. (2003) Efficient Risk Sharing within a Catastrophe Insurance Pool, *Paper presented at the 2003 NBER Insurance Project Workshop*, (October).

Major, J. A. (2004) Gradients of Risk Measures: Theory and Application to Catastrophe Risk Management and Reinsurance Pricing, *Casualty Actuarial Society Forum, Winter*. Available at: https://www.casact.org/pubs/forum/04wforum/04wf045.pdf.

Major, J. A. (2008) On a Connection between Froot-Stein and the De Finetti Optimal Dividends Models (March 2, 2007). NBER Insurance Workshop, (2008), Available at SSRN: https://ssrn.com/abstract=2606210 or https://users.nber.org/~confer/2008/INSw08/major.pdf

Major, J. A. (2009) The Firm-Value Risk Model, *SSRN Electronic Journal*. doi: 10.2139/ssrn.2610675.

Major, J. A. (2011) Risk Valuation for Property-Casualty Insurers, *Variance*, 5(2), pp. 124–140.

Major, J. A. (2018) Distortion Measures on Homogeneous Financial Derivatives, *Insurance: Mathematics and Economics*, 79, pp. 82–91. doi: 10.2139/ssrn.2972955.

Major, J. A. (2019) Methodological Considerations in the Statistical Modeling of Catastrophe Bond Prices, *Risk Management and Insurance Review*, 22(1), pp. 39–56. doi: 10.1111/rmir.12114.

Makarov, G. D. (1982) Estimates for the Distribution Function of a Sum of Two Random Variables When the Marginal Distributions Are Fixed, *Theory of Probability & Its Applications*, 26(4), pp. 803–806. doi: 10.1137/1126086.

Mango, D. (1998) An application of game theory: property catastrophe risk load, *Proceedings of the Casualty Actuarial Society*, pp. 157–186. Available at: http://www.casact.net/pubs/proceed/proceed98/980157.pdf.

Mango, D. (2005) Insurance Capital as a Shared Asset, *Astin Bulletin*, 35(2), pp. 471–486.

Mango, D., Major, J., Adler, A. and Bunick, C. (2012) Capital tranching: A RAROC approach to assessing reinsurance cost effectiveness, *Casualty Actuarial Forum* (September).

Mango, D., Major, J., Adler, A. and Bunick, C. (2013) Capital tranching: A RAROC approach to assessing reinsurance cost effectiveness, *Variance*, 7(1), pp. 82–91.

Margrabe, W. (1978) The Value of an Option to Exchange One Asset for Another, *The Journal of Finance*, 33(1), pp. 177–186.

Marinacci, M. (1999) Limit Laws for Non-additive Probabilities and Their Frequentist Interpretation, *Journal of Economic Theory*, 84(2), pp. 145–195. doi: 10.1006/jeth.1998.2479.

Marinacci, M. and Montrucchio, L. (2004) A characterization of the core of convex games through Gateaux derivatives, *Journal of Economic Theory*, 116(2), pp. 229–248. doi: 10.1016/S0022-0531(03)00258-8.

Marshall, D. (2018) An Overview of the California Earthquake Authority, *Risk Management and Insurance Review*, 21(1), pp. 73–116. doi: 10.1111/rmir.12097.

McGuinness, J. S. (1969) Is 'probable maximum loss' (PML) a useful concept?, *Proceedings of Casualty Actuarial Society*, LVI(May), pp. 31–48.

McNeil, A. J., Embrechts, P. and Frey, R. (2005) *Quantitative Risk Management: Concepts, Techniques, and Tools*. Princeton University Press. doi: 10.1198/jasa.2006.s156.

Merton, R. (1973) Theory of Rational Option Pricing, *Bell Journal of Economics*, 4(1), pp. 141–183.

Merton, R. C. and Perold, A. (1993) Theory of risk capital in financial firms, *Journal of applied corporate finance*, 6(3), pp. 16–32.

Meyers, G. G. (2003) The Economics of Capital Allocation, *The Casualty Actuarial Society Forum, Fall 2003*, pp. 391–418. Available at: http://www.casualtyactuaries.com/research/aria/meyers.pdf.

Meyers, G. G. (2020) The Chase—An Actuarial Memoir, *CAS E-Forum*, Summer.

Meyers, G. G. (1992) *An Introduction to the Competitive Market Equilibrium Risk Load Formula.* September, pp. 1–28.

Meyers, G. G. (1996) The competitive market equilibrium risk load formula for catastrophe ratemaking, *PCAS*, pp. 563–600.

Meyers, G. G. (2019a) A Cost of Capital Risk Margin Formula for Non-Life Insurance Liabilities, *Variance*, 12(2), pp. 186–198.

Meyers, G. G. (2019b) *Stochastic Loss Reserving Using Bayesian MCMC Models.* Second. CAS Monograph Series (8).

Mildenhall S. J. (2000) Application of the Option Market Paradigm to the Solution of Insurance Problems, Review of M. Wacek, *Proceedings of the Casualty Actuarial Society*, pp. 1–22.

Mildenhall, S. J. (2004) A Note on the Myers and Read Capital Allocation Formula, *North American Actuarial Journal*, 8(2), pp. 32–44. Available at: http://library.soa.org/library-pdf/naaj0402_3.pdf.

Mildenhall, S. J. (2005) Correlation and aggregate loss distributions with an emphasis on the Iman-Conover method, *Casualty Actuarial Society Forum*, Winter.

Mildenhall, S. J. (2017) Actuarial geometry, *Risks*, 5(31). doi: 10.3390/risks5020031.

Mildenhall, S. J. (2021a) Pricing seasonal peril catastrophe bonds: a simplified approach, *Variance.*

Mildenhall, S. J. (2021b) Similar risks have similar prices: an exact and useful quantification, *Insurance: Mathematics and Economics, forthcoming.*

Mitchell-Wallace, K. *et al.* (2017) *Natural Catastrophe Risk Management and Modeling - A Practitioner's Guide.* Hoboken, NJ: Wiley-Blackwell.

Möhr, C. (2011) Market-consistent valuation of insurance liabilities by cost of capital, *ASTIN Bulletin*, 41(2), pp. 315–341. doi: 10.2143/AST.41.2.2136980.

Mörters, P. and Peres, Y. (2011) *Brownian motion*, pp. 158–168. doi: 10.1088/0953-8984/23/19/194119.

Myers, S. C. and Cohn, R. A. (1987) A discounted cash flow approach to property-liability insurance rate regulation, in *Fair rate of return in property-liability insurance*, pp. 55–78. New York, NY: Springer.

Myers, S. C. and Read Jr., J. A. (2001) Capital allocation for insurance companies, *Journal of Risk and Insurance*, 68(4), pp. 545–580. Available at: http://www.jstor.org/stable/2691539.

National Association of Insurance Commissioners (2016) *Receiver's Handbook for Insurance Company Insolvencies.* NAIC. Available at: http://store.naic.org.

Obersteadt, A. (2017) NAIC Enhanced P/C RBC Formula for Catastrophe Risk Charges.

Øksendal, B. K. and Sulem, A. (2007) *Applied stochastic control of jump diffusions.* Springer.

Panning, William H (2013) Managing the Invisible: Identifying value-maximizing combinations of risk and capital. North American Actuarial Journal 17.1: 13-28.

Perold, A. (2005) Capital allocation in financial firms, *Journal of Applied Corporate Finance*, (February). Available at: http://onlinelibrary.wiley.com/doi/10.1111/j.1745-6622.2005.00051.x/full.

Phelps, R. (1993) *Convex functions, monotone operators and differentiability.* Second. New York: Springer-Verlag.

Phillips, R. D., Cummins, J. D. and Allen, F. (1998) Financial pricing of insurance in the multiple-line insurance company, *Journal of Risk and Insurance*, 65(4), pp. 597–636. doi: 10.2307/253804.

Powell, L. S. (2017) What it means to be a mutual. doi: 10.1515/9783110185522.90.

Powers, M. R. (2007a) Using Aumann-Shapley values to allocate insurance risk: the case of inhomogeneous losses. *North American Actuarial Journal* 11.3: 113-127.

Powers, M. R. (2007b) Sharing responsibility: what they didn't teach you in kindergarten, *Journal of Risk Finance*, 8(2), pp. 93–96. doi: 10.1108/15265940710732305.

Powers, M. R. and Zanjani, G. (2013) Insurance risk, risk measures, and capital allocation: navigating a copernican shift, *Annual Review of Financial Economics*, 5(1), pp. 201–223. doi: 10.1146/annurev-financial-110112-120955.

Puccetti, G. and Ruschendorf, L. (2012) Computation of sharp bounds on the distribution of a function of dependent risks, *Journal of Computational and Applied Mathematics*, 236(7), pp. 1833–1840. doi: 10.1016/j.cam.2011.10.015.

Quiggin, J. (2012) *Generalized expected utility theory: The rank-dependent model*. Springer Science & Business Media.

Quirin, G. D. and Waters, W. R. (1975) Market efficiency and the cost of capital: the strange case of fire and casualty insurance companies, *The Journal of Finance*, 30(2), pp. 427–445. doi: 10.1111/j.1540-6261.1975.tb01820.x.

Raviv, B. A. (1979) The design of an optimal insurance policy, *The American Economic Review*, 69(1), pp. 84–96.

Risk Margin Working Group of the International Actuarial Association (2009) *Measurement of Liabilities for Insurance Contracts: Current Estimates and Risk Margins*. International Actuarial Association (April), p. 210.

Robbin, I. (1992) *The Underwriting Profit Provision*. Casualty Actuarial Society Study Note.

Robbin, I. (2007) IRR, ROE, and PVI/PVE, *Casualty Actuarial Society Forum*, Winter, pp. 189–256.

Robert, C. Y. and Therond, P.-E. (2014) Distortion risk measures, ambiguity aversion and optimal effort, *ASTIN Bulletin*, 44(02), pp. 277–302. doi: 10.1017/asb.2014.3.

Rockafellar, R. T. and Royset, J. O. (2014) Random variables, monotone relations, and convex analysis, *Mathematical Programming*, 148(1-2), pp. 297–331. doi: https://doi.org/10.1007/s10107-014-0801-1.

Rockafellar, R. T. and Uryasev, S. (2002) Conditional value-at-risk for general loss distributions, *Journal of Banking & Finance*, 26(7), pp. 1443–1471.

Rockafellar, R. T. and Uryasev, S. (2013) The fundamental risk quadrangle in risk management, optimization and statistical estimation, *Surveys in Operations Research and Management Science*, 18(1-2), pp. 33–53. doi: 10.1016/j.sorms.2013.03.001.

Rockafellar, R. T., Uryasev, S. and Zabarankin, M. (2006) Generalized deviations in risk analysis, *Finance and Stochastics*, 10(1), pp. 51–74. doi: 10.1007/s00780-005-0165-8.

Rothschild, M. and Stiglitz, J. E. (1970) Increasing risk: I. A definition, *Journal of Economic Theory*, 2(3), pp. 225–243. doi: 10.1016/0022-0531(70)90038-4.

Royden, H. L. (1988) *Real analysis*. Third edition. New York: Macmillan Publishing Company.

Ruhm, D. L. *et al.* (2005) Elicitation and Elucidation of Risk Preferences, *CAS Forum*, Fall, pp. 1–28. Available at: https://www.casact.com/pubs/forum/05fforum/05f01.pdf.

Rüschendorf, L. (1982) Random variables with maximum sums, *Advances in Applied Probability*, 14(3), pp. 623–632. doi: 10.2307/1426677.

Ryff, J. V. (1967) Extreme points of some convex subsets of L1(0, 1), *Proc American Mathematical Society*, 18(6), pp. 1026–1034. doi: 10.3732/ajb.

Ryff, J. V. (1970) Measure preserving transformations and rearrangements, *Journal of Mathematical Analysis and Applications*, 31(2), pp. 449–458. doi: 10.1016/0022-247X (70)90038-7.

Salzmann, R. and Wüthrich, M. V. (2010) Cost-of-capital margin for a general insurance liability runoff, *ASTIN Bulletin*, 40(August 2013), pp. 415–451. doi: 10.2143/AST.40.2.2061123.

Samanthi, R. G. M. and Sepanski, J. (2019) Methods for generating coherent distortion risk measures, *Annals of Actuarial Science*, 13(2), pp. 400–416. doi: 10.1017/S1748499518000258.

Sato, K.-I. (1999) *Levy processes and infinitely divisible distributions*. Cambridge: Cambridge University Press, p. 486. doi: 10.2307/3621820.

Saumard, A. and Wellner, J. A. (2014) Log-concavity and strong log-concavity: a review, *Statistics Surveys*, 8, pp. 45–114. doi: 10.1214/14-SS107.

Schlesinger, H. (2012) The theory of insurance demand, *Handbook of Insurance* (February), pp. 167–184. doi: 10.1007/978-1-4614-0155-1.

Schmeidler, D. (1986) Integral representation without additivity, *Proceedings of the American Mathematical Society*, 97(2), pp. 255–255. doi: 10.1090/S0002-9939-1986-0835875-8.

Schmeidler, D. (1989) Subjective probability and expected utility without additivity, *Econometrica*, 57(3), pp. 571–587.

Schmidli, H. (2007) *Stochastic control in insurance*. Springer Science & Business Media.

Segal, U. (1992) The independence axiom versus the reduction axiom: Must we have both?. In *Utility theories: Measurements and applications*. Dordrecht, the Netherlands: Springer. 165-183. 10.1007/978-94-011-2952-7_7.

Shapiro, A. (2012) On Kusuoka representation of law invariant risk measures, *Mathematics of Operations Research*, 38(1), pp. 142–152. doi: 10.1287/moor.1120.0563.

Shapiro, A., Dentcheva, D. and Ruszczyski, A. (2009) *Lectures on Stochastic Programming* (May). doi: 10.1137/1.9780898718751.

Shapley, L. S. (1953) A value for N-person games, in Kuhn, H. W. and Tucker, A. W. (eds) *Contributions to the theory of games*. Princeton, NJ: Princeton University Press, pp. 307–317. doi: 10.7249/p0295.

Sherris, M. (2006) Solvency, capital allocation, and fair rate of return in insurance, *Journal of Risk and Insurance*, 73(1), pp. 71–96. Available at: http://onlinelibrary.wiley.com/doi/10.1111/j.1365-2966.2006.00166.x/full.

Shimko, D. C. (1992) The valuation of multiple claim insurance contracts, *The Journal of Financial and Quantitative Analysis*, 27(2), p. 229. doi: 10.2307/2331369.

Shiryaev, A. N. (1996) *Probability*. Second. New York: Springer-Verlag.

Shiu, Y. M. (2011) Reinsurance and capital structure: Evidence from the United Kingdom non-life insurance industry, *Journal of Risk and Insurance*, 78(2), pp. 475–494. doi: 10.1111/j.1539-6975.2010.01387.x.

Simon, L. J. (1979) *Total Rate of Return and the Regulation of Insurance Profits*. Casualty Actuarial Society.

Skeel, D. A. Jr. (2018) The empty idea of "Equality of Creditors", *Faculty Scholarship*, 1724. Available at: https://scholarship.law.upenn.edu/faculty_scholarship/1724.

Solberg, H. J. (1957) The profit factor in fire insurance rates, *The Journal of Insurance*, 24(2), p. 24. doi: 10.2307/250229.

Sommer, D. W. (1996) The impact of firm risk on property-liability insurance prices, *Journal of Risk and Insurance*, 63(3), pp. 501–514.

Stoyanov, J. M. (2013) *Counterexamples in probability*. Third edition. Mineola, NY, USA: Dover Books.

Strassen, V. (1965) The existence of probability measures with given marginals, *The Annals of Mathematical Statistics*, 36(2), pp. 423–439.

Struppeck, T. (2015) *Life Contingencies Study Note for CAS Exam S*. Casualty Actuarial Society, pp. 1–14. Available at: https://www.casact.org/library/studynotes/ExamS-Contingencies-Study-Note-0115.pdf.

Svindland, G. (2010) Continuity properties of law-invariant (quasi-)convex risk functions on L^∞, *Mathematics and Financial Economics*, 3(1), pp. 39–43. doi: 10.1007/s11579-010-0026-x.

Svindland, G. (2014) Dilatation monotonicity and convex order, *Mathematics and Financial Economics*, 8(3), pp. 241–247. doi: 10.1007/s11579-013-0112-y.

Tasche, D. (1999) Risk contributions and performance measurement, *Report of the Lehrstuhl fur mathematische Statistik, TU Munchen*, pp. 1–26.

Tasche, D. (2001) Conditional expectation as quantile derivative, *Arxiv preprint math/0104190* (Theorem 1), pp. 1–12. Available at: http://arxiv.org/abs/math/0104190.

Tasche, D. (2002) Expected shortfall and beyond, *Journal of Banking and Finance*, 26(7), pp. 1519–1533. doi: 10.1016/S0378-4266(02)00272-8.

Tasche, D. (2004) Allocating portfolio economic capital to sub-portfolios, *Economic Capital: A Practitioner's Guide, Risk Books*, Ashish Dev, ed. London: Risk Books. 275-301.

Tsanakas, A. (2009) To split or not to split: capital allocation with convex risk measures, *Insurance: Mathematics and Economics*, 1(2), pp. 1–28. doi: 10.1016/j.insmatheco.2008.03.007.

Tsanakas, A. (2014) Risk measures and economic capital for (re)insurers, in *Encyclopedia of quantitative risk analysis and assessment*, Brian S. Everitt and Edward L. Melnick; John Wiley & Sons, Ltd. (9), pp. 1591–1601. doi: 10.1002/9781118445112.stat03582.

Tsanakas, A. and Barnett, C. (2003) Risk capital allocation and cooperative pricing of insurance liabilities, *Insurance: Mathematics and Economics*, 33(2), pp. 239–254. doi: 10.1016/S0167-6687(03)00137-9.

Tsanakas, A. and Desli, E. (2003) Risk measures and theories of choice, *British Actuarial Journal*, 9(04), pp. 959–991. doi: 10.1017/S1357321700004414.

Tsukahara, H. (2009) One-parameter families of distortion risk measures, *Mathematical Finance*, 19(4), pp. 691–705. doi: 10.1111/j.1467-9965.2009.00385.x.

Van Heerwaarden, A. E., Kaas, R. and Goovaerts, M. J. (1989) Properties of the Esscher premium calculation principle, *Insurance: Mathematics and Economics*, 8(4), pp. 261–267. doi: 10.1016/0167-6687(89)90001-2.

Van Slyke, O. E. (1999) *Actuarial considerations regarding risk and return in property-casualty insurance pricing*. Arlington, VA: Casualty Actuarial Society, p. 179.

Venter, G. G. (1991) Premium calculation implications of reinsurance without arbitrage, *ASTIN Bulletin*, 21(02), pp. 223–230. doi: 10.2143/ast.21.2.2005365.

Venter, G. G. (2004) Capital allocation survey with commentary, *North American Actuarial Journal*, 8:2, pp. 96–107. doi: 10.1080/10920277.2004.10596139.

Venter, G. G., Major, J. A. and Kreps, R. E. (2006) Marginal decomposition of risk measures, *ASTIN Bulletin*, 36(2), pp. 375–413. doi: 10.2143/AST.36.2.2017927.

Wang, R. (2016) Regulatory arbitrage of risk measures, *Quantitative Finance*, 16(3), pp. 337–347. doi: 10.1080/14697688.2015.1070193.

Wang, R. and Zitikis, R. (2021). An axiomatic foundation for the Expected Shortfall. Management Science 67.3: 1413–1429. doi: 10.2139/ssrn.3423042.

Wang, S. (1995) Insurance pricing and increased limits ratemaking by proportional hazards transforms, *Insurance: Mathematics and Economics*, 17(1), pp. 43–54. doi: 10.1016/0167-6687(95)00010-P.

Wang, S. (1996) Premium calculation by transforming the layer premium density, *ASTIN Bulletin*, 26(01), pp. 71–92. doi: 10.2143/AST.26.1.563234.

Wang, S. (1998a) Aggregation of correlated risk portfolios: models and algorithms, *Proceedings of the Casualty Actuarial Society*, pp. 848–939. Available at: http://www.casact.com/pubs/proceed/proceed98/980848.pdf.

Wang, S. (1998b) Implementation of proportional hazards transforms in ratemaking, *PCAS*, 85, pp. 940–979. Available at: http://casualtyactuaries.com/pubs/proceed/proceed98/980940.pdf.

Wang, S. (2002) A universal framework for pricing financial and insurance risks, *ASTIN Bulletin*, 32(2), pp. 213–234. doi: 10.2143/AST.32.2.1027.

Wang, S. (2003) Equilibrium pricing transforms: new results using Buhlmann's 1980 economic model, *Astin Bulletin*, 33(01), pp. 57–73. doi: 10.1017/S0515036100013301.

Wang, S. S. (2000) A class of distortion operators for pricing financial and insurance risks, *The Journal of Risk and Insurance*, 67(1), pp. 15–36. doi: 10.2307/253675.

Wang, S. and Young, V. (1998) Ordering risks: expected utility theory versus Yaari's dual theory of risk, *Insurance: Mathematics and Economics*, 22(2), pp. 145–161. doi: 10.1016/S0167-6687(97)00036-X.

Wang, S., Young, V. and Panjer, H. (1997) Axiomatic characterization of insurance prices, *Insurance: Mathematics and Economics*, 21(2), pp. 173–183. doi: 10.1016/S0167-6687(97)00031-0.

Wen, M. M. *et al.* (2008) Estimating the cost of equity for property-liability insurance companies, *Journal of Risk and Insurance*, 75(1), pp. 101–124. doi: 10.1111/j.1539-6975.2007.00250.x.

Winter, R. A. (1994) The dynamics of competitive insurance markets, *Journal of Financial Intermediation*, 3(4), pp. 379–415. doi: 10.1006/jfin.1994.1011.

Wirch, J. L. and Hardy, M. R. (1999) A synthesis of risk measures for capital adequacy, *Insurance: Mathematics and Economics*, 25(3), pp. 337–347. doi: 10.1016/S0167-6687(99)00036-0.

Yaari, M. E. (1987) The dual theory of choice under risk, *The Econometric Society*, 55(1), pp. 95–115.

Young, V. R. (2006) Premium principles, in *Encyclopedia of actuarial science*, Jozef L. Teugels, Bjørn Sundt eds. John Wiley & Sons, Ltd.

Zanjani, G. (2002) Pricing and capital allocation in catastrophe insurance, *Journal of Financial Economics*, 65(2), pp. 283–305. doi: 10.1016/S0304-405X(02)00141-1.

Zhang, J. (2002) Subjective ambiguity, expected utility and choquet expected utility, *Economic Theory*, 20(1), pp. 159–181. doi: 10.4324/9780203195390.ch8.

Index

Pricing Insurance Risk: Theory and Practice, First Edition. Stephen J. Mildenhall and John A. Major.

b

c

k

l

m

S